THE

100

BEST

STOCKS

YOU CAN BUY

2003

John Slatter

Adams Media Corporation

Avon, Massachusetts

Dedication

To Beverly, Sarah, Carol, Melanie, Ron, and Steve.

Acknowledgments

Writing a book is far easier than finding a publisher. My first book, *Safe Investing*, didn't find a home until I latched on to my dutiful agent, Edythea Ginis Selman. Edy knows how to find a publisher, and she knows how to convince the editor that I am worth paying a living wage.

My publisher, Adams Media, has treated me like a king. That could be because the editor is Jill Alexander, an easy person to do business with.

Published by
Adams Media Corporation
57 Littlefield Street, Avon, MA 02322 U.S.A.
www.adamsmedia.com

ISBN: 1-58062-753-6

Printed in the United States of America.

J I H G F E D C B A

This book is not designed or intended to provide or replace professional investment advice. Readers should invest with care, including seeking specific professional advice, since investments by nature involve significant risk and can result in financial losses. The past performance of the investments reported in this book does not guarantee or predict future performance.

Cover design by Mike Stromberg.

This book is available at quantity discounts for bulk purchases.
For information, call 1-800-872-5627

Visit our exciting small business Web site: www.businesstown.com

Table of Contents

Part I
The Art and Science of Investing in Stocks

Is This the Right Investment Book for You?

The last time I stopped by the investment section of my local bookstore, there was no shortage of books about investing in the stock market. Fortunately, several copies of the 2002 edition of *The 100 Best Stocks You Can Buy* were prominently displayed.

However, I saw only one lonely soul trying to find a book to his liking. I was tempted to suggest that mine was the best one on the shelf. But I refrained. I recalled that on my previous trip to the bookstore I had made a similar suggestion and was totally ignored. He didn't even look up to see who was offering him this sage advice. I was tempted to report the recalcitrant cad to the manager but thought better of it.

Since you have the book in your hands and are wondering whether this is the one for you, let me give you a song and dance that will convince you that your search has ended; you don't need to look any further.

To begin, let me congratulate you on making the decision to educate yourself on the intricacies of the stock market. Many people totally ignore the importance of saving money for the future. It could be that they believe their company 401(k), along with Social Security, will do the job. The odds are that you will need more, particularly if you work for a firm that insists your 401(k) should be stuffed with your employer's company stock.

If you want to build a solid portfolio, it makes better sense to buy stocks on a regular basis—at least once a year. I suggest setting aside at least 10 percent of your gross income every year for stock purchases. And don't skip a year because you don't like the antics of the stock market at that particular time. Forecasting the market is a no-no. You can't do it—nor can anyone else.

Why People Don't Read about Investing

One reason that people don't read about investing is because they are overwhelmed by the complexity of the financial scene. I heartily concur—it *is* overwhelming. That's because there are thousands of mutual funds, common stocks, preferred stocks, certificates of deposit, options, bonds, annuities, and assorted investment products.

Even if you simply confined your search to the stocks listed on the New York Stock Exchange, the task would be daunting, since some 3,000 stocks are traded there. Or you might decide to "Let George do it," by investing in mutual funds. There, too, you will encounter infinite decisions, since there are over 14,000 mutual funds—most of which underperform such market indexes as The Dow Jones Industrial Average (called the Dow, Dow Jones, or DJIA) or the Standard & Poor's 500 (S&P 500).

If you are like many buyers of my books, you are not a sophisticated investor. You have a good job, have an income that is well above average, and you are serious about your career. That means that you spend time improving yourself by reading trade journals and taking courses at a local college.

Why Not Burn the Midnight Oil?

In other words, your day is already taken up with reading. How can you possibly start poring over annual reports, Standard & Poor's reports, *Fortune*, *Value Line Investment Survey*, *The Wall Street Journal*, *Forbes*, *BusinessWeek*, *Barron's*, and a half-dozen books on the stock market? Easy. Drink lots of coffee and stay up until two in the morning.

If you object to this routine, you will be better off with my book, since I try to make investing a lot simpler than you thought it would be. For one thing, my style of writing is easy to understand. At least that's what people tell me.

Incidentally, I am one of the few authors who take calls from readers. My address and phone number are on page 368. I assume you will confine your calls to regular business hours, based on Eastern Time, since I live in Vermont.

Whenever I buy a book, I always check to see if the writer has good credentials. For my part, I have been on the investment scene for a good forty years. I started as a plain vanilla stockbroker, and then became editor of a publication devoted to mutual funds, followed by several years as a securities analyst for a brokerage firm. I spent a few years as a portfolio manager and started operating my own firm, managing portfolios on a fee basis for investors with assets of $100,000 or more.

During these years, I did a lot of writing, first for *Barron's Financial Weekly*, and later for such publications as *Physician's Management* and *Better Investing*. During the same period, I wrote tons of reports on stocks for the brokerage firms that paid my salary. In recent years, I have written nine books: *Safe Investing*, *Straight Talk About Stock Investing*, and seven editions of *The 100 Best Stocks You Can Buy*.

I also wrote two great novels, but no publisher seems to agree that they are great, so I am not currently getting royalties on them.

As I mentioned above, the number of stocks and mutual funds out there is infinite. Besides the 3,000 stocks on the New York Stock Exchange, plus the thousands of mutual funds, there are also thousands of stocks listed on the NASDAQ and thousands more traded on markets in Europe, Asia, Latin America, and Canada.

The beauty of my book is that I whittle the number of stocks you need to know about down to 100. Among that 100 are four types of stocks, depending on your particular temperament. The types are stocks for Income, Growth and Income, Conservative Growth, and Aggressive Growth. There are about twenty-five in each category.

Diversification, the First Rule of Investing

Of course, there is no need to confine your investing exclusively to one category. A well-diversified portfolio could have half a dozen from each sector. Incidentally, diversity is the key to investing. Whenever you concentrate on one type of stock, such as technology, energy, banks, utilities, or pharmaceuticals, you expose yourself to extra risk. Don't do it. Let me emphasize that again—don't do it.

When I was a portfolio strategist in Cleveland a few years ago, I examined portfolios submitted to our firm for analysis. About 100 percent of them were not diversified. They were typically concentrated in only three industries: public utilities, banks, and oil.

Before you make up your mind which stocks to buy, you will want to collect some information. If you have access to a brokerage house, you can easily get a copy of a report prepared by *Value Line Investment Survey*. You can also subscribe yourself, but be prepared to spend over $500 a year for this service, which covers about 1,700 well-known stocks. A less-expensive alternative is the same service limited to 600 stocks. Still another good source is Standard & Poor's tear sheets, which can be obtained from a broker or library. Finally, most brokerage houses have a staff of analysts that turns out reports on a multitude of stocks.

My Sources of Information

A final source of information is this book, which is updated every year. I believe that my write-ups are valuable in ways that the other sources are not. When I first began writing this series of books, I obtained my information from each company's annual report, as well as from the two services mentioned above. Now, I go much further afield. On a daily basis, I collect information on these companies from such sources as *Barron's*, *Forbes*, *Better Investing*, *BusinessWeek*, and other monthly investment publications. In addition, I consult well-known newspapers across the country, including *The Boston Globe*, *The New York Times*, as well as papers in Chicago, Philadelphia, Atlanta, Denver, St. Louis, Houston, Milwaukee, Los Angeles, Detroit, San Francisco, Miami, and Dallas.

Whenever I see an article on one of my companies, I clip it out and file it for future reference and examine it again when I sit at my computer to prepare a report. Using this vast collection, I sift through the facts to find reasons why this stock is attractive. I also look for factors that have a negative tone. In other words, I don't want to give you a purely one-sided view of this stock. By contrast, if you read the company's annual report, you will only hear about the attributes of the company and not about its problems and deficiencies.

Similarly, if you read a report from a brokerage house, it is rarely negative. The analyst normally tells you to buy—rarely to sell. One reason for this is the tie brokerage houses have to these companies that can lead to underwriting and corporate finance deals that are extremely lucrative. If the analyst tells investors to avoid the stock, the company may decide to avoid the brokerage house and give its business to someone else.

Obviously, I have no reason to be anything but unbiased.

Forty Years of Experience Is the Key

Finally, the 100 stocks have to be selected. The publisher is not the one who picks the stocks. I do. My forty years of varied experience on the investment scene give me an edge in this regard. And, of course, I am intimately involved in stock selection from a personal perspective. I have a large portfolio of stocks, over sixty at present, which have made my wife and me millionaires.

If you would like to reach the same comfortable plateau, why not invest $14.95 and start reading?

Oh, and here's one more thing. If you read the rest of these introductory chapters, you will see that I have provided a helpful glossary that explains all the terms you will need to know to understand the fundamentals of investing.

I also have a chapter on asset allocation that will tell you what percentage of your holdings should be in stocks and how much in such fixed-income vehicles as bonds and money-market funds. Finally, there also are chapters on the common mistakes made by investors, an article on new developments in IRAs, and still another on how to analyze stocks. Lastly, there is a short chapter that focuses on the four essentials of successful investing. You'll be surprised at how simple investing can be if you read this chapter.

Why Invest in Stocks?

Investing is a complex business. But, then, so is medicine, engineering, chemistry, geology, law, philosophy, photography, history, accounting—you name it. In fact, investing is so intimidating that many intelligent individuals avoid it. Instead, they stash their money in certificates of deposit (CDs), annuities, bonds, or mutual funds. Apparently, they can't face buying common stocks. This is too bad, because that's precisely where the money is made. You don't make money every day, every week, or even every year. But over the long term, you will make the most out of your investment dollars.

Look at the Facts

One persuasive study contends that common stocks will make money for you in most years. This study, done by the brokerage firm Smith Barney, looked at the thirty-five one-year periods between 1960 and 1995.

The study computed total return, which adds capital gains and dividends. Over that span, stocks (as represented by the Standard & Poor's 500 index) performed unsatisfactorily in only eight of those thirty-five years. In other words, you would have been better off in money-market funds during those eight years. Common stocks would have been more successful in twenty-seven of those thirty-five years.

Investing for the Long Term

Investing, however, is not a one-year endeavor. Most investors start their programs in their forties and fifties, which means they could be investing over a twenty-, thirty-, or forty-year period.

If we look at the relative returns of different investments over five-year periods—rather than one-year periods—the results are even more encouraging. During the years from 1960 through 1994, there were thirty-one such periods. In only two of those five-year periods did the total return of the Standard & Poor's-based portfolio become negative.

Let's move ahead to all ten-year holding periods. There were twenty-six in that span. Exactly 100 percent worked out profitably. Equally important, the returns to the investor were impressive in all of these one-, five-, and ten-year periods. The one-year periods, for instance, gave you an average annual total return of 11.1 percent; for five-year periods, it was 10.5 percent, and for ten-year periods, it was 10.2 percent.

Based on this study, we can say with confidence that over a lifetime of investing, an investor will reap a total annual return of 10 percent or more. If you compare this with the amount you could earn by owning CDs, annuities, government bonds, or any other conservative investment, the difference is considerable.

Some Profitable Comparisons

Let's see how that difference adds up. Suppose you invested $25,000 in a list of common stocks at the age of forty, and your portfolio built up at a 10 percent compound annual rate. By the time you reached sixty-five, your common stock nest egg would be worth $270,868.

Now, let's say you had invested your money in government bonds, yielding 6 percent. The same $25,000 would be worth only $107,297, which is a difference of $163,571. Neither of these calculations has accounted for income taxes or brokerage commissions.

Now, let's look at the timid soul who invested $25,000 in CDs at age forty and averaged a return of 4 percent. By age sixty-five, that investment would be worth a paltry $66,646.

Why Doesn't Everyone Buy Common Stocks?

That's a good question, and I'm not sure I can provide you with a satisfactory answer. Part of the reason may be ignorance. Not everyone is willing to investigate the field of common stocks. These noninvestors may be too preoccupied with their jobs, sports, reading, gardening, travel, or whatever. Then, there are those who are heavily influenced by family members who have told them that stocks are too speculative and better left to millionaires. (Of course, that's how many of these millionaires became millionaires.)

Even if you are convinced that I may be right about the potential of stocks, you are probably wondering how anyone can possibly figure out which stocks to buy, since there are tens of thousands to choose from. That, in essence, is the purpose of this book.

A Real-Life Example

If you are a newcomer to investing, you may still doubt that you are capable of building a portfolio of stocks that will make you rich. Not all stocks are going to live up to their early promise, no matter how much time you devote to making a selection. On the other hand, even if you pick your stocks blindfolded, you will have some winners. Let's suppose that you want to invest $100,000 in twenty stocks, or $5,000 in each. Some will work out and some won't.

Hypothetically, it does not seem unreasonable to project that ten of these stocks will just plug along, making you neither rich nor poor. Suppose we assume that these ten stocks will appreciate (rise in value) an average of only 7 percent per year over the next ten or twenty years. Toss in a 2 percent annual dividend and the total return adds up to 9 percent per year. That is not exactly

riches, since stocks over the last seventy-five years have averaged about 11 percent.

At any rate, here is what your $50,000 will be worth at the end of ten years and twenty years:

$118,368 $280,221

Next, let's look at the three stocks that performed above your wildest dreams. They appreciated an average of 15 percent per year. Add in a modest annual dividend of only 1 percent, and you have a total return of 16 percent.

Assuming you invest $5,000 in each of these three stocks, that $15,000 will be worth over the next ten- and twenty-year periods:

$66,172 $291,911

So far, so good. Now, for the bad news. Two of your stocks hit the skids and never recovered. Total results for the $10,000 invested in these losers is: zero.

$00,000 $00,000

Finally, five of your twenty stocks do about average. They appreciate an average of 9 percent per year and have an average yearly dividend of 2 percent. That's a total return of 11 percent. Since you have five stocks in this category, your total investment is $25,000. Here is what you end up with ten and twenty years from now:

$70,986 $201,558

If we add up these various results, the final figures make you look reasonably rich:

$255,525 $773,690

By contrast, had you acted in a cowardly manner and invested exclusively in CDs, you would have only the following at the end of the two periods:

$162,889 $265,330

One final note. If you figure in taxes, you look even better, since the capital gains (on your stocks) are taxed at a much lower rate than ordinary income (which applies to CDs). And, you wouldn't even have to worry about capital gains on your stocks if you elected not to sell them.

For Busy Investors, a Strategy That Rarely Fails

As far as I know, I'm one of the few writers who gives readers the opportunity to call if they have any questions. That's why my telephone number is on page 368. When you consider the tens of thousands of investors who read my books, very few actually call. And when they do, they are startled and surprised that I usually answer the phone myself—no secretary to screen out malcontents, deadbeats, and cranks.

One of the readers who called a few weeks ago was Horst Graben, a CPA from Wyoming.

"I liked your book, Mr. Slatter, and I read every word. In fact, I actually read it twice, since there are a lot of succulent morsels to digest."

"In other words," I said, "You are *not* calling to complain."

"Well, yes and no," he said. "With 100 stocks to pick from, I am having trouble deciding which ones to buy—and when to sell them if they falter."

I thought for a moment and then said, "Most investors find buying a lot easier than selling. Too often, they let a stock sag down week after week, and suddenly they realize it's down 40 percent, and they grit their teeth, hoping it will start back up again. Usually, it doesn't."

"So what should I do?" Horst Graben asked.

"If you are going to manage your own portfolio, you have to be prepared to keep track of your stocks. That means you have to read quarterly and annual reports. It also means reading such publications as the *Wall Street Journal*, the *New York Times*, *Forbes*, *Barron's*, *BusinessWeek*, *Fortune*, and *Better Investing*."

"I was afraid you would say that," he said. "The only problem I have is time. I'm particularly busy during tax season; I work seven days a week. And even during the rest of the year I have journals to read and other business commitments. As you might have guessed, I'm a CPA with a busy practice. Reading all that investment stuff is out of the question."

"I can understand your plight, Mr. Graben. Most successful people are busy. That's why they're successful. They spend fifty or sixty hours a week making sure they stay successful."

"Are you telling me to forget about stocks and put my money in mutual funds or certificates of deposit?"

"Absolutely not," I assured him. "I have a systematic approach to stock selection that is made to order for people like you. However, I am reluctant to divulge this strategy unless you promise not to tell a soul about it—not even your wife. Are you prepared to do this?"

"Well, let me think. If you tell me how I can manage my investments without having to do a lot of research and study, and in exchange you are insisting that I keep the strategy a secret. No one is to know. Okay, I agree."

"Now that I know I can trust you, here goes," I said. "It involves investing exclusively in the thirty stocks that make up the Dow Jones Industrial Average." Then, I read him the current components of the index, including their ticker symbols:

Alcoa (AA)
American Express (AXP)
AT&T (T)
Boeing (BA)

Caterpillar (CAT)
Citigroup (C)
Coca-Cola (KO)
Disney, Walt (DIS)
DuPont (DD)
Eastman Kodak (EK)
ExxonMobil (XOM)
General Motors (GM)
General Electric (GE)
Hewlett- Packard (HWP)
Home Depot (HD)
Honeywell (HON)
Intel (INTC)
International Business Machines (IBM)
International Paper (IP)
Johnson & Johnson (JNJ)
McDonald's (MCD)
Merck (MRK)
Microsoft (MSFT)
3M Company (MMM)
Morgan, J. P. (JPM)
Altria Group (MO)
Procter & Gamble (PG)
SBC Communications (SBC)
United Technologies (UTX)
Wal-Mart (WMT)

"That sounds like a great list," he said. "In other words, I concentrate on these thirty stocks, instead of the 100 in your book. Is that what you are saying?"

"Right. These are some of the world's greatest blue-chip stocks. Not all of them will be winners, but enough of them will so you will end up a millionaire." Then, I went on to outline how to implement the Dow thirty strategy.

The reason the strategy rarely fails is because it entails investing exclusively in the thirty stocks that make up the Dow Jones Industrial Average. Most investors judge their results by this average. It follows that if you invest in all thirty stocks, your performance will approximate that of this well-known index.

Incidentally, if you forget the names of these thirty stocks, you can refresh your memory by consulting the *Wall Street Journal* any day of the week. Look in the third section (*Money and Investing*) on page 3.

Are You Ready to Be Mediocre?

Buying these thirty stocks may seem like a simplistic and cowardly approach to investing, since you are guaranteed that you will be merely average, or mediocre. And who wants to be mediocre? Most mutual funds would be delighted to be. Only a small percentage have been average in the past. The vast majority have been below average.

Nothing Is Perfect

To be sure, this method of managing a portfolio has some shortcomings:

• You will miss out on such growth stocks and high-flyers as Yahoo!, America OnLine, Harley-Davidson, Pfizer, Illinois Tool Works, Interpublic, Cisco Systems, Dell, and Lucent.

• You may end up owning a few lackluster performers such as Texaco, Eastman Kodak, Bethlehem Steel, Woolworth, and International Paper. Three of those stocks, incidentally, are no longer in the index: Texaco, Bethlehem Steel, and Woolworth. Nor are Chevron or Westinghouse (now CBS). They were replaced in 1997 by Hewlett-Packard, Johnson & Johnson, Wal-Mart, and Travelers (now Citigroup). This move markedly improved the quality of the Dow Jones Industrial Average—it added four super growth stocks to the index. In 1999, moreover, four new stocks were added: Microsoft, SBC Communications, Home Depot, and Intel, which improved the growth prospects of the index.

• You could achieve the same objective by investing in an index fund.

In Defense of My Strategy

In my view, the reasons why this strategy has merit can be summed up as follows.

On the face of it, investing seems incredibly complex because of the thousands of alternatives. In the realm of mutual funds, for instance, there are more than 12,000 to choose from. What's more, there is no strategy that leads you to the best ones. Nor are lists gleaned from financial magazines particularly helpful.

If you elect to invest in stocks, the field is even more crowded. Among the stocks listed on the New York Exchange are some 3,000 stocks. If you venture into the over-the-counter market (or Nasdaq), the choices are vast, at least 5,000. And we haven't even mentioned the immense field of foreign equities.

That's why it makes sense to find a simple—yet effective—way to invest in common stocks. The thirty stocks in the Dow Jones Average give you a playing field that is not nearly as overwhelming or complex as the above alternatives. And these companies are well managed and unlikely to disappear. To be sure, they don't always thrive, but they have the size and financial strength to make a comeback. They can afford to cast aside inept CEOs and replace them with executives with proven track records.

Best of all, thirty stocks is a number that you can keep track of. They are not obscure and are well-covered by Wall Street analysts and the *Wall Street Journal*, as well as by such periodicals as *Barron's*, *Forbes*, and *Fortune*. If you concentrate your attention on these stocks, you can bypass the other 3,000 stocks. It makes sense that most investors can become familiar with these thirty stocks and be able to determine which ones are best, based on the ample information available from the media, brokerage houses, investment manuals, and annual reports.

An important reason to concentrate on these thirty companies relates to their size. Most of them are very large companies. If you like small companies, however, this list is not for you. On the other hand, I am not convinced that small companies are the way to go. At least one authority presents solid evidence that you are usually better off with large companies. Of course, there are years in which the reverse is true.

The authority I am citing is Kenneth L. Fisher, founder, chairman, and CEO of Fisher Investment, Inc. For the past fifteen years, he has been a regular contributor to *Forbes* magazine. In an article in one of my favorite publications, *Better Investing* (June 2000), Mr. Fisher says: "On average, small stocks beat big stocks by 1.18 percent annually from 1926 through 1999. But this is highly deceptive. That entire advantage disappears completely if you eliminate two very similar years, 1933 and 1944—the very first years of the twentieth century's two biggest bull markets. Otherwise, big and small cap have done exactly the same."

Mr. Fisher goes on to say, "Eliminate three multiyear runs at the start of the century's three biggest bull markets (1933–1934, 1942–1945, and 1975–1976) and in the rest of history big cap beat small cap by 2.2 percent per year—quite opposite to popular belief."

Finally, he goes on to say, "Early in bull markets, small stocks do best. Other times and throughout bear markets, big stocks lead."

You'll be happy to learn that many of the thirty Dow stocks are discussed in the 2003 edition of *The 100 Best Stocks You Can Buy*.

Not every investor, of course, has sufficient funds to buy all thirty stocks. On the other hand, good diversification can be achieved by owning fifteen or twenty. In any event, there is no need to buy the entire portfolio on day one. If you set aside $5,000 a year and start at age forty, you can buy one stock each year. By the time you reach sixty-five, you will own twenty-five stocks. From then on, sit back and live off the dividends. In many instances, the dividends will increase every year, helping you keep pace with inflation.

The thirty stocks in the Dow are not always the same. In 1999, for instance, four new stocks were added and four were deleted. On average, about one stock is replaced each year. This is your cue to sell the stock that is tossed out, replacing it with new blood. Because of the low turnover, your taxes on capital gains are minimal, as are your brokerage charges.

Buying an index fund has become popular in recent years, as investors have observed that managed mutual funds don't often do as well. However, not everyone is satisfied to be average. If you invest in the thirty Dow stocks, you can use your ingenuity to pick the fifteen or twenty with the best prospects, casting aside the ones that don't impress you.

A $100,000 Package to Consider

If you want to play a more active part in selecting your stocks, here is an approach that might appeal to you. Let's say you have $100,000 to invest. Set aside $10,000 in a money market fund. Invest the rest as follows:

Pick out the ten stocks that you think are going to be big winners and invest $4,000 in each one, for a total of $40,000. Next, pick the ten that you think may also do better than average. Invest $3,000 in each, for a total of $30,000. Finally, invest $2,000 in the ten stocks that you think will be also-rans. That brings your overall total to $90,000 in stocks and $10,000 in cash.

This Strategy Saves You Money

Picking stocks can also save you money, as compared with mutual funds. The average fund charges 1.5 percent a year. By managing your own portfolio, you can avoid this expense ratio.

Many of the Dow stocks, incidentally, will permit you to buy stock directly from the company, thus sidestepping a commission broker. Once you own a few shares of such stocks as ExxonMobil or Procter & Gamble, you can purchase more by merely mailing in $500 or $1,000, which will be invested without a commission.

The DRIP (dividend reinvestment plan) has some shortcomings. For one thing, you can never be sure what price you will pay, since your check may not be invested for a week or more after you mail it in. The same is true when you decide to cash in some shares.

Even more troublesome are the tax consequences when you sell your shares. To calculate your cost basis, you have to tabulate the price paid with each dividend and for each payment mailed in. If you haven't kept meticulous records, the chore might be daunting, to say the least.

In a Nutshell

When I finished explaining my Dow thirty idea to Horst Graben, he said, "It sounds like an interesting idea. Let me try to summarize what you have said. As I see it, the idea of buying these thirty stocks is to make it easier for me to keep track of the stocks I plan to buy.

"It also assures me that I will be investing in many of the nation's leading companies, such as GE, ExxonMobil, Merck, Procter & Gamble, and IBM. In other words, no speculating. Since I am busy taking care of clients, it gives me more time to devote to their welfare, and thus makes them happy with my services. Anything else?"

"I think you have the picture, Horst. And don't forget the tax implications. Since the stocks in the Dow stay pretty much the same year after year, you probably won't have to sell more than one or two stocks a year—and they're usually ones that haven't done well, so the tax bite won't be onerous.

"One final word. Remember your solemn promise not to mention this ingenious scheme to anyone!"

"You have my word as a CPA."

Nine Mistakes That Investors Make

Every time I take my spiffy chariot in for a grease job or repairs I have to sit in the waiting room watching a T.V. program that someone else likes and I don't. For that reason, I always take along a good book. The trouble is that the cacophony on the T.V. interferes with my concentration.

The last time I found myself suffering in the waiting room I came up with the answer: talk to one of the other customers who are also enduring the mindless drivel. Of course, I wouldn't want my wife to find out who I was talking with, so please don't let her find out about Valira del Nord.

The reason that Mrs. del Nord (a tall, middle-aged, and well-dressed woman) was willing to break the ice was because I had displayed prominently on the floor next to my chair a copy of my latest book, *The 100 Best Stocks You Can Buy*. I never venture out of the office without a copy because you never know who might bite and buy one.

She spotted the title and said, "I see you like reading about the stock market. My husband and I used to invest, but lately we are a bit fed up with what's been happening. We're ready to switch back to certificates of deposit—I think they're called CDs."

"That's a shame," I said. "I always tell my clients that common stocks are the best place to put your money—not CDs."

"Your clients?"

"Yes, I manage people's accounts when I'm not writing books on the stock market."

"Apparently you get your ideas from books like the one by your chair. Isn't that plagiarism?"

"You're right. If you steal something from another author, you can get in trouble. But this book happens to be one I wrote, so there should be no problem."

"Wow!" she said. "Maybe I should buy an autographed copy of your book, and then I'll find out what we're doing wrong? My name is Valira del Nord. I assume you're John Slater."

"Not exactly, it's Slatter, but I'll forgive you if you buy a copy of the book—no checks please! As far as what you're doing wrong, my latest book doesn't go into that in any great detail, but I do have some ideas on the subject. If you have the time, I'll give you the latest scoop."

"I think I have the time," said Mrs. del Nord. "It seems to take an eternity to get something done here. I really dread having to get the car fixed, but my husband says it's my job. He's too busy. Maybe I should buy the book for him and make him do the waiting the next time."

"Assuming I get around to writing a new chapter," I said. "I think I'll call it "The Nine Big Blunders That Investors Make." How does that sound?"

"That might be a bit strong, but I think you're on the right track. What's blunder number one?"

"*Failure to diversify*. Nearly everyone gets fixated on one or two sectors of the market, such as banks, utilities, oil stocks, or technology. There are over seventy different industries to choose from—at least according to Value Line, but no one seems to care."

"Maybe that's what happened to us, Mr. Slattery. We had about a dozen technology stocks, plus three or four mutual funds. We made it big in 1999, but 2000 and 2001 were disasters."

I thought of telling her that my name was not Slattery, but I decided it probably didn't matter. After all, some people really go off the deep end and call me Snyder or Slaughter. Whatever. As long as they buy the book, I'm happy.

"When I worked for a brokerage house in Cleveland," I said, "one of my duties was to analyze portfolios for the firm's customers, those who had assets of $100,000 or more. In nearly all instances, these people thought they were well diversified, since they often owned twenty or more stocks. However, those twenty stocks typically included half a dozen utilities and a similar number of banks and oil companies. What's even worse, a few of those investors had nearly all their money tied up in one stock. Such inattention to diversification merely invites disaster."

"In other words," Mrs. del Nord said, "if something happens to one of those sectors, you can end up bleeding at the mouth."

"How aptly put," I said. "I like that. I think I'll put it in my next book."

"My husband and I have been bleeding at the mouth and have not been sure what to do about it. Do you have the answer?"

"Of course. That's why I write books, since investors expect that I know everything about everything. If they ever find out the truth, book sales will plummet. Meanwhile, let me outline the best way to achieve adequate diversification."

"I assume you will force me to buy a book if you give me all this free advice."

"I think 'force' is a bit strong— 'coerce' might be a better word. Well, here goes. For starters, I think twenty stocks is a good number to shoot for. Some experts would disagree. Their thinking is that you dilute your results by owning that many stocks. They say you should work like a beaver to find five or ten great stocks and put all your money in them. By contrast, if you own twenty stocks, the second ten will be much less attractive and will pull down your results."

"I can see that you don't agree."

"Exactly. I agree, however, that you should make a concerted effort to pick good stocks by doing your homework— reading such publications as *Value Line*, the *Wall Street Journal*, *BusinessWeek*, *Fortune* magazine, *Better Investing*, company annual reports, and Standard & Poor's tear sheets."

"That sounds like a lot of work. There must be an easier way."

"If you were going to buy a home, would you make an effort to look at a couple dozen before you settled on the right one?"

"I see what you mean. If we want to be millionaires, we have to pay the price. It makes me tired to think about it."

"Maybe the service manager will pop out of his hole and announce that your car is ready. Then, you won't have to listen to me any more."

"Good thought, but he's not due for at least an hour. Listening to you is at least better than watching the idiot box."

"Now that we have covered diversification, let's move on," I said. "The next blunder that people make is *paying too much for a stock*."

"What's too much?" Mrs. del Nord asked.

"A good way to determine if a stock is overpriced is to calculate the P/E ratio. Technology stocks are a good example. Many of them are growing at a fast clip, perhaps 20 or 30 percent a year. But the price tag may be fifty, seventy-five, or even 100 times earnings. That's fine as long as growth doesn't start to slow down—as it eventually does. Let's say that earnings per share have been climbing at 30 percent a year and suddenly fall to only 20 percent a year. Inevitably, the price of the stock will plunge. In 2000 and 2001, any number of hot stocks fell precipitously."

"I think you just struck a raw nerve," said Valira del Nord.

"Most of our stocks that unraveled were those with a high P/E. By the way, exactly how do you calculate the P/E?"

"That's a good question. Unfortunately, there is no good answer. Most analysts divide the current price of the stock by the earnings per share (EPS) that they expect in the next twelve months. For instance, if the stock is trading at $89 and the estimated earnings per share are $2.75, you divide that into $89 and your P/E is 32.4, which is a bit on the high side. Many pharmaceutical stocks have multiples in that range."

"I thought you said there was no good way to calculate the P/E ratio," said Mrs. del Nord, with a quizzical look on her face.

"Exactly. My method of calculating the price-earnings multiple is to use the *actual* earnings—not the estimated earnings. According to academics who do research on such things, the estimates made by analysts are often very wide of the mark. What's even worse, they tend to be far too high—rarely are they too low."

"So you use actual earnings. Right?"

"I prefer to use earnings recorded for the most recent twelve months," I said. "They're readily available—either in the Standard & Poor's *Stock Guide* or in *Value Line*. Let's say that the company in the above example actually earned only $2.25, rather than $2.75. If you divide $2.25 into $89, you get a P/E ratio of 39.6—that's a lot higher than 32.4, the one calculated by the analyst."

"I'm still a bit confused," said Mrs. del Nord. "What is your upper limit on P/E?"

"In most instances you should compare the price-earning multiple to the market, such as the Dow Jones Average or the Standard & Poor's Average. If stocks are selling for twenty-two times earnings, for instance, I might be willing to pay thirty, but I would balk at a P/E of forty, fifty, or seventy-five—no matter how fantastic the company might seem."

"Would you pardon me a minute, Mr. Slattery, while I go into the shop and see if they have started to work on my car?"

When she came back, I said, "From the look on your face, I can assume that the mechanic is still out to lunch. Maybe you had better get a cup of coffee and listen to the rest of my nine blunders. Here's number three."

She took my advice and started on her coffee. "Wow, this container is hot! I wish someone would come up with a plastic cup that didn't put you in the hospital. Sorry, Mr. Slaughter. Go ahead. I have plenty of time for lesson three. The service manager told me they don't have the part my car needs, so he has to put out an all-points bulletin to see if anyone in Vermont can rescue me."

"Maybe they can rescue me at the same time," I said. "Back to blunder number three: *Don't buy a stock with a high payout ratio.* In other words, examine what percentage of earnings per share are paid out in dividends. For instance, if the company earns $4 a share and pays out $3, that's too much. I would much prefer a company that paid out less than 50 percent—30 or 40 percent would be even better."

"I don't think that applies to us. Most of the tech stocks we own don't pay a dividend at all."

"I'm not sure that's the best answer either," I said. "Companies that don't pay a dividend are often very speculative. They can be extremely volatile. I think you have already found that out," I said.

"Don't remind me!"

"Next, let's look at blunder number four—*too much trading.* Many investors get impatient and sell their stock after a modest increase in price. When a stock goes from $30 to $45, they think it's time to take a profit—before it falls back to $30.

They reason that you can't lose money by taking a profit."

"That makes sense to me," said Valira del Nord.

"I suppose it might work out in some instances, but it is usually a better strategy to let your profits run and cut short your losses. That way your big winners will be able to help you offset your small losers."

At that moment the service manager emerged and accosted Mrs. del Nord. "Sorry for the long delay, but your car is ready."

"It looks like you won't be able to find out about the other blunders," I said. "Maybe you better buy my book so that you can hone your skills in picking stocks."

"But you said you wouldn't take a check," she said, picking up her purse and heading for the cashier's window.

"I've just changed my policy," I blurted out. "After all, what are friends for?" It was too late; she left me with another unsold book.

I guess that means that I have to continue enumerating my nine blunders for my faithful readers. Mistake number five is *don't fail to read the company's quarterly and annual reports*. The CEO and other officers don't always tell you the whole truth about the company, but they are not likely to distort the truth. If they do, you had better sell the stock. By reading the company's reports you can determine if you still want to remain a shareholder.

Blunder number six is *failing to subscribe to periodicals* that may shed light on what's going on with the companies in your portfolio. Reading the *Wall Street Journal*, *Forbes*, *Barron's*, and *BusinessWeek* will keep you up to date on recent developments, such as new products, changes in management, acquisitions, and analysts' opinions.

You Can't Predict the Market

Still another shortcoming (blunder number seven) to avoid is *failing to invest in stocks after a long decline*. There is no way to predict how long a bear market will last. It could be a few months, as it was in 1987, or it could be two years, as it was in 1973 and 1974. If you are still building a portfolio, you should be investing new money on a regular basis, such as every six months or once a year. If you are setting aside 10 percent of your income, don't suddenly decide to make it 5 percent because you are convinced that the market is headed for a dismal year. You aren't that smart—nor am I. A good rule to follow is to invest when you have the money, not when someone on *Wall Street Week* says, "Next year will be a good one for stocks."

This brings us to mistake number eight—*failure to develop an appropriate asset allocation strategy*. This is covered in considerable detail in a separate chapter, so I will not repeat myself here.

Recordkeeping

The final blunder is *failure to keep adequate records*. You should have a filing cabinet that holds a folder for each stock. The first thing you should put in that file is the confirmation slip for the purchase of the stock, which should have been sent to you by your broker. Then, when you sell the stock, you will know what you paid for it so that you can tell your accountant. He in turn will tell the IRS, and you won't have to go to jail.

However, if you do end up in the slammer, I hope you will still keep buying the new editions of my book. And one last thing, if you run into Valira del Nord, would you put in a good word for me? Maybe you can convince her that she should buy the book. She really needs it.

Some Thoughts on Analyzing Stocks

Ideally, a stock you plan to purchase should have all of the following characteristics:

- A rising trend of earnings, dividends, and book value per share.
- A balance sheet with less debt than other companies in its particular industry.
- An S&P rating of B+ or better.
- A P/E ratio no higher than average.
- A dividend yield that suits your particular needs.
- A stock that insiders are not selling in significant quantities.
- A below-average dividend pay-out ratio.
- A history of earnings and dividends not pockmarked by erratic ups and downs.
- Companies whose return on equity is 15 or better.
- A ratio of price to cash flow that is not too high when compared to other stocks in the same industry.

Where to Get Information

If you are going to concentrate your efforts on the thirty Dow stocks, you must do some reading. Most people don't want to own all thirty stocks. In addition, you will probably find some stocks not to your liking. Let's say you are opposed to tobacco—then you may want to omit Altria Group from your portfolio. Or, you may think that traditional retailers, such as Sears & Roebuck, are not going to do well against such companies as Wal-Mart; Bed, Bath & Beyond; or Home Depot. Similarly, a cyclical company like International Paper might appear too stodgy for an aggressive investor.

Because the Dow stocks are large and prominent, there is no shortage of information about them. In any given day, the *Wall Street Journal* will have a story about one or two Dow stocks. The same might be said for the *New York Times*. If you are serious about doing your homework, it would be wise to clip out these articles and file them away for future reference. You will also see articles on these companies in such publications as *Barron's*, *Better Investing*, *Forbes*, *BusinessWeek*, and *Fortune*.

There are two well-known advisory services that you won't want to ignore: Standard & Poor's publishes "tear sheets" on thousands of companies. Of course, your only interest will be in the thirty Dow stocks. These tear sheets are available in public libraries and brokerage houses.

And don't forget to check *Value Line Survey*. It reviews 1,700 companies on a regular basis. Every thirteen weeks, your Dow Stocks are updated. This service costs over $500 a year, but is readily available in brokerage offices and libraries.

In this modern age, you may also be tempted to seek out information on the Internet. Here is a sampling of what you can check:

- *www.briefing.com* reports upgrades and downgrades on stocks by full-service brokers and gives a detailed report on the market three times daily. It also offers in-depth comments on several stocks during the day.
- *www.hoovers.com* provides profiles of thousands of companies, as well as financial data and links to company home pages.
- *www.investorama.com* provides more than 8,000 links to other investment Web sites.
- *www.zacks.com* provides consensus earnings predictions for the coming quarter, current year, and next year. It also shows whether company insiders are buying or selling.

The Four Essentials of Successful Investing

If you want to be rich at sixty-five, here are the factors to bear in mind.

First, start young. Many people wait until age fifty before they realize what has happened. Let's assume you want to have $1 million by age sixty-five. That may not be enough, but it's a lot more than most people have when they decide to retire from the world of commerce and frustration.

If you start at age thirty-five and can realize an annual return of 10 percent compounded, you will have to put aside $6,079 each year. If you delay until you are forty-five, it will mean you have to set aside $17,460 each year. If you start at age fifty-five, the amount gets a little steep—$62,746!

Invest Mostly in Stocks, not Bonds

It takes commitment, even if you start early, to save for the future. But if you buy bonds, CDs, or a money market fund, the task is even tougher. Let's try the different ages again, but this time assuming a compound annual return of 6, instead of 10, percent.

If you start at thirty-five and want to have a million bucks at sixty-five, it will mean plunking $12,649 into a CD each year—that's a lot more than the first illustration, which required an annual payment of $6,079. If you start at age forty-five, the annual contribution will have to be $27,185. Finally, those who start their programs at age fifty-five and pick fixed-income vehicles will be forced to set aside $75,868 each year.

Don't Be a Spendthrift

An important ingredient of successful investing is discipline. Of course, it pays to earn an above-average salary. If you make $30,000 a year and have four children, you are not likely to end up rich. Sorry about that.

On the other hand, there are plenty of people who make great incomes and still don't own any stocks. The reason: They can always find things to buy.

Successful investors not only make a good income, but they are thrifty shoppers. For instance, do you *need* a new car every two years? I happen to be rich, and I buy used cars. Not rusted-out jalopies—normally, I buy Buicks that are three years old.

If you want to find out how people get rich, you should get *The Millionaire Next Door* by Thomas J. Stanley and William D. Danko. Typically, millionaires are extremely careful how they spend their money, and they invest in good-quality common stocks with very infrequent trading.

Picking the Right Investments

The final factor is picking the right stocks or mutual funds. Surprisingly, this is the *least* important factor. That's because no one knows how to do it consistently. There are mutual funds with good records, but those managers are rarely able to duplicate their performance year after year. However, that shouldn't deter you from trying. You will pick your share of winners if you do your homework and exercise patience. Finally, make sure you don't make any big bets. I prefer to own twenty or more stocks, with no more than 10 percent in any one industry.

In brief, here are the four rules:
- Start early in life to invest.
- Invest in common stocks.
- Invest enough to make it worthwhile, such as 10 percent of your income. You can only do this if you are thrifty.
- Study this book and do enough reading to ensure you pick stocks that have the potential to make you rich.

Basic Terminology

If you are new to the investment arena, you may have difficulty understanding parts of this book. To get you over the rough spots, I have listed some common expressions that appear frequently in books on investing. You will also encounter them in the *Wall Street Journal*, *Forbes*, *BusinessWeek*, *Barron's*, and other periodicals devoted to investing.

This is not a glossary but merely a brief list of terms that are essential for understanding this book. If you would like a more complete glossary, refer to either of my previous books: *Safe Investing* (Simon & Schuster, 1991) or *Straight Talk About Stock Investing* (McGraw-Hill, 1995).

Analyst

In nearly every one of the 100 articles, you will note that I refer to "analysts" and what they think about the prospects for a particular stock. Analysts are individuals who have special training in analyzing stocks. Typically, they have such advanced degrees as M.B.A.s or C.F.A.s. Many of them work for brokerage houses, but they may also be employed by banks, insurance companies, mutual funds, pension plans, or other institutions. Most analysts specialize in one or two industries. A good analyst can tell you nearly everything there is to know about a particular stock or the industry it's part of.

However, analysts can be dead wrong about the future action of a stock. The reason is surprises. Companies are constantly changing, which means they are acquiring, divesting, developing new products, restructuring, buying back their shares, and so forth. When they make a change and announce this change to Wall Street, the surprise can change the course of the stock. In short, analysts can be helpful, but don't bet the store on what they tell you.

As you can see, analysts are usually intelligent, hardworking, and conscientious. Even so, they don't always succeed in guiding you to riches. Perhaps the biggest beef most people have is the tie that analysts have to the companies they follow. They know these people well and may be reluctant to say anything negative.

One reason for this is economic. Most brokerage firms make a ton of money from their investment banking division. If the analyst antagonizes the company, that company may give its investment banking business to a firm that says nice things rather than pointing out warts and all.

This reluctance to see no evil and speak no evil can be seen when you examine the number of times that analysts advise investors to sell. According to the research firm First Call, more than 70 percent of the 27,000 recommendations outstanding in November 2000 were strong buys or buys. Fewer than 1 percent were sells or strong sells. To recap: of the 27,000 recommendations, 26.6 percent were holds, 36.8 percent were buys, 35.7 percent were strong buys, and a mere 0.9 percent were sells or strong sells. I rest my case.

Annual Report

If you own a common stock, you can be certain that you will receive a fancy annual report a couple of months after the close of the year. If the year ends December 31, look for your annual report in March or April. If the fiscal year ends some other time of the year, such as September 30, the annual report will appear in your mailbox two or three months later.

Not all investors read annual reports, but they might be better off if they did. Although most companies will not list their problems, you can usually get a pretty good idea how things are going. In particular, read the report by the president or CEO. It's usually one, two, or three pages long and is written in language you can understand.

If you want detailed information on the company's various businesses, the annual report will often overwhelm you with details that may be difficult to fathom. If you are really curious about what they are trying to say, feel free to call the investor contact. I have provided the phone number of this person in all one hundred stocks listed. Have a list of questions ready, and call during the person's lunch hour, leaving your name and phone number. This sneaky little strategy means the cost of the call back will be paid by the company, not you. By the way, don't assume you will be intimidated by the investor contact. Investor contacts are usually quite personable and helpful.

Asset Allocation

This is not the same as diversification. Rather, it refers to the strategy of allocating your investment funds among different types of investments, such as stocks, bonds, or money-market funds. In the long run, you will be better off with all of your assets concentrated in common stocks. In the short run, this may not be true, since the market occasionally has a sinking spell. A severe one, such as that of 2000–2002, can cause your holdings to decline in value 20 percent or more. To protect against this, most investors spread their money around. They may, for instance, allocate 50 percent to stocks, 40 percent to bonds, and 10 percent to a money-market fund. A more realistic breakdown might be 70 percent in stocks, 25 percent in bonds, and 5 percent in a money-market fund.

Balance Sheet

All corporations issue at least two financial statements: the balance sheet and the income statement. Both are important. The balance sheet is a financial picture of the company on a specific date, such as December 31 or at the end of a quarter.

On the left side of the balance sheet are the company's assets, such as cash, current assets, inventories, accounts receivable, and buildings. On the right side are its liabilities, including accounts payable and long-term debt. Also on the right side is shareholders' equity. The right side of the balance sheet adds up to the same value as the left side, which is why it is called a balance sheet.

In most instances, corporations give you figures for the current year and the prior year. By examining the changes, you can get an idea of whether the company's finances are improving or deteriorating.

Bonds

Entire books have been written on the various kinds of bonds. A bond, unlike a stock, is not a form of ownership. A bond is a contractual agreement that means you have loaned money to some entity, and that entity has agreed to pay you a certain sum of money (interest) every six months until that bond matures. At that time, you will also get back the money you originally invested—no more, no less. Most bonds are issued in $1,000 denominations. The safest bonds are those issued by the U.S. government. Not since the War of 1812 has there been a default on government bonds. The two advantages of bonds are safety and income. If you wait until the maturity date, you will be assured of getting the face value of the bond. In the meantime, however, the bond will fluctuate, because of changes in interest rates or the creditworthiness of the corporation. Long-term bonds, moreover, fluctuate far more than short-term bonds. But enough about bonds. This book is about stocks.

Capital Gains

When you buy common stocks, you expect to make money in two ways: capital gains and dividends. Over an extended period of time, about half of your total return will come from each sector. If the stock rises in value and you sell it above your cost, you are enjoying a capital gain. The tax on long-term capital gains is less than it is on dividends—a maximum of 20 percent if the stock is held for twelve months.

Chief Executive Officer (CEO)

The executive of a company who reports to the board of directors. That corporate body can terminate the CEO if he or she fails to do an effective job of managing the company. In some instances, the CEO may also have the title of either president or chairman of the board, or both.

Closed-End Investment Company

A managed investment portfolio, similar to a mutual fund, which is generally traded on a stock exchange. The price fluctuates with supply and demand, not because of changes in the assets within the trust. An open-end investment trust, or mutual fund, changes in size as investors buy new shares or surrender their shares for cash. A closed-end trust, by contrast, does not permit new money to be invested, nor can shares be redeemed by the company. Thus, the number of shares remains the same once the trust begins trading. One feature of the closed-end trust is worth mentioning: they often sell at a discount to their asset value. An open-end trust always sells at precisely its asset value.

Common Stocks

We might as well define what a common stock is, since this whole book is devoted to them. All publicly owned companies—those that trade their shares outside of a small group of executives or the founding family—are based on common stocks. A common stock is evidence of partial ownership in a corporation. Most of the stocks described in this book have millions of shares of their stock outstanding, and the really large ones may have in excess of 100 million shares. When you own common stock, there are no guarantees. If the company is successful, it will probably pay a dividend four times a year. These dividends may be raised periodically, perhaps once a year. If, however, the company has problems, it may cut or eliminate its dividend. This can happen even to a major company, such as IBM, Goodyear, or General Motors. As I said, there are no guarantees.

Investors who own common stock can sell their shares at any time. All you do is call your broker, and the trade is executed a few minutes later at the prevailing price—which fluctuates nearly every day, sometimes by a few cents or sometimes two or three points.

Current Ratio

The current ratio is calculated by dividing current assets by current liabilities. Current assets include any assets that will become cash within one year, including cash itself. Current liabilities are those that will be paid off within a year. A current ratio of 2 is considered ideal. Most companies these days have a current ratio of less than 2.

Diversification

Since investments are inherently risky, it pays to spread the risk by diversifying. If you don't, you may be too heavily invested in a stock or bond that turns sour. Even well-known stocks such as Alcoa, International

Paper, Eastman Kodak, and American Express can experience occasional sinking spells.

To be on the safe side, don't invest more than 5 percent of your portfolio in any one stock. In addition, don't invest too heavily in any one sector of the economy. A good strategy is to divide stocks among twelve sectors: basic industries, capital goods/technology, capital goods, consumer growth, consumer cyclical, consumer staples, credit cyclical, financial, energy, transportation, utilities, and conglomerates.

Here's a rule of thumb that will keep you out of trouble: Invest at least 4 percent in each sector but not more than 12 percent. That means that you should own at least twelve stocks so that you have representation in all twelve sectors.

Dividends

Unlike bonds, common stocks may pay a dividend. Bonds pay interest. Most dividends are paid quarterly, but there is no set date that all corporations use. Some, for instance, may pay January 1, March 1, July 1, and September 1. Another company may pay February 10, May 10, August 10, and November 10. If you want to receive checks every month, you will have to make sure you buy stocks that pay dividends at different times of the year. The Standard & Poor's *Stock Guide* is a source for this information, as is the *Value Line Survey*. Most companies like to pay the same dividend every quarter until they can afford to increase it. Above all, they don't like to cut their dividends, since investors who depend on this income will sell their shares, and the stock will decline in price. If you use good judgment in selecting your stocks, you can expect that your companies will increase their dividends nearly every year.

Dividend Payout Ratio

If a company earns $4 per share in a given year and pays out $3 to its shareholders, it has a payout ratio of 75 percent. If it pays out only $1, the payout ratio is 25 percent. A low payout ratio is preferred, since it means that the company is plowing back its profits into future growth.

The Dividend Reinvestment Plan

Unless you are retired, you might like to reinvest your dividends in more shares. Many companies have a dividend reinvestment plan (also known as a DRIP) that will allow you to do this, and the charge for this service is often minimal. Most of these companies also allow you to mail in additional cash, which will be used to purchase new shares, again at minimal cost.

In recent years, a few companies have created "direct" dividend reinvestment plans. Unlike most plans, direct plans enable you to buy your initial shares directly from the company. To alert you to which companies have direct plans, I have inserted the word *direct*. Companies having such plans include ExxonMobil, McDonald's, Procter & Gamble, Merck, and Lilly. Incidentally, you can rarely buy just one share. Many companies have a minimum amount, such as $500.

This may sound like a good way to avoid paying brokerage commissions, but there are some drawbacks to bear in mind. For one thing, you can't time your purchases, since it may be a week or more before your purchase is made.

Even worse is calculating your cost basis for tax purposes. By the time you sell, you may have made scores of small investments in the same stock, each with a different cost basis. Make sure you keep a file for each company so that you can make these calculations when the time comes. Or, better still, don't sell.

Dollar Cost Averaging

Dollar cost averaging is a systematic way to invest money over a long period, such as ten, fifteen, or twenty years. It entails investing the same amount of money regularly, such as each month or each quarter. If you do this faithfully, you will be buying more stock when the price is lower, and less stock when the price is higher. This tends to smooth out the gyrations of the market. Dollar cost averaging is often used with a mutual fund, but it can just as easily be done with a company that has a dividend reinvestment plan (DRIP).

Hedge Fund

In some respects, hedge funds are similar to mutual funds, but there are significant differences. For one thing, the minimum investment may be $1 million or more. More recently, these stiff entrance barriers have been whittled down in a few instances to as low as $50,000.

The manager of a hedge fund is typically permitted to employ strategies forbidden to a traditional mutual fund, including borrowing money, selling short, or using options. A hedge fund has an appeal to speculative investors, since the gains can be impressive—assuming you are willing to put up with extra risk.

According to Donna Rosato, writing for *The New York Times*, "There are nearly 6,000 hedge funds worldwide, up from 880 a decade ago. Investors poured $144 billion into the funds in 2001, pushing assets up to $563 billion, 38 percent above the total of the previous year, according to a Hennessee Group survey.

"As more investors turn to hedge funds, so do money managers in pursuit of more lucrative pay. Hedge fund managers often earn at least 20 percent of portfolio gains above a specified minimum, perhaps 8 percent. In contrast, most mutual fund managers do not receive performance fees and charge an average of 0.5 percent to 1 percent in annual management fees."

Ms. Rosato goes on to say, "Managers

of hedge funds have more flexibility than many of their mutual fund counterparts to use techniques like short-selling, leverage, and derivatives to profit in both rising and falling markets. Hedge funds can seek safety in cash; many mutual funds, by contrast, are required to keep a certain portion of assets invested at all times."

Income Statement

Most investors are more interested in the income statement than they are in the balance sheet. They are particularly interested in the progress (or lack of it) in earnings per share (EPS). The income statement lists such items as net sales, cost of sales, interest expense, and gross profit. As with the balance sheet, it makes sense to compare this year's numbers with those of the prior year.

Inflation-Indexed Treasury Bonds

Conventional bonds—those that pay a fixed rate of return, such as 5 percent—have one big drawback: They are vulnerable to rising interest rates. For example, if you buy a bond that promises to pay you 5 percent for the next fifteen or twenty years, you will lose principal if interest rates climb to 7 percent. The reason is that new bonds being issued give investors a much better return. Thus, those that pay only 5 percent will sag in price until they hit a level that equates them to the new bonds that pay 7 percent. The loss of principal, moreover, is much greater with long-term bonds, such as those due in fifteen, twenty, or thirty years.

By contrast, short-term bonds, those coming due in three or four years, are much less volatile because you can often hold the bonds until the maturity date. Thus, you are certain to receive the full face value. Of course, you can do the same thing with a twenty-year bond, but twenty years is a long time.

The way to beat this disadvantage is

to buy the relatively new bonds being issued by the U.S. government, since they are indexed to inflation. For this reason, you are unlikely to lose principal. To be sure, they pay less initially, currently 3.8 percent. But the ultimate return may be much better if inflation continues to impact the economy.

Suppose you invested $1,000 in inflation bonds at the current yield of 3.8 percent. If consumer prices rose 2.5 percent over the next year, your principal would climb to $1,025, and you would earn interest equal to 3.8 percent on this growing sum. Thus, if you spent the interest but didn't cash in any bonds, you would enjoy a rising stream of income while keeping your principal's spending power intact.

One thing to bear in mind: With inflation-indexed Treasury bonds, you have to pay federal income taxes each year on both the interest you earn and also the increase in the bonds' principal value. One way to take the sting out of this tax is to use these bonds in a tax-deferred account, such as an IRA.

Despite the tax implications, inflation bonds may be useful outside an IRA. Because these bonds don't perform as erratically as conventional bonds, they can be a good place to park money you may need if something unexpected comes along, such as a medical bill not fully covered by insurance. If inflation-indexed bonds ring a bell, ask the teller at your bank to get you started. She won't charge you a fee, and there is no red tape.

Investment Advisor

Investors who do not have the time or inclination to manage their own portfolios may elect to employ an investment advisor. Most advisors charge 1 percent a year. Thus, if you own stocks worth $300,000, your annual fee would be $3,000. Advisors differ from brokers,

since they do not profit from changes. Brokers, by contrast, charge a commission on each transaction, which means they profit from changes in your portfolio. Advisors profit only when the value of your holdings increases. For instance, if the value of your portfolio increases to $500,000, the annual fee will be $5,000. You, of course, will be $200,000 richer.

Moving Average

Some investors use the moving average to time the market. The strategy is to buy a stock when it is selling above its moving average and selling when it falls below. A popular moving average is the 200-day version. A dotted line is drawn, taking the average price of the stock over the previous 200 days. The actual price of the stock is plotted on the same graph. Studies show that this method of timing the market does not work on a consistent basis.

PEG Ratio

The PEG ratio is supposed to be helpful in determining if a stock is too expensive. It is calculated by dividing the price-earnings ratio by the expected earnings growth rate. Let's say the P/E ratio of American International Group is 34.39, which is calculated by dividing the price ($98) by the expected EPS in 2001 of $2.85. Meanwhile, the earnings per share in the 1989–1999 period expanded from $0.67 to $2.18, a compound annual growth rate of 12.52 percent. When you divide 34.39 by 12.52, the PEG ratio is 2.75. According to Michael Sivy, a writer for Money magazine, "Stocks with a PEG ratio of 1.5 or less are often the best buys."

By that rule, you would avoid American International Group. Curiously, Mr. Sivy includes AIG on his list of "100 Stocks for Long-Term Investors," published in January 2001. By his calculation, AIG had a PEG ratio at that time of 2.5.

Once again, I am a doubting Thomas. Who is to say what a company's future growth rate will be? You can easily determine what it has been in the past. And that may give you some indication of the future, but it is far from reliable. The P/E ratio is also a slippery number, since you are expected to base it on the EPS for the year ahead. I prefer to base it on the most recent twelve months, since that is a figure that does not depend on a crystal ball.

Preferred Stock

The name sounds impressive. In actual practice, owning preferred stocks is about as exciting as watching your cat take a bath. A preferred stock is much like a bond. It pays the same dividend year in and year out. The yield is usually higher than a common stock. If the company issuing the preferred stock does well, you do not benefit. If it does poorly, however, you may suffer, since the dividend could be cut or eliminated. My advice is: Never, never buy a preferred stock.

Price–Earnings Ratio (P/E)

This is a term that is extremely important. Don't make the mistake of overlooking it. Whole books have been written on the importance of the P/E ratio, which is sometimes referred to as "the P/E" or "the multiple."

The P/E ratio tells you whether a stock is cheap or expensive. It is calculated by dividing the price of the stock by the company's earnings per share over the most recent 12 months. For instance, if you refer to the Stock Guide, you will see that Leggett and Platt had earnings of $2.23. At the time, the stock was selling for $52. Divide that figure by $2.23 and you get a P/E of 23.32.

In most instances, a low P/E indicates a stock that Wall Street is not too excited about. If they like a stock, they will bid it up to the point where its P/E is quite high,

let's say twenty-five or thirty. Coca-Cola is such a stock. In this same Stock Guide, Coca-Cola had annual earnings per share of $1.59. Based on the price of the stock at that time (it was $75), that works out to a P/E ratio of 47.17. Of course, Coca-Cola is extremely well regarded by investors and is expected to do well in the future—but is it really worth forty-seven times earnings?

Stock Split

Corporations know that investors like to invest in lower-priced stocks. Thus, when the price of the stock gets to a certain level, which varies with the company, they will split the stock. For instance, if the stock is $75, they might split it three-for-one. Your original 100 shares now become 300 shares. Unfortunately, your 300 shares are worth exactly the same as your original 100 shares. What it amounts to is this: Splits please small investors, but they don't make them any richer. One company, Berkshire Hathaway, has never been split. It is now worth a huge amount per share: over $60,000. It also pays no dividend. The company is run by the legendary Warren Buffett. He has made a lot of people very wealthy without a stock split or dividend.

Technician

There are two basic ways to analyze stocks. One is *fundamental*; the other is *technical*.

Fundamental analysts examine a stock's management, sales and earnings potential, research capabilities, new products, competitive strength, balance sheet strength, dividend growth, political developments, and industry conditions.

Technicians, by contrast, rarely consider any of these fundamental factors. They rely on charts and graphs and a host of other arcane statistical factors, such as point-and-figure charts, breadth indicators, head-and-shoulders formations, relative strength ratings, and the 200-day-moving average. This technical jargon is often difficult to fathom for the average investor. Among professional portfolio managers, the fundamental approach predominates, although some institutions may also employ a technician.

The question is: Do technicians have the key to stock picking or predicting the trend of the market? Frankly, I am a skeptic, as are most academic analysts. Among the nonbelievers is Kenneth L. Fisher, the longtime columnist for *Forbes* magazine who I mentioned earlier. His columns are among my favorites. Here is what Mr. Fisher says about technicians. "One of the questions I hear most often is, 'Can charts really predict stock prices?' Naturally, there is only one answer: a flat 'No.'"

Mr. Fisher goes on to say: "There is virtually nothing in theory or empiricism to indicated anyone can predict stock prices based solely on prior stock price action. Nevertheless, a big world of chartists continues to exist, amplified by recent Internet day trading. Yet the world of investors with long-lasting success is devoid of them."

Such eminently successful portfolio managers as Peter Lynch and Warren Buffett, for instance, don't resort to charts and other technical mumbo jumbo.

Yield

If your company pays a dividend, you can relate this dividend to the price of the stock in order to calculate the yield. A $50 stock that pays a $2 annual dividend (which amounts to 50 cents per quarter) will have a yield of 4 percent. You arrive at this figure by dividing $2 by $50. Actually, you don't have to make this calculation, since the yield is given to you in the stock tables of the *Wall Street Journal*. Here are some typical yields from mid-2001. Coca-Cola, 1.5 percent; ExxonMobil, 2.0 percent; General Electric, 1.3 percent; Illinois Tool Works, 1.2 percent; Kimberly-Clark, 1.8 percent; and Minnesota Mining and Manufacturing, 2.0 percent. Although the yield is of some importance, you should not judge a stock by its yield without looking at many other factors.

Some Good News about IRAs

When the phone rang on Sunday evening at 9:30, I wondered who could be calling me at such an ungodly hour. It was none other than Harris Tottle, one of my fans in Oregon.

"Is this the famous John Slatter?"

"Who is this?"

"My name is Harris Tottle. I'm calling from Oregon. I just finished reading your great book, and I have a few questions."

"Before you go any further, Mr. Tottle, this is Sunday evening in Vermont, and I'm watching a good movie on television. I would be happy to talk with you any weekday during business hours. Could you call back then?"

"I only have a few questions, Mr. Slatter. I really need your erudite and sapient advice. Okay?"

"I'm sorry, but I don't want to continue."

"Here's my first question. It concerns my IRA."

I hung up the phone and went back to my program. I didn't even say goodbye. I was surprised when Harris Tottle called me again the following Wednesday afternoon. It must have been the noon hour in Oregon.

"Hi, Mr. Slatter. This is Harris Tottle, your pertinacious admirer from Oregon. Let me apologize for calling you Sunday evening. Here in Oregon it was still daylight, so I figured it would be okay. I'm really interested in getting your sagacious thoughts on my IRA, since your book didn't have any information. How come you left it out?"

"I'm rather surprised that you called back, Mr. Tottle. I think I hung up on you the last time you called. I guess I must

have been in a foul mood. Sorry about that. My book concentrates on how to buy stocks, Mr. Tottle. I am not a financial planner, so I rarely cover subjects on personal finance or those that don't pertain to stocks and portfolio strategy. In other words, I don't have a CFP designation. However, I am quite familiar with IRAs, since my wife and I both have one—well stocked with common stocks, of course. As you may have found out, the IRA sphere is really getting complicated. There are now six versions, which I don't have time to go into in any detail. Each has its own rules. If you have a pen, here they are:

- Deductible
- Nondeductible
- Roth
- Rollover
- Simple
- SEP

"What's your next question?"

"I've heard that Congress passed a new law a couple years ago, the Tax Relief Act of 2001," said Mr. Tottle. "In their infinite wisdom and altruism, they increased the amount you can invest in an IRA each year. Do you have any numbers that you can share with me?"

"According to the new law," I said, "the amount you can contribute to a traditional deductible and traditional nondeductible IRA and Roth IRA was increased in 2002 to $3,000 each year. In 2005 through 2007, this amount jumps to $4,000, and once again for 2008, to $5,000. That's the good news. The bad news is that the act is scheduled to expire after 2010, at which time it reverts back to pre-Tax Act status."

"Thanks, that takes care of that item.

Next, I have been told by an insurance agent that I should invest in a variable annuity with the extra cash I have sitting in my IRA. Somehow, that strikes me as a bit fishy. It sounds as though he wants to deracinate me. What do you think, Mr. Slatter?"

"I've heard that complaint many times before. According to Rick Bloom, a fee-based financial advisor and money manager who writes for *The Detroit News*, 'A variable annuity never belongs within an IRA. The reason is that you pay extra administrative fees on a year-by-year basis, and they are unnecessary. You pay fees to receive tax deferral. Since this is already within an IRA, you already have tax deferral, and thus you are paying for nothing except a modest death benefit. In addition, you are limiting your investment options unnecessarily.'

"And Mr. Bloom is not the only writer who tells people to avoid this grievous blunder. I happened to have a column written by Avrum D. Lank who writes for the *Milwaukee Journal Sentinel*. Here's what he has to say, 'Annuities are life insurance products designed to hold stocks, bonds and mutual funds, while deferring taxes on the dividends, interest and capital gains they earn. The management fees and projected returns of annuities take the value of this deferral into account. But taxes are already deferred on the earnings of any stock, bond or mutual fund you put in an IRA, so it makes little sense to pay extra for the same features in an annuity. Unlike a CD sold by a bank, there is no federal deposit insurance on an annuity.'"

"This phone call will cost me a fortune, but I think you are giving me some great advice, even though you don't have many fancy degrees. Here's another question: Can you give me a brief rundown on the Roth IRA?"

"I don't have one myself, but they make a lot of sense for some people. However, bear in mind that if you are filthy rich, you can't contribute to one. You are out of this ball game if your annual family adjusted gross income is over $160,000."

"Keep going—that's not me," Harris Tottle said.

"In my opinion, if you are eligible to open a Roth IRA, it should be near the top of your list of savings options. Of course, you must be aware that the funds you put in a Roth IRA are not deductible. On the other hand, you can withdraw money tax free if the plan is at least five years old and you are at least age fifty-nine and a half. And there is no tax or penalty to worry about. When you get down to it, the Roth IRA makes a great emergency fund. This helps make up for the nondeductible feature. More important, you can take money out when you retire with no tax to pay. By contrast, a withdrawal from a traditional IRA is taxed as if it were ordinary income—even if you are retired and regardless of age."

"I think my time is about up, since this is my lunch hour—and my boss can turn ugly when I try to stretch it beyond the one-hour mark. I want to thank you for your help, Mr. Slatter."

When our conversation was about to close, I said, "Whenever I talk to someone, I usually ask them why they bought my book. After all, Borders or Barnes & Noble have scores of books on the stock market."

"To tell you the truth, Mr. Slatter, I didn't actually *buy* your book. Nathan Forrest Bedford, a local librarian, recommended it to me. According to the indefatigable librarian, *The 100 Best Stocks You Can Buy* is the best investment book he's aware of. So I simply checked it out and read it with great alacrity. You really have a way of explaining the stock market so that even a rank novice like me can understand it."

"You've made my day, Mr. Tottle. Since you liked the book so much, I'm wondering if you might do me a favor and buy a few copies and give them as birthday presents to your friends and relatives?"

The line went dead. That's the last I ever heard of Mr. Harris Tottle of Oregon. What a pity.

Without doubt, my buddy from the West Coast was right about my omitting a rundown on the realm of the IRAs. In case you are still with me, here are a few more tidbits on the subject. Unfortunately, Harris Tottle didn't stay around long enough to take advantage of this extra lore. However, assuming Nathan Forrest Bedford tells him about the 2003 edition, he will find out eventually when the new edition pops up on his library shelf.

The Tax-Deferral Feature Really Counts

For starters, using an IRA, rather than a taxable brokerage account, makes a lot of sense because of its tax-shelter feature. Let's assume you set aside $3,000 each year (the 2002 maximum, if under age fifty), here is how much your IRA will be worth, assuming you are in a 27 percent tax bracket. Let's also assume your plan earns an average of 7 percent per year. This may appear to be on the low side, in view of the great returns of the past couple of decades. However, there are people (Warren Buffet, for one) who think it is unrealistic to expect a repeat of that fabulous period.

In an IRA in a Taxable Account

Years Invested	IRA	Taxable Account
5 years	$18,459	$17,426
10 years	$44,351	$39,710
15 years	$80,664	$68,204
20 years	$131,595	$104,639
30 years	$303,219	$210,806

To be sure, these numbers don't take into account the taxes you will have to pay on withdrawals from a non-Roth account when you tell the boss to jump in the lake—you've had enough of the rat race. That will depend on your tax bracket during retirement, as well as the tax structure in effect at that time. On the other hand, the Roth IRA keeps your investments from the clutches of the IRS, regardless of tax brackets and IRS policy—assuming Congress doesn't stab you in the back with a new twist on the Roth IRA sometime in the next twenty or thirty years.

What to Put into Your IRA

Some people use CDs or mutual funds. Based on my aversion to these two investments, you should not be surprised that I favor common stocks. In the early years, it will not be possible to achieve adequate diversification. After all, if your account is worth $3,000, or even $6,000, you can't buy shares in twenty or thirty different stocks. Your commissions would be far too high.

In any event, broad diversification is not necessary if you are only thirty-five or forty years of age. You have plenty of time to build a portfolio, one stock at a time. If you start your program at age forty, for instance, and buy one stock a year, you will have twenty-five lusty stocks by age sixty-five.

Should Bonds Be in Your IRA?

One other thing you may wonder about. Assuming you have a few bonds to cushion the ups and downs of the market, should they be in the IRA or in a taxable account? Some so-called experts recommend putting bonds in the tax shelter, so you won't have to keep the IRS happy. They contend that common stocks should be outside, since most don't pay very hefty dividends. That sounds like good sense, but I beg to differ.

It is true that stocks are not handing out very generous dividends these days, but they do promise handsome capital gains. If you buy a stock for $40 a share today and it climbs to $120 in the next five or ten years, you may decide to sell and switch to another budding winner. If that stock is in your IRA, there will be no tax to pay—and it could be substantial. In a taxable account, you will be reluctant to sell, not wanting to pay the IRS its pound of flesh. Too many investors fail to sell a stock because they don't want to pay the tax. In an IRA, by contrast, you won't be inhibited.

Which IRA Is Better?

Taxes are a key factor in deciding which IRA you should own. If you are in a high bracket now and expect to be in a lower one when you retire, the traditional IRA makes sense if you are eligible for a tax deduction when you make your contribution. If, however, you think your tax bracket will be the same or higher than it is now, then the Roth will work better. If you can't make up your mind, there is no reason why you can't split the difference and have one of each. In that event, your total annual contribution is still limited to $3,000, or whatever the maximum is at the time you invest.

What to Expect When You Retire

If you have the old-fashioned IRA that gave you an initial tax deduction, you will pay the income taxes when you reach seventy-and-a-half years of age. The government insists that you start taking assets out. It's up to you as to which assets will be withdrawn. It can be cash, bonds, stock, or any combination thereof. But you will be taxed on the entire amount withdrawn (reduced by a portion of any nondeductible

contributions) as if it were ordinary income.

In the past, the amount that you had to take out was based on a formula relating to your life expectancy or that of you and your beneficiary. It was a bit complicated, and you had some choices. Now, as of 2002, the whole ball game is changed—fortunately to your benefit. Not everyone was happy with the old arrangement, since the amount withdrawn might have been more than you really needed. The new numbers will make you happy, since you can stretch out your payments and thus take out a smaller amount each year.

The shift in life expectancy rules is substantial. For a seventy-year old man, for instance, life expectancy is now stretched out to 26.2 years, as compared with sixteen years under the old rules. And each year the man lives, the expectancy is adjusted, so if he takes minimum distributions every year, he never runs out of money.

Here's an example: For a person seventy-five years old and not married, the old rules required you to withdraw $80,000 if your IRA was worth a million dollars at that time. The new rules have whittled this down to $45,872. You may find it hard to believe that the publicans in Washington have actually done you a favor.

Please note: To ensure accuracy, I asked three experts to view my comments on IRAs. Two were lawyers, one a CPA. Two preferred to remain anonymous, but not the one named below:

Glenn A. Jarrett, Esq., CFP
Unsworth Powell Barra Orr &
    Bredice PLC
Essex Junction, Vermont

Some Simple Formulas for Asset Allocation

Serious investors spend a lot of time deciding which stocks or mutual funds to buy. I can't quarrel with that. If you are going to invest $10,000 in Merck, Illinois Tool Works, Praxair, Leggett & Platt, or United Technologies, you shouldn't do it without some research and thought.

On the other hand, some financial gurus maintain that it is far more important to make an effort to achieve an effective approach to asset allocation. They believe that you should place your emphasis on how much of your portfolio is invested in such sectors as:

Government bonds
Corporate bonds
Municipal bonds
Convertible bonds
Preferred stocks
Large-capitalization domestic stocks
Small-capitalization domestic stocks
Foreign stocks
Foreign bonds
Certificates of deposit
Annuities
Money-market funds

There are probably a few other categories you could include in your portfolio, but I think that examining this list gives you an idea of what is meant by asset allocation.

To illustrate the importance of asset allocation, look at 1998. You may recall that the long bull market temporarily aborted in mid-July of that year. Prior to that time, the big blue chip stocks had been making heady progress. Beneath the surface, however, the small and medium-size stocks were already in their own bear market. Thus, if you had avoided these smaller companies in the first six months of 1998, you would have sidestepped the devastation that was taking place in this sector.

After mid-July, however, the big stocks—particularly the financial stocks such as J. P. Morgan, Travelers (now Citigroup), and American Express—took a real tumble. The best place to be during this period was in U.S. government bonds. Once again, we are talking about asset allocation and how it can help or hurt you.

My Approach to Asset Allocation

From the comments made so far, you can see that asset allocation, like everything else in the world of finance, can get rather complex and confusing. It is no wonder that many people don't delve into this arcane realm. That's where John Slatter comes to the rescue. My idea of investing is to make it simple. After all, there are just so many hours in the day. If you are still gainfully employed, you probably work eight hours a day making a living. In the evenings, you may spend a few hours a week reading journals and other material so that you don't get fired. Obviously, that doesn't leave much time for studying the stock market.

For my part, I don't invest in many small-cap stocks, foreign stocks, bonds, convertibles, preferred stocks, or most of the other stuff on my list. I prefer to invest mostly in big-cap stocks (such as ExxonMobil, GE, Merck, IBM, Procter & Gamble, and Johnson & Johnson) and money-market funds (a safe alternative to cash).

This reduces my categories to two, not a dozen. All you have to do is decide what percentage of your portfolio is in stocks. The rest is in a money-market fund. Of course, the *percentage* is vitally important.

A Few Alternatives to Consider

Some people may be shocked that I am not concerned about foreign stocks. One firm I once worked for insisted that we strive to invest 20 percent of each investor's portfolio in foreign stocks, such as Schlumberger, Repsol, Royal Dutch Petroleum, British Telecommunications, or Elf Aquitaine.

I have no objection to such stocks, but I see no urgency to adhere to a rigid percentage. For one thing, foreign stocks are more difficult to research. Their annual reports are far less revealing than those put out by corporations here at home. They also have different and less informative accounting.

In any event, the United States has hundreds of great companies. We are the envy of the world when it comes to business. The Japanese—at least for a decade or two—tried to convince people otherwise. But they have spent that last several years wallowing in a serious recession.

As far as bonds are concerned, they don't have a particularly impressive record. Except for a year here or there, common stocks have always been a better place to be. What's more, the return on bonds today is not much better than the rate you can get on a money-market fund.

One more thing: Bonds, even U.S. Treasuries, have an element of risk; they decline in value when interest rates go up. Long-term bonds, moreover, slide precipitously when rates shoot up.

I don't want to spend too much time discussing the shortcomings of the rest of the list. I would prefer to point out the virtues of major stocks, such as McDonald's, Wal-Mart, Hewlett-Packard, Caterpillar, Boeing, Alcoa, Eli Lilly, 3M Company, and Walt Disney.

Blue chip companies are not likely to go bankrupt. To be sure, they have their troubles, but they are big enough to hire a CEO who can bring them back to life. Among the thirty companies in the Dow Jones Industrial Average, for instance, such companies as IBM, Eastman Kodak, AT&T, Sears, United Technologies, and AlliedSignal were restructured in recent years by a few dynamic executives.

Major corporations are also found in most institutional portfolios such as mutual funds, pension plans, bank trust departments, and insurance companies. One reason they like these big-capitalization stocks is liquidity. Since institutions have huge amounts of cash to invest, they feel comfortable with these stocks. The reason: The number of shares outstanding is huge, which means they won't disturb the market when they buy or sell. By contrast, if a major institution tries to invest a million dollars in a tiny Nasdaq company, the stock will shoot up several points before they complete their investing. It could be just as disruptive when they try to get out. As a consequence, major companies are in demand and are not left to drift. On the other hand, there are thousands of small companies that no one ever heard of. The only investors who can push them up are individuals—not institutions.

Another reason I like big companies is because they can afford to hire top-notch executives and they have the resources to allocate to research and marketing. In addition, their new products, acquisitions, management changes, and strategies are discussed frequently in such publications as the *Wall Street Journal*, the *New York Times, Barron's, Fortune, Forbes*, and *BusinessWeek*, all of which I subscribe to.

How Much Should You Invest in Stocks?

When it comes to deciding on the percentage you should devote to common stocks, there are several alternatives that should be considered. All have some merit, and none are perfect.

In fact, there is no such thing as a perfect formula for asset allocation. It depends on such factors as your age and your temperament. It might also depend on what you think the market is going to do. If it's about to soar, you would want to be fully invested. But if you think stocks are poised to fall off a cliff, you might prefer to seek the safety of a money-market fund.

Forget about Everything Else and Buy Only Stocks

Believe it or not, there are some investors who are convinced that common stocks—and common stocks alone—are the royal road to riches. A good friend of mine has never bought anything but stocks, and he's been doing it for many years. He even went through the severe bear market of 1973–1974, when stocks plunged over 40 percent. He wasn't exactly happy to see his stocks being ground to a pulp, but he hung on. Today, he is a millionaire many times over. He's now sixty years old, still a comparatively young investor. His name is David A. Seidenfeld, a businessman in Cleveland.

Dave got his start by listening to the late S. Allen Nathanson, a savvy investor who wrote a series of magazine articles on why common stocks are the best way to achieve great wealth. Dave Seidenfeld recently collected these essays and published them as a hardcover book, *Bullishly Speaking*, which is available in bookstores.

If you start investing early, such as in your forties, this method can work. If you systematically invest, setting aside 10 or 15 percent of your earnings each year and doing it through thick and thin, you won't need any bonds, money-market funds, or any of the other alternatives that financial magazines seem to think you must have. You will arrive at retirement with a large portfolio that will enable you to live off the dividends.

However, if you arrived late to the investment party—let's say in your late fifties or early sixties—you may not be able to sleep too well if you rely entirely on common stocks. After all, stocks have their shortcomings, too. They tend to bounce around a lot, and they can cut their dividends when things turn bleak.

Some Options to Consider

If you are an ultraconservative investor, I suggest you invest only 55 percent of your portfolio in common stocks. To be sure, when the stock market is marching ahead, as it has in recent years, you won't be able to keep pace. But if it falters and heads south for a year or two, your cautious approach will keep you out of the clutches of insomnia. Frankly, I don't think such a timid approach is the best way to approach asset allocation. However, I worked for a firm a few years ago that used this formula on nearly everyone. As far as I know, there weren't too many people complaining.

A better way to handle the uncertainty is to invest 70 percent in stocks, with the rest in a money-market fund. Once you decide on a particular percentage, stick with it. Don't change it every time someone makes a market forecast. These market forecasts don't work often enough to pay any attention to them. To my knowledge, no professional investor has a consistent record in forecasting. Every once in a while, one of these pundits makes a correct call at a crucial turning point, and from that day on, every one listens intently to the pronouncements of this person—until the day the pronouncement is totally wrong. That day always comes.

My Favorite Formula for Asset Allocation

I think age is the key to asset allocation. The older you are, the less you should have in common stocks. If you are age sixty-five, you should have sixty-five percent in common stocks, with the rest in a money-market fund. If you are younger than sixty-five, add 1 percent per year to your common stock sector. As an example, if you are sixty years old, you will have seventy percent in stocks.

If you are older than sixty-five, deduct 1 percent a year. Thus, if you are age seventy, you will have only 60 percent in stock. When you reach eighty, you will be 50–50. And if you are much younger than sixty-five, let's say forty-five, you will have 85 percent in stocks.

If you are not sure what this all means, here is a table breaking down the two percentages by age:

Age	Stocks	Money-Market Funds
40	90%	10%
45	85	15
50	80	20
55	75	25
60	70	30
65	65	35
70	60	40
75	55	45
80	50	50
85	45	55

Part II

100 Best Stocks You Can Buy

The following table lists the 100 stocks discussed in this book along with a brief description of each.

The ticker symbol is given so that you can easily look up the stock on the Internet or so you can use the quote machine in your broker's office. If you call your broker on the phone, it makes it easier if you know the ticker symbol, since your broker may not.

In the table, "Industry" refers to one of the company's main businesses. This is not always easy to express in one or two words.

For instance, United Technologies is involved in such industries as aircraft engines, elevators, and air conditioning equipment. To describe the company succinctly, I arbitrarily picked the designation, "aircraft engines."

Similarly, General Electric presents an even more daunting problem since it owns NBC and makes appliances, aircraft engines, medical devices, and a host of other things.

The designation "Sector" indicates the broad economic industry group that the company operates in, such as Transportation, Capital Goods, Energy, Consumer Cyclicals, and so forth. As described elsewhere, a properly diversified portfolio should include at least one stock in each of the twelve sectors. However, I see no problem in having stocks in nine or ten sectors.

"Category" refers to one of the following: Income (Income); Growth & Income (Gro Inc); Conservative Growth (Con Grow) or Aggressive Growth (Aggr Gro). As above, it might make sense to have some representation in each category, even though you have a strong preference for only one.

I have not included the page numbers because of space limitations. In any event, it is easy enough to find a particular stock, since they appear alphabetically in the book.

Company	Symbol	Industry	Sector	Category
—A—				
Abbott Laboratories	ABT	Med Supplies	Cons Staples	Con Grow
Air Products	APD	Chemical	Basic Ind	Con Grow
Alberto-Culver	ACV	Cosmetics	Cons Staples	Con Grow
Alcoa	AA	Metals	Basic Ind	Aggr Gro
Altria Group (formerly Philip Morris)	MO	Tobacco	Cons Staples	Income
AmerisourceBergen *	ABC	Drug Service	Cons Staples	Aggr Gro
Anheuser-Busch *	BUD	Beer	Cons Staples	Con Grow
AvalonBay *	AVB	REIT	Financial	Income
Avery Dennison	AVY	Adhesives	Basic Ind	Con Grow
—B—				
Baldor Electric	BEZ	Elect Equip	Cap Goods	Gro Inc
Bank of New York	BK	Bank	Financial	Con Grow
Banta *	BN	Printing	Cons Services	Gro Inc
Baxter Int'l	BAX	Med Supplies	Cons Staples	Aggr Gro
Becton, Dickinson *	BDX	Med Supplies	Cons Staples	Con Grow
Bemis Company *	BMS	Packaging	Basic Ind	Con Grow

Block, H&R *	HRB	Income Tax	Financial	Con Grow
Boeing	BA	Aerospace	Cap Goods	Aggr Gro
Boston Properties	BXP	REIT	Financial	Income
BP p.l.c.	BP	Oil	Energy	Gro Inc
Bristol-Myers Squibb	BMY	Drugs	Cons Staples	Con Grow
—C—				
Cardinal Health	CAH	Health care	Cons Staples	Aggr Gro
Cedar Fair	FUN	Entertain.	Cons Staples	Income
Cintas *	CTAS	Uniforms	Cons Cyclical	Aggr Gro
Citigroup	C	Bank, Ins.	Financial	Con Grow
Clayton Homes	CMH	Housing Credit	Cyclic	Aggr Gro
Clorox	CLX	Household Pd	Cons Staples	Gro Inc
Coca-Cola	KO	Beverages	Cons Staples	Con Grow
Colgate-Palmolive	CL	Household Pd	Cons Staples	Con Grow
ConAgra	CAG	Food	Cons Staples	Income
Costco Wholesale	COST	Wholesale	Cons Cyclical	Aggr Gro
—D—				
Delphi Corporation	DPH	Automotive	Cons Cyclical	Con Grow
DeVry *	DV	Schools	Cons Services	Aggr Gro
Dominion Resources	D	Utility	Utilities	Income
Donaldson *	DCI	Filtration	Cap Goods	Con Grow
Duke Energy	DUK	Energy	Utilities	Gro Inc
DuPont	DD	Chemicals	Basic Ind	Gro Inc
—E—				
Eaton Vance *	EV	Mutual Funds	Financial	Con Grow
Ecolab *	ECL	Cleaning	Basic Ind	Aggr Gro
Elect. Data Syst.*	EDS	Comp Soft	Cap Goods-Tech	Con Grow
Emerson	EMR	Elect Equip	Cap Goods	Con Grow
Equity Office Properties	EOP	REIT	Financial	Income
Ethan Allen	ETH	Furniture	Credit Cyclical	Aggr Gro
ExxonMobil	XOM	Oil	Energy	Gro Inc
—F—				
FedEx Corporation	FDX	Air Freight	Transportation	Aggr Gro
Fortune Brands *	FO	Consumer Prod	Cons Cyclical	Gro Inc
—G—				
Gannett	GCI	Publishing	Cons Services	Con Grow
General Dynamics	GD	Defense	Cap Goods-Tech	Aggr Gro
General Electric	GE	Elect Equip	Cap Goods	Con Grow
General Motors	GM	Automobile	Cons Cyclical	Gro Inc
Goodrich *	GR	Aerospace	Conglomerate	Aggr Gro
—H—				
Health Care Prop *	HCP	REIT	Financial	Income
Home Depot *	HD	Hardware	Cons Cyclical	Aggr Gro
Hormel Foods *	HRL	Food	Cons Staples	Con Grow
—I—				
Illinois Tool Works	ITW	Machinery	Cap Goods	Con Grow
Intel	INTC	Computers	Cap Goods-Tech	Aggr Gro
Int'l Business Mach	IBM	Computer	Cap Goods-Tech	Aggr Gro
—J—				
Jefferson Pilot	JP	Insurance	Financial	Gro Inc
Johnson Controls	JCI	Elect Equip	Cap Goods	Con Grow
Johnson & Johnson	JNJ	Med Supplies	Cons Staples	Con Grow

—K—

Kimberly-Clark	KMB	Tissues	Basic Ind	Gro Inc
Kimco Realty	KIM	REIT	Financial	Income

—L—

Lilly, Eli	LLY	Drugs	Cons Staples	Aggr Gro
Lockheed Martin *	LMT	Aerospace	Cap Goods-Tech	Aggr Gro
Lowe's Companies	LOW	Retail	Credit Cycl	Con Grow
Lubrizol	LZ	Oil Additives	Basic Ind	Income

—M—

McCormick & Co.	MKC	Spices	Cons Staples	Con Grow
McGraw-Hill	MHP	Publishing	Cons Services	Con Grow
MDU Resources	MDU	G&E Utility	Utilities	Gro Inc
Medtronic	MDT	Med Devices	Cap Goods-Tech	Aggr Gro
Merck	MRK	Drugs	Cons Staples	Con Grow
Microsoft	MSFT	Comp Soft	Cap Goods-Tech	Aggr Gro
3M Company	MMM	Diversified	Cap Goods-Tech	Gro Inc

—N—

National City	NCC	Bank	Financial	Gro Inc
Nordson	NDSN	Machinery	Cap Goods	Con Grow

—P—

PepsiCo	PEP	Beverages	Cons Staples	Con Grow
Pfizer	PFE	Drugs	Cons Staples	Aggr Gro
Piedmont Nat'l Gas	PNY	Nat'l Gas	Utilities	Income
Pitney Bowes	PBI	Postage Mtrs	Cap Goods-Tech	Gro Inc
Praxair	PX	Indust Gases	Basic Ind	Con Grow
Procter & Gamble	PG	Household Pd	Cons Staples	Con Grow

—S—

Safeway	SWY	Grocery	Cons Staples	Aggr Gro
SBC Communications	SBC	Telephone	Utilities	Gro Inc
Sherwin-Williams *	SHW	Paint	Credit Cyclical	Gro Inc
Stryker	SYK	Medical Sup	Cons Staples	Aggr Gro
Sysco Corporation	SYY	Food Distrib.	Cons Staples	Con Grow

—T—

Target *	TGT	Retail	Cons Cyclical	Aggr Gro
Tenet Healthcare *	THC	Health Care	Cons Services	Aggr Gro

—U—

UnitedHealth *	UNH	Health Care	Cons Services	Con Grow
United Technologies	UTX	Aircraft Eng	Cap Goods-Tech	Con Grow

—V—

Varian Medical	VAR	Med Devices	Cap Goods-Tech	Aggr Gro
Vectren	VVC	Gas & Elect	Utilities	Gro Inc
Verizon	VZ	Telephone	Utilities	Gro Inc

—W—

Wachovia *	WB	Bank	Financial	Gro Inc
Walgreen	WAG	Drug stores	Cons Staples	Aggr Gro
Wal-Mart *	WMT	Retail	Cons Cyclical	Aggr Gro
Washington Real Est.	WRE	REIT	Financial	Income
Weingarten Realty *	WRI	REIT	Financial	Income
WellPoint Health *	WLP	Health Ins.	Financial	Aggr Gro
WGL Holdings	WGL	Natural Gas	Utilities	Income
Wyeth	WYE	Drugs	Cons Staples	Con Grow

* New in this edition.

CONSERVATIVE GROWTH

Abbott Laboratories

100 Abbott Park Road □ Abbott Park, Illinois 60064-6400 □ (847) 937-8945 □ Dividend reinvestment plan
is available: (847) 937-7300 □ Web site: www.abbott.com □ Ticker symbol: ABT □ S&P rating: A+ □ Value
Line financial strength rating: A++

In 2002, the Ross Products Division of Abbott Laboratories launched an infant formula supplemented with two fatty acids that function as nutritional building blocks in brain and eye development. The two fatty acids—docosahexaenoic acid (DHA) and arachidonic acid (ARA)—are found in small amounts in breast milk.

Internationally, Ross has been selling infant formula products supplemented with DHA and ARA for some time. With the 2002 approval by the Food and Drug Administration, Ross can now penetrate the domestic market with these two fatty acids supplements in order to make their formula more closely mimic breast milk.

"We are always listening to health care professionals and parents, and some of them have told us that because DHA and ARA are in breast milk, they want a Ross product supplemented with DHA and ARA," said Ann Bair, vice president, Infant Formula Marketing. "By introducing an additional Similac With Iron product with added DHA and ARA, we are responding to this request. Parents can be reassured that today's Similac With Iron supports visual and mental development like that of the breast-fed infant."

Ross Products has been a leader in infant nutrition for more than seventy years. Ross's Similac With Iron is the leading infant formula among physicians.

Company Profile

Abbott Laboratories is one of the largest diversified health care manufacturers in the world. The company's products are sold in more than 130 countries, with about 40 percent of sales derived from international operations. ABT has paid consecutive quarterly dividends since 1924.

Abbott's major business segments include Pharmaceuticals & Nutritionals (prescription drugs, medical nutritionals, and infant formulas) and Hospital & Laboratory Products (intravenous solutions, administrative sets, drug-delivery devices, and diagnostic equipment and reagents).

The company's leading brands are:

• AxSym systems and reagents (immunodiagnostics)
• Biaxin/Biaxin XL/Klalcid/Klaricid (macrolide antibiotic)
• Depakote (bipolar disorder; epilepsy; migraine prevention)
• Depakote ER (migraine prevention)
• Ensure (adult nutritionals)
• Isomil (soy-based infant formula)
• MediSense glucose monitoring products
• Similac (infant formula)
• Ultane/Sevorane (anesthetic)

Revenue growth in Abbott's infant formula and diagnostics businesses has slowed in recent years. However, new drugs (such as the antibiotic clarithromycin), new indications (including the BPH claim for Hytrin), the launch of disease-specific medical nutritionals, and cost cutting (diagnostics and hospital supplies) continue to boost the company's profits.

Shortcomings to Bear in Mind

■ In its biggest acquisition to date, Abbott

Laboratories bought the drug business of the German chemicals giant BASF AG for $6.9 billion in 2001. BASF's Knoll Pharmaceuticals has developed a promising rheumatoid arthritis treatment, a drug referred to as D2E7. Analysts believe it could be a blockbuster, with annual sales of $1 billion or more. The drug is expected to be commercially available in 2003.

Prior to the purchase of Knoll, Abbott had come under fire from analysts for not having a major blockbuster drug, either in the works or on the market. Its top-selling drug has been Depakote, which treats bipolar disorder and generates $700 million a year in annual sales. Abbott's joint venture with Takeda Chemical Industries benefits from more than $2 billion in annual sales of Prevacid, but Abbott splits those profits with its Japanese partner.

On a more negative note, not everyone is convinced that Abbott's acquisition of Knoll Pharmaceuticals was a wise move. According to Mark Tatge, writing for *Forbes Magazine*, "But does the $6.9-billion deal really make it a better company? It almost quintuples Abbott's debt and adds only $400 million to operating income."

Still another analyst, Carol Levenson, research director at Gimme Credit in Chicago, said, "If ever we've seen a defensive acquisition, surely this must be it. Presumably a company with $7.5 billion in debt looks less appetizing than one with $1.6 billion."

For its part, Standard & Poor's said in late 2001, "The shares moved higher in recent months, boosted by strength in leading medical products stocks and faster-than-expected integration of Knoll Pharmaceuticals. Despite initial dilution, Knoll should play an important role in fueling Abbott's projected robust EPS

growth over the coming years. Knoll is rejuvenating ABT's research and development pipeline with new drugs for arthritis and heart disease and should also provide aggregate cost savings of $500 million over the 2001–2003 period."

- In late 2001, *Value Line Survey* was less than enthusiastic about Abbott: "We think there are better investment alternatives in the health care sector. Prospective pressures on Prevacid are certainly a serious concern."

Reasons to Buy

- In financial strength, Abbott has an impressive showing:
  - Market capitalization: Ranked thirty-three out of 500 in the *Fortune* 500 largest domestic corporations.
  - Earnings growth: twenty-eight consecutive years of double-digit growth (excluding onetime event in 1999).
  - Dividend growth: 310 consecutive quarterly dividends since 1924 (double-digit yearly increases for the past twenty-six years).
  - Free cash flow: About $1 billion.
  - Profits: Ranked twenty-three out of 500 among *Fortune* 500 largest domestic corporations.
  - Return on revenue: Ranked twenty-three out of 500 among *Fortune* 500.
  - Return on shareholders' equity: Ranked thirty-eight in the *Fortune* 500.
- Abbott is the leader in rapid testing in both hospitals and doctors' offices. Abbott produces tests for strep, pregnancy, and a microbe that causes ulcers. The company's Determine test line is self-contained, low-cost, and easy to use. Since its acquisition of MediSense, Inc., in 1996, the company's blood glucose monitoring systems have been well received by diabetic patients.

- In a move to enhance its drug-discovery capabilities, Abbott Laboratories purchased a biotech firm in 2002. Researchers from the University of Illinois at Urbana–Champaign founded BioDisplay Technologies. BioDisplay has technology that enables Abbott to shorten the time it takes to discover new drugs. This technology enables scientists to express vast numbers of antibodies on the surface of a single yeast cell. Researchers then can create a library of a million different mutated antibodies in days—and then select the most promising ones. "The whole idea is to develop a way to pick a needle out of a haystack," said David Kranz, a biochemistry professor at the University of Illinois. "What we are trying to do is pull out the needle, or the best antibody, in the haystack. The haystack is all sorts of different antibodies."

- Like all pharmaceutical companies, Abbott has a host of drugs under investigation. Several of the promising cancer drugs are "noncytotoxic" agents with relatively benign side effects, unlike most chemotherapy drugs that cause adverse reactions such as hair loss and nausea. A number of these new experimental drugs are designed to create "the ability to live with cancer, not die from it, and to stabilize the disease," said Perry Nisen, Abbott's divisional vice president of Oncology Development.

    For instance, several Abbott oncology drugs target the process of angiogenesis, the tendency of a tumor to develop new blood vessels and a new blood supply. One promising drug, called ABT-510, appears to inhibit growth of bladder-cancer tumors. "It's the only angiogenesis inhibitor that I know of that shrinks tumors," Dr. Nisen said.

- In a 2002 move to bolster its line of genetic tests for detecting various types of cancers, Abbott acquired Vysis, Inc., a biotech company that produces tests that detect genetic changes in cells. Prior to the acquisition, Abbott's existing molecular diagnostic tests had been largely used for infectious diseases. "Not only does this help in the diagnosis of cancer, but also in selecting therapy," said Ed Michael, Abbott's vice president of Diagnostic Assays and Systems. "There are not a lot of real world examples where you have a diagnostic that is linked to the therapeutic."

Total assets: $23,298 million
Current ratio: 1.06
Common shares outstanding: 1,554 million
Return on 2001 shareholders' equity: 17.6%

		2001	2000	1999	1998	1997	1996	1995	1994
Revenues (millions)		16285	13746	13178	12513	11889	11018	10012	9156
Net income (millions)		1550	2786	2446	2334	2079	1874	1689	1517
Earnings per share		.99	1.78	1.57	1.50	1.32	1.18	1.06	.94
Dividends per share		.82	.76	.68	.60	.54	.48	.42	.38
Price	High	57.2	56.2	53.3	50.1	34.9	28.7	22.4	16.9
	Low	42.0	29.4	27.9	32.5	24.9	19.1	15.4	12.7

CONSERVATIVE GROWTH

Air Products and Chemicals, Inc.

7201 Hamilton Boulevard □ Allentown, PA 18195-1501 □ (610) 481-5775 □ Direct dividend reinvestment plan is available: (877) 322-4941 □ Web site: www.airproducts.com □ Listed: NYSE □ Fiscal year ends September 30 □ Ticker symbol: APD □ S&P rating: A- □ Value Line financial strength rating: B++

Air Products got its start in helium in the 1950s, when the federal government hired the company to extract this "noble gas" from natural gas deposits in the Midwestern United States—currently the world's main source of helium. Nearly fifty years later, Air Products is the world's leading helium producer.

Helium has the lowest melting and boiling point of any element. It is colorless, odorless, and noninflammable. Helium is used in light-air balloons and to make artificial "air" (with oxygen) for deep-sea divers. It is also used in welding, semiconductors, and lasers. In addition, liquid helium is used in cryogenics, a branch of physics that studies materials and effects at temperatures approaching absolute zero.

In fiscal 2000, the company tripled its processing capacity at its Liberal, Kansas, facility to more than one billion standard cubic feet per year.

The helium market is expected to expand by at least 6 percent per year, a rate that suggests Air Products will need another expansion in their Kansas complex about every two years. And by supplying helium to high-growth markets such as laser welding, semiconductor manufacturing, and fiber-optics manufacturing, Air Products is growing faster than the market. The company's KeepCOLD Cryogen Fill Services Program supplies more than 4,500 MRI customer sites around the world. Finally, Air Products owns Gardner Cryogenics, a world leader in manufacturing liquid helium and liquid hydrogen distribution and storage equipment.

Company Profile

Air Products and Chemicals, Inc., is a leading supplier of industrial gases and related equipment, specialty and intermediate chemicals, and environmental and energy systems. It has operations in thirty countries.

A diverse base of customers in manufacturing, process, and service industries use Air Products' industrial gas and chemical products.

In the environmental and energy businesses, Air Products and its affiliates own and operate facilities to reduce air and water pollution, dispose of solid waste, and generate electric power.

Industrial Gases

The markets served by the Air Products Industrial Gases operation include chemical processing, metals, oil and gas production, electronics, research, food, glass, health care, and pulp and paper. Principal products are industrial gases, such as nitrogen, oxygen, hydrogen, argon, and helium, as well as various specialty, cutting, and welding gases.

• APD is a world leader.

• Its products are essential in many manufacturing processes.

• Gases are produced by cryogenic, adsorption, and membrane technologies.

• They are supplied by tankers, on-site plants, pipelines, and cylinders.

• International sales, including the company's share of joint ventures, represent more than half of Air Products' gas revenues.

Chemicals

The markets served by the Air Products Chemicals operation include adhesives, agriculture, furniture, automotive products, paints and coatings, textiles, paper, and building products. Its principal products are emulsions, polyvinyl alcohol, polyurethane and epoxy additives, surfactants, amines, and polyurethane intermediaries.

- APD has a leadership position in over 80 percent of the markets served.
- Markets include a wide range of attractive, diversified end uses that reduce overall exposure to economic cycles.
- World-scale, state-of-the-art production facilities and process technology skills ensure consistent, low-cost products while enhancing long-term customer relationships.
- International sales, including exports to over 100 countries, represent about 40 percent of APD's business.

Environmental and Energy Systems

The markets served by Air Products Environmental and Energy Systems operation include solid waste disposal, electrical power generation, and air-pollution reduction.

- Facilities, owned and operated with partners, dispose of solid waste, reduce air pollution, and generate electrical power.
- Strong positions are built by extending core skills developed in the industrial gas business.
- Forces driving this market are environmental regulations, demand for efficient sources of electrical power, utility deregulation, and privatization. Principal products are waste-to-energy plants, electric power services, and air pollution-control systems.

Equipment and Services

The markets served by Air Products Equipment and Services operation include chemicals, steel, oil and gas recovery, and power generation.

- Cryogenic and noncryogenic equipment is designed and manufactured for various gas-processing applications.
- Equipment is sold worldwide or manufactured for Air Products industrial gas business and its international network of joint ventures.

Highlights of 2001

- Achieved record sales of $5.7 billion.
- Maintained return on capital in a difficult economic environment.
- Increased its quarterly dividend for the nineteenth consecutive year.
- Acquired Messer Griesheim's German respiratory home-care business.
- Divested two cogeneration facilities, consistent with the company's management goal of freeing up resources for higher-growth opportunities.
- For the second consecutive year, the American Chemical Council named Air Products the safest large-scale chemical manufacturer in North America.
- For the second consecutive year, *InternetWeek* named Air Products one of the top 100 e-business leaders in the United States.

Shortcomings to Bear in Mind

- Air Products has a rather leveraged balance sheet. Its common stock represents only 54 percent of capitalization. My preference is for common stock to represent 75 percent of capitalization.

Reasons to Buy

- Revenues for four of the company's growth engines—electronics, the chemical and processing industries (CPI), medical, and Asia—grew at double-digit rates in 2001. What's more, APD holds leading global market positions in electronics and hydrogen, currently the two most attractive markets for industrial gases.

- The company's electronics group offers customers total service and solutions. Air Products leads the market by offering a wide array of specialty gases, specialty chemicals, and services such as the company's much-heralded Megasys Total Gas and Chemical Management. The company's sales to the electronic sector have expanded at an average annual rate of 18 percent over the last five years, exceeding $1 billion in 2001.
- APD's CPI division is the world's leading supplier of HyCO products (hydrogen, carbon monoxide, and syngas, a mix of hydrogen and carbon monoxide). The company has increased its capacity tenfold in the last ten years, and about 75 percent of its volume is delivered to major global refining and chemical centers via APD's pipelines.

Air Products' technical leadership, operational expertise, and established franchises make the company the first choice of customers in the petrochemical, refining, specialty chemical, and life-sciences industries. Air Products is also NASA's sole supplier of liquid hydrogen for space shuttle launches.

Total assets: $8,084 million
Current ratio: 1.49
Common shares outstanding: 215 million
Return on 2001 shareholders' equity: 17.6%

		2001	2000	1999	1998	1997	1996	1995	1994
Revenues (millions)		5717	5467	5020	4919	4638	4008	3865	3485
Net income (millions)		519	533	451	489	429	416	368	264
Earnings per share		2.37	2.46	2.09	2.22	1.95	1.69	1.62	1.03
Dividends per share		.78	.74	.70	.64	.58	.54	.51	.48
Price	High	49.0	42.2	49.3	45.3	44.8	35.3	29.8	25.2
	Low	32.2	23.0	25.7	33.2	25.2	21.9	19.4	18.8

CONSERVATIVE GROWTH

Alberto-Culver Company

2525 Armitage Avenue □ Melrose Park, Illinois 60160 □ (708) 450-3005 □ Web site: www.alberto.com □ Dividend reinvestment plan is not available □ Fiscal year ends September 30 □ Listed: NYSE □ Ticker symbol: ACV □ Standard & Poor's rating: A+ □ Value Line financial strength rating: B++

For almost forty years, the Alberto-Culver Company, a pioneer on the global package goods stage, has carried the flag from country to country, continent to continent. Today, the company sells its products, such as Alberto VO5 and St. Ives Swiss Formula, in 120 countries, with manufacturing facilities in Sweden, the United Kingdom, Australia, Argentina, Mexico, Puerto Rico, and Canada, as well as here at home.

Following the acquisitions in Argentina and Chile in 1999, Alberto-Culver added to its lineup in 2000 with its Swedish subsidiary, Cederroth International's, acquisition of Soraya in Poland. The acquisition included the Soraya factory, sales organization, and popular skin-care line. In addition to a base in Poland, Soraya gives the company an additional resource for expanding its business throughout Eastern Europe, which it sees as an excellent future growth platform for its products.

Company Profile

Alberto-Culver is a leading developer and manufacturer of personal-care products, primarily hair care, retail food, household items, and health and hygiene products.

Alberto-Culver is comprised of three strong businesses built around potent brands and trademarks:

• Alberto-Culver USA develops innovative brand-name products for the retail, professional beauty, and institutional markets. Personal-use products include hair fixatives, shampoos, hairdressings, and conditioners sold under such trademarks as Alberto VO5, Bold Hold, Alberto, Alberto Balsam, Consort, TRESemme, and FDS (feminine deodorant spray).

Retail food product labels include SugarTwin, Mrs. Dash, Molly McButter, Baker's Joy, and Village Saucerie.

Household products include Static Guard (antistatic spray) and Kleen Guard (furniture polish).

• Alberto-Culver International has carried the Alberto VO5 flag into more than 120 countries. From that solid base, the business has built products, new brands and businesses focused on the needs of each market.

• Sally Beauty Company is the engine that drives Alberto-Culver. With over 2,400 outlets in the United States, the United Kingdom, Canada, Puerto Rico, Japan, and Germany, Sally is the largest cash-and-carry supplier of professional beauty products in the world.

The typical Sally Beauty store averages 1,800 square feet and is situated in a strip shopping center. It carries more than 3,000 items. About 75 percent of Sally Beauty's sales are to small beauty salons and barbershops, with the rest being made to retail customers.

Sally is the only U.S. national player in cash-and-carry beauty supplies that are sold primarily to professionals. It is the market leader by a wide margin. Sally capitalizes on its dominance in that niche, which provides beauty professionals the opportunity to purchase products from a wide selection of vendors at wholesale prices without having to manage and carry inventory in their stores.

The company's products do not have a common origin. They have come to Alberto-Culver in diverse ways. For instance, the original Alberto VO5 Hairdressing was a small regional brand that the company acquired because it felt it had national sales potential.

In another instance, the FDS products and its mousse products had counterparts in the marketplace in Europe. Consequently, ACV brought the ideas to the United States and introduced its products to an American audience.

In another realm, the company's research and development team developed Mrs. Dash, Static Guard, and Consort internally because its customers identified a need that these products met.

In yet another instance, SugarTwin and TRESemme were acquired by the company as tiny brands and were then grown to the strong positions they hold today.

Perhaps the company's most important acquisition—after the original purchase of Alberto VO5 Hairdressing—was the purchase of the Sally Beauty Company, originally a chain of twelve stores, many of which were franchised.

Today, the chain has over 2,400 company-owned stores, including units in Great Britain, Germany, and Japan. Sally is the largest distributor of professional beauty supplies in the world.

Sally's primary customer is the salon and barber professional who can find at Sally an unmatched selection of professional beauty supplies available at discount prices. In addition to the supplies they need, these professionals find in Sally a valuable source of information about trends and products that they can take back to their customers.

One of the keys to Sally's success is the ability to quickly get product from warehouse to shelf. This process starts with proprietary point-of-sale (POS) registers in each Sally store that record and report each sale. Sally is now investing millions of dollars to add a second POS register to each store to enhance its ability to serve customers.

Shortcomings to Bear in Mind

■ Over the past forty-five years, the company has experienced steady growth. However, it can't match the stylish image of some competitors. Indeed, retailers often relegate its bargain-basement products to the bottom shelf—eye level, of course, would be a better place to catch the consumer's attention. And professional hair stylists turn their noses up at its old standbys, such as Alberto VO5, TRESemme, and St. Ives Swiss Formula.

"They've got good products, but they are not linked with the current expression of high style," said Brian Hurley, president of Fairman, Schmidt & Hurley, an adverting agency that is familiar with hair-care advertising.

These pejorative comments don't seem to faze CEO Howard Bernick. "We have stood the test of time. We've been hearing predictions of our demise from so-called financial experts, but we keep going from record year to record year."

■ Sally Beauty Company experiences domestic and international competition from a wide range of retail outlets, including mass merchandisers, drug stores, and supermarkets, all carrying a full line of health and beauty products. In addition, Sally competes with thousands of local and regional beauty supply stores and full-service dealers selling directly to salons through both professional and distributor sales consultants as well as cash-and-carry outlets open only to salon professionals. Sally also faces competition from certain manufacturers that employ their own sales forces to distribute professional beauty products directly to salons.

Reasons to Buy

■ Alberto-Culver continued its winning streak in fiscal 2001, despite the recession. In fact, said CEO Bernick, "Most people don't stop washing their hair or bathing during tough times." Perhaps the key to the company's ability to weather economic slumps is based on the prices it puts on its merchandise—well below its illustrious competition. In the words of Mr. Bernick, "We are very pleased to report that our fiscal 2001 sales grew 11 percent, to $2.49 billion, from $2.25 billion in fiscal 2000. Net earnings grew close to 14 percent, to $110.4 million. This marked our tenth consecutive year of record sales and earnings. During the ten-year span, our sales have almost tripled, while our earnings have almost quadrupled."

■ Alberto-Culver's success has not gone unnoticed. Barron's, the leading weekly financial newspaper, said in early 2002, "Alberto-Culver's growth is all the more remarkable because of its many large and small rivals in the personal-care business. The big competitors include Avon Products, Procter & Gamble, and Gillette." Barron's went on to say, "As things now stand in the industry, the distribution end of the business is clearly dominated by Alberto-Culver. Most other distributors have fallen short of the success of Sally Beauty and Beauty Systems, frequently giving up by selling out to Alberto-Culver."

- Alberto-Culver has survived—and grown—by staying true to its low-cost niche. In the past couple of years, the company freshened up the forty-five-year-old brand, Alberto VO5, with new herbal shampoos that sell for as little as $0.99 a bottle. By contrast, Clairol's Herbal Essences sell for six times as much.

  The company also introduced facial creams for St. Ives, such as one that includes retinol, an antiwrinkle ingredient. In 2001, moreover, the company expanded its TRESemme line of haircare products with a new shampoo and conditioner designed to hold more moisture in the hair.

- Alberto VO5 Hairdressing remains by far the number-one brand in its category and the best-selling hairdressing in the world. VO5 is among the market leaders in the United States, Great Britain, Scandinavia, Canada, Mexico, Australia, and Japan.

- In over 120 countries, Alberto-Culver International markets or manufactures many of the consumer brands that it markets in the United States, including Alberto VO5 and St. Ives Swiss Formula brands.

  In addition, some of the company's international units offer products unique to their markets. In the Scandinavian countries, for example, ACV is the market leader in a wide range of toiletries and household products. In the United Kingdom, the company is a market leader in hairstyling products. What's more, it has introduced several items in the hair-coloring segment. Finally, in Canada, Alberto-Culver produces the top-selling Alberto-European styling line, and its SugarTwin artificial sweetener is number one in its category.

Total assets: $1,517 million
Current ratio: 2.25
Common shares outstanding: 57 million
Return on 2001 shareholders' equity: 16.1%

		2001	2000	1999	1998	1997	1996	1995	1994
Revenues (millions)		2494	2247	1976	1835	1775	1590	1358	1216
Net income (millions)		110.4	97.2	86.3	83.1	75.6	62.7	52.7	44.1
Earnings per share		1.91	1.83	1.51	1.37	1.25	1.06	.94	.79
Dividends per share		.32	.29	.26	.24	.20	.18	.16	.14
Price	High	46.3	43.5	27.9	32.4	32.6	25.0	18.3	13.7
	Low	36.9	19.4	21.6	19.8	23.6	16.3	12.9	9.7

AGGRESSIVE GROWTH

Alcoa, Inc.

201 Isabella Street at 7th Street Bridge □ Pittsburgh, PA 15212-5858 □ (212) 836-2674 □ Dividend reinvestment plan is available: (800) 317-4445 □ Web site: www.alcoa.com □ Listed: NYSE □ Ticker symbol: AA □ S&P rating: B+ □ Value Line financial strength rating: A

The January 2002 issue of *Money* magazine featured Alcoa as the best investment for 2002—only one of eight stocks named. In addition to praise for the company's management and ability to cut costs, the article cited Alcoa's ten-year history of 31 percent annual increases in earnings, while the average S&P 500 stock gained only 11 percent annually. The company also earned praise for its 154 percent five-year return on investment, compared with the S&P 500's 64 percent. The magazine refers to Alcoa as "a growth machine."

The China Connection

In addition to a number of relatively small alliances, acquisitions, and divestitures, Alcoa undertook a major growth initiative in 2001. The company began a long-term strategic relationship with Chalco (Aluminum Corporation of China).

In the words of CEO Alain J. P. Belda, this move "establishes us strongly in the fastest-growing aluminum market in the world. Our future participation as a 50 percent partner in Chalco's Pingguo primary aluminum and alumina facility will support our plans for further growth in fabricated products in China. We anticipate future mutually beneficial joint ventures with Chalco."

Though Alcoa had a large presence in Australia, it had relatively minor operations in China, including production of bottle tops, aluminum foil, sheet, and strip products in Shanghai. Analysts said Alcoa serviced some customers in China from Australia and, by setting up operations in China, Alcoa can now cut out expensive shipping costs.

Company Profile

Alcoa (formerly Aluminum Company of America), founded in 1888, is the world's leading integrated producer of aluminum products. The company is active in all major aspects of the industry: technology, mining, refining, smelting, fabricating, and recycling.

Alcoa's aluminum products and components are used worldwide in aircraft, automobiles, beverage cans, buildings, chemicals, sports, and recreation, and a wide variety of industrial and consumer applications, including such Alcoa consumer brands as Alcoa wheels, Reynolds Wrap aluminum foil, and Baco household wraps.

Related businesses include packaging machinery, precision castings, vinyl siding, plastic bottles and closures, fiber-optic cables, and electrical distribution systems for cars and trucks.

Since aluminum is expensive and has difficulty competing against steel—even though it has some admirable qualities—it might appear to be a rare element. Not so.

Aluminum is an abundant metal, in fact, the most abundant metal in the earth's crust. Of all the elements, only oxygen and silicon are more plentiful. Aluminum makes up 8 percent of the crust. It is found in the minerals of bauxite, mica, and cryolite, as well as in clay.

Until about 100 years ago, aluminum was virtually a precious metal. Despite its abundance, it was very rare as a pure metal because it was so difficult to extract from its ore. This is because aluminum is a reactive metal that cannot be extracted by smelting with carbon.

Displacement reactions were tried to solve the extraction enigma, but finally metals such as sodium or potassium had to be used, making the cost prohibitive. Electrolysis of the molten ore was tried, but the most plentiful ore, bauxite, contains aluminum in the chemical form of an oxide, which does not melt until it reaches 2,050 degrees centigrade.

Charles Hall in the United States and Paul Heroult in France, both working independently, discovered the solution to the problem of extracting aluminum from its ore. The method now used is called the Hall-Heroult process.

I won't bore you with the steps taken to effect this result. The important fact to remember is that it is far from cheap. Even so, it can be done economically enough to make aluminum the second most widely used metal. However, it is not likely to replace iron and steel any time soon. Iron makes up more than 90 percent of the metals used in the world.

The main cost in the Hall-Heroult process is electricity. So much energy is required that aluminum smelters have to be situated near a cheap source of power, normally hydroelectric.

The price of entry into the business is high enough to discourage most upstarts from taking the plunge.

On the other hand, this frustrating effort to produce commercial aluminum is worth the cost, since the white metal has a number of valuable attributes, including the following:

- It has a low density.
- It is highly resistant to corrosion.
- It is lightweight—one-third the weight of steel.
- It is an excellent reflector of heat and light.
- It is nonmagnetic.
- It is easy to assemble.
- It is nontoxic.
- It can be made strong with alloys.
- It can be easily rolled into thin sheets.
- It has good electrical conductivity.
- It has good thermal conductivity.
- Aluminum doesn't rust.

Shortcomings to Bear in Mind

- Alcoa is not immune to the ups and downs of the economy, and 2001 was no exception. In the words of Mr. Belda, "We operated in a deteriorating environment. Demand in our markets weakened as a consequence of the U.S. recession, the European slowdown, and the continued recession in Japan. London Metal Exchange prices for aluminum decreased by 13 percent, from a closing price of $1,550 a metric ton on January 2, 2001, to $1,355 at closing on December 28, 2001. The price decrease occurred despite a 4 percent reduction in global output, as reported by the International Aluminum Institute, between December 2000 and December 2001.

"Power shortages in the U.S. and Brazil reduced Alcoa's own output by 7.6 percent of our total consolidated annual capacity. All of Alcoa's major markets were affected by the economy—aerospace, automotive, housing and construction, packaging, and industrial."

Alcoa, like many others, took steps to minimize the red ink. According to Mr. Belda, "We did what you have to do in circumstances like these. We contained capital expenditures, paid down debt, controlled expenses, and closed high-cost facilities.

"Several of these actions were started in the second half of year 2000. As a consequence, we will have reduced our workforce by some 10,000, or 8 percent; permanently closed eighteen locations, mostly in Europe and the U.S.; and reduced our costs by $348 million. Our actions blunted the impact of greatly reduced market activity but could not eliminate it."

Reasons to Buy

- Despite an extremely challenging business environment, 2001 proved to be the second-best year in the company's history, in terms of earnings before special charges, and the fourth-best year after such charges. As compared with the Dow Jones Industrial Average, which had a total shareholder return of minus 5.4 percent, Alcoa's total shareholder return was a plus 7.8 percent.

Net income for the year was $980 million, or $1.05 per share, including special after-tax charges of $355 million, or $0.41 per share, compared with $1.484 billion, or $1.80 per share in 2000. Excluding special charges, earnings for 2001 were $1.263 billion, or $1.46 per share. This was a drop of 42 percent on a postspecial items basis and 19 percent on a prespecial items basis.

- Work is proceeding on schedule to test and improve a revolutionary smelting technology of Alcoa's that uses inert anodes instead of carbon anodes. If it proves to be feasible on a commercial scale, the new process promises to increase smelter capacity and lower production costs. It also would benefit the environment, because the principal emission is oxygen, rather than carbon dioxide and sulfur derivatives. Test cells are operating in Europe and North America. It is expected that significant tonnage will be converted to inert anodes for full-scale testing by year-end 2002.

- During periods when the aluminum industry suffers through a protracted slump in aluminum prices, Alcoa has seen its profits rise. Part of that is due to the effects of recent acquisitions. But much of the improvement can be traced to a new corporate philosophy, called the "Alcoa Business System." Essentially, it calls for plants to produce more aluminum, produce it faster, and not let it sit on the docks for too long. The new production processes are "deceptively simple and seemingly obvious," says one analyst. But, on top of other cost-cutting efforts already in the works, they are helping Alcoa weather what otherwise might be a dismal year. As aluminum prices recover—either because of growing demand or because excess capacity is shuttered—Alcoa stands to see earnings jump dramatically. Analysts say that each penny increase in the LME price of aluminum boosts Alcoa's per-share earnings by about 12 cents. LME refers to the spot price of aluminum ingots on the London Metals Exchange. Normally, the prevailing world price of aluminum is an important determinant of aluminum companies' profits. From 1982 through 1995, Alcoa's earnings and the LME price moved in lock step. Since then, however, the LME price has dropped while Alcoa's earnings have held steady or drifted up. According to the company's chief financial officer, Richard Kelson, "We are breaking away from the LME pricing."

- Automakers Nissan and Daimler-Chrysler and truck-maker Freightliner are featuring components made of Alcoa's enhanced 6022 alloy in their 2002 cars and trucks. The new alloy provides improved strength, formability, and corrosion resistance.

  Nissan is using the alloy for hoods and deck lids in its 2002 Altima, named Car of the Year at the North American International Auto Show. Daimler-Chrysler employs it for hoods in both the 2001 and 2002 Concorde and LHS vehicles. Freightliner also used Alcoa sheet in 2002 for the newest member of its heavy-duty truck line. Ford's redesigned Explorer and 2002 models of the Dodge Ram 4x2 and 4x4 pickup trucks feature an Alcoa aluminum steering knuckle, the component that attaches the wheel to the vehicle's steering and suspension system.

Total assets: $28,355 million
Current ratio: 1.36
Common shares outstanding: 858 million
Return on 2001 shareholders' equity: 8.3%

	2001	2000	1999	1998	1997	1996	1995	1994
Revenues (millions)	22859	22936	16323	15340	13319	13061	12500	9904
Net income (millions)	908	1484	1054	859	759	555	796	193
Earnings per share	1.05	1.80	1.41	1.22	1.09	.79	1.11	.27
Dividends per share	.60	.50	.40	.38	.25	.33	.23	.20
Price High	45.7	43.6	41.7	20.3	22.4	16.6	15.1	11.3
Low	27.4	23.1	18.0	14.5	16.1	12.3	9.2	8.0

INCOME

Altria Group
(formerly Philip Morris Companies Inc.)

120 Park Avenue □ New York, N.Y. 10017-5592 □ (917) 663-3460 □ Dividend reinvestment plan is available: (800) 442-0077 □ Listed: NYSE □ Web site: www.philipmorris.com □ Ticker symbol: MO □ S&P rating: A □ Value Line financial strength rating: A

Today's smokers, shivering in the winter cold outside their smoke-free office buildings, should be glad they weren't living in Constantinople in the early 1600s. That's when Murad IV, ruler of the vast Ottoman Empire, had an even nastier habit than tobacco. He roamed the city's streets in disguise, "feigning an urgent craving for a smoke, then beheading any good Samaritans who offered relief," reports Iain Gately in his entertaining *Tobacco: A Cultural History of How an Exotic Plant Secured Civilization.* In just fourteen years, Murad personally killed or had put to death more than 25,000 suspected smokers.

The above is from a book review written by John Carey for *BusinessWeek.* Here is more:

"Tobacco's ability to calm nerves, suppress hunger, and provide a moment of calm during the horror of the trenches made it 'as indispensable as the daily ration,' said U.S. General John J. Pershing. President Franklin D. Roosevelt even declared tobacco an essential wartime material. By 1949, the percentage of British men who were hooked on the weed rose to 81 percent.

"Today, smoking's foes have regained strength in the U.S.—perhaps too much, Gately seems to believe. 'To the 1.2 billion smokers in the world, tobacco is not just a killer, but a pleasure, a comforter, and a friend,' he argues."

Company Profile

Operating in nearly 200 countries, the Altria Group is the largest consumer packaged-goods company in the world. Altria is also the largest domestic cigarette manufacturer and the nation's largest food processor (Kraft). Finally, Miller Brewing is the nation's second-largest brewer.

As noted, the Altria Group is primarily a tobacco company, with such major brands as Marlboro (the top-selling brand in the United States), Merit, Virginia Slims (the bestselling women's cigarette), Benson & Hedges, and Parliament. Altria has a 49.4 percent share of the domestic tobacco market. Outside the United States, the company also has well-known brands, such as L & M and Lark.

The company's other large operation is food, as a result of prior acquisitions of General Foods (1984) and Kraft (1988). Some well-known names include Jell-O, Shake 'n Bake, Lender's Bagels, Philadelphia Cream Cheese, Post cereals, Velveeta, Kool-Aid, Miracle Whip, Oscar Mayer, Cracker Barrel cheese, Tang, and Maxwell House coffee.

Ranking third is the company's beer business, featuring such brands as Miller Lite, Miller Genuine Draft, Miller, Icehouse, Red Dog, Lowenbrau, Meister Brau, and Milwaukee's Best. During 1997, Miller sold its equity interest in Molson Breweries in Canada and 49 percent of its ownership of Molson USA, which holds the rights to import, market, and distribute the Molson and Foster's brands in the United States. Currently, Miller holds a 21 percent share of the domestic beer market.

Finally, Altria also has a stake in financial services (Philip Morris Capital Corp.).

Shortcomings to Bear in Mind

- An analyst writing for Argus Research Corporation has a concern worth noting. "We must urge caution with this sector, however. To begin with, the retreat of advertising leaves national brands all the more vulnerable to competition from private-label brands, a threat we have discussed repeatedly in recent months. Private-label goods are much better bargains, and Americans will now reach for them more often."

- As most investors are aware, the Altria Group is being besieged by the many pressures facing the U.S. tobacco industry: public smoking restrictions, possible excise tax hikes, congressional hearings, negative media coverage, and litigation. Still, we should remember that the company's tobacco segment has faced similar threats before and has overcome them. Finally, it's important to note that over the past forty years, the tobacco industry has rarely lost or paid to settle a smoking-health product liability case.

  More recently, however, that seems to be changing. In 1999, a jury in San Francisco awarded $1.5 million in damages to compensate a former smoker with lung cancer, the largest such award against the tobacco industry and the first against the Altria Group. The verdict, following a monthlong Superior Court trial, served abrupt notice to the tobacco industry that it remains vulnerable to suits brought by individual smokers, despite a $206-billion settlement with states in 1998 that ended their efforts to recoup health outlays linked to smoking-related illnesses.

- The European Union (EU), whose fifteen member nations make up one of the world's biggest tobacco markets, agreed on a law that will significantly enlarge health warnings on cigarette packages and make them much more explicit. Under the law, to take effect in the countries of the EU by October 2002, the warnings must cover at least 30 percent of the pack's surface, up from as little as 4 percent. The law will also require more graphic warnings, such as "Smokers die younger," and could eventually allow individual EU governments to demand that manufacturers place on the pack color photos showing how smoking-related diseases can ravage the body.

Reasons to Buy

- Despite the company's success in the tobacco realm, it cannot claim the same success with its Miller beer operation. However, that may be changing. The company's new CEO, Louis C. Camilleri, said in early 2002, that the Miller unit is starting to improve. Excluding discontinued brands, Miller's shipments in the final quarter of 2001 were up 3.2 percent. Mr. Camilleri said, "We're not oblivious to the consolidation in the beer industry. We will pursue any options that are in the best interest of shareholders."

- In a demographic study sponsored by Sanford C. Bernstein & Co., it was found that young smokers, those between the ages of eighteen and twenty-four, have a strong preference for Marlboro, Camel, and Newport. Among these, Marlboro, the leading brand of Altria, was the clear winner, with a whopping 78 percent preference. This is a key finding, since smokers typically carry their preferences with them as they mature.

- The Altria Group's outstanding brands, marketing, and infrastructure have made the company the market leader in tobacco in the United States and in thirty other major markets around the world. They have also won the company first place positions in eighteen of its twenty most profitable food categories in North America and in more than forty of its major coffee, confectionery, cheese, and powdered soft drink businesses.

- Despite the never-ending strife against antismoking forces, Altria has been a most successful company. Unlike many other huge companies, the Altria Group is growing at a consistent and impressive pace. In the 1991–2001 period, earnings per share climbed from $1.51 to $3.87, a compound annual growth rate of 9.9 percent. Similarly, dividends per share expanded from $0.64 to $2.32, a growth rate of 13.7 percent.

- Kraft is one of the largest coffee companies in the United States. Major brands include Maxwell House, Yuban, Sanka, Maxim, and General Foods International Coffees. The company's coffee business has been gaining both volume and market share in a highly competitive environment. This performance was attributable to the success of Kraft's licensing agreement to roll out Starbuck's coffee to grocery customers, as well as the introduction of Maxwell House Slow Roast coffee.

- Including Nabisco, the Altria Group has ninety-one brands that each generated $100 million or more in revenues in 2000. Of these brands, fifteen generated $1 billion or more, led by Marlboro.

- Perry H. Roth, an analyst with Value Line Survey, said at the end of 2001, "The company remains the leading player in the domestic tobacco arena. U.S. cigarette retail share now stands at 50.7 percent, an increase of 50 basis points from the end of June (2001). The company is even more dominant in the premium market, with a retail share of 61.8 percent. Altria owes much of its domestic tobacco success to the still-rising popularity of its Marlboro brand,

one of the best-marketed and promoted consumer brands in the history of the United States."

- Despite the recession and the threat from deranged terrorists, tobacco stocks have done well. From a low of $18.7 in early 2000, the Altria Group has been as high as $53.9 in 2001. You might wonder why. According to an article in *Time Magazine* written by Daren Fonda, "Tobacco stocks have surged for good reason: nothing beats the weed when it comes to generating cash. A $3.15 pack of Marlboros reaps $1.40 in revenues for Philip Morris, says analyst David Adelman. That's a 44 percent operating margin, a figure any Internet firm would envy."

- Although the Altria Group derives a majority of its sales and earnings from tobacco, it also has a solid contribution from food. In 2001, Kraft reported worldwide volume increase of 32.5 percent. Reported operating companies income, moreover, shot up 26.9 percent, to $6 billion. However, it should be borne in mind that this huge increase was due primarily to the acquisition of Nabisco in December of 2000. Assuming Kraft owned Nabisco for all of 2000, Kraft worldwide volume for the full year increased a much less impressive 2.5 percent. This increase reflected the success of new products and higher volume in developing markets.

- For Altria as a whole, 2001 was a good year—despite the effect of the recession, terrorist attacks, and the negative impact of a strong dollar. Operating revenues increased 11.9 percent, to $89.9 billion; operating income increased 7.7 percent, to $17.5 billion; net earnings were up modestly, 0.6 percent, to $8.6 billion; and diluted earnings per share rose 3.2 percent, to $3.87.

Total assets: $79,067 million
Current ratio: .72
Common shares outstanding: 2,185 million
Return on 2001 shareholders' equity: 52.5%

	2001	2000	1999	1998	1997	1996	1995	1994
Revenues (millions)	89900	80356	78596	74391	72055	69204	66071	65125
Net income (millions)	8900	8520	7675	5372	6310	6303	5478	4725
Earnings per share	3.87	3.71	3.19	2.20	2.58	2.56	2.17	1.82
Dividends per share	2.32	1.97	1.84	1.68	1.60	1.47	1.22	1.01
Price High	53.9	45.9	55.6	59.5	48.1	39.7	31.5	21.5
Low	38.8	18.7	21.3	34.8	36.0	28.5	18.6	15.8

AGGRESSIVE GROWTH

AmerisourceBergen Corporation

Post Office Box 959 ◻ Valley Forge, PA 19482 ◻ (610) 727-7000 Ext. 7118 ◻ Dividend reinvestment program is not available ◻ Fiscal year ends September 30 ◻ Listed: NYSE ◻ Web site: www.amerisourcebergen.net ◻ Ticker symbol: ABC ◻ S&P rating: Not rated ◻ Value Line financial strength rating: B

AmerisourceBergen buys pharmaceuticals from manufacturers, warehouses them, and then distributes them, along with value-added services, to both retail and institutional pharmacies nationwide.

AmerisourceBergen was created in August of 2001 through the merger of AmeriSource Health Corporation and Bergen Brunswig Corporation.

Combining the two national pharmaceutical supply companies made great practical sense. Bergen was strong in the West; AmeriSource was strong in the East and Midwest.

Both serviced large numbers of independent community pharmacies, regional drug stores, and food chains with innovative services and programs. AmeriSource was a leader in the acute-care hospital business, while Bergen was a leader in the alternate-care and institutional pharmacy markets and had a large and growing specialty distribution business.

Finally, the two companies shared few of the same customers and both had strong reputations for customer service.

According to CEO Robert E. Martini, "One of the motivations for the merger was the capture of significant cost-saving opportunities. When we announced the merger, we stated that $125 million in annual synergies would be captured by the end of the third year, fiscal 2004.

"After the transaction closed, additional savings were identified, and we revised that estimate to $150 million by the end of year three. The savings will accrue from three broad areas:

• distribution, network rationalization, and operations enhancements.

• elimination of redundancies, primarily in back-office functions.

• procurement efficiencies.

"With little overlap in customers and our long-standing commitment to customer service, we will continue to field the largest sales force in the industry."

Company Profile

AmerisourceBergen is the largest pharmaceutical services company in the United States dedicated solely to the pharmaceutical supply chain. It is the leading distributor of pharmaceutical products and services to the hospital systems/acute care market, alternate care facilities, independent community pharmacies, and regional drug store and food merchandise chains. The company is also a leader in the institutional pharmacy marketplace.

Revenues are broken down as follows: independent community drug stores (30 percent); regional drug store chains (18 percent); the hospital/acute care market (31 percent); and the alternate site (mail-order facilities, nursing homes, clinics and other nonacute care facilities) (21 percent).

Among the company's operations are the following divisions:

• Independent community pharmacies can take advantage of either Good Neighbor Pharmacy or Family Pharmacy, two branded pharmacy programs that offer group purchasing, advertising, and private-label products.

• HBC Source provides competitively priced over-the-counter (those sold without a prescription) and health and beauty aid products.

• AmerisourceBergen Specialty Group (ABSG) is the company's fastest-growing specialty distribution business. It provides products to doctors and clinics, based on disease type. With annual revenue approaching $2 billion, ABSG is the second leading pharmaceutical service provider to oncologists (physicians who treat cancer), and a leader in the distribution of blood plasma and in the vaccine market. ABSG also provides inventory management and distribution services to biotech pharmaceutical manufacturers and will play a major role in the company's future growth.

• PharMerica is the second-largest provider to pharmacy services to the long-term care and alternate care markets. It also has a rapidly growing business providing an array of pharmacy services to the workers' compensation marketplace, where PharMerica is the leader.

• Rita Ann, the company's cosmetic distribution business, adds a full line of cosmetics, cosmetic accessories, sundries, and hosiery from more than 200 manufacturers.

• The American Health Packaging division has a 150,000-square-foot facility that repackages drugs from bulk to unit dose, unit of use, blister pack, and standard bottle sizes.

AmerisourceBergen employs more than 13,000 people and has over 25,000 customers. The company serves its customers nationwide through twenty-one drug distribution facilities and three specialty products distribution facilities.

Shortcomings to Bear in Mind

■ *Standard & Poor's Stock Reports* expressed some reservations in a report issued in early 2002. "Gross margins are likely to continue to narrow, albeit gradually, in light of competitive pricing and increased penetration of large accounts, which demand cheaper pricing, partly offset by increased usage of generic drugs."

On a more positive note, the S&P report points out, "The company's long-term forecast of revenue growth in excess of 15 percent and EPS growth of better than 20 percent, starting in FY 02, continues to look achievable. In part, this reflects favorable demographic trends and industry fundamentals, improved economies of scale, and the realization of synergies."

Reasons to Buy

■ In fiscal 2001 (ended September 30, 2001), the company enjoyed stellar performance. Diluted earnings per share (which adjusts for the conversion of convertible bonds and preferred stock) climbed to a record $2.31, a gain of 22 percent over the prior year.

Return on committed capital (ROCC), according to Mr. Martini, is "Our most important measurement because it best reflects our ability to create shareholder value over the long term." In 2001, it was 26.7 percent, "well above our 20-percent long-term target. On a pro forma basis, revenue in our pharmaceutical distribution segment reflected a strong year for both former companies. AmeriSource revenue was up 20 percent, and Bergen Brunswig increased 11 percent. In our PharMerica segment, which includes our institutional pharmacy and workers' compensation fulfillment businesses, pro forma revenue increased 6 percent."

- AmerisourceBergen commands a leading position in a strong industry. In the words of Mr. Martini, "Some industry experts expect the pharmaceutical industry to grow revenues at an annual rate of nearly 14 percent over the next five years. This growth is driven by more than $57 billion in worldwide pharmaceutical company research for new drugs and an increasing research for new drugs and an increasing U.S. population over 65 years of age, which accounts for an estimated two-thirds of total health care expenditures.

  "About $35 billion of branded pharmaceuticals will come off patent in the next five years. As the largest purchaser of generic pharmaceuticals in the U.S., we have a great opportunity to influence market share in this market."

- At the heart of ABC's distribution system are the most modern and automated facilities in the industry. Currently, AmerisourceBergen distribution centers process an average of $623 million in annual revenue, with some facilities running at more than $1.5 billion a year. The industry average is about $600 million per year.

  When the consolidation is complete, the company's distribution centers will average about $1.8 billion in revenue annually (based on revenue growth of 15 percent annually), with the biggest facilities processing more than $2 billion in sales. The result, says Mr. Martini, "will be the largest and the lowest-cost distribution systems in the industry."

- In March of 2002, Eric Coldwell, an analyst with Prudential Financial, said this about ABC: "We believe that AmerisourceBergen is a well-managed, high-quality distributor that now has the scale, scope, and financial might to compete head-on with its two national peers. In our opinion, Amerisource-Bergen is a simple story: Integrate, cut costs, and grow."

- A generic purchasing program for independent pharmacies and chain drug stores capitalizes on Amerisource-Bergen's position as the number one buyer of generic pharmaceuticals in the United States. Customers entrust AmerisourceBergen to make the generic product selection based on generic value.

- Several studies by independent groups in 2001 rated former AmeriSource number one in customer service among national distributors, with former Bergen Brunswig close behind.

Total assets: $10,291 million
Current ratio: 1.36
Common shares outstanding: 104 million
Return on 2001 shareholders' equity: 12.1%

	2001	2000	1999	1998	1997	1996	1995	1994
Revenues (millions)	16191	11645	9760	8575	7816	5552	4669	4182
Net income (millions)	124	99	71	50	47	43	28	def
Earnings per share	2.10	1.90	1.38	1.04	0.97	0.92	0.77	def
Dividends per share	Nil	—	—	—	—	—	—	—
Price High	72.0	53.7	41.4	40.4	33.2	22.9	17.1	NA
Low	40.1	12.0	11.0	22.2	20.6	13.9	9.9	NA

CONSERVATIVE GROWTH

Anheuser-Busch Companies, Inc.

One Busch Place □ St. Louis, Missouri 63118 □ (314) 577-2000 □ Dividend reinvestment plan is available: (888) 213-0964 □ Web site: www.budweiser.com □ Listed: NYSE □ Ticker symbol: BUD □ S&P rating: A □ Value Line financial strength rating: A++

"Anheuser-Busch had another outstanding year in 2001, selling over 107 million barrels of its beer brands worldwide and delivering 12 percent earnings per share growth," said August A. Busch III, chairman of the board and president. In a difficult economic environment, Anheuser-Busch continues to realize dependable earnings growth, and the company now has achieved 13 consecutive quarters of double-digit earnings per share growth.

Mr. Busch went on to say, "Anheuser-Busch is a simple, straightforward consumer-products company, and with our significant competitive strengths, we have been able to achieve these consistently strong results.

"Strong growth in domestic revenue per barrel has driven significantly enhanced profit margins, increasing return on capital employed another 70 basis points in 2001. (100 basis points are the same as one percent.) In addition, the international beer segment once again made a considerable contribution to earnings per share growth in 2001, through the strong performance of the company's

equity partner Grupo Modelo, Mexico's largest brewer, and significant increases in volume and profits on the sales of Anheuser-Busch products overseas."

Mr. Busch also commented on 2002, "Our consistent increases in revenue per barrel over the past three years reflect the company's sharp focus on profit margin growth and earnings. For 2002, the outlook for continued increases in revenue per barrel remains favorable. Anheuser-Busch's gross profit margins increased 120 basis points in the fourth quarter of 2001 and 100 basis points for the year, while operating margins increased 100 basis points during the fourth quarter and 110 basis points for the full year."

Company Profile

Anheuser-Busch's operations and resources are focused on beer, adventure park entertainment, and packaging. Anheuser-Busch also has interests in aluminum beverage container recycling, malt production, rice milling, real-estate development, turf farming, creative services, metalized paper label printing, and transportation services.

Here are some comments on a few of the most important operations.

Bacardi Silver

Bacardi Silver leverages the heritage, resources, and commitment to quality of two industry leaders. Anheuser-Busch, the world's largest brewer, and Bacardi U.S.A., importer of the world's number one distilled spirit, each bringing more than 130 years of experience to this alliance.

Produced, marketed, and exclusively distributed by Anheuser-Busch, Bacardi Silver is a clear malt beverage made with the flavors of Bacardi rum and citrus that features a crisp, refreshing taste. Bacardi rum is a component in the flavor of Bacardi Silver.

Anheuser-Busch Companies, Inc.

Anheuser-Busch, the world's largest brewer, operates fourteen breweries, twelve in the United States and two overseas. The company currently brews about thirty beers for sale in the United States. Here is a brief descriptions of some of them.

Budweiser Family

Budweiser—Brewed and sold since 1876, "The King of Beers" has been the world's bestselling beer since 1957. It is distributed in more than seventy countries. Budweiser leads the U.S. premium beer category, outselling all other domestic premium beers combined.

Bud Light—Introduced nationally in 1982, Bud Light is brewed with a malt-and-hops ratio different from Budweiser for a distinctly crisp taste with fewer calories. It became the country's number-one light beer in 1994 and has grown at a double-digit pace for the past eight years.

Bud Ice—Introduced in 1994, Bud Ice is a smooth-tasting ice beer. Combined with Bud Ice Light, Bud Ice is one of the country's top-selling ice beers.

Bud Ice Light—Introduced in 1994, Bud Ice Light has fewer calories (only 112 calories per twelve-ounce serving) than Bud Ice.

Michelob Family

Michelob—Super-premium Michelob was developed in 1896 as a "draught beer for connoisseurs."

Michelob Golden Draft—Introduced in 1991 and distributed in select U.S. markets.

Michelob Golden Draft Light—Also made its debut in 1991.

The above beers are the most important, but by no means the entire list. The company also has a stake in light beers, nonalcoholic brews, a line sold under the Busch label, and malt liquors, among others.

Anheuser-Busch Entertainment Operations

Busch Entertainment Corporation, the company's family entertainment subsidiary, is one of the largest adventure park operators in the United States. Its parks are situated throughout the country. They include SeaWorld Orlando, Busch Gardens Tampa Bay, Adventure Island, SeaWorld San Diego, Busch Gardens Williamsburg, Water Country USA, SeaWorld San Antonio, and Discovery Cove.

Anheuser-Busch Packaging

Anheuser-Busch is one of the largest U.S. manufacturers of aluminum beverage containers and the world's largest recycler of aluminum beverage containers.

Shortcomings to Bear in Mind

- The company's balance sheet is too leveraged for my taste. It has more debt than common equity. Only about 42 percent of the capitalization is in the form of common stock. I would prefer 75 percent.
- At the end of 2001, NBC decided to give liquor companies a chance to advertise their wares on television. According to

Thomas Lee, who writes for the *St. Louis Post Dispatch*, this move "could represent the distilled-spirits industry's first serious challenge to the market dominance and the brand power of brewers—including St. Louis-based Anheuser-Busch Co.—which have relied heavily on national TV advertising.

"By purchasing commercials on a national network, makers of vodka, rum, and whiskey will go head-to-head with beer and wine makers, creating a vastly more competitive marketplace and possibly overwhelming the consumers," experts say.

"'This is a big issue for brewers,' said Bill Finnie, a former director of strategic planning for A-B, who now works as a consultant for Grace Advisors. 'This impacts the very relationship between beer versus liquor.'

"For more than 50 years, brewers enjoyed a strategic marketing advantage over liquor companies: Beer could be advertised on television; liquor could not."

Reasons to Buy

- BUD has a solid, but not spectacular, record of growth. In the 1991–2001 period, earnings per share (EPS) advanced from $0.81 to $1.99, a compound annual growth rate of 9.4 percent. In that span, EPS declined only once (in 1995, from $0.97 to $0.95). In the same stretch, dividends per share climbed from $0.27 to $0.69, a growth rate of 9.8 percent, far surpassing the rate of inflation.
- *Value Line's* analyst Kenneth A. Nugent commented, in a report issued at the end of 2001, "Foreign investments are likely to continue to lift earnings both short and long term. During the first nine months of this year, A-B's international beer volume grew by almost 7 percent, thanks to solid volume growth in Canada and China. And we are confident that Grupo Modelo, which should boost 2001 company-wide sales by about $260 million, will continue to lift BUD's fortunes going forward, thanks to market leadership and strong exports to the United States."
- In a report published in February of 2002, *Standard & Poor's Stock Reports* said, "We continue our accumulate recommendation on the shares, reflecting a positive earnings growth outlook due to a favorable domestic beer pricing environment and expected gains in equity income. BUD should also benefit from a favorable demographic shift over the next decade, with strong growth in the 21-to-27-year-old population."
- For the fourth straight year, the company grabbed the top spot in *USA Today's* Super Bowl Ad Meter. Anheuser-Busch's "Satin Sheets" ad was the most popular, according to *USA Today's* Ad Meter. The winning spot features a Bud Light-loving guy whose wife lures him with a bottle but quickly loses him to some slick satin sheets that send him flying out the window.
- In February of 2002, the company announced the rollout of its premium-flavored malt beverage, Bacardi Silver. "It is with great anticipation and excitement that we unveil Bacardi Silver, an innovative product that we believe will appeal to contemporary adult consumers," said August A. Busch IV, group vice president, Marketing and Wholesale Operations.

Bacardi Silver is being supported by a marketing budget of nearly $60 million. It includes advertising and media, sales promotion items, and merchandising. Media support includes national television, print, radio, outdoor, and Internet advertising.

Total assets: $13,085 million
Current ratio: 1.02
Common shares outstanding: 889 million
Return on 2001 shareholders' equity: 40%

	2001	2000	1999	1998	1997	1996	1995	1994
Revenues (millions)	12911	12262	11704	11246	11066	10884	10341	12054
Net income (millions)	1705	1552	1402	1233	1179	1123	986	1032
Earnings per share	1.99	1.69	1.47	1.27	1.18	1.11	.95	.97
Dividends per share	.69	.64	.58	.54	.50	.46	.42	.38
Price High	46.9	49.9	42.0	34.1	24.1	22.5	17.0	13.8
Low	36.8	27.3	32.2	21.5	19.3	16.2	12.7	11.8

GROWTH AND INCOME

AvalonBay Communities, Inc.

2900 Eisenhower Avenue, Suite 300 ◻ Alexandria, Virginia 22314 ◻ (703) 317-4632 ◻ Dividend reinvestment program not available ◻ Web site: www.avalonbay.com ◻ Listed: NYSE ◻ Ticker symbol: AVB ◻ S&P rating: Not rated ◻ Value Line financial strength rating: B+

AvalonBay is a real estate investment trust that caters to the "carriage trade." Its core customers—many of whom can afford to own a home—have chosen to rent for lifestyle reasons. These "discretionary renters" represent the fastest-growing segment in the market. Management contends that they are "attracted to our communities because we provide more than just shelter. The company's communities are fresh and contemporary—at an average age of 6.7 years at the end of 2001—the youngest portfolio in the industry.

"Our purpose is to enhance the lives of our residents. We accomplish this through our professional associates, high-quality amenities and convenient locations near centers of arts, entertainment, and shopping, ultimately providing our residents the time to do the things most important to them—time to work, time to play, time to indulge . . . and we call that *Time Well Spent*."

What Is a REIT?

Real estate investment trusts (REITs) are dedicated to owning and, in most cases, operating a portfolio of real-estate properties to generate profits for its shareholders. To qualify for REIT status, a company's assets must be primarily long-term real estate, and its income must be primarily derived from rents on real estate.

A REIT is generally not taxed at the corporate level on net income to the extent net income is distributed to the REIT's stockholders. REITs currently must pay out at least 90 percent of their net income in dividends to shareholders.

● Funds from operations (FFO) is, according to most REITs, generally considered to be an appropriate measure of the operating performance of a REIT. That's because it provides investors an understanding of the ability of the company to incur and service debt and to make capital expenditures.

Funds from Operations (FFO)

FFO is an accounting term peculiar to the REIT industry. It is often used instead of earnings as a guide to how well the company is doing. However, it does not represent cash generated from operating activities in accordance with generally accepted accounting principles (GAAP). Therefore, it should not be considered an alternative to net income as an indication of performance.

Company Profile

AvalonBay Communities, Inc., headquartered in Alexandria, Virginia, currently owns or holds an ownership interest in 141 apartment communities containing 41,191 apartment homes in eleven states and the District of Columbia, of which fifteen communities are under construction and three are under reconstruction. AvalonBay is in the business of developing, redeveloping, acquiring, and managing luxury apartment communities in high barrier-to-entry markets of the United States. These markets are in the Northeast, mid-Atlantic, Midwest, Pacific Northwest, Northern California, and Southern California regions of the nation.

In the words of management, "We operate in premier markets—developing, acquiring and managing luxury apartment communities—led by a seasoned management team with a proven track record of creating significant shareholder value and consistently achieving financial performance well above the multi-family sector and REIT industry averages. Our high-quality portfolio is uniform in quality, yet diverse in product type. Our communities include garden and townhouse, mid-rise and high-rise communities.

"The average age of these communities, as of December 31, 2001, is only 6.7 years, and they are geographically distributed across 17 markets."

Shortcomings to Bear in Mind

- *Value Line Survey* expressed a few negative thoughts in a January 2002 report. The analyst, Adam Rosner, said, "Significant declines in occupancy have occurred in northern California (accounts for 30 percent of net operating income) due to higher unemployment levels and corporate bankruptcies. Also, operating margins have narrowed slightly, due to increased operating expenses, which will likely put pressure on the bottom line."

- As of early 2002, AvalonBay had cut back on its new development projects—at least temporarily. Development levels, moreover, have declined since the heady days of 1999, and the company has delayed development on projects in Washington and California. On the other hand, a few projects are under way in some high-demand regions of the Northeast.

- Investors looking for high yield may not be attracted to AvalonBay, since it combines growth with income—and has a track record to support it. In the 1996–2001 period, earnings per share advanced from $1.48 to $3.12, a compound annual growth rate of 16.1 percent. That's why I have labeled this REIT a growth and income stock.

- The vacancy rate for higher-end apartments throughout the country rose to 5.8 percent in the final quarter of 2001, up from 3.5 percent in the same quarter of the prior year. According to Reis, Inc., a New York research firm, the vacancy rate had risen to 6.3 percent in March of 2002. For its part, AvalonBay began offering as much as one month's free rent in some of its Seattle and Northern California buildings in 2001, and in 2002 the company added some apartments in metropolitan New York and Boston.

Reasons to Buy

- Led by a seasoned management team, AvalonBay has consistently achieved strong funds from operations (FFO). Since 1994, the company has, for the most part, outperformed equity REITs, the S&P 500, the Russell 2000, the NASDAQ Composite, and U.S. Treasury ten-year notes.

- AvalonBay's goal is to be the market leader in each of the markets in which it operates. According to management, "This market-leader position often provides us with the first look at land in our chosen markets."
- By using a highly integrated team of local real estate experts to identify strategic land opportunities, AvalonBay has created value through development of forty-five communities since 1994. AvalonBay has one of the industry's largest development pipelines, currently consisting of thirty-four development rights that provide a platform for creating value through external development growth. These development rights, if pursued, would add about 9,900 upscale apartment homes at a budgeted cost of $1.9 billion.
- Over the years, the National Association of Home Builders (NAHB) has continually recognized AvalonBay through the Pillars of the Industry Awards program. This award program, conducted annually, recognizes companies that demonstrate the highest standards in multifamily housing design and management and who promote a positive image of the multifamily housing industry. Named Property Management Company of the Year and Development Firm of the Year, AvalonBay's corporate and property specific awards shine amongst the multifamily housing industry leaders. AvalonBay Communities, Inc., is proud to be recognized by the National Association of Home Builders (NAHB) in several prestigious categories. These awards include the following:
  - 1996 Property Management Firm of the Year
  - 1998 Best Mid- or High-Rise Development of the Year
  - 1998 Development Firm of the Year
  - 1999 Development Firm of the Year

- 1999 Best Rehabilitation of a Multifamily Property
- 1999 Best Mid- or High-Rise Apartment Community
- 1999 Best Mid- or High-Rise Development of the Year
- 2000 Best Multifamily Community by a REIT

- The company is not standing still. New properties are being added and less attractive ones liquidated. Here are two that were completed in the final quarter of 2001:

  Avalon on the Sound, a luxury high-rise community containing 412 apartment homes, was developed in a joint venture partnership in which AvalonBay holds a 25 percent interest. Avalon on the Sound, conveniently located in downtown New Rochelle, New York, adjacent to a Metro-North rail station, was completed approximately one month ahead of schedule for a total construction cost of $92.5 million. Monthly average rents per home are approximately $2,470.

  Avalon Belltown, a luxury mid-rise community containing 100 apartment homes, is conveniently located just two blocks from the Seattle waterfront, six blocks from the world-famous Pike Place Market, and less than eight blocks from the downtown Seattle business and financial district. Avalon Belltown was completed on schedule at a total construction cost of $18.7 million, and monthly average rents per home are approximately $1,660.

- In 2001, the company sold seven communities with 2,551 apartment homes for a gross sales price of $242.1 million, compared with an initial value of $63.3 million. Through these sales, the company disposed of properties in several noncore markets, including Portland, Oregon, and Hartford, Connecticut. Using the proceeds, AvalonBay invested in new development and redevelopment sectors that it believes to be high barrier-to-entry markets.

■ The company has been strengthening its balance sheet by paying off the balance on its line of credit. With about 50 percent of its capitalization in common equity, AvalonBay's balance sheet is somewhat stronger than the industry average, leaving the company well able to cover interest and fixed charges.

Total assets: $4,664 million
Current ratio: 0.52
Return on 2001 equity: 8%
Common shares outstanding: 68 million

		2001	2000	1999	1998	1997	1996	1995	1994
Revenues (millions)		642	573	504	371	170	125		
Net income (millions)		216	170	142	98	65	46		
Funds from operations		4.15	3.70	3.22	2.87	2.77	2.17		
Earnings per share		3.12	2.53	1.55	1.35	1.59	1.48		
Dividends per share		2.56	2.24	2.06	2.00	1.94	1.90		
Price	High	51.9	50.6	37.0	39.3	40.6	36.0		
	Low	42.4	32.6	30.8	30.5	32.1	22.6		

CONSERVATIVE GROWTH

Avery Dennison Corporation

150 North Orange Grove Boulevard □ **Pasadena, CA 91103-3596** □ **(626)-304-2204** □ **Direct Dividend reinvestment plan is available: (800) 756-8200** □ **Web site: www.averydennison.com** □ **Listed: NYSE** □ **Ticker symbol: AVY** □ **S&P rating: A+** □ **Value Line Financial Rating: A**

Avery Dennison Corporation announced in early 2001 that it had established Avery Dennison Medical, a new business unit in the company's Worldwide Specialty Tape Division.

Avery Dennison Medical will operate as a full-line supplier, building on its core competencies in manufacturing, converting, and research and development to create specialized adhesives and proprietary technologies for the wound-care, surgical, ostomy, electro-medical, and diagnostic markets.

"Our specialty tapes are already used by some of the largest medical product innovators in the industry," said Philip M. Neal, chief executive officer of Avery Dennison. "The health care industry is constantly looking for new products that will reduce costs and improve patient outcomes."

"Highly specialized wound-care products that reduce the time required for care or improve the quality of patient comfort will win," added Mr. Neal. "Advances in medical technology have resulted in new, minimally invasive surgical procedures that have created increased demand for advanced, over-the-counter health care products as patient care shifts from the hospital to the home environment."

The demand for advanced health care management products is projected to expand annually at double-digit rates. Key factors driving growth include longer life spans and new medical technologies that reduce mortality and morbidity as well as enhance quality of life.

Company Profile

Avery Dennison is a global specialty chemical company as well as an industrial and consumer-products company. Its pioneering pressure-sensitive technology is an integral part of products found in virtually every major industry. The company was formed in 1990 with the merger of Avery International Corporation and Dennison Manufacturing Corporation.

The company's primary businesses are organized into two sectors under a decentralized management structure.

The Pressure-Sensitive Adhesives and Materials Sector manufactures adhesives and base materials for industrial and commercial applications.

The Consumer and Converted Products Sector manufactures self-adhesive products for the office and home, including desktop printer labels and cards, markers, and organization and presentation products, as well as a variety of self-adhesive industrial labels, fastening devices, self-adhesive postage stamps, battery tester labels, and other specialized label products for global markets. The company employs more than 17,400 people in 200 manufacturing and sales facilities that produce and sell Avery Dennison products in eighty-nine countries.

The company is best known for its Avery-brand office products, Fasson-brand self-adhesive base materials, peel-and-stick postage stamps, industrial and security labels, retail tag and labeling systems, self-adhesive tapes, and specialty chemicals. Well-known products include the United States Postal Service's self-adhesive stamps and Duracell's battery-testing labels.

Under the Avery Dennison and Fasson brands, the company makes papers, films, and foils coated with adhesive and sold in rolls to printers. The company also makes school and office products (Avery, Marks-A-Lot, Hi-LITER), such as notebooks, three-ring binders, markers, fasteners, business forms, tickets, tags, and imprinting equipment.

Shortcomings to Bear in Mind

- At the end of 2001, *Value Line Survey* pointed out some problems and rated the stock below average in the "Timeliness" category. "We think the slowdown in the rate of construction of new domestic retail stores may hurt the company's volumes. In addition, the economic conditions in some of Avery's foreign markets, particularly Europe, have weakened in the last few months, which should hurt sales."

Reasons to Buy

- Avery Dennison acquired Dunsirn Industries, Inc., in early 2001. Dunsirn is a leading provider of nonpressure-sensitive materials to the narrow web printing industry. Dunsirn, based in Neenah, Wisconsin, also provides high-quality, contract slitting, and distribution services for paper, film, textile, nonwoven, and specialty roll materials.

"Avery Dennison's roll materials capabilities will expand overnight with the additional technical expertise, sales channel, and distribution infrastructure that Dunsirn brings to us," said Mr. Neal. "Our global reach will enable us to grow the business by introducing Dunsirn products to international markets, while our Fasson customers will benefit from the convenience of purchasing roll materials, both pressure-sensitive and non-pressure-sensitive, from a single source."

- The dividend has been increased for twenty-five consecutive years. In the last ten years (1991–2001), dividends advanced from $0.38 to $1.23, a compound annual growth rate of 12.5 percent.

In the same period, earnings per share expanded from $0.51 to $2.47, a growth rate of 17.1 percent.

- Self-adhesive labels imprinted with bar codes have greatly increased the speed and accuracy of baggage sorting—as well as a multitude of other tasks. For instance, they're used for inventory control, product tracking, distribution, and logistics management. What's more, you'll find them everywhere, from airports to hospitals, warehouses, retail stores, and packages ordered on the Internet.

- The company's Fasson-brand materials set the industry standard for variable information printing applications. They ensure superior bar-coding, which translates into accurate scanning. Also, they stay stuck to a wide variety of surfaces, even in harsh environments.

- In another sector, Avery Dennison automotive products decorate, seal, identify, and secure items throughout millions of automobiles. The automotive industry uses the company's specialty self-adhesive tapes instead of nuts, bolts, and other fasteners. What's more, that industry uses Avery's labels to carry all kinds of important information—from part numbers to safety warnings—on components like air bags and radiator covers.

    These products can also enhance a car's appearance, inside and out, with attractive exterior graphics, including decorative striping, and interior laminates such as wood-grain films.

    In addition, Avery Dennison Avloy Dry Paint film is changing the way the automotive industry thinks about finishing plastic-based car parts. Major manufacturers are using the company's performance films more and more as an alternative to spray-painting—on everything from side moldings to spoilers. And with good reason. Avery Dennison Avloy film looks great and is durable, cost-effective, and friendly to the environment.

- Although Avery Dennison is well known for its office products, the company is now expanding beyond the office with useful, creative, and fun products for making personalized items right at home. These include greeting cards, banners, posters, flyers, and T-shirts.

- Even the wine industry is being attracted to Avery products.

    For wine label designers, the possibilities are endless. According to management, "Wineries love the production efficiencies—hundreds of domestic wineries are using pressure-sensitive labels already—and Avery Dennison is leading the way worldwide."

    Avery Dennison's Decorating Technologies Division worked with E&J Gallo Winery to create a new Avery Dennison Clear ADvantage heat-transfer label for a new line of wines known as Wild Vines. Gallo selected the Avery Dennison labeling process because of its unique capability in achieving a frosted-bottle look.

- Nor has the company ignored the Internet. The Avery Web site enhanced consumer awareness and demand for Avery-brand products. The site, which drew several million hits in 2000, provides free Avery Wizard and Avery LabelPro software, which once downloaded creates an instant base of new customers.

- The company now has an European Films Center in Gotha, Germany, the largest label film facility outside North America, to meet rapidly growing demand for Fasson pressure-sensitive label materials throughout Europe.

- The company's Fasson Roll Specialty business has achieved double-digit growth, creating innovative, customized solutions—such as dissolvable labels, holographic films, and unique wall covering materials—that incorporate pressure-sensitive adhesive technology.

■ South of the border, Avery has been aggressively pursuing its Latin American growth strategy. This strategy includes the acquisition of a prominent pressure-sensitive materials business in Colombia and substantial majority ownership in its label materials operation in Argentina, significantly strengthening the company's market presence of its roll materials business in this expanding region.

■ Across the Pacific, despite economic turmoil in some Asian nations, the company's label materials operation in Asia Pacific continues to grow, reflecting the rapid growth of consumer products markets in the region. Sales of the company's pressure-sensitive materials have been growing in China at a double-digit pace.

■ In 2001, Polaroid Corporation and Avery Dennison introduced an instant photo identification badge kit that contains everything needed to produce cut-and-paste photo ID badges. Included in the kit is a Polaroid Pocket ID instant camera as well as easy-to-print-and-format name badges, provided by Avery.

Total assets: $2,819 million
Current ratio: 1.03
Common shares outstanding: 110 million
Return on 2001 shareholders' equity: 27.7%

	2001	2000	1999	1998	1997	1996	1995	1994
Revenues (millions)	3803	3894	3768	3460	3346	3222	3114	2857
Net income (millions)	243	284	215	223	205	174	143	109
Earnings per share	2.47	2.85	2.55	2.15	1.94	1.61	1.34	.99
Dividends per share	1.23	1.11	1.13	.87	.72	.62	.56	.50
Price High	60.5	78.5	73.0	62.1	45.8	36.5	25.1	18.0
Low	43.3	41.1	39.4	39.4	33.4	23.8	16.6	13.3

GROWTH AND INCOME

Baldor Electric Company

5711 R. S. Boreham Jr. Street ▫ Fort Smith, Arkansas 72908 ▫ Dividend reinvestment plan is available: (800) 509-5586 ▫ Web site: www.baldor.com ▫ Listed: NYSE ▫ Ticker symbol: BEZ ▫ S&P rating: A ▫ Value Line financial strength rating: B++

What sets Baldor apart, analysts believe, is its innovative approach to the business of manufacturing industrial motors. For one thing, Baldor offers a broad selection of motors. What's more, it produces motors in small lot sizes that only fit the needs of a small group of customers. About a third of what it sells are custom products.

Second, the company is a domestic manufacturer. Even so, Baldor's margins are about the same as most of its competitors. Some of these rivals, moreover, also include higher-margined mechanical transmissions linkage products. What's more, Baldor has the highest margins of any domestic industrial motor manufacturer.

Analysts think part of the explanation relates to Baldor's fragmented customer base—it has over 8,000 customers. Additionally, the company sells only a modest volume into the consumer market, where the customers are large and can exercise significant pricing leverage.

Third, Baldor doesn't have its own sales force. Instead, it relies on independent sales representatives who are paid on commission. Each of these agents has an exclusive territory and sells all of Baldor's products in that region. In addition, the mix of Baldor's business is more heavily weighted to distributor sales—50 percent of sales, compared with 33 percent for the industry. This is a plus factor because distributors tend to concentrate on the replacement market, which is more recession-resistant than the original-equipment realm.

Company Profile

With annual sales of just only $558 million, Baldor Electric Company is a pygmy among giants. Baldor makes electric motors that power pumps, fans, conveyor belts, and all the other automated components that keep modern factories humming. It competes successfully against much larger firms such as Reliance Electric, Emerson Electric, and General Electric. But what Baldor lacks in size, it more than makes up for in flexibility and profitability.

Baldor Electric designs and manufactures a broad product line to serve its customers' diverse needs. Industrial AC and DC electric motors, ranging from 1/50 through 800 horsepower, are the mainstay of the company's products.

Baldor's line of Standard-E motors are designed to meet the efficiency requirements of the Energy Policy Act. Baldor's premium efficient Super-E motors are widely recognized as offering some of the highest efficiencies. These higher efficiencies translate into lower operating costs to the motor end-user.

Baldor also offers customers a wide range of "definite-purpose" motors. Examples include Baldor's Washdown Duty motors, which are ideal for food processing and other wet environments. Baldor's Chemical Processing line of cast-iron motors are built for the harsh environment of mills and processing plants. Baldor Farm Duty motors meet the rugged outdoor requirements in the agricultural market. Also included are broad lines of brake, pump, and gear motors, explosion-proof, and C-Face motors.

The fastest-growing segment of Baldor's product line is adjustable-speed drives. The company offers DC SCR controls, AC inverters, and vector control, and a wide range of servo and positioning products. Baldor markets Matched Performance by offering customers matched motor and control packages with lab-tested performance.

Baldor recently introduced the Baldor SmartMotor, an integrated motor and adjustable-speed control. Now available from one to ten horsepower, this breakthrough new product is easy to install and offers many performance advantages.

Shortcomings to Bear in Mind

- Up until 2001, Baldor Electric could boast of a long string of earnings increases. But, the bubble burst in 2001, as it did for most businesses in that hectic year. Earning per share declined from $1.34 to $.65 on a 10 percent decline in sales. It is not likely that 2002 will see a return to the levels of 2000.

Reasons to Buy

- On the other hand, 2002 should be better, according to CEO John McFarland. "We think 2002 will be much better! Let's look at some reasons why.

"First, there are some strong, positive trends in the U.S. economy. We have low inflation, low interest rates, rising consumer confidence, low inventories, low energy prices (except electricity), and increasing government spending.

"While 2001 was a bad year at Baldor for sales and profits, it was a good year in many other ways. We have been working 'smart' during these tough times."

Mr. McFarland went on to say, "We have reduced our costs by eliminating three plants and mechanizing some undesirable jobs. We have also been successful in reducing our material costs and reducing our energy consumption. We have made some good investments in equipment for better productivity. We have also increased our investment in training. The skills of our people are vital to our success."

- Studies indicate that it pays for employers to spend time and money on training, as Mr. McFarland points out. "We have been recognized by *Fortune* magazine for our efforts on the education of our employees, and our commitment to education is as strong as ever.

"In addition to employee education, Baldor's customer education classes continued to be well attended in 2001, with more than 7,000 graduates in the past 10 years. Our customer classes cover everything from basic understanding of motors and drives to advanced hands-on training requiring prerequisite classes. Our customers learn to apply and sell our products in these very popular training classes."

- Baldor offers the industry's broadest line of stock motors and drives. It offers more than 6,000 stock motor and drive products, now including servo motors and MINT motion control products. In 2001, BEZ added new standby and portable generators.

Baldor products are available at more locations than any other brand. Its thirty-nine district offices across North America offer immediate availability of Baldor products to thousands of distributors in the U.S., Canada, and Mexico.

- Baldor has the shortest lead times on custom motors—as short as two weeks. According to a spokesman, "Our unique Flex Flow manufacturing process lets us produce any order in any quantity, quickly and efficiently. In addition to short manufacturing lead times, Baldor's Mod-Express department allows us to provide numerous modifications to stock motors and drives in a matter of hours. This service helps customers needing immediate non-stock products."

- Baldor Electric is the industry leader in energy efficiency, dating back to the 1929s—long before others were even talking about it. In the words of a company spokesman, "Today, our line of Super-E premium efficient motors range from 1 through 1500 horsepower and rank among the highest motor efficiencies produced. Baldor was the first motor manufacturer to meet the Consortium for Energy Efficiency levels across the board."

- Over the last two decades, Baldor has risen from the "other" category to the position of "most preferred" as industry's choice for electric motors. This distinction is awarded from data collected through independent surveys by industrial trade journals covering a wide variety of industry segments.

- According to the company's 2001 annual report, "Industrial plants that install and use Baldor Super-E premium efficient motors can reduce their electricity bills. In addition, the installation of variable frequency drives on many motor applications will further reduce the electricity consumption.

"Baldor is the industry leader, offering motors with the highest efficiency available and a full line of variable frequency drives to complement our Super-E motors."

- The 2001 annual report also states, "In 2001, more than 500 new stock products were developed. Some of the new products included a new line of cooling tower motors, new MSHA-(Mining Safety and Health Administration) approved motors, larger explosion-proof motors, new MINT motion controllers, improvements in our washdown motors, expansion in our larger AC motors, and new generators for poultry house applications. We also developed a wide variety of custom motors for numerous OEM customers, meeting specific applications and performance requirements, positioning Baldor as the Value provider in the motors, drives and generators industry."

- Baldor Electric spends thousands of hours every year talking with customers to see how the company is perceived. Baldor consistently receives high grades. In recent surveys, for instance, 82 percent of those interviewed named Baldor first when asked, "What motor line do you prefer?"

- Alan G. House, an analyst with *Value Line Investment Survey*, said in January of 2002, "a clean balance sheet, healthy new-product pipeline, and adept management team position the company well for the long run. Baldor's strong balance sheet makes future acquisitions a strong possibility."

Total assets: $458 million
Current ratio: 3.24
Common shares outstanding: 34 million
Return on 2001 shareholders' equity: 8.6%

	2001	2000	1999	1998	1997	1996	1995	1994
Revenues (millions)	558	621	577	589	558	503	473	418
Net income (millions)	23	46	44	45	40	35	32	26
Earnings per share	.65	1.34	1.19	1.17	1.09	.97	.84	.70
Dividends per share	.52	.49	.43	.40	.35	.29	.26	.21
Price High	25.2	22.5	21.7	27.2	23.8	18.8	19.9	13.6
Low	18.0	14.9	17.0	10.1	18.2	13.9	12.9	10.6

CONSERVATIVE GROWTH

The Bank of New York Company, Inc.

One Wall Street □ New York, New York 10286 □ (212) 635-1569 □ Direct Dividend reinvestment plan is available: (888) 643-4269 □ Web site: www.bankofny.com □ Listed: NYSE □ Ticker symbol: BK □ S&P rating: A □ Value Line financial strength rating: A

The Bank of New York Company is not like any bank you have ever heard of. The company is most accurately described as a leading global trust bank, rather than a traditional lending institution that is more vulnerable to changes in interest rates and economic conditions.

For many years, BK has maintained a consistent strategy of focusing on high-growth, fee-based businesses that has transformed the bank from a traditional commercial bank into the world's premier financial asset servicer.

Today, BK is a market leader in many

businesses that focus on servicing securities issuers and all forms of investors and intermediaries. The company's well-diversified franchise has become an integral part of the infrastructure for the global capital markets. What's more, the breadth of its products and services allows BK to build client relationships through many different avenues in all markets and regions throughout the world.

This strategic transformation is evident in the increased earnings contribution from BK's fiduciary and securities servicing businesses. These high-growth, fee-based businesses now comprise 55 percent of total normalized earnings, up from 27 percent in 1995. Traditional banking activities, which comprised 73 percent of total earnings in 1995, now make up only 45 percent of normalized earnings. Finally, the bank's continued focus on fee-based businesses resulted in noninterest income growing to 66 percent of total normalized revenue in 2001, up from 64 percent in 2000 and 47 percent five years ago.

Company Profile

BK is one of the largest bank holding companies in the United States, with total assets of more than $77 billion at the end of 2001. BK does not dominate the New York landscape. Even so, the bank is thriving after several years of shuffling its businesses and swallowing a string of small, niche-oriented acquisitions.

While largely sitting out the recent merger wave that is reshaping the banking group, BK has carved out a growing and highly profitable role as one of the nation's major processors of basic securities transactions. In fact, analysts say it resembles a processor more than a bank, especially considering its relatively modest consumer banking operation.

The company provides a complete range of banking and other financial services to corporations and individuals worldwide through its core businesses. These services include securities and other processing, corporate banking, retail banking, trust, investment management, and private banking and financial market services.

The company's principal subsidiary, the Bank of New York, is one of the largest commercial banks in the United States. Alexander Hamilton founded it in 1784, and it is the nation's oldest bank operating under its original name.

The bank is an important lender to major domestic and multinational corporations and to midsize companies nationally. It is the leading retail bank in suburban New York. The bank is also the largest provider of securities-processing services to the market and a respected trust and investment manager. It also provides cash-management services to corporations located primarily in the mid-Atlantic region.

Shortcomings to Bear in Mind

- BK is often considered a low-profile, conservative institution. It is a linchpin in the critical business of clearing securities trades and sending money between banks. However, its financial systems were among the most severely disrupted in the September 11 terrorist attacks. At some point during that fateful week, BK had more than $100 billion in transfers backed up in its system, including $30 billion owed to both Citigroup and J. P. Morgan Chase.

BK handles about 12 percent of funds transfers in the United States—or about $900 billion on a typical day—with the rest of the market divided between other major banks such as Citibank, Bank of America, J. P. Morgan, and Deutsche Bank AG. BK also clears, on an average day, as much as $1 trillion in government securities, a field in which the only other major player is J. P. Morgan.

On a more positive note, as soon as the attacks occurred, the bank activated its disaster recovery plan. Its government securities clearing backup site is in New Jersey, as is the backup data center for the funds transfer business.

Reasons to Buy

- Despite the problems of 2001, BK fared well in that turbulent year. In the words of CEO Thomas A. Renyi, "On a reported basis, we recorded net income of $1.34 billion and diluted earnings per share of $1.81. On a normalized basis, diluted earnings per share rose 5 percent to $2.01, from the $1.92 earned last year. Net income was $1.49 billion, an increase of 4 percent over the $1.43 billion earned last year."

- Securities Servicing and Global Payment Services is the bank's largest and fastest-growing business segment, contributing 61 percent of total fee revenue in 2001. Fee revenues from these businesses grew to $2.05 billion in 2001, compared with $1.91 billion the prior year.

  According to the BK 2001 annual report, "We are the market leader in many of the businesses in this segment, with specialized services and expertise required to help institutions worldwide mitigate risk, maximize performance, manage costs, and realize new opportunities.

  "Through the infrastructure we provide to the capital markets, we support broker/dealers and other market participants with essential services such as securities clearance, securities lending, collateral management and liquidity. We provide critical back-office functions for issuers of securities, including all types of fixed-income securities, equities, American depositary receipts and exchange-traded funds."

- BK has consistently invested in the technology necessary to improve its processing efficiency and accommodate incremental volume. As an example, BK designed a personal-computer-based information delivery system called Workstation. It enables the bank's processing customers to access a range of securities-related data captured by the bank from their own offices. Software the bank has developed, moreover, has allowed the bank to adapt this technology for use in virtually all of its securities-processing businesses.

- In the field of American depositary receipts (ADRs), BK holds a pre-eminent position. Domestic banks create ADRs to represent stocks issued by corporations abroad. Whenever you invest in a foreign company, you get an ADR, rather than the actual certificate of the foreign company.

  BK expanded its market leadership position in depositary receipts during 2001 by winning 68 percent of all new sponsored depositary receipt appointments, adding ninety-two programs from twenty-six countries. BK is the world leader in public-sponsored depositary receipt programs, with a market share of 66 percent, representing 1,400 programs from seventy countries.

- The bank is also the market leader for innovative, high-quality corporate trust services. BK was ranked as the number one trustee in the United States, administering a portfolio of 80,000 trust and agency appointments, representing more than $1 trillion in outstanding securities for over 30,000 clients worldwide. According to a company spokesman, "We are a recognized leader in trust services for several debt products, including mortgage- and asset-backed securities, corporate and municipal debt, derivative securities, and international debt offerings."

- Continuing a long-term strategy, the company announced nine acquisitions in 2001. BK expanded its corporate trust business by acquiring the corporate trust operations of U.S. Trust. It expanded its brokerage and clearing capabilities through the acquisition of Westminster Research Associates. In another sector, the bank enhanced its stock purchase and stock option capabilities with the acquisition of Mavricc Management Systems.

The bank has completed more than seventy acquisitions since 1994, most of them related to the company's securities servicing businesses. Acquisitions are used to enhance "our product offering, expand our geographic reach, and consolidate scale business, such as corporate trust, clearing services and global custody," according to the 2001 annual report.

- BK has a solid record of growth. In the past eleven years (1990–2001), earnings per share climbed from $0.50 to $1.92, a compound annual growth rate of 13 percent. I used eleven years, since earnings per share were depressed in 1991, which would have given the percentage gain an unrealistic boost. In the same eleven-year period, dividends advanced from $0.27 to $0.72, a growth rate of 9.3 percent.
- For the second consecutive year, BK was named Best Custody Bank by *Global Finance*. *Global Custodian* ranked the company number one by for its technology, Internet access, value-added custody services, securities lending, and other custodial areas.

Total assets: $77,785 million
Return on average assets: 1.92%
Common shares outstanding: 737 million
Return on 2001 shareholders' equity: 23.8%

		2001	2000	1999	1998	1997	1996	1995	1994
Loans (millions)		37291	39262	38881	38340	36577	36105	36931	32291
Net income (millions)		1492	1429	1282	1192	1104	1020	914	749
Earnings per share		1.92	1.85	1.67	1.53	1.36	1.21	1.08	.93
Dividends per share		.75	.66	.58	.54	.49	.42	.34	.28
Price	High	58.1	59.4	45.2	40.6	29.3	18.1	12.3	8.3
	Low	40.2	29.8	31.8	24.0	16.4	10.9	7.1	6.2

GROWTH AND INCOME

Banta Corporation

225 Main Street □ Post Office Box 8003 □ Menasha, Wisconsin 54952 □ (920) 751-7713 □ Dividend reinvestment program not available □ Web site: www.banta.com □ Listed: NYSE □ Ticker symbol: BN □ S&P rating: B+ □ Value Line financial strength rating: B+

In its March 4, 2002, issue, *Fortune* magazine named Banta Corporation as one of its "Most Admired Companies" in America. The list was compiled following extensive research and analysis.

A select group of 10,000 executives, directors, and analysts rated the ten largest companies in each of the fifty-eight industries, based on eight attributes. In the printing industry, Banta ranked first in the employee talent attribute and second in use of corporate assets, social responsibility, financial soundness, long-term investment value, and quality of products and services.

"We are honored to be included in this prestigious list for the second consecutive year," said Donald Belcher, chairman and chief executive officer of Banta. "It's especially gratifying to receive this recognition, since the input that prompts the rankings come from our peers, industry analysts and others outside of Banta. For more than 100 years, we have focused our energies on advancing the eight attributes on which the list is based."

Company Profile

Banta is much more than a leading provider of printing and digital imaging services. The supply-chain management business, the fastest-growing segment of Banta's operations, offers important value-added products and services to support the growth of Banta's core printing businesses.

Although you probably never gave it much thought, the last time you opened a carton containing a new computer, VCR, or other piece of electronic gear, there was a good chance that Banta printed the instruction booklet, installation guide, warranty cards, and other printed matter inside. Banta also probably provided the how-to video or audio tape, supplied the software kit, including diskettes, and provided all of the packaging, whether plastic, cardboard, or paper.

Banta Corporation is a market leader in two primary businesses: printing, and supply-chain management. The company has more than thirty-five operations in North America, Europe, and Asia. Founded in 1901, Banta became a public company in 1971.

Business, trade, and special-interest magazine publishers turn to Banta for the production of nearly 800 titles. Three modern facilities provide a focused production environment for printing and mailing short- to medium-run publications.

It publishing market products include the following:

- Educational, trade, juvenile, professional, and religious books
- Business, trade, association, and consumer special-interest magazines
- Journals and newsletters
- Technical manuals
- Calendars
- Directories
- Multimedia kits
- Instructional games
- CD-ROMs
- Video and audio cassettes
- Web sites

Banta provides a full spectrum of direct marketing materials and personalization technologies that maximize the effectiveness of direct-response print. The company is the leader in the production and distribution of specialty and retail catalogues.

Finally, Banta holds a leadership position in each of its market segments.

Banta Health care products extends the company's reach beyond the traditional printing and digital-imagining segments. Three manufacturing facilities produce sterile and nonsterile products used in hospitals, outpatient clinics, and dental offices. These specialized products are composed of paper, nonwoven materials, and polyethylene film. The product line also extends to related applications in the foodservice industry, such as disposable bibs, tablecloths, and gloves.

Shortcomings to Bear in Mind

- I find it difficult to find much wrong with this company. It has experienced steady growth and pays a solid dividend. The only shortcoming it may have is that it is not growing at a pace that would appeal to an aggressive investor.

If you have a conservative outlook, this stock should appeal to you.

- On the other hand, no company is perfect. The 2001 slump in advertising hurt the company. In the fourth quarter of that year, page counts for Banta's special-interest magazines fell 16 percent, compared with the same period of the prior year. For the full year, moreover, the reduction was 10 percent. On a more positive note, despite the page reductions and an unusually high incidence of magazine attrition, Banta increased the number of magazines it produces to just over 800, gaining new customers and titles and increasing its market share.

Reasons to Buy

- In the past ten years (1991-2001), earnings per share (EPS) advanced from $0.96 to $2.31, a compound annual growth rate of 9.2 percent. During that span, EPS declined twice, but the decline was modest. In the same period, dividends per share rose from $0.25 to $0.62, a growth rate of 9.5 percent. During those years, the dividend increased every year. To be sure, these numbers are not particularly impressive. However, the price-to-earnings ratio of Banta is extremely low, compared to the market.

- In an interview conducted by *The Wall Street Transcript* in mid-2001, Mr. Belcher answered this question: "How do you perceive your standing as far as your competition goes?"

    Mr. Belcher said, "We're certainly among the top rank of printers in this country. We're very much a niche player. We focus on two segments: one is the publishing segment where we print soft-cover books and special-interest magazines. Our books include educational materials and trade books, and our specialty magazines are short- to medium-run publications that focus on hobbies, professions and other special interests.

    "Our second print sector is direct marketing, where we produce catalogs and direct mail. So, we're very much a niche player, and we are a leader in each of those categories. We don't try to compete across the board. And in terms of industry prominence, we certainly place ourselves among the top echelon of printers in North America.

    "In supply-chain management, we're operating on a global basis now, with the blue chip companies of the technology world. Among our larger clients are Compaq, Microsoft, Cisco, Dell, Oracle, IBM and Sun Microsystems. Again, we rank in the top echelon of those competitors that are providing outsourcing services to the technology sector."

- Mr. Belcher explained why his company favors working with special-interest magazines. "These magazines are attractive to advertisers because the specialized readerships allows them to target their messages to their best prospects. As a result, special-interest magazines are less prone to advertising cycles. "This has been one of our fastest-growing print markets, and we see that growth continuing for us through both market growth and by taking market share, which we have effectively done over the years. Our customers realize that we really specialize in producing short- to medium-run monthly magazines and, as a result, provide the value-added services and print schedule fidelity that are essential to their businesses."

- He went on to explain why Banta does well in direct marketing. "Direct marketing is the fastest-growing print category. The material that shows up in your mailbox seems to increase instead of reduce, and that's an area which is projected to continue growing in the 6 percent to 7 percent annual range over the next several years."

- Supply-chain management has been a key factor in Banta's growth. Commenting on this business, Mr. Belcher said, "Supply-chain management is our global growth engine. This is a business where the underlying trends for outsourcing services, which are really what we provide in supply-chain management, are very strong. More and more companies, particularly in technology—but other industries as well, are looking for companies to help take over all or part of their manufacturing and distribution processes, so that they can concentrate on their own core competencies. Industry forecasts indicate that the demand for these services will expand at a more than 30 percent compound annual growth rate over the next several years.

  "Banta has grown very rapidly in this business. Our supply-chain business was about $35 million in revenue five years ago, and we should be in excess of $350 million this year (2001). We are confident that growth in the future will continue to be very, very exciting for us."

- Mr. Belcher went on to say, "In the supply-chain management area, I would say we are extremely well positioned with technology companies. One of the things that we are working on very hard right now is looking to find other related industries where we can bring this same outsourcing solution to capitalize on our particular strengths.

"One very good product example is medical devices. A company we are working with right now manufactures diabetic testing kits. We source the various materials for the kit, assemble and test the devices and then provide the packaging, distribution and fulfillment requirements for our customer. Those are the same type of services that we are providing for companies like Compaq, Microsoft, Dell, Cisco, IBM, and several other key players in the technology arena."

- Finally, Mr. Belcher points out that Banta has a solid financial structure. "We have always prided ourselves on maintaining a very strong financial position and a strong balance sheet. Right now (in mid-2001), our debt to total capital is a little over 30 percent. That gives us lots of room to increase our financial leverage to pursue acquisitions, which we hope to be able to do over the next few months and years.

  "We also have a very solid return on equity. One of the things we're working to do is to help investors see that Banta is much more than just a great printing company. We have a growth engine in addition to our cash engine of print, and that growth engine is our supply-chain management sector which we believe deserves a much higher multiple. It will become a larger part of our corporation going forward."

Total assets: $820 million
Current ratio: 2.12
Common shares outstanding: 25 million
Return on 2001 shareholders' equity: 14.5%

	2001	2000	1999	1998	1997	1996	1995	1994
Revenues (millions)	1453	1538	1278	1336	1202	1084	1023	811
Net income (millions)	50	59	54	53	52	51	54	47
Earnings per share	2.31	2.35	2.02	1.80	1.73	1.63	1.75	1.55
Dividends per share	.62	.60	.52	.51	.47	.44	.37	.35
Price High	31.0	25.7	27.4	35.3	29.9	30.7	30.1	25.7
Low	22.5	17.2	16.8	21.8	21.6	20.5	19.0	18.0

Baxter International, Incorporated

One Baxter Parkway □ Deerfield, Illinois 60015 □ (847) 948-2875 □ Dividend reinvestment program available: (800) 446-2617 □ Web site: www.baxter.com □ Listed: NYSE □ Ticker symbol: BAX □ S&P rating: B □ Value Line financial strength rating: A+

Fifty years ago, people with end-stage renal disease (ESRD), or kidney failure, faced certain death. There was no treatment that could replicate the function of the kidneys—to remove toxins, waste, and excess water from the bloodstream. Nor were transplants an option a half century ago.

There is no cure for end-stage renal disease. Without either dialysis or a kidney transplant, a person with ESRD will die.

In 1956, Baxter introduced the first commercial hemodialysis (HD) machine, making life-saving dialysis therapy possible for thousands of people suffering from kidney failure.

Today, there are approximately a million dialysis patients worldwide. About 86 percent of them use HD as their primary therapy. The other 14 percent use peritoneal dialysis (PD), a newer, home-based therapy pioneered by Baxter in the late 1970s. Today, Baxter is a world leader in providing products and services to people with ESRD, serving patients in more than 100 countries.

Dialysis treatment rates are expected to grow significantly in developing countries in the years ahead, if economic growth continues. In Latin America, for instance, dialysis treatment rates are expected to double over the next several years. That's because of an aging population, increasing health-care coverage, and better diagnosis of kidney disease.

Company Profile

Baxter dates back to 1931, when it was the first producer of commercially prepared intravenous solutions. The company is now a leading producer of medical products and equipment, with an emphasis on products and technologies associated with the blood and circulatory system. Sales abroad account for more than 50 percent of revenues.

In 2000, the company spun off its cardiovascular business as a separate publicly traded company. As it is now constituted, Baxter operates three divisions.

Medication Delivery

2001 Sales: $2.93 billion

This division manufactures a range of products used to deliver fluids and drugs to patients. These products provide fluid replacement, nutrition therapy, pain management, antibiotic therapy, chemotherapy, and other therapies.

The company provides intravenous (IV) and irrigating solutions in flexible, plastic containers; premixed liquid and frozen drugs for IV delivery; IV access systems and tubing sets; electronic IV infusion pumps; solutions, containers, and automated compounding systems for IV nutrition; IV anesthesia devices and inhalation agents; and ambulatory infusion systems.

BioScience

2001 Sales: $2.79 billion

The BioScience division produces therapeutic proteins from plasma and through recombinant methods to treat hemophilia, immune deficiencies, and other blood-related disorders. These include coagulation factors, immune globulins, albumin, wound-management products, and vaccines. Baxter also has a stake in blood-collection containers and automated blood-cell separation and collection systems. These products are used by hospitals, blood banks, and plasma-collection centers to collect and process blood components for therapeutic use or for processing into therapeutic products, such as albumin. Therapeutic blood components are used to treat patients undergoing surgery, cancer therapy, and other critical therapies.

Renal

2001 Sales: $1.94 billion

The Renal division provides a range of renal dialysis products and services to support people with kidney failure. The company is the world's leading manufacturer of products for peritoneal dialysis (PD), a home dialysis therapy. These products include PD solutions, container systems, and automated machines that cleanse patients' blood overnight while they sleep. Baxter also manufactures dialyzers and instrumentation for hemodialysis (HD). Baxter's Renal Therapy Services (RTS) operates dialysis clinics in twelve countries outside the United States, while Renal Management Strategies, Inc. (RMS), works with U.S. nephrologists to provide a kidney-disease management program to health care payers.

Baxter continues to develop new PD solutions to better manage specific patient needs. One example is Extraneal, which improves the removal of excess fluids and toxins from patients with end-stage renal disease. Introduced in Europe in 1997 and approved in twenty-eight countries, Extraneal today is being used by more than 6,000 European patients—more than a third of Baxter's European PD population—and is currently under regulatory review in the United States.

Shortcomings to Bear in Mind

- Growth in earnings per share is rather pedestrian. In the 1991–2001 period, earnings per share increased from $1.02 to $1.09, a compound annual growth rate of only 0.7 percent. In the same ten-year span, dividends edged up from $0.37 to $0.58, a growth rate of 4.6 percent. What's more, the $0.58 dividend has been paid in each of the past four years.

- In the summer of 2001, Baxter said that its dialysis filters appear to have played a role in the deaths of dialysis patients in several countries. The company's announcement came as government health authorities were investigating the deaths of fifty-one patients in connection with Baxter's recalled dialysis filters—forty-seven in Croatia, Spain, and elsewhere overseas, and two each in Nebraska and Texas. Baxter concluded that a processing fluid used in routine testing in its manufacturing operation in Ronneby, Sweden, may have played a role in many of the deaths. The fluid, a chemical known as 5070, is used to test for leaks, but somehow was not fully removed from all dialyzers, the company said.

  In November of that year, Baxter agreed to pay $289,000 to each of the families of the dialysis patients whose deaths were linked to the flawed dialysis filters. "Our goal is to do the right thing," said CEO Harry Jansen Kramer Jr. "While nothing we do will replace the loss these families have experienced, we understand their need to bring closure to the tragedy. Our hope is that this settlement helps to minimize the distress to the families involved."

Reasons to Buy

- Late in 2001, Baxter purchased the assets of a small company that has exclusive rights to the technology for a unique and proprietary recombinant erythropoietin (Epo) drug for the treatment of anemia. This product, known as Epoetin Omega, has characteristics that are distinctly different from other Epos.

Since Epoetin Omega was first launched, it has been used by thousands of patients and more than 1,000 individuals have participated in clinical trials. The epoetin class of drugs represents the largest single category in the total dialysis product market, which includes equipment, disposables, and pharmaceuticals. Global sales were nearly $5 billion in 2000 and are expected to more than double in size by 2005.

"We are pleased to be moving forward so quickly with our entry into the pharmaceutical arena related to treating kidney disease and associated illnesses, which is the strategic business direction we announced in March (2001). The acquisition of Epoetin Omega marks the first step for Baxter's renal business in this new marketplace. It also positions Baxter in a unique role as the only company offering a complete and complementary portfolio of dialysis-related products," said Alan L. Heller, Baxter senior vice president and president of its Renal business.

- As we enter the twenty-first century, the growing, aging population is creating unprecedented, explosive growth in medical conditions that occur more frequently and grow more acute with age. Baxter manufactures and markets products and services that are used to treat patients with many of these conditions, including cancer, trauma, hemophilia, immune deficiencies, infectious diseases, kidney disease, and other disorders.

The company also makes products that are used in the treatment of patients undergoing most surgical procedures. All of these conditions can cause severe physical, emotional, and financial burdens to patients and their families. Baxter's role is to help alleviate these burdens by developing innovative technologies that improve the patient's quality of life and medical outcome and lower the overall cost of patient care. The majority of Baxter's businesses are pioneers in their field, with more than 70 percent of sales coming from products with leading market positions.

- Injury or trauma is the leading cause of death for people under age forty-four. Many trauma victims receive Baxter products—IV solutions, plasma-volume expanders, blood-transfusion products, and other products for fluid replenishment and blood-volume stabilization.

- In early 2002, Baxter bought Fusion Medical Technologies, Inc., a company that develops products used to control bleeding during surgery. "The acquisition of Fusion expands and enhances our strong portfolio of bio-therapeutic solutions for surgery and tissue repair," said Thomas Glanzmann, president of Baxter BioScience. "Fusion's expertise in collagen and gelatin-based products complements Baxter's strength in fibrin-based technologies. With the combination, we will be able to offer surgeons an array of solutions to seal tissue, enhance wound healing, and manage hemostasis—now including bleeding."

- In a report issued in February of 2002, the analyst for Argus Research Corporation said, "We believe the company is well-positioned to continue delivering solid growth in the future as it continues to pursue a host of growth initiatives, including development of new recombinant proteins, vaccines, drug delivery platforms, oncology, pathogen inactivation, renal products and continued expansion of its protein manufacturing capabilities."

- Standard & Poor's Stock Reports said in early 2002, "We believe Baxter is one of the more compelling names in our health care universe, and the stock remains attractive at current levels. Baxter has a robust pipeline of new products which should help accelerate the revenue and earnings growth rate meaningfully through 2005."

- According to Christopher Helman, writing for *Forbes* magazine in April 2002, "John Schroer, president of hedge fund Itros Capital Management, is particularly jazzed about Baxter's booming hemophilia drug. Factor VIII provides a blood component absent in hemophiliacs that allows blood to clot normally. The drug is in great demand by the nation's 40,000 hemophiliacs. Many take Factor VIII prophylactically before participating in risky activities like sports. Baxter sold $750 million of the drug last year (2001) and is on target to sell $1.3 billion in 2003. The drug's operating margins are 50 percent, double those of the company's total product line."

Total assets: $9,663 million
Current ratio: 1.60
Common shares outstanding: 590 million
Return on 2001 shareholders' equity: 24%

	2001	2000	1999	1998	1997	1996	1995	1994
Revenues (millions)	7663	6896	6380	6599	6138	5438	5048	9324
Net income (millions)	612	740	779	731	652	575	485	596
Earnings per share	1.09	1.24	1.34	0.55	0.53	1.06	0.67	1.06
Dividends per share	0.58	0.58	0.58	0.58	0.57	0.59	0.56	0.51
Price High	55.9	45.1	38.0	33.0	30.1	24.1	22.4	14.4
Low	40.1	25.9	28.4	24.3	19.9	19.9	13.4	10.8

CONSERVATIVE GROWTH

Becton, Dickinson, and Company

1 Becton Drive □ Franklin Lakes, New Jersey 07417-1880 □ (201) 847-7178 □ Direct dividend reinvestment plan is available: (800) 919-3111 □ Web site: www.bd.com □ Fiscal year ends September 30 □ Ticker symbol: BDX □ S&P rating: A □ Value Line financial strength rating: A+

Becton, Dickinson has the technology to help reduce the medical errors that have received attention of late. A U.S. government scientific panel found that about 75,000 hospital patients die each year from medical mistakes. Yet only 9 percent of the facilities have invested in equipment to address the problem.

For its part, Becton, Dickinson is offering two hand held devices, based on 3Com's Palm Computing technology. One tracks drugs from the initial order through their administration. The other serves a similar purpose for specimen collection, testing and patient file management.

Company Profile

Becton, Dickinson is a medical technology company that manufactures a broad range of supplies, devices, and systems for use by health care professionals, medical research institutions, industry, and the general public.

Becton, Dickinson focuses strategically on achieving growth in three worldwide business segments.

• BD Medical Systems accounted for 53 percent of sales and 59 percent of operating profits in fiscal 2001. It includes hypodermic products specifically designed for diabetes care, prefilled drug-delivery systems, and infusion therapy products. The segment also includes specialty blades and cannulas for ophthalmic surgery procedures, anesthetic needles, critical care systems, elastic support products, and thermometers.

• BD Biosciences accounted for 16 percent of sales and 13 percent of operating profit in 2001. The segment sells clinical and industrial microbiology products, flow cytometry systems for cellular analysis, tissue culture labware, hematology instruments, and other diagnostic systems, including immuno-diagnostic test kits.

• BD Clinical Laboratory Solutions accounted for 31 percent of sales and 28 percent of operating profits in fiscal 2001. This segment sells clinical and industrial microbiology products, sample collection products, specimen management systems, hematology instruments, and other diagnostic systems, including immuno-diagnostic test kits. Finally, this part of Becton, Dickinson has a stake in consulting services and customized, automated bar-code systems for patient identification, and point-of-care data capture.

The company's products are marketed here at home through independent distribution channels and directly to end-users. Outside the United States, products are sold through independent distribution channels, sales representatives, and, in some markets, directly to end-users.

Becton, Dickinson generates close to 50 percent of its revenues outside the United States. Demand for health care products and services continues to be strong worldwide, despite the ongoing focus on health care cost containment around the world. The health care environment favors good continued growth in medical delivery systems as a result of new products and opportunities.

In particular, the domestic market is poised for broad-scale conversion to advanced protection devices due to the growing awareness of benefits of protecting health care workers against accidental needle-sticks and a high level of current legislative and regulatory activity favoring conversion.

Shortcomings to Bear in Mind

■ Nearly half of the company's sales come from abroad. This exposes Becton, Dickinson to the risks associated with foreign current rates, which could create increased volatility in reported earnings. On the other hand, Becton, Dickinson has done a good job of managing foreign currency exposure, and the impact on earnings has typically been limited to only 1 or 2 percent.

■ Recent tensions between India and Pakistan as well as India and China regarding nuclear testing could interfere with the company's aggressive expansion into these densely populated markets. This might come through domestic or United Nations economic sanctions. However, analysts believe that any sanctions would exclude companies that provide medical supplies.

Reasons to Buy

■ According to a company spokesman, "We are a leader in a number of platforms in the Biosciences segment. In the last few years, we made key acquisitions in the areas of immunology, cell biology, and molecular biology. Growth in research products is driven by the expansion in genomic research and increased pharmaceutical and government spending in this area.

"In the Clinical Laboratory Solutions' segment, we have strong marketing positions. We also have opportunities for further growth in this segment. For example, nearly half of the world's population lives in medical markets that do not currently use evacuated blood collection systems, one of our principal products in this segment."

- Becton, Dickinson made solid progress in fiscal 2001, ended September 30, 2001. According to CEO Edward J. Ludwig, "Among financial highlights, 2001 revenues increased approximately 4 percent over 2000 (7 percent at constant foreign exchange rates) and net income, in line with expectations, was $438 million (before the cumulative effect of an accounting change), or $1.63 per share.

  "The revenue increases reflect growth in all three worldwide segments; in particular, sales of our safety-engineered products exceeded our projections, and BD Biosciences showed strength across the board. Additional revenue drivers included Pharmaceutical Systems and contributions from our two new clinical diagnostic platforms, BD Phoenix and BD Probe Tec ET."

- Mr. Ludwig also commented on the company's safety-engineered product line. "With the introduction of products such as our new BD Integra retracting needle syringe, we are embarking on our fourth generation of safety-engineered products. This legacy not only underscores our leadership in the field, it also points out BD's ability to continually innovate in mature market categories such as syringes, hypodermic needles, catheters and blood-collection devices."

- Mr. Ludwig also gave investors a glimpse of what lies ahead. "Looking further into the future, we have a range of genuinely exciting technologies and product platforms under development, particularly in the area of advanced drug delivery. This opportunity is especially compelling because these drug delivery systems are coming of age at the dawn of the biotechnology era. Large molecule biotechnology-based drugs today most often must be injected, as opposed to ingested. Early tests indicate that the delivery systems we have under development could significantly increase the effectiveness of such drugs. When added to the drug discovery role played by BD Biosciences and the diagnostics performed by BD Clinical Laboratory Solutions, BD is poised to participate in every phase of the biotechnology revolution, from drug discovery through diagnostics to drug delivery."

- Becton, Dickinson has been growing at a solid pace. In the 1991–2001 period, earnings per share climbed from $0.61 to $1.63, a compound annual growth rate of 10.3 percent—without a dip in earnings in any of those years. In the same ten-year span, dividends per share expanded from $0.15 to $0.38, a growth rate of 9.7 percent.

- The company has been repositioning the newly formed Bioscience/Diagnostics business towards faster-growing markets through new technologies. In the past, Becton, Dickinson has been strong in two markets: clinical microbiology, and flow cytometry for clinical and research applications.

  In the microbiology market, the company is trying to leverage its strong market position by introducing new technology platforms. These include a new automated microbiology system as well as the new Probetec DNA analyzer.

  In flow cytometry, Becton, Dickinson is trying to compete more broadly (both in research and clinical diagnostics), relying partly on acquisitions. For instance, the acquisition of Biometric Imaging (BMI) broadened the company's technology platform in cellular analysis. In addition, the purchase of Clontech Laboratories, a rapidly growing maker of reagents and tools used in the study of molecular biology (such as genomics), added research products for gene expression analysis.

- Domestic sales of insulin needles and syringes are expected to increase in the high single digits during the next few years, fueled by the estimated five percent annual growth in the number of Americans suffering from diabetes plus by the trend toward multiple insulin injections. Recent scientific studies have shown that the use of multiple daily injections of insulin reduces the severity of the disease's longer-term deleterious effects. Becton, Dickinson, which accounts for about 90 percent of the domestic insulin syringe market, has entered into an arrangement with Eli Lilly, the largest domestic producer of insulin products, and Boehringer Mannheim, a major manufacturer of glucose monitoring devices, to provide information to diabetics regarding the best manner in which to control their disease. Over time, this program should accelerate the trend toward multiple daily insulin injections. The company is also reviewing a number of noninvasive techniques to monitor glucose levels in diabetics. This device could reach the market before the end of the decade and further enhance the company's overall position in the diabetic sector.

- With a strong base of proprietary technology, Becton, Dickinson holds a leading worldwide market position in peripheral vascular access devices for infusion therapy and is an important supplier of components and procedural kits for regional anesthesia.

- Becton holds a strong market position in hypodermic needles and syringes and prefallible systems and offers a wide array of safety products for medication delivery in many areas of the world.

- The company's use of computer-aided design and manufacturing technology enables Becton to bring quality products to market faster and at a lower cost. One such technology is stereo lithography, which uses a laser system to quickly create a three-dimensional physical object from a computer-aided design model. Engineers can use this extremely accurate model as a prototype, improving both the quality of the product design and the speed of the product development process.

Total assets: $4,802 million
Current ratio: 1.38
Common shares outstanding: 258 million
Return on 2001 shareholders' equity: 20.8%

	2001	2000	1999	1998	1997	1996	1995	1994
Revenues (millions)	3754	3618	3418	3117	2810	2770	2712	2560
Net income (millions)	438	393	386	360	315	283	252	227
Earnings per share	1.63	1.49	1.46	1.37	1.21	1.06	.90	.75
Dividends per share	.38	.37	.34	.29	.26	.23	.21	.19
Price High	39.3	35.3	44.2	49.6	27.8	22.8	19.0	12.5
Low	30.0	21.8	22.4	24.4	20.9	17.7	12.0	8.5

Bemis Company, Inc.

222 South Ninth Street, Suite 2300 □ Minneapolis, MN 55402-4099 □ (612) 376-3030 □ Dividend reinvestment program is available: (612) 376-3030 □ Listed: NYSE □ Web site: www.bemis.com □ Ticker symbol: BMS □ S&P rating: A □ Value Line financial strength rating: A+

The key to market leadership is cutting-edge technology and innovation, based primarily upon material science. At Bemis' Flexible Packaging operations, differing grades of polymers, such as polyethylene, polystyrene, polypropylene, nylon, and polyester, are combined in a variety of ways to create films that are stronger, shinier, clearer, abuse-resistant, peelable, easier to print, sterilizable, and easier to process on machinery.

What's more, the company's recent acquisition of a shrink-packaging business introduced a patented technology that was not previously available to Bemis. The combination of this shrink film technology and "our material science expertise creates sizable opportunities for a variety of new innovations for our Flexible Packaging operations," said a company spokesman.

"Our research and development efforts go beyond the laboratory to the manufacturing floor, designing films that work better on even the newest high-speed machinery. We go into customer plants to design innovative solutions for their packaging and marketing needs. Bemis consistently devotes a significant effort to the development of new products and processes that will keep us at the forefront of the industry and keep our customers anticipating the next generation of packing innovation."

Company Profile

Dating back to 1858, Bemis is a leading manufacturer of flexible packaging and pressure-sensitive materials. More than 75 percent of the company's sales are packaging related.

Flexible packaging refers to product packaging that can be easily bent, twisted, or folded. The opposite is rigid packaging, which includes things like glass and plastic bottles, metal cans, and cardboard boxes. Examples of flexible packaging include candy bar wrappers, pouches for shredded cheese, bread bags, and dog food bags.

Flexible packaging is an attractive means of packaging a wide variety of products because of its light weight, its strength, and the way it can be used in small amounts in most applications. That results in lower costs for the package itself and gives the consumer less material to dispose of after the package is used.

The primary market for the company's products is the food industry, which accounts for over 65 percent of sales. Other markets include medical, pharmaceutical, chemical, agribusiness, printing and graphic arts, as well as a variety of other industrial end uses. Bemis holds a strong position in many of its markets and actively seeks new market segments where its technical skill and other capabilities provide a competitive advantage.

Bemis has a strong technical base in polymer chemistry, film extrusion coating and laminating, printing and converting, and pressure-sensitive adhesive technologies. These capabilities are being integrated to provide greater innovation and accelerated growth in the company's core businesses.

Business Segments
Flexible Packaging
Bemis is the leading manufacturer of

flexible packaging in North America. The company provides multinational and North American food and consumer products companies with packaging solutions that protect contents during shipment, extend shelf life, and offer attractive, consumer-friendly designs. Over 60 percent of Flexible Packaging sales are printed film materials. The balance is sold as plain film for retail and institutional food as well as a variety of other markets.

This segment breaks down into three smaller pieces:

- High Barrier Products (42 percent of sales) includes controlled and modified atmosphere packaging for food, medical, personal care, and nonfood applications consisting of complex barrier, multilayer polymer film structures, and laminates. Primary markets are processed and fresh meat, liquids, snacks, cheese, coffee, condiments, candy, pet food, personal care, and medical packaging.

- Polyethylene Products (26 percent of sales) include mono-layer and co-extruded polymer films that have been converted to bags, roll stock, or shrink wrap. Primary markets are bakery products, seed, retail, lawn and garden, ice, fresh produce, frozen vegetables, shrink wrap, tissue, and sanitary products.

- Paper products (9 percent of sales) include multiwall and single-ply paper bags, balers, printed paper roll stock, and bag closing materials. Primary markets are pet products, seed, chemicals, dairy products, fertilizers, feed, minerals, flour, rice, and sugar.

Pressure-Sensitive Materials

Bemis is a major worldwide manufacturer of pressure-sensitive adhesive-coated materials for a variety of markets. Under the brand name MACtac, Bemis delivers advanced product performance to the pressure-sensitive industry. Examples include labeling for cold temperature food packaging, harsh environment conditions, wet manufacturing processes, miniature electronic components, tamper evident packaging, and technologically advanced fastener applications.

This segment is divided as follows:

- Roll Label Products (11 percent of sales) include unprinted rolls of pressure-sensitive adhesive coated papers and film. These products are sold to converters who print labels for bar coding, product decoration, identification, safety marking, and product instructions. Primary markets are food packaging, personal care product packaging, inventory control labeling, and laser/ink jet printed labels.

- Graphics and Distribution Products include unprinted rolls or sheets of pressure-sensitive adhesive-coated papers and films. Offset printers, sign makers, and photo labs use these products on short-run and/or digital printing technology to create labels, signs, or vehicle graphics. Primary markets are sheet printers, shipping labels, indoor and outdoor signs, photograph and digital print over-laminates, and vehicle graphics.

- Technical and Industrial products include pressure-sensitive adhesive-coated tapes used for mounting, bonding, and fastening. Tapes sold to medical markets feature medical-grade adhesives suitable for direct skin contact. Primary markets are batteries, electronics, medical, and pharmaceuticals.

Shortcomings to Bear in Mind

■ Joseph A. Beyrouty, an analyst with *Value Line Survey*, said in early 2002, "The pressure-sensitive business faces a weak market. As a result, its plants are being under-utilized, and its costs are high relative to sales. Further, pricing and volume weakness caused by the ailing economy continues to plague this division's earnings."

Mr. Beyrouty also pointed out, "Bemis entered into a swap agreement to effectively lower interest payments. The agreement provides Bemis Company with a hedge against $350 million worth of debt. Currently, the swap and favorable Fed rate cuts saved the company a little over $1 million in interest expense during the third quarter of 2001. Unfortunately, a disappointing joint venture in Brazil, coupled with negative translation effects, more than offset savings in interest expense in 2001."

Reasons to Buy

- Bemis has a solid record of growth. In the 1991–2001 period, earnings per share expanded from $1.03 to $2.64, a compound annual growth rate of 9.9 percent. What's more, there were no dips along the way. That's particularly noteworthy in view of the recession that took place in 2001. The dividend in the same ten-year span advanced from $0.42 to $1.00, and was raised every year during that period.

- Bemis has been active on the acquisition front. In late 2001, the company acquired Duralam, Inc., a maker of films for packaging meat, cheese, candy, and other foods, for $69 million. A year earlier, Bemis purchased the specialty plastic films business (with sales of about $150 million per year) of Viskase Companies, Inc. It paid $228 million in cash. The Viskase line gave Bemis immediate access to important fresh meat markets and was a natural extension of its position in processed meat, cheese, and poultry. Finally, the company also purchased the flexible packaging business of Arrow Industries (with annual sales of about $33 million) during 2000.

- *Standard and Poor's Stock Reports* spoke favorably of Bemis in a report issued in early 2002. "We expect capacity to continue to grow, while inventories decline, as BMS uses excess cash primarily to pay down debt (37 percent of capital at December 31, 2001). The company should benefit from lower interest rates and more value-added products for the food sector in flexible packaging (nearly 80 percent of sales)."

- "Bemis delivered solid results in 2001 despite facing some significant challenges," said Jeff Curler, president and CEO of Bemis. "During 2001, we successfully integrated new strategic businesses into our current operations, maintaining profit margins and customer service levels during the transition. We have added capacity where growth opportunities are imminent, and we have made manufacturing improvements in our pressure-sensitive materials business, which we expect to lead to improved results in 2002."

- "Our attention to maintaining a world-class manufacturing organization has rewarded our customers with competitive edge and flexibility in packaging options," said a company spokesman. "Over the past five years, Bemis has devoted substantial resources to improving capacity and expanding world-class operating facilities to meet the increasing demand for sophisticated barrier films.

  "Since the majority of the packages we sell in the Flexible Packaging business are printed, graphics capabilities are a significant source of expertise and competitive edge for Bemis. We are vertically integrated, offering customers our graphic design and color separation expertise. Bemis manufacturing operators work directly with graphic designers to create the highest-quality printed package. Our state-of-the-art printing presses significantly improve our manufacturing efficiencies with robotics to reduce press idle-time during change over to new colors."

Total assets: $1,889 million
Current ratio: 2.39
Common shares outstanding: 53 million
Return on 2001 shareholders' equity: 15.5%

		2001	2000	1999	1998	1997	1996	1995	1994
Revenues (millions)		2293	2165	1918	1848	1877	1655	1523	1390
Net income (millions)		140	131	115	111	108	101	85	73
Earnings per share		2.64	2.44	2.18	2.09	2.00	1.90	1.63	1.40
Dividends per share		1.00	.96	.92	.88	.80	.72	.64	.54
Price	High	52.5	39.3	40.4	46.9	47.9	37.6	30.0	25.8
	Low	28.7	22.9	30.2	33.5	33.6	25.6	23.0	20.5

CONSERVATIVE GROWTH

H&R Block, Incorporated

4410 Main Street □ Kansas City, MO 64111 □ (816) 701-4443 □ Dividend reinvestment plan is available: (816) 701-4443 □ Web site: www.hrblock.com □ Listed: NYSE □ Fiscal year ends April 30 □ Ticker symbol: HRB □ S&P rating: A- □ Value Line financial strength rating: A

Tax changes keep H&R Block's business humming. In the spring of 2002, another flood of tax changes prompted H&R Block to join forces with EarthLink to offer a comprehensive range of Internet-based tax tools available on the taxpayer's home computer.

EarthLink, one of the nation's leading Internet services providers, is helping to mitigate the guesswork and frustration from the tax-preparation process. It now does this by providing its subscribers with direct access to H&R Block's latest online tax services. Under this arrangement, EarthLink subscribers can now access H&R Block's vast array of online tax solutions.

"By teaming up with H&R Block, we combine the reliable source of financial services and information with the convenience of a fast, stable Internet connection," said Jon Irwin, EarthLink's executive vice president of Customer Experience. "EarthLink subscribers can simply log on to their Personal Start Page, and in seconds they can access information regarding the latest tax laws. They also can receive tax advice and confidently prepare,

review, and file their taxes—right from their home or office computer."

Company Profile

Founded in 1955, H&R Block provides a wide range of financial services through more than 10,400 offices situated in the United States, Canada, Australia, and the United Kingdom. Operations fall under five headings, as the following sections describe.

U.S. Tax Operations

This segment consists of the company's traditional tax business, which served 16.9 million taxpayers in fiscal 2001—more than any other company. Tax-related service revenues include fees from company-owned tax offices and royalties from franchised offices. At the end of fiscal 2001, there were 9,072 H&R Block offices located in the United States.

In addition to its regular offices, the company offers tax return preparation services at 484 H&R Block Premium offices for taxpayers with more complicated returns.

This segment also participates in the refund-anticipation loan products offered by third-party lending institutions to tax clients. This segment includes the company's tax preparation software Kiplinger TaxCut from H&R Block, other personal productivity software, online tax preparation through a tax preparer (where the client fills out an online tax organizer and sends it to a tax preparer for preparation), online do-it-yourself-tax preparation, online professional tax review, and online tax advice through the *www.hrblock.com* Web site.

International Tax Operations

This segment has a stake in providing local tax return preparation, filing, and related services. It consists of 1,378 company-owned and franchised offices in Canada, Australia, and the United Kingdom.

In addition, there are franchise offices in nine countries that prepare U.S. tax returns for U.S. citizens living abroad. This segment served 2.3 million taxpayers in fiscal 2001. Tax-related service revenues include fees from company-owned tax offices and royalties from franchised offices.

Mortgage Operations

This operation is engaged in the origination, servicing, and sale of nonconforming and conforming mortgage loans. Through a network of mortgage brokers, Mortgage Operations offers a flexible product line to borrowers who are creditworthy but who do not meet traditional underwriting criteria. Conforming mortgage loan products, as well as the same flexible product line available through brokers, are offered through H&R Block Financial Centers and H&R Block Mortgage Corporation retail offices.

Investment Services

This segment has a stake in offering full-service investment advice through H&R Block Financial Advisors, Inc., a full-service discount securities broker. Financial planning and investment advice are offered through H&R Block Financial Centers, H&R Block Financial Advisors offices, and tax offices. Stocks, bonds, mutual funds, and other products and securities are offered through a nationwide network of registered representatives at the same locations.

Business Services

Business Services provides accounting, tax, and consulting services to business clients, as well as tax, estate planning, financial planning, wealth management, and insurance services to individuals.

The business services operation consists essentially of RSM McGladrey, Inc., (RSM). In fiscal 2002, RSM purchased and integrated assets of regional firms Messina, Ceci, Archer & Company, and Fisk & Robinson. Finally, an investment banking firm, EquiCo., was acquired in November of 2001.

Shortcomings to Bear in Mind

- During 2001, several insiders—such as corporate executives and board members—sold part of their holdings in the company. Very few were buyers during this same period.
- A negative comment from Pallavi Gogoi who writes for *BusinessWeek*, "Even the booming tax business—which makes up 55 percent of Block's revenues and profits—is likely to slow," he said in March of 2002. "Revenues from tax preparation are expected to be up 13 percent this fiscal year and next but will return to more typical 6 percent growth by 2004."

    Mr. Gogoi also said, "Block isn't as powerful in the do-it-yourself market for tax prep—largely an online business dominated by Intuit, Inc. It accounts for only 5 percent of revenues, and its market share has been flat for three years."

- The company's accounting and consulting operations are suffering from the decline in business spending and could take a hit from the Arthur Andersen fallout. Detroit's Olde Discount Corporation, a broker H&R Block bought for $850 million in 1999, is hurting because of the slump in the stock market. Finally, the mortgage boom is likely to run out of steam when interest rates start to climb.

Reasons to Buy

- At least one investor is not too concerned about the future of H&R Block. The legendary Warren E. Buffett bought 8.4 percent of HRB in 2001 and added 230,000 shares in early 2002. Since he is the world's richest person, maybe it can be assumed he knows more about H&R Block than some of the skeptics.
- *Standard & Poor's Stock Reports* is in Mr. Buffett's camp. In early 2002, the analyst said, "We see revenues climbing in the mid-double digits for both FY 02 (Apr.) and FY 03 as confusing tax law changes and increased advertising take effect, leading to greater demand for professional help. We also expect newer products to add appeal.

   "Margins for FY 02 should widen 70–80 basis points on cost controls, despite a marketing blitz to increase brand relevance to an underrepresented middle income market. In addition, the growth of mortgages and business services, which are relatively recession-resistant, will likely further diversify earnings."

- The company produced record earnings in fiscal 2001, despite a challenging environment. In the words of Frank J. Cotroneo, senior vice president and Chief Financial Officer, "We attained our goal and saw our U.S. tax margin increase from 22.4 percent last year (2000) to 26.2 percent this year. In addition, the pre-tax margin within our mortgage operations improved to 33.4 percent, from 24.9 percent the prior year."

   Mr. Cotroneo went on to say, "This year we repurchased 6.8 million shares of H&R Block stock within our twelve-million repurchase allocation. We are increasing our quarterly cash dividend 7 percent and implementing a two-for-one split of our common stock. A strengthening stock price during a time of general market uncertainty suggests that investors acknowledge the value of our business strategy and recognize our company's strong financial performance and progress executing it."

- A key element in the recent success of H&R Block is the company's CEO, Mark A. Ernst. Ever since the forty-three-year-old former American Express executive joined the company in 1998, he has been hell-bent on diversifying into other financial services. What's more, he is undeterred by the failure of his predecessors' moves into legal services or the ill-timed sales of Internet service provider CompuServe Corporation for $1.3 billion in 1998 when critics said it was worth twice that.

   Investors quickly voted their confidence in Mr. Ernst's actions. After languishing for years, the stock climbed 117 percent in 2001 at a time when the S&P 500 average sagged nearly 12 percent.

Total assets: $4,122 million
Current ratio: 1.14
Common shares outstanding: 183 million
Return on 2001 shareholders' equity: 34.8%

	2001	2000	1999	1998	1997	1996	1995	1994
Revenues (millions)	3002	2452	1645	1307	1916	861	1326	1215
Net income (millions)	277	252	238	174	48	125	107	164
Earnings per share	1.52	1.28	1.18	.81	.23	.59	.51	.77
Dividends per share	.54	.51	.43	.40	.52	.64	.61	.55
Price High	46.4	24.8	29.8	24.5	22.9	21.1	24.4	24.4
Low	18.3	13.5	19.0	17.7	14.0	11.8	16.7	16.5

AGGRESSIVE GROWTH

The Boeing Company

100 North Riverside Plaza ◻ Chicago, Illinois 60606-1596 ◻ Listed: NYSE ◻ (312) 544-2140 ◻ Dividend reinvestment plan is available: (888) 777-0923 ◻ Web site: www.boeing.com ◻ Ticker symbol: BA ◻ S&P rating: B ◻ Value Line financial strength rating: A

Boeing has been gradually adopting "lean" manufacturing strategies since the early 1990s. However, the company was not the first to emulate the Japanese approach. Domestic car companies made similar moves a decade earlier. The basic philosophy of the strategy is to make it easier for workers to boost output using less space and fewer movements.

Since late 1998, when Boeing began applying lean activities on its newest model, the 777, the time it takes to assemble the major components into a finished aircraft has dropped from seventy-one days to thirty-seven. The impact can be seen in the operating margins of the commercial airplane division—Boeing's largest and the source of 61 percent of its revenue.

In 1998, the unit's profit margin was a puny 1 percent. In 2002, it surpassed 10 percent. Although some of the gain comes from the company's increasing unwillingness to get into a price war with Airbus, executives also say that lean manufacturing has made a big impact.

"The whole concept is to look for quantum leaps in efficiency, to the tune of 50 percent," says David Swain, president of the Phantom Works division. "We are looking for whole new ways to build airplanes."

Company Profile

Founded eighty-six years ago by William E. Boeing, The Boeing Company is the leading aerospace company in the world, as measured by total revenues. The holder of more than five thousand patents, Boeing is the world's largest manufacturer of commercial jetliners and military aircraft and provides related services worldwide.

Boeing is also NASA's largest contractor. The company's capabilities and related services include helicopters, electronic and defense systems, missiles, rocket engines, launch systems, and advanced information and communications systems. Boeing has customers in 145 countries.

Boeing's military aircraft include the F/A-18 Hornet strike fighter, the F-15E Eagle fighter-bomber, the C-17 Globemaster

III transport, and the AH-64D Apache Longbow helicopter.

Boeing's space operations include communications satellites, Delta rockets, and the Space Shuttle (with Lockheed Martin). Finally, the company is also the prime contractor for the International Space Station.

Boeing's defense and space operations primarily makes the F-18 fighter jet for the U.S. Navy, the E-3 Airborne Warning and Control System (AWACS), the 767-based AWACS, and CH-47 helicopter. The company also has important development programs: the Joint Strike Fighter, the Airborne Laser, the F-22 fighter, and the expendable launch vehicle. Finally, the unit also makes Delta rockets, which are primarily used to carry commercial and military satellites.

Shortcomings to Bear in Mind

- Boeing is hoping to transform itself from an aerospace manufacturer into a comprehensive aerospace-manufacturing-and-services provider. Over the past decade, a number of developments have taken a toll on the company's profits. Not only have earnings been erratic, but return on equity has been far from impressive. These troublesome factors include mature and volatile markets, accelerating competition, and the commodity nature of jets, rockets, and satellites. Some analysts believe that Boeing is attempting to mimic GE's highly successful business model of using new-equipment sales as a platform for selling high-margin, long-term maintenance contracts. However, only time will tell whether this strategy will work.

  As part of the strategy, the company abandoned its long-time headquarters in Seattle in 2001 and moved to Chicago. According to Harry Stonecipher, Boeing's vice chairman, "Within five years, commercial aircraft will only account for about 50 percent of this company's revenues." He added that commercial aircraft sales in 2000 accounted for nearly two-thirds of Boeing's revenues. Mr. Stonecipher said that new sales in aircraft services and financial deals by Boeing Capital will grow at an annual rate of at least 15 percent.

- Four Boeing planes went down in the September 11 terrorists attacks; air travel declined precipitously; the company's stock sank and lost half of its value since May of 2001; and management had to lay off 30,000 workers. On top of that, Boeing lost out to Lockheed Martin in October of 2001 for the biggest defense contract ever—for the joint strike fighter—wiping out years of development and $1 billion in projected revenue for 2002 alone.

- Since the Boeing 717 entered service in 1999, the company had booked 137 firm orders (as of late 2001) for the jet and delivered eighty-six. This is far fewer than the 200 units it was estimated Boeing and its suppliers had to produce to break even on the program.

  However, pressure from existing and potential airline customers, including some airlines in emerging markets in China, might persuade Boeing to keep its beleaguered 717 jetliner program operating instead of shutting it down, as many in the aerospace industry have predicted.

  Customers who use the midrange airplane rave about its performance and operating costs, but it has also been criticized as being too expensive for a 100-seat airplane. The jetliner lists for between $31 million and $34 million, but most customers have been paying about $25 million—a price that some airline executives say is still about $5 million too high.

Reasons to Buy

- Boeing's chief competitor, Airbus Industries, is developing a super jumbo jet. For its part, Boeing says it will focus on a new, near-supersonic jet that the company says will be able to fly 20 percent faster than today's conventional planes without boosting operating costs. This move allows Boeing, the world's largest manufacturer of commercial jets, to stake out a fundamentally different view of the future of commercial aviation than that of Europe's Airbus. While Airbus is betting more than $12 billion that airlines want super jumbo jets that can carry more than 600 passengers on long trips to a given destination, Boeing is convinced there is much larger demand for smaller, faster planes that take people directly to their destination.
- The airline industry has not fared well since the terrorist attacks on September 11, 2001. On the other hand, the defense industry stands to benefit. Boeing is particularly well positioned to gain, according to one defense analyst. He contends that Boeing's F-15 Eagle, F/A-18E and F Super Hornet, and AV-8B Harrier production lines are still up and running.
- Boeing won a major contract in March of 2002 to develop an entire network of new weapons, communications systems, and intelligence-gathering sensors. The Pentagon hopes they will one day revolutionize the way the Army fights wars.

  The overall value of these contracts could top $10 billion as elements of future Combat Systems are deployed over the next decade. For the first time, the Army is asking a single contractor to oversee development of a range of new technologies and weapons that would bring the service into the digital age.
- Boeing may not admit it, but its new finance unit (created early in 2001),

aspires to be a GE Capital clone. Boeing Capital is moving aggressively to help its parent not only sell more aircraft and expand into aerospace, but also move into financing such big-ticket items as oil rigs, barges, and cargo ships. Boeing Capital was created as part of the company's diversification strategy.

"Clearly we believe in the concept of a financial-service company," says Boeing Capital President James F. Palmer. "One doesn't have to look any further than GE to see what they have been able to do. The key question is: 'How do you grow at a profitable rate?'"

The crux of BA's growth plan is to stick to financing airplanes and heavy equipment. Mr. Palmer also sees new opportunities in commercial satellite financing—particularly now that Boeing owns Hughes Satellite Company.

- Boeing builds about 85 percent of the world's jetliners, and an estimated $74 billion a year is spent to keep them flying. However, up until recently, Boeing was giving away its engineering drawings to third-party service providers. No longer. It is now making an across-the-board push into maintenance, modifications, financing, air-traffic control, and even pilot training. "This could be big stuff," said Cai von Rumohr, an aerospace analyst with SG Cowen. Already, more than 20 percent of Boeing's military revenues emanate from activities like maintaining Air Force bases, and its Web site for spare parts generated revenues of $400 million a year. In a sign of how far the services push might go, Boeing agreed to buy thirty-four used 757s from British Airways, convert them into freighters, and lease them to carrier DHL with a fixed hourly maintenance fee.
- Boeing began installing new landing aids in the cockpits of thousands of its jetliners in 2002. The additional feature is

designed to give pilots earlier and more clear-cut warnings if an aircraft is following a wrong trajectory approaching an airport, or if it is likely to land too short or too far down a runway to safely slow down and turn off at an appropriate spot. Boeing crash studies indicate that in the past ten years, 51 percent of all major accidents involving Western-built jetliners occurred during the final approach and landing. "It is the single most important thing we can do in the short term to improve safety," said Bob Myers, the Boeing manager in charge of the project. The goal is to give cockpit crews extra time to gauge the momentum of aircraft during the hectic last few minutes of the flight and adjust the rate of descent, or to abort a landing if necessary.

■ At the end of 2001, Congress reached an agreement on a $22 billion plan for the Air Force to lease 100 Boeing 767s that will be converted into midair refueling planes. The deal calls for the planes to be leased for ten years.

■ Boeing finished 2001 on a high note. In the fourth quarter, it delivered 144 commercial jet transports, bringing the total for the year to 527 planes, or five more than the revised estimate of 522 following the September 11 attacks.

Total assets: $48,344 million
Current ratio: .79
Common shares outstanding: 798 million
Return on 2001 shareholders' equity: 21%

	2001	2000	1999	1998	1997	1996	1995	1994
Revenues (millions)	58198	51321	57993	56154	45800	22681	19515	21924
Net income (millions)	2721	2513	2309	1120	632	976	393	856
Earnings per share	3.41	2.44	2.49	1.15	.63	1.42	.58	1.26
Dividends per share	.68	.59	.56	.56	.56	.55	.50	.50
Price High	69.8	70.9	48.5	56.3	60.5	53.8	40.0	25.1
Low	27.6	32.0	31.6	29.0	43.0	37.1	22.2	21.1

INCOME

Boston Properties, Incorporated

111 Huntington Avenue □ Boston, Massachusetts 02199 □ Listed: NYSE □ (617) 236-3463 □ Dividend reinvestment plan is available: (888) 485-2389 □ Web site: www.bostonproperties.com □ Ticker symbol: BXP □ S&P rating: Not rated □ Value Line financial strength rating: Not rated

Boston Properties is one of the premier business-office real estate companies, with Class A office buildings situated in markets that are difficult to enter, such as Boston, New York, Washington, and San Francisco. Erecting new office buildings is difficult because of the physical constraints of these particular cities, coupled with stringent approval processes and the complexity of the building process. Yet the demand for office space continues unabated, causing rents to climb.

Company Profile

Boston Properties is a fully integrated, self-administered, and self-managed real estate investment trust that develops, redevelops, acquires, manages, operates, and owns a diverse portfolio of Class A office properties in the United States, concentrated in four core markets—Boston, Washington, D.C., midtown Manhattan, and San Francisco. As of year-end 2001, Boston properties owned 147 properties totaling 40.8 million square feet. The overall occupancy rate for properties in service at year-end 2001 was 95.3 percent.

Founded by Mortimer B. Zuckerman and Edward H. Linde, Boston Properties completed its initial public offering in June of 1997. As of the end of 2001, the company had twelve properties under development totaling 4.9 million square feet.

Among the company's largest properties are the following: Embarcadero Center in San Francisco, with 3.93 million net rentable square feet; The Prudential Center in Boston, with 2.14 million square feet; and Carnegie Center in Princeton, New Jersey, with 1.85 million square feet.

At the other extreme are such smaller properties as Three Cambridge Center in Cambridge, Massachusetts, with 107,484 net rentable square feet; The Arboretum in Reston, Virginia, with 95,584 square feet; 17 Hartwell Avenue in Lexington, Massachusetts, with 30,000 square feet; and 560 Forbes Boulevard in South San Franciso, CA, with 40,000 square feet.

Boston Properties, Inc. is a self-administered and self-managed real estate investment trust (REIT) that develops, redevelops, acquires, manages, operates, and owns a diverse portfolio of Class A office, industrial, and hotel properties.

Class A office buildings are generally considered those that have excellent locations and access and that attract high-quality tenants, are well maintained, and professionally managed.

The company is one of the largest owners, acquirers, and developers of Class A office properties in the United States.

Founded in 1970, the company's primary focus is office space. However, its property portfolio also includes hotels and industrial buildings.

Since becoming a public company in June of 1997, Boston Properties has experienced rapid growth by acquisitions in excess of $4 billion of office properties in existing and complementary markets. The company's expanding asset base is comprised of 144 properties, totaling 37.1 million square feet. To support its continued growth, Boston Properties raised over $800 million of equity through a secondary stock offering in January of 1998, $140 million in May of 1999, and $634 million in October of 2000.

What Is an Equity REIT?

As opposed to mortgage REITs, which lend money to property owners, equity REITs make their money by owning properties. Equity REITs allow you to invest in a diversified collection of apartment buildings, hospitals, shopping centers, hotels, warehouses, and office buildings.

Like mutual funds, REITs are not taxed themselves, providing they pay out at least 95 percent of their taxable income. That translates into fat dividends for shareholders, as REITs pass along the rents and other income they collect. Dividend yields are typically 6 percent or more. "Put it all together, and you are looking at a double-digit total return. Over the long haul, the return should be lower than traditional stocks, but higher than bonds," says Chris Mayer, a real estate professor at the University of Pennsylvania's Wharton School.

Kevin Bernzott, an investment adviser in Camarillo, California, views REITs as a stock/bond hybrid. "If you select quality REITs, they kick off a highly predictable stream of income, and eventually you may get some price appreciation. We plug them into the bond portion of the portfolio. They're almost like a bond with an equity kicker."

Shortcomings to Bear in Mind

- Some investors might be concerned that Boston Properties is not well diversified, since most of its properties are situated in only four cities. Also, the company's holdings are essentially concentrated in office buildings, to the exclusion of such sectors as retail shopping centers, apartment buildings, and industrial parks.
- *Standard & Poor's Stock Reports* had some negative thoughts. In 2001, they said, "vacancy rates jumped to double-digit levels in markets where the trust has office concentrations, such as Boston and San Francisco. Although BXP's year-end vacancy rates of 7.7 percent and 6.5 percent in these respective cities were better than the market, they represent a significant deterioration from prior-year levels of 0.7 percent and 2.1 percent.

 "Asking rents have been declining commensurately, and we expect higher insurance and security expenses to weigh on earnings."

Reasons to Buy

- As noted above, Boston Properties is not well diversified geographically. Instead, it concentrates on four cities.
  - San Francisco is the nation's west coast financial center. It is home to leading financial institutions, investment management firms, venture capitalists, law firms, consultants, and other business services.

   A combination of factors, including a talented, highly educated labor pool and exceptional "quality of life," continues to draw and to keep the most successful businesses in San Francisco.

   In San Francisco, new supply is projected to be limited by several factors, including legislated growth restrictions and lack of sites that can be developed in the core financial district.

- New York City is the nation's leader in financial services and international business and a worldwide center of commerce, finance, and culture. The city's extensive infrastructure includes the largest mass transit system in the nation. The media and financial services sectors, particularly financial, legal, communications, and other specialty businesses, are the economic engines that drive demand for office space, most markedly in midtown Manhattan.
- The area including northern Virginia and suburban Maryland, in addition to the District of Columbia, is the nation's fifth-largest metropolitan area and third-largest office market, after New York and Chicago. The economy of the entire region benefits enormously from the presence, stability, and funding of the federal government. It is home to one of the most highly educated workforces, the highest concentration of scientists and engineers, and the second-largest concentration of high technology firms in the country.

   Business service and government consulting industries, particularly knowledge-based enterprises such as information technology management and data communications firms, have been the driving engines of growth. Fairfax County, Virginia, has become the technology center of the region, while Montgomery County, Maryland, is experiencing the emergence of specialized research companies—reflecting proximity to and increased funding from the National Institutes of Health and the U.S. Food and Drug Administration—and strengthening the overall economic growth and diversity of the area.
- The greater Boston area draws upon both stable and established companies

as well as the emergence of a large number of small to midsize firms in four industry groups: financial services, health care, high technology, and knowledge creation, including research and development, consulting, and education.

Economic growth in this seventh-largest metropolitan area is powered by a number of factors, including the following: the diverse mix of companies; the presence of leading universities and medical research institutions; the availability of local venture and growth capital; the vitality of the city of Boston as a business, cultural, and residential center; and major improvements in the transportation infrastructure that are currently underway.

- The company's management believes prospects for internal growth are strong, in light of the REIT's high-quality portfolio, and the fact that its properties are situated in desirable locations in markets that are experiencing rising rents, low vacancy rates, and increasing demand for office and industrial space.

Internal growth prospects are also bolstered by the fact that the company's properties are in markets in which supply is usually limited by the lack of available sites and by the difficulty in obtaining the necessary approvals for developing vacant land. These high barriers to entry argue for the trust's ability to obtain strong increases in rental revenue in the years ahead.

- Boston Properties has always followed a conservative strategy of entering into long-term leases with tenants of strong financial standing. This means that in any given year, the turnover with its existing portfolio is moderate. More specifically, in 2001, leases terminated on only 7.5 percent of the space in existing buildings. In 2002, only 8.3 percent terminated.

- Boston Properties has long been recognized for its ability to create value through the development of its own properties, as opposed to the purchase of others. While notable acquisitions have been an important part of its impressive growth, the company has also demonstrated that high returns can be achieved by employing its team of skilled professionals to create projects from the ground up. Boston Properties has fully staffed development and construction operations in each of its markets. The company, moreover, has more development project in the works today than at any other office REIT.

Total assets: $7,254 million
Current ratio: NA
Return on 2001 equity: 8.9%
Common shares outstanding: 91 million

	2001	2000	1999	1998	1997	1996	1995	1994
Revenues (millions)	1033	879	787	514	140*			
Net income (millions)	201	146	114	93	35.2			
Earnings per share	2.24	2.05	1.72	1.53	.70			
Funds from operations	3.57	3.31	2.89	2.50	1.96			
Dividends per share	2.27	1.96	1.75	1.66	1.62			
Price High	43.9	44.9	40.8	41.6	36.2			
Low	34.0	29.0	30.9	33.4	30.3			

* Statistical information only available since the company went public in 1997.

GROWTH AND INCOME

BP p.l.c.

Britannic House, 1 Finsbury Circus □ London EC2M 7BA, United Kingdom □ (212) 451-8034 □ Dividend reinvestment program not available □ Web site: www.bp.com □ Listed: NYSE □ Ticker symbol: BP □ S&P rating: Not rated □ Value Line financial strength rating: A++

For many years to come, global energy needs will be met mainly by hydrocarbons (such as coal and oil), but the mix is rapidly shifting towards natural gas. Not surprisingly, the share of natural gas in BP's production has been climbing significantly. The company continues to search for, discover, and develop new sources of oil and natural gas to meet the world's energy needs.

Looking into the future, natural gas is an important bridge between oil and such nonpolluting solutions as fuel cells and renewable sources. Natural gas is a lower-carbon source of energy, producing greenhouse gas emissions that are 40 percent lower than those of coal. Discovered gas resources are almost equivalent in energy content to all the world's current oil reserves.

The application of technology to "our first LNG (liquified natural gas) plant in Trinidad set new cost standards," said a company spokesman. "We are developing processes that will cut costs further and also reduce emissions from future LNG plants.

"We are also investing in renewable energy technologies. BP is a global leader in solar power, accounting for nearly one-fifth of the world solar market. In 2001, we launched a project that will provide power to 150 isolated villages in the Philippines.

"In addition, we are making selective investments in wind power generation on BP's operational sites, such as the Nerefco refinery in the Netherlands."

Working with the city of London, BP p.l.c. is helping to introduce hydrogen fuel cell buses to the U.K. capital by 2003. The company will build and manage the supply network for the hydrogen fuel cell. Vehicles that use this fuel will make little noise and produce no emissions other than water vapor.

Company Profile

Because of the recession and unsettling terrorist activity, 2001 proved to be a year of transition for BP p.l.c. The generally tight markets of 2000 and early 2001 gave way to a more balanced oil market and a relatively weak U.S. natural gas market.

BP serves millions of customers every day, providing fuel for mobility, energy for light and heat, and petrochemicals. The company has some 110,000 employees working in more than 100 countries to create choices and satisfy energy needs of a growing world population. The following provides a glimpse of BP p.l.c. at the end of 2001.

● The company's production increased by 5.5 percent over 2000. On average, BP produced 1.93 billion barrels of crude oil each day in 2001 and 8.6 billion cubic feet of natural gas.

● BP's hydrocarbon reserves stood at 16.3 billion barrels of oil equivalent.

● In 2001, the company was selling natural gas in twenty-four countries, with average sales volumes of 18.8 billion cubic feet a day, compared with 14.5 billion cubic feet a day the prior year.

● BP had increased annual sales of solar power capacity, to fifty-five megawatts, or 30 percent more than in 2000.

- The company had interests in twenty-one refineries, with a throughput of 2.9 million barrels of crude oil a day.
- It was selling an average of 160 million gallons of fuel a day through 26,800 service stations and other commercial channels.
- BP's convenience store sales revenues exceeded $3.2 billion a year.
- The company had 55 petrochemicals sites worldwide.

Shortcomings to Bear in Mind

- In 2001, the company found out that it was not immune to adversity. In the oil sector, prices were 15 percent below the levels seen in 2000. What's more, refinery margins were weak; retailing was "fiercely competitive," said CEO Sir John Browne. "And in the chemicals sector, margins were at levels below those seen at the bottom of the previous business cycle."
- Two of Alaska's most controversial offshore oil ventures are the target of fervent environmental criticism because they are the first U.S. offshore production projects to use undersea pipelines. Situated in BP's Arctic Ocean Northstar fields, which hold between 140 million and 150 million barrels of crude oil each, these fields could eventually help steady Alaska's falling production and ease a long decline in U.S. domestic output. The projects should add more than 120,000 barrels per day to Alaska's output, which has fallen nearly 10 percent over the last year to below 920,000 barrels per day, its lowest level since 1950. In its defense, a BP spokesman said, "We designed a pipeline that, if operated properly, should never leak." On the other hand, critics who oppose the dominance of oil over the environment in the region believe that undersea pipelines in the Arctic's Beaufort Sea

are vulnerable to seasonal ice floes known to scour the ocean floor.

- According to Robert Mitkowski Jr., an analyst with *Value Line Investment Survey*, "BP will be hard-pressed to top its performance of the Nineties. The company attained super-major status in the oil business by buying Amoco and ARCO. But, although finances are formidable, BP doesn't enjoy quite the balance sheet strength of an ExxonMobil or a Royal Dutch/Shell. That puts it at a slight disadvantage when it comes to expansion. Having less cash on hand than its peers might hold back share repurchases, too, which, in turn, could keep corporate returns a step behind its immediate competitors. BP compensates by innovating more to increase its efficiency and global reach."

Reasons to Buy

- In 2001, BP p.l.c. invested about $13 billion of new capital in its operations, much of it to provide for future growth.
- The company improves the quality of its portfolio by regularly reviewing its assets. BP disposes of those assets that have more value to others and acquires new ones with the right strategic fit. For example, the purchase of a majority stake in Veba Oil of Germany in early 2002 makes BP the biggest fuel and convenience retailer in the world's third-largest economy.

  In 2001, with the sale of two refineries in the United States, the company completed the $10 billion of planned disposals resulting from the merger of BP and Amoco. In the words of a company spokesman, "We are making significant investments to maintain and grow our natural gas production in the USA. We are expanding our supply of gas to the U.S. market from operations in Canada, Trinidad, and the

USA. We are also focusing our chemicals business on core products."

- The company has been actively developing key resources. For example, engineering and design work on the Thunder Horse project and Mardi Gras pipeline is well under way in the Gulf of Mexico. According to a spokesman, "We have also begun detailed engineering and planning work for the Baku-Tbilisi-Ceyhan pipeline to transport oil from the Caspian Sea to global markets. Agreement has also been reached with the governments of Azerbaijan, Georgia, and Turkey for the development of a parallel gas pipeline. We are making major new investments in China in petrochemicals and retail fuel operations, with more than 200 service stations now open."

- In the United Kingdom, where the company is the leading fuel retailer, "Our ambition is to become the number one convenience retailer as well," said Graham Sims, Business Unit Leader, Western Europe Retail. "The BP Connect concept, which now numbers seventy-two stores in the UK, will help us achieve this ambition. Connect represents a totally new approach for the industry, and our new store at Hornchurch, near London, is arguably the world's more environmentally friendly service station—utilizing 100 percent green energy sources and offering customers a range of organic and fair trade products."

- BP Amoco holds extensive leases in the federal waters of the Gulf of Mexico. It is one of the three largest acreage holders in the Gulf and the leading acreage holder in the Gulf's deepwater portion. Onshore, the company operates some 470 natural gas wells and 330 oil wells.

The Houston region's offshore production currently totals about 240,000 barrels of oil equivalent a day. Production onshore in the region is more than 365,000 barrels of oil equivalent a day. These figures will rise sharply as offshore projects under development come onstream.

- Many people in the oil patch consider the company's CEO, Sir John Browne, age fifty-four, to be the industry pacesetter. A decade ago, BP, then British Petroleum, was a struggling midsize company short on earnings and clout. But Browne, who was promoted to chief executive in 1995, has been instrumental in transforming it into the world's number two oil company, behind ExxonMobil. His $57-billion acquisition of Amoco in 1998 triggered a massive wave of industry consolidation. Browne then bought Atlantic Richfield in 1999 for $25 billion.

These groundbreaking moves are more than paying for themselves. According to an *Argus Company Report*, "With its high-profile acquisition of Atlantic Richfield (ARCH), we think BP is now in a position to reap the rewards of owning ARCO's very lucrative refining and marketing position on the West Coast. In addition, the company will profit from ARCO's huge natural gas reserves in Southeast Asia. Moreover, through well-defined synergies attached to the ARCO merger that are only now coming to the fore, the company is currently positioned to harvest about $2.3 billion a year in total cost savings going forward."

Total assets: $103,544 million
Current ratio: 1.06
Common shares outstanding: 22,442 million
Return on 2001 shareholders' equity: 9.2%

	2001	2000	1999	1998	1997	1996	1995	1994
Revenues (millions)	148062	148062	83566	68304	71274	76490	57047	50667
Net income (millions)	13178	12555	6204	4468	4628	4114	2070	2001
Earnings per share	2.13	3.49	1.92	1.39	2.44	2.18	1.13	1.08
Dividends per share	1.29	1.22	1.52	1.21	1.12	.92	.77	.52
Price High	55.2	60.6	62.6	8.7	46.5	35.9	26.0	21.3
Low	42.2	43.1	40.2	36.5	32.4	23.6	18.9	14.6

CONSERVATIVE GROWTH

Bristol-Myers Squibb Company

345 Park Avenue □ New York, N.Y. 10154-0037 □ Listed: NYSE □ (212) 546-4103 □ Dividend reinvestment plan is available: (800) 356-2026 □ Web site: www.bms.com □ Ticker symbol: BMY □ S&P rating: A □ Value Line financial strength rating: A++

In 2001, Bristol-Myers agreed to pay $1 billion to buy 19.9 percent of ImClone, a biotech company that makes Erbitux, a controversial drug to treat colorectal cancer. It later paid another $200 million to ink the deal and promised to pay an additional $800 million if the drug passes FDA scrutiny.

In exchange, Bristol-Meyers would be entitled to 40 percent of the domestic profits from the sale of Erbitux. Unfortunately, in December of 2001, the FDA stunned both ImClone and Bristol-Myers by refusing to review the cancer-drug application, citing problems in the pivotal clinical trial. As a consequence, Bristol-Myers wrote off $735 million of its $1.2 billion investment in early 2001—and admitted it may have to write off even more.

In February of 2002, Bristol-Myers said it wanted to "fundamentally restructure" its relationship with ImClone, including changing its top management. "We are taking this action because we believe Erbitux has great potential to treat cancer patients, and we want to move the

process forward as quickly as possible," said Bristol Meyer's CEO Peter A. Dolan.

For its part, ImClone rejected Bristol-Myers's proposal to fundamentally restructure their $2 billion partnership, saying the deal was not in the best interest of its shareholder.

In an editorial in *The Wall Street Journal*, the paper suggested that perhaps the FDA should reconsider its decision. The writer said, "We wish they'd also think of the morality of serving patients. For amid all the recriminations, the consensus remains that Erbitux could be a revolutionary and life-saving drug. Bristol-Myers CEO Peter Dolan wouldn't still be bullying ImClone for more of the Erbitux profits if he didn't think so. And Germany's Merck KGaA, which owns rights to the drug outside of North America, announced this week (mid-February 2002) it expects European approval next year. Some 10,000 people have asked for the 'compassionate' pre-approval use of Erbitux, many of them desperately ill."

In March of 2002, the two companies agreed to new terms that will give Bristol-Meyers greater control and reduce its payments to ImClone. Under the new arrangement, the $300 million payment will be replaced by a payment of $140 million now and $60 million a year from now, not contingent upon any action by the FDA. The $500 million payment will now be split into two parts, with $250 million being paid when Erbitux is approved to treat its first type of cancer and $250 million when it is approved for an additional use.

Company Profile

Bristol-Myers is a global leader in chemotherapy drugs and ranks near the top in cardiovascular drugs and antibiotics. Heart drugs include Pravachol, a cholesterol-reducing agent, and Capoten/Capozide and Monopril, which are antihypertensive preparations. Through a joint venture with Sanofi, SA, Bristol-Myers produces Plavix, a platelet aggregation inhibitor for the prevention of stroke, heart attack, and vascular diseases, as well as Avapro, an angiotensin II receptor blocker that treats hypertension. Principal anticancer drugs consist of Taxol, Paraplatin, VePesid, and Platinol.

The company features a wide variety of anti-infective drugs, including Duricef/Ultracef, Cefzil, and Maxipime antibiotics and Videx and Zerit AIDS therapeutics.

The company's nutritionals encompass infant formulas, such as Enfamil and ProSobee, vitamins, and nutritional supplements.

Highlights of 2001

For the full year on a continuing-operations basis, sales increased 7 percent (or 9 percent if foreign exchange is excluded), to $19.4 billion. This includes sales from the $7.8-billion DuPont pharmaceuticals acquisition in October of 2001.

Diluted earnings per share increased to 2.41.

"2001 was a critical year of transformation for Bristol-Myers Squibb, as we moved aggressively to become a more pharmaceuticals-focused company," said Peter R. Dolan. "We spun off our Zimmer orthopedic implants business, acquired the DuPont pharmaceuticals business, and sold our Clairol hair care business to Procter & Gamble. We also invested in a promising pipeline of new pharmaceutical products, including a number of first- or possibly best-in-class compounds with blockbuster potential that we expect to submit for filing by the end of 2002." The industry defines "blockbuster" as a drug that has annual revenues of more than $1 billion.

Shortcomings to Bear in Mind

- Analysts look for the company's earnings to dip modestly in 2002. They attribute the shortfall to the declining sales of Glucophage, used to treat diabetes. With the loss of patent protection in 2002, the company faces the onslaught of competition from generic copies made by Ivax, Barr, and Watson.

In order to salvage something from the patent loss, the company tried to create a new drug by combining XR with Glucophage, but the ploy met with modest success. The lower-priced generic pills won the skirmish.

On a more positive note, the company had this to say in early 2002: "The entire Glucophage (metformin) franchise continued its strong growth rate, with sales increasing 42 percent, to $2,682 million. Glucophage IR sales increased 18 percent, to $2,049 million, while Glucovance, and Glucophage XR Extended Release tablets had sales of $330 million and $303 million respectively."

- Still another drug under siege from generics is BuSpar, used to treat anxiety. *Value Line Survey* predicts that sales will fall by 65 percent in 2002, to $130 million. BuSpar went off patent in April of 2001.
- In 2001, sales of the company's leading cancer drug, Taxol, decreased 25 percent, to $1,197 million. In 2000, the company's patent expired on Taxol.
- Not everyone was happy with Bristol-Myers's purchase of DuPont's drug business in mid-2001 for $7.8 billion. "The deal is very expensive and disappointing since they didn't get the crown jewels," said Trevor Polischuk, an analyst with Lehman Brothers, Inc. He said that DuPont's drug business was worth no more than $5 billion without Cozaar and Hyzaar, two drugs used to treat hypertension.

Reasons to Buy

- Peter R. Dolan, age forty-five, often regarded at the next CEO of Bristol-Myers Squibb, took that post in May of 2001, replacing Charles A. Heimbold, age sixty-seven, who retired. Mr. Dolan joined the company in 1988 and became president in early in 2000.

  Peter Dolan first achieved recognition by convincing consumers to buy more JELL-O when he was with General Foods (now part of the Altria Group, formerly Philip Morris). Mr. Dolan said his consumer marketing expertise will serve him well, now that drug companies can no longer rely on selling their drugs primarily by having their salespeople hand out samples and leave product literature with the medical profession. These days, pharmaceutical companies are reaching out to consumers through advertising as well. Nor are they neglecting to use their blandishments on the governments and the managed-care companies that pay for most drugs.

  Mr. Dolan has shown that his marketing talents can create higher sales in the pharmaceutical realm. As president of Mead Johnson Nutritional Group of Bristol-Myers in 1995, he boosted Enfamil to the number one infant formula in the United States by advertising it to mothers, in addition to promoting it to pediatricians.

  Analysts are convinced that the new CEO has exceptional credentials. "What Peter Dolan brings to the table is his global view, his strength of being a strategic thinker and planner," said Richard Lawrence, pharmaceutical analyst for Parker Hunter, Inc. "He's an aggressive, young CEO that wants to leave his mark—his own mark—and he's going to want to do it early on and get some momentum behind the company in the next few years."

- Several key pharmaceutical products had excellent results in 2001:
  - Worldwide sales of Pravachol, a cholesterol-lowering agent and the company's largest-selling product, increased 20 percent, to $2,173 million.
  - Sales of Plavix, a platelet aggregation inhibitor, had excellent growth, increasing 50 percent in 2001, driven in part by positive results of the CURE study in unstable angina to prevent recurrent ischemic events. This study was published in the prestigious *New England Journal of Medicine* in August of 2001.
  - Sales of Avapro, an angiotensin II receptor blocker for the treatment of hypertension, increased 34 percent, to $510 million.
  - Sales of Serzone, a novel antidepressant, increased 14 percent, to $409 million.

- Bristol-Myers Squibb has paid a dividend to its shareholders for an unbroken sixty-nine years—since becoming a public company in 1933. What's more, the company has increased the dividend each year since 1972. Earnings per share, moreover, have also done well, climbing from $0.99 in 1990 to $2.44 in 2001, for a compound annual growth rate of 9.4 percent.

- Sustagen, a nutritious, flavored milk-substitute for preschool and school-age children and pregnant or lactating mothers, is particularly popular in Latin America and Asia. As Mead Johnson seeks to standardize the product's formulation, Sustagen has become a cornerstone of the division's efforts to globalize its business.

- Bristol-Myers Squibb has more than fifty drugs in development, including treatment for cancer, hypertension, diabetes, obesity, heart failure, coronary thrombosis, stroke, hepatitis, infectious diseases, migraine, inflammation, pain, and skin disorders.

- In mid-2001, Bristol-Myers bought the pharmaceutical business of DuPont for $7.8 billion. DuPont's bestselling drug in 2000 was Sustiva, with sales of $386 million. Sustiva is a widely used part of the powerful combination therapy for treating AIDS. For its part, Bristol-Myers sells Zerit and Vides, which are also important parts of the AIDS therapy. DuPont has three AIDS drugs

in development, and Bristol-Myers also has AIDS therapies in its pipeline. Mr. Dolan said that DuPont also has several promising drugs under development with "blockbuster potential."

- In mid-2001, Bristol-Myers sold its Clairol hair-coloring business for $4.9 billion. The deal with DuPont a month later gives "credibility to Bristol's statements that it would concentrate on the pharmaceutical business," said analyst Bob Kirby of Edward Jones.

- A key ingredient for pharmaceutical companies is research. In the past, Bristol-Myers Squibb has not been in the same league with such industry leaders as Lilly, Merck, and Pfizer. Now, that seems to be changing. Peter Ringrose, a research superstar hired away from Pfizer in 1997, has led the way. After about five years on the job, Dr. Ringrose told analysts, "I'm ready and eager to be judged." Over the next year, he said in late 2001, the company expects to file for regulatory approval for five new drugs, including the schizophrenia treatment Aripiprazole, the antibiotic Besquinolone (related to Cipro), and the antihypertensive Vanlev. "The strategy is dead on, and they've got the right person in Peter Ringrose," said Richard Evans, an analyst with Sanford C. Bernstein & Company.

Total assets: $24,635 million
Current ratio: 1.34
Return on 2001 equity: 43.5%
Common shares outstanding: 1935 million

	2001	2000	1999	1998	1997	1996	1995	1994
Revenues (millions)	19087	18216	20222	18284	16701	15065	13767	11984
Net income (millions)	4736	4309	4167	3630	3205	2850	2600	2331
Earnings per share	2.44	2.16	2.06	1.80	1.61	1.42	1.28	1.15
Dividends per share	1.10	.98	.86	.78	.76	.75	.74	.73
Price High	73.5	74.9	79.3	67.6	49.1	29.1	21.8	15.3
Low	48.5	42.4	57.3	44.2	26.6	19.5	14.4	12.5

Cardinal Health, Incorporated

7000 Cardinal Place ❑ Dublin, Ohio 43017 ❑ (614) 757-5592 ❑ Dividend reinvestment plan is not available ❑ Web site: www.cardinal.com ❑ Listed: NYSE ❑ Fiscal year ends June 30 ❑ Ticker symbol: CAH ❑ S&P rating: A ❑ Value Line financial strength rating: B++

New York-Presbyterian Hospital is the largest hospital in the nation's largest city. It has more than 2,000 beds and treats nearly a million patients a year. The hospital is under constant pressure to reduce its costs. It turned to Cardinal Health to help reduce inventory and labor costs.

Cardinal is this hospital's primary supplier of pharmaceuticals and medical-surgical and laboratory products and services. The company also provides cost-saving solutions in many interrelated areas.

Cardinal brought all of its capabilities together for this important customer. Working together, Cardinal and New York-Presbyterian implemented solutions such as the following:

- Just-in-time delivery of supplies
- Supply-standardization review
- Pharmaceutical inventory management systems
- Automated dispensing systems for pharmaceuticals and supplies
- Electronic interfaces with various hospital systems

The hospital has experienced real savings resulting from these programs, including reducing inventory in the central pharmacy by 37.5 percent, increasing pharmacy inventory turns from twelve to twenty, reducing supply inventory by $3.5 million, and reducing labor costs by $1.2 million.

Cardinal Health's record of outstanding performance has given the company its pre-eminence in health care supply procurement and distribution. Each Cardinal business consistently outperforms

its competitors because of its leadership position and superior resources available under the Cardinal Health umbrella.

What's more, Cardinal boasts strong management, superior service levels, industry information sharing, greater operating leverage, and a lower cost of capital.

Cardinal has long delivered strong revenue and operating income growth, while maintaining a solid balance sheet. By leveraging its infrastructure to operate more efficiently, operating earnings growth consistently outpaces revenue growth.

Analysts at Deutsche Banc Alex. Brown, moreover, "expect this trend to continue, as the company further integrates its acquisitions. Indeed, both return on sales and return on committed capital reached record levels" in fiscal 2001.

The Deutsche Banc Alex. Brown report went on to say, "In our view, Cardinal distinguishes itself from its competition by providing consistently superior service to its customers. Significantly, Cardinal is also an innovator, continually adding incremental services and instituting more efficient ways of conducting business."

Company Background

Cardinal Health provides innovative products and services to tens of thousands of customers in the health care industry. By working with its customers to address challenges they face in the fast-changing health care environment, the company maintains market-leading positions in pharmaceutical formulation, manufacturing, packaging and distribution; medical-surgical product manufacturing and distribution; and automation and information services.

Cardinal operates a family of businesses that offer many complementary products and services to its health care manufacturer and provider customers. The company segregates its operations into four primary business segments that reflect the products they provide and the customers they serve.

Pharmaceutical Distribution and Provider Services (51 percent of fiscal 2001 operating earnings) offers pharmaceutical and specialty product distribution, repackaging, retail pharmacy franchising, hospital pharmacy management, and other services to health care providers. In fiscal 2001, revenues and operating earnings from this segment both grew 31 percent, and return on committed capital reached 29 percent while generating $492 million in cash flow.

Medical-Surgical Products and Services (26 percent of operating earnings) manufactures and distributes a comprehensive array of medical-surgical and lab products used by hospitals, surgery centers, physicians' offices, and long-term care facilities. In 2001, revenues expanded 19 percent for this business, and operating earnings rose 20 percent. Return on sales increased to 7.49 percent, and return on committed capital reached 32 percent, with cash flow at the $393 million level.

Pharmaceutical Technologies and Services (13 percent of fiscal operating earnings) provides comprehensive services to pharmaceutical manufacturers and biotechnology companies, including proprietary drug delivery technologies and contract manufacturing processes, integrated packaging services, as well as sales and marketing. On sales of $1.2 billion, this segment had revenue and earnings gains of 9 percent in 2001. It achieved strong cash flow and a return on committed capital of 27 percent despite being

dealt a complicated hand with a changing market for protease inhibitors and nutritionals, expansion, and addition of new plants, coupled with the planning and construction of a new pharmaceutical technologies and services center.

Automation and Information Services (10 percent of operating earnings) develops automated systems for dispensing pharmaceuticals and medical-surgical supplies as well as a variety of information systems used by health care providers and manufacturers. In this business, the company's operating earnings expanded 22 percent in 2001, with a gain in revenues of 17 percent. Return on sales reached nearly 36 percent, a new record.

Highlights of Fiscal 2001

- The company achieved earnings per share of $2.07, up 21 percent, on sales of $38.7 billion, up 28 percent; raised return on committed capital to 30 percent; and generated $871.7 million in cash flow. This is the fourteenth consecutive year in which earnings per share have advanced by more than 20 percent.
- Cardinal spent nearly $3 billion on thirteen acquisitions in 2001. According to CEO Robert D. Walter, "Each acquired company met our standard of being outstanding by itself, fitting closely into our strategy, making Cardinal collectively stronger for the future."
- The two largest acquisitions in fiscal 2001 were Bindley Western Industries and Bergen Brunswig Medical, distributors of pharmaceuticals and medical-surgical products, respectively. Mr. Walter said, "We are confident that the synergies from all acquisitions will generate more than $130 million in annual earnings over the next three years. Our confidence comes from the fact that we understand these businesses and have a tremendous amount of experience in successfully integrating the over forty

acquisitions we have made over the past twenty years."

Shortcomings to Bear in Mind

- The health care industry is subject to constant change as a result of product innovation, cost pressures, competitive pressures, and new legislation.
- Because Cardinal has been so consistently successful, it is a difficult stock to buy at a reasonable price. Typically, it sells at a P/E of 30 or more.

Reasons to Buy

- People over the age of fifty make up the fastest-growing demographic category of the population. Today, they represent 27 percent of the U.S. population, and in just five years their numbers will increase 13 percent, totaling 85 million. This category of consumers spends $610 billion on health care, uses 74 percent of all pharmaceuticals, represents 65 percent of hospital-bed days, and accounts for 42 percent of physician visits.
- Health care is an enormous industry, representing about 14 percent of the domestic gross domestic product. With an aging population, there is a solid long-term demand for everything that Cardinal does. For example, during the next five years, more than $34 billion of branded pharmaceuticals face patent expiration. Cardinal's Pharmaceutical Distribution and Provider Services businesses should benefit from this trend because sales of generic products tend to be more profitable for the company than sales of equivalent branded products.

At the other end of the spectrum, Cardinal's Pharmaceutical Technologies and Services businesses are well positioned to assist branded manufacturers in the development of new or reformulated pharmaceutical products to help replace sales of products losing patent protection. In addition, the government appears poised to pass some form of Medicare drug benefit for seniors that should encourage greater consumption of pharmaceuticals, especially generics.

- Cardinal Health provides manufacturers with highly efficient and economical distribution services essential for its products. Cardinal handles all of the logistics, inventory, and receivables management as well as administrative activities involved in delivering pharmaceutical products to more than 26,000 pharmacy locations every day.

For its pharmacy customers, Cardinal consolidates orders for products, potentially from hundreds of manufacturers, into pharmacy-specific deliveries of the right products to the right place at the right time.

- Cardinal's operations include full-line drug distribution as well as several specialty pharmaceutical distribution businesses that address specific customer or manufacturer requirements. These businesses include the nation's leading pharmaceutical repackaging operation (currently used by six of the ten largest retail chains in the country), a leading blood plasma and specialty drug distributor, and a company that provides full-service, third-party logistics to manufacturers.

This group includes three additional businesses, complementary to distribution, for pharmacy providers.

Medicine Shoppe International is the country's leading franchiser of independent retail pharmacies, with about 1,300 of apothecary-style pharmacies in the United States and nine other countries. Medicine Shoppe offers a successful, alternative business format for retail pharmacists who prefer to own their own stores.

For hospitals, Owen Health care offers pharmacy and materials-management services that help customers control costs while enhancing the quality of patient care.

The recently formed Cardinal Health Staffing Network assists Cardinal retail and hospital pharmacy customers with their staffing needs as they face a growing shortage of pharmacy profes- sionals. Through these businesses, Car- dinal Health has become one of the largest employers of pharmacists in the nation, with more than 2,200 pharma- cists on its staff.

Total assets: 14,642 million
Current ratio: 1.63
Common shares outstanding: 449 million
Return on 2001 shareholders' equity: 19.3%

	2001	2000	1999	1998	1997	1996	1995	1994
Revenues (millions)	38660	25247	21481	12927	10968	8862	7806	5790
Net income (millions)	943	730	574	283	221	160	85	63
Earnings per share	2.07	1.71	1.37	1.13	.90	.73	.60	.47
Dividends per share	.09	.07	.06	.05	.04	.04	.04	.03
Price High	77.3	70.0	55.5	50.9	35.0	26.0	17.2	14.3
Low	56.7	24.7	24.7	31.0	22.9	15.5	12.3	9.8

INCOME

Cedar Fair, L. P.

One Cedar Point Drive ❑ Sandusky, Ohio 44870-5259 ❑ (419) 627-2233 ❑ Dividend reinvestment plan is available: (800) 278-4353 ❑ Web site: www.cedarfair.com ❑ Listed: NYSE ❑ Ticker symbol: FUN ❑ S&P rating: Not rated ❑ Value Line financial strength rating: B+

Every year, Cedar Fair invests in new rides and attractions that will attract more visi- tors to the company's six amusement parks and five water parks. For instance, at Dorney Park & Wildwater Kingdom, situ- ated near Allentown, Pennsylvania, the company saw attendance in 2001 shoot up to a record 1.5 million guests, up 16 per- cent over the prior year.

CEO Richard L. Kinzel attributes the jump in attendance at Dorney Park to its new Talon roller coaster, a world-class sus- pended coaster with a 135-foot-tall first hill and a terrifying fifty-eight mile-an-hour first drop. "These results once again demonstrated the drawing power of a great new attraction," he said.

In 2002, the centerpiece of Cedar Point's capital program will be the world's tallest and fastest "double impulse" roller coaster. Cedar Point is situated on Lake Erie between Toledo and Cleveland, Ohio. "This new thrill ride, named Wicked Twister, will be Cedar Point's fif- teenth roller coaster, and it will be the eighth world-record-breaking ride the park has introduced since 1989," said Mr. Kinzel.

Wicked Twister will use linear induc- tion motors (LIM) to smoothly launch pas- sengers out of the coaster's station at a maximum speed of seventy-two miles per hour in 2.5 seconds, propelling them up the ride's first 215-foot-tall tower before briefly pausing and then reversing and accelerating up a second 215-foot tower. The coaster will continue to propel its pas- sengers up and down its U-shaped steel track a total of five times—forward three times and backward twice—during an intense forty-second ride.

Commenting on Cedar Point's other big capital projects for the 2002 season, Mr. Kinzel said, "In 2002, we will also be focusing our capital spending on families with the introduction of a Peanuts-themed ice show that will feature Snoopy and four other popular Peanuts characters.

"Wicked Twister will reinforce the park's position as the thrill ride capital of the world, and 'Snoopy Rocks! On Ice' will introduce a brand new type of family entertainment to the park. Including the $13 million in capital expenditures for the 2002 season, Cedar Fair will have invested more than $120 million in Cedar Point over a five-year period."

Company Profile

Cedar Fair, L. P., owns and operates six amusement parks, five major water parks, three resort hotels, several year-round restaurants, a marina, and an RV campground. The company's parks attract more than 10 million visitors a year.

Cedar Fair prides itself on the growth of its roller coasters. Cedar Point alone boasts fourteen—more than any other park in the world. All told, Cedar Fair parks have thirty-eight roller coasters, including some of the tallest, steepest, and highest-rated coasters ever built.

Cedar Fair's Six Parks

Cedar Point, which is located on Lake Erie between Cleveland and Toledo, is one of the largest amusement parks in the United States; it serves a total market area of 22 million people.

Valleyfair, located near Minneapolis/St. Paul, draws from a total population of 8 million people in a multistate market area.

Dorney Park and Wildwater Kingdom is located near Allentown, Pennsylvania; it serves a total market area of 35 million people in the Northeast.

Worlds of Fun/Oceans of Fun, in Kansas City, Missouri, draws from a total market area of 7 million people.

Knott's Berry Farm, near Los Angeles, is one of several major year-round theme parks in southern California. It serves a total market area of 20 million people as well as a large national and international tourist population.

Michigan's Adventure and Oasis Water Park, the company's newest parks, were acquired in 2001.

How They Operate

The parks are family-oriented, providing clean and attractive environments with exciting rides and entertainment. Except for Knott's Berry Farm (which is open all year), the operating season is generally from May through September.

The parks charge a basic daily admission price that provides unlimited use of virtually all rides and attractions. Admissions accounted for 50 percent of revenues in 2000, with food, merchandise, and games contributing 41 percent and accommodations the other 9 percent.

Shortcomings to Bear in Mind

- About two-thirds of the company's revenue is derived from the Midwest and mid-Atlantic regions. Adverse economic conditions in these regions could hurt attendance at Cedar Fair parks. On the other hand, the acquisition of Knott's Berry Farm lessens this risk somewhat.
- When you file your income tax, you may find that Cedar Fair has failed to send you the usual paperwork. One year, I didn't get mine till mid-March (in 2002, on March 16th). I had already given my accountant the rest, and he had completed my return before I realized my blunder. Unfortunately, it was back to square one—at my expense. Also, since

Cedar Fair operates in several states, you may find you have to pay a few of them some tax money. Otherwise, it is a great stock.

- Cedar Fair's results in 2001 were hurt by a slack economy. Dorney Park, as mentioned above, had a good year. According to Mr. Kinzel, "We were pleased with the solid season at our newest park, Michigan's Adventure, which finished the year with post-acquisition attendance of just over 400,000, right in line with our expectations. Meanwhile, results at our other three parks were negatively impacted by the weak economy and the lack of a major new attraction. For the year, attendance at Cedar Point was down nearly 9 percent, to 3.1 million guests; attendance at Valleyfair decreased 8 percent, to 1.1 million; and attendance at Worlds of Fun was down 3 percent to slightly more than 900,000. At our only year-round park, Knott's Berry Farm, attendance finished the year down 4 percent, at 3.6 million, due mostly to a drop in tourism in the southern California market that began well before the September 11 terrorist attack in the East."

Reasons to Buy
- Both Cedar Fair and Knott's Berry Farm are recent recipients of the Applause Award, the industry's highest honor for "foresight, originality, and sound business development." And for the third consecutive year, Cedar Fair received the prestigious "Golden Ticket Award" for being named the Best Amusement Park in the World, in an international survey conducted by *Amusement Today*, a newspaper that ranks the "best of the best" in the amusement industry.

The company's parks also placed four coasters in the Top Roller Coaster ranking: Magnum, number one; Millennium Force, number two, and Raptor, number five. Dorney Park's Wildwater Kingdom, moreover, ranked as the number-three water park in the *Amusement Today* survey.

- Cedar Fair's parks are well run and boast profit margins that are the highest in the industry.
- At Cedar Point, more than a third of the park's visitors, the highest ever, spent the night as part of their visit to the park. To build this momentum, said Mr. Kinzel, "We are adding an upscale camping complex, called Lighthouse Point, to our popular Camper Village RV campground. Lighthouse Point will feature upscale cabins, cottages, and RV campsites, as well as a swimming pool, fishing pier, and other amenities."
- According to one analyst, Cedar Fair's management team "exhibits both strength and depth." The general managers at the five parks have an average tenure of nearly twenty-five years with the company.
- Cedar Fair operates in an industry with high barriers to entry, with scant likelihood of new competition. The absence of direct competition gives the parks pricing power in their regions, bolstering profit margins.
- For the 2002 season, the company is investing $14 million with the addition of Xcelerator, a new world-class roller coaster that will be the fourth major thrill ride added to the park since its acquisition by Cedar Fair in late 1997.

"This new coaster will be one of the largest single investments in Knott's Berry Farm's history, and it will bring a whole new level of thrill riding to the park," said Mr. Kinzel. Designed and manufactured by Intamin International of Switzerland, Xcelerator will launch riders smoothly from zero to eighty-two miles per hour in only 2.3 seconds and then climb to a height of 205 feet before spiraling down a 130-foot inverted drop. "Xcelerator will continue to build upon the momentum we have established at Knott's through strategic capital spending over the past four years, and it will further increase the park's level of recognition in the very attractive and competitive southern California market."

Total assets: $764 million
Current ratio: 0.15
Partnership units: 51 million
Return on 2001 partners' capital: 23%

	2001	2000	1999	1998	1997	1996	1995	1994
Revenues (millions)	477	473	438	420	264	250	218	198
Net income (millions)	58	78	86	84	68	74	66	61
Earnings per share	1.13	1.50	1.63	1.58	1.47	1.59	1.45	1.37
Dividends per share	1.58	1.50	1.40	1.29	1.26	1.20	1.14	1.06
Price High	25.0	20.9	26.1	30.1	28.3	19.5	18.6	18.3
Low	17.8	17.4	18.4	21.8	17.7	16.1	14.1	13.4

AGGRESSIVE GROWTH

Cintas Corporation

Post Office Box 625737 ◻ Cincinnati, Ohio 45262-5737 ◻ (513) 573-4013 ◻ Dividend reinvestment plan is not available ◻ Web site: www.cintas.com ◻ Fiscal year ends May 31 ◻ Listed: NASDAQ ◻ Ticker symbol: CTAS ◻ S&P rating: A+ ◻ Value Line financial strength rating: B++

In the spring of 2002, Cintas Corporation, the leader in corporate identity uniforms for such industries as hotels and airlines, announced that it had acquired Omni Services, Inc., a wholly owned subsidiary of Filuxel SA. Omni Services, with annual revenues of about $320 million, is one of the leading uniform rental companies in the United States, serving more than 90,000 customers throughout thirty-one states.

Robert J. Kohlhepp, chief executive of Cintas, said, "We have always had a great deal of respect for the Omni organization, and we are delighted to join forces with them. Each year, the majority of Cintas and Omni's new business comes from companies that have never used our services before. We estimate there are over 85 million people who need our uniforms, and there are more than 5 million businesses that can use our ancillary services.

"The combined sales and marketing teams of Cintas and Omni will continue their focus on developing that potential market. The combination of our two great companies will also benefit our existing customers with an enhanced product and service offering making us an even more valuable resource."

Upon completion of the acquisition, Cintas will have the following:

• Annual revenues exceeding $2.5 billion.

• Uniform rental locations covering thirty-nine states and four Canadian provinces.

• In excess of 500,000 customers being served on a regular basis, usually weekly.

• More than 5 million individuals wearing Cintas uniforms.

• Significant synergies from combining the operations.

• Additional products and services to offer customers.

This acquisition is not a new strategy for Cintas. In past years, a key part of the company's growth strategy has been through acquisitions. For example, in fiscal 1999, Cintas made several acquisitions. One of them, Unitog, the fifth-largest domestic uniform rental company, was the largest in Cintas's history. In fiscal 1998, the company made nine acquisitions, highlighted by the purchases of Uniforms To You and Mechanics Uniform Service. Finally, in fiscal 2001, the company made two minor acquisitions.

Company Profile

Cintas designs, manufactures, and implements corporate identity uniform programs, which it rents, or sells to customers throughout the United States and Canada. The company also provides ancillary services, including entrance mats, sanitation supplies, first aid products and services, and cleanroom supplies. Cintas provides its award-winning design capability and top-quality craftsmanship to the high end of the market—hotels, airlines, cruise ships, and the like. The company delivers the proper uniform to anyone in any job classification, from the doorman to the cocktail waitress in a hotel; from the mechanic to the pilot at the airlines; even to people working in the retail sector.

According to a Cintas spokesman, "Companies like Albertson's use Cintas uniforms to identify their employees to their customers. An employee who wears a clean, crisp, and attractive uniform is always viewed as more professional than someone in ordinary work clothes. Uniforms also complement a company's esprit de corps by building camaraderie

and loyalty. Bottom line—we don't just sell uniforms—we sell image, identification, teamwork, morale, pride, and professionalism." Put another way, Cintas believes that when people *look* good, they *feel* good. And when they feel good, they work better. What's more, their improved attitude results in a decline in absenteeism and turnover.

Shortcomings to Bear in Mind

■ Although Cintas has a superb long-term record, it was unable to cope with the recession and other events in 2001. In the first nine months of fiscal 2002, sales were up, but the advance was only 4.4 percent over the comparable period of the prior year. Similarly, net income inched ahead only 4.8 percent in the same nine-month period. To be sure, this performance was far better than most companies during the same stretch.

In the third quarter of 2002, moreover, rental revenue was up 6 percent, compared with the same quarter in 2001. However, other services revenue, which includes the sale of uniforms as well as the sale of other products and services, declined 12 percent. In the words of Mr. Kohlhepp, "Since the tragic events of September 11, our uniform sales customers—which include hotels, airlines, auto rental, and entertainment businesses—have delayed their uniform purchases because of weakness in their business. Although we are disappointed in the sales-side of our uniform business, we believe there is a pent-up demand for new uniforms, which we will benefit from as the economy gains strength."

On the other hand, all is not gloom and doom. The business that the company obtains from the airline, lodging, and automobile-related sectors makes up only 5 percent of Cintas revenue.

For his part, Mr. Kohlhepp looks at things this way: "On the positive side, we continue to add new customers at a record rate. Our new business is increasing at a mid-teens rate ahead of last year. We also have a strong balance sheet and healthy cash flow. We believe this financial strength, as well as our strong management team, will enable us to weather this economic storm and emerge as a stronger force in our industry."

Reasons to Buy

- Fiscal 2001, ended May 31, 2001, was another record-breaker:
  - Sales were $2.2 billion, an increase of 2.6 times in four years, or a compound annual growth rate of 27 percent.
  - Profits were $223 million, an increase of 2.4 times in four years, or a compound annual growth rate of 25 percent.
  - Increased customer base by more than 50,000 new uniform customers.
  - Expanded uniform rental presence into ten new cities.
  - Ranked number one among outsourcing services businesses in *Fortune* magazine's 2001 survey, "America's Most Admired Companies."
  - Recognized as one of the world's most valuable companies in the *BusinessWeek* "Global 1000."
  - Recognized in the elite list of "America's Finest Companies" by the Staton Institute, for the eleventh consecutive year.
  - Won three of the "Top 10" Image of the Year Awards—the uniform industry's highest honor for uniform design.
  - First uniform supplier to receive Ford Motor Company's Q1 Award for quality distinction.
- For those considering investing in Cintas, here are some factors to bear in mind.

- Cintas is the largest company in its industry.
- Cintas has grown for thirty-two consecutive years, through all economic cycles. During this thirty-two-year span, the company's sales have expanded by a compound annual rate of 24 percent. What's more, profits have climbed even better, at a thirty-two percent annual pace.
- Cintas is the industry's market leader.
- Most of the company's executives have the majority of their net worth invested in Cintas stock.

- Cintas's frequent contact and its close relationship with its customers "presents us with the opportunity to offer many ancillary products and services. We look for the opportunity to provide services that are very important but are small details that can be easily neglected by our customers—things like entrance mats, hygiene supply services, and first aid services. These small details can be easily delegated to us, since we are already delivering the customer's uniforms weekly anyway," said a company spokesman.

- Many large corporations are re-engineering all aspects of their business, and they are consolidating their source of supply of products and services. They prefer to deal with fewer suppliers to reduce purchasing and administrative costs. They often prefer to do business with Cintas because the company is a complete uniform service, whether the customer wants to rent, lease, or buy their uniforms. In addition, Cintas also provides online ordering, inventory control, and paperless systems.

- Robert M. Greene, CFA, an analyst with *Value Line Investment Survey*, said, "Cintas remains a strong player in an attractive market. The uniform-rental industry has typically grown faster than the overall economy, and we expect this trend to continue. Moreover, Cintas, helped by its previously mentioned ability to bring new customers into the industry and an active and successful acquisition program, has consistently grown faster than its publicly traded peers."

Total assets: $1,752 million
Current ratio: 3.72
Common shares outstanding: 170 million
Return on 2001 shareholders' equity: 19.6%

	2001	2000	1999	1998	1997	1996	1995	1994
Revenues (millions)	2161	1902	1752	1198	840	730	615	523
Net income (millions)	222	193	139	123	91	75	63	53
Earnings per share	1.30	1.14	.82	.79	.64	.53	.45	.38
Dividends per share	.19	.15	.12	.12	.10	.08	.07	.06
Price High	53.3	54.0	52.3	47.5	28.3	21.2	16.0	12.1
Low	33.8	23.2	26.0	26.0	17.0	13.9	11.2	9.9

CONSERVATIVE GROWTH

Citigroup, Incorporated

399 Park Avenue □ New York, New York 10043 □ (212) 559-4658 □ Dividend reinvestment plan is not available □ Web site: www.citigroup.com □ Listed: NYSE □ Ticker symbol: C □ S&P rating: A □ Value Line financial strength rating: A

In 2001, Citigroup bought Grupo Financiero Banamex-Accival SA (also known as Banacci)—one of Mexico's blue-chip stocks—for $12.5 billion in cash and stock. The deal provides a major boost to Citigroup's aspirations in emerging markets, which CEO Sanford I. Weill believes will be a key driver of the company's growth and profitability in the next five years.

The acquisition of Banacci, one of Mexico's largest financial companies, and parent of the 1,379-branch bank Banamex, the country's second largest bank, also counters the aggressive inroads of Spanish banks in that country. These branches, coupled with Citigroup's existing 197 outlets, now form a vast network of 1,576 branches.

"Citigroup was able to acquire the best banking franchise in Mexico," said Brent Erensel, a bank stock analyst at Deutsche Banc Alex. Brown. "Banamex gains the Citigroup's funding advantage and wide product mix, and Citigroup gains a dominant position in a fertile banking market."

The deal makes Citigroup the largest bank in a country that remains severely lacking in financial services for the average citizen. Mexico's treasury secretary, Francisco Gil Diaz, noted that it was hard for ordinary people in Mexico to obtain a loan or a mortgage. The deal "should help restore credit," he said, and is a tremendous vote of confidence in the country.

Citigroup, the biggest financial-services company in the United States, also intends to use both the Banamex and Citibank brand names to increase Citigroup's presence among Hispanic immigrants to the U.S. "This is not just about growth of the Mexican market, but the fast growth of the Hispanic population in the U.S.," said Mr. Weill.

Citigroup has been in Mexico since 1929 and has been a favorite institution of the Mexican elite. When the country nationalized the banks, including Banamex, in 1982, most foreign banks were sent packing. But not Citigroup. It was allowed to remain in Mexico.

Company Profile

In one of the largest corporate mergers in history, Citigroup was formed in late 1998, combining Citicorp (a large bank) with Travelers Group (a major insurance company). Citigroup is now the nation's largest financial-services firm.

Melding traditional banking and insurance businesses together on a scale never attempted, the company's goal is to serve the financial needs of the widest possible audience on a global scale. Operations break down as described in the following sections.

The Global Consumer Segment

This segment includes branch and electronic banking, consumer lending services, credit card and charge card services, personalized wealth-management services for high-net-worth clients, as well as life, auto, and homeowners insurance.

Several specialized units include mortgage banking, which creates mortgages and student loans across North America; cards, which offers products such as MasterCard, VISA, Diners Club, and private-label credit cards. It has some 53 million cardmember accounts; consumer finance services, which maintains 980 loan offices in forty-five states; and insurance, which offers annuities and various life and long-term-care insurance to individuals and small businesses.

The Global Corporate and Investment Bank Segment

This segment provides investment advice, financial planning, and retail brokerage services, banking, and other financial services and commercial insurance products throughout the United States and in ninety-eight foreign countries.

The segment includes Salomon Smith Barney, which offers investment banking services such as underwriting of fixed-income and equity securities. Specialized units include emerging markets, which offers cash-management, short-term loans, trade services, project finance, and fixed-income issuance and trading to countries outside North America, Western Europe, and Japan; global relationship banking, which offers cash-management, foreign exchange, securities custody, and structured products to multinational companies; and commercial lines, which provides property and casualty insurance through brokers and independent agencies throughout the United States.

Global Investment Management and Private Banking

The Global Investment Management and Private Banking segment includes asset management services provided to mutual funds, institutional, and individual investors, as well as personalized wealth-management services for high-net-worth clients. This group is comprised of the SSB Citi Asset Management Group and the Citibank Private Bank.

The SSB Citi Asset Management Group includes Salomon Brothers Asset Management, Smith Barney Asset Management, and Citibank Global Asset Management. These businesses offer a broad range of asset-management products and services from global investment centers around the world, including mutual funds, closed-end funds, managed accounts, unit investment trusts, variable annuities, and personalized wealth-management services to institutional, high-net-worth, and retail clients.

Shortcomings to Bear in Mind

- In 2001, the problems in Argentina hurt Citigroup, and there may be more bad news in the offing. Some analysts cautioned that the company could take further hits from Argentina's meltdown, depending on how quickly that country finds a viable economic plan. "They took a few body blows from Enron and Argentina but still made the numbers," said Michael Mayo, analyst at Prudential Securities. "But I wouldn't be surprised if they needed to set aside additional reserves for Argentina before this is over."
- Citigroup's Citibank, the nation's largest credit card issuer, agreed in early 2002 to pay $1.6 million as part of a settlement with twenty-seven states over the way telemarketing firms sell products and services to the banking company's customers. Citibank customers had complained the telemarketing firms used deceptive sales pitches, which resulted in charges for products and services they did not knowingly agree to buy, according to Wisconsin attorney general James Doyle.

Reasons to Buy

- At the end of 2001, Citigroup signaled its desire to make more acquisitions as it unveiled plans to raise billions of dollars by spinning off its Travelers Property Casualty insurance unit. Citigroup's CEO, who bought into Travelers in 1992 and built up his now-global financial empire with a series of big deals (culminating in a merger with Citicorp in 1998), looks to cash out of a historically volatile business at an opportune time, according to analysts.

"Over history, the returns in the P&C business aren't as high as the returns that we can achieve in some of our other businesses," Mr. Weill said. Specifically, Mr. Weill said he was most interested in increasing Citigroup's activities in emerging markets such as China, consumers' financial services, and wealth management.

To be sure, the move marks a turnaround from Mr. Weill's recent acquisition binge. On the other hand, it is hardly a dismantling of the huge financial conglomerate. Travelers Property Casualty contributes about 10 percent of Citigroup's income. What's more, it has long lagged behind other Citigroup divisions in terms of profitability.

Mr. Weill said he planned to sell 20 percent of the commercial, auto, and home insurance business through a stock offering in early 2002. (It was sold in March of 2002.) Analysts said such a move could raise between $4 billion and $6 billion. The rest would be given to Citigroup shareholders.

- In 2001, the company acquired European American Bank (EAB) from ABN AMRO Bank N.V. for $1.6 billion, plus the assumption of $350 million in preferred stock. Headquartered in Uniondale, Long Island, EAB is one of Long Island's largest banks. It has $11.5 billion in deposits, $15.4 billion in assets, and ninety-seven branches, including sixty-seven in Long Island's Nassau and Suffolk counties and thirty in the five boroughs of New York City.
- Citigroup has established teams of executives worldwide, including six in Japan alone, who are dedicated to finding new purchases in conjunction with the executives in charge of individual businesses there. Further streamlining in Citigroup's regional management structure is also being considered, a move that may make the acquisitions process smoother.

- The Internet will play a significant role in the growth of the cards business. Citibank cards are among those most frequently used for Internet purchases today, and the company's goal is to be the payment vehicle of choice for online shoppers. Citigroup already offers online account management, an Internet-only credit account, an online shopping mall that provides savings exclusively to Citibank cardholders, and CitiWallet for convenient and secure Internet shopping. As consumers grow more comfortable shopping and paying over the Internet, they will be more inclined to use the company's online financial services, such as banking and brokerage.
- Citigroup recently dislodged Merrill Lynch & Company as Wall Street's biggest underwriter of stocks and bonds. For the first time in more than a decade, Merrill lost what are the financial world's most-coveted bragging rights—the equivalent on Wall Street of the final baseball standings.

    The ascendancy of Citigroup's Salomon Smith Barney unit at the end of 2001 is a striking example of how banks have made inroads into some of Wall Street's bread-and-butter businesses, in part because of their willingness to package investment-banking services with lines of credit vitally needed by many big clients.

- Enron's demise and the Argentina debacle cost Citigroup almost $700 million, before taxes, in the fourth quarter of 2001. Even so, the giant financial institution still posted a 36-percent rise in net income for the period. The results, analysts said, show again how Citigroup's breadth, combined with a clampdown on expenses, is paying off for the firm despite rough times for the economy.
- Citigroup is by far the world's largest card company, with 97 million cards in force worldwide. Cards are the hub of the consumer sector. A credit card is usually among the client's first services purchased from Citigroup, and it therefore becomes the basis for introducing clients to products from the company's other divisions.

    Cards are often the first product the consumer business introduces when it enters a new country, as was the case in 1999 with Egypt. In newer Citigroup consumer markets, such as Hungary, Poland, and Turkey, the card business supplies the company's growth and its broadest appeal to customers.

Total assets: $1,051 billion
Common shares outstanding: 5,145 million
Return on 2001 shareholders' equity: 20.4%

	2001	2000	1999	1998	1997*	1996	1995	1994
Revenues (millions)	83625	77694	57237	48936	47782			
Net Income (millions)	14284	13519	9947	6342	7751			
Earnings per share	2.75	2.62	2.15	1.33	1.59			
Dividends per share	.60	.52	.41	.12	.09			
Price High	57.4	59.1	43.7	26.6				
Low	44.7	35.3	24.5	14.3				

* Because of the merger with Travelers in 1998, no other statistics are available for prior years.

Clayton Homes, Inc.

Post Office Box 15169 □ Knoxville, Tennessee 37901 □ (865) 380-3206 □ Web site: www.clayton.net □
Dividend reinvestment plan is available: (800) 937-5449 □ Fiscal year ends June 30 □ Listed: NYSE □ Ticker
symbol: CMH □ S&P rating: A- □ Value Line financial strength B++

Among the eight members of Clayton's board of directors, three have the last name of Clayton. James L. Clayton is Chairman of the Board; Kevin T. Clayton is CEO; and B. Joe Clayton is CEO of Clayton Automotive Group. Each is an owner of company stock. For his part, James L. Clayton owns 27.9 percent of Clayton Homes common stock.

This concentration of power in the hands of the Clayton clan may smack of nepotism, but I prefer to think that the family's large stake in the business will keep them hustling to make Clayton Homes a success—as it certainly has in the past.

Company Profile

Clayton Homes, Inc., is a vertically integrated manufactured housing company headquartered in Knoxville, Tennessee. Employing more than 6,500 people and operating in thirty-three states, the company builds, sells, finances, and insures manufactured homes. It also owns and operates residential manufactured housing communities.

The company makes a wide variety of single- and multisection manufactured homes. They are factory-built, completely finished, constructed to be transported by trucks, and designed as permanent, primary residences when sited.

The company's homes range in price from $10,000 to $75,000. They vary in size from 500 to 2,400 square feet.

The Manufacturing group is a leading producer of manufactured homes, with twenty plants supplying homes to 1,012 independent and company-owned retail centers.

The Retail group sells, installs, and services factory-built homes. At the end of fiscal 2001, there were 297 company-owned retail centers in twenty-three states.

Financial Services provides financing and insurance for home-buyers at company-owned and selected independent retail sales centers through Vanderbilt Mortgage and Finance, a wholly owned subsidiary.

The Communities group owns and operates eighty-one manufactured housing communities, with 21,121 home sites in twelve states.

Highlights of 2001

- Awarded Manufacturer of the Year by the Manufactured Housing Institute for the second consecutive year.
- Received Industry Best House Award at the company's newest plant in Hodgenville, Kentucky.
- Expanded Vanderbilt's mortgage servicing to $4.3 billion.
- Added five properties in the Communities Group; increased total sites by 953, to 21,121.
- Expanded interactive Internet training to accommodate, on-site, all 6,500 team members.
- Achieved Financial Services' year-end delinquency target of 2.1 percent.
- Generated $128 million in free cash-flow during an industry downturn.
- Fiscal 2001 was the company's twenty-seventh consecutive profitable year, with

revenues of $1.2 billion and net income of $107 million.

- The company's market share in 2001 increased to 11.1 percent, up from 8.9 percent the prior year.
- The Manufacturing Group remained profitable in 2001, with no plant closings, while 28 percent of the industry's factories closed during the prior two years. As industry shipments fell 34 percent, Clayton's home production declined only 26 percent.
- Industry-wide, retail unit sales declined 31 percent for the year. By contrast, Clayton Retail significantly outperformed the other participants. The company's strategic inventory management process implemented early in the year produced the desired results, as the number of units on hand decreased by 1,812, or 23 percent. This effort improved cash flow by $37 million.

Shortcomings to Bear in Mind

- Cautious investors should be aware of the highly cyclical nature of the manufactured housing industry.

Reasons to Buy

- Growth among the company's four groups has varied from quarter to quarter and year to year, but the synergies involved in this very-difficult-to-execute concept have enabled the company to consistently achieve records. While one group is undergoing a period of slower growth, another group is enjoying high growth. The challenge of balancing and maintaining the model should not be underestimated—especially since other industry leaders have taken multiple charges to restate their securitization models. On the other hand, Clayton Homes has taken a conservative approach to growth and risk management.

- Despite a dip in earnings in fiscal 2001, the company has an impressive record of growth. In the most recent ten-year period (1991–2001), earnings per share advanced from $0.24 to $0.77, a compound annual growth rate of 12.4 percent.
- The Community Group capitalizes on every aspect of profitable vertical integration. Residents may choose a quality home from the company's Manufacturing group, select an attractive home site in the community, and secure their mortgage and insurance from the Clayton Financial Services Group.
- The Communities group best exemplifies the company's unique brand of vertical integration. When the group sells a home, profit is realized from five different components of the transaction, including manufacturing, retailing, financing, insuring, and leasing the home site.
- Clayton's finance subsidiary, Vanderbilt Mortgage & Finance, enjoys a sterling reputation. As one competitor commented, "It's a class act." Clayton's retail managers—unlike most salespeople—make money, not simply by selling homes, but also by sharing in the profit and losses on the associated loans. If a loan goes bad, the sales manager "eats 40 percent to 50 percent of the loss," according to a company spokesman.
- In 2001, Value Line Survey commented on Clayton Homes: "Clayton's prospects through 2004–2006 are more attractive, as the company has weathered the storm much better than its competitors, and we look for this pattern to continue over the coming years."
- *Standard & Poor's Stock Report* commented in late 2001 that, "The company has generally posted impressive earnings consistency in light of the highly cyclical nature of the manufactured housing

industry. Clayton strives for steady long-term growth through a disciplined operating strategy. It refuses to overpay for factories and sales centers during industry upturns, and prides itself on snaring additional capacity at bargain prices during tougher industry times."

■ At the end of 2001, Salomon Smith Barney raised its rating on Clayton from "outperform" to "buy." "Demand for housing remains strong because the U.S. population is growing," said Stephen Kim, Salomon's housing analyst. "Also, builders have reduced the number of homes started without first securing a buyer, and more are using options to control land instead of buying it outright, reducing expenses. This is a dramatically different industry than it was a decade ago."

Total assets: $1,654 million
Current ratio: 11.4
Common shares outstanding: 138 million
Return on 2001 shareholders' equity: 9.8%

		2001	2000	1999	1998	1997	1996	1995	1994
Revenues (millions)		1151	1293	1344	1128	1022	929	758	628
Net income (millions)		107	144	155	138	120	107	87	69
Earnings per share		.77	1.03	1.06	.92	.80	.72	.59	.47
Dividends per share		.06	.06	.06	.06	.06	.05	.03	Nil
Price	High	17.6	13.1	15.4	18.1	15.6	14.5	15.0	11.5
	Low	10.0	7.7	8.3	10.7	10.1	9.9	6.8	6.6

GROWTH AND INCOME

The Clorox Company

1221 Broadway □ Oakland, California 94612 □ (510) 271-7000 □ Web site: www.clorox.com □ Dividend reinvestment plan is available: (888) 259-6973 □ Fiscal year ends June 30 □ Listed: NYSE □ Ticker symbol: CLX □ Standard & Poor's rating: A □ Value Line financial strength rating: A+

Over the years, the name Clorox has become synonymous with household bleach. No wonder. Since the company introduced its first pint of Clorox bleach in the 1920s, The Clorox Company has come to dominate the domestic bleach market, with a nearly 70 percent share.

Today, Clorox has evolved into a diversified consumer-products company whose domestic retail products include many of the best-known brands of laundry additives, home cleaning and automotive-appearance products, cat litters, insecticides, charcoal briquettes, salad dressings, sauces, and water-filtration systems.

Company Profile

In 1913, a group of Oakland businessmen founded the Electro-Alkaline Company, a forerunner of The Clorox Company. The company originally produced an industrial-strength liquid bleach. It was sold in five-gallon crockery jugs to industrial customers in the San Francisco bay area.

A household version of Clorox liquid bleach was developed in 1916 and distributed in sample pint bottles. Demand for the product grew, and its distribution was gradually expanded nationally until it became the country's bestselling liquid bleach.

Clorox was a one-product company for its first fifty-six years, including the eleven years from 1957 through 1968, when it was operated as a division of The Procter & Gamble Company. Following its divestiture by Procter & Gamble in 1969, the company has broadened and diversified its product line and expanded geographically. Today, Clorox manufactures a wide range of products that are marketed to consumers in the United States and internationally. It is also a supplier of products to food service and institutional customers and the janitorial trades.

Although the company's growth in the first few years after divestiture came largely through the acquisition of other companies and products, strong emphasis is now being given to the internal development of new products.

The company's line of domestic retail products includes many of the country's best-known brands of laundry additives, home cleaning products, cat litters, insecticides, charcoal briquettes, salad dressings, sauces, and water-filtration systems. The great majority of the company's brands are either number one or two in their categories.

Included in Clorox products are such well-known names as Formula 409, Liquid-Plumr, Pine-Sol, Soft Scrub, S.O.S., Tilex, Armor All, Kingsford charcoal, Match Light, Black Flag insecticides, Fresh Step cat litter, Hidden Valley salad dressing, and Kitchen Bouquet.

Clorox's Professional Products unit is focused on extending many of the company's successful retail equities in cleaning and food products to new channels of distribution, such as institutional and professional markets and the food-service industry.

Internationally, Clorox markets laundry additives, home cleaning products, and insecticides, primarily in developing countries. What's more, Clorox is investing heavily to expand this part of its business. Overall, Clorox products are sold in more than seventy countries and are manufactured in thirty-five plants at locations in the United States, Puerto Rico, and abroad.

Shortcomings to Bear in Mind

- Clorox reported sales of $3.9 billion for the fiscal year ended June 30, 2001. This represented a decrease of 4.4 percent. Contributing to the drop in sales was the 6.6 percent decline in Homecare and Cleaning, from $1.63 billion to $1.52 billion. There were also decreases in sales in Specialty Products (down 2.6 percent, to $1.78 billion).

  Most of the company's sales in 2001 were in its domestic market, where revenues were $3.17 billion, or 81.2 percent of the total. Clorox's revenues in 2001 declined in the United States 8.3 percent, to $3.17 billion. On a more positive note, international sales climbed 16.9 percent in 2001, to $734 million.

- In a report issued by *Value Line Investment Survey*, an analyst said, "We expect increased competition in several businesses: notably bags and wraps, cat litter, and auto care. Moreover, the company faces tough economic conditions in Latin America."

Reasons to Buy

- In the company's annual report, CEO G. Craig Sullivan painted a brighter outlook for Clorox. "The conversion of our namesake bleach to Ultra Clorox liquid bleach, with an improved whitening formula, was completed in March 2001. This was an important project involving hundreds of Clorox people working together to bring the conversion in on time and under budget. The results? Additional shelf space at more than 85 percent of retailers, and in the fourth quarter, the highest market share for Clorox bleach in nearly four years.

"Despite only modest volume growth for the total U.S. specialty projects segment, the seasonal, auto care, and cat litter businesses each posted mid-single-digit volume gains. Kingsford charcoal achieved another record year of volume, and market share reached an all-time high, exceeding 65 percent. Also, the introduction of our new Armor All protectant and cleaning wipes generated significant incremental volume for the brand. The food products business showed the signs of a slowing and intensely competitive salad dressing category, resulting in decreased consumption of Hidden Valley dressings.

"While the cat litter business closed on a high note, it began the year with some missteps in execution that negatively impacted volume and profit. By the third quarter, our efforts to restore executional excellence started to pay off with Scoop Away and Fresh Step cat litters, which were relaunched with product improvements and new advertising, and new packaging for Scoop Away. Together, Fresh Step and Scoop Away market shares improved sequentially each quarter in fiscal 2001."

- In a report issued by Goldman Sachs in late 2001, an analyst said that the "worst is behind the company. Management has clearly realized its past mistakes and has put in place programs to reinvigorate growth. In the near term, higher levels of marketing spending, coupled with selective list price reductions, are aiding volume. A much more aggressive focus on cost reduction will continue to aid margins."

- In fiscal 2001, Clorox introduced its response to the needs of the modern driver with the launch of STP 6,000 Mile Oil Extender, a new premium oil additive that enables users to drive up to

6,000 miles between oil changes. The introduction of the new additive comes on the heels of extensive qualitative research showing the number one undelivered benefit consumers seek from an oil additive is extending their oil change interval. In addition, a recent survey shows that nearly 55 percent of Americans worry more about changing their oil on a regular basis than other routine car maintenance tasks.

STP 6,000 Mile Oil Extender became available in stores nationwide late in 2000 carrying a price tag of $6.99 for the fifteen-ounce bottle. According to the company, "The major benefit that this product brings to users is that Oil Extender maintains the viscosity of the motor oil while boosting the level of the oil's performance additives. By boosting these ingredients, STP 6,000 Oil Extender provides an extra level of protection in your motor oil."

- In fiscal 2001, the company announced an agreement with Brita GmbH of Germany to acquire full control of Brita water filtration products in North and South America, including the exclusive use of the Brita trademark, full rights to develop and market new products under the Brita name, and all business assets in the region.

"The buyout of the joint venture will enhance the ability of Brita Products to pursue new business opportunities, and improve its operating efficiency in the Americas," according to Scott Weiss, Clorox's general manager for Brita Products. He added that the two Brita entities will continue to share marketing, research, and development information.

- Clorox continues to expand where the company sees an opportunity to enter a market with a competitive advantage. Once Clorox acquires a business, it expands it by modernizing plants. What's more, the company builds mass through line extensions and strategic acquisitions.

Clorox also upgrades packaging and leverage marketing expertise gained in the United States by putting it to use in a new country with the company's just-acquired brands. In sum, that's how Clorox built leadership positions in the majority of its worldwide markets.

Total assets: $3,995 million
Current ratio: 1.03
Common shares outstanding: 237 million
Return on 2001 shareholders' equity: 20.2%

		2001	2000	1999	1998	1997	1996	1995	1994
Revenues (millions)		3903	4083	4003	2741	2533	2218	1984	1837
Net income (millions)		384	420	391	298	249	222	201	180
Earnings per share		1.63	1.75	1.63	1.41	1.21	1.07	.95	.84
Dividends per share		.84	.80	.72	.64	.58	.53	.48	.47
Price	High	40.85	56.4	66.5	58.8	40.2	27.6	19.8	14.9
	Low	29.95	28.4	37.5	37.2	24.3	17.5	13.8	11.8

CONSERVATIVE GROWTH

The Coca-Cola Company

One Coca-Cola Plaza □ Atlanta, Georgia 30311 □ (404) 676-8054 □ Dividend reinvestment plan is available: (888) 265-3747 □ Web site: www. coca-cola.com □ Listed: NYSE □ Ticker symbol: KO □ S&P rating: A- □ Value Line financial strength rating: A++

Douglas Daft, CEO of Coca-Cola, has drawn on the lessons he learned in his previous post as head of the company's Asian operations. His mantra is, "Think local, act local." Daft wants to sell more products suited to local tastes under existing U.S. brands (such as Minute Maid juices, PowerAde sports drinks, and Dasani water) or new ones tailored to local markets (such as a drink in Japan called Tea Water Leafs).

This strategy is based on two facts about the global market. One is that Coke controls half of carbonated drink sales around the world but only 18 percent of the total nonalcoholic beverage market. On that basis alone, there's simply much more room for Coke to expand in noncarbonated drinks. Second, outside the U.S., noncola drinks are far more popular than colas.

For an example of how Mr. Daft has changed things at Coke, let's take a look at one of the tiny countries in the Baltic region, such as Estonia. In mid-2001, Coke decided it had to act fast to counter the surging popularity of *kvass*, a beverage made from stale bread, sugar, and yeast—not exactly a concoction that might appeal to someone in Boston, Denver, Milwaukee, or Atlanta. To deal with the problem, Coke bought the Baltic producers of this ancient Russian thirst-quencher.

The local Coke producer struck a deal with Tallinn-based AS Osel Foods and acquired the rights to the Estonian *kvass* brand name, Linnuse Kali, and the Latvian brand name, Pilskalna. With *kvass* threatening to surpass cola in the Baltic region, Coca-Cola concluded that it couldn't fight the Estonians' and Latvians' rediscovered taste for the brownish, ciderlike drink Russians have quaffed for more than 300 years. The beverage gets its name from the Slavic word for "ferment."

"This is the essence of our 'think local' strategy," said Aki Hirvonen, the marketing manager for Coca-Cola Baltic Beverage Ltd. After Osel Foods started selling *kvass* in 1998, its market share expanded eightfold, to 32 percent in Latvia. Coke and *kvass* now have a fifth each of the Baltic soft-drink market.

Company Profile

The Coca-Cola Company is the world's largest producer and distributor of soft-drink syrups and concentrates. Company products are sold through bottlers, fountain wholesalers, and distributors in nearly 200 countries. The company's products represent about 48 percent of total soft-drink unit-case volume consumer worldwide. (A unit-case is equal to twenty-four eight-ounce servings.)

Trademark Coca-Cola accounts for about 68 percent of the company's worldwide gallon shipments of beverage products (excluding those distributed by The Minute Maid Company).

The company's allied brands account for the remaining 32 percent of gallon sales. These brands are Sprite, Diet Sprite, TAB, Fanta, Fresca, Mr Pibb, Hi-C, Mello Yello, Barq's, PowerAde, Fruitopia, and specialty overseas brands.

The company's operations are managed in five operating groups and The Minute Maid Company. Excluding those products distributed by The Minute Maid Company, the company's unit case volume by region is as follows: North America Group, 31 percent; Latin America Group, 25 percent; Greater Europe Group, 21 percent; Middle and Far East Group, 19 percent; and Africa Group, 4 percent.

The Minute Maid Company, headquartered in Houston, Texas, is the world's largest marketer of juice and juice-drink products.

Major products of The Minute Maid Company include the following:

- Minute Maid chilled ready-to-serve and frozen concentrated citrus and variety juices, lemonades, and fruit punches.
- Hi-C brand ready-to-serve fruit drinks.
- Bright & Early breakfast beverages.
- Bacardi tropical fruit mixes.

Highlights of 2001

- Reported earnings of $1.60 per share, up from $0.88 in 2000.
- Driven by international volume growth of 5 percent, worldwide volume expanded by 4 percent in 2001.
- Noncarbonated beverages grew 22 percent, drive by strong performance in waters, juices and juice drinks, and sports drinks.
- Full-year cash flow was robust, with over $4 billion of cash from operations and over $3 billion in free cash flow.
- Return on capital improved to 27 percent.

Shortcomings to Bear in Mind

- Coca-Cola took two steps backward in 2001. It lost market share for its top brand, Coke Classic, and gave up some of its lead in the domestic soft drink industry. To be sure, the company is the clear leader in sales of soft drinks in the United States—and by a wide margin. Even so, Pepsi-Cola gained ground in 2001, partly on the strength of its new products. It now holds a 31.6 percent share of the market.

For its part, Coke still holds a commanding lead, with a 43.7 percent share, down by 0.4 points from the prior year. The last time Coke lost share to its archrival was in 1988. As for Coke Classic itself, its share at 19.9 percent makes it the leader in the cola sector.

These numbers were compiled by *Beverage Digest/Maxwell*, which estimated the size of the soft drink industry in 2001 at $61.7 billion.

- Coke is the ultimate global company, selling $20 billion worth of beverages in nearly 200 countries. Its mission seems simple—sell more drinks to more people in more countries. But the execution can be difficult. The soda market here at home, by far the company's largest, is stagnant. Overseas markets, and especially the developing ones that Coke depends on for growth, are volatile.

And the theory that everyone, everywhere, will someday be drinking as much of the company's sodas as Americans do now—425 cups per person per year—doesn't seem to hold water. Coke also has been slow to recognize consumers' shift away from soda and toward an array of juices, sports drinks, teas, coffees, and bottled waters. Of late, however, it has been making some bold moves to catch up.

Reasons to Buy

- In 2001, Coca-Cola strengthened its position as the leading marketer of carbonated soft drinks and noncarbonated beverages in the world. In 2001, consumers in nearly 200 countries bought 17.8 billion cases of the company's beverages.
- The company forecasts accelerating carbonated soft drink growth, led by Coca-Cola. In summary, this what management sees:
  - Over the next five years, carbonated soft drinks will be the largest category for growth among all nonalcoholic beverages in the world.
  - Carbonated soft drinks continued as the largest growth category for the company during 2001, generating about 250 million cases of growth.
  - Coke, Diet Coke, Sprite, and Fanta remain the company's largest brands.
  - Diet Coke and Fanta contributed the most growth to the company

throughout 2001, both growing at 6 percent.

- New brands—carbonated and noncarbonated—launched in key countries around the globe accounted for about 40 percent of the company's growth in 2001.
- In 2001, Coca-Cola Company realized growth rates of 62 percent, 18 percent, and 13 percent in waters, juices and juice drinks, and sports drinks, respectively.
- In 2001, the company sold nearly a billion cases of juices and juice drinks throughout the world, led by Minute Maid and Hi-C, as well as a number of local brands.
- Coca-Cola's water business grew sharply during 2001 and is now selling over 570 million cases worldwide, led by such brands as Dasani in the United States, Ciel in Mexico, and Bonaqua in Europe.

- CEO Daft is decentralizing management. To get closer to local markets, he is reassigning hundreds of headquarters people to far-flung outposts. And, rolling back the overambitious expansion plans of Mr. Ivester, he is biting the bullet on poorly performing ventures in the Baltics and Japan—which will cost $813 million in write-downs.

The speed at which Coke's CEO is moving to bring change to Coke is winning him plaudits from observers, analysts, and influential investors in the company. The changes, those around him say, have been needed for years and are only the beginning. "I'm very impressed thus far not only with the quality of the management shifts, but the implications they have for the organization and the message it sends," said one analyst.

- Coke is not content merely to sell its flagship beverage. It is well aware that the noncarbonated beverage market is expanding at a heady clip. In late 2001, the company bought Odwalla, Inc., a small beverage company based in California that sells its juices in more than thirty states. Now a part of The Minute Maid Company, Odwalla markets flash-pasteurized juices and blends such as C Monster, Mo' Beta, Rooty Fruity, and Viva Las Veggies.

At the time of the transaction, Don Short, president and CEO of The Minute Maid Company, said, "Under the leadership of Stephen Williamson and his team, Odwalla's talented and proven people have built unique brands with loyal followings. Odwalla, as the North American leader in the super premium juice category, is a key component of Coca-Cola's strategy for building category leaders and profitable growth in new beverage categories."

Super-premium juices are one of the fastest-growing beverage categories.

Odwalla offers an appealing range of juices, vegetable drinks, fortified beverages, smoothies, shakes, soy, and lactic beverages; impressive chilled direct store distribution capabilities—and a culture of innovation.

For Coca-Cola, the deal means a bigger slice of the "good-for-you beverage area," said John Sicher, editor of *Beverage Digest*, an industry publication. "It's a smart deal for Coke," he said. "It's easier to take a small brand that already has some real consumer following and make it into a bigger brand than to start from scratch."

The Odwalla deal was not an isolated event. In recent months, Coke has acquired Planet Java, a maker of coffee drinks, and Mad River Traders, Inc., which distributes New Age teas, juices, lemonades, and sodas.

Total assets: $20,834 million
Current ratio: .87
Common shares outstanding: 2,487 million
Return on 2001 shareholders' equity: 34.7%

		2001	2000	1999	1998	1997	1996	1995	1994
Revenues (millions)		20092	19889	19805	18813	18868	18546	18018	16172
Net income (millions)		3969	2177	2431	3533	4130	3492	2986	2554
Earnings per share		1.60	.88	.98	1.42	1.64	1.40	1.19	.99
Dividends per share		.72	.68	.64	.60	.56	.50	.44	.39
Price	High	62.2	66.9	70.9	88.9	72.6	54.3	40.2	26.7
	Low	42.4	42.9	47.3	53.6	50.0	36.1	24.4	19.4

CONSERVATIVE GROWTH

Colgate-Palmolive Company

300 Park Avenue □ New York, New York 10022-7499 □ Listed: NYSE □ (212) 310-3072 □ Dividend reinvestment plan is available: (800) 756-8700 □ Web site: www.colgate.com □ Ticker symbol: CL □ S&P rating: A □ Value Line financial strength rating: A++

The U.S. Surgeon General recently cited oral disease as a "silent epidemic," of which the primary victims are inner city children. Initially designed to improve the oral health of urban youngsters in the United States, Colgate's Bright Smiles, Bright Futures program has expanded to address oral care needs in eighty countries.

In the midst of expanding the company's reach, Colgate dental vans are stopping in cities across the country. New York, Houston, Atlanta, Chicago, and Los Angeles are examples of the many cities where children benefit from the expertise of volunteer dental professionals. Colgate's partnership with retail giants such as Wal-Mart and Kmart reaches children and their families outside stores across the United States. Each year, this campaign reaches 5 million children in the United States as well as another 49 million around the world.

Company Profile

Colgate-Palmolive is a leading global consumer products company, marketing its products in over 200 countries and territories under such internationally recognized brand names as Colgate toothpaste and brushes, Palmolive, Mennen Speed Stick deodorants, Ajax, Murphy Oil Soap, Fab, and Soupline/Suavitel, as well as Hill's Science Diet and Hill's Prescription Diet.

With 75 percent of its sales and earnings coming from abroad, Colgate is making its greatest gains in overseas markets.

Travelers, for instance, can find Colgate brands in a host of countries.

• They'll find Total toothpaste, with its proprietary antibacterial formula that fights plaque, tartar, and cavities, in more than seventy countries.

• The Care brand of baby products is popular in Asia.

• Colgate Plax makes Colgate number one in mouth rinse outside the United States.

• The Colgate Zig Zag toothbrush, popular in all major world regions outside the United States, helps make Colgate the number one toothbrush company in the world.

• Axion is an economical dishwashing paste popular in Asia, Africa, and Latin America.

Shortcomings to Bear in Mind

■ In the fourth quarter of 2001, Colgate's per-share earnings inched ahead from $0.46 to $0.49. Sales, however, performed below normal and were essentially flat. In most years, the company's quarterly sales rise between 2 percent and 3 percent. The culprit was foreign currency translations, which had a negative impact. Sales from abroad must be translated into U.S. dollars. When the dollar is strong, as it has been of late, the translation hurts Colgate.

In the past, Colgate has outperformed most consumer-products makers. But its large overseas business was not a help in 2001. The company's business comes largely from abroad. Only 25 percent is done in North America.

Reasons to Buy

■ For the full year of 2001, Colgate fared well—particularly in relation to most companies that felt the impact of a recession and the threat of terrorism. Colgate's global unit volume increased 5 percent in 2001. What's more, operating profit and operating profit margins increased in every operating division worldwide. In the words of Reuben Mark, chairman and CEO, "With weak economic conditions around the world, this was a strong finish to a strong year. The combination of sharply higher gross margin and excellent overhead control allowed us to provide a healthy increase in total marketing spending worldwide, while also meeting our profit expectations."

Mr. Mark went on to say, "In each of the last six years, Colgate has delivered double-digit earnings-per-share increases in conjunction with strong worldwide volume growth and gross profit margin improvement. In the year 2002, we again expect excellent growth and gross profit margin increases which will support another double-digit improvement in EPS."

- Aggressive new product activity continued in 2001, with a record twenty-one new introductions. Keeping up with its fast launch pace, Colgate U.S. had already announced several new products by January of 2002, including Softsoap Naturals moisturizing body wash enriched with pure milk proteins and natural milk extracts; Colgate Active Angle toothbrush; Lady Speed Stick Clean Glide deodorant; and new Softsoap Rainforest Series liquid hand soap.

- Technology-based new products and veterinary endorsements are driving growth at Hill's, the world's leader in specialty pet food. Hill's markets pet foods mainly under two trademarks: Science Diet, which is sold through pet supply retailers, breeders, and veterinarians; and Prescription Diet for dogs and cats with disease conditions. Hill's sells its products in eighty-five countries.

Recent introductions gaining wide acceptance are Science Diet Canine and Feline Oral Care, Science Diet Canine Light Small Bites, and new Prescription Diet Canine b/d, a clinically proven product that reduces the effects of canine aging.

Hill's International growth was strong in 2001 across Europe, South Pacific, and Latin America. Science Diet Canine, Feline Oral Care, Prescription Diet Canine, and Feline z/d for allergic animals contributed to gains, as did enhanced merchandising programs.

- In early 2002, *Value Line Survey's* analyst Jeremy S. Marks, said, "A number of recently introduced products should allow the company's oral care segment to continue to prosper: Colgate Total plus Whitening toothpaste, Colgate 2 in 1 liquid toothpaste and mouthwash, and Colgate Actibrush battery-powered toothbrush have been strong performers

in the oral care segment, and are likely to continue to do well in the coming year.

"Led by these products (among others), Colgate's market share in the U.S. toothpaste segment is now an impressive 34.3 percent. This is a full 3 percentage points above the year-ago number. Management looks to build on this recent success with Colgate Fresh Confidence toothpaste and Colgate Motion battery-powered toothbrush (both among the record twenty products introduced in 2001), and additional product rollouts in 2002."

- In an issue of *BusinessWeek* dated January 14, 2002, an article about Colgate said, "In a year of high-profile CEO dismissals, it's remarkable that the same man has been running Colgate-Palmolive Co. since 1984. Experience working through previous slumps may have helped Reuben Mark, 62, keep the company on track. So has his relentless focus on developing new products and getting them to markets around the world with lightning speed. In 2000, Colgate pulled 38 percent of its revenues from goods launched in the past five years. That's up from 27 percent in 1996."

- In a recent issue of Argus Research Corporation, the analyst said, "We remind investors how relatively well-positioned Colgate is to resist the challenge of private-label goods, the scourge of the consumer staples sector as a whole. Colgate's product lines are in private label's sights, to be sure. But they are not sitting at point-blank range, as are iconic cereal brands, tissues, or basic foods. Consequently, Colgate CEO Reuben Mark is confident the company will post at least 5 to 6 percent volume growth once again in 2002."

- Colgate has a solid and consistent growth record. In the 1991–2001 period, earnings per share advanced from $0.64 to $1.89, a compound annual growth rate of 11.4 percent. In the same ten-year stretch, dividends climbed from $0.26 to $0.68, a compound growth rate of 10.1 percent, or far above the inflation rate.

- Colgate concentrates research expenditures on priority segments that have been identified for maximum growth and profitability. For example, the fast-growing liquid body-cleansing category has benefited from continuous innovation. As a result, European sales of Palmolive shower gel have nearly tripled during the past four years. The latest innovation, Palmolive Vitamins, uses unique technology to deliver two types of Vitamin E to the skin, thus providing both immediate and long-lasting protection.

In another sector, focused research and development at Colgate's Hills subsidiary has resulted in a superior antioxidant formula that helps protect pets from oxidative damage, including damage to the immune system. This discovery led to a significant nutritional advance of Hill's Science Diet dry pet foods, introduced in the United States in 2000. The product has gained an excellent reception from vets, retailers, and their customers, aided by national media advertising. Hill's scientists have also developed a new Prescription Diet brand formulation that nutritionally helps avoid food-related allergies.

- Adding to region-specific initiatives is the company's vast consumer intelligence. Every year Colgate interviews over 500,000 consumers in more than thirty countries to learn more about their habits and usage of the company's products.

- Colgate's global reach lets the company conduct consumer research in countries with diverse economies and cultures to create product ideas with global appeal. The new product development process begins with the company's Global Technology and Business Development groups. These groups analyze consumer insights from various countries to create products that can be sold in the greatest possible number of countries. Creating "universal" products saves time and money by maximizing the return on research and development, manufacturing, and purchasing. To assure the widest possible global appeal, potential new products are test-marketed in lead countries that represent both developing and mature economies.

- To best serve its geographic markets, Colgate has set up regional new-product innovation centers. From these centers, in-market insight from thousands of consumer contacts is married with research and development, technology, and marketing expertise to capitalize on the best opportunities. Early on, the consumer appeal, size, and profitability of each opportunity are assessed. Once a new product concept is identified, it is simultaneously tested in different countries to assure acceptance across areas. Then commercialization on a global scale takes place rapidly.

A prime example is Colgate Fresh Confidence, a translucent gel toothpaste aimed at young people seeking the social benefits of fresh breath and oral health reassurance. The process from product concept to product introduction in Venezuela took only one year. Within another six months, Colgate Fresh Confidence had been expanded throughout Latin America and began entering Asia and Europe. Today, less than a year after its first sale, Colgate Fresh Confidence is available in thirty-nine countries and is gaining new Colgate users among the targeted age group. Colgate Fresh Confidence, moreover, has expanded even faster than Colgate Total, the most successful toothpaste introduction ever.

Total assets: $7,252 million
Current ratio: 1.12
Common shares outstanding: 552 million
Return on 2001 shareholders' equity: NMF*

	2001	2000	1999	1998	1997	1996	1995	1994
Revenues (millions)	9428	9358	9118	8972	9057	8749	8358	7588
Net income (millions)	1147	1064	937	849	740	635	541	580
Earnings per share	1.89	1.70	1.47	1.31	1.14	1.05	.90	.96
Dividends per share	.68	.63	.59	.55	.53	.47	.44	.39
Price High	64.8	66.8	58.9	49.4	39.3	24.1	19.3	16.3
Low	48.5	40.5	36.6	32.5	22.5	17.2	14.5	12.4

* NMF means no meaningful figure.

INCOME

ConAgra Foods, Incorporated

One ConAgra Drive □ Omaha, Nebraska 68102-5001 □ (402) 595-4154 □ Dividend reinvestment plan is available: (800) 214-0349 □ Web site: www.conagra.com □ Listed: NYSE □ Fiscal year ends last Sunday in May □ Ticker symbol: CAG □ S&P rating: A □ Value Line financial strength rating: A

ConAgra Foods acquired International Home Foods Corporation in fiscal 2001 for about $2.9 billion, including $1.3 billion in debt. This move enhanced the company's diversification by adding such products as Chef Boyardee pasta products, PAM cooking spray, Gulden's mustard, Bumble Bee Tuna, and other well-known shelf-stable products. International Home Foods' product portfolio is a good fit for ConAgra and should create immediate value for the company.

Twenty years ago, ConAgra had minimal presence in value-added foods and a limited number of recognizable brands. Today, ConAgra is known for household-branded foods such as Healthy Choice, Butterball, Banquet, Hunt's, Orville Redenbacher's, Reddi-wip, Slim Jim, and Armour. ConAgra has twenty-seven brands with retail sales in excess of $100 million each.

Company Profile

ConAgra Foods, Inc., is one of the world's most successful food companies. As North America's largest foodservice manufacturer and second-largest retail food supplier, ConAgra is a leader in several segments of the food business.

ConAgra has uniquely positioned its assets to take advantage of meals prepared at home as well as in such foodservice institutions as schools, hospitals, and restaurants. Food products generate more than $20 billion in sales and $1.5 billion in operating profit. As a result of a constantly improving business mix, more than 75 percent of the company's profits are generated from sales of branded and value-added products. Less than 25 percent of the company's food profits come from commodity operations.

ConAgra's operations broke down as follows in fiscal 2001 (in millions of dollars):

	Sales	Operating Profit
Packaged Foods	$8,681.7	$1,139.2
Refrigerated Foods	13,212.1	437.8
Agricultural Products	5,300.4	281.0
Total	27,194.8	1,858.0

Packaged Foods

In this segment, shelf-stable foods include a host of major brands, including Hunt's, Healthy Choice, Wesson, Orville Redenbacher's, Slim Jim, Act II, Peter Pan, Van Camp's Beanee Weenee, Manwich, Hunt's Snack Pack, Swiss Miss, Knott's Berry Farm, Chun King, La Choy, Rosarita, Gebhardt, Wolf Brand, Pemmican, Penrose, and Andy Capp's.

Under foodservice products are such major brands as Lamb Weston, Fernando's, Casa de Oro, Holly Ridge, and Rosarita.

In the frozen food sector are such major brands as Healthy Choice, Banquet, Marie Callender's, Kid Cuisine, MaMa Rosa's, Papa G's, Gilardi's, The Max, Morton, Patio, Chun King, and La Choy.

Finally, Packaged Foods also has a substantial stake in dairy case products such as Parkay, Blue Bonnet, Fleischmann's, Move Over Butter, Egg Beaters, Healthy Choice, County Line, Reddi-wip, and Treasure Cave.

Refrigerated Foods

In this sector, the company is involved in the production and marketing of fresh and branded processed meats, beef and pork products, and chicken and turkey products for grocery, foodservice, institutional, and special market customers.

Major brands include Butterball, Healthy Choice, Armour, Eckrich, Swift Premium, Decker, Ready Crisp, Cook's, Hebrew National, Monfort, Country Pride, To-Ricos, Texas BBQ, Brown 'N Serve, Golden Star, and National Deli.

Agricultural Products

This segment includes basic grain processing, food ingredients, and the value-added business of crop inputs and yield-enhancement services. The Food Ingredients group and its Flour Milling Company are the processing and milling components of the Agricultural segment. Major businesses include flour milling, specialty food ingredients manufacturing, oat and corn milling, dry edible bean processing and merchandising, and barley malting.

In the United Agri Products segment, principal activities include the distribution of crop input (seeds, fertilizer products, crop protection chemicals, and information systems), in the United States, Argentina, Bolivia, Canada, Chile, Ecuador, France, Mexico, Peru, South Africa, Taiwan, the United Kingdom, and Zimbabwe.

In the Trade Group segment, the company's principal activities are marketing bulk agricultural commodities throughout the world. Major businesses are grain procurement and merchandising, food-related commodity trading, and commodity services.

Shortcomings to Bear in Mind

- In a report issued by Standard & Poor's in late 2001, the analyst said, "Profits for the agricultural products segment will likely decline, reflecting high energy costs and soft international demand for grain and fertilizer. Refrigerated foods profits should be mixed, as strength in beef and pork outweighs the impact of challenging poultry market conditions."

  On the other hand, the S&P analyst pointed out that, "the packaged food segment should generate strong operating profit growth, as the company continues to become a more important supplier to the fast-growing foodservice industry."

- ConAgra's balance sheet contains more debt than I would like.

  Capitalization is about 49 percent common equity, well below the 75 percent that I would prefer. Coverage of debt interest is below six times, at 5.1.

- ConAgra—along with many other companies—had a rough year in fiscal 2001. Earnings skidded 17.3 percent. The main culprits were higher energy costs, increased marketing spending, and a sluggish domestic economy. These trends persisted into fiscal 2002.

Reasons to Buy

- ConAgra is the most diversified food company in the world, with more than seventy brands, along with meat processing, grain milling, and trading operations across major sectors.
- One way to judge a company is to examine its return on shareholders' equity. In this regard, ConAgra gets high marks. In fiscal 2001, return on equity was an impressive 26.9 percent.
- At the end of 2001, ConAgra Foods merged its Australian grain business with rival Grainco Australia Ltd, giving ConAgra greater access to supplies from the world's third-largest wheat exporter.

  "This joint venture allows CTG (ConAgra Trade Group) and Grainco Australia to participate in a larger grain marketing business within Australia," said Greg Heckman, ConAgra Trade Group's president.

  Australia ships about 16 percent of world trade in wheat and is also the biggest exporter of barley used to make beer and the second-biggest canola exporter.

- In fiscal 2001, ConAgra Foods introduced a host of new products, including Homestyle Bakes from Banquet; Jolly Rancher Gels; Orville Redenbacher's Chocolate Sensations; Act II Corn-on-the-Cob Popcorn; new Healthy Choice items; new Marie Callender's items; Hunt's Family Favorites; Butterball gravy, broth, and stuffing; Armour Guaranteed Tender Pork; Treasure Cave Gorgonzola Cheese Crumbles; Reddi-wip Light; among others.

- In recent years, income stocks have been difficult to find. For its part, ConAgra is an ideal dividend stock, with a generous yield and a dividend that has been boosted on a regular basis, with annual increases dating back before 1985. In the past ten years (1991–2001), the per-share dividend climbed from $0.22 to $0.86, an impressive compound annual growth rate of 14.6 percent.

- In the first quarter of fiscal 2002, net income grew 57 percent to $188 million; sales climbed 8 percent to $7.6 billion; and operating profits rose 20 percent to $528 million. The quarterly per-share dividend was raised to an annual rate of $0.94, up from $0.86.

Total assets: $16,481 million
Current ratio: 1.06
Common shares outstanding: 524 million
Return on 2001 shareholders' equity: 26.9%

	2001	2000	1999	1998	1997	1996	1995	1994
Revenues (millions)	27195	25386	24594	23841	24002	24822	24109	23512
Net income (millions)	683	801	696	628	615	545	496	437
Earnings per share	1.33	1.67	1.46	1.36	1.34	1.17	1.03	.91
Dividends per share	.86	.79	.69	.61	.53	.46	.42	.35
Price High	26.2	24.4	34.4	33.6	38.8	27.4	20.9	16.6
Low	17.5	15.1	20.6	22.6	24.5	18.8	14.9	12.8

AGGRESSIVE GROWTH

Costco Wholesale Corporation

999 Lake Drive □ Issaquah, WA 98027 □ (425) 313-8203 □ Dividend reinvestment plan is not available □ Web site: www.costco.com □ Listed: NASDAQ □ Fiscal year ends Sunday nearest August 31 □ Ticker symbol: COST □ S&P rating: B □ Value Line financial strength rating: B++

Costco's strategy of retailing has grown in popularity among consumers and small-business owners in recent years. As a consequence, it has taken market share from such traditional retailers as supermarkets and drug stores. As the leader in its field, Costco should be able to strengthen its position further by broadening its line of products and services, coupled with further penetration into new markets, both at home and abroad.

A reputation for merchandising excellence and quality are a hallmark of Costco operations. These attributes have not gone unnoticed. The American Customer Satisfaction Index survey conducted by the University of Michigan Business School showed that Costco had the highest customer satisfaction rating of any domestic traditional national retailer.

Company Profile

Costco is the largest wholesale club operator in the United States (ahead of Wal-Mart's Sam's Club). Costco operates a chain of membership warehouses that sell high quality, nationally branded, and selected private label merchandise at low prices to businesses purchasing for commercial use, personal use, or resale. The company also sells to individuals who are members of selected employee groups.

Costco's business is based on achieving high sales volumes and rapid inventory turnover by offering a limited assortment of merchandise in a wide variety of product categories at very competitive prices.

As of December 2001, the company operated a chain of 385 warehouses in thirty-five states (284 locations), nine Canadian provinces (sixty locations), the United Kingdom (eleven locations, through an 80-percent-owned subsidiary), Korea (five locations), Taiwan (three locations, through a 55-percent-owned subsidiary) and Japan (two locations). The company also operates twenty warehouses in Mexico through a 50-percent joint venture partner.

Costco units offer discount prices on nearly 4,000 products, ranging from alcoholic beverages and computer software to pharmaceuticals, meat, vegetables, books, clothing, and tires. Food and sundries account for 60 percent of sales. Certain club memberships also offer products and services, such as car and home insurance, mortgage services, and small-business loans.

A typical warehouse format averages about 132,000 square feet. Floor plans are designed for economy and efficiency in the use of selling space, the handling of merchandise, and the control of inventory.

Merchandise is generally stored on racks above the sales floor and is displayed on pallets containing large quantities of each item, reducing labor required for handling and stocking.

Specific items in each product line are limited to fast-selling models, sizes, and colors. Costco carries only an average of about 3,500 to 4,500 stock keeping units (SKUs) per warehouse. Typically, a discount retailer or supermarket stocks 40,000 to 60,000 SKUs. Many products are offered for sale in case, carton, or multiple-pack quantities only.

Low prices on a limited selection of national brand merchandise and selected private-label products in a wide range of merchandise categories produce high sales volume and rapid inventory turnover. Rapid inventory turnover, combined with operating efficiencies achieved by volume purchasing in a no-frills self-service warehouse facility, enables the company to operate profitably at significantly lower gross margins than traditional retailers, discounters, or supermarkets.

The company buys virtually all of its merchandise from manufacturers for shipment either directly to the warehouse clubs or to a consolidation point (depot) where shipments are combined so as to minimize freight and handling costs.

Highlights of 2001

- Sales of $34.8 billion, reflecting an 8 percent increase over the prior year.
- Record expansion of thirty-nine warehouse openings, including seven relocations, six openings in existing markets, and twenty-six openings in a number of new markets.
- On the negative side, earnings were below the company's original operating budget and 5 percent below the prior year. CEO Jim Sinegal blamed this sluggish growth on "a weakened economy, both domestically and abroad; currency dilution in all six non-U.S. countries in which we operate; and significant costs related to our major ramp-up in warehouse club expansion."
- In terms of expansion, fiscal 2001 represented the largest financial commitment to growth in Costco's corporate history. Nearly $1.5 billion was expended during the year—including more than $1 billion for new warehouses and relocations and over $150 million on remodeling efforts to upgrade and expand the company's existing base of more than 300 warehouses.
- On the merchandise front, new initiatives included the domestic rollout of

the company's Special Order Kiosk program, whereby Costco is able to offer its members, on a special-order basis, up to 40 percent savings on big-ticket items, such as Kohler and Grohe bathroom fixtures, Sealy mattresses, high-performance tires, and brand-name furniture, among hundreds of additional products.

- In 2001, the company continued the rollout of its ancillary departments, such as pharmacy and optical shops and gasoline stations; introduced several new Kirkland Signature items, such as clothing, baby formula, health products, and frozen food and delicatessen items; and added several important new merchandise vendors, including Titleist, Levi, Thomasville, Elizabeth Arden, and Sony computers.
- Sales of warehouses opened for at least one year were up 4 percent in 2001, which is significant considering that the average Costco warehouse does over $100 million in annual sales.

Shortcomings to Bear in Mind

- The Standard & Poor's financial strength rating is below average, at B. However, Value Line gives the company an average B++ rating.
- The wholesale club industry proved to be vulnerable to an economic slowdown, even though it sells basics, because of its business-membership exposure. What's more, the company's competition has stepped up its presence and is modeling itself more closely to the Costco strategy.
- Not everyone agrees that Costco is going to continue its winning ways. According to one analyst, "Costco is settling into a period of slower top-line growth. Over the past several years, Costco has consistently been able to generate double-digit comparable-store sales gains. However, given the slowdown in the pace of economic activity and the level of consumer spending, we are not surprised to see this streak snap."

- Insiders, such as officer and board members, have been selling shares of Costco for the past year or so.

Reasons to Buy

- Costco warehouses generally operate on a seven-day, sixty-eight-hour week, and they are open somewhat longer during the holiday season. Generally, warehouses are open between 10:00 A.M. and 8:30 P.M., with earlier closing hours on the weekend. Because these hours of operation are shorter than those of traditional discount grocery stores and supermarkets, labor costs are lower relative to the volume of sales.

- The health of Costco's business can be measured not only by the record of sales and profit but also by the record number of new members and membership renewal rates that remain at the highest level in the company's history. Further, Costco can point to the cleanest inventory levels and best inventory turn rates in its history. In addition, Costco has experienced strong expense control at every level of the company, as well as strong financial and procedural controls that enable the company to achieve the lowest inventory shrinkage numbers (a polite word for theft) of any major retailer in the world. Finally, the company boasts a strong balance sheet.

- Costco has a major alliance with American Express Company, whereby Costco accepts American Express cards in all domestic Costco locations. The company says that American Express "has similar customer philosophies to Costco; a great degree of member/customer loyalty; and overall, an upscale consumer and small business focus. We believe that the card acceptance and co-branded card issuance are the first of many unique and strategic business opportunities that will benefit both Costco and American Express, along with the millions of members and cardholders of our two companies."

- Costco's policy generally is to limit advertising and promotional expenses to new warehouse openings and occasional direct mail marketing to prospective new members. These practices result in lower marketing expenses as compared to typical discount retailers and supermarkets.

  In connection with new warehouse openings, Costco's marketing teams personally contact businesses in the region that are potential wholesale members. These contacts are supported by direct mailings during the period immediately prior to opening.

- Costco knows when a deal is too good to pass up. That's why the company is buying merchandise from Internet retailers. According to Richard Galanti, the firm's chief financial officer, "So many of these e-commerce companies, quite frankly, are using incredible valuations to sell stuff at ridiculous prices. We actually buy some things below cost from some of them."

- In 2001, Costco boasted an 86 percent membership renewal rate, the highest in the company's history.

- For the past year or two, Costco has been testing a food factory in a Seattle store that produces smoked meats and tortilla chips, bottles a private-label sports drink, and makes fresh-squeezed orange juice behind glass walls so customers can watch. However, there are no immediate plans to try the factory in any of its other warehouses.

- In fiscal 2001, according CEO Jim Sinegal, the company had "particularly strong sales in our pharmacy, optical, and food court departments; and at fiscal year end, had 139 high-volume gas stations in operation. The combined sales of these ancillary departments in fiscal 2001 exceeded $3 billion—nearly 10 percent of our total sales—and grew at over twice the rate of total company sales growth."

Total assets: $10,090 million
Current ratio: 0.95
Common shares outstanding: 451 million
Return on 2001 shareholders' equity: 13.2%

	2001	2000	1999	1998	1997	1996	1995	1994
Revenues (millions)	34797	32164	27456	24269	21874	19566	18247	16481
Net income (millions)	602.1	631.4	545.3	459.8	350.9	248.8	217.2	190.9
Earnings per share	1.29	1.35	1.18	1.02	.82	.61	.53	.44
Dividends per share	Nil	—	—	—	—	—	—	—
Price High	46.4	60.5	46.9	38.1	22.6	13.0	9.8	10.8
Low	29.8	25.9	32.7	20.7	11.9	7.3	6.0	6.3

CONSERVATIVE GROWTH

Delphi Corporation
(Formerly Delphi Automotive Systems Corporation)

5725 Delphi Drive □ Troy, MI 48098-2815 □ (877) SEEK-DPH □ Direct dividend reinvestment plan is available: (800) 818-6599 □ Web site: www.delphiauto.com □ Listed: NYSE □ Ticker symbol: DPH □ S&P rating: Not rated □ Value Line financial strength rating: B

In 2001, Delphi introduced 122 new products, such as diesel common rail-fuel systems, receivers for satellite radio, and sophisticated sensor and connection systems. According to CEO J. T. Battenberg III, that's just the beginning.

"We are very excited about the increasing demand for Delphi's expertise, knowledge, and technology in other markets, including commercial vehicles, aftermarket, consumer appliances, medical, telecommunications, personal computing, aerospace, and defense.

"Our technology pipeline is filled with new ideas and innovations, including the planned introduction of 350 new products and processes over the next three years. These introductions are supported by our ongoing commitment—$1.7 billion in 2001—to engineering, research, and development innovation to keep the pipeline full. It's an exciting future!"

Company Profile

Delphi Corporation is the world's largest and most diversified supplier of components, integrated systems, and modules to the automotive industry. Delphi's primary mission is providing products directly to automotive manufacturers. A wholly owned subsidiary of General Motors prior to February 1999, Delphi was spun off to GM shareholders in May 1999.

Delphi delivers the broadest range of high-technology solutions worldwide for its customers in the areas of safety, performance, comfort, and aesthetics. It is through the company's approach to new technology and product development that Delphi has established its leadership position while maintaining the tradition of individual product excellence. Today, Delphi's products are organized into three synergistic business sectors, including an aftermarket division (aftermarket refers to products sold for repair and replacement, rather than for cars being manufactured).

Electronics & Mobile Communications Sector

As Delphi's fastest-growing sector, Electronics & Mobile Communications designs products to enhance safety, comfort, and security, as well as to bring entertainment, information, and connectivity to the vehicle.

Mobile multimedia products include telematics, such as wireless phones, but also the OnStar communications system now being expanded beyond Cadillacs into the entire GM fleet. Equally important are rear-seat entertainment systems, including video consoles and DVD players.

Safety, Thermal & Electrical Architecture Sector

This sector offers a comprehensive portfolio of vehicle interior, safety, and occupant-protection products; heating and cooling systems to manage vehicle compartment temperatures; and power and signal distribution systems for advanced electronic management of power, signal, and data communications.

The sector coordinates product development in the rapidly expanding cockpit and interior modules market. The sector's Advanced Safety Interior Systems, Gold Dot Connection Systems, and Advanced Thermal Management Systems are just a few of Delphi's high-tech products.

The following sections describe the products in this sector.

To help improve safety, Delphi has developed its Advanced Safety Interior suite of products. This evolving portfolio of technologies is designed to provide protection in front, side, and rear collisions, as well as when a vehicle rolls over. Technologies include anticipatory crash, rollover, and occupant-characteristic sensing systems; head and side airbags; variable airbag inflation; adaptive seatbelt restraints; active knee bolster; adaptive force-limiting pedals; and an energy-absorbing steering column.

Gold Dot Connection Systems are flexible printed materials with shaped planar contacts that simplify high-speed, high-density data connections. The technology can be used in a wide variety of applications, including computer instrumentation and emulation, automotive, and military uses. Current applications include telecommunication applications, from cellular phones to network switches and routers.

Dynamics & Propulsion Sector

This sector provides technologies for superior automotive ride and handling performance, including advanced suspension, brake, drive line, and steering products. It also offers complete gas and diesel engine management systems to improve fuel efficiency and increase environmental responsiveness. These include air and fuel systems, ignition systems, sensors, and exhaust after treatment.

This sector is rapidly transforming its product portfolio from traditional mechanical systems to electronically enhanced systems. The infusion of electronics and the implementation of lean manufacturing principles in this sector provide great opportunities to enhance the company's margins. "X-by-Wire" Systems, Energen, and MagneRide are just three product systems in this sector.

Aftermarket Division

One exciting area that should double its sales in the next five years is Delphi's Aftermarket Operation. Launched in 1999, Delphi's newest division is enhancing its brand and sales in the aftermarket. With aftermarket activities on four continents, Delphi is set to deliver the same quality and technological expertise that go into its original equipment products under the new Delphi Aftermarket brand.

Delphi produces a wide variety of aftermarket products, which fall under five key categories: under car (such as shocks/struts), thermal systems (such as air conditioning systems), energy/engine management systems (such as alternators and batteries), electronics (such as audio and security systems), and remanufactured products.

Shortcomings to Bear in Mind

- In a report issued in early 2002, *Standard & Poor's Stock Reports* said, "The worst is likely past for DPH, but with a weak economy, pricing pressures, and limited earnings visibility, we do not advise adding to existing positions."
- The automotive business is traditionally very cyclical. You can expect years of great prosperity, as well as those when the industry sinks into the doldrums. In this connection, the company can be vulnerable to higher interest rates, since people often buy cars on the installment plan. Lenders are quick to raise their rates when interest rates are boosted.

Reasons to Buy

- According to Mr. Battenberg, "Change is evident within the company too, where we continue to transform Delphi away from traditional, low-margin, mostly mechanical businesses toward high-technology, electronically enhanced and higher margin products and systems. In 2001, we divested or closed seventeen product lines, businesses, and facilities, and we made significant progress in improving the performance of several businesses in our portfolio.

  "These actions are helping us reduce our operating costs and improve our earnings power. At the same time, we bought growth businesses into our portfolio. We acquired Eaton's Vehicle Switch & Electronics Division to strengthen our switch and electronics portfolio and broaden our solutions capability.

  "We bought Automotive Technical Resources, Inc., to further develop comprehensive service support and share our electronics expertise with automotive technicians and repair facilities.

Already one of the top suppliers of automotive connection systems, we purchased Specialty Electronics to expand our reach into new markets for connectors and connection systems."

- Competition is formidable and includes Bosch, Siemens, Motorola, and Visteon. On the other hand, analysts point out that Delphi's insider position with GM, as well as GM's growing web of relationships with global OEMs (such as Saab, Suzuki, Isuzu, Subaru, and Fiat) represent a real advantage.
- Ford Motor Company recognized Delphi in 2001 as the only company to win both its Gold and Silver World Excellence Awards for being one of its top performing suppliers in the world for 2000.
- Delphi earned five Shingo Awards for manufacturing excellence in 2001. Evidence of Delphi's high-quality global manufacturing footprint was recognized at sites in Mexico and the United States.
- Delphi received a "Technology Innovation Award" from the French publication *Automobile* magazine. It was the first time in twenty-three years an automotive supplier earned this prestigious award.
- With thirty-two technical engineering centers around the world, Delphi's promise of engineering expertise and global reach has become a reality as these centers provide advanced products, processes, and manufacturing support for all of Delphi's global customers.

  In 2001, Delphi China achieved record-breaking annual sales—an increase of almost 30 percent over 2000. With the Chinese government's implementation of tight emission control standards, environmentally friendly products like Delphi's Engine Management Systems and catalytic converters are in demand.
- Delphi offers a wide range of technologies that improve a vehicle's efficiency

and, as a result, make them more environmentally friendly. In the words of a company spokesman, "For example, our diesel common rail direct injection system improves fuel use by over 30 percent.

"In Europe, where diesel-powered engines are predicted to account for more than 40 percent of European new car sales by 2005, we have approximately 15 percent of the diesel injection market. During this time, we will be producing nearly 2 million units per year for Renault, Ford, Hyundai-Kai, and PSA Peugeot Citroen."

- Delphi's newly developed Passive Occupant Detection System, which is being supplied for Jaguar and four other Ford and Lincoln-Mercury vehicles, enables vehicle manufacturers to improve the effectiveness of air bag protection through smart deployment or suppression of the passenger's air bag.

- In early 2002, Justin Hellman, an analyst with *The Value Line Investment Survey* said, "The company's long-term prospects are bright, in our view, thanks to its position as the leading electronic supplier in the auto parts industry. Over the next few years, the rollout of new products and technologies, such as a hands-free mobile Internet service platform for vehicles, a detection system designed to improve airbag protection, and an advanced onboard climate-control system, should enable Delphi to broaden its customer base and gain market share."

Total assets: $18,602 million
Current ratio: 1.28
Common shares outstanding: 560 million
Return on 2001 shareholders' equity: NM

	2001	2000	1999	1998	1997	1996	1995	1994
Revenues (millions)	26088	29139	29192	28479	*	—	—	—
Net income (millions)	def	1094	1083	def	—	—	—	—
Earnings per share	def	1.94	1.91	def	—	—	—	—
Dividends per share	.28	.28	.21	—	—	—	—	—
Price High	17.5	21.1	22.3	—	—	—	—	—
Low	9.5	10.5	14.0	—	—	—	—	—

* Since Delphi was a recent spin-off from General Motors, the usual information is not available for this table.

AGGRESSIVE GROWTH

DeVry Incorporated

One Tower Lane ◻ Oakbrook Terrace, IL 60181 ◻ (630) 574-1931 ◻ Dividend reinvestment plan is not available ◻ Web site: www.devry.com ◻ Listed: NYSE ◻ Fiscal year ends June 30 ◻ Ticker symbol: DV ◻ S&P rating: B+ ◻ Value Line financial strength rating: B++

When DeVry University announced that it was building a new campus at Westminster, near Denver, in the spring of 2002, the Westminster City Manager, Brent McFall said, "We hear consistently from local employers that one of their greatest challenges is filling skilled positions. Having DeVry here will be a great benefit both to Westminster and other regional businesses who are seeking a well-educated technology workforce."

DeVry will offer courses in higher

education opportunities in business and technology in the Denver metro area. "The new campus will offer classrooms with networked multimedia equipment, specialized technology laboratories, and a technical library complete with computer workstations and will be capable of supporting a student body of nearly 3,000 students," said Timothy Campagna, the president of DeVry University's Colorado campuses.

The New Economy Index by Milken Institute ranks Colorado number three in the nation among high-tech growth. The index criteria include percentage of advanced degrees in the state.

In the spring of 2001, DeVry Institutes posted its thirty-first consecutive term of increases in total undergraduate student enrollment. This solid growth is made possible by continued new student demand, driven by a number of favorable trends. These include a growing number of graduating high school seniors, a higher percentage of high school students seeking post-secondary education, and increasing numbers of students over age twenty-five pursuing higher education.

Company Profile

DeVry is one of the largest publicly held, international, higher-education companies in North America. It is the holding company for DeVry University and Becker Conviser Professional Review.

DeVry University is composed of an undergraduate division (DeVry Institutes) and a graduate school division (Keller Graduate School of Management). These operations provide rigorous academic preparation for careers in technology, business, and management and deliver undergraduate, graduate, and lifelong learning programs that combine proven educational technologies with employer input and workplace applications. The DeVry University system emphasizes teaching and service to a diverse and geographically dispersed student population.

Founded in 1931, DeVry Institutes have provided career-oriented, technology-based bachelor and associate degree programs to high school graduates in the United States and Canada for more than seventy years. The institutes are situated at twenty-three campuses (three of which are in Canada), with more than 47,000 full- and part-time students.

The Keller Graduate School, founded in 1973, provides practitioner-oriented, graduate management degree programs leading to a master's degree. It awards master's degrees in business administration, accounting and financial management, information systems management, human resource management, project management, and telecommunications management. At the end of fiscal 2001, Keller classes were offered to more than 6,683 students at forty-two locations in the United States, including the Online Education Center.

Shortcomings to Bear in Mind

- Like most companies with a stellar record of growth, DeVry typically has a P/E ratio well above the market.
- DeVry is not without competition. The country has thousands of colleges, universities, and business schools eagerly looking for students.

Reasons to Buy

- Since the company's initial public offering in June of 1991, DeVry's success has included a record of more than 20 percent growth in net income from operations annually, an accomplishment that less than a dozen public companies achieved during that decade.
- Nor was 2001 an exception. DeVry again delivered strong, consistent results in fiscal 2001. Revenues advanced to $568 million from $505 million. Tuition

revenue was up a hefty 18.1 percent over the prior year. Net income expanded 20.9 percent to $57.8 million. Earnings per share climbed 20.6 percent, while margins also continued to increase. The company completed 2001 with no long-term debt and higher cash balances, despite record capital expenditures for expansion, improvements, and the acquisition of Stalla Seminars.

- The momentum was still in evidence in the first half of fiscal 2002. Despite the recession and other negative factors, revenues advanced to $321.3 million in the six-month period, up from $276.4 million in a comparable period of the prior year.

The revenue increase reflects higher total enrollment at DeVry Institutes, an increase in course-takers at Keller Graduate School of Management (KGSM), and an increase in enrollment at Becker Conviser Professional Review, as well as higher tuition rates. The number of course-takers at KGSM for the 2001 November term increased 19 percent, to 8,823, compared to 7,416 for the same term a year earlier.

- During the second quarter of fiscal 2002, DeVry continued its expansion with the opening of a new DeVry Institute in the Washington, D.C., area and a new KGSM education center located in Houston, Texas. Further, the company is on track to open its twenty-fourth undergraduate campus in the greater Philadelphia area to house both a DeVry Institute as well as a KGSM center. The Philadelphia-area DeVry Institute is scheduled to begin offering classes in the summer of 2002. It marks the company's entrance into the state of Pennsylvania.

What's more, DeVry plans to open its second Florida undergraduate campus in November of 2002. In February of 2002, Keller Graduate School

of Management started operations in Charlotte, North Carolina, its forty-seventh location.

- In fiscal 2001, DeVry met its expansion goals for both the undergraduate and the graduate/professional segments. The company's Tinley Park campus, opened in July of 2000, is the third DeVry location in the Chicago area. The first Florida campus opened in Orlando in November of 2000. These additions brought the total number of undergraduate campuses to twenty-one by the end of that year. During 2001, the company began development of two new campuses, one in the Seattle area, which opened in July 2001, and one in Arlington, Virginia, which began serving the Washington, D.C., metro area in late 2001.

Keller Graduate School of Management (KGSM) opened six sites in fiscal 2001, for a total of forty-two U.S. sites, including the Keller Online Education Center. The facilities in Irving, Texas; Bellevue, Washington; and Columbus and Cleveland, Ohio, establish KGSM's presence in three new states, increasing the total to fourteen. What's more, the company is strengthening the graduate school's presence in existing markets with the opening of its second center in Orlando and the fifth in the Atlanta area.

- In 2001, DeVry launched its first DeVry University Center to better serve the growing adult-learner population. At this location, DeVry Institutes and KGSM offer select undergraduate and graduate degree programs in a format convenient for working adults, which allows students the option to combine online with on-site course work.

- DeVry became the first private, for-profit institution in Canada to be provincially accredited to grant baccalaureate degrees. In February of 2001, the province of Alberta authorized

DeVry/Calgary to offer bachelor of technology degree programs in electronics, engineering, technology, and computer information systems, as well as a bachelor of business operations degree program.

- In the company's graduate and professional operations, KGSM received approval in Missouri for its seventh graduate degree program, the master's in public administration. KGSM also receive approval in eight states for a certificate in entrepreneurship within its MBA program. Two new graduate certificates in educational management, approved in the state of Illinois, were launched in September 2001.

- In January of 2001, Becker Conviser Professional Review acquired Stalla Seminars, a leading provider of Chartered Financial Analyst (CFA) review courses and materials. Stalla Seminars,

acquired for $8.6 million in cash, develops and markets exam preparation materials for the CFA professional certification, as administered by the Association for Investment Management and Research.

To become a CFA, an analyst or portfolio manager must take a series of three all-day examinations, which are very rigorous and difficult to pass without help from teachers such as those provided by Stalla Seminars. The exams, which have a higher failure rate, are spaced a year apart, and successive tests cannot be taken until the previous test is passed, each in its proper order.

Like all of the acquisitions DeVry seeks, Stalla Seminars meets the company's high standards for quality and is expected to bolster earnings of the Becker Conviser operation.

Total assets: $392 million
Current ratio: 0.94
Common shares outstanding: 70 million
Return on 2001 shareholders' equity: 22.7%

		2001	2000	1999	1998	1997	1996	1995	1994
Revenues (millions)		567	505	419	352	307	259	227	211
Net income (millions)		57.8	47.8	38.8	30.7	24.2	19.2	14.9	12.2
Earnings per share		.82	.68	.55	.44	.36	.29	.22	.18
Dividends per share		Nil	—	—	—	—	—	—	—
Price	High	40.2	41.5	31.9	30.6	16.5	12.7	7.0	4.2
	Low	22.8	16.1	15.6	14.0	9.5	6.4	3.8	2.9

INCOME

Dominion Resources, Inc.

Post Office Box 26532 ◻ Richmond, Virginia 23261-6532 ◻ Listed: NYSE ◻ (804) 819-2150 ◻ Direct dividend reinvestment plan is available: (800) 552-4034 ◻ Web site: www.dom.com ◻ Ticker symbol: D ◻ S&P rating: B ◻ Value Line financial strength rating: B++

Dominion's history of additions to its domain through acquisitions continued in 2001. Late in the year, the company bought Louis Dreyfus Natural Gas Corporation for

$2.3 billion, including cash, stock, and assumed debt. Louis Dreyfus, based in Oklahoma City, is among the group of oil and gas exploration and production companies whose natural gas reserves are likely to be coveted by larger energy companies.

Analysts said the Louis Dreyfus acquisition was an adroit move, since the company's goal is to obtain about one-quarter of its operating income from gas and oil production. Both are nonregulated, unlike its electric utility, which is regulated by state commissions who are often more sympathetic to customers than utilities.

With the addition of Louis Dreyfus Natural Gas Corporation, Dominion's E&P (exploration and production) unit now owns more than 4.6 trillion cubic feet equivalent of proved reserves, an increase of more than 60 percent, and will produce more than 450 billion cubic feet annually, an increase of more than 40 percent. When added to Dominion's existing 22,000-megawatt electric generation portfolio, Dominion has daily energy production capability of more than 3 trillion BTUs.

Over the next three years, Dominion—already one of the nation's largest traders of gas and electricity— expects the acquisition of Louis Dreyfus Natural Gas to help double its energy trading and sales volumes over 2000 levels. The company expects gas trading volumes to increase from 1.2 trillion to 2.4 trillion cubic feet annually and electricity trading volumes to increase from 136 million megawatt-hours to 265 million megawatt-hours annually.

Company Background

Dominion is a holding company headquartered in Richmond, Virginia. Its principal subsidiaries are the following.

• Virginia Electric and Power Company, a regulated public utility engaged in the generation, transmission, distribution, and sale of electric energy with a 30,000-square-mile region in Virginia and northeastern North Carolina.

The company sells electric power to about 2.1 million retail customers (including government agencies) and to wholesale customers such as rural electric cooperatives, municipalities, power marketers, and other utilities.

• Consolidated Natural Gas Company (CNG) was acquired on January 28, 2000. CNG operates in all phases of the natural gas industry in the United States, including exploration for and production of oil and natural gas, as well as natural gas transmission, storage, and distribution.

Its regulated retail gas distribution subsidiaries serve about 1.7 million residential, commercial, and industrial gas-sales and transportation customers in Ohio, Pennsylvania, and West Virginia.

Its interstate gas transmission pipeline systems service each of its distribution subsidiaries, nonaffiliated utilities, and end-use customers in the Midwest, the mid-Atlantic, and Northeast states.

CNG's exploration and production operations are conducted in several of the major gas and oil producing basins in the United States, both onshore and offshore, and in Canada.

The company's other major subsidiaries are the following:

• Dominion Energy (DEI) is engaged in independent power production and the acquisition and production of natural gas and oil reserves. In Canada, DEI has a stake in natural gas exploration, production, and storage.

• Dominion Capital, Inc. (DCI) is Dominion's financial services subsidiary. DCI's primary business is financial services, which includes commercial lending and residential mortgage lending.

Shortcomings to Bear in Mind

■ Dominion's aggressive acquisition strategy has one drawback: it has increased the company's debt, resulting in a leveraged balance sheet. Common equity represents only about one-third of capitalization. Coverage of bond interest, moreover, is only 2.7 times. I would prefer at least 3 or 4 times.

Reasons to Buy

- Dominion is the largest producer of BTUs in the Midwest, Northeast, and mid-Atlantic regions of the United States, home to 40 percent of the nation's demand for energy. The company built an even larger position in this region when it completed its $1.3-billion acquisition (2001) of the 1,954-megawatt Millstone Nuclear Power Station, situated in Connecticut on Long Island Sound.

  Adding Millstone to the company's growing generation fleet boosted its combined utility and nonutility capacity by 10 percent. According to Thomas Capps, Dominion's CEO, "We should see at least an extra five cents in earnings per share each year in the first two years of ownership—and even greater annual contributions beyond that. In 2001, we brought on line nearly 700 megawatts of additional gas-fired generation in Virginia and at our Elwood facility in Illinois, expanding what long-timers call 'iron in the ground.'

  "In the years immediately following this, Dominion's power generation team has nearly 3,850 megawatts of new capacity either under construction or on the drawing boards. We've secured turbines and identified site possibilities for another 2,400 megawatts. In total, we hope to have nearly 9,000 new megawatts in service by 2005, most of it gas-fired. Gas from our own production company delivered by our own pipeline will fire four of these facilities in Ohio, Pennsylvania, and West Virginia."

- The Consolidated Natural Gas acquisition made Dominion Resources the fourth-largest domestic electric and natural gas utility, with over $9 billion in annual revenues. The merger could realize cost savings gains of $150 million to $200 million by 2002.

- Dominion Resources is committed to continuing its $2.58 annual dividend. In the view of management, dividends are an important, if neglected, component of total return. Maintaining the dividend is important to many shareholders who depend on dividends for income.

  Some Wall Street pundits say a company intent on share-price growth can't afford to reward its investors with cash. Mr. Capps does not agree. "Unless the laws of gravity change, our share price should rise with rising earnings. And the percentage of earnings we pay as dividends will go down—something Wall Street will view favorably. At the end of 2001, our payout was about 72 percent of total earnings. Over time, we'll work to have earnings growth move that in the neighborhood of 50 to 55 percent."

- In the telecommunications and technology realm, the company is fortunate to have in-house expertise at Dominion Telecom that opens new opportunities. Dominion Telecom plans to invest about $700 million over the next two to three years to expand its fiber-optic network. The company will use this expanded network—planned to span more than 9,000 route miles—to provide Internet, video conferencing, and other broadband services. In the words of Mr. Capps, "Yes, we're looking to be a niche player. We aren't interested in going toe-to-toe with the national telecoms. But we see a real opportunity in offering telecom capacity to Cleveland, Buffalo, Toledo, and other underserved cities in our core energy markets."

- Investors are sometimes critical of company officials who don't own many shares of their own company. They ask the disturbing question: "How can they expect me to invest in their company when they don't have enough confidence to buy stock themselves?"

If you own Dominion Resources, you won't have this concern. Under voluntary guidelines adopted by the board of directors, Dominion's officers are expected to own company shares in amounts totaling from three to eight times their base salaries. This is a major obligation that requires most officers to borrow money.

According to Mr. Capps, "Loans to purchase these shares come due in five years, and our dividends help pay the interest. We're all personally on the hook if, in the interim, we have not made sound business decisions and grown the company profitably.

■ At the end of 2001, Dominion began construction of a new $800 million electric generating facility in Falls Township, Virginia. When completed in 2004, the Fairless Works Energy Center will occupy a forty-five-acre site with the USX Industrial Park. The facility will produce 1,200 megawatts of power. According to Mr. Capps, "The Fairless Works Energy Center will provide a much-needed new source of clean-burning electric generation capacity to meet growing demand for power from Pennsylvanians and their neighbors in the region."

■ In a report issued by Argus Research Corporation in December of 2001, the analyst said, "We continue to recommend that investors buy shares of Dominion Resources for three primary reasons: strong earnings growth, a balanced and integrated strategy, and a solid management team. We expect Dominion to produce sustainable double-digit earnings growth over the next several years due to its diverse asset base, disciplined hedging, and strategic acquisitions.

"We think Dominion's earnings are sustainable due largely to the company's prudent hedging strategy. The company indicated that it has hedged 85 percent to 90 percent of its power output through 2003. In addition, Dominion has sold forward capacity from power plants that are currently under construction. Unlike some other companies, which wait for a plant to be completed to sell power, Dominion sells the power as soon as capital is approved for the project."

Total assets: $34,369 million
Current ratio: .72
Common shares outstanding: 263 million
Return on 2001 equity: 7.1%

	2001	2000	1999	1998	1997	1996	1995	1994
Revenues (millions)	10968	9260	5520	6086	7678	4842	4652	4491
Net income (millions)	544	436	639	400	604	515	469	520
Earnings per share	2.15	2.50	2.99	1.72	3.00	2.65	2.45	2.81
Dividends per share	2.58	2.58	2.58	2.58	2.58	2.58	2.58	2.55
Price High	70.0	67.9	49.4	48.9	42.9	44.4	41.6	45.4
Low	55.1	34.8	36.6	37.8	33.3	36.9	34.9	34.9

CONSERVATIVE GROWTH

Donaldson Company, Incorporated

1400 West 94th Street ▢ Post Office Box 1299 ▢ Minneapolis, Minnesota 55431 ▢ (952) 887-3753 ▢
Dividend reinvestment plan is available: (612) 887-3131 ▢ Web site: www.donaldson.com ▢ Fiscal year ends
July 31 ▢ Listed: NYSE ▢ Ticker symbol: DCI ▢ S&P rating: A+ ▢ Value Line financial strength rating: B++

You can expect to see Donaldson Company's filtration products on the heavy-duty truck traveling the interstate highway or on the construction equipment on the side of the road. "After all, that's where our company began," said CEO William G. Van Dyke.

"But you aren't as likely to expect our filters in the camera that captures memories of your daughter's birthday party. Or in the backup generator providing electricity to your computer center or office.

"Donaldson filters and related products are in many unexpected places—in products you see, touch, and use every day. Our long-term, focused investment in filtration technology has created the leverage to carry us into new product lines, new markets, and new geography. This diversification in end markets, linked by a common technology base, has enabled us to smooth out the ups and downs of the various market segments and to achieve our twelfth consecutive year of double-digit earnings growth—no small feat in these turbulent economic times.

"We're proud of our progress so far. Our industrial businesses are approaching our goal of 50 percent of total revenues, and our international businesses make up almost 38 percent of total revenues, with operations in nineteen countries. "Donaldson holds more than 370 U.S. patents and related patents filed around the world, and our employees are constantly developing new ways to utilize superior filtration and acoustic technology for products that are still years away from market."

Company Profile

Donaldson Company is a leading worldwide provider of filtration systems and replacement parts. Founded in 1915, Donaldson is a technology-driven company committed to satisfying customers' needs for filtration solutions through innovative research and development.

The company's product mix includes air and liquid filters as well as exhaust and emission-control products for mobile equipment; in-plant air-cleaning systems; air intake systems for industrial gas turbines; and specialized filters for such diverse applications as computer disk drives, aircraft passenger cabins, and semiconductor processing.

The company has two reporting segments engaged in the design, manufacture, and sale of systems to filter air and liquid and other complementary products.

● The Engine Products segment makes air intake systems, exhaust systems, and liquid filtration systems. The company sells to original-equipment manufacturers (OEMs) in the construction, industrial, mining, agriculture, and transportation markets, independent distributors, OEM dealer networks, private-label account, and large private fleets.

● Industrial Products consist of dust, fume, and mist collectors, static and pulse-clean air filter systems of industrial gas turbines, computer disk-drive filter products, and other specialized air-filtration systems. Donaldson sells to various industrial end-users, OEMs of gas-fired turbines, and OEMs and users requiring highly purified air.

Sales to General Electric, its largest customer, accounted for 12 percent of sales in 2001. Caterpillar is also a major customer. In 1999, sales to Caterpillar amounted to 11 percent of the company's total revenues.

The company operates plants throughout the world. Of these, fourteen facilities are in the United States, three in the United Kingdom, and there are two each in Germany, Japan, China, South Africa, and Mexico. Finally, the company has one plant in each of the following countries: Australia, France, Hong Kong, Italy, Belgium, and India.

Shortcomings to Bear in Mind

- In 2001, the North American heavy-truck market experienced a sickening sinking spell. As a consequence, Donaldson suffered from a drop in truck and automotive revenue of close to 50 percent. Fortunately, the company's widely diversified portfolio structure "meant the drop in these applications would slow, but not cripple, the company," said Mr. Van Dyke. Thus, despite the loss of business in this volatile sector, sales and earnings for the company advanced once again, as they have for more than a decade.

Reasons to Buy

- Donaldson has an enviable record of growth. In the past ten years (1991–2001), earnings per share advanced from $0.42 to $1.66 (with no dips along the way), a compound annual growth rate of 14.7 percent. In the same span, dividends climbed from $0.07 to $0.30, a compound annual growth rate of 15.7 percent.

  Despite this fine record of growth, the stock sells at a very reasonable price/earnings multiple.
- In 2002, the company's string of good earnings continued. In the first six months, net earnings totaled a record $40.5 million, up 16 percent from the

same period of the prior year. However, the revenue stream slackened a bit, down 2.9 percent, partly because of the weakness of the yen and the South African rand. Foreign currency translation reduced revenue by 1.1 percent.

- Donaldson is a key player in the booming gas turbines business, an industry that's striving to keep pace with the world's immense demand for power. DCI entered this market more than thirty years ago with the first self-cleaning filter system. Today, Donaldson holds the leadership position in air filtration systems worldwide, working with all the makers of large and small turbines, including GE, Siemens, Westinghouse, and Solar. What's more, the company experienced yet another record year in 2001, with sales in this segment up more than 66 percent over the prior year.

  From permanent solutions like gas turbines to backup power sources, Donaldson is uniquely positioned to capitalize on the insatiable demand for energy with filtration technology that protects a broad spectrum of power generation. For example, diesel generators are providing much-needed backup power to computer centers, office buildings, hospitals, and municipalities. They are often the sole sources of power for remote locations in the Third World. As the key supplier of air and liquid filters to Caterpillar's diesel generator business, the industry leader, "our diesel generator business was up 28 percent over last year, and we expect 20 percent annual growth over the next five years," said Mr. Van Dyke.
- More than 21 million U.S. workers are exposed to poor indoor air quality, not to mention many millions more around the world. "We're doing our part to clean the air with dust-collection systems that filter harmful particles and fumes, enhancing conditions for

employees, products, and manufacturing proceeds," said Mr. Van Dyke.

"In 2001, we introduced the Torit Downflo Oval (DFO) dust-collection system, which offers a revolutionary oval cartridge filter, redesigned cabinet, and an enhanced cleaning system applicable to thousands of businesses in the powder, metal, woodworking, and processing industries worldwide.

"For our customers, this patented system means more effective and efficient filtration, while requiring less floor space. One metalworking customer, using the new DFO, was able to more than double production capacity. Their 'old' dust collector was extremely undersized because of restricted floor space, and thus several of their steel cutting tables could run at only 40 percent capacity. Our new, smaller DFO fit into the available space and enabled them to ramp up to full production. Customer acceptance has been excellent, with over 300 DFO units already sold."

■ Long before NAFTA, Donaldson realized the geographic and market advantages of working in Mexico. From a relative modest start twenty years ago, "our presence has grown to include three manufacturing plants," said Mr. Van Dyke. "Our new 200,000-square-foot facility in Monterey will enable us to bring more gas turbine filter production in-house and expand our capacity to meet increasing customer demands. The facility, our fourth plant worldwide devoted to gas turbines, will produce filter housings, inlet ducting, and silencing products.

"We're also expanding our Aguascalientes facility, where 200 employees manufacture 5 million air, liquid, and oil filters a year.

"In addition to producing large volumes of filters for shipment to the United States and Mexico, our Mexican facilities also serve our European and South American customers."

■ In fiscal 2002, the company announced a major development contract with a leading Japanese automobile manufacturer to apply fuel cell-filtration science to fuel cell-powered automobiles, helping accelerate their commercialization. The first commercialized fuel cell vehicles will begin appearing in 2003. Donaldson FC3 products filter intake air and mitigate acoustics in fuel cells, helping a wide range of products—from cell phones to automobiles—make the leap from the laboratory to the marketplace.

The Donaldson FC3 business has more than twenty-five nondisclosure agreements with fuel cell manufacturers in Europe, North America, and Japan.

"Fuel cell developers, including automobile manufacturers, are recognizing the need for intake-air—or cathode-side—filtration to ensure fuel cell reliability and performance," said Richard Canepa, director of the Donaldson FC3 business unit. "In all corners of the world, ambient air contains contaminants that can compromise the fuel cell system durability, life, and performance. By incorporating current, state-of-the-art, proprietary FC3 technologies, we are making fuel cell-specific products that are cost-effective and available today."

Donaldson is working with the Los Angeles National Laboratory to lead fuel cell filtration development. The company has established FC3 offices in North America, Japan, and Europe and is working with multiple fuel cell manufacturers and fuel cell-powered product developers to make the technology a commercially viable power source for a wide range of transportation, residential, and portable applications.

Total assets: $707 million
Current ratio: 1.89
Common shares outstanding: 44 million
Return on 2001 shareholders' equity: 25.2%

	2001	2000	1999	1998	1997	1996	1995	1994
Revenues (millions)	1137	1092	944	940	833	759	704	594
Net income (millions)	75.5	70.2	62.4	57.1	50.6	43.4	38.5	32.0
Earnings per share	1.66	1.51	1.31	1.14	.99	.84	.73	.59
Dividends per share	.30	.28	.24	.20	.18	.15	.14	.13
Price High	40.3	28.9	25.9	26.8	27.7	17.0	14.0	13.1
Low	24.5	18.8	17.1	13.5	15.3	12.0	11.3	10.0

GROWTH AND INCOME

Duke Energy Corporation

526 South Church Street □ Charlotte, North Carolina 28202-1904 □ Listed: NYSE □ (704) 382-8695 □ Direct dividend reinvestment plan is available: (800) 488-3853 □ Web site: www.duke-energy.com □ Ticker symbol: DUK □ S&P rating: A- □ Value Line financial strength rating: A+

By 2010, domestic demand for natural gas is expected to expand from 22 trillion to 30 trillion cubic feet per year—mostly to fuel electric generation. The Department of Energy estimates $1.5 trillion will be invested in new pipelines and gas infrastructure over the next fifteen years. Duke Energy is increasing its share of that business by developing new gas projects in high-growth eastern U.S. markets.

In the Southeast, natural gas usage is growing at an annual rate of more than 4 percent, twice the national average. To open the region to natural gas supplies from the Gulf Coast, Duke Energy Gas Transmission (DEGT) purchased the East Tennessee Natural Gas Company and connected its pipelines to Duke Energy's own Texas Eastern system. Further expansion is planned via the Patriot Extension, which will bring natural gas to southwest Virginia for the first time and introduce a competitive gas supply to North Carolina.

In New England, Duke Energy is a partner in the Maritimes & Northeast Pipeline, completed in 1999. Originating offshore of Nova Scotia, the pipeline is fueling new merchant plants and expanding its reach into the Boston area with the current Hubline project.

Company Background

Duke Energy Corporation is an integrated energy and energy-services provider with the ability to offer physical delivery and management of both electricity and natural gas throughout the United States and abroad. Duke Energy provides these and other services through the following seven business segments.

• Franchised Electric generates, transmits, distributes, and sells electric energy in central and western North Carolina and the western portion of South Carolina (doing business as Duke Power or Nantahala Power and Light).

• Natural Gas Transmission, through its Northeast Pipelines, provides interstate transportation and storage of natural gas for customers primarily in the mid-Atlantic and New England states.

• Field Services gathers, processes, transports, and markets natural gas and produces and markets natural gas liquids (NGL). Its operations are conducted primarily through Duke Energy Field Services,

LLC (DEFS), a limited-liability company that is about 30 percent owned by Phillips Petroleum. Field Services operates gathering systems in eleven states that serve major gas-producing regions in the Rocky Mountains, Permian Basin, Mid-Continent, and Gulf Coast regions.

• North American Wholesale Energy's (NAWE's) activities include asset development, operation and management, primarily through Duke Energy North America, LLC (DETM). DETM is a limited liability company that is about 40 percent owned by Exxon Mobil Corporation. NAWE also includes Duke Energy Merchants, which develops new business lines in the evolving energy commodity markets. NAWE conducts its business throughout the United States and Canada.

• International Energy conducts its operations through Duke Energy International, LLC. Its activities include asset development, operation, and management of natural gas and power facilities, energy trading, and marketing of natural gas and electric power. This activity is confined to the Latin American, Asia-Pacific, and European regions.

• Other Energy Services provides engineering, consulting, construction, and integrated energy solutions worldwide, primarily through Duke Engineering & Service, Inc., Duke/Fluor Daniel, and Duke Solutions.

• Duke Ventures is comprised of other diverse businesses, primarily operating through Crescent Resources, Inc., DukeNet Communications, LLC, and Duke Capital Partners (DCP). Crescent develops high-quality commercial, residential, and multifamily real estate projects and manages land holdings primarily in the southeastern United States. DukeNet provides fiber-optic networks for industrial, commercial, and residential customers. DCP, a newly formed, wholly owned merchant finance company, provides financing,

investment banking, and asset management services to wholesale and commercial energy markets.

Shortcomings to Bear in Mind

■ Public utilities are sensitive to changes in interest rates. This is partly because they often borrow money to finance new plants. Higher interest rates shove up the cost of these funds. High interest rates can also cause investors to sell their shares in order to invest their money where the return is greater.

Reasons to Buy

■ In 2002, Duke paid $8.5 billion to acquire Westcoast Energy, Inc., a Canadian firm based in Vancouver, British Columbia. Westcoast Energy is a leading North American energy company with assets of about $15 billion. The company's interests include natural gas gathering, processing, transmission, storage and distribution, as well as power generation. Westcoast Energy adds $10 billion to Duke's assets. It is expected to add $.04 a share to profits in 2002 and $0.10 in 2004.

■ "The attraction of the Duke story is attractive franchises in attractive markets, and their ability to increase their earnings as more of their business becomes unregulated," said Julie Hollinshead, an analyst with Munder Capital Management.

■ According to Barron's, "Another plus for Duke is the region where it transmits power. In North and South Carolina, Duke benefits from the healthy transmission grid in the Southeast. In more heavily populated areas in the United States, power companies' hands are somewhat tied: they can increase their output, but the transmission lines are more congested," says Claude Cody, who includes Duke among his top holdings in the AIM Global Utilities Fund.

- In 2002, Duke/Fluor Daniel was awarded contracts by Duke Energy North America to perform engineering, procurement, and construction services for three natural gas-fired, combined-cycle, merchant power generation facilities with a combined capacity of 2,420 megawatts. "This brings our portfolio of active EPC (engineering, procurement, and construction) projects to more than 16,000 megawatts of fossil-fueled power generation," said Jeff Faulk, president and CEO of Duke/Fluor Daniel.

  Duke/Fluor Daniel provides comprehensive engineering, procurement, construction, commissioning, and operating plant services for fossil-fueled electric power generating facilities throughout the world. The partnership of Duke Energy and Fluor Corporation makes one of the largest power contractors in the world. It also has the largest domestic market share for the engineering and construction of natural gas-fired power projects.

- Duke Energy entered into a major transaction with Phillips Petroleum in 2000. The companies are the nation's two top producers of natural gas liquids (NGL), such as propane and butane. Duke and Phillips combined their gas-gathering and processing operations. Duke owns 70 percent of the new company. Duke says the combination enables the company to release more value from its natural gas operations, which it believes have been undervalued by the market. "It will be more highly valued (in a separate company) than it was as part of our consolidated business," said Richard Priory, chairman of Duke Energy. Duke said the new venture should help the company meet its goal to increase earnings per share by 8 percent to 10 percent a year.

  For their part, analysts said the natural-gas operations of both companies are considered well run and solid performers that will only increase in value when combined. Those assets include fifteen gas-processing plants, owned by Phillips in Texas, New Mexico, and Oklahoma, and fifty-two plants owned by Duke in Wyoming, Colorado, Kansas, Oklahoma, New Mexico, Texas, and Canada.

- Duke Power is uniquely positioned to capitalize on its expertise in designing, building, and operating generating facilities. Duke is one of only a few domestic utilities that has historically designed, built, and operated its own power plants. The expertise Duke gained in those areas over the years has been retained through Duke Engineering & Services, Inc., and Duke/Fluor Daniel (DE&S).

- Duke Power meets its customers' needs for electricity primarily through a combination of nuclear-fueled, fossil-fueled, and hydroelectric generating stations.

  Over the past twenty years, Duke's fossil-fueled generating system has consistently been cited by *Electric Light & Power* magazine as the country's most efficient fossil system as measured by heat rate. Heat rate is a measure of the efficiency with which the energy contained in a fossil fuel such as oil, natural gas, or coal is converted into electricity. A low heat rate means Duke burns less fossil fuel to generate a given quantity of electricity, lowering operating costs and helping keep rates competitive.

- Duke Power offers attractive incentive rates for businesses to relocate and expand within its service territory. Duke's Economic Development Rate awards an initial 20 percent discount during the first year for industrial customers who expand their electricity consumption by one megawatt and either hire a minimum of 75 new employees or invest at least $400,000 in capital upgrades. Several dozen companies have qualified for the program.

- In 2001, Duke Energy made a pact with California's Department of Water Resources to sell about $4 billion worth of electricity to the power-starved state over a nine-year period. Duke Energy said deliveries totaling 550 megawatts would begin January 1, 2002, increasing to 800 megawatts on January 1, 2003, and lasting through December 31, 2010.

One megawatt powers about 1,000 homes.

- Duke Energy made an agreement to supply natural gas to Ivanhoe's iron-pellet plant at Port Latta, Tasmania, in 2001. The agreement enables Ivanhoe to convert its pellet plant furnaces from oil to the cleaner-burning natural gas. For Duke, the deal secures an underpinning load for the company's Tasmanian Gas Pipeline, which began converting the pellet plant to natural gas in 2002.

Total assets: $58,176 million
Current ratio: .96
Common shares outstanding: 777 million
Return on 2001 shareholders' equity: 12.1%

	2001	2000	1999	1998	1997	1996	1995	1994
Revenues (millions)	59503	49318	21742	17610	16309	4758	4677	4279
Net income (millions)	1884	1757	1383	1260	974	730	715	639
Earnings per share	2.64	2.10	1.80	1.72	1.26	1.69	1.63	1.44
Dividends per share	1.10	1.10	1.10	1.10	1.08	1.04	1.00	.96
Price High	47.7	45.2	32.7	35.5	28.3	26.5	23.9	21.5
Low	32.4	22.9	23.4	26.6	20.9	21.7	18.7	16.4

GROWTH AND INCOME

E. I. duPont de Nemours & Company

1007 Market Street □ Wilmington, DE 19898 □ (302) 774-4994 □ Dividend reinvestment plan is available: (888) 98-DUPONT □ Web site: www.dupont.com □ Listed: NYSE □ Ticker symbol: DD □ S&P rating: B+ □ Value Line financial strength rating: A++

DuPont launched a fuel cell business in 2001 to pursue growth in the emerging proton-exchange membrane fuel cell market. The company intends to apply its integrated expertise in polymer, coatings, and electro-chemicals technology.

DuPont's goal is to become the leading supplier of materials and components to the emerging worldwide fuel cell market. What's more, DuPont is seeking a strong presence in what it believes will be a $10-billion market for fuel cells by the year 2010.

A fuel cell is a device that converts chemical energy to electrical energy. It

does this by using a fuel and an oxidizer (a substance that removes electrons in a chemical reaction). Compared with a battery, a fuel cell's electrodes remain largely unchanged during its operation, whereas a battery's electrodes are gradually used up. Fuel cells are more efficient than conventional electric generators, which cannot convert all the heat that is sent to them. Fuel cells produce less waste heat. On the other hand, fuel cells are extremely expensive and are used only where price is not a factor, such as in a space shuttle.

DuPont opened a multimillion-dollar fuel cell technology center in 2000 near its headquarters in Wilmington, Delaware. The company is also working in partnership with others in the industry to improve the capabilities, availability, and economic feasibility of fuel cell technology.

"Increasing global energy requirements and the desire for new alternative energy sources in many markets make fuel cells an exciting new growth opportunity for DuPont," said Richard J. Angiullo, Vice President and General Manager of DuPont Fluoroproducts. "We intend to be a leader in applying integrated materials science and expertise to develop new, cleaner, and more convenient energy sources for people around the world."

Company Profile

Although DuPont is the largest domestic chemical company, it is much more besides. With annual revenues of $25 billion, DuPont links its fortunes to a host of business sectors, including agricultural chemicals, industrial and specialty chemicals, titanium dioxide, fluorocarbons, nylon, polyester, aramid and other fibers, polymer intermediates, films, resins, adhesives, electronic products, automotive paints, coatings, and pharmaceuticals (sold in 2001 to Bristol-Myers Squibb).

The company operates 200 manufacturing and processing facilities in forty countries.

In its fibers segment, DuPont has a diversified mix of specialty fibers produced to serve end uses such as high-strength composites in aerospace, active sportswear, and packaging.

Polymers consists of engineering polymers, elastomers, and fluoropolymers.

DuPont's diversified businesses include agricultural products, coal, electronics, films, and imaging systems.

In its chemical operations, DuPont is primarily focused on brand-name downstream materials rather than on commodity items. They include Stainmaster carpet, Lycra, Spandex and Dacron polyester fiber, Teflon and Silverstone nonstick systems, as well as DuPont automotive paints.

DuPont is also the largest agrochemical producer in the United States and Asia.

Shortcomings to Bear in Mind

- An analyst writing for Argus Research Corporation in early 2002 was not encouraging. The report said, "The more newsworthy information concerns DuPont's outlook for 2002 and 2003. Few companies have their hands in as many fires as DuPont, depending as it does on the auto industry, flooring, agriculture, apparel, the electronics industry, pharmaceuticals, and homebuilding for its earnings. DuPont can therefore serve as a partial proxy for the state of America's industrial economy as a whole.

"Given the sharp 1.2 percent increase in the Conference Board's Index of Leading Indicators for December 2001 (figures released January 22), one might expect things to be looking up for DuPont. But that is not the impression the company gave in its conference call with Wall Street analysts on January 23. In fact, we infer from DuPont's comments that the economic recovery is not so close at hand as the Conference Board's numbers would have us believe. DuPont's management called the year 2002 'at least as challenging as 2001,' and 'less clear than year 2003, because the timing and pace of the economic recovery remain unclear, as is the value of the dollar.'

"These are worrisome admissions indeed. First, DuPont's customers buy products quite a few months in advance. If an economic recovery were on the way, the company would have an early view of it. If DuPont cannot see it, it probably is not there. Second, the company is pessimistic concerning foreign currencies. We infer from this that the prospects for Europe in particular (25 percent of DuPont's 2001 revenue) are dark."

Reasons to Buy

■ Not everyone agrees with the pessimistic report issued by Argus. According to a mid-2001 article in *Barron's*, the prestigious weekly investment publication, "But some contrarians remain optimistic. They claim that the company's planned sale of its drug unit shows that DuPont is beginning to execute. DuPont should also benefit when the economy recovers. And the stock is trading at a reasonable valuation.

"The company has no expectations from the Street, in general," observes Clay Hoes, a basic-materials analyst at American Express. "How much worse can it get?"

■ DuPont and Sabanci Holding announced in 2001 the completion of an agreement to further expand their multiregional alliance for industrial nylon. The fifty-fifty venture, DUSA International, is the world's leading global supplier of heavy decitex nylon industrial yarn and tire cord fabric.

"DUSA International will operate as one global business dedicated to meeting the needs of its customers in tires, mechanical rubber goods, cordage, and webbing better than any other nylon supplier," said Peter Hemken, chief executive of the new company. "This combination offers many benefits, among them the scale and resources to invest, renew, and add value to our offerings for customers."

■ Achieving sustained, profitable growth in today's global marketplace requires clear competitive advantage. DuPont defines that advantage as being number one or two in both market position and technology in its chemicals and specialty businesses that are global in scope. About two-thirds of the company's businesses are already positioned as global leaders by this measure. Among them are Lycra, titanium dioxide, agricultural products, fluoroproducts, nonwovens, aramids, and photopolymers. DuPont has some others, such as polyester, finishes, and ethylene copolymers that are very strong regionally. For these, the company is pursuing creative ways to achieve a strong global position.

■ Research and development is essential to DuPont's growth strategy, and the company continues to use its technological strength to add superior competitiveness. DuPont expects research and development to revolutionize the productivity of its manufacturing assets. A third of DuPont's revenue growth is targeted to come from new products. Research programs balance near- and long-term opportunities. The company's agricultural products pipeline includes fourteen new crop protection chemicals. Two other promising drugs are in the DuPont Merck research pipeline. Other development programs are focusing on the commercialization of new products and processes from a radical new catalyst system for polyolefins and a series of new technologies for polyester. Both polyesters and polyolefins are large markets that are growing rapidly and that represent potential for DuPont, based on new technologies.

■ Fluorine chemistry is a core DuPont technology. The company buys fluorspar, a naturally occurring mineral, and converts it into fluorochemicals, which can also be further upgraded into fluoropolymers. Fluoroproducts are particularly valuable because of their unique inertness, lubricity, and heat-transfer properties.

The largest and fastest-growing segment is Teflon wire and cable jacketing polymers. They provide flame- and smoke-resistance that allows low-cost plenum installations for the rapidly growing local area network (LAN) market. Teflon, however, is more expensive than polyvinylidine polymers. On the other hand, Teflon can be high speed-melt extruded as a coating. This eliminates the need for an overlay wrap.

Additional reasons to buy include the following:
- DuPont has paid dividends annually since 1904.
- A new generation of herbicides is contributing to increased earnings at DuPont's agricultural chemicals division.
- DuPont is the world market-share leader in most of its businesses, including nylon, polyester, specialty fibers, titanium dioxide (which serves to make certain substances opaque, such as paint, paper, and plastic), thermoplastics, and other products.
- The company has more than forty research and development and customer service labs in the United States and more than thirty-five labs in eleven other countries.
- DuPont is different from most other chemical companies in two ways: its strong brand franchises (such as Stainmaster, Lycra, and Teflon) and its ownership of Conoco, which contributes 40 percent of overall sales. Thus, DuPont can differentiate itself from the commodity-type chemical companies, since most of the DuPont's chemical products are downstream specialties with 50 percent of sales abroad.

In addition, the company's business mix has only a tiny portion that can be deemed primary ethylene derivatives, and only about 16 percent of total sales are to construction and automotive markets—with only about half of that being in the more cyclical United States.

What's more, even within the automotive segment, the largest business is refinish paint, which is fairly insensitive to the OEM auto cycle. In elastomers, DuPont expects 20 percent growth over the next five years from its new joint venture with Dow Chemical. And, within the construction market, analysts believe market-share gains are being made by the new Stainmaster carpet products, as well as by Corian and Tyvek. DuPont has number one or two positions in virtually every business it is in.

- DuPont has been strengthening its balance sheet. The company's sale of its pharmaceutical business to Bristol-Myers Squibb in 2001 closed for $7.8 billion in cash. The company can use the after-tax proceeds to reduce long-term debt.
- In early 2002, DuPont said that it plans to spin off its textiles and interiors business, which makes Lycra fabrics and Stainmaster carpets. DuPont Textiles and Interiors will be the world's largest integrated fibers company, with estimated annual sales of $6.5 billion, or about 23 percent of total DuPont sales in 2001. "It's a pretty bold move," said John Moten, an analyst with Deutsche Banc Alex. Brown. "But I had expected something dramatic from the company. "I've often argued they need to shrink to grow, and this is a step."

Total assets: $39,426 million
Current ratio: 1.27
Common shares outstanding: 1,025 million
Return on 2001 shareholders' equity: 9.5%

	2001	2000	1999	1998	1997	1996	1995	1994
Revenues (millions)	24726	28268	26918	24767	45079	43810	42163	39333
Net income (millions)	4339	2314	7690	2860	4087	3636	3293	2777
Earnings per share	1.19	2.73	2.58	2.54	3.61	3.24	2.91	2.04
Dividends per share	1.40	1.40	1.40	1.37	1.23	1.12	1.02	.91
Price High	49.9	74.0	75.2	84.4	69.8	49.7	36.5	31.2
Low	32.6	38.2	50.1	51.7	46.4	34.8	26.3	24.1

CONSERVATIVE GROWTH

Eaton Vance Corporation

255 State Street □ Boston, MA 02109 □ (617) 482-8260 □ Dividend reinvestment plan is not available □ Fiscal year ends October 31 □ Web site: www.eatonvance.com □ Listed: NYSE □ Ticker symbol: EV □ S&P rating: A □ Value Line financial strength rating: A

Mutual funds—and there are a staggering 12,000 or more to choose from these days—tend to ignore taxes when they brag about their performance. Eaton Vance doesn't. In March of 1996, Eaton Vance introduced Eaton Vance Tax-Managed Growth Fund, one of the first equity mutual funds managed specifically for superior after-tax returns.

A year or so later, the company expanded its family of tax-managed funds—sold under the banner *Mutual Funds for People Who Pay Taxes*—to include a broad range of investment strategies, including emerging growth, value, and international investing. The company also created a related series of innovative privately placed equity funds for qualified affluent investors, and it hired the portfolio managers, research analysts, and sales staff to capture its share of the fund market that invests outside of tax-deferred retirement plans (such as IRAs and 401(k) plans). These efforts paid off.

Today, Eaton Vance has the largest family of mutual funds actively managed for superior after-tax returns. At the end of fiscal 2001 (ended October 31, 2001), assets under management in the company's

tax-managed equity funds totaled $21.5 billion, and total managed equity funds had grown to 57 percent of total assets under management, rising from 24 percent at the end of fiscal 1996.

Unlike investors in most mutual funds, shareholders of Eaton Vance tax-managed funds have earned essentially all of their investment returns free of the burden of annual tax payments. They pay only when they sell their fund shares.

The company has become the acknowledged innovator and leader in tax-managed investing, with the broadest family of tax-managed equity funds and tax-free municipal bond funds, all aimed at higher-net-worth investors who care about the impact of taxes on their investment returns. Assets in these funds currently exceed $28 billion, giving Eaton Vance the top ranking in actively managed tax-efficient funds.

In March of 2002, Eaton Vance announced the introduction of three new tax-managed equity mutual funds: Eaton Vance Tax-Managed Mid-Cap Core Fund, Eaton Vance Tax-Managed Equity Asset Allocation Fund, and Eaton Vance Tax-Managed Small-Cap Value Fund.

"According to industry statistics, approximately half of all 89 million U.S. investors hold assets outside qualified plans, representing potentially billions of dollars in funds that are subject to tax," said Thomas E. Faust Jr., Eaton Vance Corporation executive vice president and the firm's chief investment officer. "With the SEC now requiring after-tax performance disclosure, and shareholders increasingly seeking ways to maximize returns in uncertain markets, Eaton Vance is responding to a very real demand among investors and their financial professionals for a family of funds that emphasize both superior pre- and after-tax returns."

Company Profile

Eaton Vance conducts its investment management business through two wholly owned subsidiaries: Eaton Vance Management, and Boston Management and Research. It also has two majority-owned subsidiaries: Atlanta Capital Management Company LLC, and Fox Asset Management LLC.

In fiscal 2001, the company expanded its investment focus beyond mutual funds by targeting two major potential growth sectors: managing assets for institutions, including pension plans and endowments; and managing individual portfolios for higher-net-worth clients who want a more customized form of asset management than that provided by mutual funds.

At the end of fiscal 2001, equity assets under management represented 57 percent of total assets under management; fixed-income assets (such as bonds) were 26 percent; and floating-rate assets were 17 percent.

Over $30 billion of the company's assets under management, or 54 percent of the total, is contained in tax-managed equity funds, municipal bonds funds, and taxable separate accounts, all managed for superior after-tax returns.

Shortcomings to Bear in Mind

- The mutual fund industry is highly competitive, since there are thousands of mutual funds to choose from. And investors are fickle. They often buy the fund with the best recent record. Then they are surprised when it ranks last the next year. So they sell out and get a new one. Even though some mutual funds do a good job, investors don't necessity benefit because of their impatience. They fail to follow my strategy of "buy and hold."

Reasons to Buy

- Eaton Vance has transformed its business dramatically in recent years. Not only has it introduced a host of innovative mutual funds and expanded its team of portfolio managers and research analysts, it has developed several creative private equity funds, diversified its investment management services beyond mutual funds, and delivered improved investment performance to its clients. The result has been a significant increase in market share and outstanding returns for Eaton Vance shareholders.

- Eaton Vance's stock price per share appreciated 13 percent in fiscal 2001, from $24.9 at October 31, 2000, to $28.1 a year later. During the same period, the S&P 500 Index dropped 25 percent, and the NASDAQ Composite Index plummeted 50 percent.

- Assets under management in 2001 increased 15 percent, to $56.6 billion.

- On September 30, 2001, after an exhaustive search, Eaton Vance acquired a 70 percent interest in Atlanta Capital Management Company LLC, based in Atlanta, Georgia. The company also acquired 80 percent of Fox Asset Management LLC, based in Little Silver, New Jersey. These acquisitions added $6.1 billion and $1.8 billion, respectively, to Eaton Vance's assets under management.

Atlanta Capital and Fox are leading investment management firms focusing, respectively, on growth and value investing. They complement the strengths of Eaton Vance and provide new opportunities to broaden the company's mix of asset management disciplines, clients, and distribution channels.

Both firms are established institutional investment manager and managers of investor portfolios through broker/dealer separately managed account programs—the two markets that Eaton Vance has targeted. Both firms have excellent investment performance records and growing market share. Eaton Vance intends to accelerate this growth by devoting substantially greater marketing resources to these businesses than Atlanta Capital and Fox could provide on their own.

- Eaton Vance has increased its dividend for twenty-one consecutive years, and the company increased it by 21 percent in 2001.
- The company has a strong balance sheet with little debt.
- According to *Strategic Insight*, Eaton Vance ranks twenty-second by long-term mutual fund assets under management, out of some 600 asset management firms in the fund industry. The company has gained market share steadily over the last four years, climbing from thirty-seventh in 1997.
- As of December 31, 2001, the performance of the company's flagship Tax-Managed Growth Fund beat that of the S&P 500, both before and after taxes, ranking it in the top 20 percent of comparable funds for the trailing one-, three-, five-, and ten-year periods.
- In 2001, Eaton Vance outperformed most of the mutual fund industry in terms of asset growth, market share gains, earnings progress, and stock price performance.

- In a report issued by *Standard & Poor's Stock Reports* in early 2002, the analyst said, "We believe EV merits a premium valuation relative to its group, in light of its stellar growth in managed assets and operating cash flow. In addition, financial stocks in general should benefit in coming periods from a benign interest rate environment. We expect the acquisition of a number of investment management companies in recent quarters to help focus investor attention on small independent asset management companies such as EV."
- Eaton Vance's concept of comprehensive wealth management addresses the three stages of a family's investment requirements: creating and growing wealth, protecting and preserving wealth, and, ultimately, distributing the wealth. The company's tax-managed equity funds, municipal bond funds, and its many other investment products target the first two stages.

To assist investors and their advisers in the tax-efficient distribution of accumulated wealth, in the spring of 2000, Eaton Vance introduced The U.S. Charitable Gift Trust, a tax-exempt public charity approved under the Internal Revenue Code.

The trust provides a way to serve the burgeoning breadth, wealth, and generosity of private philanthropy in the United States. As a donor-advised fund, the trust accepts charitable gifts of cash or appreciated securities from donors, providing them an immediate income tax deduction, reducing the size of their taxable estate, and creating both a family tradition of giving and a legacy that lives long after them. Using the trust, donors thus have many of the advantages of a private foundation for charitable giving, while avoiding the expensive legal, accounting, and administrative costs of a foundation.

Total assets: $675 million
Current ratio: NA
Common shares outstanding: 70 million
Return on 2001 shareholders' equity: 41.7%

	2001	2000	1999	1998	1997	1996	1995	1994
Revenues (millions)	486	430	349	250	201	181	168	218
Net income (millions)	116	116	52	30	40	36	30	28
Earnings per share	1.60	1.58	0.71	0.41	0.52	0.47	0.36	0.38
Dividends per share	0.25	0.20	0.16	0.13	0.11	0.09	0.08	0.08
Price High	39.2	32.9	20.0	12.5	9.6	6.2	4.9	4.7
Low	26.5	18.1	9.3	8.7	5.2	3.2	3.4	3.1

AGGRESSIVE GROWTH

Ecolab Incorporated

Ecolab Center ▢ 370 Wabasha Street North ▢ St. Paul, MN 55102 ▢ (651) 293-2809 ▢ Dividend reinvestment program available: (651) 293-2809 ▢ Web site: www.ecolab.com ▢ Listed: NYSE ▢ Ticker symbol: ECL ▢ S&P rating: A ▢ Value Line financial strength rating: B++

Ecolab has a highly skilled research and development team that continues to turn out innovative new products. According to a company spokesman, "Never content with the status quo, we strive for constant improvement, so far earning nearly 2,600 patents worldwide. And we boast the industry's most sophisticated research and development facilities—where break-throughs happen every day."

In the spring of 2002, for example, Ecolab launched a revolutionary foaming hand-soap system for the janitorial and building service contractor markets. The EpiSoft foaming Lotion Soap System combines exceptional quality soap in a sleek dispenser.

Cutting-edge technology is the key to the EpiSoft success story. Its patented antidrip dispenser prevents wasteful spills with an auto retraction device that keeps unused soap inside the dispenser. The unique reservoir system holds up to seventy additional washes, which allows the soap container to drain completely before being replaced, lessening waste while ensuring a continuous supply of foaming soap.

"Ecolab's ongoing focus on research and development gives us a great competitive advantage," said Tim Mulhere, Ecolab's vice president and general manager of the Professional Products Division. "EpiSoft combines superior foam and cleansing ingredients with innovative dispensing technology, which the janitorial segment hasn't been exposed to in the past."

The silky EpiSoft foam lathers faster and rinses more easily than conventional liquid soaps. Additionally, the superior quality and fresh scent of the foam encourages more frequent hand washing, which is the number one way to help reduce cross-infection and resulting illness and absenteeism.

Number One in the World

According to the company's CEO, Allan Schuman, "When it comes to delivering premium commercial cleaning and sanitizing solutions on a truly global basis, Ecolab is the one. No other company comes close to rivaling our worldwide reach or the extraordinary breadth of products, systems and services we offer.

"We meet the varied and specialized needs of thousands of diverse businesses and institutions in North America, Europe, Asia, Latin America, Africa, the Middle

East—the list of countries in which we do business reads like an atlas. In 2001, we took decisive actions to ensure that Ecolab remains number one in the world for many years to come."

Company Profile

Founded in 1923, Ecolab is the leading global developer and marketer of premium cleaning, sanitizing, pest elimination, maintenance, and repair products and services for the world's hospitality, institutional, and industrial markets.

In the early years, Ecolab served the restaurant and lodging industries and has since broadened its scope to include hospitals, laundries, schools, retail, and commercial property, among others.

The company conducts its domestic business under the following segments.

• The Institutional Division (67 percent of sales) is the leading provider of cleaners and sanitizers for ware washing, laundry, kitchen cleaning, and general housecleaning as well as product-dispensing equipment, dishwashing racks, and related kitchen sundries to the foodservice, lodging, and health care industries. It also provides products and services for pool and spa treatment.

• The Food & Beverage (12 percent) offers cleaning and sanitizing products and services to farms, dairy plants, food and beverage processors, and pharmaceutical plants.

• The Kay Division (6 percent) is the largest supplier of cleaning and sanitizing products for the quick-service restaurant, convenience store, and food retail markets.

Ecolab also sells janitorial and health care products: detergents, floor care, disinfectants, odor control, and hand care (4 percent) under the Airkem and Huntington brand names; textile care products (3 percent) for large institutional and commercial laundries; vehicle care products for rental, fleet, and retail car washes (2 percent); and water-treatment products for commercial, institutional, and industrial markets (1 percent).

Other domestic services include institutional and commercial pest elimination and prevention (7 percent) and the GCS commercial kitchen equipment repair services (4 percent).

Around the world, Ecolab operates directly in nearly seventy countries. International sales account for 22 percent of sales. In addition, the company reaches customers in more then 100 countries through distributors, licensees, and export operations. To meet the global demands for its products, Ecolab operates more than fifty state-of-the-art manufacturing and distribution facilities worldwide.

Highlights of 2001

■ In the words of Mr. Schuman, "Thanks to our acquisition of the remaining 50 percent of our European joint venture, Ecolab is now one seamless company worldwide. For the first time since the former Henkel-Ecolab was established more than ten years ago, we are now one Ecolab in Europe, North America, and around the globe."

■ Sales from wholly owned operations increased 4 percent to a record $2.4 billion. Mr. Schuman said, "Investments in our sales-and-service force, new products and services, aggressive sales incentives, and strategic acquisitions were key drivers of the gain as we fought the sliding economy. Due to the timing of the acquisition's closing date, Henkel-Ecolab's 2001 results have been accounted for as equity income, consistent with prior years."

■ Income was $188 million, a decline of 5 percent from income before unusual items of $198 million in 2000. Diluted earnings per share eased 3 percent, to $1.45. Productivity gains and cost controls partially offset the difficult economic climate of 2001.

- Mr. Schuman pointed out, "We outperformed the S&P 500 for the second consecutive year, and we've now beaten the index nine out of the past eleven. Our stock price opened 2001 at $43.19 and closed at $40.25, off 7 percent. While this was our first such annual decline since 1994, we still outperformed the 12 percent stock price decline of the S&P 500."

Shortcomings to Bear in Mind

- Wall Street seems well aware that Ecolab has a bright future, since it has tagged it with a lofty multiple, close to thirty times earnings.
- *Standard & Poor's Stock Reports*, in a report issued in early 2002, pointed out, "While we still view ECL as a strong company with attractive long-term growth prospects and cash flow, we are concerned that an association with the travel and hotel sectors will limit near-term market performance."

Reasons to Buy

- Over the past ten years (1991–2001) earnings per share (EPS) advanced from $0.48 to $1.45, a compound annual growth rate of 11.7 percent. During that stretch, EPS declined only once, and then only modestly, from $1.49 in 2000 to $1.45 in 2001. In the same ten-year period, dividends climbed from $0.18 to $0.52, a growth rate of 11.2 percent. What's more, the dividend was boosted every year except 1992.
- *Value Line Investment Survey* is convinced that Ecolab is headed in the right direction. Its analyst, Frederick L. Harris III, said in the spring of 2002, "The company's 2005–2007 prospects look bright. It has been able to increase earnings at a steady clip over the years, largely due to aggressively cross-selling its various divisions' complementary products. We think this strategy will

continue to pay off nicely."

- In the fall of 2001, the company's GCS Service Division acquired Commercial Parts & Service, a provider of kitchen equipment repair services and parts with branches in Indiana, Kentucky, Tennessee, and Mississippi. GCS now covers nearly every major domestic restaurant market, with the broadest national independent service capability in the country.
- Mr. Schuman said, "The largest and best-trained sales-and-service organization only got better in 2001. In addition to more than 2,500 European associates added through the Henkel-Ecolab acquisition, we added more than 300 new associates to our field organization, which now totals more than 10,000 members. Simply put, our global service coverage is unmatched by anyone, anywhere."
- In January of 2002, the company acquired Chicago-based Audits International, a provider of food safety services since 1982, and launched a new service: EcoSure Food Safety Management. According to Mr. Schuman, "A natural extension of our growing service offerings, EcoSure evaluates food safety procedures of restaurants, hotels, supermarkets, and other foodservice and hospitality establishments."
- For the second year in a row, the company was designated one of America's "100 Best Corporate Citizens" by *Business Ethics* magazine. In addition, the company was the first recipient of the International Dairy Foods Association Supplier Excellence Award, which Ecolab received in late 2001 at the Worldwide Food Expo in Chicago. Mr. Schuman said, "Judged on superior service to customers, product/service innovations that assist customers, and demonstrated dedication to the food industry, we were very pleased to be recognized with this award."

Total assets: $2,525 million
Current ratio: 1.12
Common shares outstanding: 128 million
Return on 2001 shareholders' equity: 23.0%

	2001	2000	1999	1998	1997	1996	1995	1994
Revenues (millions)	2355	2264	2080	1888	1640	1490	1341	1208
Net income (millions)	188	209	176	155	134	113	99	85
Earnings per share	1.45	1.58	1.31	1.15	1.00	.88	.75	.63
Dividends per share	.53	.49	.42	.38	.34	.29	.26	.23
Price High	44.2	45.7	44.4	38.0	28.0	19.8	15.9	11.8
Low	28.5	28.0	31.7	26.1	18.1	14.6	10.0	9.6

CONSERVATIVE GROWTH

Electronic Data Systems Corporation

5400 Legacy Drive □ Plano, Texas 75024-3199 □ (972) 604-6000 □ Dividend reinvestment plan is not available □ Web site: www.eds.com □ Listed: NYSE □ Ticker symbol: EDS □ S&P rating: A □ Value Line Financial Rating: A+

According to John P. Larson, portfolio manager in the Milwaukee office of Wells Fargo investment management, by the late 1990s Electronic Data Systems (EDS) had become a big, lumbering company that had lost its way. In an interview conducted by Kathleen Gallagher, a business writer for *The Milwaukee Journal Sentinel*, Mr. Larson said, "Growth was slowing and margins were coming under pressure. They had all these independent business units going in different directions, and they weren't managing customer relationships particularly well."

Then, Chairman and Chief Executive Officer Richard H. Brown took over in 1999 and began restructuring the company. He reduced the number of business units and got all remaining units to go to clients with a consistent sales approach.

Mr. Larson thinks the company is well positioned to take advantage of the continuing trend to outsource that he believes will have companies renting computer time, storage capability, and software.

EDS, unlike many of its smaller competitors, can offer its customers "end-to-end" solutions, from initial consulting to running the most outsourced functions, according to Mr. Larson.

"Customers are saying 'we can go to EDS or fifteen other vendors to get the same services, but we'd have to line up those fifteen vendors."

Finally, Mr. Larson contends "In strong economies, EDS's consulting business helps clients develop growth strategies, then implement them, often with EDS outsourcing services. But in down economies, EDS's outsourcing services can still help clients control costs, improve productivity, curtail discretionary spending, and convert fixed costs to variable costs."

Company Profile

EDS was founded by Ross Perot in 1962, then bought by General Motors in 1984 and spun off as EDS in 1996.

EDS, the leading global services company, provides strategy, implementation, and hosting for clients managing the business and technology complexities of the digital economy. The company's comprehensive portfolio of services, which spans the range from the boardroom to the back office, is managed through the five following market-facing lines of business.

Business Process Management

This line provides complete business process outsourcing, including customer relationship management, financial process management, and administrative process management.

E Solutions

E Solutions provides the consulting and solutions that enhance performance of digital businesses. E Solutions combines diverse electronic business and solutions consulting offerings into a single organization, creating a bridge between EDS's management consulting and information technology (IT) outsourcing and business process management.

Information Solutions

Information Systems is the company's traditional IT outsourcing business. It includes network and system operations, data management, applications development, and field services, as well as internal hosting and Web site management. Information Solutions services include centralized systems management, distributed systems management, communications management, and applications services.

Management Consulting (A. T. Kearney)

Addresses CEO-level concerns through strategy, organization, operations, IT, and executive search services. A.T. Kearney, a global management consulting arm, became a subsidiary in 1995. A.T. Kearney serves clients through practice teams focused on major industries, including automotive, consumer products, retail, financial institutions, pharmaceuticals, and transportation.

PLM Solutions

This business line offers the most robust product lifestyle management portfolio, including product development, manufacturing planning, product data management, and collaborative commerce offerings supported by a broad set of product-driven services.

Some Distinctive Features of EDS

EDS offers the following distinctive features:

- Serves more than 9,000 accounts in infrastructure, consulting, outsourcing, and more than 24,000 clients in product life-cycle management.
- Holds the largest IT contract in U.S. government history, the $6.9 billion Navy/Marine Corps Intranet.
- Provides hosting services for about 6,500 clients worldwide, managing about 50,000 servers in 140 company-owned and client-owned data centers.
- Supports more than 3 million desktops around the world.
- Enables more than 13 billion business, consumer, and government transactions every day.
- Processes 2.4 billion ATM transactions annually, placing EDS among the top five third-party processors in the United States.
- Is the largest mortgage processing outsourcer in the world, handling about 2.4 million mortgages a year.

Shortcomings to Bear in Mind

- In late 2001, Ken Brown wrote an article for *The Wall Street Journal* that said, "Name a Texas company that does significant off-balance-sheet financing and whose earnings have soared even as its cash flow has sunk and whose level of disclosure is criticized by some investors and analysts.

    "Try Electronic Data Systems, the big Plano technology outsourcing and consulting company founded by Ross Perot. No one believes EDS is another Enron, its fallen neighbor 250 miles to the south, but some investors and analysts are negative on the stock and feel EDS's gains will be limited unless it can clear up several important financial issues. The company is trying to do just that, improving its disclosure and actively rebutting company critics."

Reasons to Buy

- On a more positive note, Mr. Brown said, "EDS fans see an efficiently run company with a big backlog of business that will carry it well into the future in an industry that itself is growing at a healthy rate. Jim Benson, an analyst at the Oakmark funds, a big EDS shareholder, expects the percentage rise in earnings to be in the mid-teens for the next several years, something relatively rare for a company its size. 'How many companies have 15 percent compound growth expectations locked in due to a backlog over the next two to three years?' he asks. 'You can probably count them on one hand.'"

- At the end of 2001, *Value Line Survey* rated the stock above average in the Timeliness category. The analyst commented, "We look for share earnings to increase at a mid-teen annual pace in the next few years, on the strength of firm volume gains, and gradually rising margins."

- EDS has been building its business through acquisitions. In July of 2001, the company acquired the airline infrastructure outsourcing business of Sabre for about $670 million. The company also acquired a German company, Systematics, for cash and stock valued at $570 million. In mid-2001, EDS acquired Structural Dynamics Research Corporation for $950 million in cash.

- An analyst with Standard & Poor's said, "The number of new contracts has risen significantly over the past two years, and the backlog and pipeline are at very strong levels." S&P also pointed out that, "Revenues will benefit further from the company's focus on e-business service opportunities."

- In a move that could bolster the sale of copyrighted digital content such as movies and music over the Internet, EDS announced in 2002 that it will run an e-commerce network for SSP Solutions, Inc. Under the agreement, EDS will host and manage SSP's Trusted Assurance Network, which is designed to offer digital rights management for online content providers, including entertainment companies, banks, and hospitals. The SSP system uses Wave System Corporation's (WAVX.0) Embassy microprocessor and software that encrypts content, allowing only authorized people to view it.

Total assets: $16,353 million
Current ratio: 1.69
Common shares outstanding: 474 million
Return on 2001 shareholders' equity: 23.9%

		2001	2000	1999	1998	1997	1996	1995	1994
Revenues (millions)		21543	19226	18534	17022	15236	14441	12422	9960
Net income (millions)		1387	1091	954	840	942	1006	939	822
Earnings per share		2.86	2.29	1.92	1.70	1.91	2.07	1.96	1.71
Dividends per share		.60	.60	.60	.60	.60	.60	.52	.48
Price	High	72.5	76.7	70.0	51.3	49.6	63.4	52.6	39.5
	Low	50.9	38.4	44.1	30.4	25.5	40.8	36.9	27.5

Emerson Electric Company

8000 W. Florissant Avenue □ **Post Office Box 4100** □ **St. Louis, Missouri 63136-8506** □ **(314) 553-2197** □ **Dividend reinvestment plan is available: (888) 213-0970** □ **Web site: www.gotoemerson.com** □ **Listed: NYSE** □ **Ticker symbol: EMR** □ **Fiscal year ends September 30** □ **S&P rating: A+** □ **Value Line financial strength rating: A++**

Emerson—better known for selling electric motors, refrigeration components, and industrial tools—has been positioning itself to cash in on the booming demand for reliable backup power systems for computer networks.

With the country's power grid quickly reaching its capacity, outages are no longer a rare occurrence. And when power goes out, Emerson components kick in, switching the power from one source to another and regulating voltage. Emerson also provides diesel generators and fuel cells that generate temporary electricity. These products have become must-buys for any corporation that uses the Internet for conducting business. "The potential for Emerson is huge," said Edward Whitacre, CEO of SBC Communications and an Emerson board member.

One of the key ways that Emerson is entering more and faster-growing markets is through technology investment. The company's leading areas of technology spending are now electronics, communications, and software.

In the words of Chairman Charles F. Knight, "I view this as an important shift, given the opportunities for product differentiation and the increased value proposition for customers that these technologies provide. Customers are responding enthusiastically to the intelligence embedded in our products, as well as to our new software and service offerings."

Company Profile

Emerson is a leading manufacturer of a broad list of intermediate products, such as electrical motors and drives, appliance components, and process-control devices. The company also produces hand and power tools, as well as accessories.

Founded 108 years ago, Emerson is not a typical high-tech capital goods producer. Rather, the company makes such prosaic things as refrigerator compressors, pressure gauges, and the In-Sink Erator garbage disposal—basic products that are essential to industry.

Emerson operates in the following five segments.

• Emerson Industrial Automation provides integral horsepower motors; alternators; electronic and mechanical drives; industrial valves; electrical equipment; specialty heating, lighting, testing, and ultrasonic welding and cleaning products for industrial applications. Key growth drivers for the segment include the embedding of electronics into motors and other equipment to enable self-diagnosis and preventative maintenance functionality, as well as alternators for diesel and natural gas generator sets to create reliable distributed power solutions. The Industrial Automation segment is the company's largest, with revenues of $3.0 billion in fiscal 2001, or 19.4 percent of the company's overall revenues of $15.5 billion. Earnings of this segment in 2001 were $400 million, a decrease of 14 percent, due to the steep downturn in industrial capital goods spending, divestitures, and a stronger U.S. dollar.

• Emerson Process Control offers control systems and software; analytical instrumentation; measurement devices;

and valves and other control equipment for customers in oil and gas, chemical, power, water and wastewater, food and beverage, pharmaceutical, and other industries. Key growth drivers include Emerson's innovative PlantWeb technology, which redefines plant architecture, and new solution and service opportunities created by Emerson's unique ability to apply its technology to specific customer needs. In 2001, this segment had earnings before interest and income taxes of $360 million in 2001, a 28 percent increase from the prior year, reflecting broad strength across virtually all areas of the business, coupled with rationalization of the cost structure completed over the past two years.

• Emerson Heating, Ventilating, and Air Conditioning (HVAC) offers compressors, thermostats, temperature controls, hermetic terminals, and valves for HVAC and refrigeration systems. A key driver of this business is the Copeland Scroll compressor, a revolutionary technology that is more energy efficient, reliable, and quiet than competing traditional technologies. Scroll also has created entirely new compression markets outside of HVAC, such as microturbine gas boosters for distributed power generation. HVAC is the smallest segment of Emerson. In 2001, earnings decreased $35 million, or 9 percent, to $347 million. This segment was hurt by lower domestic demand for air conditioning and refrigeration products in all markets.

• Electronics and Telecommunications, through Emerson Network Power, delivers comprehensive solutions for highly reliable power. Offerings include AC UPS Systems, DC power systems, precision air-conditioning systems, embedded and power supplies, transfer switches, and site monitoring systems and services for the fast-growing communications and Internet infrastructure markets. Additionally, fiber-optic conduit and connectivity products support the global expansion of broadband communications. Key drivers include the rapid build-out of wireless, broadband, and other data and voice services, as well as the increasing need for dependable backup power to support the utility grid. In 2001, Electronics and Telecommunications had earnings of $359 million, a decrease from the prior year, when it earned $447 million. The weakness can be traced to the impact on profits resulting from the decline in sales volume and higher costs for the rationalization of operations.

• Appliance and Tools includes the Emerson Storage Solutions, Emerson Tools, Emerson Appliance Solutions, and Emerson Motors brand platforms. Customer offerings feature an extensive range of consumer, commercial, and industrial storage products; market-leading tools; electrical components and systems for appliances; and the world's largest offering of fractional horsepower motors. Key growth drivers include professional-grade tools serving the fast-growing home center market, as well as advanced electrical motors, which create entirely new market opportunities for Emerson. This part of the company had earnings in 2001 of $503 million, for a decrease of 13 percent. The company blamed this shortfall on a decrease in volume and the Vermont American divestiture.

Shortcomings to Bear in Mind

■ Long celebrated as a model of stable, consistent earnings growth, Emerson has lost some of its luster on Wall Street. In the words of CEO David N. Farr, here's what happened to Emerson in fiscal 2001, after racking up a long record of gains in earnings and dividends.

"Fiscal 2001 was among the most challenging years in Emerson's long history. Not since the early 1960s have so many sectors been simultaneously impacted by such a sudden economic downturn. While our business and geographic diversity have historically helped buffer economic swings, the breadth of this downturn has been exceptional.

"We responded to this environment in several ways. First, we accelerated cost cutting and restructuring, investing in actions such as facility consolidations and product line rationalizations to improve Emerson's long-term cost structure. Second, we maintained investments in our industry-leading, technology-based products and services, which drive over half of Emerson's total sales. This commitment will help increase our lead over competitors who cannot keep up during tough times. And finally, we continued repositioning into faster-growth areas worldwide through acquisitions and divestitures."

Reasons to Buy

- In the process business, Emerson is the only company with a scalable, intelligent process automation architecture that is commercially available. According to Mr. Farr, "We call our technology PlantWeb, and since its launch in 1998, it has been selected over legacy process automation systems on more than 2,000 occasions. Virtually all major customers in the oil and gas, refinery, chemical, pharmaceutical, and other process industries have embraced PlantWeb."

- In 2001, Emerson took advantage of the recession to accelerate creation of a single global integrated Network Power business and to emerge a stronger leader. The recent purchase of Avansys Power (the largest private acquisition in China by a foreign company) supports the company's global integration and extends its leadership. Mr. Farr says that, "Avansys Power also creates opportunities for

other Emerson operations, elevating our total presence in Asia. This region is important because it contains more than 50 percent of the world's population and more than 25 percent of world gross domestic product. More than 22,000 Emerson employees reside in Asia, supporting sales of approximately $1.7 billion, including Avansys. While this is a strong presence, we clearly have substantial opportunities to grow.

"As Avansys illustrates, we continue to use acquisitions and divestitures to reposition Emerson into faster-growth markets. Since 1998, Emerson has announced divestitures of eleven slower-growing, non-core operations with annual sales of about $1.5 billion."

- Emerson has one of the greatest growth records of all time. For forty-three consecutive years, earnings per share have increased at a compound annual pace of 11 percent. Dividends have done slightly better, with a forty-four-year record, coupled with a compound growth rate of 12 percent. In 2001, this string was snapped, as earnings were hurt by a serious recession. However, the dividend was increased, thus preserving that impressive record.

- Technology is fundamental to Emerson's sales growth. As a consequence, the company has been increasing its investment in Engineering & Development, notably in such sectors as communications, software, and electronics. Engineering & Development investment, moreover, has risen every year since 1973.

- Over the years, Emerson has enjoyed its share of recognition. *BusinessWeek*, for instance, named Emerson's Knight (chairman) and Farr (CEO) among the Top Managers of 2000. *Fortune's Investor's Guide* included Emerson among "Seven Stocks That are Ready to Run."

Total assets: $15,046 million
Current ratio: 0.99
Common shares outstanding: 428 million
Return on 2001 shareholders' equity: 20.2%

	2001	2000	1999	1998	1997	1996	1995	1994
Revenues (millions)	15480	15545	14270	13447	12299	11150	10013	8607
Net income (millions)	1032	1422	1314	1229	1122	1018	908	789
Earnings per share	2.40	3.30	3.00	2.77	2.52	2.28	2.03	1.76
Dividends per share	1.54	1.43	1.31	1.18	1.08	.98	.89	.78
Price High	79.6	79.8	71.4	67.4	60.4	51.8	40.8	33.0
Low	44.0	40.5	51.4	54.5	45.0	38.8	30.8	28.2

INCOME

Equity Office Properties Trust

Two North Riverside Plaza, Suite 2100 ▢ Chicago, Illinois 60606 ▢ Listed: NYSE ▢ (800) 692-5304 ▢ Direct dividend reinvestment plan is available: (312) 466-3508 ▢ Web site: www.equityoffice.com ▢ Ticker symbol: EOP ▢ S&P rating: Not rated ▢ Value Line financial strength rating: B+

Equity Office Properties, a leading REIT that invests in office buildings, bought Spieker Properties, Inc., in the summer of 2001. Spieker is the largest commercial real estate owner on the West Coast. It added 25 million square feet to Equity Office Property's 124 million square feet across the country. At $7.2 billion, the purchase—for cash, stock, and assumed debt—was the biggest domestic transaction in real estate history.

According to Credit Suisse First Boston Corporation, "the Spieker merger improves Equity Office Property's all-important return on invested capital." What's more, said the Credit Suisse analyst, the merger will "increase the amount of free cash flow and improve overall balance sheet ratios." In this same report, the analyst also pointed out that Equity Office Properties can now "lay claim to being the number one office player in Boston, Chicago, San Francisco, Silicon Valley, Seattle, Portland, and Atlanta."

Company Profile

Equity Office Properties Trust is the nation's largest publicly held owner and manager of office properties. With a total market capitalization of about $27 billion, Equity Office owns and manages 128 million square feet of primary Class A office space in 774 buildings in thirty-seven major metropolitan areas across the country. The company serves more than 6,800 businesses, including many of the most recognized companies in America. The company's buildings are situated in such cities as Boston (fifty-five buildings), Chicago (thirty), San Francisco (twenty-eight), New York (six), Seattle (twenty-one), Washington, D.C. (twenty-five), Atlanta (forty-five), San Jose/Silicon Valley (thirty-seven), Los Angeles (thirteen), and Denver (fifteen). All told, these top ten markets are responsible for 77.6 percent of the company's operating income.

The company's origins date back to 1976 when Samuel Zell, now chairman of Equity, founded an integrated real estate management and acquisition organization. The company's portfolio was consolidated and taken public in July 1997. Since its initial public offering (IPO), the company has nearly quadrupled in size, growing from

32.2 to 125 million square feet through strategic acquisitions, including the $4.3 billion Beacon Properties, Inc., merger in December 1997 and the $4.5 billion Cornerstone Properties merger in June 2000.

Office buildings are structures used primarily for the conducting of business, such as administration, clerical services, and consultation with clients and associates. Class A office buildings are generally considered those that have excellent locations and access, that attract high-quality tenants, that are well maintained and professionally managed. They also achieve the highest rent, occupancy, and tenant retention rates within their markets.

Acquisitions

Acquisitions have played an integral part in the company's growth. Equity Office Properties Trust significantly expanded its operations in late 1997 with the acquisition of Beacon Properties for $4.3 billion, adding 130 properties and 21 million square feet to its holdings. In 1999, the Trust completed six acquisitions, investing $393 million and acquiring ten office properties containing 589 spaces. In mid-2000, it completed the acquisition of Cornerstone Properties for $2.7 billion. Cornerstone is an office REIT that owns eighty-six office properties in the United States, totaling over 18.5 million square feet. Finally, its largest acquisition, as noted above, was Spieker Properties.

What Is an Equity REIT?

Equity REITs make their money by owning properties, as opposed to mortgage REITs, which lend money to property owners. Equity REITs allow you to invest in a diversified collection of apartment buildings, hospitals, shopping centers, hotels, warehouses, and office buildings.

Like mutual funds, REITs are not taxed themselves, providing they pay out at least 95 percent of their taxable income.

That translates into fat dividends for shareholders, as REITs pass along the rents and other income they collect. Dividend yields are typically 6 percent or more. "Put it all together, and you are looking at a double-digit total return. Over the long haul, the return should be lower than traditional stocks, but higher than bonds," says Chris Mayer, a real estate professor at the University of Pennsylvania's Wharton School.

Kevin Bernzott, an investment adviser in Camarillo, California, views REITs as a stock-bond hybrid. "If you select quality REITs, they kick off a highly predictable stream of income, and eventually you may get some price appreciation. We plug them into the bond portion of the portfolio. They're almost like a bond with an equity kicker."

Shortcomings to Bear in Mind

- The leasing of real estate is highly competitive. Equity Office's properties compete for tenants with similar properties situated in its markets, primarily on the basis of location, rent charged, services provided, and the design and condition of improvements.

  The company also experiences competition when attempting to acquire interests in desirable real estate, including competition from domestic and foreign financial institutions, other REITs, life insurance companies, pension trusts, trust funds, partnerships, and individual investors.

- Many investors buy shares in real estate investment trusts to achieve high income. In this regard, they may be disappointed with Equity Office Properties Trust, since its dividend yield is below the REIT industry average. "Nevertheless," said *Standard & Poor's Stock Reports*, "EOP is a well-run REIT and can be considered one of the blue chips of the industry. The trust's chairman,

Sam Zell, is one of the most successful U.S. real estate investors. Equity Office Property's geographically diversified portfolio insulates it from regional recessions and overbuilding, and provides it with certain economies of scale. The REIT is also conservatively capitalized, with a high interest coverage ratio and a solid debt-to-total-capitalization ratio."

- Adam Rosner, an analyst with *Value Line Survey*, said in early 2002, "The current slowdown in the real estate markets will likely affect operations. Given the high unemployment levels, as well as corporate bankruptcies, it is likely that office vacancies will increase, and new space will not be absorbed quickly. Occupancy at the same-store portfolio has declined somewhat in recent months. However, current occupancy levels are about 94 percent, which is still respectable."

Reasons to Buy

- Equity Office Properties is well positioned to sustain this growth, according to Timothy H. Callahan, the company's CEO. "We believe that on average, our existing rents are more than 30 percent below current market rents. We expect to realize this embedded growth as new leases are signed at current market-level rents. Over the next five years, approximately 11 percent to 13 percent of our leases expire annually, giving us strong growth potential. The nature of this primary revenue stream—long-term leases with over 6,800 businesses across all industries—helps insulate Equity Office from economic downturns. Finally, our geographic diversity also mitigates our exposure to regional downturns."
- In 2001, Equity Office Properties Trust was named to *Fortune* magazine's Most Admired list as the number one company in the real estate sector. EOP also scored among the top five percent among companies in all industries.
- In early 2002, *Standard & Poor's Stock Reports* commented, "External growth is likely to come from acquisitions. When acquiring parking facilities, management seeks facilities that have limited competition, minimal or no rental rate restrictions, and a superior location near or affiliated with airports, commercial business districts, entertainment projects or health care facilities."
- In an article appearing in *The Wall Street Journal* in November of 2001, Tom Lauricella said, "Real-estate investment trusts, the securities most widely owned by real-estate funds, have an extremely low correlation to broad stock market gauges and to bonds, meaning that REITs may zig when others zag, or vice versa.

  "In fact, researchers at Chicago-based Ibbotson Associates recently published a study showing that the correlation between REITs and other stocks is roughly half the correlation between stocks and bonds. 'As an asset class, REITs have some unique characteristics,' said Peng Chen, Ibbotson's director of research."
- Equity's clients are mostly *Fortune* 500 corporations that sign long-term leases, guaranteeing that revenues will flow even during an economic downturn. "Equity Office has the nameplate properties in big cities," said Bill Schaff, manager of Berger Large Cap Value Fund. "The nameplate properties are always filled."
- Michael Arndt, writing for *BusinessWeek* on December 31, 2001, said, "Today's best bets, say the pros, are industry leaders such as Equity Office Properties Trust. They have top-notch management teams, strong balance sheets, and such geographically diverse portfolios that they can weather downturns handily,

whether it's the burst dot-com bubble in San Francisco or the blow from terrorism in Manhattan.

"Although new-lease rents are down from the 2000's peak across the United States, Equity Office Properties, for instance, was still raising rents by an average of $4.50 per square foot in late 2001. How's that possible? Tenants whose leases are up for renewal typically have been paying rates set ten years ago. Even today's lower rents are higher than they were back then."

Total assets: $18,794 million
Current ratio: NA
Return on 2001 equity: 10%
Common shares outstanding: 414 million

	2001	2000	1999	1998	1997	1996*	1995	1994
Revenues (millions)	3130	2264	1942	1680	752			
Net income (millions)	618	473	442	357	282			
Earnings per share	1.55	1.53	1.52	1.24	1.11			
Funds from operations	3.20	2.86	2.57	2.33	0.89			
Dividends per share	1.90	1.74	1.58	1.38	0.56			
Price High	33.2	33.5	29.4	32.0	34.7			
Low	26.2	22.9	20.8	20.2	21.0			

* Statistical information only available since the company went public in 1997.

AGGRESSIVE GROWTH

Ethan Allen Interiors, Inc.

Ethan Allen Drive □ Danbury, Connecticut 06811 □ (203) 743-8234 □ Web site: www.ethanallen.com □ Dividend reinvestment plan is not available □ Fiscal year ends June 30 □ Listed: NYSE □ Ticker symbol: ETH □ S&P rating: B+ □ Value Line financial strength rating: B+

Ethan Allen is now selling its wares over the Internet. In an effort to extend its reach and supplement traditional marketing efforts, the company has expanded and redesigned its Web site to allow for the direct sale of more than 5,000 home-furnishing products.

Analysts believe the company is uniquely positioned to leverage its widely recognized brand name and favorable reputation to swiftly develop a valuable e-commerce endeavor. What's more, Ethan Allen's extensive distribution network and integrated retail structure provides it with a competitive advantage in servicing online customers.

Most other furniture producers have been reluctant to establish an Internet retail presence—such a move would alienate its retail and wholesale customers. For its part, Ethan Allen has no such fears, since its furniture is marketed exclusively through its own network of stores.

Company Profile

Ethan Allen, one of the ten largest manufacturers of household furniture in the United States, sells a full range of furniture products and decorative accessories through a network of 312 retail stores, of which eighty-four are company-owned. The rest are owned and operated by independent dealers. However, all stores sell Ethan Allen products exclusively. Retail stores are located in the United States, Canada, and Mexico, with more than eighteen located overseas. The company has eighteen manufacturing facilities, including three sawmills, located throughout the United States. In addition, Ethan Allen has six regional distribution centers situated throughout the United States.

The company's stores (it prefers the term "galleries") are scattered across the country, with outlets in nearly every state. However, Ethan Allen has more than a dozen outlets in such states as California, Texas, and Florida. There is a also a concentrated cluster of Ethan Allen stores along the Eastern Seaboard in such states as New Jersey, Connecticut, and Massachusetts.

Within this fragmented industry, the company has the largest domestic furniture retail network of those using the gallery concept. Comparable-store sales have benefited from a repositioning of the product mix to appeal to a broader consumer base and a program to renovate or relocate existing stores, coupled with more frequent advertising and promotional campaigns.

Ethan Allen is pursuing an aggressive growth strategy, including investments in technology, employee training, and new stores. A number of strategies have enhanced margins, such as manufacturing efficiencies, lower interest expense, and a strengthening of the upholstery and accessory lines.

With an efficient and flexible vertically integrated structure, a strong, dedicated retail network, an impressive 95-percent brand-name recognition rate, and a sixty-eight-year reputation for exceptional quality and service, Ethan Allen is uniquely positioned as a dominant force in the home furnishings industry.

As Ethan Allen enters the new millennium, the company's philosophy of design remains the same as when the company was founded sixty-eight years ago. Styles may have changed from colonial to eclectic, but the company's commitment to exceptional quality, classical design elements, innovative style, and functionality will continue to position Ethan Allen as a preferred brand for years to come.

In keeping with the way today's consumers live, the company has organized its product programs into two broad style categories. "Classic" encompasses more historically inspired styles, from early European and French influences to designs from the eighteenth and nineteenth century masters. "Casual," on the other hand, captures a clean, contemporary line and an updated country aesthetic.

Shortcomings to Bear in Mind

- This stock is labeled "aggressive growth," because it has a high beta coefficient of 1.45. A beta coefficient of 1 indicates a stock that fluctuates with the market. High betas are indicative of stocks that can be volatile.
- The stock of Ethan Allen can be sensitive to the cyclical whims of furniture demand. For instance, when interest rates rise, the furniture industry is hurt along with housing starts.

Reasons to Buy

- The company employs a showcase gallery concept. Products are displayed in complete room ensembles, including furnishings, wall decor, window treatments, floor coverings, accents, and accessories. Ethan Allen believes the gallery concept leads to higher sales, as it encourages customers to buy a complete home collection, including case goods (furniture made of wood, rather than upholstered), upholstery, and accessories. This concept also offers designers an opportunity to offer additional services.

- Ethan Allen benefits from vertical integration. Because the company controls many aspects of its operations, it is self-sufficient, efficient, and cost-effective. Ethan Allen management makes business decisions on everything from sales events to manufacturing locations. That way, the company can position its strategies based on what works best. In other words, the company has eliminated the middleman and the resulting waste and it is therefore able to avoid bottlenecks. This translates into productivity, increased efficiency, satisfied customers, and steadily climbing profits.

- Ethan Allen's new stores are situated in high-traffic shopping areas for customer convenience. Many existing stores have been relocated to better-traveled retail routes. For example, in 2000, management relocated its Akron, Ohio, store less than one mile from its previous location. The company expanded its square footage to take advantage of the more accessible location. By making these changes, the store increased traffic by an impressive 66 percent. In just a few months, moreover, sales were up 50 percent.

- In the realm of advertising, the company allocated over $70 million in a multimedia campaign using a combination of TV, radio, and direct mail, e-mail, and print advertising that breaks through the clutter and establishes a strong preference for the Ethan Allen brand.

  The company's message is being conveyed to the public in a variety of ways. Its television campaign spans twenty-seven weeks of the year, much during prime time. Ethan Allen also boasts the largest direct mail campaign in its industry, with more than 70 million direct mail pieces each year.

  Once inside the store, the customer is offered a complimentary copy of *The Treasury of American Home Interiors*, which contains the company's complete product line, enabling the customer to continue shopping at home. Finally, the company's Web site now allows customers to shop and learn about the Ethan Allen brand on the Internet twenty-four hours a day.

- Ethan Allen's new Simple Finance Plan is an impressive consumer payment program. The company's innovative approach to financing, both from its revolving credit card and its installment loan programs, continues to drive new business to Ethan Allen's stores. The installment loan program, launched in fiscal 2000 in partnership with a leading financial institution, provides no risk to the company's retailers or Ethan Allen. It offers unsecured installment loans of up to seven years from $2,000 to $50,000 at a fixed annual percentage rate of 9.99 percent. Over $445 million in credit lines has been approved, making Ethan Allen products within reach of thousands of customers through affordable monthly payment plans.

- To stay competitive in the global marketplace, Ethan Allen allocated $48.2 million to capital expenditures in 2001. Major improvements were made in domestic facilities, including expansion projects at the company's case goods locations at Andover, Maine; Orleans, Vermont; and Beecher Falls, Vermont.

  In addition, the company invested in its upholstery plants, adding more work cells to ensure that workflow is managed more efficiently and production is faster. What's more, the company realigned its case goods production so that each product is made closer to its sources of raw materials.

  In 2001, Ethan Allen purchased a state-of-the-art facility in Dublin, Virginia. Its single-story floor plan is well suited to the company's needs and was engineered to optimize product flow-through. The plant has 450,000 square feet of manufacturing space and 120,000 square feet of warehouse distribution space, as well as computerized machinery, and a skilled, well-trained workforce. The plant is able to produce a wide range of case goods.

- Operating a store in today's environment is a complicated business if management doesn't have the right structure in place. Ethan Allen is convinced that "You need to be able to keep the store beautiful and inspiring, help customers select the right products, train and motivate the sales staff, grow a complicated custom business, make accessory house calls and anticipate customer service requests—all at the same time."

To respond to these demands, Ethan Allen began testing new ways to staff its stores. For example, at its corporate headquarters in Danbury, Connecticut, management looked at its needs—especially on high-traffic weekends—and created an environment to better support the designers who were working on the front lines.

First, the company established the right sales management structure, so that designers were able to obtain the training and direction they needed to build their businesses. Then, Ethan Allen added specialists in the soft goods and accessories areas to help designers sell more of the complicated product programs. In addition, the company also added a merchandise manager to keep the store beautiful and a customer service specialist to address delivery and service issues.

Since this structure has been in place, traffic in the Danbury store increased about 19 percent. During that same period, the store's written business jumped up 35 percent.

- Running a custom business that offers hundred of frames, thousands of fabrics, and endless combinations in a challenge in itself. Running it profitably is even harder. At Ethan Allen, the company does it by marrying state-of-the-art technology with smart work processes and trained processionals.

For instance, new technology like the fabric-cutting machine in operation at the company's Maiden, North Carolina, facility is changing the way Ethan Allen does business. Using a computerized mapping system and automated cutting mechanism, the machine can cut perfectly matched pieces on a very complicated fabric pattern with precision and accuracy. In addition to eliminating the cost of human error, the machine allows the company to triple its output using fewer people. Plans are under way to install this technology in Ethan Allen's other upholstery plants.

Total assets: $619 million
Current ratio: 2.69
Common shares outstanding: 38.7 million
Return on 2001 shareholders' equity: 18.6%

	2001	2000	1999	1998	1997	1996	1995	1994
Revenues (millions)	904	856	762	693	572	510	476	437
Net income (millions)	80	91	81	72	49	28	23	23
Earnings per share	1.98	2.20	1.92	1.63	1.11	.65	.52	.51
Dividends per share	.16	.16	.12	.09	.06	.01	Nil	Nil
Price High	42.3	33.8	37.8	44.4	28.6	13.0	8.3	10.7
Low	26.5	20.5	24.7	15.7	12.3	6.5	5.7	6.5

ExxonMobil Corporation

5959 Las Colinas Boulevard □ Irving, Texas 75039-2298 □ (972) 444-1000 □ Direct Dividend reinvestment program available: (800) 252-1800 □ Web site: www.exxonmobil.com □ Listed: NYSE □ Ticker symbol: XOM □ S&P rating: A- □ Value Line financial strength rating: A++

The use of petroleum and other forms of fossil fuels is not likely to become obsolete, despite the burgeoning growth of the Internet and high technology. For its part, ExxonMobil is convinced that energy savings on the manufacturing and production side will be offset by "energy consuming purchases" made by workers with more money to spend.

"That means more houses, bigger houses, more cars, faster cars," according to Kathleen B. Cooper, chief economist with Exxon Mobil. "All you have to do is look around North Dallas—and a lot of other cities around the United States—and you can see that that's going on. And obviously, this means more energy use."

To be sure, online buying may cut down on trips to the local mall, a potential energy savings. "But what it will also require is a lot more of those UPS trucks driving around the neighborhood delivering goods."

Ms. Cooper admits that the use of solar and wind power will grow rapidly over the next two decades. Even so, those forms of energy will remain minuscule as a percentage of the total energy supply in the United States and throughout the world, less than one half of one percent.

Company Profile

Mobil Corporation ceased to exist at the end of November 1999, after government regulators approved the company's $81-billion acquisition by Exxon, reuniting the two largest pieces of the Standard Oil monopoly nearly ninety years after trustbusters split them apart. As a result of this merger, Exxon Mobil has passed Royal Dutch Petroleum as the world's largest petroleum company, in terms of oil and gas reserves.

The Federal Trade Commission, following an eleven-month review, overcame its initial skepticism about the deal and blessed it, having forced the companies to shed as much as $2 billion in service stations and other assets. Commenting on the decision, Exxon CEO Lee R. Raymond said the two companies were creating "the world's premier petroleum and petrochemical company" and estimated that savings from the merger would exceed the $2.8 billion over three years that the companies had originally anticipated.

Merger Requirements of Federal Trade Commission

The chemicals and technology businesses of both companies were not affected.

The bulk of the divestitures came in the refining and marketing sectors. In the United States, ExxonMobil was required to sell one refinery; this represented about 2 percent of the company's refining capacity. The remaining worldwide refining network leads the industry, with fifty refineries and total capacity of 6.4 million barrels a day.

In addition, ExxonMobil was required to divest some 770 company-owned or leased service stations in the United States and to assign contracts to new suppliers. These changes affected more than 1,600 stations owned by branded distributors and others. In Europe, Mobil was required to sell its 30-percent interest in the

BP/Mobil joint-venture fuels business as well as its 28-percent interest in the German joint-venture marketing company, Aral.

These divestitures should be viewed in the context of the more than 45,000 remaining Exxon, Mobil, and Esso stations worldwide. Here at home, despite the refinery and service station divestitures, ExxonMobil's combined refining and marketing business is far stronger than either one of the companies had before.

Shortcomings to Bear in Mind

- ExxonMobil ended 2001 on a down note. In the fourth quarter of that year, net income slid to $2.68 billion, or $0.39 per share, compared with $5.22 billion, or $0.75 per share, in the same period of 2000. Revenue, moreover, tumbled 26 percent, to $47.3 billion, down from $64.14 billion in the prior year. The company blamed the weak showing on a slump in crude oil prices, which sagged 38 percent during the fourth quarter. In the same period, natural gas prices plunged 59 percent. Despite the poor results, ExxonMobil said that it would boost capital spending by 10 percent in 2002.
- The CEO of ExxonMobil has a rather tarnished image. In an August 2001 article in The Wall Street Journal, Thaddeus Herrick wrote, "Like his predecessors, ExxonMobil Corp. Chairman and Chief Executive Lee Raymond keeps a relatively low profile. He's reluctant to grant interviews and make public appearances. But ever since he assailed the Kyoto initiative to combat global warming in a speech a few years ago, Mr. Raymond has been inextricably linked to the issue.

  "Add to that his disdain for gay rights and his unflinching responses to critics of ExxonMobil's business in repressive regimes, and Mr. Raymond comes off as a strikingly politically incorrect character for a modern-day, big-company CEO."

Reasons to Buy

- In late 2001, ExxonMobil said a consortium it leads planned to invest $12 billion to develop energy reserves off Russia's Pacific coast, beginning a long-awaited project that will mark the biggest foreign investment to date in Russia's energy sector.

  Situated off Sakhalin Island just north of Japan, the Sakhalin 1 project will strengthen Russia's lucrative oil and gas trade with Asia's growing energy consumers.

  Sakhalin 2, a nearby project led by Royal Dutch/Shell, began producing oil in 1999. Both projects spent more than five years fighting geological and legal hurdles before getting under way. The Sakhalin 1 fields contain an estimated 2.3 billion barrels of oil and 17 trillion cubic feet of gas. ExxonMobil and its partners will invest an initial $4 billion to begin pumping oil by 2005.
- In the important "upstream sector," Mr. Raymond believes that "our exploration and production portfolio of complementary assets is the best in the industry. We are the world's largest private-sector producer of oil and gas combined, and we continue to expand our excellent position in many of the world's most exciting and rapidly emerging oil and gas areas."
- With 17 billion cubic feet of sales a day, ExxonMobil is the world's largest non-government marketer of natural gas. These sales, many of which are underpinned by long-term contracts, produce a strong positive cash flow and provide a solid platform for growth. The company markets gas in North and South America, Europe, the Middle East, and Asia/Pacific, with pipeline and liquid

natural gas (LNG) sales in more than twenty-five countries—in some regions for more than seventy-five years.

ExxonMobil has access to a diverse portfolio of both mature gas fields and new gas development totaling 57 trillion cubic feet of proved gas reserves and more than 180 trillion cubic feet of discovered resources, providing a solid base for profitable growth. The company is actively pursuing opportunities to develop and bring to market very large resources in areas such as the Middle East, Africa, Russia, Asia, Alaska, Eastern Canada, Bolivia, and Europe. The company's proprietary LNG, gas-to-liquids, gas pipeline, and power generation technologies, coupled with gas marketing expertise, are key to commercializing large remote gas resources in many areas around the world.

- ExxonMobil has an ownership interest in fifty refineries in twenty-seven countries, with 6.4 million barrels of distillation capacity a day. Seventeen of these refineries have lube base-stock manufacturing facilities with a capacity of 156,000 barrels a day. ExxonMobil operates thirty-four refineries, with the balance operated under joint-venture agreements.

- ExxonMobil markets gasoline and other fuel products at more than 45,000 branded service stations in 118 countries. Its affiliates serve aviation customers at 700 airports in eighty countries, marine customers at 150 ports in sixty countries and some 1 million industrial and wholesale customers in fifty countries. The company markets three of the best-known brands in the world, Exxon, Mobil, and Esso.

- In a recent edition of *Value Line Survey*, the analyst said, "ExxonMobil is better positioned than any other oil company to weather the global business slowdown. Even assuming roughly a 10 percent dip in profits for 2001 and 2002, the company should still produce annual earnings in the $12 to $15 billion range. Reinvestment of those funds will go a long way toward helping the company hold onto, and possibly extend, its leadership position in the oil industry."

- Argus Research Corporation had some good words to say about the company is a report issued in early 2002. "Over the longer term, ExxonMobil's efficiency in replacing reserves, financial flexibility, and diversification of geographic and operational exposure should continue to make the company one of the top two or three players in the international integrated oil and gas business. As for refining and marketing, Exxon focuses on those products where it has a strong marketing presence, including premium gasoline and top-of-the-line motor oils. And, in the chemical sector, ExxonMobil deals from a position of strength. It is the world's second-largest petrochemicals operation and the company's strong focus on cutting overhead and making well-planned capacity expansions is another foundation for strong company-wide profitability down the road."

- In 2001, Exxon Mobil said it had completed an expansion at the Yanpet joint venture petrochemical complex at Yanbu, Saudi Arabia. Included in the expansion is a second 800,000-ton-per-year cracker, a new 535,000-ton-per-year polyethylene plant, and a new 410,000-ton-per-year ethylene glycol plant. Yanpet is a fifty/fifty joint venture between Mobil Yanbu Petrochemical Company, a subsidiary of Exxon Mobil, and Saudi Basic Industries Corporation.

Total assets: $144,521 million
Current ratio: 1.17
Common shares outstanding: 6,841 million
Return on 2001 shareholders' equity: 20.0%

	2001	2000	1999	1998	1997	1996	1995	1994
Revenues (bil)	213	233	185	106	120	117	108	101
Net income (millions)	15320	16910	8380	6440	8155	6975	6380	4611
Earnings per share	2.21	2.41	1.19	1.31	1.64	1.40	1.28	.92
Dividends per share	.91	.88	.84	.82	.81	.78	.75	.73
Price High	45.8	47.7	43.6	38.7	33.6	25.3	21.5	16.8
Low	35.0	34.9	32.2	28.3	24.1	19.4	15.1	14.0

AGGRESSIVE GROWTH

FedEx Corporation

942 South Shady Grove Road □ Memphis, Tennessee 38120 □ (901) 818-7468 □ Web site: www.fedex.com □ Direct purchase only, no dividend paid: (800) 524-3120 □ Fiscal year ends May 31 □ Listed: NYSE □ Ticker symbol: FDX □ Standard & Poor's rating: B □ Value Line financial strength rating: B++

The U.S. Postal Service said in early 2001 that it had struck a seven-year, $6.3-billion alliance with FedEx for air delivery of priority, express, and first-class mail. The service began in August of 2001.

With the Postal Service expected to lose more than $1 billion in 2001, Postmaster General William J. Henderson said, tapping FedEx's fleet of more than 600 planes will give consumers better service at lower cost.

The United States Postal Service had been searching for a company to handle its express and priority mail. That job had previously been handled primarily by Emery Worldwide Airlines. But postal officials said that the deal with Emery had been too costly and inefficient.

Under the new pact, FedEx carries up to 3.5 million pounds of Postal Service mail a day, or the capacity of about thirty wide-body DC-10 airplanes. To meet the demand, FedEx had to hire some 500 new pilots and about 1,000 new mechanics and cargo handlers.

Company Profile

FedEx Corporation (formerly FDX Corp.) is the world's leading provider of guaranteed express delivery services. Using a $4 million inheritance as seed money, Frederick W. Smith founded FedEx in 1971 when he was only 27.

The company offers a wide range of express delivery services for the time-definite transportation of documents, packages, and freight. FedEx also offers commercial and military charter services. The company operates in the United States, France, England, Canada, and Japan.

FedEx provides same-day service, overnight, and deferred delivery services for documents, packages, and freight, using a network of 53,700 ground vehicles, 640 aircraft, and 50,000 drop-off boxes. In fiscal 2001 (ended May 31, 2001), FedEx Express accounted for 91 percent of the company's revenues. About 72 percent of FedEx's revenues are from domestic services, with about 76 percent express delivery and 24 percent lower-yielding deferred delivery.

FedEx reported sales of $19.6 billion in the fiscal year ended May 31, 2001. This represented an increase of 8 percent over the previous year.

Shortcomings to Bear in Mind

- According to management, "We are a very capital-intensive business. To do what we do takes big wide-bodied planes—and lots of them. It takes trucks and vans and large, costly operating hubs, both across America and abroad. It takes a lot of information and telecommunications devices, whether it be scanners and radios in the trucks or what-have-you."

  On the other hand, FedEx's global network is now more or less complete, and that will make a big difference, not least because investors can expect the pace of capital spending to decline sharply.

- Over the years, the relationship between FedEx managers and some of its 4,000 pilots has been strained, in part because of CEO Fred Smith's opposition to unions.

  "We had started with the dream that if the company rose to Fred's vision, we'd be at the top as well," said Don Wilson, a twenty-eight-year company veteran who helped organize the FedEx Pilots Union in 1992. "The company has exceeded beyond what anyone expected, but our pay and benefits have not," Mr. Wilson said.

  On the other hand, the company has had a reputation as a great place to work, with employees claiming they "bleed purple and orange"—the company's colors—and living by Smith's mantra: "People, service, profit." FedEx has repeatedly been on *Fortune* magazine's list of the "100 Best Companies to Work For" and its lists of best places for minorities and women to work.

- FedEx hasn't added to earnings in three years, as it digested nine acquisitions that transformed it from an overnight package-delivery company to a comprehensive package-delivery and trucking operation.

Reasons to Buy

- FedEx became the Official Worldwide Delivery Service Sponsor of the National Football League (NFL), beginning in the fall of 2000. The three-year agreement gave FedEx NFL marketing rights domestically and worldwide. FedEx also is now an official sponsor of the thirty-two NFL teams, the Super Bowl, and the Pro Bowl.

  The company also sponsors the following:

- FedEx Field, the home of the NFL's Washington Redskins.
- The FedEx Orange Bowl, host of the 2000 college football national championship game.
- The FedEx St. Jude Classic, which raises money for the St. Jude's Children's Research Hospital.
- The FedEx Championship Series, the country's premier open-wheel racing circuit (CART).
- America's men's and women's Olympic basketball teams.
- The Ferrari Formula One racing team in Europe.
- FedEx is more sensitive to shifts in the economy than such cyclical companies as paper and chemicals. As sales pick up for retailers, they order more goods, which flow back to companies that supply such things as boxes and bags. As a consequence, FedEx quickly feels the benefits of an economic recovery. That's because a shipping company obtains more business as soon as retailers order more goods.
- Increasingly, businesses are seeking strategic, cost-effective ways to manage their supply chains—the series of transportation and information exchanges required to convert parts and raw materials into finished, delivered products. According the management: "Experience tells us that customers prefer one supplier to meet all of their distribution

and logistics needs. And FedEx has what it takes: Our unique global network, operational expertise and air route authorities cannot be replicated by the competition. With FedEx, our customers have a strategic competitive weapon to squeeze time, mass, and cost from the supply chain."

- In a deal worth $1.2 billion, FedEx bought American Freightways Corporation in 2000. It extended the reach of the company's less-than-truckload (LTL) freight business to forty-eight states, up from eleven (through Viking Freight, mostly on the West Coast). At the time of the acquisition, American Freightways was the fourth-largest LTL carrier in the United States. By combining its operations with Viking Freight, FedEx now has the nation's second-largest less-than-truckload carrier. "By joining forces, this new FedEx LTL freight group can sell a more complete package of multiregional services and capture business that previously went to the competitors," said Douglas G. Duncan, who became president and CEO of the new FedEx freight group overseeing American and Viking.

- In an effort to make it easier to return merchandise using the Internet, FedEx significantly expanded the capabilities of its system that enables customers and merchants to process package returns electronically. In 2000, the company announced that its NetReturn system (then three years old) would let customers print a shipping label generated on a home computer.

   The system also provides the customer with nearby drop-off locations for the return package. Up until then, the return service required parcel pickup by FedEx, which often made the system inconvenient. FedEx made this move, hoping the enhancements would make its system more appealing to current

users such as Apple Computer and Hewlett-Packard, as well as to fend off UPS when that company rolled out its online-returns system in the early part of 2001. This move by FedEx is an indication that shipping companies and retailers are trying to find ways to avoid repeating the problems of the prior Christmas, when many online retailers were unable to cope with the avalanche of gift returns.

- FedEx, the world's largest express transportation company, and Tianjin-based Datian W. Air Service Corporation announced in mid-2000 the formation of a joint venture in Beijing. According to the company, this is a "joint venture dedicated to providing unparalleled international express services for customers with shipping requirements to and from China. Federal Express-DTW Co. Ltd. represents the first joint venture in FedEx's global network, bringing together two powerhouses in the express transportation industry. With a strong network and a proven track record in the Chinese marketplace, Datian is an ideal partner for FedEx."

- When a large corporation decentralizes shipping, it's like a computer's circuitry firing at random: interesting pyrotechnics, but not very productive. That's why Unisys chose to harness the buying power of hundreds of sales offices, service locations, and manufacturing sites by using FedEx transportation management services. Unisys employees simply call a toll-free number staffed by Caliber Logistics. Caliber distribution experts rely on FedEx to ship everything from critical replacement parts to Unisys enterprise servers directly to the customer site. Each shipping decision reflects the most appropriate and cost-effective delivery solution.

- What the stock market seems to be overlooking right now is that for all the books and computers and corduroy britches consumers buy from today's Internet retailers, someone has to deliver the goods. In millions of instances, that someone is FedEx. This helps explain how FedEx has been able to keep growing.

- FedEx has invested heavily in recent years to develop an international infrastructure. It presently can reach locations accounting for 90 percent of world gross domestic product, with twenty-four or forty-eight hour service. International delivery services for documents and freight have been growing faster than domestic business in recent years.

Total assets: $13,340 million
Current ratio: 1.06
Common shares outstanding: 298 million
Return on 2001 shareholders' equity: 10.9%

	2001	2000	1999	1998	1997	1996	1995	1994
Revenues (millions)	19629	18257	16773	15703	11520	10274	9392	8480
Net income (millions)	663	688	531	526	348	308	282	204
Earnings per share	2.26	2.32	2.10	1.75	1.51	1.35	1.25	.92
Dividends per share	Nil	—	—	—	—	—	—	—
Price High	53.5	49.8	61.9	46.6	42.3	22.5	21.5	20.2
Low	33.2	30.6	34.9	21.8	21.0	16.7	14.7	13.4

GROWTH AND INCOME

Fortune Brands, Incorporated

300 Tower Parkway □ Lincolnshire, Illinois 60069 □ (847) 484-4400 □ Dividend reinvestment plan is available: (800) 225-2719 □ Web site: www.fortunebrands.com □ Listed: NYSE □ Ticker symbol: FO □ S&P rating: B- □ Value Line financial strength rating: A

"In a difficult economic environment that got the best of many other companies, Fortune Brands more than held its own in 2001," said the company's chief executive officer Norman H. Wesley in early 2002. "We gained share in key markets and developed industry-leading new products. We made major strategic progress, especially in our spirits and wine business. We also substantially strengthened an already attractive balance sheet.

"Let me underscore that in addition to our $311 million in free cash, our major strategic initiatives delivered 1 billion dollars in proceeds in 2001. That cash enabled us to cut our debt in half and buy back 7.5 million shares in 2001. The strength of our balance sheet is a power resource as we look to drive shareholder value even higher in 2002.

"As Fortune Brands enters 2002, our prospects are excellent. We feel the disciplined strategy that delivered another year of solid performance positions us well to succeed in an economic environment that remains uncertain."

Company Profile

Fortune Brands owns companies with leading consumer brands in home products, office products, golf equipment, and spirits and wine. These brands include familiar names like Moen, Titleist, Jim Beam, Master Lock, Swingline, Day-Timer, FootJoy, Cobra, Kensington, ACCO, Wilson Jones, and Geyser Peak.

In 1998, total sales exceeded $5 billion.

Named Fortune Brands only since 1997, the company was formerly known as American Brands. It was incorporated in Delaware in 1985 as a holding company with subsidiaries in the above-mentioned businesses, as well as others in which it no longer has holdings.

Fortune Brands' roots were planted decades ago. In 1966, a former New Jersey-incorporated subsidiary changed its name to American Brands and began a diversification program with the acquisition of Sunshine Biscuits. The diversification extended to the distilled spirits business in 1967 with the acquisition of the company now known as Jim Beam Brands Worldwide. The first home and office brands—including Swingline, Master Lock, and Wilson Jones—were acquired in 1970. The 1976 acquisition of Acushnet, with its premier Titleist brand, led the charge into the golf business. In the ensuing years, a wide range of businesses and brands were both acquired and divested to promote the goal of enhanced shareholder value.

In 1994, American Brands, by then a wide collection of businesses with annual net sales totaling more than $15 billion, began a fundamental transformation to focus solely on growing categories in which the company was a leader—home, office, golf, and distilled spirits. The company made significant divestitures in 1994, and in 1997, the company spun-off its remaining noncore subsidiary. With its fundamental transformation complete, the company changed its name to Fortune Brands in June of 1997.

Today, fifteen brands have annual sales exceeding $100 million each. Moen, Titleist, and Jim Beam, Fortune's three largest brands, account for more than a quarter of sales. More than 80 percent of sales come from brands that are number one or two in their markets, and more than 25 percent of sales come from new products. For two successive years, the company has been recognized by *Fortune* magazine's prestigious annual survey of executives, directors, and securities analysts as the most admired company in the world in its category. The 1999 survey proclaimed Fortune Brands as one of the top five U.S. "National Champions" and as one of the top three companies in the world in innovativeness.

Shortcomings to Bear in Mind

- If the economy remains soft in 2002, it is likely that the company's office products units will see its sales decline as much as 6 percent.

Reasons to Buy

- In February of 2002, Home Depot selected Fortune Brands to supply its entire line of kitchen and bath cabinets for its 1,200 home improvement stores. "We are delighted to expand our relationship with the Home Depot and to combine our strength in semicustom cabinetry with the well-known Thomasville brand name," said Rich Forbes, president of MasterBrand Cabinets, Fortune Brands' cabinet unit. "Under the Thomasville name, we'll offer Home Depot customers high-quality semicustom cabinetry in a wide array of finishes and door styles that can meet virtually any kitchen design need."
- The company's spirit and wine segment is not subject to the ups and downs of the economy. According to Lars L. Bainbridge, writing for Value Line Survey, "And by leveraging its strong brand position with new products, incremental price hikes, and enhanced marketing efforts, the segment should be able to continue increasing the top line."
- At the end of 2001, *Standard & Poor's Stock Reports* had this to say about Fortune Brands: "We acknowledge

that several of FO's business units are facing pressures from a soft economy, but we believe the company is well managed and will recover soundly when the economy rebounds. In addition to attractive valuation, the shares should benefit from a favorable distribution agreement with Vin & Sprit of Sweden, creating the second-largest spirits distributor in the United States."

■ Kolorfusion International, Inc., announced in February of 2002 that a license agreement had been negotiated with Moen, Inc., a wholly owned subsidiary of Fortune Brands. Kolorfusion is the owner of process patents for three-dimensional product decoration invented in France by Jean-Noel Claveau. The company's technology is considered a major breakthrough for product finishing, as the process actually transfers any design with any colors into a product's coating or directly into the plastic or aluminum itself, no matter what the shape. The result is a fully decorated product as durable as the coating or part.

The license allows Moen to install and utilize Kolorfusion's patented process on their faucet and bath products. "Having licensed this process, we can now truly provide unique designs and customization to our customers," said David Lingafelter, vice president of marketing for Moen.

■ Since the company shed its tobacco business at the end of 1944 and changed its name from American Brands to Fortune Brands, earnings have performed well, advancing from $0.99 to $2.49, a compound annual growth rate of 16.6 percent.

■ In the fall of 2001, Fortune Brands announced that its Jim Beam Brands Worldwide unit had sold its U.K.-based Scotch whiskey business. The sale of the business, consisting of the Invergordon private-label and bulk Scotch operations and several regional brands in the United Kingdom, further sharpens Jim Beam Brands' global strategic focus on fast-growing, high-return premium and super-premium spirits and wine brands.

The selling price for the Scotch business was about $290 million in cash. The sale had no effect on the U.S. or international distribution of the Jim Beam Brands portfolio of premium and super-premium brands that includes Jim Beam bourbon, Knob Creek small batch bourbon, DeKuyper cordials, Vox vodka, and Geyser Peak wines. Jim Beam Brands will retain global ownership of After Shock, a fast-growing premium liqueur brand marketed in the United Kingdom, and will also hold a perpetual license in the United States to The Dalmore, recently named the world's finest single malt Scotch at the International Wine & Spirit Competition.

"This sale is another very positive strategic development for our Jim Beam Brands spirits and wine business," said Mr. Wesley. "On the heels of our creative distribution partnership with ABSOLUT vodka, this move will enable Jim Beam Brands to intensify its strategic focus on the premium and super-premium spirits and wine market, the fastest-growing segment in the industry. The U.K. Scotch business, while successful, offered lower returns and lower growth than our core spirits and wine business, and simply didn't fit with our strategic focus.

"This transaction will also further enhance Fortune Brands' financial flexibility to drive shareholder value higher. We'll evaluate our highest return opportunities for the use of the proceeds, including strategic acquisitions and attractive share repurchases," Wesley added.

Earlier in 2001, Jim Beam Brands moved aggressively to strengthen its clout in the premium and super-premium market and reduce its distribution costs by teaming up with the maker of ABSOLUT vodka for joint distribution of the two companies' spirits and wine brands. "Just four months after beginning operations, the Jim Beam-ABSOLUT partnership is already a distribution powerhouse," said Jim Beam Brands President and CEO Rich Reese. The partners now distribute the second-highest volume portfolio in the United States through their Future Brands LLC joint venture. They are also partners for distribution in key markets outside the United States through the Maxxim joint venture. Invergordon's private-label and bulk products are not distributed by Maxxim.

Total assets: $5,764 million
Current ratio: 1.35
Common shares outstanding: 152 million
Return on 2001 shareholders' equity: 17%

	2001	2000	1999	1998	1997	1996	1995	1994
Revenues (millions)	5674	5844	5525	5241	4844	4712	4928	NA*
Net income (millions)	336	366	340	294	242	182	186	NA
Earnings per share	2.49	2.29	1.99	1.67	1.41	1.04	.99	NA
Dividends per share	.97	.93	.89	.85	.41	NA	NA	NA
Price High	40.5	33.3	45.9	42.3	38.0	NA	NA	NA
Low	28.4	19.2	29.4	25.3	30.4	NA	NA	NA

*NA: Not available because the company was restructured, and its tobacco business was eliminated.

CONSERVATIVE GROWTH

Gannett Company, Inc.

7950 Jones Branch Drive □ McLean, Virginia 22107 □ (703) 284-6918 □ Dividend reinvestment plan is available: (800) 778-3299 □ Web site: www.gannett.com □ Listed: NYSE □ Ticker symbol: GCI □ S&P rating: A □ Value Line financial strength rating: A++

As the Internet continues to be a growing part of people's lives, more Gannett newspapers are jumping into the World Wide Web. What's more, the online pioneers continue to enhance content and add new products, including those stemming from Gannett's participation in Classified Ventures and www.CareerPath.com.

As leading information providers for their communities, the company's newspapers are aware that fresh information is essential to success online. FLORIDA TODAY's Space Online (www.spaceonline.com), for instance, covers space shuttle launches, literally as they blast off. Reporters with laptop computers file stories from the beach at Cape Canaveral, supplying live news online within moments of a launch.

Company Profile

Founded in 1906 by Frank E. Gannett and associates, Gannett was incorporated in 1923 and listed on the New York Stock

Exchange in 1967. Gannett is an international news and information company that publishes ninety-nine daily newspapers in the United States. The combined paid daily circulation is 7.7 million. This includes *USA Today*, the nation's largest-selling daily newspaper, with a circulation of 2.3 million, available in sixty countries.

The company also owns a variety of nondaily publications in the United States and *USA Weekend*, a weekly newspaper magazine. In the United Kingdom, Gannett subsidiary Newsquest plc publishes nearly 300 titles, including fifteen daily newspapers. Gannett also operates twenty-two television stations in the United States.

Operations Worldwide

Gannett is an international company with headquarters in Arlington, Virginia, and operations in forty-three states, the District of Columbia, Guam, the United Kingdom, Germany, and Hong Kong.

Newspapers

Gannett is the largest domestic newspaper group, in terms of circulation. The company's ninety-nine daily newspapers in the United States have a combined daily paid circulation of 7.8 million. They include *USA Today*, with a circulation of about 2.3 million. *USA Today* is available in sixty countries.

In addition, Gannett owns a variety of nondaily publications and *USA Weekend*, a weekly newspaper magazine of 23.6 million circulation delivered on Sundays in 591 Gannett and non-Gannett newspapers.

Newsquest plc, a wholly-owned Gannett subsidiary acquired in mid-1999, is one of the largest regional newspaper publishers in England, with a portfolio of more than 300 titles. Its publications include fifteen daily newspapers with a combined circulation of about 600,000. Newsquest also publishes a variety of nondaily publications,

including *Berrow's Worcester Journal*, the oldest continuously published newspaper in the world.

Broadcasting

The company owns and operates twenty-two television stations covering 17.7 percent of the United States.

On the Internet

Gannett has more than 100 Web sites in the United States and the United Kingdom, including *www.USATODAY.com*, one of the leading newspaper sites on the Internet.

Other Ventures

Other company operations include Gannett News Service; Gannett Retail Advertising Group; Gannett TeleMarketing, Inc.; Gannett New Business and Product Development; Gannett Direct Marketing Services; Gannett Offset, a commercial printing operation; Gannett Media Technologies International; and Telematch, a database marketing company.

Shortcomings to Bear in Mind

- Some people consider newspapers a dying medium. In 1990, for instance, 113 million Americans read dailies; today, only 76.6 million do. Classified ads, which account for 27 percent of Gannett's annual revenues, seem destined to move to the Internet.

- The company's television operations finished 2001 on a weak note. In the fourth quarter of 2001, television revenues declined 23 percent, to $180.1 million, down from $233.2 million in the same quarter of the prior year. The revenue decline reflected the weak advertising environment and the difficult comparison with 2000's fourth quarter, which benefited from strong election-related ad spending, plus an extra week. Finally, television operating cash flow decreased to $91.2 million, from $131.8 million in the fourth quarter of 2000.

- A campaign to gain new readers on college campuses is carried out by *USA Today* with the distribution of thousands of copies of the paper. Gannett seeks to sell these bulk copies to colleges, which in turn distribute them in dorms and activity centers. However, not everyone is happy with this ploy. In particular, students who publish newspapers are trying to stymie the idea, since they, too, benefit from advertising dollars. They fear that they will lose advertising revenue as well as readers. For instance, in late 2001, students at the University of Louisiana at Lafayette followed the advice of their campus newspaper and voted down a proposal to distribute bulk copies of the local Gannett paper, the *Daily Advertiser*. Similarly, at Vanderbilt University in Nashville, *USA Today* officials twice tried to convince university administrators to sign onto their program. But administrators declined, largely because of concerns about the biweekly student newspaper, the *Hustler*. An editorial cartoon in the college paper pictures a Gannett executive standing beside a drawing-board presentation tiled "Invade Vanderbilt."

Reasons to Buy

- At the end of 2001, Gannett had more than 100 domestic publishing-related Web sites, including *www.USATODAY.COM*, one of the most popular newspaper sites on the Web. The company also has Web sites in all of its nineteen television markets. In December of 2001, Gannett's consolidated domestic Internet audience share was 9 million unique visitors reaching 8 percent of the Internet audience, according to Nielsen/Net Ratings. For the year, the company generated

about $71 million in revenues from Internet activities, up from $63 million the prior year.

- The uneven newsprint market, which began 2001 with an announced price increase of $50 per metric ton, turned in Gannett's favor. Supply and demand would not support the higher prices and, in fact, resulted in significant downward pressure on prices. Gannett is now buying newsprint at some of the lowest prices in ten years.

- Gannett Broadcasting's television stations are local market leaders. KARE-TV in Minneapolis-St. Paul, Minnesota; KSDK-TV in St. Louis, Missouri; and KUSA-TV in Denver, Colorado are the top three stations in the nation for late local news in the key selling demographic of adults aged twenty-five to fifty-four in the November 2001 ratings.

KPNX-TV in Phoenix, Arizona, joins them in the top ten in the country. WBIR-TV in Knoxville, Tennessee; WCSH-TV in Portland, Maine; and WMAZ-TV in Macon, Georgia; are tops among the nation's medium-sized smaller markets.

WGRZ-TV in Buffalo, New York; KTHV-TV in Little Rock, Arkansas; and WLTX-TV in Columbia, South Carolina, three stations purchased in the 1990s and all with a history of under-performance, made great strides in 2001. WGRZ went from third to first place in late news for the first time in the station's history. KTHV ranked number two in all news time periods with adults aged twenty-five to fifty-four.

- Although earnings declined modestly in 2001, the company has a solid record. 2001 was the only year in the past ten that earnings dipped. In the 1991–2001 period, earnings per share advanced from $1.00 to $3.12, a compound annual growth rate of 12.1 percent. In the same period, however, dividends did not do nearly as well, rising from $0.62 to $0.89, a growth rate of only 3.7 percent.

■ Newspapers and other advertisers were hurt by the lack of advertising revenues in 2001 and into 2002. Since the recession has been officially declared dead, it's only a matter of time before advertising revenues begin to perk up. That should bode well for Gannett's newspapers and television stations. It's amazing, in fact, how well Gannett coped with the recession, since earnings per share only declined from $3.63 to

$3.12. In that period, it outstripped its peer group.

■ Most of the company's newspapers are the only daily publication in their respective cities. To be sure, that doesn't mean they have a monopoly on advertising, since there are other ways to advertise, such as television, radio, and direct mail. Still, newspapers have always been an important advertising medium, and it always helps to be the only game in town.

Total assets: $13,096 million
Current ratio: 0.94
Common shares outstanding: 265 million
Return on 2001 shareholders' equity: 14.5%

	2001	2000	1999	1998	1997	1996	1995	1994
Revenues (millions)	6344	6222	5260	5121	4730	4421	4007	3824
Net income (millions)	831	972	919	816	713	531	477	465
Earnings per share	3.12	3.63	3.26	2.86	2.50	1.89	1.71	1.62
Dividends per share	.89	.86	.82	.78	.74	.71	.68	.67
Price High	71.1	81.6	83.6	75.1	61.8	39.4	32.4	29.5
Low	53.0	48.4	60.6	47.6	35.7	29.5	24.8	23.1

AGGRESSIVE GROWTH

General Dynamics Corporation

3190 Fairview Park Drive □ Falls Church, Virginia 22042-4523 □ (703) 876-3195 □ Dividend reinvestment plan is not available □ Web site: www.generaldynamics.com □ Listed: NYSE □ Ticker symbol: GD □ S&P rating: B+ □ Value Line financial strength rating: A+

According to an article in *Fortune* magazine (November 12, 2001), General Dynamics is Wall Street's favorite defense contractor. The author, Andy Serwer, said, "No, this stock isn't for everybody. For the most part, General Dynamics is in the war business (70 percent of sales), and some investors have a problem with that. But generally Wall Street loves General Dynamics. Unlike other defense contractors, says Chris Mecray of Deutsche Banc

Alex. Brown, "General Dynamics management runs this company for shareholder interest rather than just for national security. The CEO is a careful and deliberate caretaker of shareholder money."

The CEO is sixty-year-old Nick Chabraja (*cha-BRAH-ya*), a "sharp-witted lawyer. Chabraja, a deal dude, has been part of a management team that has bought nineteen businesses over the past seven years."

Company Profile

With headquarters in Falls Church, Virginia, General Dynamics has leading market positions in shipbuilding and marine systems, business aviation, information systems, and land and amphibious combat systems. The company has four primary business groups.

Marine Systems

General Dynamics Marine Systems has the broadest range of integration, design, engineering, and production skills in naval shipbuilding. Marine Systems is the U.S. Navy's leading supplier of combat vessels—including nuclear submarines, surface combatants, and auxiliary ships. The group also manages ready-reserve and prepositioning ships and builds commercial vessels.

Aerospace

Gulfstream Aerospace group is the world's leading designer, developer, manufacturer, and marketer of midsize and intercontinental business jet aircraft. The group is also a major provider of maintenance and refurbishment services for a wide variety of business jets. The Aerospace group is comprised of Gulfstream Aerospace and General Dynamics Aviation Services.

Gulfstream Aerospace has produced more than 1,200 aircraft for customers around the world since 1958. It offers a full range of aircraft products and services, including the ultra-long-range Gulfstream V, the Gulfstream IV-SP, Gulfstream 200, Gulfstream 100, Gulfstream Shares, Gulfstream Financial Services, Gulfstream Lease, Gulfstream Pre-Owned Aircraft Sales, Gulfstream Charter Services, Gulfstream Management Services, and Gulfstream ServiceCare. Late in 2000, Gulfstream announced its new aircraft—the Gulfstream V-SP.

General Dynamics Aviation Services provides airframe, avionics, engine, and refurbishment work at five service locations in the United States. Its expertise covers the wide variety of business jet aircraft operating today.

Information Systems and Technology

General Dynamics Information Systems group provides defense and select commercial customers with the infrastructure and systems-integration skills they need to process, communicate, and manage information effectively. It has established a global presence in specialized data acquisition and processing, in advanced electronics, and in the total battlespace information management systems that are key to military superiority in the twenty-first century. It also provides telecommunications solutions and data management services for the commercial market.

Combat Systems

General Dynamics Combat Systems is becoming the world's preferred supplier of land and amphibious combat system development, production, and support. Its product line includes a full spectrum of armored vehicles, light-wheeled reconnaissance vehicles, suspensions, engines, transmissions, guns and ammunition-handling systems, turret and turret-drive systems, and reactive armor and ordnance.

Shortcomings to Bear in Mind

- General Dynamics is one of the companies that makes business jets, along with Textron, Raytheon, France's Dassault Aviation, and Canada's Bombardier. With all the fear of flying, more corporations are giving serious thought to taking the risk out of flying by owning their own jets. However, there is a downside to that option. According to an article in *Barron's* (November 19, 2001), "For all their advantages, business jets have always had one big problem: They are very expensive. A new midsized jet, like a Dassault Falcon 50, which seats nine passengers very comfortably, costs $19 million. Add another $800,000 a year for maintenance, fuel and landing fees, plus another few hundred thousand for pilots, flight attendants, and other costs, and the annual tab can easily come to $1 million, assuming 500 hours—9.6 hours a week—in the air. And that doesn't include the cost of capital that's tied up in the plane itself."

Reasons to Buy

- On a more positive note, the *Barron's* article quoted above outlined the reasons why it believed good times were ahead for makers of private jets. "Even before September 11, the market for private jets was gaining altitude. The U.S. fleet of private-jet aircraft hit 8,000 last year (2000), up from 5,000 in 1990. And despite the slack U.S. economy, which has caused many orders to be delayed or cancelled, the waiting time for a $45 million Bombardier Global Express is forty months. For a $40 million Gulfstream V, it's twelve to fifteen months."

- In the *Los Angeles Times*, another writer said, "For costs ranging from millions of dollars for sole ownership of a new jet to $5,000 an hour for a charter, companies can purchase the peace of mind of knowing who's on board, what's in the luggage, and who's piloting the aircraft." Not least, with commercial air travelers now advised to allow at least two hours to board a domestic flight, lost time is also a factor. "The business they are losing is the CEOs, the CFOs, the executive VPs," said Kevin Mitchell, chairman of the Business Travel Coalition, a Pennsylvania advocacy group. "The fliers with a high impact on the bottom line, that's

who they're losing. That's the trend, and it's strong. And September 11 just made it stronger."

- In 2002, Gulfstream Aerospace was awarded a $49.8 million contract to supply one Gulfstream V business jet to the National Center for Atmospheric Research (NCAR). The modified aircraft will be used in a wide variety of environmental research missions supported by the National Science Foundation (NSF). Mission requirements will take full advantage of the Gulfstream's exceptionally high altitude, endurance, range, payload, and low operating costs. Named HIAPER, for High-Performance, Instrumented, Airborne Platform for Environmental research, the aircraft will be manufactured at Gulfstream's facility in Savannah, Georgia, and is scheduled to enter service in 2005.

  "The Gulfstream V HIAPER enables us to investigate essential questions concerning the earth's changing climate that have previously been beyond our grasp," said Timothy Killeen, Director, NCAR. "These involve clouds, greenhouse gas concentrations, aerosol plumes, temperature, and other environmental factors."

- In 2002, Gulfstream Aerospace confirmed an order with a potential value of $1.5 billion from Avolar, a UAL Corporation subsidiary. UAL is the parent of United Airlines, the second-largest domestic carrier. The order is for twenty-four Gulfstream 200 business jet aircraft, with options for forty-three more. In addition, Gulfstream and Avolar entered into a long-term maintenance contract. The total value of the order, options, and maintenance agreement exceeds $2 billion. The first deliveries of Gulfstream 200s will be made in 2002 and, with options, will extend through 2007.

"We are impressed by the Gulfstream 200," said Stuart Oran, Avolar president and CEO. "It's a high-performance business jet aircraft with an optimal combination of cabin size, performance, and reliability. Another important factor in our decision was Gulfstream's strong reputation for providing high levels of service and support."

- In 2001, the company bought Galaxy Aerospace Company, a producer of midsize aircraft, giving General Dynamics a presence in the fastest-growing segment of the business jet market. "This acquisition gives General Dynamics immediate presence in the super midsize and midsize market," said CEO Nicholas Chabraja. "It greatly expands our competitive position—without the expense and time of product development."

- At the end of 2001, the U.S. Army awarded GM GDLS Defense Group, a joint venture between General Motors and General Dynamics Land Systems, a delivery order worth $48 million for ten Mobile Gun System vehicles to equip its new Brigade Combat Teams. The Mobile Gun System consists of a 105mm tank cannon mounted on a low-profile turret integrated on the General Motors Interim Armored Vehicle (IAV) chassis. The IAV is a full-time four-wheel drive, selective eight-wheel drive, armored vehicle weighing about nineteen tons. It can attain speeds of sixty-two miles an hour on the highway and has a maximum range of 312 miles.

A year earlier, the U.S. Army awarded GM GDLS Defense Group a six-year contract with an estimated total value of $4 billion to equip its new Brigade Combat teams with a family of eight-wheeled armored vehicles. The contract is to equip up to six Brigade Combat teams, or 2,131 vehicles, through a series of delivery orders.

- In August of 2001, General Dynamics bought Motorola's Integrated Information Systems Group for $825 million. "This acquisition strengthens our position in communications and information technology for military and government customers," said Mr. Chabraja. "This is a business we know, and we believe it will achieve a full potential as part of General Dynamics."

Based in Scottsdale, Arizona, the group has 3,000 employees, including 1,100 engineers. Most of the Motorola unit's work is for defense-related customers, including the U.S. Department of Defense, NASA, the Central Intelligence Agency, and the North Atlantic Treaty Organization.

Total assets: $11,015 million
Current ratio: 1.13
Common shares outstanding: 202 million
Return on 2001 shareholders' equity: 20.5%

	2001	2000	1999	1998	1997	1996	1995	1994
Revenues (millions)	12163	10359	8959	4970	4062	3581	3067	3058
Net income (millions)	943	900	715	364	316	270	247	223
Earnings per share	4.65	4.48	3.54	2.86	2.50	2.14	1.96	1.76
Dividends per share	1.10	1.02	.96	.87	.82	.82	.75	.70
Price High	96.0	79.0	75.4	62.0	45.8	37.8	31.5	23.8
Low	60.5	36.3	46.2	40.3	31.6	28.5	21.2	19.0

General Electric Company

3135 Easton Turnpike □ Fairfield, CT 06431 □ (203) 373-2468 □ Direct dividend reinvestment plan is available: (800) 786-2543 □ Web site: www.ge.com □ Ticker symbol: GE □ S&P rating: A+ □ Value Line financial strength rating: A++

When legendary General Electric CEO Jack Welch retired a couple years ago, a number of exceptional executives were poised to take the reins. However, there could be only one winner. Two that didn't get the nod resigned and took CEO positions elsewhere.

The winner was Jeffrey R. Immelt, then forty-four, president and chief executive of GE Medical Systems, a $7-billion segment of General Electric (GE). The division, based in Waukesha, Wisconsin, is a world leader in medical diagnostic technology and information systems. Mr. Immelt took over that division in 1997 and has increased profits by 20 percent a year.

Effective at the end of November 2000, Mr. Immelt became president and chairman-elect. In announcing the GE board's decision, Mr. Welch described Immelt as "a natural leader, and ideally suited to lead GE for many years."

Immelt joined GE in 1982. After a brief stint in corporate marketing, he held a series of jobs in the company's plastics division. Immelt moved to appliances in 1989, before becoming GE's vice president of Consumer Service in 1991 and then vice president for Marketing and Product Management.

The transition at the top was smoothed by Robert Wright and Dennis Dammerman, two GE vice-chairmen with extensive experience with the company's broadcasting and finance operations, assuring investors that Mr. Immelt would have qualified tutors to indoctrinate the new CEO with the GE operations he knows least.

Company Profile

General Electric, a superbly managed company, provides a broad range of industrial products and services. Under the stewardship of CEO Jack Welch, GE has transformed itself from operating as a maker of diverse industrial equipment to being a provider of a broad range of commercial and consumer services.

In 1980, manufacturing operations generated about 85 percent of operating profits; currently, services operations generate 70 percent of total operating profits. GE Capital (the company's enormous financing arm, and the world's largest non-bank financial operation) alone generates nearly 30 percent of operating profits.

General Electric is one of the world's largest corporations, with 2001 revenues of more than $126 billion. Although GE can trace its origins back to Thomas Edison, who invented the light bulb in 1879, the company was actually founded in 1892.

The company's broad diversification is clearly evident if you examine its components. Operations are divided into two groups: the product, service, and media businesses, and GE Capital Services (GECS).

Product, service, and media include eleven businesses: aircraft engines, appliances, lighting, medical systems, NBC, plastics, power systems, electrical distribution and control, information services, motors and industrial systems, and transportation systems.

GECS operates twenty-seven financial businesses clustered in equipment management, specialty insurance, consumer services, specialized financing, and mid-market financing.

Shortcomings to Bear in Mind

- *Standard & Poor's Stock Reports* forecasts progress in the years ahead, but the analyst has some reservations. "Despite the deteriorating global economy, we believe GE will still be able to grind out a 10 percent to 13 percent rise in EPS for 2002. GE's vaunted cost-cutting programs, and 10 percent to 20 percent revenue hikes in GE's power turbine, medical equipment and financing segments, should more than offset weak near-term aerospace, consumer, industrial, and commercial demand for the company jet engines, appliances, plastics, and NBC advertising.

  "However, we forecast that over the next decade, average annual EPS growth may slow to 9 percent to 10 percent and average return on equity (ROE) may drop to 15 percent. We believe that the sheer size of GE may make it very difficult for the company to match historical revenue and EPS growth rates and ROE. Ironically, increasing sales contributions from GE enormous financing and leasing segment (50 percent of revenues) may hamper long-term profitability."

- Acquisitions have been a key factor for GE's relentless advance in recent years. Jeanne G. Terrile, an analyst with Merrill Lynch, estimated in mid-2001 that about 40 percent of annual compound revenue growth from 1985 through 2000 came from acquisitions. The company typically makes at least 100 acquisitions each year, most of them by GE Capital. As a result, that segment of GE has become the world's largest nonbank financial services concern, with $370 billion in assets.

  According to an article by Matt

Murray in the *Wall Street Journal*, GE must keep on making scads of acquisitions. "More than many other multinational companies, GE depends on acquisitions, lots of them, to help fuel its growth."

An analyst with Edward Jones, a St. Louis brokerage firm, concurs. Commenting on the pace of acquisitions needed, Bill Fiala said, "It will become more challenging. In five years, if their growth record stays on track, this is going to be a company that's making $25 billion a year, and the cash flow from their businesses is going to grow even faster. The pace of acquisitions is going to have to double over the next five years to keep the double-digit growth alive."

Value Line Survey takes issue with that type of thinking. The advisory service had some good things to say about GE in early 2002. "Part of the growth plan is to remain acquisitive. With more than $10 billion in cash, GE is targeting several buyouts that could potentially add $100 billion in industrial revenues. Recent deals include GE Capital's intent to purchase real estate firm Security Capital Group for $4 billion, NBC's offer to buy a San Francisco station for $230 million, and GE Industrial Systems' plan to acquire electronic security company Interlogix, for $777 million in cash and stock."

Reasons to Buy

- In its 2001 annual report, General Electric reacted to the Enron accounting debacle by adding sixteen more pages of detail and explanation. What's more, it broke out twenty-six businesses, up from twelve segments the prior year. It devoted a remarkable amount of attention to its accounting practices and the use of special-purpose entities that move assets off the balance sheet.

- GE paid $5.3 billion to acquire Heller Financial, a big domestic specialty lender, in mid-2001. Denis Nayden, chairman and CEO of GE Capital, said the takeover would lead to a "significant increase" in GE Capital's corporate finance business by adding Heller's international factoring operations, based in France. "The deal gives us a real chance to be a player in that game across Europe," Said Mr. Nayden. In addition, he said that the acquisition gives GE a niche business in health care finance and strengthens GE Capital's presence in the market for small- and medium-sized corporate borrowers. Of the three specialty finance groups that changed hands in the first half of 2001, Heller was the most profitable.
- The key to GE's business plan is the requirement that businesses be first or second in market share in their industries. Those that fail to achieve this status are divested.
- Over the years, General Electric has been honored on many occasions, including the following:
  - Global Most Admired Company— *Fortune* (1998, 1999, 2000)
  - World's Most Respected Company— *Financial Times* (1998, 1999, 2000)
  - America's Most Admired Company— *Fortune* (1998, 1999, 2000, 2001)
  - America's Greatest Wealth Creator— *Fortune* (1998, 1999, 2000).
  - First—*Forbes* 100 (1998, 1999, 2000)
  - First—*BusinessWeek* 1,000 (1999)
  - First—*BusinessWeek*'s 25 Best Boards of Directors (2000)
  - Fifth—*Fortune* 500. If ranked independently, thirteen GE businesses would appear on the *Fortune* 500.
- Jack Welch, GE's previous CEO, developed a defect-reduction program called Six Sigma. Six Sigma contributes mightily to GE's earning growth. Think of sigma as a mark on a bell curve that measures standard deviation. Most companies have between 35,000 and 50,000 defects per million operations, or about 3 sigma. For GE, a defect could be anything from the misbilling of an NBC advertiser to faulty wiring in locomotives. Four years ago, engineers determined that the company was averaging 35,000 defects per million operations—or about 3.5 sigma. (The higher the sigma, the fewer the errors.) That was a better-than-average showing, but not enough for Welch's relentless mind. He became maniacal about hitting his goal of reducing defects to the point where errors would be almost nonexistent: 3.4 defects per million, or 6 sigma.
- Despite its huge size, GE continues to demonstrate growth. In the 1991–2001 period, earnings per share climbed from $0.43 to $1.41, a compound annual growth rate of 12.6 percent. (The company, moreover, has had twenty-five consecutive annual earnings increases.) In the same ten-year span, dividends per share advanced from $0.17 a share to $0.64, a growth rate of 14.2 percent.
- NBC has moved aggressively to expand into cable television. The network has stakes in seventeen cable networks, including CNBC, Court TV, and the History Channel. NBC has also moved swiftly in recent years to introduce new entertainment and new channels in Europe, Asia, and Latin America.
- In 2001, Jay Leno agreed to a new contract with NBC that will extend his tenure as host of the network's "Tonight" show for another five years. Mr. Leno succeeded Johnny Carson in 1992. After a period when he trailed his late-night rival, David Letterman, Jay Leno has been the consistent leader in late-night shows, and his ratings in 2001 are better than the prior year.

- Argus Research Corporation rated GE a Buy in early 2002. Its analyst said, "In an exceptionally difficult environment of global recession that impacted nearly all of the multiple geographies and product segments in which the company participates, Buy-rated General Electric Co. reported double-digit EPS growth in the fourth quarter of 2001 and for the full year.

"The outlook going forward is highly positive for the company, which is modeling operations to include no recovery in the global economy in 2002. General Electric time and time again has demonstrated a knack for turning everyone else's crisis into its own opportunities, as it did in acquiring high-quality assets on the cheap in Asia during the 1997–1998 crisis."

Total assets: $437 billion
Current ratio: 0.87
Common shares outstanding: 9,935 million
Return on 2001 shareholders' equity: 25.0%

	2001	2000	1999	1998	1997	1996	1995	1994
Revenues (millions)	125913	129853	111630	100469	54515	46119	43013	60109
Net income (millions)	13684	12735	10717	9296	8203	7280	6573	5915
Earnings per share	1.41	1.27	1.07	0.93	0.83	0.73	0.65	0.58
Dividends per share	.64	.57	0.48	0.42	0.36	0.32	0.28	0.25
Price High	53.6	60.5	53.2	34.6	25.5	17.7	12.2	9.1
Low	28.5	41.6	31.4	23.0	16.0	11.6	8.3	7.5

GROWTH AND INCOME

General Motors Corporation

100 Renaissance Center □ Detroit, Michigan 48243 □ (313) 667-1667 □ Dividend reinvestment plan is available: (800) 331-9922 □ Web site: www.gm.com □ Listed: NYSE □ Ticker symbol: GM □ S&P rating: B □ Value Line financial strength rating: B++

After years of insisting it didn't need a "car guy" to fix its lineup of mostly lackluster cars and trucks, General Motors (GM) named Robert A. Lutz in late 2001 as vice-chairman and Head of Product Development. Mr. Lutz, age seventy, the former president of Chrysler, is known for championing distinctive vehicles such as the Jeep Grand Cherokee, Dodge Viper, and the PT Cruiser.

The Swiss-born former Marine pilot is not exactly a dull fellow. Blunt-spoken and brash, he flies a Soviet-era jet for fun and has an extensive personal garage stocked with collectible cars. In the past, Mr. Lutz has been critical of the quality of many cars produced by Detroit and called a new crop of concept vehicles at a recent auto show "angry kitchen appliances."

GM's move to put Bob Lutz on the payroll was touted as the finale to a run of big hires, including former Ford Chief Financial Officer John M. Devine as finance chief, along with some big-name stylists. "Wagoner is getting all the cards in order," said Stephen Girsky, an auto analyst with Morgan Stanley Dean Witter.

General Motors' CEO G. Richard Wagoner is also relatively new to the corner office at Detroit's largest automaker. However, he's a career GM executive, not a transplant from outside.

According to *BusinessWeek*, Mr. Lutz "offers several skills GM's design team has been lacking: a keen eye for winning design and willingness to speak out."

"GM still has too many bland, me-too vehicles," said Saul Rubin, an analyst at UBS Warburg. "That's where Lutz could make a difference."

In his quest to get the job done, Bob Lutz is pushing aside years of past GM practice in order to give the company's designers more clout in the process of developing new models. And he is breaking down bureaucratic barriers that often stifled innovative ideas in the past. Finally, the new "car guy" is overhauling the cumbersome and often flawed process that General Motors marketers use to figure out what consumers wanted from new models.

Company Profile

General Motors Corporation, founded in 1908, is the world's largest vehicle manufacturer. GM designs, manufactures, and markets cars, trucks, automotive systems, heavy-duty transmissions, and locomotives worldwide.

Other substantial business interests include Hughes Electronics Corporation and General Motors Acceptance Corporation.

GM cars and trucks are sold in close to 190 countries, and the company has manufacturing, assembly, or component operations in more than fifty countries.

General Motors' Operations

General Motors North American Operation manufactures vehicles for the following nameplates: Chevrolet, Pontiac, Oldsmobile (to be discontinued), Buick, Cadillac, GMC, and Saturn.

General Motors International Operations meets the demands of customers outside North America, with vehicles designed and manufactured for the following nameplates: Opel, Vauxhall, Holden, Isuzu, and Saab.

General Motors Acceptance Corporation provides a broad range of financial services, including consumer vehicle financing, full-service leasing and fleet leasing, dealer financing, car and truck extended-service contracts, residential and commercial mortgage services, and vehicle and homeowners' insurance. GMAC's business spans thirty-three markets around the world.

General Motors Locomotive Group manufactures diesel-electric locomotives, medium-speed diesel engines, locomotive components, locomotive services, and light-armored vehicles to a global customer base.

Allison Transmission Division is the world's largest producer of heavy-duty automatic transmissions for commercial-duty trucks and buses, off-highway equipment, and military vehicles.

Shortcomings to Bear in Mind

- Although some key people have been brought in from outside, such as Bob Lutz as head of product development, some observers, including David Welch of *BusinessWeek*, are wondering "Will it be enough? While the outside hires—a rarity for GM in the past— demonstrate a new aggressiveness on Wagoner's part to fix GM, the carmaker has a ways to go. It will be a few years before Lutz's creations hit dealer showrooms. Until then, Wagoner is betting that GM's launches in the next couple of years, combined with cost cuts enforced by Devine, will keep GM in the black."

- Some investors are wondering why GM has found tough sledding on the Continent. For one thing, its overcapacity problems are even more conspicuous in Europe, where competition is intense. "The main problem is that continental automakers like Volkswagen, Peugeot, and Renault have got their act together," said John Casesa, an analyst with Merrill Lynch.

  Also, GM fell behind on a European favorite: diesel engines. "Diesels have been an important part of the picture in Europe for some time," said John Devine, GM's chief financial officer. "They're running roughly 40 percent of the mix right now, and in many countries it's higher than that. And for the last couple years, we have been short on diesels—but we're catching up."

- The Chevrolet Camaro and the Pontiac Firebird, two GM vehicles that helped define "muscle cars" for generations of American teenagers, died at the age of thirty-five in 2002. Like all muscle cars, the Camaro and Firebird were hit by the oil embargoes and clean-air restrictions of the early 1970s, which led to a switch to a less-responsive engine, not the kind that appeal to macho drivers.

  Launched in 1966 as a response to the popular Ford Mustang, the Camaro and Firebird twins and their high-performance Z28 and Trans Am variants met their demise because of changing industry economics. Marketing large numbers of 300-horsepower sports coupes to men under age thirty-five became close to impossible. Even if those youthful buyers could afford the $25,000 to $35,000 price tag, they would be further penalized by hefty insurance premiums. They "have literally been stopped dead in their tracks," said Jim Wangers, an auto industry analyst and former advertising executive who helped spur sales of the Firebird in

1966. In September 2002, GM closed the Canadian plant where two models were built, ending production after more than 6.6 million vehicles had come off assembly lines.

Reasons to Buy

- General Motors is no longer an also-ran. It is closing the gap with its rivals. For most of the 1990s, Ford dominated the market for big pickups and SUVs, while GM, busy investing cash to revamp its aging car line, remained a perennial laggard. But thanks to improved styling, the freshest products on the market, and aggressive pricing, GM has already grabbed the lead in full-size SUVS and pickups. Thanks to its popular new Chevy Tahoe, General Motors is taking market share in full-size SUVs, where profits are $10,000 to $15,000 per vehicle. Now, it's out to beat a suddenly vulnerable Ford in Detroit's largest market: midsize SUVs, long ruled by Ford's popular Explorer.

- In March of 2002, GM reported that its bread-and-butter Chevrolet division outsold archrival Ford division for the first time in more than a decade.

- In October of 2001, General Motors agreed to spin off its Hughes Electronics subsidiary tracking stock prior to GM's merger with EchoStar Communications. As part of the transaction, GM received $4.2 billion in cash and an 11-percent ownership in the combined company, for a total of $26 billion. The cash infusion helped General Motors shore up its balance sheet, since the company continues to burn through cash at the rate of about $3 billion a year.

- For the first time in years, many Wall Street analysts are recommending General Motors stock in 2002. According to Scott Hill, an analyst with Sanford C. Bernstein, "GM is doing all the right things right now."

- In a late 2001 issue of Argus Research, the analyst spoke favorably of General Motors' prospects: "GM has been able to avoid many of the problems that have beseeched Ford (recalls, lawsuits, product launch delays, and major management shakeups) and Daimler-Chrysler (merger issues, cash flow problems, and talent defection) over the past twelve months. The appointment of Bob Lutz as chairman of GM North America has fired up the troops at GM as the 'ultimate car guy' replaces Ron Zarrella, formerly (and once again) of Bausch & Lomb."

- Skeptics like to point out that General Motors is losing market share. One such critic says that the company's market share "has been drifting now for around three decades, from about 50 percent to a little above 28 percent in 2001. In answer to this, Mr. Wagoner said, "In fairness, you have to remember that our share of the U.S. car market alone is about 28 percent. Our second-place competitor, Ford, has only 18 percent, and DaimlerChrysler has 9.3 percent."

- In the all-important truck market, General Motors has taken the lead from Ford, thanks to hot-selling SUVs like the Chevrolet TrailBlazer and Tahoe, which have dramatically upgraded engines and interiors.

- Just a few years ago, Cadillac was the number one luxury car. By 1997, it had lost that distinction to Lincoln. Three years later, moreover, it had sagged even further to the number-three slot. General Motors, for its part, is determined to reverse the slide and is pledged to invest $4.3 billion over the next three or four years to get Cadillac back into the winner's circle. That amounts to 15 percent of GM's capital budget, aimed at a division that brings in a paltry 4 percent of GM's revenues.

  By 2004, there will be as many as nine models, up from five. Among them are a car-based sports utility vehicle in 2002 as well as the 2001 Cadillac version of the Chevy Avalanche and the all-new Catera sport utility sedan. While the old Catera was modeled on the stodgy European Opel Omega, the new Catera is being completely redesigned. The new Cadillacs will not only be sportier, but they will be equipped with more powerful engines, better handling, and the edgy styling of the Evoq concept car, Cadillac's new two-seat roadster which will be in the showrooms in 2003 under a yet-to-be-determined name. "This is the best strategy Cadillac has had in two decades," said Christopher W. Cedergren, an analyst at marketing firm Nextrend, Inc.

Total assets: $324 billion
Current ratio: 0.73
Common shares outstanding: 556 million
Return on 2001 shareholders' equity: 6.0%

	2001	2000	1999	1998	1997	1996	1995	1994
Revenues (millions)	177268	175332	176558	161315	153782	164069	168829	154951
Net income (millions)	502	4452	6002	2956	6698	4668	6932	5659
Earnings per share	1.77	6.68	8.53	5.21	8.70	5.72	7.28	6.20
Dividends per share	2.00	2.00	2.00	2.00	2.00	1.60	1.10	.80
Price High	67.8	94.6	94.9	76.7	72.4	59.4	53.1	65.4
Low	39.2	48.4	59.8	47.1	52.3	45.8	37.4	36.1

The Goodrich Company

2730 West Tyvola Road □ Four Coliseum Center □ Charlotte, North Carolina 28217 □ (704) 423-5517 □
Dividend reinvestment plan is available: (800) 524-4458 □ Web site: www.goodrich.com □ Listed: NYSE □
Ticker symbol: GR □ S&P rating: B+ □ Value Line financial strength rating: B+

If the world's largest aircraft needs to be evacuated in an emergency, critical systems must work without fail. No wonder Airbus (the huge European aircraft manufacturer—and Boeing's only major competitor) turned to Goodrich, the leading global supplier of aircraft evacuation systems, to meet the design demands for its new super-jumbo jet, the A380.

The task was daunting: eighteen slides for each eighty-foot-high twin-deck plane—more in number and size than ever before. Six seconds for the slides to inflate. Ninety seconds for up to 650 passengers to evacuate. Fortunately, by having the right concepts, processes, and technologies, Goodrich was up to the challenge.

What started as a Goodrich BRITE innovation program (see following) became a technological differentiation that drove the A380 win. "Our unique inflation device resulted in a system 10 percent lighter than existing slides—a critical factor for such a large aircraft," said Christine Probett, president of Aircraft Interior Products. "A passion for Lean processes also drove operational excellence, slashing design time, improving quality and lowering costs."

This Lean manufacturing showcase has garnered national attention, with Goodrich recently named for the second year as one of *IndustryWeek's* "Best Plants in America."

Ms. Probett went on to say, "With the Airbus Order, Goodrich is launching the next generation of evacuation systems. This is a major strategic win for us, based on our innovative technologies and our demonstrated manufacturing and service process excellence."

The BRITE Program

"Our goal is to develop a continuing stream of advanced products and processes," said Dr. Jerry Lee, Goodrich's senior vice president of Technology and Innovation. "This requires not only incremental but also distinctive, game-changing technologies, and a culture that encourages new ideas. Our innovation initiative is the catalyst that helps us take giant leaps in that direction."

A cornerstone of Goodrich's innovation initiative is its BRITE program, which provides millions of dollars annually to business units who compete successfully for these resources, based on the breakthrough potential and commercial promise of their ideas.

"Our ability to innovate and create new technologies and products is at the center of our success," said Dr. Lee. "The BRITE program ensures that our best ideas are funded and managed to reach the market profitably. It has won broad acceptance throughout the company because it produces concrete results. I am constantly amazed at the number of great ideas we see each year."

Company Profile

Once synonymous with automobile tires, Goodrich has emerged as one of America's leading multi-industry companies with an enviable record of profitable growth. Today's Goodrich is a leader in aerospace systems and services, as well as engineered industrial products.

In 1999, Goodrich and Coltec Industries completed a $2.2 billion merger that significantly boosted Goodrich's aerospace business and added engineered industrial products to the portfolio.

Goodrich employs about 23,000 people in 180 facilities across twenty countries. It ranks about 300 in *Fortune* magazine's list of America's largest companies.

The Aerospace segment is made up of Aerostructures and Aviation Technical Services, Landing Systems, Engine and Safety Systems, and Electronic Systems. These groups serve commercial, military, regional, business, and general aviation markets.

Engineered Industrial Products is a single business group. This group manufactures industrial seals, gaskets, packing products, self-lubricating bearings, diesel, gas and dual fuel engines, air compressors, spray nozzles, and vacuum pumps.

Goodrich spun off its engineered industrial products business to shareholders in the second quarter of 2002. It sold its Electronic Materials Division to Sumitomo Bakelite Company, Ltd., in August of 2001.

Shortcomings to Bear in Mind

- As you might expect, not everyone agrees with me that this is a great stock. For its part, the *Standard & Poor's Stock Reports* said in its March 2002 report, "Although we believe Goodrich's aerospace businesses will be able to generate respectable, if not spectacular, return on equity (ROE), it remains to be seen whether Goodrich will be able to post sustainable, outsized cash earnings-per-share growth. Goodrich maintains dominant shares in several key aircraft component markets. However, long-term demand for new large-passenger jets, as well as maintenance, repair and overhaul (MRO) services, by far Goodrich's

largest end-markets, are projected to expand only at modest rates."
- If you are looking for a rising dividend, you won't like Goodrich. It has paid the same $1.10 per share each year since 1991.
- Goodrich does not exhibit steady growth in its earnings per share. Rather, there is a great deal of variability in recent years, plus two years when the company lost money (1991 and 1992).

Reasons to Buy

- For the last five years, Goodrich has delivered the following:
  - Record earnings per share every year, averaging 26 percent growth **
  - 8 percent average annual sales growth
  - 19 percent average annual operating income growth **
  - 20 percent average annual return on equity **
  - ** From continuing operations and excluding special items
- "Our proven track record is driven by key company strengths," said Rick Schmidt, senior vice president and chief financial officer. "As an early and aggressive participant in aerospace industry consolidation, we have established market leadership positions with proprietary technology and products that drive a strong, profitable aftermarket." (Aftermarket refers to follow-up business, such as service, spare parts, and repairs.)

  Mr. Schmidt went on to say, "Our evolution from a collection of small, component businesses to a portfolio of advanced systems, products, and services has made Goodrich a high value-added supplier, enjoying tier-one status with global customers."
- Mr. Schmidt emphasized the importance of free cash flow—the cash flow that

remains after taking into account all cash flows including fixed-asset acquisitions, asset sales, and working capital expenditures. "Free cash flow is the lifeblood of our financial performance, providing the resources to support our internal growth and acquisition strategies, as well as dividend payments to shareholders.

"That's why we have placed increased emphasis on cash flow, and our operations are focused on furthering the progress we made in 2001. Our goal is to significantly increase our free cash flow during 2002 and to upgrade internal processes to sustain cash conversion at greater than 80 percent of net income over the long term."

- When Goodrich merged with Coltec Industries in 1999, the company created a full-service landing gear powerhouse with enhanced capabilities and opportunities as a total systems integrator. This move paid off in 2001, with $10 billion in contract wins, including significant commercial and military landing gear awards for the Airbus A380 and the Lockheed F-35 Joint Strike Fighter.

"Our combined experience and expanded engineering and systems integration capabilities are without question the reasons why we won these two contracts," said Brian Gora, president of Goodrich's Landing Gear Division. "Goodrich is the strongest systems supplier for the global landing gear business, supporting any aircraft manufacturer anywhere in the world."

- Aerospace original equipment revenues are traditionally cyclical, as manufacturer's production schedules change in response to new aircraft orders. However, about 43 percent of Goodrich sales are from the "aftermarket," which includes spare parts and services to commercial airlines, military, and other aircraft owners.

This business is driven by factors that are different from those that affect the aircraft manufacturing cycle, most notably fleet sizes, aircraft utilization rates, and equipment aging characteristics. As a result, the aftermarket helps Goodrich keep revenues on an even keel despite normal cycles.

"As an airplane ages, it requires more services and parts, "said Bob Gustafson, vice president and general manager, Aftermarket Services of Goodrich's Aerostuctures business. "This means revenues from the sale of parts and services are stable and predictable over a long period of time."

Bob estimated that his division alone supports nearly 6,000 aircraft currently in use in the world market, and that the average age of those aircraft is only six years. "Goodrich made a deliberate decision to invest in the infrastructure required to support the aftermarket early in the life cycle of our commercial programs. Consequently, we're been experiencing excellent growth."

- *Fortune* magazine ranked Goodrich as one of the "Most Admired" aerospace companies. Goodrich is also included on *Forbes* magazine's "Platinum List" of America's best big companies.

Total assets: $4,638 million
Current ratio: 1.66
Common shares outstanding: 102 million
Return on 2001 shareholders' equity: 13.7%

		2001	2000	1999	1998	1997	1996	1995	1994
Revenues (millions)		4184	4364	5538	3951	3373	2239	2409	2199
Net income (millions)		177	286	170	228	113	106	118	66
Earnings per share		1.65	2.68	1.53	3.04	1.53	1.97	2.15	1.12
Dividends per share		1.10	1.10	1.10	1.10	1.10	1.10	1.10	1.10
Price	High	44.5	43.1	45.7	56.0	48.2	45.9	36.3	24.2
	Low	15.9	21.6	21.0	26.5	35.1	33.4	20.8	19.5

INCOME

Health Care Property Investors, Inc.

4675 MacArthur Court, Suite 900 □ Newport Beach, CA 92660 □ Listed: NYSE □ (888) 604-1990 □ Direct dividend reinvestment plan is available: (800) 524-4458 □ Web site: www.hcpi.com □ Ticker symbol: HCP □ S&P rating: Not rated □ Value Line financial strength rating: B+

Why Invest in Health Care REITS?

The demographics of an aging domestic population support the continued growth of health care REITs. America is growing older: the first of 81 million Baby Boomers began turning fifty in 1996.

Life expectancies are also increasing. The number of people aged sixty-five and older is expected to increase over the next twenty years and should become the fastest-growing population segment.

The proclivity of people over sixty to need and use medical services is a compelling indicator of the growth potential for the health care industry. Health care is now the nation's largest industry, representing 14 percent of gross domestic product.

Company Profile

Dating back to 1985, Health Care Property Investors (HCP) is a self-administered real estate investment trust (REIT) that invests exclusively in health care real estate throughout the United States.

A REIT is a corporation or business trust that invests in real estate for the benefit of its stockholders. A REIT is generally not required to pay corporate income taxes, provided it distributes at least 90 percent of its net taxable income to its stockholders in the form of dividends. The REIT status was established to enable small investors to own real estate without a large capital commitment.

HCP is the nation's largest and most diversified health care REIT—by the type of facility, number of properties, geographic area, operator, and tenant.

The company's real estate investments, as of year-end 2001, consisted of 429 facilities totaling 21.5 million square feet and situated in forty-two states. These properties include 7,000 units, 650 tenants, and ninety health care operators. The company focuses on purchasing newer health care facilities (the average facility age is seventeen years) and emphasizes existing buildings over new construction.

The company has an experienced professional management team with an average tenure of fifteen years. Health Care Property Investors has the highest investment grade bond ratings of all health care REITs.

The company's investments include 176 long-term care facilities, ninety-four congregate care and assisted-living facilities, eighty-six medical office buildings, twenty-one acute-care hospitals, nine freestanding rehabilitation facilities, six health care laboratory and biotech research facilities, and thirty-seven physician group practice clinics. The company leases its single-tenant buildings to health care operators on a long-term basis, and its multitenant buildings to health care providers under various market terms.

As of year-end 2001, the company's annualized revenues broke down as follows:

- Acute-care hospitals: 26%
- Long-term care facilities: 27%
- Medical office buildings: 20%
- Congregate care/assisted living facilities: 15%
- Physician group practice clinics: 5%
- Rehabilitation hospitals: 5%
- Laboratory and biotech research: 2%

Shortcomings to Bear in Mind

- REITs have a history of performing well during market turbulence, such as we saw in 2000 and 2001. But if stocks in general perform well, as they did in 1999, REITs are less likely to follow suit. In 1999, for instance, HCP declined from a high of $33.1 to a low of $21.7. In the two years that followed, however, the stock more than made up for its slump in 1999, climbing as high as $39 in that span.
- According to the company's 2001 annual report, "As we review the past several years, we realize that certain trends in the industry continue to evolve slowly. Many of the issues we faced a year ago remain today, while other factors are now just shaping our investment climate.

   "As expected, the environment for nursing homes, hospitals, and ancillary hospital buildings continued to improve. However, just when we thought nursing homes might be sailing into smoother

waters, 'sunset' or automatic termination dates for the 1999 Amendment to the Balanced Budget Act now appear looming for the fall of 2002. Industry lobbyists are again scrambling to preserve the funding originally promised to nursing home operators. Changes in nursing home reimbursement may impact our investment goals."

Reasons to Buy

- In the year ended December 31, 2001, the company provided a 32.4 percent total return to stockholders. From inception in 1985 through year-end 2001, the company posted an annual average total return to investors of 17.4 percent. This compares very favorably with other equity REITs.
- HCP has a record of sixty-five consecutive quarterly dividends increases, with no reductions. Many companies increase their dividends annually, but very few quarterly.
- The company is acquisition-minded. In 2001, for instance, HCP invested $240 million in new properties, thus exceeding the prior two years. Included in these purchases were eight skilled nursing facilities, nine assisted-living centers, nine medical office buildings, six laboratory buildings, and one hospital. All told, these outlays comprised a total of 987 skilled nursing beds, 1,118 assisted-living units, 415,226 square feet of medical office space, 432,248 square feet of laboratory space, and 78,754 square feet of hospital space.
- In order to fund this expansion, the company had to seek capital. According to CEO Kenneth B. Roath, "With more than $200 million in new equity raised during 2001, the company was far more successful in obtaining new capital than we anticipated at the start of the year. We raised new equity capital principally in three ways. In May

we issued approximately four million new shares of company common stock, yielding $133 million in net proceeds to the company.

"We introduced a new Dividend Reinvestment and Stock Purchases Plan in the spring that contributed another $29 million in new equity over the remainder of the year. Later in the year we completed a large DownREIT transaction, where nonmanaging membership units contributed most of the balance of the equity. These transactions brought the combined total of new equity to slightly more than $200 million."

Mr. Roath went on to say, "We successfully increased the size of our revolving line of credit from $310 million to $395 million, and brought five new banks into our line. The revolving line of credit is an important component of our financing strategy.

"We value our relationships with our lead banking institutions: The Bank of New York, Wells Fargo Bank, Bank of America, and Wachovia Securities. The bank line allows us to 'warehouse' acquisitions before raising long-term capital. As of December 31, 2001, we had $108 million outstanding under our bank line."

- The company is sound financially, with very little debt. In early 2002, Mr. Roath said, "Looking forward, we are cautiously optimistic about delivering significant improvement results to stockholders in 2002. The company is in the best financial position we have been in over the past several years, with debt to total market capitalization at only 30 percent. We are poised to expand into new investments without the need to raise new equity capital."

- During 2001, Health Care Property Investors continued to actively manage its portfolio. According to a spokesman, "We divested non-core or underperforming assets, which raised a total of $29 million. We sold four vacant buildings during the year, and released forty-seven properties, twenty-two of which were leased to Kindred Health care, which successfully emerged from bankruptcy a much stronger tenant. We have currently identified several additional buildings for sale or release. Success with the sale or release of these buildings would improve the company's FFO." (FFO is short for "funds from operations," the most commonly accepted and reported measure of real estate investment trust operating performance. FFO is equal to a REIT's net income, excluding gains or losses from property sales or debt restructuring, plus real estate depreciation and after adjustments for unconsolidated partnerships and joint ventures.)

Total assets: $2,431 million
Current ratio: NA
Return on 2001 equity: 10%
Common shares outstanding: 54 million

	2001	2000	1999	1998	1997	1996	1995*	1994
Revenues (millions)	332	330	225	162	129	120		
Net income (millions)	121	109	78	87	63	61		
Earnings per share	1.78	2.14	2.22	2.46	2.21	2.12		
Funds from operations	3.32	3.32	3.22	3.06	2.84	2.76		
Dividends per share	3.10	2.94	2.78	2.62	2.46	2.30		
Price High	39.0	30.4	33.1	40.0	40.4	37.8		
Low	29.3	23.1	21.7	28.3	31.9	30.5		

* Data prior to 1996 is not available.

The Home Depot, Incorporated

2455 Paces Ferry Road, NW □ Atlanta, Georgia 30339 □ (770) 384-2666 □ Direct dividend reinvestment plan is available: (800) 577-0177 □ Web site: www.homedepot.com □ Fiscal year ends Sunday closest to January 31 of following year □ Listed: NYSE □ Ticker symbol: HD □ S&P rating: A+ □ Value Line financial strength rating: A++

Arthur Blank, Home Depot's sixty-year-old chairman and cofounder, takes nothing for granted. "We're in the relationship business, not the transaction business," he says. "People can buy this merchandise somewhere else. The challenge is always remembering to walk in the customer's footsteps, not our own."

Customers, in fact, are responsible for 70 percent of Home Depot's 50,000 items. Among them are items like precut Venetian blinds, tool rentals, Christmas, trees, and pretzels. And now Home Depot is selling large appliances. After a two-year test, Home Depot decided to start selling washer-dryers and refrigerators in all of its stores. Maximizing its gross profit bang-per-invested-buck, Home Depot decided to stock only 60 percent of the appliance line. It struck a deal with General Electric to ship the other 40 percent directly to the customer's home.

Company Profile

Founded in 1978, The Home Depot—or Big Orange—is the world's largest home improvement retailer. It operates 1,348 retail outlets, including 1,220 Home Depot stores in the United States, seventy-eight Home Depot stores in Canada, and four Home Depot stores in Mexico. The company also operates forty-one EXPO Design Centers, four Villager's Hardware stores, and one Home Depot Floor Store outlet.

Home Depot is credited as being the innovator in the home improvement retail industry by combining the economies of

scale inherent in a warehouse format with a level of customer service unprecedented among warehouse-style retailers.

Home Depot stores cater to do-it-yourselfers, as well as home improvement, construction, and building maintenance professionals.

Each Home Depot store stocks about 40,000 to 50,000 different kinds of building materials, home improvement supplies, and lawn and garden products. New Home Depot stores in the United States and Canada range from 105,000 to 115,000 square feet, with an additional 15,000- to 25,000-square-foot garden center.

The stores have design centers staffed by professional designers who offer free in-store consultation for home improvement projects that range from lighting to computer-assisted design for kitchens and bathrooms.

Home Depot offers installation services of select products, ranging from single items such as carpet to more extensive projects such as kitchen cabinets. The company is also testing the At-Home Services program, which will offer complete installation of roofing, siding, and window products in limited markets.

Home Depot has been publicly held since 1981 and is included in the S&P 500.

Shortcomings to Bear in Mind

■ Like most successful companies, Home Depot sells at a lofty price/earnings multiple. In the event of a disappointing quarter, the stock could hit an air pocket.

- According to analysts, the only possible threat to Home Depot's dominance in hardware retailing is Lowe's Companies of Wilkesboro, North Carolina. Lowe's is half the size of Home Depot in sales and store count. On the other hand, don't forget that Big Orange has already obliterated its shares of competitive chains, not to mention scads of mom-and-pop hardware emporiums.

Reasons to Buy

- Despite the recession and other negative factors, Home Depot finished 2001 with a flourish. The fourth quarter was particularly impressive, as profits shot up 53 percent. The company earned $710 million, compared with $465 million in the year-earlier period. For all of 2001 (ended February 3, 2002), sales advanced to $53.55 billion, up from $45.74 billion. Earnings per share climbed to $1.30, compared with $1.11 in the same period of 2001. Commenting on the strong finish, CEO Bob Nardelli said, "In light of today's economic conditions, Home Depot ended the year in a very strong financial condition, with equity of $18 billion, a debt-to-equity ratio under 7 percent, and a record $2.5 billion in cash."

- The U.S. home improvement industry continues to grow, as new and existing home sales reach record levels, home ownership rates increase, and existing houses and their owners age. In addition, the quality of home life has become more important to many homeowners, prompting them to make improvements or enhancements to kitchens, bathrooms, and other frequently used rooms. All of these factors spell opportunity for Home Depot.

  The company intends to capture these opportunities in new and existing Home Depot stores, which will continue to drive consistent sales and earning growth for the foreseeable future. In the longer term, increasing the company's sales in other segments of the industry will become progressively more important to support of a consistent growth pattern.

- When General Electric selected its new CEO in late 2000, two of the highly regarded candidates who were not chosen to succeed Jack Welch were motivated to leave the company. Among them was Robert L. Nardelli, age fifty-three, who had been president and CEO of GE Power Systems, that company's largest industrial business and a maker of power generators. Among the reasons cited for choosing Nardelli as their new CEO, Home Depot cited Mr. Nardelli's strong track record at General Electric, along with what it called his "uncanny ability to develop managerial talent and motivate employees to perform exceptionally well."

  Gerard Roche, senior chairman of Heidrick & Struggles International, handled the search for Home Depot. Mr. Roche said that he suggested Mr. Nardelli to Home Depot because he knew the General Electric executive was a charismatic leader who inspired his troops—an important trait for a retailer that takes pride in its strong corporate culture and attention to the needs of hourly workers. "His GE troops would die for him," Mr. Roche said. "He's taken a lot of ragtag teams and built them into the best in the country."

- The company is taking steps to increase its share of the professional business customer market. In some respects, this has been a balancing act for Home Depot, since do-it-yourself customers are still the company's most important customers, and the company is committed to continuing to serve their needs. However, Home Depot is also focusing on gaining more sales from the pros already shopping in its stores. According to management, "As we refine the tests we are conducting today to expand our professional programs to more stores, we expect this customer segment will drive incremental sales."

- Home Depot's profit margins have been increasing of late. Flexing its buying power, the company continues to call in suppliers to demand better terms and more attractive merchandise. It is also buying more goods directly from foreign suppliers, shutting out middlemen. In addition, the company says it is reducing losses from shoplifting and has expanded a tool-rental program.

- In 2002, Home Depot was named sixth in *Fortune* magazine's list of America's Most Admired Companies for the second consecutive time. The company was also named Most Admired Specialty Retailer for the ninth consecutive time.

- Home Depot is opening new stores at a fast clip. On February 7, 2002, for instance, the retailer opened seventeen new outlets, the largest one-day store rollout in the company's twenty-three-year history. The previous record for one day was thirteen on November 16, 2000. "It's interesting to note that the 200 stores we will open this year are more stores than the company opened in its first thirteen years," said Mike Folio, senior vice president of real estate.

- Mr. Nardelli looks for Home Depot to increase earnings growth by 18 percent to 20 percent per year through the year 2004. Skeptics wonder whether in a flat economy, "isn't this too aggressive a target?"

Mr. Nardelli answers, "We've got over $17 billion of assets, and I think we have an obligation to drive more sales per square foot of existing assets. How will we do that? By gaining share. The industry's top five competitors have about 17 percent of the market. There's 83 percent of the market that represents opportunity.

"So how do we attract that customer base? One of the ways is services. We're the largest retailer of carpeting in the United States, and we want to be the largest installer. Our tool-rental business is having phenomenal growth. While we're number one in home improvement, I want to make sure we're number one in every segment of home improvement."

- In early 2002, *Value Line Survey* had some favorable comments on Home Depot. Its analyst, Carrie Galeotafiore, said, "We believe Home Depot should maintain its leadership position in the retail homebuilding supply industry, thanks to a few compelling opportunities. The company is moving forward with the rollout of its tool rental program, which is slated to be in over 600 and 1,300 stores in 2002 and 2004, respectively. What's more, Home Depot will continue to target the professional market via its Pro Service Initiative, and through the launch of its 'HD Supply' test program this year. The initiative is aimed at larger commercial and industrial customers (HD's current pro base consists mainly of smaller-scale contractors)."

Total assets: $21,385 million
Current ratio: 1.56
Common shares outstanding: 2,339 million
Return on 2001 shareholders' equity: 18.9%

		2001	2000	1999	1998	1997	1996	1995	1994
Revenues (millions)		53553	45738	38434	30219	24156	19536	15470	12477
Net income (millions)		3044	2581	2320	1614	1160	938	732	604
Earnings per share		1.30	1.11	1.00	.71	.52	.43	.34	.29
Dividends per share		.17	.16	.11	.08	.06	.05	.04	.03
Price	High	53.7	70.0	69.8	41.3	20.2	13.2	11.1	10.7
	Low	30.3	34.7	34.6	18.4	10.6	9.2	8.1	8.1

CONSERVATIVE GROWTH

Hormel Foods Corporation

1 Hormel Place ◻ Austin, MN 55912-3680 ◻ (507) 437-5007 ◻ Dividend reinvestment plan is available: (877) 536-3559 ◻ Fiscal year ends on the last Saturday of October ◻ Listed: NYSE ◻ Web site: www.hormel.com ◻ Ticker symbol: HRL ◻ S&P rating: A ◻ Value Line financial strength rating: A

In recent years, Hormel Foods has transformed itself from a pure meatpacker, selling products primarily on a commodity basis (that is, not any different from its competitors), to more of a classic packaged foods company, developing value-added, branded products.

This strategic metamorphosis boosted the company's sales and profitability. In the past ten years, for example, Hormel's profit margin climbed from 3 percent to 4.4 percent in fiscal 2001. Similarly, its operating margin advanced from 6 percent in 1991 to 9.5 percent in the latest fiscal year. Finally, sales, during that ten-year span, moved ahead from $2.8 billion to $4.1 billion.

Having found the key to success, Hormel is not about to shift gears. According to *Value Line Survey*, "the company should continue to roll out new branded products, similar to last year's introduction of the Hormel Add-Ons brand of deli wafers sliced meats and cheeses, which supported sales growth in the refrigerated foods segment.

"We also expect the company to shore up its grocery products business by leveraging its signature brands, such as Spam luncheon meat and Hormel chili, and expanding its newer lines of olive oil and ready-to-serve ethnic foods."

Company Profile

Founded by George A. Hormel in 1891 in Austin, Minnesota, Hormel Corporation is a multinational manufacturer of consumer-branded meat and food products, many of which are among the best known and trusted in the food industry. The company, according to management, "enjoys a strong reputation among consumers, retail grocers, and foodservice and industrial customer for products highly regarded for quality, taste, nutrition, convenience, and value."

The company's larger subsidiaries include Jennie-O Turkey Store, the nation's largest turkey processor; Vista International Packaging, Inc., a manufacturer of casings; and Hormel Foods International Corporation, which markets Hormel products throughout the world.

The company's business is reported in four segments: Refrigerated Foods (accounting for 54 percent of total Hormel

Foods sales in 2001 and 27 percent of operating profits); Grocery Products (22 percent and 45 percent); Jennie-O Turkey Store (20 percent and 22 percent); and all other (4 percent and 6 percent).

The company's products include hams, bacon, sausages, franks, canned luncheon meats, stews, chilies, hash, meat spreads, shelf-stable microwaveable entrees, salsas, and frozen processed meats.

These selections are sold to retail, foodservice, and wholesale operations under many well-established trademarks that include the following: Black Label, by George, Cure 81, Always Tender, Curemaster, Di Lusso, Dinty Moore, Dubuque, Fast'n Easy, Homeland, Hormel, House of Tsang, Jennie-O-Kid's Kitchen, Layout Pack, Light & Lean 100, Little Sizzlers, May Kitchen, Old Smokehouse, Peloponnese, Range Brand, Rosa Grande, Sandwich Maker, Spam, and Wranglers.

These products are sold in all fifty states by a Hormel Foods sales force assigned to offices in major cities throughout the United States. Their efforts are supplemented by sales brokers and distributors.

The headquarters for Hormel Foods is in Austin, Minnesota, along with its Research and Development division and flagship plant. Company facilities that manufacture meat and food products are situated in such states as Iowa, Georgia, Illinois, Wisconsin, Nebraska, Oklahoma, California, and Kansas. In addition, various companies perform custom manufacturing of selected Hormel Foods products that adhere to stringent corporate guidelines and quality standards.

Hormel Foods International Corporation (HFIC), a wholly owned subsidiary in Austin, has established a number of joint venture and licensing agreements in such countries as Australia, China, Colombia, Costa Rica, Denmark, England, Japan, Korea, Mexico, Panama, the Philippines,

Poland, Spain, among others. HFIC exports products to more than forty countries.

Highlights of 2001

- Sales in the year ended October 27, 2001, climbed 12.2 percent, to a record $4.1 billion. However, physical volume increased only 6.2 percent despite managed reductions in commodity pork processing levels.

  In the same period, the company reported total earnings of $182.4 million, an increase of 7.2 percent. Reported earnings of $1.30 per share, an increase of 8.3 percent over 2000.

- Through significant acquisitions, the company achieved scale and industry leadership positions in two categories, turkey and managed health care foods. According to CEO Joel W. Johnson, "they have outstanding prospects. These are important steps in our effort to grow high-potential product categories."

- Mr. Johnson goes on to say, "Our strategy to emphasize branded, value-added products continued to gain momentum in fiscal 2001. Sales of branded foods accounted for 78 percent of total fiscal 2001 sales, compared with 76 percent in fiscal 2000 and 58 percent in fiscal 1995."

- The company's pace of innovation continued to accelerate in 2001, as products introduced in the last five years accounted for 31 percent of sales.

- Hormel Foods was one of the few food companies ranked on *Forbes* magazine's list of 400 Best-Managed Companies.

Shortcomings to Bear in Mind

- *Standard & Poor's Stock Reports* was not too keen on Hormel Foods in a report issued at the end of 2001. "We continue our Hold recommendation on the shares, reflecting our concerns over high pork prices and weakness in the foodservice segment due to the slowing economy. Sales growth has benefited from acquisitions and aggressive advertising and merchandising programs, but margins are being impacted by higher-than-expected raw material costs. While the company's procurement agreements with hog producers have helped limit margin erosion, a continuation of high pork prices remains a concern."

- Although Hormel had a good year in fiscal 2001, its Grocery Products, which consists primarily of processing, marketing, and sale of shelf-stable food products sold predominantly in the retail market, slipped 3 percent below the prior year. According to management, the disappointing showing for this sector "was due to higher fiscal 2001 costs for raw materials overall, which were up 15.9 percent from 2000, and heavy Y2K purchasing in the first quarter of fiscal 2000."

Reasons to Buy

- On a more positive note, the other two main segments turned in solid results. Refrigerated Foods, which consists of processing, marketing, and sale of branded and unbranded pork products for retail, foodservice, and fresh consumer markets, advanced a healthy 9.2 percent in 2001.

  The star performer, however, was the Jennie-O Turkey Store, whose business consists primarily of processing, marketing, and sale of branded and unbranded turkey products for the retail, foodservice, and fresh consumer markets, saw its tonnage volume increase 29.3 percent in fiscal 2001. What's more, sales advanced 42.9 percent for the year. Operating profits, moreover, climbed a spectacular 76.4 percent that year.

- Over the past ten years (1991–2001), earnings per share advanced from $0.57 to $1.30, a compound annual growth rate of 8.6 percent. In the same span,

dividends climbed from $0.15 to $0.37, a growth rate of 9.4 percent. To be sure, these are not dazzling growth rates, but they are steady and consistent. Thus, I have put Hormel Foods into the conservative growth category. As further confirmation of this, the beta coefficient is incredibly low, at .50. That means you can expect this stock to hold up well when the economy is weak, but also to lag behind when things are booming.

- Sales of the company's value-added branded products have grown at a compound annual rate of 5.1 percent since 1995. According to management, "these products deliver the greatest value to consumers and shareholders." Branded products accounted for 78 percent of total sales in fiscal 2001.

- Hormel's Always Tender meat products are growing at a good clip. In its first six months on the market, the Always Tender brand of products has "developed a loyal following" and has achieved a 94 percent average annual sales growth. According to the company, these products "are bringing to the meat case all the great taste and convenience customers have come to expect from the Hormel brand."

- Value-added products are also helping the Jennie-O Turkey Store. This segment now offers a broad selection of value-added branded products such as Thanksgiving Tonight oven-roasted turkey breast, which "delivers holiday flavor and everyday convenience."

  Demand for value-added turkey items, moreover, is growing faster than that for traditional products.

- Developing new products takes some effort. For Hormel, it means asking customers "about features that make their lives better." A case in point is the award-winning kid-friendly plastic packaging "of our popular Kid's Kitchen brand of microwave-ready foods."

Total assets: $2,163 million
Current ratio: 2.10
Common shares outstanding: 139 million
Return on 2001 shareholders' equity: 18.3%

	2001	2000	1999	1998	1997	1996	1995	1994
Revenues (millions)	4124	3675	3358	3261	3257	3099	3046	3065
Net income (millions)	182	170	160	122	106	88	120	118
Earnings per share	1.30	1.20	1.09	.81	.70	.58	.79	.77
Dividends per share	.37	.35	.33	.32	.31	.30	.29	.25
Price High	27.3	21.0	23.1	19.7	16.5	14.0	14.0	13.4
Low	17.0	13.6	15.5	12.8	11.8	9.7	11.4	9.4

CONSERVATIVE GROWTH

Illinois Tool Works, Inc.

3600 West Lake Avenue □ Glenview, Illinois 60025-5811 □ (847) 657-4104 □ Dividend reinvestment plan is available: (888) 829-7424 □ Web site: www.itwinc.com □ Listed: NYSE □ Ticker symbol: ITW □ S&P rating: A+ □ Value Line financial strength rating: A

Although 2001 was not a banner year for Illinois Tool Works, prospects are looking up in 2002. For instance, Precor, Inc., the company's leading fitness equipment brand, bolted out of the gate in early 2002, with January sales exceeding comparable 2001 figures by double digits.

"One month doesn't make a year, but we're very optimistic about our business in 2002," said Paul J. Byrne, president of Precor. "We've set aggressive goals and are off to a great start to achieve them."

Precor's commercial division registered a 30 percent sales increase, setting an all-time sales record for the division serving club, education, government, and corporate markets. On the home fitness front, Precor retail sales were up 10 percent over 2001, following a robust holiday season.

Founded in 1980, Precor is headquartered northeast of Seattle in Woodinville, Washington, with international offices in the United Kingdom, Germany, and Hong Kong. One of the largest fitness equipment manufacturers in the United States, Precor sets the standard for innovation and excellence in fitness equipment product quality and customer service.

Company Profile

Illinois Tool Works is a multinational manufacturer of highly engineered fasteners, components, assemblies, and systems. Illinois Tool's businesses are small and focused, so they can work more effectively in a decentralized structure to add value to customers' products.

The company has subsidiaries and affiliates in forty countries on six continents. More than 500 ITW operating units are divided into several business segments, as the following sections describe.

Premark International, Inc.

In 1999, the company made its biggest purchase yet—Premark International, Inc.—a $2.7-billion conglomerate that makes everything from industrial food equipment to gym equipment to residential flooring and appliances.

The Street did not take kindly to this huge acquisition. The day after the announcement, the stock dropped 8 percent, closing at $73.69 on September 10, 1999. More than a year later, the stock was still under siege, as it sagged below $50. No one seemed to notice that 90 percent of Premark's revenue came from nonconsumer goods, making it, at least in management's view, a good fit for Illinois Tool.

Engineered Products—North America

Businesses in this segment are located in North America. They manufacture short lead-time components and fasteners, and specialty products such as adhesives, resealable packaging, and electronic component packaging.

Engineered Products—International

Businesses in this segment are located outside North America. They manufacture short-lead-time components and fasteners and specialty products, such as electronic component packaging and adhesives.

Specialty Systems—North America

Businesses in this segment operate in North America. They produce longer-lead-time machinery and related consumables as well as specialty equipment for applications such as industrial spray coating, quality measurement, and static control.

Specialty Systems—International

Operations in this segment do business outside North America. They have stakes in longer-lead-time machinery and related consumables as well as specialty equipment for industrial spray coating and other applications.

How Illinois Tool Works Got Started

Founded in 1912, Illinois Tool Works' earliest products included milling cutters and hobs used to cut gears. Today, Illinois Tool is a multinational manufacturer of highly engineered components and systems.

In 1923, the company developed the Shakeproof fastener, a patented, twisted tooth-lock washer. This product's success enabled Illinois Tool to become the leader in a new industry segment—engineered metal fasteners.

Illinois Tool soon expanded the Shakeproof line to include thread-cutting screws, preassembled screws, and other metal fasteners.

By the late 1940s, the line had grown to include plastic and metal/plastic combination fasteners. Today, Illinois Tool units produce fasteners for appliance, automotive, construction, general industrial, and other applications.

After World War II, the company also expanded into electrical controls and instruments, culminating in the formation of the Licon division in the late 1950s. Today, Illinois Tool units provide a wide range of switch components and panel assemblies used in appliance, electronic, and industrial markets.

In the early 1960s, the newly formed Hi-Cone operating unit developed the plastic multipack carrier that revolutionized the packaging industry. Hi-Cone multipacks today are used to package beverage, food, and a variety of other products.

Also in the 1960s, the company formed Buildex to market existing Shakeproof fasteners as well as a line of masonry fasteners to the construction industry. Today, Buildex manufactures fasteners for drywall, general construction, and roofing applications.

In the mid-1980s, Illinois Tool acquired Ramset, Phillips Drill (Red Head), and SPIT, manufacturers of concrete anchoring, epoxy anchoring, and powder actuated systems; and Paslode, maker of pneumatic and cordless nailers, staplers, and systems for wood construction applications. Today, the construction industry is the largest market served by Illinois Tool Works.

In the 1970s, Illinois Tool purchased Devcon Corporation, a producer of adhesives, sealants, and related specialty chemicals. Today, the company's engineered polymers businesses offer a variety of products with home, construction, and industrial applications.

In 1986, Illinois Tool acquired Signode Packaging Systems, a multinational manufacturer of metal and plastic strapping stretch film, industrial tape, application equipment, and related products. Today, Illinois Tool offers a wide range of industrial packaging systems, including Dynatec hot-melt adhesive application equipment.

In 1989, Illinois Tool Works acquired Ransburg Corporation, a leading producer of finishing equipment.

Illinois Tool expanded its capabilities in industrial finishing with the purchase of DeVilbiss Industrial/Commercial division in 1990. Today, DeVilbiss and Ransburg manufacture conventional and liquid electrostatic equipment, while Gema Volstatic (acquired with the Ransburg and DeVilbiss purchases) produces electrostatic powder coating systems.

The company acquired the Miller Group in 1993. Miller is a leading manufacturer of arc welding equipment and related systems. Miller's emphasis on new product development and innovative design fits well with Illinois Tool's engineering and manufacturing strategies.

Shortcomings to Bear in Mind

■ The recession caught up with Illinois Tool Works in 2001.

Net income of $805.7 million was 16 percent below the prior year. Diluted earnings per share of $2.63 were 17 percent below 2000. The operating revenue of $9.3 billion was modestly (2 percent) below the prior year. Finally, operating income slid 17 percent in 2001 to $1.3 billion.

■ The stock has historically traded at a premium to the market, but based on its exceptional performance over the years, the price would appear to be warranted.

With some 500 businesses, Illinois Tool offers investors wide diversification by product line, geographic region, and industry. This helps insulate the company from weakness in any one sector. Over the years, this has resulted in consistent performance despite the cyclicality of the automotive and construction sectors.

Reasons to Buy

■ Acquisitions are likely to remain a key component of the company's growth strategy. Illinois Tool has grown steadily over the years largely by taking underperforming businesses and turning them into solid performers.

In most years, the company completes a dozen or two "bottom-up" acquisitions—companies that are directly related to or integrated into an existing product line or market. These transactions, typically representing more than $1 billion in combined revenues, are normally initiated by operating management for both North American and international businesses. According to management, "Looking ahead, our pipeline of potential acquisitions remains full."

A second type of acquisition, which the company undertakes far less frequently, is a major, or "top-down" proposition. These transactions are identified by senior management and represent entirely new businesses. Illinois Tool completed the largest transaction of this type in its history when it merged with Premark in 1999.

This merger brought the company nearly eighty decentralized businesses with products marketed in more than 100 countries. Two principal lines of business—commercial food equipment and laminate product used in construction—represent about $2.5 billion in revenues. Their products have strong brand names, such as Hobart, Wilsonart, Traulsen, Vulcan, and Wittco, established market positions, good distribution channels, and benefit from value-added engineering—all the things Illinois Tool Works looks for in a successful acquisition.

■ Illinois Tools' record of sustained quality earnings is the result of a very practical view of the world. The company relies on market penetration—rather than price increases—to fuel operating income growth. What's more, the company's conservative accounting

practices serve as a reliable yardstick of financial performance. These results then generate the cash needed to fund Illinois Tool's growth—through investing in core businesses and through acquisitions.

■ Illinois Tool Works has an impressive record of growth. In the 1991–2001 period, earnings per share climbed from $0.81 to $2.63, an annual compound growth rate of 12.5 percent. In the same ten-year stretch, dividends advanced from $0.21 to $0.82, for a growth rate of 14.6 percent.

Total assets: $9,696 million
Current ratio: 2.08
Common shares outstanding: 305 million
Return on 2001 shareholders' equity: 13%

		2001	2000	1999	1998	1997	1996	1995	1994
Revenues (millions)		9293	9984	9333	5648	5220	4997	4152	3461
Net income (millions)		806	958	841	810	587	486	388	278
Earnings per share		2.63	3.15	2.99	2.67	2.33	1.97	1.65	1.23
Dividends per share		.82	.76	.63	.54	.46	.36	.31	.28
Price	High	72.0	69.0	82.0	73.2	60.1	48.7	32.8	22.8
	Low	49.2	49.5	58.0	45.2	37.4	26.0	19.9	18.5

AGGRESSIVE GROWTH

Intel Corporation

2200 Mission College Boulevard □ Santa Clara, California 95052-8119 □ (408) 765-1480 □ Dividend reinvestment plan is available: (800) 298-0146 □ Web site: www.intc.com □ Listed: NASDAQ □ Ticker symbol: INTC □ S&P rating: A □ Value Line financial strength rating: A++

According to the Pew Internet & American Life Project, during the 2001 holiday season, 29 million people spent an average of $392 each purchasing gifts online, up from 20 million people who each spent an average of $330 on online holiday gifts in 2000. That represents a growth in online holiday gift sales from $6.6 billion to $11.4 billion, a year-to-year increase of about 72 percent.

This increase in Internet shopping came in the midst of an otherwise

lackluster holiday retail season, counteracting predictions by some that the days of the Web were numbered in the wake of the dot-com shakeout. "This is only one example of evidence that the Internet is alive and well and on its way to becoming the preeminent medium for commerce, information, and entertainment," said Intel's chairman, Andrew S. Grove, in 2002. "The Internet is in its infancy, and we have just begun to envision its multitude of uses."

Company Profile

It has been about three decades since Intel made technology history with the introduction of the world's first microprocessor. The computer revolution that this technology spawned has changed the world. Today, Intel supplies the computing industry with the chips, boards, systems, and software that are the "ingredients" of computer architecture. Industry members use these products to create advanced computing systems.

Intel Architecture Platform Products

Microprocessors, also called central processing units (CPUs), or chips, are frequently described as the "brains" of a computer, because they control the central processing of data in personal computers (PCs), servers, workstations, and other computers. Intel offers microprocessors optimized for each segment of the computing market. Chipsets perform the essential logic functions that surround the CPU in computers, and they support and extend the graphics, video, and other capabilities of many Intel processor-based systems. Motherboards combine Intel microprocessors and chipsets to form the basic subsystem of a PC or server.

Wireless Communications and Computing Products

These Intel products are component-level hardware and software. They focus on digital cellular communications and other applications that need both low-power processing and reprogrammable, retained memory capability (flash memory). These products are used in mobile phones, hand held devices, two-way pagers, and many other products.

Networking and Communications Products

Intel system-level products consist of hardware, software, and support services for e-business data centers and building blocks for communications access solutions. These products include e-commerce infrastructure appliances; hubs, switches, and routers for Ethernet networks; and computer telephony components. Component-level products include communications silicon components and embedded control chips designed to perform specific functions in networking and communications applications, such as telecommunications, hubs, routers, and wide area networking. Embedded control chips are also used in laser printers, imaging, storage media, automotive systems, and other applications.

Solutions and Services

These Intel products and services include e-commerce data center services, as well as connected peripherals and security access software.

Intel's Major Customers

- Original equipment manufacturers of computer systems and peripherals.
- PC users, who buy Intel's PC enhancements, business communications products, and networking products through reseller, retail, and OEM channels.
- Other manufacturers, including makers of a wide range of industrial and telecommunications equipment.

Shortcomings to Bear in Mind

■ Advanced Micro Devices (AMD) is a major reason that Intel is trying to compete with more technical weapons. In 2000, AMD actually beat Intel to market with the first one-gigahertz chip. Although AMD's fastest chip now operates at just 1.4 gigahertz, some benchmark tests indicate that Athlon chips at that clock speed can still outperform an Intel Pentium 4 running at 1.7 gigahertz.

From a competitive point of view, there's no question they want to distance themselves from AMD," said analyst Mark Edelstone of Morgan Stanley.

According to Molly Williams, a reporter for *The Wall Street Journal*, "Intel has been battling AMD with aggressive price cuts, which are also designed to help boost demand and accelerate a transition to the Pentium 4. AMD has been gaining market share, mostly in the retail market and laptops, but still has to win significant sales from the largest makers of PCs for the corporate market.

"That is part of the reason AMD is looking to educate users about the performance of its Athlon chips. In an advertising campaign that will begin in the fourth quarter (of 2001), AMD plans to emphasize that even at lower speeds, Athlon is competitive with Pentium 4."

Reasons to Buy

- "Looking at the fallout from failed online businesses over the past couple of years has led some naysayers to dismiss the importance of the Internet," said Intel Chairman Andy Grove in 2002. "But I believe that claims of the demise of the Internet, like Mark Twain said about news of his death, have been greatly exaggerated. While economics and other factors have currently slowed the deployment of the Internet infrastructure, data show that Internet use has continued to accelerate. Our industry is poised for significant expansion in the future as the Internet evolves, and Intel is well positioned to be at the center of that evolution."
- Intel announced in 2001 that its engineers had made a chip that combines the central functions of wireless devices into one piece of silicon, a device that will lead to smaller and faster consumer products. Other semiconductor makers have produced these so-called systems on a chip, but Intel claims it has done so without sacrificing computing speed.

Analysts said no other company appears to have developed anything similar yet. "I wouldn't call it a breakthrough product, but it is moving in the right direction," said Sean Badding, senior analyst at The Carmel Group, a market research firm. "Intel knows the market better than anyone, in my mind. They are now fulfilling a market that they believe will be on the upward trend the next couple of years."

- In March of 2002, Intel said it had developed ultra small memory circuitry with an advanced production technology that will be ready for the market in 2003. The company said that it had fabricated a dime-sized test chip with 330 million transistors, or 50 percent more than its most complex design to date. The chip, known as SRAM (for static random access memory), can store 52 million bits of data, compared with 32 million for chips produced by its competitors. Data is stored in cells that are a mere one micron small, or half the size of previous circuitry. A micron is one millionth of a meter.
- In 2001, Intel signed an agreement to supply Germany's Siemens AG with $2 billion in chips for mobile phones during the next three years. Intel is now Siemens's primary flash-memory chip supplier. Flash-memory chips are an essential component of advanced mobile phones because they retain stored data even when the phone is turned off.

The deal allows Intel to lock in a good price for flash-memory chips—then in short supply—before supply catches up with demand and prices fall. In 2000, major flash-memory chip producers couldn't meet the demands of mobile phone producers.

- In 2001, Intel introduced the first Pentium 4 processors based on the company's industry-leading 0.13-micron technology. Available at speeds of 2.2 gigahertz and 2 gigahertz, the new processors are the world's fastest, bringing the industry's highest performance to today's most demanding PC applications.

- In 2001, the company launched the industry's first suite of wireless networking products based on the IEEE 802.11a specification. Intel's new products include wireless hubs, adapters, and software that allow businesses and consumers to connect to corporate networks and the Internet five times faster than with wireless products based on the 802.11b specification.

- In 2001, Intel announced that its Intel StrataFlash memories will be used by leading manufacturers of digital set-top boxes for cable, satellite, and antenna-operated television. Vendors include Scientific-Atlanta, Motorola Broadband Communications Sector, Thomson Multimedia, and Hughes Network Systems.

- In the same year, Intel Online Services announced a new automated service technology that extends the company's managed services capabilities and adds remote management and other productivity improvements. Open Control Technology gives customers and systems integrators shared management and flexible control of e-business solutions, whether they are located in an Intel Online Service data center, a customer data center, or another third-party facility.

- In a cost-cutting move, IBM stopped selling desktop PCs in the United States with AMD microprocessors and might also drop AMD processors from its computers sold in Asia. IBM's desktops will now carry only Intel's processors. "With the low margins on PCs, it doesn't make sense for us to invest in two sets of chip platforms, " said a spokesman for IBM's PC division.

- An analyst writing for *Standard & Poor's Stock Reports* said in 2002, "Despite a difficult sales environment, we believe Intel's strong fundamentals remain intact, and that the shares warrant holding. Through its manufacturing prowess, the company has a competitive advantage over its peers. Future growth is enhanced by Intel's ability to further penetrate the market for higher-end platforms, and by its leverage of web-based processes to reduce its cost structure. In light of the company's dominance in the microprocessor industry, and based on our belief that new products offer opportunities for solid EPS growth over the long term, we see a good long-term story at INTC."

Total assets: $44,395 million
Current ratio: 2.72
Common shares outstanding: 6,712 million
Return on 2001 shareholders equity: 9%

		2001	2000	1999	1998	1997	1996	1995	1994
Revenues (millions)		26539	33726	29389	26273	25070	20847	16202	11521
Net income (millions)		1291	10535	7314	6178	6945	5157	3491	2562
Earnings per share		.19	1.51	1.17	.89	.97	.73	.50	.37
Dividends per share		.08	.07	.05	.04	.03	.03	.02	.02
Price	High	38.6	75.8	44.8	31.6	15.5	17.7	9.8	4.6
	Low	19.0	29.8	25.1	16.4	15.7	6.3	4.0	3.5

AGGRESSIVE GROWTH

International Business Machines Corporation

New Orchard Road ❏ Armonk, New York 10504 ❏ (914) 499-7777 ❏ Direct dividend reinvestment plan is available: (888) IBM-6700 ❏ Web site: www.ibm.com/investor ❏ Listed: NYSE ❏ Ticker symbol: IBM ❏ S&P rating: B ❏ Value Line financial strength rating: A++

While Microsoft and America Online battle for control of the consumer Internet, International Business Machines (IBM), under the direction of CEO Louis Gerstner, has quietly been constructing its own grand plan to rule the lucrative world of corporate computing. The idea is to put Big Blue at the forefront of a movement in which companies farm out their computing needs to utility-like providers.

Instead of having to constantly buy, maintain, and upgrade the latest technology, IBM envisions a simpler world in which companies would buy computer power and programs on an as-needed basis, just as they do electricity from power companies. IBM is investing billions to turn the vision into reality.

The company is spending $4 billion to add fifty hosting centers worldwide that will serve as its e-sourcing hubs. It is also striking up partnerships with telecommunications and hosting companies like Qwest Communications International, Inc., as well as AT&T, in order to create the Internet network to deliver services. What's more, IBM scientists are busy at work in "e-utility" labs developing the computing environments to bring Mr. Gerstner's dream to fruition.

Company Profile

Big Blue is the world's leading provider of computer hardware. IBM makes a broad range of computers, including PCs, notebooks, mainframes, and network servers. The company also develops software (number two, behind Microsoft) and peripherals. IBM derives about one-third of its revenues from an ever-expanding service arm that is the largest in the world. IBM owns Lotus Development, the software pioneer that makes the Lotus Notes messaging system.

The company's subsidiary, Tivoli Systems, develops tools that manage corporate computer networks. Finally, in an effort to keep up with the times, IBM has been making a concerted effort to obtain a slice of Internet business.

Shortcomings to Bear in Mind

- The personal computer and hard disk drive operations are weak, and customers of the company's microelectronics business have reduced purchases. Nor is IBM immune to the global economic slowdown, which was hurt further by the terrorist attacks on September 11, 2001.

- In late 2001, the Argus Research Corporation said, "While there is some good news in IBM's earnings picture, we need to note that not all is well. One aspect of IBM's business is its exposure to the financial service and insurance sector, where technology spending has weakened quite a bit. As well, the economic environment both at home and overseas is much less favorable than earlier this year."

On a brighter note, Argus went on to say, "To IBM's advantage is the fact that its largest business is now services. While winning new contracts in this business may be difficult, we note that IBM has a huge backlog of business in this space that will keep their revenue sufficient in this area for quite some time."

- The legendary CEO Louis V. Gerstner had been at the helm of IBM for a span of eight years when he retired in favor of Samuel J. Palmisano, Gerstner's right-hand man during that period. Although it may be too early to tell, it is likely that the company's style and image may be in for a transformation. People who have watched the two men say their management styles are very different. Mr. Gerstner is imposing and autocratic. His successor is regarded as gregarious and overtly competitive. "Mr. Palmisano has the potential to be a visible, charismatic leader," said Thomas Bittman, a former IBM manager. In view of the remarkable results turned in by Mr. Gerstner, however, it would be hard to believe that the new CEO will be able to match the performance of his mentor.

Reasons to Buy

- Sony Corporation hired IBM in 2001 to develop and produce a high-performance microprocessor for Sony's next generation of consumer electronics, including the PlayStation 3. This deal was a major win for IBM's semiconductor business, which had sales of $3.5 billion to external customers in 2000. The Sony pact could bring IBM revenue of between $2 billion and $4 billion over three years, beginning in 2004.

- IBM introduced a new family of microchips in 2001. They are intended to reduce sharply the size, power requirements, and cost components in Internet appliances and portable consumer electronic devices. The company said the new chips would enable its customers to design Internet devices using, on average, one-tenth the number of microchips in current products.

- Although IBM is well known as the titan of computer hardware, it is the Global Services division that is proving to be the company's star performer. While sales for the rest of Big Blue are barely inching ahead, the services division is averaging more than a 10 percent sales growth a year. That has helped pull up overall growth at IBM to about 5 percent per year.

- In an aggressive move to build a dominant position in the $8-billion market for database software, IBM made its biggest acquisition in six years in 2001. The company acquired Informix Corporation's database-software business for $1 billion.

  The move gives IBM a significant market-share lead over Oracle Corporation, which in recent years has been a close rival of IBM in the database sphere.

  In Informix, IBM has acquired an enterprise with about $800 million in annual revenue. It has some 100,000 customers, compared with IBM's database customer list of about 400,000. "We are buying a great database team and a great set of skills to win the database war," said Janet Perna, General Manager of IBM's Software Data Management Solutions. "The company that's got the best talent and the most customers is going to win this."

- In 2001, IBM invested $1 billion in the Linux operating system because it's the best answer to competing private standards and increasing demands on the Internet. With predictions of a thousand-fold increase in Internet traffic in the next few years, the networked world will be "several orders of magnitude more complicated than anything we know today," said IBM's CEO, Louis Gerstner. He went on to say that the proliferation of wireless devices as well as demands on Web servers amount to a prescription for meltdowns. "We're headed for a wall," he said. This means more viruses, hacker attacks, and security problems at a time when voice, data, dial tone, and switching are converging, he said. Mr. Gerstner said IBM decided to invest in Linux because it's growing faster than the mainstay operating system, Microsoft's Windows NT.

- IBM, still the world's foremost computer manufacturer, is no longer merely a computer vendor. Although hardware accounts for about 43 percent of revenues, the company has focused on such key sectors as services (which accounts for 37 percent of sales—a big jump from only 15 percent in 1994), and software (about 14 percent).

- Considered key growth engines, services and software have gained momentum. IBM has leveraged its unique capabilities in offering e-business solutions, well aware that the Internet is emerging as a business tool in streamlining everything from supply-chain management to customer service.

- IBM said that it will be a prime supplier of advanced chips and components to the main builder of China's Internet system, Huawei Technologies Company. Huawei, founded in 1988, is China's primary maker of routers and optical data-transmission systems used by telecommunications companies. The multiyear agreement, made in late 2000, could enhance IBM's chances of selling a broader range of computer products, including server computers, as China increases its use of the Internet. "We view Huawei as a very significant customer, and this establishes a stronghold for our technology in the Asia-Pacific region," said Steve Longoria, IBM's director of marketing for network processing.

- Competing against everyone from Electronic Data Systems to Big Four accounting firms to boutique shops offering only Web services, IBM has emerged as the world's largest purveyor of technology services, according to *BusinessWeek*. It counsels customers on technology strategy, helps them prepare for mishaps, runs all their computer operations, develops their applications, procures their supplies, trains their employees, and even gets them into the dot-com realm.

- IBM launched a security system that it expects will set the industry standard for protecting confidential documents, such as those used in the growing sector of electronic commerce. Unlike previous security measures that rely on software "fireballs" that filter out unauthorized users of information, IBM has developed a security chip embedded within the computer hardware, which adds additional levels of security. "People from outside your organization can get at your software," said Anne Gardner, General Manager of Desktop Systems for IBM. "People from the outside can't get to your hardware."

- IBM scientists intend to spend the next five years building the fastest computer in the world, 500 times faster than anything in existence today. The machine, dubbed Blue Gene, will be turned loose on a single problem. The computer will try to model the way a human protein folds into a particular shape that gives its unique biological properties, so as to understand the nature of consciousness, the origins of sex, the causes of disease, and many other mysteries.

The company is paying for the Blue Gene project, as it does many ambitious pure-science ventures, in hopes of being able to spin off new knowledge into products for the fast-growing market in biological computing. What's more, IBM research scientists relish the opportunity to sink their teeth into a daunting problem such as how proteins fold up into working molecular machines.

"Nature does this day in and day out, second by second, and has done it for billions of years," said Sharon Nunes, a senior manager in computational biology at IBM. "We really want to understand the fundamental why and how."

■ In a joint effort with a German company, Infineon Technologies AG, IBM plans to make semiconductor chips that will extend battery life in hand held instruments. By using the new chips, a laptop computer could be left in standby mode for months—or even years—without running down the battery.

Today's batteries, by contrast, give up the ghost within eight or ten hours.

According to analysts, IBM was among the first in the race to develop an innovative technology known as Magnetic Random Access Memory, or MRAM. It uses magnetic, rather than electronic, charges to store bits of data. MRAM has the promise of storing more information and using less battery power than traditional Dynamic Random Access Memory, or DRAM, used in most computer devices.

Total assets: $88,313 million
Current ratio: 1.21
Common shares outstanding: 1,723 million
Return on 2001 shareholders' equity: 38.0%

	2001	2000	1999	1998	1997	1996	1995	1994
Revenues (millions)	86866	88396	87548	81667	78508	75947	71940	64052
Net income (millions)	7495	8093	7712	6328	6093	5429	6334	2965
Earnings per share	4.35	4.44	4.12	3.29	3.01	2.76	2.76	1.23
Dividends per share	.55	.51	.47	.44	.39	.33	.25	.25
Price High	124.7	134.9	139.2	95.0	56.8	41.5	28.7	19.1
Low	83.8	80.1	80.9	47.8	31.8	20.8	17.6	12.8

GROWTH AND INCOME

Jefferson Pilot Corporation

P. O. Box 21008 □ Greensboro, NC 27420 □ (336) 691-3382 □ Dividend reinvestment plan is available: (800) 829-8432 □ Web site: www.jpfinancial.com □ Listed: NYSE □ Ticker symbol: JP □ S&P rating: A+ □ Value Line financial strength rating: A+

Jefferson Pilot launched a new advertising campaign in 2001 that represents a significant departure from the company's previous advertising. For the first time, Jefferson Pilot advertisements are appearing on such prime-time network television shows as *Frasier*, *The West Wing*, *Law and Order*, *Dateline*, and *60 Minutes*. The campaign was developed to bolster Jefferson Pilot's national name recognition.

Built around the theme, "Financial Freedom, It Has Its Advantages," the advertisements are designed to capture viewers' attention through humor. The first commercial to appear, for example, featured a man shattering his alarm clock with a golf club, suggesting that Jefferson Pilot has helped provide the financial freedom that allows him to sleep in.

Company Profile

Jefferson Pilot has two business segments: insurance, and communications. Within the insurance segment, Jefferson Pilot offers individual life insurance products, annuity and investment products, and group insurance products through these principal subsidiaries: Jefferson Pilot LifeAmerica Insurance Company, Jefferson Pilot Securities Corporation, Jefferson Pilot Financial Insurance Company, Benefit Partners, and Jefferson Pilot Life Insurance Company.

Major products in the life insurance sector are universal life insurance, variable life insurance, and term life insurance. In the annuity and investment sector, Jefferson Pilot markets single-premium and flexible-premium deferred annuities, immediate annuities, equity indexed annuities, variable annuities, mutual funds, and asset management programs. Finally, in the group operation (Benefit Partners), the principal products are group term life insurance, group disability income insurance, and group dental insurance.

Within the communications segment, Jefferson Pilot operates television broadcasting stations (three) and radio broadcasting stations (seventeen) and provides sports and entertainment programming. These operations are conducted through Jefferson Pilot Communications Company.

Highlights of 2001

- According to CEO David A. Stonecipher, "Annualized new premium sales of life insurance products grew almost 20 percent, excluding large-case single-premium BOLI business. Sales of annuities grew more than 10 percent overall, even with a decline in variable annuity sales. Growth of earnings per share (before realized investment gains of 7 percent) was below both our historical trend and our goal of 10 percent annual growth—though it was good in view of the challenges presented by the economy in 2001.

"Jefferson Pilot felt the effect of the nation's recession in our communications business, and our life insurance and annuity and investment products business experienced some earnings pressure, including the adverse effect of the September 11 terrorist attack.

- For the year, our earnings per share (before realized investment gains) increased to $3.06, from $2.86 in 2000. Net income per share (including realized investment gains) increased to $3.34, from $3.28. Cash dividends paid per share increased more than 11 percent."

Shortcomings to Bear in Mind

- In 2001, investment product sales through the company's broker dealer (primarily mutual funds) were down 24 percent, a response to the public's diminished appetite for products related to the stock market.
- Jefferson Pilot Communications Company faced a difficult economic environment in 2001. Advertising spending throughout the economy was down sharply, and the company's radio and television properties, as well as JP Sports, experienced lower revenues. For the year, broadcast cash flow declined to $74 million from $90 million in 2002. According to Mr. Stonecipher, "We remain optimistic, however, about the future of our properties. All of our radio and television stations are in superior markets with above-average potential, and our competitive position is very strong in each market."
- Gerard Feenan, an analyst with *Value Line Investment Survey*, had some lukewarm observations at the beginning of 2002. "The stock price has languished in recent years, reflecting a moderation in earnings growth from the company's historic pace. Our projections suggest only modest appreciation potential to 2004–2006."

Reasons to Buy

- The year 2001 capped a five-year record of progress "in which we take great pride," said Mr. Stonecipher. Achievements included the following:
  - Earnings per share (before realized investment gains) expanded at a compound annual rate of nearly 14 percent.
  - Return on equity has been at a consistently high level and was over 16 percent in 2001.
  - Cash dividends per share increased every year, growing at close to a 12 percent rate in that five-year stretch.
  - Jefferson Pilot's share price grew at a compound annual rate of 13 percent, well outpacing the S&P 500.
- Fixed annuity sales were strong in 2001, up 17 percent, and lapse trends improved significantly. The result was a solid increase of 8 percent in the company's fixed annuity assets, an important determinant of future earnings potential of Jefferson Pilot's Annuity and Investment Products segment. On the negative side, variable annuity sales declined in response to the market's lower level of interest in products tied to stock prices. On the other hand, overall annuity sales increased 10 percent in 2001.
- Jefferson Pilot's Benefit Partners group of life and disability business produced outstanding results in 2001. Sales of life, disability, and dental insurance products increased 25 percent. What's more, earnings grew an impressive 36 percent, to $44 million. The loss ratio improved. The expense ratio, driven by cost savings continuing to emerge from the Guarantee Life acquisition in 1999, also declined.
- Today, Jefferson Pilot is a focused provider of financial products and services to increasingly upscale markets. Jefferson Pilot creates and administers a portfolio of competitive financial products in centralized, very efficient operations, and distributes them via diversified sales channels.
- Jefferson Pilot is focused on the high end of the financial services market. The company is using its capability in variable universal life, as well as its broker dealer, Jefferson Pilot Securities Corporation, to service agents and clients in the estate planning and well-preservation market. This is reflected in the average size of Jefferson Pilot's life sale, which ranks the company among the top-tier life companies serving the affluent market. Demographic projections indicate strong growth over the next two decades in both the over-sixty-five population and the forty-five-to-fifty-four age range, providing tremendous potential for retirement-planning and wealth-preservation products and services in that target market.
- Jefferson Pilot's annuity management has capitalized on the favorable market conditions by adding new products, including popular multiyear rate guaranteed contracts; by responding quickly and aggressively to changing interest rates; and by focusing more effectively on all of the elements necessary to be a performance leader in the dynamic annuity marketplace.
- Jefferson Pilot views the Internet as a very substantial opportunity. With a surging percentage of domestic households now connected to the Internet, and with online banking established as a viable consumer product, there is no question as to the potential of the Internet as a medium.

  According to management, "Certain of our product may achieve direct distribution via the Internet, but the real opportunity, we believe, is to upgrade our service levels and strengthen our relationship with our clients."

- The company had an enviable record of growth in the 1991–2001 period. Earnings per share advanced from $1.02 to $3.34, a compound annual growth rate of 12.6 percent. What's more, the record was consistent, with no dips along the way. In the same ten-year stretch, the per-share dividend climbed from $.32 to $1.07, a compound growth rate of 12.8 percent.
- The company has capitalized on a consolidation trend under way in the life insurance business to add to its core life insurance business. In 1995, Jefferson Pilot acquired the life insurance and annuity business of Kentucky Central Life and Health Insurance Company. Also in 1995, the company acquired Alexander Hamilton Life Insurance Company of America from Household International. In 1997, Jefferson Pilot purchased the life insurance unit of Chubb Corporation. At the end of 1999, the company acquired The Guarantee Life Companies, Inc.

- In the spring of 2002, *Standard & Poor's Stock Reports* had a favorable view of Jefferson Pilot. "The shares of this leading variable and universal variable life insurer have trended upward since late 2001. This strength reflects a number of factors, including an expected increase in demand for life insurance in the wake of the September 11 terrorist attacks. The stock's recent strength also likely reflects investor belief that sales of variable life insurance products and communications revenues (that is, advertising spending) will benefit from a rebound in equity markets and the economy. We are also encouraged by JP's expanded distribution capabilities, particularly through non-agent channels."

Total assets: $28,996 million
Common shares outstanding: 150 million
Return on 2001 shareholders' equity: 16.2%

	2001	2000	1999	1998	1997	1996	1995	1994
Revenues (millions)	3330	3238	2460	2610	2578	2125	1569	1334
Net income (millions)	513	512	470	418	370	291	255	230
Earnings per share	3.34	3.29	2.95	2.61	2.32	1.82	1.58	1.40
Dividends per share	1.07	.96	.86	.77	.69	.62	.56	.50
Price High	49.7	50.6	53.1	52.3	38.6	26.5	21.4	16.3
Low	38.0	33.3	40.8	32.4	22.9	20.1	15.0	12.9

CONSERVATIVE GROWTH

Johnson Controls, Inc.

Post Office Box 591 ◻ Milwaukee, Wisconsin 53201-0591 ◻ (414) 228-1200 ◻ Direct dividend reinvestment plan is available: (800) 828-1489 ◻ Fiscal year ends September 30 ◻ Web site: www.jci.com ◻ Ticker symbol: JCI ◻ S&P rating: A+ ◻ Value Line financial strength rating: A

Johnson Controls bought a battery manufacturer, Hoppecke Automotive of Brilon, Germany, in 2001. The transaction expanded the company's reach in the battery market and gave Johnson Controls access to new battery technology. The acquisition was the second in the past two years for the battery unit of Johnson Controls, the leading supplier of automotive batteries in the Western hemisphere.

A year earlier, Johnson Controls bought Gylling Optima from a Swedish company. Optima batteries employ a new technology that ensures that batteries won't spill or leak if they are ruptured or punctured.

With these two deals, the company's goal was to have a stake in the emerging technology to make batteries that serve vehicles with 42-volt electrical systems, a major improvement over conventional 14-volt systems. Converting to the 42-volt system will help automakers enhance fuel economy by at least 10 percent. When more power is generated by a car's electrical system, there is less drain on its engine.

The number of cars and light trucks with 42-volt systems is expected to surge ahead in the years ahead. In 2002, global production of vehicles with 42-volt systems is estimated to reach the 46,000 mark. By 2009, moreover, as many as 10 million vehicles will come off assembly lines with the higher-voltage electrical systems, according to a forecast by Standard & Poor's. What's more, S&P believes that one-third of light vehicles made in North America, Europe, and Japan will use the 42-volt system by 2010.

Company Profile

Johnson Controls, Inc. is a global market leader in automotive systems and facility management and control. In the automotive market, it is a major supplier of seating and interior systems and batteries. For nonresidential facilities, Johnson Controls provides building control systems and services, energy management, and integrated facility management.

Automotive Systems Group

- Johnson Controls Automotive Systems Group is the global market leader in seating and interior systems for light vehicles, including passenger cars and light trucks.

- Systems supplied include seating, overhead, door, instrument panels, storage, electronics, and batteries.

- All systems are sold to the original equipment automotive market. However, the automotive replacement market is the major course of sales for batteries.

- Major customers include Auto-Zone, Costco, DaimlerChrysler, Fiat, Ford, General Motors, Honda, Interstate Battery Systems of America, John Deere, Mazda, Mitsubishi, Nissan, NUMMI, Peugeot, Renault, Sears, Toyota, Volkswagen, and Wal-Mart.

- The group has 275 locations worldwide.

Controls Group

- The Controls business is a leader in supplying systems to control heating, ventilating, air conditioning (HVAC), lighting, security, and fire management for buildings. Services include complete mechanical and electrical maintenance.

- The business is a world leader in integrated facility management, providing facility management and consulting services for many Fortune 500 companies. The company manages more than one billion square feet worldwide.

- Customers worldwide include education, health care, industrial, government, and office buildings.

- The group has 300 locations worldwide.

Shortcomings to Bear in Mind

- The company's large exposure to the automotive industry often worries investors. While it is difficult to argue that such concerns are unfounded, some analysts are convinced that they are overemphasized. For one thing, during periods of economic weakness, Johnson Controls' earnings have typically held up considerably better than those of most auto suppliers. On the other hand, there is no doubt that car sales trends are subject to sharp ups and downs.

- *Value Line Survey* had some negative comments on Johnson Controls at the end of 2001. "Johnson Controls' financial outlook has weakened. North American auto production in the coming quarters will likely fall further from reduced levels, as fragile consumer confidence and rising unemployment, exacerbated by the terrorist attacks, hurt domestic retail sales, one-third of which are automotive-related."

Reasons to Buy

- Over the past ten years, 1991–2001, the company's earnings per share increased without interruption, climbing from $1.06 to $5.11, an impressive annual compound growth rate of 17.0 percent. In the same ten-year span, dividends advanced from $.62 to $1.24, a more modest growth rate of 7.2 percent. However, the dividend payout ratio is extremely favorable, at only 24 percent. A low payout ratio is characteristic of a company with solid growth prospects.

- According to David Leiker, an auto analyst with Robert W. Baird & Company, "On average, auto suppliers get about 60 percent of their revenue from the big three automakers. But less than half of Johnson Controls' total revenue comes from GM, Ford, and DaimlerChrysler." The industry does about 5 percent to 10 percent of its business with transplants—foreign companies that are making cars in North America. Mr. Leiker believes that Johnson Controls gets about 25 percent of its automotive business from transplants, which means it is picking up market share because foreign brands are taking share away from domestic brands.

- Integration of electronics into vehicle interiors is one of the company's specialties,

ranging from global positioning systems to digital compasses and Homelink. The company, moreover, is continuously developing new products and holds more patents than any other automotive interior supplier.

- The company's automotive business is expected to expand in the years ahead as automakers continue outsourcing seating and interior systems in North America and Europe, as well as in emerging global markets.

What's more, the company's development of innovative features and application of new technologies for the automotive interior will strengthen the company's leadership position, as Johnson Controls makes its customers' vehicles more comfortable, convenient, and safe.

- In the company's automotive business, its strategy is to supply larger modules, and over time, deliver complete interiors to its automotive customers. Johnson Controls is well on the way toward achieving this goal, having received its initial orders in 2000 to provide complete interiors for future vehicle models.

- Nearly every automotive system the company makes today includes electronics. New products are electronics-based, such as the company's AutoVision, in-vehicle video system, and PSI tire pressure-sensing system. What's more, electronics are a part of its seats and other interior systems as well. Innovative use of electronics creates new features and functions for car interiors, as well as new ways for the company's automaker customers to differentiate their vehicles.

- Industry studies estimate that 75 percent of all tires are improperly inflated. The company's PSI system uses a radio-frequency transmitter in each tire, which sends air pressure information to an in-vehicle electronic display.

- The annual market for automotive electronics in North America will reach a total of $28 billion by 2004. To help meet this demand, Johnson Controls management says, "We're expanding and accelerating our electronics capabilities and creating new partnering programs with leading electronics firms."

- According to a spokesman for the company, "With more than 110 years of experience in the controls industry, Johnson Controls understands buildings better than anyone else. That's why tens of thousands of commercial, institutional, and government building owners and managers around the world turn to Johnson Controls to improve the quality of buildings' indoor environments by maximizing comfort, productivity, safety, and energy efficiency."

- The company engineers, manufactures, and installs control systems that automate a building's heating, ventilating, and air conditioning, as well as its lighting and fire-safety equipment. Its Metasys Facility Management System automates a building's mechanical systems for optimal comfort levels while using the least amount of energy. In addition, it monitors fire sensors and building access, controls lights, tracks equipment maintenance and helps building managers make better decisions.

- Building systems at some companies are critical to achieving their corporate missions. In the pharmaceutical industry, for example, the failure of a building's equipment or staff to maintain the proper laboratory conditions could mean the loss of years of new drug research and development. In a bank's data center, moreover, the failure of cooling equipment could shut down computer systems, delaying millions of dollars in transactions every minute.

- The company's Controls Group does business with more than 7,000 school districts, colleges, and universities as well as over 2,000 health care organizations. These customers benefit from performance contracting, a solution that lets them implement needed facility repairs and updates without upfront capital costs. Performance contracting uses a project's energy and operational cost savings to pay its costs over time. For instance, using a performance contract, Grady Health System in Atlanta was able to complete energy efficiency upgrades that will generate $20 million in savings over the next ten years.

- At the end of 2001, Johnson Controls purchased Scientech Security Systems, based in Idaho Falls, Idaho. Scientech operates and maintains a wide variety of life/safety systems, including access control, security command and control, alarm and video surveillance, intrusion detection, and fire protection. In the words of Mark Filteau, vice president and general manager of Johnson Controls Government Systems, "This acquisition strengthens our offerings for security solutions, particularly for the federal government marketplace." Johnson Controls already offers its Cardkey security systems with its Metasys and other building systems.

Total assets: $9,912 million
Current ratio: 0.98
Common shares outstanding: 93 million
Return on 2001 shareholders' equity: 17%

	2001	2000	1999	1998	1997	1996	1995	1994
Revenues (millions)	18427	17155	16139	12587	11145	10009	8330	6870
Net income (millions)	478	472	387	303	265	235	196	165
Earnings per share	5.11	5.09	4.13	3.25	2.85	2.14	1.80	1.49
Dividends per share	1.24	1.12	1.00	.92	.86	.82	.78	.72
Price High	82.7	65.1	76.7	61.9	51.0	42.7	34.9	30.9
Low	48.2	45.8	49.0	40.5	35.4	31.3	22.9	22.4

CONSERVATIVE GROWTH

Johnson & Johnson

One Johnson & Johnson Plaza □ New Brunswick, N.J. 08933 □ (800) 950-5089 □ Dividend reinvestment plan is available: (800) 328-9033 □ Web site: www.jnj.com □ Listed: NYSE □ Ticker symbol: JNJ □ S&P rating: A+ □ Value Line financial strength rating: A++

Standard & Poor's Stock Reports, a leading statistical and advisory service, had some good things to say about Johnson & Johnson in a report issued in early 2002. "We expect 2002 sales to increase 11 percent. Drug sales will benefit from continued growth in Procrit treatment for anemia, Duragesic transdermal patch for chronic pain, and Remicade anti-inflammatory agent. We also see greater contributions from newer drugs such as Aciphex antiulcer, Topamax antiepileptic, and Reminyl for Alzheimer's disease. Higher sales are forecast for ALZA Corp., acquired in June 2001. We also see continued strength for medical devices, driven by new products such as drug-coated coronary stents, as well as growth in established orthopedic and diagnostic lines."

This assessment is not surprising, in view of the company's outstanding showing in 2001. Leading the uptrend was Johnson & Johnson's pharmaceutical division (which accounted for 41 percent of company sales), with $14.85 billion in sales, for a gain of 17.3 percent for the year. On the home front, sales were ahead

a lusty $21.3 percent. Abroad, results were hampered by currency translations but advanced 9.3 percent nonetheless.

Among products that made a hefty contribution were the following: Procrit/Eprex, with sales of $3.43 billion, up 27 percent; Risperdal, an antipsychotic, with 2001 sales of $1.85 billion, for a gain of 15 percent for the year; Duragesic with sales of $875 million, up an astounding 33 percent; Topamax, with revenues of $477 million in 2001, up a whopping 55 percent.

Company Profile

Johnson & Johnson is the largest and most comprehensive health care company in the world, with 2001 sales of $33 billion.

The company offers a broad line of consumer products, ethical—or prescription—drugs, and over-the-counter drugs, as well as various other medical devices and diagnostic equipment.

The company has a stake in a wide variety of endeavors: anti-infectives, biotechnology, cardiology and circulatory diseases, the central nervous system, diagnostics, gastrointestinals, minimally invasive therapies, nutraceuticals, orthopaedics, pain management, skin care, vision care, women's health, and wound care.

Johnson & Johnson has 194 operating companies in fifty-one countries, selling some 50,000 products in more than 175 countries.

One of Johnson & Johnson's premier assets is its well entrenched brand names, which are widely known in the United States as well as abroad. As a marketer, moreover, Johnson & Johnson's reputation for quality has enabled it to build strong ties to health care providers.

Its international presence includes not only marketing, but also production and distribution capability in a vast array of regions outside the United States.

One advantage that Johnson & Johnson's worldwide organization offers is markets, such as China, Latin America, and Africa, that offer growth potential for mature product lines.

The company's well-known trade names include Band-Aid adhesive bandages; Tylenol; Stayfree; Carefree and Sure & Natural feminine hygiene products; Mylanta; Pepcid AC; Neutrogena; Johnson's baby powder, shampoo, and oil; and Reach toothbrushes.

The company's professional items include ligatures and sutures, mechanical wound closure products, diagnostic products, medical equipment and devices, surgical dressings, surgical apparel and accessories, and disposable contact lenses.

Shortcomings to Bear in Mind

■ *Value Line Survey* points out the negative impact of coming competition. "Amgen's Aranesp could be a serious threat to the company's top line for 2003 and beyond. Aranesp is the second-generation version of erythropoietin (which J&J markets as Procrit/Eprex, and Amgen markets as Epogen). Presently, Procrit/Eprex is J&J's top seller, garnering more than

$2.7 billion in sales in 2000. Amgen, which recently filed an application with the FDA for cancer-related anemia, may receive clearance to market Aranesp by late 2002. Doctors appear favorably disposed to Aranesp (which would likely be priced comparable to Procrit/Eprex), due to its more convenient dosing regimen."

■ Because of its stunning record, Johnson & Johnson is priced rather generously, typically at thirty times earnings or more. It might pay till someone says something nasty about the stock, pushing it down a notch or two.

Reasons to Buy

■ Research is the name of the game for drug companies. For its part, Johnson & Johnson invested $3.6 billion in research and development in 2001, up a tidy $486 million over the prior year.

■ Johnson & Johnson acquired Alza Corporation in 2001 for $10.5 billion. The deal will add about $700 million to the company's pharmaceutical business. Alza developed the bestselling time-release delivery of the NicoDerm anti-smoking patch, which is sold by Glaxo-SmithKline p.l.c.

Alza also makes time-release capsules that enable patients to take pills less often, as well as systems that use electricity to push drugs through the skin. In addition, Alza will contribute to Johnson & Johnson's line with such products as Concerta, a once-a-day remedy for attention deficit hyperactivity disorder; Ditropan XL for urinary incontinence; and the cancer drug Doxil.

The Alza products are expected to immediately benefit from Johnson & Johnson's deep pockets and worldwide marketing reach that are likely to produce more revenue for the drugs than if Alza sold them on its own.

- The FDA approved Johnson & Johnson's new drug for Alzheimer's disease in 2001. Reminyl, which became available in May of 2001, was approved to treat mild-to-moderate Alzheimer's cases. The Alzheimer's Association estimates that four million Americans suffer from progressive neurological disease. The association believes that if no cure is found, as many as 14 million more Americans will develop Alzheimer's by the middle of the century. Reminyl was shown to be effective in improving or helping to stabilize patients' ability to think and perform daily tasks in studies involving more than 2,650 subjects.

  Initially, the company launched the sale of Reminyl in the United States, the United Kingdom, Denmark, and Sweden. Over a dozen other countries have also granted approval.

- Taking advantage of the Internet, Johnson & Johnson is determined to become the best-connected health care company in the world. In the words of CEO Ralph S. Larsen, "We anticipate the Internet will enable us to change the ways we conduct business within and among our 194 companies, helping us to capture economies of scale while maintaining our decentralized management structure."

  The company is pursuing strategies based on three principles:

  - Using the Internet to create new ways of connecting with its customers, including physicians, hospitals, consumers, and retail partners.
  - Transforming Johnson & Johnson's core business processes—redesigning the ways the company works—in order to take full advantage of the Internet technology to save time, money, and improve quality.
  - Creating a Web-savvy culture throughout "our entire employee base around the world, recognizing that the Internet is an important tool in everything we do—at work and at home."

- Stents, the tiny metal scaffolds that transformed the care of heart patients in the 1990s, are on the threshold of a major advance that may put an end to one of cardiology's most baffling enigmas.

  Each year, about 700,000 patients in the United States undergo angioplasty, in which a balloon is used to clear an obstruction in a coronary artery and a stent is deployed to keep it open. Unfortunately, a high percentage of patients who undergo these procedures—some 15 to 20 percent—develop serious problems within six months, as the stent develops restenosis (arterial scarring).

  Now, heart researchers and stent makers are developing a new generation of stents that not only prop open the artery but that deliver drugs to the site of the blockage in an effort to keep the vessel open. Research studies suggest that stents coated with a drug called rapamycin put a stop to restenosis. Rapamycin is an immune-system suppressant drug marketed by American Home Products. Johnson & Johnson has licensed the drug, which it calls Sirolimus, for use with stents. It halts the replication of certain cells that, as part of the body's response to injury, are involved in the proliferation of scar tissue.

  Johnson & Johnson is well along in the development of its "pharma stent," which is coated with rapamycin. The company is widely regarded as being well ahead of competitors in a race to bring similar coated devices to market.

  In 1994, Johnson & Johnson initiated a new era in heart treatment with its first stent, which dominated the market for three years. But its days of glory were short-lived when rivals invaded its domain with better technology.

Now, however, the company is poised to make a comeback. Analysts and physicians are convinced that Johnson & Johnson's Cordis unit is about to reclaim much of its former market share for angioplasty devices. Among other recent accomplishments, Cordis received FDA approval for the Checkmate System for gamma radiation of in-stent restenosis, coupled with its acquisition of Atrionix, which brings Johnson & Johnson a company with promising technology for treating atrial fibrillation—a condition for which, until now, there has been no effective treatment.

"We're predicting that J&J is going to be the leader in this field for a few years," said William O'Neill, director of cardiology at William Beaumont Hospital, Royal Oak, Michigan.

■ A new contact lens made by Johnson & Johnson promises to clear the fuzzy vision of aging Americans who would rather squint than be caught wearing bifocals. Johnson & Johnson is heavily marketing Acuvue Bifocal disposable contact lenses to the 80 million people who have presbyopia, a vision problem that usually begins shortly after forty. Caused by a loss of flexibility in the eye, presbyopia makes it hard to thread a needle, read a newspaper, or focus on a computer screen. The Acuvue Bifocal lenses are paper-thin and can be worn continuously for seven days or during waking hours for two weeks. Designed with five invisible concentric rings that bring distant and near objects into focus, they allow wearers to shift focus back and forth easily. They cost about $13 to $14 a pair.

■ The company can boast of impressive world leadership in the following ways:
● It is the largest medical-device company.
● It is the eighth-largest pharmaceutical company.
● Johnson & Johnson has the largest:
   Over-the-counter pharmaceutical business.
   Disposable contact lens business.
   Minimally invasive surgical-equipment business.
   Surgical suture business.
   Blood-glucose monitoring business.

Total assets: $31,321 million
Current ratio: 2.54
Common shares outstanding: 3,048 million
Return on 2001 shareholders' equity: 25.0%

		2001	2000	1999	1998	1997	1996	1995	1994
Revenues (millions)		33000	29139	27471	23657	22629	21620	18842	15734
Net income (millions)		5700	4800	4167	3669	3303	2887	2403	2006
Earnings per share		1.92	1.63	1.47	1.34	1.21	1.09	.93	.78
Dividends per share		.70	.62	.55	.49	.43	.37	.32	.29
Price	High	61.0	53.0	53.5	44.9	33.7	27.0	23.1	14.2
	Low	40.3	33.1	38.5	31.7	24.3	20.8	13.4	9.0

GROWTH AND INCOME

Kimberly-Clark Corporation

P. O. Box 619100 □ Dallas, Texas 75261-9100 □ (972) 281-1478 □ Dividend reinvestment plan is available: (800) 730-4001 □ Web site: www.Kimberly-Clark.com □ Ticker symbol: KMB □ S&P rating: A- □ Value Line financial strength rating: A++

Diapers are big business for Kimberly-Clark as well as its archrival, Procter & Gamble. In 2001, Kimberly-Clark launched a redesigned line of Huggies diapers across its European markets, demonstrating the company's intention to bolster its position in the $4.6-billion European diaper market.

Research conducted by Kimberly-Clark in Europe convinced the company that a new approach was needed. It now divides diaper-age children into three groups: "Beginnings" (newborn to three months), "Freedom" (four months or more), and "Adventurers" (twelve months or more). Early indications from market research show that this will be a winner with the European consumer.

"Our new products are drier than our competitors' and are clinically proven to protect against diaper rash," said James Meyer, president of Infant & Child Care for Kimberly-Clark Europe. "More importantly, however, we believe that our new range of products and positioning now matches the way parents see the growth and development of their baby."

Product improvements in the new Huggies diaper range include a softer outer cover and leak guards for the "Beginnings" stage, greater absorbency and dryness for the "Freedom" stage, and a new super-premium, better-fitting diaper for the "Adventurers" stage.

"Since 1996, our diaper sales in Europe have more than doubled," said Mr. Meyer. "And we are confident that the new Huggies product and positioning will continue this volume and market share growth. In fact, Huggies is the fastest-growing of the top fifty non-food grocery brands in the United Kingdom."

Company Profile

Kimberly-Clark is a worldwide manufacturer of a wide range of products for personal, business, and industrial uses. Most of the products are made from natural and synthetic fibers, using advanced technologies in absorbency, fibers, and nonwovens.

The company has manufacturing facilities in forty countries and sales in more than 150. Kimberly-Clark has been one of *Fortune* magazine's "Most Admired" corporations since 1983.

The company's well-known brands include Kleenex facial and bathroom tissue, Huggies diapers and baby-wipes, Pull-Ups training pants, GoodNites underpants, Kotex and New Freedom feminine care products, Depend and Poise incontinence care products, Hi-Dri household towels, Kimguard sterile wrap, Kimwipes industrial wipers, and Classic premium business and correspondence papers.

Results in 2001

- In 2001, sales of $14.5 billion were up 3.9 percent. Excluding the negative impact of currency translation (because of the strong U.S. dollar), sales in 2001 were more than 6 percent above the prior year. Operating profit declined 10.2 percent to $2,364.8 million. However, if unusual items are ignored, operating profit decreased only 3.1 percent. Diluted earnings per share were $3.05, down from $3.31 in 2000, a decline of 7.9 percent. On the other hand, excluding onetime items, earnings per share were $3.27, a very modest decline from $3.32 in 2000.

Wayne R. Sanders, the company's CEO, said, "In 2001, Kimberly-Clark faced the most difficult business environment in recent memory. While everyone at K-C is disappointed with our performance last year, we are confident that we have been doing the right things to drive profitable growth going forward. Comprehensive marketing programs will continue to drive volume growth for our consumer products.

"While the outlook for improvement in Argentina and Brazil remains uncertain, we should benefit from improved market conditions for our business-to-business operations in North America, as the economy recovers. We're building competitive advantage to grow the top- and bottom-lines, and we're focused on increasing cash flow to help fund our growth."

Shortcomings to Bear in Mind

- If Kimberly-Clark is to succeed, it must continually battle against the relentless, determined Procter & Gamble, one of the most innovative and skillful companies in the world.
- Growth in earnings has been rather pedestrian of late. In the 1991–2001 period, earnings per share advanced from $1.59 to $3.27, a compound annual growth rate of 7.5 percent. In the same ten-year stretch, dividends expanded from $.76 a share to $1.10, a growth rate of 3.8 percent.

  However, the all-important payout ratio is indicative of a growth company. The company pays out only a third of its earnings in the form of dividends, thus a generous portion is available to invest in expansion.
- In a 2002 report, Jeremy S. Marks, an analyst with *Value Line Survey*, had

some negative comments. "Kimberly-Clark's 2002 earnings per share are unlikely to grow at management's long-term stated goal, of double-digit annual percentage gains, excluding the $0.18-a-share benefit from an accounting change related to amortization of goodwill. Increased pension expense, as a result of lower returns on retirement assets, is the main reason we figure this target will not be met. In fact, we believe pension expense will be a drag on earnings by about $60 million, or $0.12 a share, in 2002. This compares to 2000 and 2001, when income from pension assets *added* $85 million and $30 million, respectively, to annual profits. On a positive note, we expect lower raw material and energy prices, to shore up the bottom line over the coming twelve months."

Reasons to Buy

- The cornerstone of Kimberly-Clark, according to management, is "brands and technology. Let's take our successful relaunch of Kleenex Cottonelle bathroom tissue. It's a great example of how we're now applying to tissue the same formula that's worked so well for us in personal care and health care—that is, employing technology to deliver superior-performing products that win in the marketplace."

  Using a patented process first commercialized at the company's mill in Villey-Saint-Etienne, France, Kimberly-Clark has produced a tissue with superior bulk, strength, softness, and absorbency—while reducing manufacturing costs. As a result, Kleenex Cottonelle has achieved record profits for the company's premium bathroom tissue business in North America.
- As the world's foremost producer of nonwoven fabrics, Kimberly-Clark also brings sophisticated technology and

cost advantages to bear on its health care products, which include sterile wrap, surgical drapes and gowns, and other protective apparel. In fact, the company holds an impressive 25 percent of the hundreds of patents granted in the nonwoven field since 1995. In the opinion of Kimberly-Clark management, "health care is a business that continues to exceed expectations and offers enormous potential for further growth."

- In the realm of professional health care products, the company has been achieving impressive results, much of it emanating from innovative surgical gowns, drapes, and wraps. The same is true of the performance of Kimberly-Clark's nonwoven materials segment, which supplies versatile fabrics to its consumer-products operations and other businesses at a cost advantage, compared with its competition.

- One of Kimberly-Clark's strengths stems from the leadership position it holds in three core technologies—fibers, absorbency, and nonwovens. It also comes from the company's capacity in high-speed manufacturing and from its constant emphasis on innovation, productivity, and cost reduction.

- Looking at Kimberly-Clark as it is now constituted, it is a much more balanced company. Before the Scott Paper merger and other acquisitions, the company derived almost half of its revenues from diapers and other personal care products. That portion is now a third. Consumer tissue also accounts for about a third of revenues, with the balance coming from a combination of away-from-home and other products.

- Kimberly-Clark has dominance in many of its brands throughout the world. In country after country, the company's position in its product is either number one or number two. In Australia, for instance, its Snugglers diapers and Thick & Thirsty paper towels fall into this group. The same holds true in such countries as Bolivia with Bebito diapers, Intima feminine pads, Sanex paper towels, and a host of other products. Similarly, in Brazil, this distinction includes Monica diapers, Chiffon paper towels, and Neve bathroom tissue; in China, it's Comfort & Beauty feminine pads; in the Netherlands, Page bathroom tissue and paper towels; in Mexico, Kleen Bebe diapers and Petalo bathroom tissue; in Spain, Monbebe diapers; in Germany, Camelia feminine pads and Tampona tampons; in Israel, Titulim diapers, Lily feminine pads, Molett bathroom tissue and paper towels, and Iris paper napkins. The list goes on and on.

- An analyst for *Standard & Poor's Stock Reports* had this to say about Kimberly-Clark in early 2002. "In the fourth quarter (of 2001), sales growth was stronger than we expected; KMB is apparently maneuvering well in the marketplace against the intense competition.

   "Sales at the business-to-business segment, which caters to office buildings, manufacturing facilities, and hotels, were down as expected, but we anticipate gradual improvement here, in line with gains for the economy. With a solid balance sheet, strong cash flows, and a seasoned management team, we expect KMB to perform in line with the broader market, and view the shares as fairly valued."

- An analyst for Argus Research Corporation made these comments at the beginning of 2002. "KMB has loaded up a strong repertoire of new products for 2002, especially in its Personal Care segment. The company is especially excited about an improved version of Pull-Ups post-toddler underpants (called 'training pants,' they are a branch of diapers, essentially), which fit more like underwear than previous models. Surveyed consumers preferred the new version by a ratio of 2:1. Consumers in sample groups already choose Pull-Ups over the top competitor (from Procter & Gamble) by a ratio of 3:2, so we look for KMB to improve its diaper market share in the United States in the next year or two.

"The company's diapers have withstood heavy marketing campaigns for all categories of diapers from Procter & Gamble in European markets this year (2001). They finished the year with a 23 percent market share in diapers in Europe, just as they began it."

Total assets: $14,480 million
Current ratio: 0.94
Common shares outstanding: 521 million
Return on 2001 shareholders' equity: 28.5%

		2001	2000	1999	1998	1997	1996	1995	1994
Revenues (millions)		14524	13982	13007	12298	12547	13149	13789	7364
Net income (millions)		1626	1801	1609	1353	1403	1404	1104	535
Earnings per share		3.27	3.31	2.98	2.45	2.44	2.49	1.98	1.67
Dividends per share		1.10	1.07	1.03	.99	.95	.92	.90	.88
Price	High	72.2	73.3	69.6	59.4	56.9	49.8	41.5	30.0
	Low	52.1	42.0	44.8	35.9	43.3	34.3	23.6	23.5

INCOME

Kimco Realty Corporation

3333 New Hyde Park Road □ New Hyde Park, New York 11042 □ Listed: NYSE □ (516) 869-7197 □ Direct dividend reinvestment plan is available: (877) 453-1506 □ Web site: www.kimcorealty.com □ Ticker symbol: KIM □ S&P rating: Not rated □ Value Line financial strength rating: B++

Milton Cooper, Kimco's chairman, calls the Real Estate Investment Trust (REIT) Modernization Act the "Emancipation Proclamation" of the REIT sector. He believes the Act will let REITs retain a greater percentage of their earnings, as it treats taxable subsidiaries as separate businesses with the ability to retain cash flow. In addition, he notes that the Act should give REITs the ability to compete more effectively with other real estate companies and be more entrepreneurial and aggressive in their expansion and operating strategies.

The law, which became effective January 1, 2001, now enables REITs to own a taxable REIT subsidiary (TRS). The law

permits a REIT to own up to 100 percent of the stock of a TRS, which can provide services to tenants and others without jeopardizing a REIT's ability to avoid paying federal income taxes at the corporate level. To ensure that a REIT remains focused on core real estate operations, the bill contains a size limit on TRSs. Specifically, TRS securities may not exceed 20 percent of a REIT's assets, and income received from a TRS may not exceed 75 percent of a REIT's gross revenues.

Anticipating new opportunities when the REIT Modernization Act became effective on January 1, 2001, Kimco formed a subsidiary that operates as a merchant developer. The new legislation allows the subsidiary to immediately sell properties it develops and receive after-tax profits, instead of holding the assets for at least four years.

Company Profile

Kimco Realty Corporation is the largest publicly traded REIT that owns and operates a portfolio of neighborhood and community shopping centers (measured by gross leasable area). It has interests in 498 properties: 432 shopping centers, two regional malls, fifty-five retail store leases, and other projects totaling 66 million square feet of leasable area in forty-one states.

Since incorporating in 1966, Kimco has specialized in the acquisition, development, and management of well-located centers with strong growth potential. Self-administered and self-managed, the company's focus is to increase the cash flow and enhance the value of its shopping center properties through strategic retenanting, redevelopment, renovation, and expansion. Kimco's goal is also to make selective acquisitions of neighborhood and community shopping centers that have below market-rate leases or other cash flow growth potential.

A substantial portion of Kimco's income consists of rent received under long-term leases, most of which provide for the payment of fixed-base rents and a pro rata share of various expenses. Many of the leases also provide for the payment of additional rent as a percentage of gross sales.

Kimco's neighborhood and community shopping center properties are designed to attract local area customers. They are typically anchored by a supermarket, discount department store, or drugstore, offering day-to-day necessities rather than high-priced luxury items. Among the company's major tenants are Kmart, Wal-Mart, Kohl's, and TJX Companies.

Kimco's core strategy is to acquire older shopping centers carrying below-market rents. The space is then released at much higher rates.

Funds from Operations

REITs are not valued by earnings per share (EPS) but rather by funds from operations (FFO) per share. FFO is calculated by adding net income and depreciation expense and then subtracting profits from the sale of assets. If a REIT pays out 90 percent or more of its taxable income in dividends, it is exempt from paying federal income taxes. FFO per share is in excess of net income because depreciation is added in. This means that a REIT such as Kimco pays out only about 66 percent of its FFO in dividends, with the balance of 34 percent available for acquisitions and improving existing properties.

Shortcomings to Bear in Mind

- The Kmart bankruptcy was a blow for the REIT industry, including Kimco. Kmart, which operates 2,100 stores, rents seventy-five spaces from Kimco and a Kimco-led joint venture. This accounts for about 70 million square feet that Kimco owns. Kmart pays about $55 million in annual rent to Kimco and its joint venture. This represents about 12 percent of Kimco's total rent receipts. Kmart has said that it intends to close 350 stores, thirteen of which are owned by Kimco. In fact, it may consider closing others. A Kimco spokesman said the possibility that Kmart may close another ten Kimco-owned stores is a "fair estimate."

According to an article in The Wall Street Journal, written by Dean Starkman in early 2002, "Kimco is expected to weather the setback comfortably, but its vaunted reputation will sustain a dent."

Mr. Starkman also said, "A big question is who will rent these big boxes and at what rents. Kimco received about $10 a foot for the stores that are closed or are expected to close. Michael W. Mueller, an analyst with CIBC World Markets, estimates that the market for the stores has fallen to about $5 to $7 a foot."

Reasons to Buy

- Despite the recession of 2001, Kimco had a good year. Net income increased 15.4 percent, to $236.5 million. Net income per diluted share increased to $2.16, an increase of 13.1 percent. Funds from operations (FFO) rose 16.4 percent to $295.9 million. On a diluted basis, FFO advanced 11.2 percent, to $2.99 per share.

- In the spring of 2001, Milton Cooper, age seventy-two, announced that he would step down as CEO of Kimco, a company he cofounded forty years ago. However, he was replaced by an experienced executive, David B. Henry, who resigned his post at General Electric. Henry was Chief Investment Officer and Senior Vice President at GE Capital Real Estate, as well as chairman of GE Capital Investment Advisors. David Henry, age fifty-one, joined Kimco as chief investment officer with the expectation that in a year he will become Kimco's CEO.

  Mr. Cooper, who has known Mr. Henry for more than fifteen years, said, "Finding a person to entrust the future of my life's work was not easy, but I believe he is perfectly suited to lead Kimco. His impressive background and vast industry relationships will help Kimco expand its business platform and operating capabilities. He will lead our company to the next level." Although Mr. Cooper will no longer be CEO when Mr. David takes the reins, he will remain with Kimco as chairman.

- Kimco's customers include some of the strongest and most rapidly growing chains in the United States, such as Costco, Home Depot, Circuit City, Best Buy, Ames, Wal-Mart, Value City, Target, Kohl's, and Kmart.

- Nearly all of the company's revenue is contractual. This means that even when a retailer's sales slump, it does not change the rent they must pay to Kimco under the lease agreement or the value of the company's real estate.

- Knowledge of local markets and trends is crucial to success in the real estate sector. Kimco's decentralized asset management staff—situated in such cities as New York, Los Angeles, Chicago, Philadelphia, Dallas, Phoenix, Tampa, Charlotte, and Dayton—provides knowledge of real estate developments that are analyzed by professionals on the scene.

- Kimco's success comes not by accident but as the careful product of business principles that have remained firmly in place since the company was founded in the 1950s. The company invests in properties that are undervalued assets, where management knows it will be able to capitalize on the margin between the price at which it can buy the property and the price at which it can lease it. The average rent on properties in Kimco's portfolio remains below the market, providing the company with significant upside potential.

- Management is clearly aligned with shareholders as indicated by their collective 21.2 percent ownership stake in the company.

- Kimco has had a knack for opportunistic buys. In 1998, it did a sale-leaseback to take control of some 10 million square feet of space of Venture Stores real estate. It seemed like a risky move because Venture Stores was tottering. When the retailer eventually went belly-up, Kimco quickly leased the Venture units to new tenants at even higher rates.

  In a more recent move into the

bankruptcy realm, Kimco was awarded asset designation rights for thirty-four former Hechinger Stores and Builders Square locations at the end of 1999. The rights enable Kimco to direct the disposition of the positions held by the bankrupt estate. Separately, Kimco acquired fee title to seven Hechinger locations and one ground lease position.

- Kimco Realty, in a joint venture in the spring of 2001 with Simon Property Group and the Schottenstein Group, was awarded asset designation rights for all of the real estate property interests of the bankrupt estate of Montgomery Ward LLC and its affiliates. These property interests consist of 250 former Montgomery Ward department stores and other operating real estate assets. All told, the designation rights include 315 separate fee simple and leasehold property interests. These designation rights enable the venture to auction off the properties held by the bankrupt estate. According to Lorraine Mirabella, a writer for the Baltimore Sun, "Kimco has apparently lined up deals with retailers such as Target Corp., Kohl's, May Department Stores Co., and Federated Department Stores, Inc., to take over the sites—many at desirable locations—said David M. Fick, managing director of Legg Mason Wood Walker in Baltimore. Fick said he believes Kimco already has deals for at least half the Wards stores. Fick estimated that the average rents of the Wards stores ranged from $2 to $4 per square foot and could be re-leased in the $6-to-$12-per-square-foot range."

Total assets: $3,112 million
Current ratio: NA
Return on 2001 equity: 12.5%
Common shares outstanding: 96 million

	2001	2000	1999	1998	1997	1996	1995	1994
Rental Income (millions)	469	459	434	339	199	168	143	125
Net income (millions)	237	205	177	122	86	74	52	41
Earnings per share	2.16	1.91	1.64	1.35	1.19	1.07	.89	.78
Funds from operations	2.99	2.69	2.41	2.02	1.75	1.58	1.44	1.32
Dividends per share	1.96	1.83	1.62	1.31	1.15	1.04	.96	.89
Price High	34.1	29.8	27.2	27.8	24.1	23.3	18.8	17.3
Low	27.2	21.8	20.6	22.3	20.2	16.8	15.7	14.7

AGGRESSIVE GROWTH

Eli Lilly and Company

Lilly Corporate Center ▫ Indianapolis, Indiana 46285 ▫ (317) 433-8444 ▫ Direct dividend reinvestment plan is available: (800) 833-8699 ▫ Web site: www.lilly.com ▫ Listed: NYSE ▫ Ticker symbol: LLY ▫ S&P rating: A- ▫ Value Line financial strength rating: A++

Investors who own Eli Lilly have not been happy campers for the last couple of years. The price of the stock has declined from a high of $109 in mid-2000 to a low of $70 in 2001. It should be no surprise that the problem is the loss of patent protection for its flagship drug, Prozac.

Introduced in 1988, Prozac put Lilly on the map. Prozac, known generically as fluoxetine, was the first of a class of antidepressants that work by increasing the brain's supply of serotonin, a neurotransmitter that allows nerve cells in the brain to communicate with each other. It became a blockbuster because its lacks the harsh side effects of earlier depressant medicines, an advancement that spurred more doctors to prescribe it. Consequently, Prozac ended some of the taboo surrounding mental illness.

In the thirteen years that ended in August of 2001, the drug brought in sales of $23 billion, accounting for one-third of the company's revenues. But on that fateful day in 2001, a generic manufacturer, Barr Laboratories, took the ball and started running with it.

In January of 2002, Barr's chairman, Bruce L. Downey, proudly announced, "Since the launch of generic Prozac . . . nearly 80 percent of all prescriptions for Prozac have been filled with the generic product, resulting in a consumer savings of hundreds of millions of dollars." In that span, Lilly's sales of the drug has slowed to a trickle.

Although Lilly was well aware that its bonanza would not last forever, it put up a gallant struggle to keep its patent. Going back to 1996, Lilly sued generic drug makers for patent infringement, when rivals first sought FDA approval to make a generic form of Prozac. On the other hand, Barr Labs was equally dogged in its determination to wrest control away from its prestigious rival.

More recently, Barr and other generic firms took Lilly to court, insisting that it had improperly double-patented Prozac in a last-ditch effort to keep itself out of the clutches of the copycat companies. The Court of Appeals sided with Barr and its pals. Not about to give up, Lilly appealed to the U.S. Supreme Court. But that was the end of the road, since the high court did not care to pursue the matter.

Whenever a company loses patent protection on a major drug, it's not good news. Some analysts predicted that Lilly would be forced to cast its lot with another drug company, in order to stay afloat. Lilly vehemently rejected that alternative.

In view of the dismal performance of Lilly's stock in recent years, it's obvious that investors are convinced that Lilly is in deep trouble and will not be able to reward them in the manner to which they are accustomed.

They could be wrong. In fact, they *probably* are wrong.

Lilly, under the able and spirited leadership of CEO Sidney Taurel, only fifty-three years old and a thirty-one year veteran at the company, is dead set on showing the world that Lilly will emerge from the fray stronger than ever. A host of new products churned out by a huge research staff—and backed up by a dedicated and growing sales staff—are factors to bear in mind the next time you decide to avoid buying a few shares of Lilly.

Company Profile

Eli Lilly is one of the world's foremost health care companies. With a solid dedication to research and development, Lilly is a leader in the development of ethical drugs—those available on prescription.

Lilly is well known for such drugs as Prozac (to treat depression); a number of antibiotics such as Ceclor, Vancocin, Keflex, and Lorabid; and insulin and other diabetic care items. Some of its other important drugs include Gemzar (to treat cancer of the lung and pancreas); Evista (to treat and prevent osteoporosis); ReoPro (a drug used to prevent adverse side effects from angioplasty procedures); Zyprexa (a breakthrough treatment for schizophrenia and bipolar disorder); Dobutrex (for congestive heart failure); Axid (a medication that reduces excess stomach acid); and Sarafem (for the treatment of premenstrual dysphoric disorder).

Lilly also has a stake in animal health and agricultural products.

Like most drug companies, Lilly is active abroad and does business in 120 countries.

Shortcomings to Bear in Mind

- Analysts point out that new drug markets are inherently unpredictable. Says Mara Goldstein, an analyst with CIBC World Markets, "Sometimes products look good on paper, but they don't turn out that way in reality." In 1998, for instance, the company launched Evista—which can prevent and reverse osteoporosis in older women—in the hopes that it would become an overnight success. But first-year sales came in a less-than-spectacular $144 million. Mr. Taurel said it was harder than expected to convince women to buy the drug before they have symptoms of the degenerative bone disease. Michael Arndt, a writer for *Business-Week*, said, "But after Lilly tweaked its marketing effort, the drug took off, with sales expected to top $700 million this year (2001). It is a blockbuster after all."

- In early 2002, Argus Research Corporation had some reservations concerning Lilly's future. The analyst said, "Though we do not question whether Lilly will be able to do this, as the company's pipeline is one of the industry's best, the question for investors is, when is this likely to occur? Lilly has suggested that strong growth will likely resume sometime in the middle of 2003. However, this is dependent on a number of factors, including what proportion of Lilly's late-stage pipeline products pass the muster with the various regulatory agencies on their medical merits, and whether the company can resolve its seemingly mounting manufacturing difficulties."

In response to the latter concern, Mr. Taurel said, "Our number one priority is to address all the manufacturing issues raised by the FDA to its satisfaction in order to bring our innovative new products to market as quickly as possible."

Reasons to Buy

- Despite its loss of sales from Prozac in the latter half of 2001, Lilly had some major accomplishments in that fateful year. "Our sales performance, excluding Prozac, continued to be impressive, with 15 percent growth in the fourth quarter and 17 percent for the year 2001," said Mr. Taurel. "This strong sales growth continued to be driven by our five best-in-class growth products, Zyprexa, Gemzar, Actos, Humalog and Evista—which grew 32 percent for the quarter and 36 percent for the year."

- Mr. Taurel vowed not to be painted into a corner again. "The situation we had in the mid-1990s, of having 35 percent of our sales dependent on Prozac, won't repeat itself." Eight new drugs are in the pipeline for introduction in the 2002–2004 period. According to an article in *BusinessWeek*, "Lilly has the financial muscle to pay the $1 billion it can take to bring out a new drug. Lilly also has an 11,500-member sales force to push new pharmaceuticals." Sales are important, to be sure, but research is the real key. Again, according to *BusinessWeek*, Mr. Taurel "furiously ramped up new-drug development after becoming CEO and chairman in 1998. He increased the research and development budget about 30 percent, to more than $2.2 billion, hired 700 scientists in the last year (2000) alone, and in a search for the next blockbuster, ordered Lilly's 6,900 researchers not to bother with any drug unlikely to top $500 million in annual sales. The payoff: Lilly now has a medicine cabinet stocked full of promising new drugs, including treatments for schizophrenia and for sepsis—a potentially fatal form of bacterial infection."

■ Here are some of the drugs the company is banking on to restore its growth pattern in the years ahead.

Cialis

• Cialis, for the treatment of erectile dysfunction, is scheduled for introduction in late 2002. Cialis will lock horns with Pfizer's blockbuster, Viagra. Erectile dysfunction affects 30 million men in the United States alone.

  The company has joined forces with Icos Corporation whose pill, Cialis, has been successfully tested on 212 men. Research demonstrated that Cialis enhanced erections for 88 percent of men, compared with 28 percent for those taking a placebo.

  Alex Zisson, a pharmaceutical analyst with Chase H&Q, said, "Cialis looks very, very similar to Viagra. There is no market, especially a billion-dollar market, that is fully satisfied by one drug. The second and third drugs usually expand the market."

Atomoxetine

• Atomoxetine (also known as tomoxetine) is a nonstimulant to treat attention deficit disorder in children, for introduction in late 2002.

  Among hard-to-treat diseases is an affliction called attention deficit disorder, or ADD for short. ADD is often characterized by an inability to concentrate and may also include aggression and hyperactivity. Up until recently, the drug used most often was Ritalin (produced by Novartis AG), which has its share of side effects, notably its tendency to be a stimulant. The drug is also available in generic form, methylphenidate. Because of Ritalin's side effects, researchers have been trying to find a treatment for ADD that doesn't involve the use of stimulants. Now, it appears that Lilly has come up with such a drug—it's called tomoxetine. Researchers say that tomoxetine doesn't trigger sleeplessness and has relatively little tendency to suppress appetites.

  "This will open windows for patients who would otherwise not be medicated," said Joseph Biederman, the chief of pediatric psychopharmacology at Massachusetts General Hospital in Boston, who ran a study on tomoxetine in 2000.

  "The market could easily exceed $1 billion for a product like tomoxetine," said Hemant K. Shah, an independent medical-industry analyst. "Ritalin has such a bad name that it would not be that difficult to convert people to a nonstimulant."

Duloxetine

• Duloxetine is used to treat depression and could take up the slack from Prozac. Duloxetine is scheduled to go to market in late 2002. In an article appearing in *The Boston Globe* in December of 2001, the author, Liz Kowalczyk, said, "While Prozac and drugs like it increase the amount of the chemical serotonin in the brain, duloxetine and Effexor enrich the supply of *two* important mood-boosting chemicals, or neurotransmitters: serotonin and norepinephrine. Because these drugs have two different mechanisms of action, rather than one, doctors believe they may be more effective than Prozac-like drugs at improving patients' moods and might help more seriously depressed patients." Effexor, a drug sold by Wyeth, has this dual action and has been on the market since 1994, but is only recently been gaining popularity. Sales of Effexor in 2001 were $1.2 billion.

Xigris

- In November of 2001, the FDA gave the green light to Xigris, a drug used to treat septic infections. Xigris, according to Wall Street analysts, could become a blockbuster drug with annual sales of more than $1 billion. In a large clinical study, Xigris reduced deaths from severe sepsis by nearly 20 percent. In the words of Thomas M. Burton, writing for *The Wall Street Journal*, "As the first medication to treat this severe infection of the blood, Xigris has been expected to carry a hefty price tag, and Lilly estimates that the amount of Xigris given to a typically sized patient will be about $6,800."

The Journal reporter went on to say, "Sepsis often occurs in surgical and cancer patients and, in its most severe form, carries a mortality rate of about 30 percent. While it can be treated with antibiotics, the clotting and organ failure often can kill patients before the antibiotics get a chance to take effect."

Additional drugs in the Lilly pipeline include the following:

- Forteo, a bone-building agent to reverse osteoporosis, is scheduled to go on the market in 2002.
- Olanzipine and Fluoxetine, a combination used for treatment-resistant depression and psychotic depression, will seek FDA approval sometime in 2002.
- Alimta is used for the treatment of mesothelioma, a rare lung cancer linked to asbestos exposure. Lilly

expects to submit it to the FDA in mid-2002.

- PKC beta inhibitor is for the treatment of diabetic macular edema and diabetic retinopathy, the leading cause of blindness in people under the age of sixty-five. Lilly expects to seek FDA approval in 2003.

Diabetes Treatment

- As the developer of the first insulin product and one of the world's major suppliers of insulin, Lilly has long been a global leader in the field. But diabetes, which affects more than 100 million people worldwide, continues to cause severe long-term complications, suffering, lost productivity, and death.

For many patients with this disease, diabetes is also inconvenient. Diabetics have to check their blood glucose several times a day. They may have to give themselves one or more shots of insulin. And they must take insulin at least thirty minutes before a meal or risk severe complications.

Lilly believes that it has an answer that gives patients with diabetes a better quality of life—and a good deal more convenience. Humalog acts faster than traditional insulin to control blood-glucose levels. Patients take it right before a meal, compared with thirty to forty-five minutes before with current products. Humalog provides them with more freedom, better health, and fewer complications.

- During 2001, Zyprexa, Lilly's breakthrough drug for schizophrenia and bipolar mania, became the company's first product to surpass $3 billion in annual sales. This was a noteworthy accomplishment in view of its launch just five years ago and especially when coupled with increasing competition in the antipsychotic and mood-stabilization markets.

Total assets: $14,691 million
Current ratio: 1.46
Common shares outstanding: 1,124 million
Return on 2001 shareholders' equity: 39%

	2001	2000	1999	1998	1997	1996	1995	1994
Revenues (millions)	11543	10953	10003	9237	8518	7346	6764	5712
Net income (millions)	3014	2905	2721	2098	1774	1524	1307	1269
Earnings per share	2.76	2.65	2.28	1.94	1.57	1.33	1.15	1.09
Dividends per share	1.12	1.04	.92	.80	.74	.69	.66	.63
Price　High	95.0	109.0	97.8	91.3	70.4	40.2	28.5	16.6
Low	70.0	54.0	60.6	57.7	35.6	24.7	15.6	11.8

AGGRESSIVE GROWTH

Lockheed Martin Corporation

6801 Rockledge Drive ▫ Bethesda, MD 20817 ▫ (301) 897-6584 ▫ Dividend reinvestment plan is not available ▫ Web site: www.lockheedmartin.com ▫ Listed: NYSE ▫ Ticker symbol: LMT ▫ S&P rating: B ▫ Value Line financial strength rating: B

Capping a four-year, $1 billion Concept Demonstration Program, the U.S. Department of Defense selected Lockheed Martin (along with its subcontractors) over Boeing to receive up to $200 billion to build a fleet of Joint Strike Force fighters. Over the next twenty-five years, Lockheed Martin will design and build nearly 3,000 Joint Strike Fighters, a single-engine, supersonic, multirole, stealth aircraft, which will be known as the F-35. Announced in October of 2001, the contract was the largest ever awarded by the Pentagon.

The new contract positions Lockheed Martin to dominate the domestic and foreign jet fighter markets for decades to come. Scheduled to enter service in 2008, the new F-35 will replace a number of older jets, including the F-14 and F-16 fighters, the A-10, the AV-8 Harrier, and the F/A-18. To save the costs of developing more specialized planes, each of the services will receive different versions of the Joint Strike Fighters. For instance, the Navy model will be able to operate from an aircraft carrier, while the one developed for the Marines will be able to take off vertically. What's more, Lockheed will also produce a version of the F-35 for the U.K. Royal Air Force and the Royal Navy.

All variants will be supersonic and stealthy (radar-evading), and equipped with cutting-edge avionics designed to enhance the pilot's situational awareness. Range and payload will be markedly greater than those of today's fighters. Finally, the Joint Strike Fighter is designed to require significantly less maintenance and support, cutting long-term ownership costs by half.

Using highly advanced manufacturing methods that dramatically reduce the time, parts, and labor required to build each aircraft, the Lockheed Martin team will fly the first test aircraft in 2005 and deliver the first operational F-35 in 2008.

Company Profile

Lockheed Martin was created in 1995 when Lockheed Corporation merged with Martin Marietta. The new stock began trading on March 16, 1995. Lockheed Martin has a stake in the operation of advanced technology systems, products, and services. Its products and services range from aircraft, spacecraft, and launch vehicles to missiles, electronics, information systems, and telecommunications.

Areas of concentration include space and missile systems, electronics, aeronautics, and information systems. Among the company's well-known products are the following: F-16, F-22, F-117A aircraft, Trident ballistic missile systems, the C-130 military transport, and Titan launch vehicles. The company operates in five principal business segments.

Systems Integration

Lockheed Martin's Systems Integration segment has a stake in the design, development, and integration of complex systems for global defense, civil government, and commercial markets. Core operations include undersea warfare, surface warfare, and land surveillance systems; tactical missiles, air defense systems, and fire-control and sensor systems; information superiority systems; simulation and training systems; air traffic-management systems; aerospace systems and platform integration; business system solutions; and distribution technologies. The latter includes automated material handling solutions for postal systems and commercial customers.

Space Systems

Lockheed Martin's Space Systems segment designs, develops, engineers, and produces civil, commercial, and military space systems. Major products include spacecraft, space launch vehicles, and human space systems, as well as their supporting ground systems and services and strategic fleet ballistic missiles.

Aeronautics

This Lockheed Martin segment is engaged in the design, research, and development and production of combat aircraft, surveillance/command systems, reconnaissance systems, and platform systems. Major products include the F-16 fighter, the F-22 fighter, and the C-130J tactical airlift aircraft.

Technology Services

This Lockheed Martin unit provides a wide variety of management, engineering, scientific, logistic, and information services to federal agencies and other customers.

Global Telecommunications

Global Telecommunications has a stake in communications services and advanced technology solutions through three lines of business. Enterprise Solutions provides telecommunications services, managed networks, and information technology solutions in the United States and international markets. Satellite Services provides global fixed and mobile satellite services.

Finally, Systems and Technology designs, builds, and integrates satellite gateways, and provides systems integration services for telecommunications networks.

Shortcomings to Bear in Mind

■ Standard & Poor's casts some doubt on Lockheed's long-term future. In November of 2001, its analyst said, "In late 2001, the Pentagon chose LMT's design for the potentially enormous Joint Strike Fighter program. The Pentagon will initially purchase 21 JSF's over the next ten years, at a cost of $19 billion. We estimate this phase of the contract will generate middling 6 percent to 8 percent profit margins during this phase. If the program goes into full production, profit margins could rise to 15 percent." However, there are no guarantees that Congress will approve funding of the entire projected $220 billion, twenty-seven-year, 2,800-plane program.

- On November 16, 2001, *The Wall Street Journal* reported, "As the Bush administration pushes to deploy a national missile defense quickly, a key satellite system under development by Lockheed Martin Corp. is as much as $2 billion over cost and running almost three years behind schedule, according to company and government officials.

  "The Space-Based Infrared System-High, known as SBIRS-High, is a key element of what has been previously known as the National Missile Defense System, a large defense mechanism that would launch ground-based interceptors to impede an enemy missile attack. While the Pentagon now is looking at connecting a number of small and large missile-defense systems into a broad defensive plan, SBIRS-High still would be the early-warning system that would first detect that a missile had been launched at America. It would replace the twenty-five-year-old satellites currently serving this function."

- In the 1992–2001 period, earnings per share have bounced up and down, but they have made no net progress, slipping from $1.66 to $1.45. Dividends in the same span have also shown very little to write home about. The dividend in 1992 was $.52, which advanced to $.88 in 1999 and was subsequently cut in half, where it stands now.

Reasons to Buy

- In early 2002, a U.S. Air Force Milstar II military communications satellite lifted off from Cape Canaveral Air Station, Florida, aboard a Titan IVB launch vehicle. Lockheed Martin Space Systems Company built the satellite and launch vehicle. The satellite, designated Milstar II, is the U.S. Department of Defense's most technologically advanced telecommunications satellite. It is the second to carry the Medium Data Rate (MDR) payload, which can process data at speeds of 1.5 megabits per second. The Air Force transitioned to the Block II configuration with an earlier successful launch of the first Milstar II satellite. The Milstar Block II system offers a variety of enhanced communications features for the U.S. military, including added security through the use of specially designed antennas and faster data-rate transitions for users.

- In early 2002, Lockheed Martin and Boeing were chosen to team up to create a multibillion-dollar U.S. drive to build missile shields. As comanagers of the so-called national team being shaped by the Pentagon, the two companies—the two largest domestic military contractors—will have key roles in more effectively meshing the dozen or so existing missile defense programs.

  Boeing will take the lead in defining the architecture of a planned multilayered shield that could involve systems based on land, ships, in space, and on modified Boeing 747 aircraft. A second group, led by Lockheed Martin, will put the overlapping systems to work through integrated battle-management and command-control software.

  President Bush signed a defense funding bill into law in early 2002 that includes $8 billion for missile defense development to meet what he called a growing threat of intercontinental ballistic missile attack from such "rogue" states as North Korea, Iran, and Iraq.

Total assets: $27,654 million
Current ratio: 1.11
Common shares outstanding: 441 million
Return on 2001 shareholders' equity: 1.2%

		2001	2000	1999	1998	1997	1996	1995	1994
Revenues (millions)		23990	25329	25530	26266	28069	26875	22853	22906
Net income (millions)		79	432	575	1184	1300	1205	1118	955
Earnings per share		0.18	1.07	1.41	3.11	3.05	2.70	2.50	2.19
Dividends per share		.44	.44	.88	.82	.80	.80	.67	.57
Price	High	53.0	37.6	46.0	58.9	56.7	48.3	39.8	NA
	Low	31.0	16.5	16.4	41.0	39.1	36.5	25.0	NA

CONSERVATIVE GROWTH

Lowe's Companies, Incorporated

1605 Curtis Bridge Road ◻ Post Office Box 1111 ◻ Wilkesboro, North Carolina 28656 ◻ (336) 658-5239 ◻ Direct Dividend reinvestment plan available: (877) 282-1174 ◻ Web site: www.lowes.com ◻ Fiscal years end Friday closest to January 31 of following year ◻ Listed: NYSE ◻ Ticker symbol: LOW ◻ S&P rating: A+ ◻ Value Line financial strength rating: A+

In 1946, a young veteran of World War II, H. Carl Buchan, returned home to the town of North Wilkesboro to resume a role as half owner of a hardware store his wife's father incorporated in 1921. Besides miscellaneous hardware and some building materials, North Wilkesboro Hardware stocked produce and groceries, snuff, dry goods, notions, harnesses and horse collars.

Ten years later, Buchan bought the North Wilkesboro Hardware Company from brother-in-law James Lowe, with a vision of creating a chain of hardware stores. Buchan sold out all the inventory except heavy hardware and building materials. During the postwar building boom, he established a reputation for Lowe's Low Prices by cutting out wholesalers and dealing directly with manufacturers.

Lowe's soon grew into a regional chain of stores selling building supplies and big-ticket consumer durables. Although the company did have some retail customers, the majority of business came from professional contractors who built homes. The typical Lowe's store was a free-standing building situated near railroad tracks at the edge of a southern town.

With the growth of the do-it-yourself, home-improvement, and repair industry, it occurred to the company that every homeowner was a potential Lowe's customer if "we could bring ourselves up to speed as retailers. Throughout the eighties, we nurtured the growth of our homeowner customer franchise, enlarging our sales floors and expanding our merchandise offering. Consumers responded enthusiastically, and by the end of the decade, Lowe's was gaining a reputation as a home-center retailer, with a wide variety of products, friendly service, and unbeatable prices."

In the late 1980s, Lowe's began transforming from a chain of conventionally sized units into its current 150,000-square-foot prototype, which is the largest in the industry. Lowe's continues its most aggressive expansion plan ever, thriving in metropolitan markets with superstores in half of the nation's top twenty-five most populated cities.

Company Profile

Lowe's Companies, Inc. is the second-largest domestic retailer of home-improvement products serving the do-it-yourself and commercial business customers. (Home Depot is number one.) Capitalizing on a growing number of U. S. households (about 100 million), the company has expanded from fifteen stores in 1962 and now operates more than 744 stores in forty-two states. Lowe's competes in the highly fragmented, $300-billion, home-improvement industry.

The company sells more than 40,000 home-improvement products, including plumbing and electrical products, tools, building materials, hardware, outdoor hard lines, appliances, lumber, nursery and gardening products, millwork, paint, sundries, cabinets, and furniture. Lowe's has often been listed as one of the "100 Best Companies to Work for in America."

The company obtains its products from about 6,500 merchandise vendors from around the globe. In most instances, Lowe's deals directly with foreign manufacturers, rather than third-party importers.

In order to maintain appropriate inventory levels in stores and to enhance efficiency and distribution, Lowe's operates six highly automated, efficient, state-of-the-art regional distribution centers (RDCs). RDCs are strategically situated in North Carolina, Georgia, Ohio, Indiana, Pennsylvania, Washington, and Texas.

In 2000, the company broke ground in Findlay, Ohio, on an $80-million regional distribution center. Completed in October of 2001, the 1.25-million-square-foot facility employs 500 people and supplies products to some 100 stores throughout the lower Great Lakes region.

Lowe's serves both retail and commercial business customers. Retail customers are primarily do-it-yourself homeowners and others buying for personal and family use. Commercial business customers include building contractors, repair and remodeling contractors, electricians, landscapers, painters, plumbers, and commercial building maintenance professionals.

During 1999, Lowe's acquired Eagle Hardware & Garden, a thirty-six-store chain of home-improvement and garden centers in the West. The acquisition accelerated Lowe's' West Coast expansion and provided a stepping stone for the company into ten new states and a number of key metropolitan markets.

In recent years, the company has been transforming its store base from a chain of small stores into a chain of home-improvement warehouses. The current prototype store (the largest in the industry) has 150,000 square feet of sales floor and another 35,000 dedicated to lawn and garden products. The company is in the midst of its most aggressive expansion in company history. Lowe's is investing $2 billion a year and opening more than one store each week.

Shortcomings to Bear in Mind

- Despite owning 750 stores in forty states, Lowe's is still struggling to expand beyond its Southeastern roots and build a national brand. One problem is its name. Unlike Home Depot, the name does not make you think of home improvement. In fact, it might make you think of a theater chain—Loews Cineplex Entertainment Corporation of New York. The company's name, moreover, might also bring to mind Loews Corporation, a diversified concern with a stake in insurance, Lorillard cigarettes, Bulova watches, hotels, and offshore drilling.

In 2001, Lowe's decided it was time to overcome these misconceptions, launching its first network advertising campaign. In January of 2001, it began running commercials on four major networks during such prime-time shows as "Law & Order," "Who Wants to be a Millionaire?", and "Everybody Loves Raymond."

Without naming its competitor, the ads portray Lowe's as a well-lit, organized alternative to cluttered warehouse stores that frustrate shoppers. For instance, one thirty-second spot shows a woman wandering aimlessly and begins, "Yesterday, finding anything at a home-improvement store meant searching for hours. Getting dirty and lost. People accepted this. Today, there's Lowe's."

Reasons to Buy

- Lowe's ended fiscal 2001 with a flourish. The fourth quarter was particularly impressive, as profits jumped 55 percent. Part of the good tidings came to attributed to the weather in that span. Warmer temperatures in many regions prompted consumers to go outside to "slap on a fresh coat of paint or spruce up their back desk. "Clearly, the weather helped them and the entire industry," said Wayne Hood, an analyst with Prudential Securities. "I was out cutting my grass in December."

  The CEO of Lowe's, Robert Tillman, had another explanation. "This is a clear sign U. S. consumer spending, at least for products in and around the home, remains strong despite general weakness in the economy."

  Still another explanation might be that Lowe's benefited from opening more warehouse stores in major metropolitan markets, where initial sales are generally 10 percent higher than the company's store average. Some of these new metro stores, such as ones in the Boston area or New York's Long Island, are on track for more than $50 million in annual sales. The company average is about $33 million per store. Lowe's said about 65 percent of its 123 new stores for 2002 will be in metropolitan markets with a population exceeding 500,000. Lowe's had 744 stores in forty-two states at the end of 2001.

- Looking ahead to 2002, the company outlined its expectations:
  - Lowe's expects to open 123 stores in 2002, reflecting total square footage growth of 18 percent.
  - Total sales are expected to increase between 18 percent and 19 percent.
  - Gross margins are expected to improve twenty to thirty basis points. (One percent equals 100 basis points).

- To enhance its extensive line of national brands, such as DeWalt, Armstrong, American Standard, Olympic, Owens Corning, Sylvania, Harbor Breeze, and Delta, the company is teaming up with vendors to offer preferred brands exclusive to Lowe's. These include Laura Ashley, Sta-Green, Troy-Bilt, Alexander Julian, among others.

  In categories where preferred brands are not available, Lowe's has created its own brands, including Kobalt tools, Reliabilt doors and windows, and Top Choice lumber.

- Lowe's advanced to the number two spot in domestic appliance sales in 2000. However, the company is the number one seller of appliances among home-improvement centers. In its stores, Lowe's features such leading brands as Whirlpool, KitchenAid, Frigidaire, Maytag, Jenn-Air, and General Electric.

- During the 1991–2001 period, Lowe's racked up an explosive record of growth, as its earnings per share shot up from $0.09 to $1.30, a compound annual growth rate of 30.6 percent. In the same ten-year span, dividends, although very modest, advanced from $0.03 to $0.075, for a much-less-impressive growth rate of 9.6 percent. Obviously, you would not buy this stock for current income, since the yield is a tiny fraction of one percent.

- In the spring of 2002, Waverly, one of the premier home furnishing brands became exclusively available at Lowe's stores. "Waverly Home Classics" consist of a variety of classic Waverly designs in wall covering, with complementary window treatments and drapery hardware. "Our customers are looking for coordinated solutions for their home-decorating projects," said Melissa Birdsong, Lowe's director of trend forecasting and design. "The Waverly brand is among the most recognized in home decor and is an outstanding addition to Lowe's assortment of exclusive premier brands."

Total assets: $13,736 million
Current ratio: 1.67
Common shares outstanding: 774 million
Return on 2001 shareholders' equity: 15%

	2001	2000	1999	1998	1997	1996	1995	1994
Revenues (Millions)	22111	18779	15905	12245	10137	8600	7075	6110
Net Income (Millions)	1023	810	673	482	357	292	226	224
Earnings per share	1.30	1.06	.90	.68	.51	.43	.34	.35
Dividends per share	.075	.07	.06	.06	.06	.05	.05	.05
Price high	48.9	33.6	33.2	26.1	12.3	10.9	9.7	10.3
low	21.9	17.1	21.5	10.8	7.9	7.2	6.5	6.7

INCOME

The Lubrizol Corporation

29400 Lakeland Boulevard □ Wickliffe, Ohio 44092-2298 □ (440) 347-1252 □ Direct dividend reinvestment plan is available: (877) 573-3998 □ Web sites: www.lubrizol.com □ Listed: NYSE □ Ticker symbol: LZ □ S&P rating: B+ □ Value Line financial strength rating: B+

Lubrizol leads the industry in developing solutions to complex environmental and lubrication questions. The company's PuriNOx Performance Systems, for instance, is among the latest in a long line of products designed to make the world a cleaner, healthier place.

PuriNOx is a low-emission water-blend fuel product combining additive chemistry with a specialized blend unit. This clean air technology makes it easier to reduce particulate matter and nitrogen oxide emissions. By substituting this unique low-emission fuel technology for commercial diesel fuel, both old and new equipment and vehicles can immediately begin improving air quality. Field trials under way in 2001 in areas like Hong Kong and the Houston ship channel will help advance this technology.

In the spring of 2001, Lubrizol and Laketran, a mass-transit provider in Northeast Ohio, announced air-emissions reductions achieved during a six-month market demonstration in which ten Laketran buses ran on Lubrizol's PuriNOx fuel in regular service on area highways. The buses demonstrated up to 32 percent reductions in nitrogen oxide emissions and between 26 percent and 55 percent reductions in particulate emissions, compared with conventional diesel fuel.

PuriNOx is a stable blend of conventional diesel fuel, purified water, and a proprietary Lubrizol additive package. The company designed the new fuel in conjunction with Caterpillar, Inc., as an alternative to conventional diesel fuel for vehicle fleets and stationary equipment.

PuriNOx is a revolutionary system,

but it represents just one of the company's fluid technologies for a better world. Lubrizol's interests range from defoamers, which improve performances of coatings, metalworking fluids, and lubricants, to alternative fuel technologies to reduce or eliminate harmful emissions or greenhouse gases.

Company Profile

Lubrizol was founded by six men with an idea that set the stage for every Lubrizol product that followed. From the beginning, the company recognized a problem, used technology to solve it, and developed a product that was better than anything else available.

Next, Lubrizol found a way to make it easy for its customers to use the product. The result of that first idea was a product called Lubri-Graph. Designed to eliminate the squeak caused by the leaf springs in early model cars, it was sold with a ten-gallon pressurized drum dispenser that made it easy to apply.

Lubrizol is a fluid technology company concentrating on high-performance chemicals, systems, and services for transportation and industry. Lubrizol develops, produces, and sells specialty additive packages and related equipment used in transportation and industrial finished lubricants. The company creates its products through the application of advanced chemical and mechanical technologies to enhance the performance, quality, and value of the customer products in which they are used.

Lubrizol groups its product lines into two operating segments: chemicals for transportation, and chemicals for industry. Chemicals for transportation make up about 82 percent of consolidated revenues and 85 percent of segment pretax operating profit.

Lubrizol products can be found in a variety of markets, including coatings, inks, compressor lubricants, and metalworking

fluids. The company is also combining the expertise of its equipment-related businesses with chemicals for transportation and industry to provide integrated solutions for lubrication or environmental problems.

Highlights of 2001

- Revenues for 2001 were the highest in Lubrizol's history, up 4 percent over 2000 on record shipment volumes. In the words of CEO William G. Bares, "Our track record of strong cash flow continued: year-end cash flow from operations approached $200 million. However, we were disappointed that earnings of $1.84 per share for the year fell a bit below 2000 results and below our early 2001 expectations, largely due to higher raw material costs."

Mr. Bares went on to say, "In running the business, Lubrizol's fluid technologies for transportation segment tends to be more recession-resistant than many other manufacturing industries—especially in the early stages of economic downturns when vehicle mileage and maintenance, as well as product shipments, tend to remain fairly stable.

"Nevertheless, the turbulent world economy affected our results for this segment in 2001. Weakness in the Asian economy affected our transportation business all year. In addition, from September onward, demand weakened in North America and Europe.

"Compared to our transportation segment, fluid technologies for industry is more susceptible to manufacturing cycles. Our 2001 segment results show the effect of the economy on our industrial business.

"However, these setbacks were offset by new engine oil revenues we gained early in the year as a result of our industry leadership. Additionally, revenues from the late-2000 consolidation of our China joint venture compensated for market contraction in the rest of Asia."

Shortcomings to Bear in Mind

- In the 1991–2001 period, earnings per share made no progress. Rather, earnings per share were basically flat, inching up from $1.79 to $1.84—hardly a record that would lead you to regard Lubrizol as a growth company. In the same ten-year period, dividends per share moved ahead, from $0.77 to $1.04, a very modest growth rate of 3.1 percent. However, the dividend yield is far above most other stocks, which leads me to think this stock should be considered suitable for investors seeking dependable income.
- Management believes that the global growth rate for lubricant additives is about 1 percent per year. Due to changing industry market forces, such as improved engine design and longer drain intervals, the company does not expect the annual growth rate to exceed 1 percent in the future.

Reasons to Buy

- Lubrizol chemical products all have one thing in common. They do their work in the molecular world, wherever surfaces interact. It doesn't matter whether the surfaces are the parts of a diesel engine or paint on a wall. Lubrizol chemicals are designed to slip between them, helping things to work better. Lubrizol chemicals enhance performance. They improve the operating efficiency of equipment and extend its useful life. For the company's customers, that means lower maintenance costs and a reduction in scheduled downtime.
- Improving performance and extending equipment life is one part of the equation. The other is the increased demand

placed on chemical manufacturers by environmental regulations and worker health and safety. These are top priorities in all of the company's markets, so they are top priorities for Lubrizol. In addition to improving operating efficiency, Lubrizol chemicals also reduce harmful emissions. They extend the useful life of performance fluids, which results in less waste fluid for disposal. The company's antimist technologies, with applications in metalworking, coatings, inks, and the transportation industry, help keep work environments cleaner and safer and save energy and maintenance costs.

- Italy's third-largest fuel and lubricant marketer, Kuwait Petroleum Italia SpA (KPIT), is introducing Lubrizol's PuriNOx to the Italian market under the brand Q White. During 2001, KPIT leased and installed three of Lubrizol's patented blending units required to mix the finished, low-emission fuel. With no need for hardware add-ons, engine modifications, or replacements, the technology helps protect the environment by reducing smog-forming nitrogen oxides and particulate matter. "Needless to say, Lubrizol is extremely enthusiastic about this new development, which will enable us to make our low-emission diesel alternative available to the Italian market," said Alex Psaila, European PuriNOx Business Manager for Lubrizol. "The fact that KPIT is such a major marketer devoting substantial resources to marketing the technology bodes well for Europeans who are putting forth the effort to improve air quality. It will be a large-scale initiative."
- Through an exclusive agreement with Clean Diesel Technologies, Inc. (CDTI), Lubrizol became a licensed distributor and blender of CDTI's patented Platinum Plus fuel additive technology in the spring of 2001. Platinum Plus is a

platinum and cerium catalyst that, when mixed with diesel fuel, facilitates the combustion of carbon-rich particulate (soot) into carbon dioxide, thus removing particulate from the filter. Typically, particulate will combust on its own, but this only happens at temperatures higher than those generally found in diesel exhaust systems. Platinum Plus, however, lowers the temperature of particulate combustion, allowing soot to be "burned off" at normal exhaust temperatures.

■ There are two paths to growth. One is internally focused, building on long-established competencies and expanding existing strengths and technology portfolios into new market areas. However, according to Jack Kimes, president of Gateway Additive Company and Lubrizol's Global general manager for its metalworking segment, "The other path is through acquisitions. Internal growth is important to Lubrizol, but it will not be enough for us to reach the ambitious financial targets we have set. That's why we are aggressively pursuing acquisitions that are closely aligned with our strengths and vision."

Mr. Kimes went on to say, "The Gateway Additive Company was the first metalworking business Lubrizol acquired. Others, including Becker Chemie and the metalworking additive business of Alox Corporation, soon followed."

In 2001, said Mr. Kimes, "We made an acquisition, ROSS Chem, Inc., that opened up an important new product area for us. ROSS Chem specializes in defoamers, which are chemical products used in metalworking, coatings, inks, and textiles. These products are critical to fluid performance. The ROSS Chem product line complements existing Lubrizol technology and adds another dimension to our product offering."

■ In 2002, Lubrizol continued its acquisition strategy and acquired Chemron Corporation. Lubrizol and Chemron market complementary surfactant technologies to the coatings, metalworking, and oilfield markets. The acquisition extended Lubrizol's business into high-growth surfactants markets where it does not currently complete, including personal care products as well as industrial and institutional cleaners.

Total assets: $1,662 million
Current ratio: 2.92
Common shares outstanding: 51 million
Return on 2001 shareholders' equity: 12.3%

	2001	2000	1999	1998	1997	1996	1995	1994
Revenues (millions)	1845	1776	1780	1615	1669	1593	1658	1593
Net income (millions)	94	118	123	87	155	135	133	149
Earnings per share	1.84	2.22	2.25	1.55	2.68	2.23	2.08	2.26
Dividends per share	1.04	1.04	1.04	1.04	1.01	.97	.93	.89
Price High	37.7	33.9	31.4	40.2	46.9	32.4	37.4	38.6
Low	24.1	18.2	18.0	22.4	30.4	26.5	25.5	28.5

McCormick & Company, Incorporated

18 Loveton Circle □ Post Office Box 6000 □ Sparks, Maryland 21152-6000 □ (410) 771-7244 □
Web site: www.mccormick.com □ Direct dividend reinvestment plan is available: (800) 468-9716 □ Fiscal year
ends November 30 □ Listed: NYSE □ Ticker symbol: MKC □ S&P rating: A- □ Value Line financial strength
rating: B++

Standard & Poor's Stock Reports had some favorable comments on McCormick & Company in February of 2002. "MKC's financial strength continues to improve, and free cash flow generation is rising. Internal volume trends remain solid, with volume gains exceeding category growth for several core product lines. Long-term growth prospects remain bright, reflecting the company's dominant and expanding U.S. spice market share (over 45 percent), as well as its leading share of the European consumer market (over 20 percent)."

Company Profile

McCormick, the world's foremost maker of spices and seasonings, is committed to the development of tasty, easy-to-use new products to satisfy consumer demand.

When investors hear the name McCormick, they think of the spices they use every day. Indeed, McCormick is the world's largest spice company. But the company is also the leader in the manufacture, marketing, and distribution of such products as seasonings and flavors to the entire food industry. These customers include foodservice and food-processing businesses as well as retail outlets.

McCormick also has a stake in packaging. This group manufactures specialty plastic bottles and tubes for food, personal care, and other industries. Founded in 1889, McCormick distributes its products in about 100 countries.

McCormick's U.S. Consumer business, its oldest and largest, is dedicated to the manufacture and sale of consumer spices, herbs, extracts, proprietary seasoning blends, sauces, and marinades. They are sold under such brand names as McCormick, Schilling, Produce Partners, Golden Dipt, Old Bay, and Mojave.

Many of the spices and herbs that McCormick purchases are imported into the United States from the company of origin. However, significant quantities of some materials, such as paprika, dehydrated vegetables, onion, and garlic, and food ingredients other than spices and herbs originate in the United States.

McCormick is a direct importer of certain raw materials, mainly black pepper, vanilla beans, cinnamon, herbs, and seeds from the countries of origin.

The raw materials most important to the company are onion, garlic, and capsicums (paprika and chili peppers), which are produced in the United States; black pepper, most of which originates in India, Indonesia, Malaysia, and Brazil; and vanilla beans, a large portion of which the company obtains from the Malagasy Republic and Indonesia.

Shortcomings to Bear in Mind

- The company purchases certain raw materials that are subject to price volatility caused by weather and other unpredictable factors. While future movements of raw material costs are uncertain, a variety of programs help McCormick address this risk, including periodic raw material purchases and customer price adjustments. Generally, the company does not use derivatives to manage the volatility related to this risk.
- This may not be a shortcoming, except

for people who are overwhelmed when they look at the hundreds of different spices in the supermarket. Trying to find the one you want can be daunting—until someone tells you they are arranged alphabetically. I didn't realize this until recently. Whenever my wife puts spices on the list, I hunt and hunt trying to locate the product she insists I buy. No more hunting, since an obliging clerk tipped me off about the alphabetical arrangement. What a relief!

- The company does not have a strong balance sheet, since only 48 percent of capitalization is in common equity. However, coverage of bond interest is more than adequate, at 9.1 times.

Reasons to Buy

- Including fiscal 2001, McCormick has now achieved the following:
  - Twelve consecutive quarters of meeting or exceeding Wall Street earnings estimates.
  - Five consecutive years of increasing economic value added. In 2001, for instance, if you add the annual dividend and the action of the stock, the total shareholder return for that year was 18 percent. Needless to say, the rest of the market turned in a dismal performance during the same period.
  - Fifteen consecutive years of dividend increases (and seventy-seven consecutive years of dividend payments).
- The market environment for McCormick's consumer products—such as spices, herbs, extracts, proprietary seasoning blends, sauces, and marinades—varies worldwide. In the United States, for instance, usage is up, and consumers are seeking new and bolder tastes.

  Although many people use prepared foods and eat out, a *Parade Magazine* survey reports that 75 percent of families polled eat dinner together at least

four nights a week. A study conducted by *National Panel Diary* indicates that 70 percent of all meals are prepared at home, and a Canned Food Association Survey reports that 51 percent of women eighteen to sixty-four actually "scratch-cook" meals six times a week.

- In the company's industrial business, said Mr. Lawless, "Our customers are constantly seeking new flavors for their products. In this environment, the ability to identify, develop, and market winning flavors is essential. We flavor all kinds of products—spaghetti sauce, snack chips, frozen entrees, yogurt, a pack of chewing gum. In restaurants, we provide seasonings for a gourmet meal, salad dressings at a casual dining chain, and coating and sauce for a quick-service chicken sandwich.

  "To anticipate and respond to changing tastes in markets worldwide, we are investing in research and development staff, equipment, instrumentation, and facilities. These investments enable us not only to create innovative products but also to use sensory skills to make sure that the flavors we deliver are winners in the marketplace."
- McCormick has paid dividends every year since 1925. In the 1991–2001 period, dividends climbed from $0.14 to $0.40, a compound annual growth rate of 11.1 percent. In the same ten-year stretch, earnings per share advanced from $0.49 to $1.10, a growth rate of 8.4 percent.
- Worldwide, the retail grocery industry continues to consolidate, creating larger customers. What's more, in many of McCormick's markets, the company has multiyear contracts with customers to secure the shelf space for its products. McCormick's capabilities in category management and electronic data interchange, along with its high-quality products and service, also forge a link to its increasingly larger customers.

- McCormick's past successes and future potential are rooted in the strength of the McCormick name. As a consequence, the company is now experiencing a 95 percent brand-awareness rating in the United States. This leadership role in the food industry ensures that consumers will enjoy a McCormick product at nearly every eating occasion. Grocery store aisles present more than 700 well-known products from major processors that rely on McCormick for seasoning or flavor.

- In the United States, McCormick continues to roll out the Quest program (launched in 1997). Quest seeks to increase volume by encouraging retailers to reduce their prices on McCormick items. Quest prices most of the company's bestselling spice items and all of its seasoning mixes to the customer, net of discounts and allowances; the objective is to increase consumer sales. Using McCormick's category-management capabilities, the company is working with its customers to provide a wide variety of products at attractive prices. This benefits the company's customers with higher volumes sold and gives the consumer a better value, as well.

- McCormick is bent on improving its profit margins. After approaching 40 percent in the early 1990s, the company's gross profit margin declined to 34.5 percent in 1998 but bounced back to 41.0 percent in 2001. According to Mr. Lawless, "With the addition of the higher-margin Ducros business, we expect to reach a gross profit margin of 42 percent in 2003."

McCormick's cost-reduction initiatives focus on supply chain management, from procurement of materials through distribution of the manufactured product. In 2000, the company created a platform to consolidate its worldwide sourcing of spices, herbs, and certain other agricultural products to be used by its operations around the globe.

The company has also improved plant efficiencies and reduced working capital in the domestic spice-processing facility by significantly reducing the number of distinct items carried in inventory and working with customers to accept alternative product or pack size. In distribution, moreover, McCormick is joining forces with other food processors to obtain freight efficiencies.

- The company made a strategic acquisition in 2000, with the purchase of the Ducros business from Eridania Beghin-Say for $379 million. With annual sales of about $250 million, Ducros has two basic businesses: spices and herbs, and dessert aid products. Headquartered in France, the Ducros business has five manufacturing plants in France, Portugal, and Albania.

Ducros has achieved sales growth of more than 7 percent compounded annually during the last three years. Consumer products comprise 88 percent of sales, while industrial products sold to the food industry and other food processors are 12 percent of sales. In France, the Ducros name has a 96-percent brand recognition among consumers.

Robert J. Lawless, CEO of McCormick, said, "One of the company's goals is to expand by acquiring leading brands in key markets. Ducros is a business that clearly meets this strategic goal. Ducros is an ideal fit, both geographically and operationally. Together, Ducros and McCormick will hold the number one share positions in France, Spain, Portugal, Belgium, the United Kingdom, Ireland, and Switzerland and number two positions in several other key European markets."

Total assets: $1,772 million
Current ratio: 0.89
Common shares outstanding: 16 million voting,
122 million nonvoting
Return on 2001 shareholders' equity: 40.5%

		2001	2000	1999	1998	1997	1996	1995	1994
Revenues (millions)		2372	2124	2007	1881	1801	1732	1859	1695
Net income (millions)		147	138	122	106	998	83	98	108
Earnings per share		1.10	1.00	.85	.72	.65	.52	.60	.66
Dividends per share		.40	.38	.34	.32	.30	.28	.26	.24
Price	High	23.3	18.9	17.3	18.2	14.2	12.7	13.3	12.4
	Low	17.0	11.9	13.3	13.6	11.3	9.5	9.1	8.9

CONSERVATIVE GROWTH

The McGraw-Hill Companies, Inc.

1221 Avenue of the Americas □ New York, New York 10020 □ (212) 512-4321 □ Direct Dividend reinvestment program available: (888) 201-5538 □ Web site: www.mcgraw-hill.com □ Listed: NYSE □ Ticker symbol: MHP □ S&P rating: not rated □ Value Line financial strength rating: A+

In 2001, Stephen B. Shepard, editor-in-chief of McGraw-Hill's *BusinessWeek*, received The Henry Johnson Fisher Award, the highest honor awarded by the magazine industry. Under Mr. Shepard's leadership, *BusinessWeek* helped set the national agenda for business and economic issues, pioneered coverage of the New Economy, exposed the Mob on Wall Street, and broke the story of prison labor in China. What's more, circulation expanded by 40 percent, since Mr. Shepard became editor-in-chief of McGraw-Hill's flagship business publication in 1984.

During those years, moreover, *BusinessWeek* has been a National Magazine Award finalist eighteen times, winning four times. The publication also won numerous Overseas Press Club awards and three Gerald Loeb Awards for distinguished business and financial journalism, among others.

Company Profile

The McGraw-Hill Companies is a multimedia information provider. The company publishes textbooks, technical and popular books, and periodicals (*BusinessWeek*, *Aviation Week*, *ENR*, and others). McGraw-Hill holds leadership positions in each of the markets it serves.

Financial Services

• Standard & Poor's Ratings Services is the number-one rating service in the world and is applying its leadership to rating and evaluating a growing array of nontraditional financial instrument.

• Standard & Poor's Indexes, led by the S&P 500, are the world's benchmark measures of equity market performance.

• Standard & Poor's *Compustat* is the leading source of financial databases and advanced PC-based software for financial analysis.

• Standard & Poor's *MMS* supplies the world with real-time fundamental and technical analysis in the global money, bond, foreign exchange, and equity markets.

• Standard & Poor's *Platt's* is the key provider of price assessments with the petroleum, petrochemical, and power markets.

• Standard & Poor's *J. J. Kenny* produces the most comprehensive evaluating pricing information for the fixed-income investment community.

• Standard & Poor's *DRI* is the leading supplier of economics-driven information to corporate and government clients.

Educational and Professional Publishing

• The McGraw-Hill School Division stands number one in providing educational materials to elementary schools.

• Glencoe/McGraw-Hill tops the grade six through twelve segment.

• CTB/McGraw-Hill is the pre-eminent publisher of nationally standardized tests for the U.S. kindergarten through twelfth-grade market.

• Irwin/McGraw-Hill is the premier publisher of higher-educational materials in business, economics, and information technology.

• The Professional Book Group is the leading publisher of business, computing, and reference books serving the needs of professionals and consumers worldwide.

Information and Media Services

• *BusinessWeek* is the world's most widely read business publication, with a global audience of 6.3 million.

• F. W. Dodge is the leading provider of information to construction professionals.

• Sweet's Group is the premier supplier of building products information, in print and electronically.

• *Architectural Record* stands atop its industry as the official publication of the American Institute of Architects.

• *Aviation Week & Space Technology* is the world's most authoritative aerospace magazine.

• Tower Group International is the leading provider of customs brokerage and freight forwarding services.

Shortcomings to Bear in Mind

■ Although the company's performance in 2001 had a number of high points, the recession and other negative factors hurt some of McGraw-Hill's operations.

• Decreased sales in the company's computing books affected its international operations, which experienced softness in the Spanish-language market. As a result, gains in the Asia-Pacific region and Canada were offset by the weakness in the Latin American region.

• Revenue for the Business-to-Business Group, which included *BusinessWeek*, the Construction Information Group, *Platt's*, the *Aviation Week* Group, and the Health care Group, declined 14 percent in 2001.

• In the face of a recession and the terrorist attack in September, advertising pages declined 37 percent at *BusinessWeek* in 2001. For the fourth quarter, normally *Business-Week's* biggest of the year, ad pages declined 41 percent. Nevertheless, *BusinessWeek* improved market share slightly in its three-book field in 2001, and the magazine finished the year with circulation stronger than ever.

• A drop in advertising pages at the Construction Information Group's publications and reduced volume at F.W. Dodge led to a modest decline in revenue.

• The Broadcasting Group's revenue declined 17.5 percent in 2001, reflecting the economic downturn and the absence of political advertising.

Reasons to Buy

■ Offsetting some of the weaknesses noted above were some stronger performances in a few of the company's operations.

● "We demonstrated our resilience in 2001 by producing a tenth consecutive year of growth, despite an economic recession in the United States and a steep decline in advertising," said Harold McGraw III, the company's CEO. "A strong performance by Financial Services and solid growth in education, particularly in the college and university market, helped create this record."

Mr. McGraw went on to say, "Revenue at our School Education Group, which serves the elementary, high school, and children's publishing markets, grew by 24 percent. We won the year's biggest adoption, capturing more than 31 percent of the huge Texas market, but shortfalls in California math and science dampened an otherwise successful performance in the 2001 adoption market. We captured 33 percent of the state adoption market outside California." (Creating textbooks is complicated by the adoption process. Twenty-one states are referred to as "adoption states," which means that the company's proposed textbook must be approved by state officials before it can be sold to specific schools within the state. Among the major states that have this approach are California, Texas, and Florida.)

■ S&P Indexes are the foundation for a growing array of investment funds and exchange-traded products that continue to generate new revenue. McGraw-Hill receives fees based on assets and trading activity. In addition, the recent volatility of the stock market has increased the revenue stream. Currently, more than $700 billion is invested in mutual funds tied to the S&P indexes.

■ Europe contributes almost half of McGraw-Hill's international revenue, an income stream that's growing at a double-digit rate. With a push from the new Monetary Union, the European market will be a springboard for growth in many of the company's key businesses. Here are some expectations:

● European companies that once financed their growth mainly by borrowing from banks are shifting to the issuance of corporate bonds instead, while nontraditional financial instruments also boom. Those are both large opportunities for Standard & Poor's Rating Services, which has built the world's largest network of ratings professionals.

● Increases in investments by Europeans building retirement funds—the result of a transition to privately funded pension plans—will accelerate demand for global financial information. These are pluses for Standard & Poor's Financial Information Services.

● The use of English is increasing in business communications and as a second language in everyday use. These will benefit the company's educational products and the European edition of *BusinessWeek*.

● The promise of the global economy depends on educational training. This is a plus for McGraw-Hill's global publishing activities—most notably the company's business, finance, engineering, information technology, and English instruction products.

■ In the construction industry, The McGraw-Hill Construction Information Group (MH-CIG) is the foremost source of information crucial to new construction projects and planning. MH-CIG has increasingly turned to the Internet and other electronic tools to gather and distribute information.

Dodge Plans is the latest of several MH-CIG electronic products stemming from print media. It provides access—online or by CD-ROM twice weekly—to the plans, specifications, and bidding requirements for more than 60,000 new construction and renovation projects.

- The digital economy and e-commerce have the capacity to transform McGraw-Hill, adding a completely new dimension to its products and services. More than 90 percent of the company's information is already in digital form and, in each of the company's major business units, there are major efforts to create and deliver a host of new electronic services.

- The McGraw-Hill Professional Book Group publishes nearly 800 titles per year in computing, business, science, technical, medical, and reference markets. The group continues to expand by creating publishing alliances with partners such as Oracle and Global Knowledge, transforming key reference titles into Internet-based services. In addition, the Professional Book Group offers electronic products that range from Internet subscription services to CD-ROMs and is building its capabilities in on-demand publishing.

- The company launched an education Web site in 2001 that is sold to schools, teachers, and parents who have children in grade school, from kindergarten through the twelfth grade. The part-free, part-pay site, called the McGraw-Hill Learning Network, offers interactive textbooks, learning exercises, and teacher tips. It also sells school supplies, including flash cards, maps, globes, and workbooks.

Parents can log on to see their children's assignments, grades, and progress—with the aid of password protection. McGraw-Hill expects that parents will buy electronic textbooks, so their kids can leave the print books at school. Parents get access to the entire site by buying at least one electronic book per year, priced at $4.95.

The site is a centerpiece of McGraw-Hill's digital and Internet strategy. It is also the company's first big bet on the kindergarten through twelfth grade market, which has been slower to adopt electronic learning than the professional and college markets.

Total assets: $5,472 million
Current ratio: 1.06
Common shares outstanding: 193 million
Return on 2001 shareholders' equity: 24%

	2001	2000	1999	1998	1997	1996	1995	1994
Revenues (millions)	4646	4308	3992	3729	3534	3075	2935	2761
Net income (millions)	377	481	402	342	291	250	227	203
Earnings per share	1.92	2.41	2.02	1.71	1.46	1.25	1.14	1.03
Dividends per share	.98	.94	.86	.78	.72	.66	.60	.58
Price High	70.9	67.7	63.1	51.7	37.7	24.6	21.9	19.3
Low	48.7	41.9	47.1	34.3	22.4	18.6	15.9	15.6

MDU Resources Group, Inc.

Schuchart Building □ Post Office Box 5650 □ Bismarck, North Dakota 58506-5650 □ (800) 437-8000 □
Direct dividend reinvestment plan is available: (800) 813-3324 □ Web site: www.mdu.com □ Listed: NYSE □
Ticker symbol: MDU □ S&P rating: A □ Value Line financial strength rating: A+

After serving MDU Resources Group for twenty-five years, John A. (Jack) Schuchart retired in 2001 as the company's chairman. It's unlikely that his distinguished service will soon be forgotten, since MDU's headquarters in Bismarck, North Dakota, are situated in the Schuchart Building.

During the past quarter century, MDU has not only grown but transformed itself and no longer relies primarily on revenues from its public utilities, as Jack Schuchart explains:

"Essentially, we were in one line of business twenty-five years ago. The company was known as Montana–Dakota Utilities Company. It was a combination electric and natural gas utility. We also had a coal company and some income from our oil interests, but they were viewed as incidental to the utility business. We employed about 1,800 people in our operations in five states.

"From a financial point of view, we had 2.4 million shares outstanding in 1975. Today we have 65 million shares. Reported revenues in 1975 were $86.5 million. Our revenues in 2000 were nearly $2 billion, and our earnings exceeded the 1975 revenues!"

Company Profile

MDU Resources Group, Inc., is a natural resource company. The company's diversified operations, such as oil and gas and construction materials, should help MDU grow at a better rate than electric utilities that depend entirely on their electric business.

MDU Resources Group has a number of operations.

Electric Distribution

Montana–Dakota Utilities Company generates, transmits, and distributes electricity and provides related value-added products and services in the Northern Great Plains. In 2001, this operation had earnings of $18.7 million, or 12.1 percent of total corporate earnings. Those results were up 4 percent over the prior year.

Natural Gas Distribution

Montana–Dakota Utilities Company and Great Plains Natural Gas Company distribute natural gas and provide related value-added products and services in the Northern Great Plains. In 2001, earnings from natural gas distribution were $0.7 million, or 0.4 percent of MDU's total. This was an increase of 10 percent over 2000.

Utility Services

Operating throughout most of the United States, Utility Services, Inc., is a diversified infrastructure construction company specializing in electric, natural gas, and telecommunication utility construction as well as interior industrial electrical, exterior lighting, and traffic stabilization. In 2001, Utility Services was responsible for earnings of $12.9 million, or 8.3 percent of the MDU corporate total.

Utility services had a banner year in 2001, up by 115 percent.

Pipeline and Energy Services

WBI Holdings, Inc., provides natural

gas transportation, underground storage, and gathering services through regulated and nonregulated pipeline systems. WBI Holdings also provides energy marketing and management throughout the United States. Operations are situated primarily in the Rocky Mountain, Midwest, Southern, and Central regions of the United States. In 2001, WBI Holdings had earnings of $16.4 million, or 10.6 percent of the MDU total. That amounted to a decrease of 17 percent.

Oil and Natural Gas Production

Fidelity Exploration & Production Company is engaged in oil and natural gas acquisition, exploration, and production throughout the United States and in the Gulf of Mexico. This business was responsible for 2001 earnings of $63.2 million, or 40.7 percent of the corporate total. This represented another big gain for this segment, up 52 percent over the prior year.

Construction Materials and Mining

Knife River Corporation mines and markets aggregates and related value-added construction materials products and services in the western United States, including Alaska and Hawaii. It also operates lignite and coal mines in Montana and North Dakota.

In 2001, this business brought in earnings of $43.2 million, representing 27.9 percent of MDU Resources' total. That amounted to a gain of 28 percent over results in 2000.

Shortcomings to Bear in Mind

- In 2001, MDU benefited from higher oil and natural gas prices. These prices are likely to be lower in 2002.
- In a report issued early in 2002, *Standard & Poor's Stock Report* was not too enthusiastic about MDU Resources. The analyst said, "Although we still

believe MDU's diversified businesses provide a long-term hedge to natural gas price volatility, for the short term a weak economy in combination with uncertainty in the natural gas markets will continue to put pressure on the stock."

- As noted above, the company's electric utility was its poorest performer in 2001, down 4 percent from the prior year. According to management, there is a negative factor to bear in mind: "Montana–Dakota has obtained and holds valid and existing franchises authorizing it to conduct its electric and natural gas operations in all of the municipalities it serves where such franchises are required. As franchises expire, Montana–Dakota may face increasing competition in its service areas, particularly in service to smaller towns, from rural electric cooperatives.

"Montana–Dakota intends to protect its service area and seek renewal of all expiring franchises and will continue to take steps to effectively operate in an increasingly competitive environment."

Reasons to Buy

- In spite of the challenges in 2001, MDU Resources enjoyed another year of record earnings. Earnings were $155.1 million, or $2.29 per share diluted (which assumes conversion of convertible securities), compared with $110.3 million, or $1.80, in 2000. Total corporate revenues reached a record $2.2 billion, a gain of 19 percent over the prior year. Over the past five years, MDU Resources has returned a 17 percent compound annual total return to shareholders.
- In August of 2001, the company increased its dividend by 5 percent, making 2001 the eleventh consecutive year of increased dividends. What's more, MDU has an unbroken record of

paying quarterly dividends that dates back to 1937.

- MDU Resources has an established position in the coal bed natural gas fields in the Powder River Basin of Wyoming and Montana. This provides the company's natural gas and oil production segment with additional reserve potential of low-cost coal bed natural gas.

  In addition, MDU continues enhancing production from its existing gas fields in Colorado and Montana. The company's strong reserve position, both onshore and offshore in the Gulf of Mexico, provides this group a large geographic base upon which to expand.

- In 2001, for the second consecutive year, MDU Resources was named to *Forbes* magazine's "Platinum List of America's 400 Best Big Companies." To make the Platinum 400, "companies were selected based on their composite scores for long- and short-term growth and return on capital, plus other performance and valuation measure," according to *Forbes*.

- The biggest contributor to 2001's record earnings was a 64 percent increase in earnings at the natural gas and oil production segment. During that year, natural gas prices averaged 30 percent higher than 2000, while oil prices were 7 percent higher.

  Combined natural gas and oil production was up 30 percent, primarily due to an aggressive drilling program in the Powder River Basin coal beds and other operated properties in the Rocky Mountain region. According to CEO Martin A. White, "During the same time, our natural gas and oil reserves went up by 7 percent. We plan to continue growing production in 2002, but will be challenged by low natural gas and oil prices."

- The company's pipeline and energy services segment had an outstanding year

in 2001, with earnings of $16.4 million, compared with $10.5 million the year before. A significant contribution to these results stemmed from record throughput at higher-than-average rates on the pipeline and gathering systems.

MDU requested regulatory approval to build a 247-mile pipeline from the Power River Basin in Wyoming to North Dakota. The pipeline would interconnect with a number of pipelines transporting natural gas to Midwest markets.

- Similarly, the construction materials and mining segment performed well in 2001, with total earnings of $43.2 million, or 43 percent higher than the prior year. The acquisition of Bauerly Brothers in Minnesota moved the company into a new market that is currently experiencing high growth. The completion of a new cement terminal in Hawaii increased operational efficiencies in that market.

- The utility services segment also had a stellar year, with earnings of $12.9 million, a 50 percent increase over 2000. The additions of Capital Electric and Bell Electrical in Missouri, and Oregon Electric in Portland increased the company's market share and brought new and expanded services into the utility services diverse areas of expertise.

- According to Mr. White, "In 2002, we will expand outside of North America by pursuing electric generation opportunities in Brazil. Our first project is a 200-megawatt, natural gas-fired generating facility. We plan to begin production in the second quarter. We are also pursuing prudent investments in domestic independent power production in various locations, particularly those close to our industrial properties or natural gas lines."

Total assets: $2,623 million
Current ratio: 1.96
Common shares outstanding: 69 million
Return on 2001 shareholders' equity: 15.3%

	2001	2000	1999	1998	1997	1996	1995	1994
Revenues (millions)	2224	1874	1280	897	608	515	464	450
Net income (millions)	156	110	83	74	55	46	42	40
Earnings per share	2.29	1.80	1.52	1.44	1.24	1.05	.95	.91
Dividends per share	.90	.86	.82	.78	.75	.73	.72	.70
Price High	40.4	33.0	27.2	28.9	22.3	15.7	15.4	14.3
Low	22.4	17.6	18.8	18.8	14.0	13.3	11.5	11.3

AGGRESSIVE GROWTH

Medtronic, Inc.

710 Medtronic Parkway N. E. □ **Minneapolis, MN 55432-5604** □ **Listed: NYSE** □ **(763) 505-2694** □ **Dividend reinvestment plan is available: (888) 648-8154** □ **Web site: www.medtronic.com** □ **Ticker symbol: MDT** □ **Fiscal years end April 30th** □ **S&P rating: A** □ **Value Line financial strength rating: A+**

A genetically engineered bone-growth developed by Medtronic has proven effective in a clinical study of back surgery. This advance—which was announced in late 2001—may sidestep the need for patients to undergo painful hip surgery in order to transplant the bone needed to rebuild the spine.

Medtronic acquired the rights to the protein, called BMP-2, from American Home Products. A number of orthopedic surgeons believe that bone-growth protein will transform back surgery, now performed each year on about 250,000 people in the United States. Some 65 million Americans suffer from lower-back discomfort caused by the degeneration of discs, which puts pressure on nerves near the spine.

"People feel that this will revolutionize spinal surgery and the treatment of low-back pain," said Matthew F. Gornet, a spine surgeon at the Missouri Bone and Spine Center, who played a key role in conducting the study. "These people walk out of the hospital the next day."

If approved by the FDA, it would be the first bone-growth protein approved for spine surgery and the first drug ever sold by Medtronic, primarily a maker of medical devices.

Company Profile

Medtronic is the world's leading medical-technology company.

Over the past half century, Medtronic has pioneered in the development of sophisticated instruments that help restore health, extend life, and alleviate pain.

Medtronic's devices help regulate erratic heartbeats, tremors, and incontinence. About one-half of the company's revenues come from the sale of defibrillators and pacing devices, including products for slow, irregular, and rapid heartbeats.

Medtronic also has a stake in spinal implant devices, mechanical and tissue heart valves, implantable neurostimulation and drug-delivery systems, catheters, stents, and guide wires used in angioplasties.

Shortcomings to Bear in Mind

■ Like most great growth companies, Medtronic typically sells at a lofty price/earnings ratio.

Reasons to Buy

- In fiscal 2001 (ended April 30, 2001), Medtronic marked the sixteenth consecutive year of increased earnings and dividends. Annual net earnings (before onetime charges) grew to $1.28 billion, or $1.05 per share (diluted), up 17 percent from the prior year. Revenues for 2001, moreover, advanced to $5.55 billion, a 14 percent increase.

- Medtronic is a pioneer in the emerging field of medicine that promises to restore normal brain function and chemistry to millions of patients with central nervous system disorders. The company's implantable neurostimulation and infusion systems treat disorders by modulating the nervous system with electrical stimulation, chemicals, and biological agents delivered in precise amounts to specific sites in the brain and spinal cord.

  Medtronic is currently treating tremor and Parkinson tremor, as well as chronic pain and incontinence, with the implantable systems. The company is awaiting FDA approval of its Activa neurostimulator for the treatment of Parkinson's disease. It is also exploring new treatments for other diseases, including epilepsy, obsessive-compulsive disorder (OCD), depression, and movement disorders.

- At the end of 2001, Medtronic acquired Endonetics, Inc., a developer of technologies for the diagnosis and treatment of gastroesophageal reflux disease (GERD). GERD, a common disorder characterized by serious heartburn, is caused when the lower esophageal sphincter muscle becomes weak and ineffective, allowing bitter digestive acids to back up into the esophagus.

  More than 60 million American adults experience GERD and heartburn at least once a month, and about 25 million suffer every day from heartburn.

"We expect Endonetics' products to set the gold standard for patient-friendly, minimally invasive, and therapeutic techniques for the treatment of GERD," said Art Collins, Medtronic president and chief executive officer.

- In 2001, Medtronic continued to broaden its portfolio of medical devices by agreeing to pay $3.7 billion for MiniMed, Inc., a manufacturer of insulin pumps and wearable glucose monitors, and for Medical Research Group, Inc., a related, closely held company. MiniMed is the leading insulin-pump manufacturer, with an estimated 80-percent market share in the United States. The main product of MiniMed is an external pump, worn at a patient's belt, to administer insulin continuously to people with Type 1 diabetes. Type 1 diabetes affects people who are born without the ability to make insulin, whereas Type 2 patients (far more numerous) develop the affliction late in life, usually after the age of fifty.

- In 2001, the FDA approved Medtronic's InSync device for domestic marketing. It is the first electrical device ever approved for the treatment of congestive heart failure patients. Heart failure doesn't mean complete failure but rather a slow degeneration of the heart muscle. It is sometimes called congestive heart failure because the body tends to take on more fluid. That fluid can, in turn, pool in various organs, especially the lungs. This can severely hamper breathing and cause the patient to seek emergency-room treatment frequently.

  Not all heart-failure patients are candidates for the InSync device. However, the potential market is still huge, since an estimated five million people in the United States suffer from the condition. Medtronic believes that 650,000 heart-failure patients are potential purchasers of its new device. Sales of at least $100 million are forecast for InSync's first year on the market.

The approval represents a victory for Medtronic over archrival Guidant Corp., which appeared before an advisory panel on July 10, 2001, the same day as Medtronic. At that time, the panel voted favorably for InSync and six-to-two against Guidant's device.

- Since its origin, Medtronic has held a clear market leadership in cardiac pacing. This leadership comes chiefly from pacemakers designed to treat bradycardia (hearts that beat irregularly or too slow) and more recently, tachyarrhythmia (hearts that beat too fast or quiver uncontrollably, called tachycardia and fibrillation). Today, more than half the cardiac rhythm devices and leads implanted throughout the world come from Medtronic.

- The worldwide coronary vascular market is estimated at $4 billion and is expected to grow because it serves significant, unmet medical needs. Medtronic's coronary vascular products include several types of catheters used to unblock coronary arteries, stents that support the walls of an artery and prevent more blockage, and products used in minimally invasive vascular procedures for coronary heart disease, the chief cause of heart attack and angina.

- Medtronic's cardiac surgery group offers superior products to support cardiac surgeons, including tissue heart valves that are best represented by the Freestyle stentless valve, the Mosaic stented tissue valve, and the Hall mechanical valve. In addition, the company is expanding its leadership in cardiac cannulae used to connect a patient's circulatory system to external perfusion systems used in conventional and minimally invasive surgeries.

The acquisition of Avecor adds to Medtronic's well-established line of perfusion systems designed to sustain patients during open-heart surgery. These systems include market-leading oxygenators, blood pumps, arterial filters, and autotransfusion and monitoring products that are used to circulate and oxygenate the blood and regulate body temperature during procedures when the heart must be stopped while repairs are made.

Finally, Medtronic is leading the way in developing products to make cardiac surgery less invasive and, ultimately, to reduce pain, patient recovery time, and medical costs. One new product that addresses these needs is the Octopus2 tissue-stabilization system that allows the cardiac surgeon to repair blocked blood vessels while the heart is still beating.

- At the end of 2001, the FDA approved the Medtronic Kappa 900 series of cardiac pacemakers, featuring new atrial monitoring and diagnostic functions to help physicians make more precise patient-management decisions. This pacemaker represents the next generation of the Medtronic Kappa family, the world's most prescribed pacemaker. The Kappa family provides therapies that treat patients with chronic heart problems in which the heart beats too slowly to adequately support the body's circulatory needs.

In addition, the Kappa 900 now offers expanded monitoring information of the atria (upper chamber) and ventricles (lower chambers). The information is easy to interpret and enables doctors to more efficiently assess atrial rhythm control and ventricular control. The new diagnostic information can result in more confident patient-management decisions by physicians and shorter follow-up visits for patients.

Total assets: $7,039 million
Current ratio: 2.76
Common shares outstanding: 1,210 million
Return on 2001 shareholders' equity: 25.0%

	2001	2000	1999	1998	1997	1996	1995	1994
Revenues (millions)	5552	5015	4134	2605	2438	2169	1742	1391
Net income (millions)	1282	1111	905	595	530	438	294	232
Earnings per share	1.05	.90	.75	.61	.53	.46	.30	.25
Dividends per share	.20	.16	.12	.11	.10	.07	.05	.04
Price High	62.0	62.0	44.6	38.4	26.4	17.5	15.0	7.0
Low	36.6	32.8	29.9	22.7	14.4	11.1	6.5	4.3

CONSERVATIVE GROWTH

Merck & Co., Inc.

One Merck Drive □ P. O. Box 100 □ Whitehouse Station, New Jersey 08889-0100 □ (908) 423-5185 □ Direct dividend reinvestment plan is available: (800) 831-8248 □ Web site: www.merck.com □ Listed: NYSE □ Ticker symbol: MRK □ S&P rating: A+ □ Value Line Financial Rating: A++

Efforts to convince the public that drug companies are charging consumers too much are getting a great deal of publicity, particularly to benefit people on Social Security—an influential and vocal group of voters. In Vermont, for instance, people are crossing the nearby border to Montreal, where prescription drugs are far cheaper, apparently subsidized by the Canadian government. The drug companies are described as greedy monsters with little regard for those who depend on their medicines for the relief of their ailments.

To be sure, most pharmaceutical companies are doing well. However, there are other factors to bear in mind. For one thing, companies such as Merck, Bristol-Myers Squibb, and Lilly are suffering because some of their most lucrative drugs are losing patent protection. When that happens, firms that make generic versions jump in like hungry vultures and cut prices drastically. After all, they haven't invested millions of dollars in research. Understandably, this new horde of competitors wreaks havoc with the price of the drug being copied.

The best way for the drug companies to battle back is to bring out new and more effective drugs, which they are doing. But the cost of finding a new drug is staggering. In a Tufts University study from late 2001, the cost of bringing out a new drug has spiraled to $802 million. What's more, that's two and half times the cost in 1987, when it was a mere $231 million. Part of the problem revolves around the number of patients that have to use the drug during the test period. It has increased to 4,000, up from 1,300 in the early 1980s.

That's the bad news. The good news is that the stock prices of such companies as Merck and Bristol-Myers came tumbling down in 2001. Bristol-Myers fell 27.6 percent in 2001, or far worse than the percent decline of either the Dow Jones Industrial Average or the S&P 500. For its part, Merck plunged 37.2 percent. Drug stocks are noted for selling at high P/E ratios. Now they are available at multiples that take some of the bad news into account. You may find this to be a good time to add a drug company to your portfolio. In fact, adding two or three might be an even better idea.

Company Profile

Merck is a leading research-driven pharmaceutical products and services company. Directly and through its joint ventures, the company discovers, develops, manufactures, and markets a broad range of innovative products to improve human and animal health. Merck also provides pharmaceutical and benefit services through Merck-Medco Managed Care.

Human Health Products

Human health products include therapeutic and preventative drugs, generally sold by prescription, for the treatment of human disorders. Among these are elevated-cholesterol products, which include Zocor and Mevacor; hypertensive/heart failure products, including Vasotec, the largest-selling product among this group; Cozaar, Hyzaar, Prinivil, and Vaseretic; antiulcerants, of which Pepcid is the largest-selling; antibiotics, of which Primaxin and Noroxin are the largest-selling; ophthalmologicals, of which Timoptic, Timoptic-XE, and Trusopt are the largest-selling; vaccines/biologicals, of which Recombivax HB (hepatitis B vaccine recombinant), M-M-R II, a pediatric vaccine for measles, mumps, and rubella, and Varivax, a live virus vaccine for the prevention of chickenpox, are the largest-selling; HIV, comprised of Crixivan, a protease inhibitor for the treatment of human immunodeficiency viral infection in adults, which was launched in the United States in 1996; and osteoporosis, which includes Fosamax, for the treatment and prevention in postmenopausal women.

Animal Health Products

Animal health products include medicinals used to control and alleviate disease in livestock, small animals, and poultry. Crop protection includes products for the control of crop pests and fungal disease.

Merck-Medco

Merck-Medco primarily includes Merck-Medco sales of non-Merck products and Merck-Medco pharmaceutical benefit services, which consist mostly of managed prescription drug programs and programs to manage health and drug utilization.

Shortcomings to Bear in Mind

- Shares of Merck fell nearly 6 percent in mid-March of 2002, after it was announced that the company had withdrawn an application for regulatory approval of a pain reliever called Arcoxia, the successor to one of the Merck's top-selling drugs, Vioxx.

  Some analysts said that Merck might have withdrawn the application because of concerns about the drug's potential cardiovascular risks, a possible problem that slowed the growth of Vioxx sales in 2001.

- Product patents for Vasotec, Vaseretic, Mevacor, Prinivil, Prinzide, Pepcid, and Prilosec (which Merck manufactures and supplies to Astra for the U.S. market) went off patent in 2000 and 2001. On the other hand, Merck contends that its newer products "will keep us competitive." Increasingly greater percentages of the company's overall sales derive from the fourteen new drugs and vaccines it has introduced since 1995.

- The markets in which the company's business is conducted are highly competitive and, in many ways, highly regulated. Global efforts toward health care cost containment continue to exert pressure on product pricing.

  In the United States, government efforts to slow the increase of health care costs and the demand for price discounts from managed-care groups have limited Merck's ability to mitigate the effect of inflation on costs and expenses through pricing.

Outside of the United States, government-mandated cost-containment programs have required Merck to similarly limit selling prices. Additionally, government actions have significantly reduced the sales growth of certain products by decreasing the patient reimbursement cost of the drug, restricting the volume of drugs that physicians can prescribe, and increasing the use of generic products. It is anticipated that the worldwide trend for cost containment and competitive pricing will continue in the direction of the 1990s and result in continued pricing pressures.

Reasons to Buy

■ In the summer of 2002, Merck spun off its Merck-Medco operation, which manages pharmacy benefit programs for employers. According to Adrienne Carter and Lisa Gibbs, writing for *Money* magazine, this "looks like a smart move. In 1993, when burgeoning health maintenance organizations threatened to curb pharmaceutical sales, Merck bought Medco so that it would have a guaranteed distribution channel for its drugs.

"But Medco grew faster than anyone expected—which turned out to be a mixed blessing. As sales exploded from $4.1 billion in 1994 to $16 billion last year (2001), Medco's low-margin business dragged down Merck's overall net profit margin. In 2001, Medco accounted for 55 percent of Merck's revenue but only about 13 percent of profits. So Merck has decided that the two companies are worth more if separated."

■ Despite comments by some analysts, Merck is "stronger today than ever," said CEO Raymond V. Gilmartin in 2001. "Here are some of our more recent accomplishments:

● "Merck has introduced fifteen new medicines in the last five years.

● "Our key drivers of growth—Vioxx, Singulair, Cozaar/Hyzaar, and Zocor—now account for nearly 60 percent of pharmaceutical sales.

● "Looking at Merck's human health and vaccines businesses, including Merck-Medco, in the last three quarters, Merck's revenue growth ranked number one in the industry (17 percent, 18 percent, and 18 percent, respectively). In six of the last seven quarters, Merck's revenue growth has ranked either number one or number two within the industry.

● "Merck-Medco is the most successful provider of pharmacy care in the United States, serving more than 65 million people, or about one in four Americans, and saving clients roughly $1 billion per year.

● "Merck also is well positioned for the future. Our early-stage pipeline is broader and deeper than ever before. Additionally, there are several important new medicines moving through later stages of clinical development.

They include:

● "MK-663, our second COX-2 inhibitor, which is the most selective known in development. MK-663 is under study for osteoarthritis, rheumatoid arthritis, and pain.

● "Zocor/ezetimibe, from our Schering-Plough partnership, for cholesterol control.

● "Singulair/loratadine (Claritin) for allergic rhinitis, also from our Schering-Plough partnership.

● "Cancidas, the first of a new investigative class of agents for the treatment of life-threatening fungal infections. We have submitted an application for FDA approval of Cancidas.

● "Invanz, a long-acting antibiotic for the treatment of bacterial infections.

We have submitted an application for FDA approval of Invanz.

- "Substance P antagonist program for the treatment of chemotherapy-induced vomiting and depression.
- "KRP-297, licensed from Kyorin, for the treatment of type 2 diabetes.
- "Vaccines for rotavirus (childhood diarrhea and dehydration) and human papilloma virus, the cause of most cervical cancer cases."

■ Merck has been criticized because it hasn't been aggressive enough in beefing up its drug portfolio through acquisitions and licensing deals. For its part, Merck makes no apologies for focusing on drugmaking rather than deal-making. "We're distinguished by the excellence of our research," said CEO Raymond Gilmartin. "Investing in that capability is the best opportunity for us to create shareholder value."

Indeed, while many pharmaceutical companies slash research and development spending when earnings are weak, Merck pledged late in 2001 to boost its annual research and development budget by $400 million from an already impressive $2.5 billion. "Merck could have made their numbers had they chosen to hatchet research and development," said Edward Studzinski, an analyst at Oakmark. "I like that they chose to take the hit and focus on research and development rather than image and perception."

■ Vioxx was given to 8,000 patients to determine whether it produced adverse stomach irritation. In a study published in *The New England Journal of Medicine*, it was found that Vioxx reduced the risk of serious gastrointestinal complications by one half when compared with naproxen, a leading drug used to treat pain. Still another study (published in November of 2000) showed that when combined with acetaminophen (the chemical name for Tylenol), Vioxx significantly reduced moderate-to-severe acute pain after dental surgery and to a greater degree than codeine.

■ Fosamax, with annual sales of more than $1 billion, is used primarily for the treatment of osteoporosis in women, but it is also effective in the enhancement of bone density in men, according to a 2000 study in the *New England Journal of Medicine*. Osteoporosis, a disease in which bones become fragile and prone to fractures, is often regarded as a women's disease. C. Anthony Butler, an analyst with Lehman Brothers, predicts the male market will have little effect on sales in the short run, given the need to convince men and their doctors that osteoporosis is not merely a female affliction. Even so, the analyst believes that the addition of men to the consumer pool could increase the drug's annual sales to $3 billion in 2007, up from his earlier forecast of $2.5 billion.

■ In 2001, Merck purchased Rosetta Inpharmatics, Inc., a company that makes equipment and software used to speed development of gene-based drugs. Merck has long been known for its dedication to its own research prowess. But in recent years, the company has made a determined effort to bolster its ties with academics and to bring new technologies developed elsewhere into its laboratories.

"This is a longer-term purchase that will augment their research and leave them better-positioned," said Leonard Yaffe, an analyst at Banc of America Securities. "Over the next twenty years, genomics is going to become a lot more influential, so it makes sense."

Total assets: $43,706 million
Current ratio: 1.09
Common shares outstanding: 2,275 million
Return on 2001 equity: 48.7%

		2001	2000	1999	1998	1997	1996	1995	1994
Revenues (millions)		47716	40363	32714	26898	23637	19829	16681	14970
Net income (millions)		7281	6822	5890	5248	4614	3881	3335	2997
Earnings per share		3.14	2.90	2.45	2.15	1.92	1.60	1.35	1.19
Dividends per share		1.37	1.21	1.10	.95	.85	.71	.62	.57
Price	High	95.3	79.0	87.4	80.9	54.1	42.1	33.6	19.8
	Low	56.8	52.0	60.9	50.7	39.0	28.3	18.2	14.1

AGGRESSIVE GROWTH

Microsoft Corporation

One Microsoft Way ▫ Redmond, WA 98052-6399 ▫ (425) 706-3703 ▫ Dividend reinvestment plan is not available ▫ Web site: www.microsoft.com ▫ Listed: NASDAQ ▫ Fiscal year ends June 30 ▫ Ticker symbol: MSFT ▫ S&P rating: B+ ▫ Value Line financial strength rating: A++

Microsoft, in its battle with market leader Palm, Inc.—with an 80 percent share—unveiled a new version of the Pocket PC hand held computer in fiscal 2002. The device is powered by Microsoft software that boasts improved links to other Microsoft products. At a festive launch event in San Francisco, Microsoft CEO Steve Ballmer dubbed the new pocket computer a "connectivity machine."

Connections to products like Microsoft's Exchange server, which runs the popular Outlook e-mail and calendar software as well as the company's SQL Server database, are expected to help Microsoft gain market share, particularly among corporate users. Most companies' employees already use programs such as Microsoft Office at work.

Microsoft's Pocket PCs have more features than Palm's devices and are nearly as easy to use. In addition to the usual selection of address books, calendars, memo pads, and calculators, Microsoft hand held computers come with Windows Media Player for music and a broad assortment of software, including Microsoft Money, Pocket Word, and Pocket Excel

(all of which synchronize with the full desktop versions); the Pocket Streets map suite, and Microsoft Reader for e-books.

Company Profile

Microsoft is the dominant player in the PC software market. It climbed to prominence on the popularity of its operating systems software and now rules the business-applications software market. Microsoft, moreover, has set its sights on becoming the leading provider of software services for the Internet.

By virtue of its size, market positioning, and financial strength, Microsoft is a formidable competitor in any market it seeks to enter. Earnings have shown explosive growth in recent years. Earnings have been enhanced by a strong PC market in general, along with new product introductions and market-share gains.

Microsoft is best known for its operating-systems software programs, which run on close to 90 percent of the PCs currently in use. Its original DOS operating system, of course, gave way to Windows, a graphical user interface program run in conjunction with DOS, which made using a PC easier.

The company entered the business-applications market in the early 1990s via a lineup of strong offerings, combined with aggressive and innovative marketing and sales strategies. The company's Office 97 suite, which includes the popular Word (word processing), Excel (spreadsheet), and PowerPoint (presentation) software programs, is now by far the bestselling applications software package.

Shortcomings to Bear in Mind

- The U.S. Justice Department told Microsoft and eighteen states in September of 2001 that it won't seek a breakup of Microsoft. That move formally ended the historic attempt to dissolve one of the most successful companies in U.S. history as a remedy to correct damage done to the computer marketplace and prevent future harm to competition. Justice officials also said they would not pursue further proceedings on a charge that Microsoft had illegally tied its Internet browser to the Windows operating system. The government moves were taken, the Justice Department said, "to obtain prompt, effective, and certain relief for consumers."

  Rather than seek a breakup, the government said it would pursue a series of measures modeled after remedies ordered before the antitrust case went to a federal appeals court. The limitations, as outlined in the 2000 order, included the following measures.
- Companies that build computers and use Microsoft software have been given much greater flexibility to configure versions of the Windows operating system with applications from providers other than Microsoft—such as Web browsers, instant messengers, and streaming media players. The appeals court ruled that Microsoft could not commingle its operating system code with the code for its Web browser, Internet Explorer.

- Microsoft is required to make the code that links applications to the Windows operating system more accessible to independent software developers.
- Microsoft is prohibited from retaliating against business partners and developers that don't do the company's bidding or that align too closely with Microsoft competitors.

Reasons to Buy

- Microsoft Office XP was launched in the spring of 2001. According to Bill Gates, XP "empowers customers to achieve more and unleashes the next wave of productivity gains. More specifically, Office XP revolutionizes the way people collaborate with one another, access important information, and accomplish their tasks. Thanks to innovative technologies such as smart tags, Task Panes, speech/handwriting recognition, and SharePoint Team Services, Office XP offers customers new experiences and capabilities that redefine productivity."
- According to the company's 2001 annual report, "Our latest operating system, Windows XP, will enable inspiring new experiences that help people unlock the full possibilities of their PCs—from advanced communication, collaboration, and remote access to digital photos, music, video, and building home networks." Launched in the late summer of 2001, Windows XP established "a new standard in reliability and performance, offering customers the freedom to create, connect, and communicate in ways that weren't possible before."
- In the words of Stephen H. Wildstrom, who writes a column for *BusinessWeek* (one of my favorite magazines), "Microsoft's new operating system, Windows XP, was sent off to manufacturing on August 24, 2001 in a maelstrom of criticism. To hear the detractors tell it, XP will eliminate competition

in the software industry and wipe out all vestiges of personal privacy. To be sure, Microsoft has brought these troubles upon itself. For example, it picked a pointless and losing fight with Eastman Kodak, which complained Microsoft had rigged Windows to favor Microsoft's picture-handling software over Kodak's.

"Something very important has been lost in the noise, however. XP is the most significant Microsoft product for consumers and small business since Window 95 was released six years ago. With XP, Microsoft finally leaves behind the twenty-year legacy of MS-DOS and builds instead on the much more solid foundation of the business-oriented Windows NT and 2000. And where networking was always a function grafted onto Windows 95 and its progeny, XP is built from the ground up as a networking operating system."

- In fiscal 2001, Microsoft released a dozen new server applications that enable customers to rapidly build and fund flexible Web-based solutions that integrate with their existing systems. According to Bill Gates, the firm's founder and chairman, "From new releases of our messaging, database, e-commerce, and management products to offerings in mobile information access and Web content management, the Microsoft NET Enterprise Servers provide the scalability, reliability, and manageability that today's agile businesses need."

- With more than 250 million unique users worldwide each month, MSN is now one of the most popular destinations on the Internet. And with the launch of the newest version of MSN in 2002, the momentum continues. This latest offering includes a new home page design, improved performance, and several updates to help users better communicate and enjoy digital media. It also provides fast and reliable Internet access

in the United States with the new MSN Broadband service.

- Xbox is Microsoft's future-generation video game system that gives players the game experiences they have yet to imagine. With a built-in hard disk drive, Xbox delivers much richer game worlds. And with Dolby Digital 5.1 sound, gamers actually feel what's happening. Xbox is the only system designed to enable players to compete or collaborate with other players around the world through broadband online gaming.

- Microsoft push into consumers' living rooms took a big step forward in fiscal 2002 when the company announced that Charter Communications, Inc., the nation's fourth-largest cable company, would deploy Microsoft's interactive-television software in a million homes.

The deal was a major boost for Microsoft's television business, which had suffered several setbacks over the prior year. AT&T, for instance, announced earlier that year that it was scaling back plans to deploy Microsoft's advanced-TV software. What's more, AT&T also invited a rival software firm, Liberate Technologies, Inc., of San Carlos, California, to compete for some of its business.

That move of AT&T's was devastating news to Microsoft because MSFT had invested $5 billion in AT&T to get its technology into the cable boxes that sit on top of televisions in customers' homes.

Fortunately, Charter, a St. Louis company with nearly seven million customers, is now giving the same Microsoft advanced-TV software new life. Charter now uses Microsoft's technology to offer customers a premium service package, with cable television and new types of entertainment and information services, including video on demand, digital video clips to go with news and sports services, and high-speed Web surfing.

Total assets: $59,257 million
Current ratio: 3.56
Common shares outstanding: 5,382 million
Return on 2001 shareholders' equity: 17.6%

	2001	2000	1999	1998	1997	1996	1995	1994
Revenues (millions)	25296	22956	19747	14484	11358	8671	5937	4649
Net income (millions)	7785	9421	7625	4786	3454	2176	1453	1210
Earnings per share	1.80	1.70	1.39	.89	.66	.43	.29	.25
Dividends per share	Nil	—	—	—	—	—	—	—
Price High	76.2	117.1	119.9	72.0	37.7	21.5	13.7	8.1
Low	42.6	40.3	68.0	31.1	20.2	10.0	7.3	4.9

GROWTH AND INCOME

3M Company
(Formerly Minnesota Mining & Manufacturing Company)

3M Center, Building 225-01-S-15 □ St. Paul, MN 55144-1000 □ (651) 733-8206 □ Web site: www.3M.com □ Listed: NYSE □ Dividend reinvestment plan is available: (800) 401-1952 □ Ticker symbol: MMM □ S&P rating: A □ Value Line financial strength rating: A++

When GE selected a new chief executive to replace the legendary Jack Welch, other companies who were searching for their own CEO replacements immediately courted the two runners-up.

Among these companies was 3M, whose chairman, Livio D. DeSimone, was slated to retire January 1, 2001. When he took the reins of 3M in December of 2000, W. James McNerney Jr. (who headed GE's aircraft-engines division) was fifty-one years old.

Mr. McNerney said that a notably bright spot is 3M's technology business, which he described as "far broader and deeper than most people understand." One of the company's strongest performers in this realm is the electro and communications segment, which makes fiber-optic cabling systems and tiny, flexible circuits used in ink jet printers.

Within his first three weeks on the job, Mr. McNerney outlined a cost-cutting strategy that focused on four key factors. One of these was the implementation of Six Sigma—a quality control strategy he

brought with him from General Electric. To be sure, 3M is relatively inexperienced when dealing with these new programs and strategies. However, "there can be no doubt regarding their effectiveness," according to an analyst at Argus.

Company Profile

Minnesota Mining and Manufacturing— usually referred to as 3M—is a $16-billion diversified technology company with leading positions in industrial, consumer and office, health care, safety, electronics, telecommunications, and other markets. The company has operations in more than sixty countries and serves customers in nearly 200 countries.

3M has a vast array of products (more than 50,000) that includes such items as tapes, adhesives, electronic components, sealants, coatings, fasteners, floor coverings, cleaning agents, roofing granules, firefighting agents, graphic arts, dental products, medical products, specialty chemicals, and reflective sheeting.

The company's Industrial and

Consumer Sector is the world's largest supplier of tapes, producing more than 900 varieties. It is also a leader in coated abrasives, specialty chemicals, repositionable notes, home-cleaning sponges and pads, electronic circuits, and other important products.

The Life Sciences Sector is a global leader in reflective materials for transportation safety, respirators for worker safety, closures for disposable diapers, and high-quality graphics used indoors and out. This sector also holds leading positions in medical and surgical supplies, drug-delivery systems, and dental products.

3M is a decentralized organization with a large number of relatively small profit centers, aimed at creating an entrepreneurial atmosphere.

Shortcomings to Bear in Mind

- The company's new CEO has his work cut out for him, according to an analyst at *Standard & Poor's Stock Reports*. "One of McNerney's biggest challenges will be streamlining 3M's hodgepodge of over 50,000 product offerings. The company will also need to become more nimble. For example, 3M will need to pump out an increasing number of new products, especially if it wants to expand into the high-growth, but rapidly changing, hi-tech and health care markets.

  "With a research and development budget that amounts to 7 percent of revenues, 3M's main problem has not been one of innovation, but of execution. In the past, 3M's hidebound culture prevented the company from quickly developing and commercializing new offerings, which in turn seriously hampered long-term EPS and equity growth."

  But the analyst was not entirely negative. "However, McNerney also has much to work with. 3M possesses excellent brand names and maintains dominant positions in most of its markets. In addition, 3M has great global reach, as is evidenced by its international sales contributions (50 percent of revenues and 60 percent of operating profits). Moreover, the company is highly profitable: two of 3M's six business units sport profit margins greater than 20 percent; return on equity (ROE) over the last ten years averaged 23 percent."

Reasons to Buy

- 3M has many strengths, including the following:
  - Leading market positions. 3M is a leader in most of its businesses, often number one or number two in market share. In fact, 3M has created many markets, frequently by developing products that people didn't even realize they needed.
  - Strong technology base. The company draws on more than thirty core technologies—from adhesives and nonwovens to specialty chemicals and microreplication.
  - Healthy mix of businesses. 3M serves an extremely broad array of markets—from automotive and health care to office supply and telecommunications. This diversity gives the company many avenues for growth while also cushioning the company from disruption in any single market.
  - Flexible, self-reliant business units. 3M's success in developing a steady stream of new products and entering new markets stems from its deeprooted corporate structure. It's an environment in which 3M people listen to customers, act on their own initiative, and share technologies and other expertise widely and freely.
  - Worldwide presence. 3M has

companies in more than sixty countries around the world. It sells its products in nearly 200 countries.

- Efficient manufacturing and distribution. 3M is a low-cost supplier in many of its product lines. This is increasingly important in today's value-conscious and competitive world.
- Strong financial position. 3M is one of a small number of domestic companies whose debt carries the highest rating for credit quality.

■ To sustain a strong flow of new products, 3M continues to make substantial investments—about $1 billion a year—in research and development.

■ 3M is a global leader in industrial, consumer, office, health care, safety, and other markets. The company draws on its many strengths, including a rich pool of technology, innovative products, strong customer service, and efficient manufacturing.

■ The unrelenting drive toward smaller, lighter, more powerful, and more economical electronic products creates strong demand for leading-edge 3M Microflex Circuits. 3M is the world's number one supplier of adhesiveless flexible circuitry. 3M microflex circuits connect components in many of the world's ink-jet printers. They also link integrated circuits to printed circuit boards efficiently and reliably, making it possible to develop even smaller cellular phones, portable computers, pagers, and other electronic devices.

■ 3M supplies the automotive market with a wide variety of products, including high-performance tape attachment systems; structural adhesives; catalytic converter mounts; decorative, functional and protective films; and trim and identification products.

■ The Life Sciences Sector produces innovative products that improve health and safety for people around the world. In consumer and professional health care, 3M has captured a significant share of the first-aid market with a superior line of bandages. 3M Active Strips Flexible Foam Bandages adhere better to skin—even when wet—and 3M Comfort Strips Ultra Comfortable Bandages set new standards for wearing comfort. Under development are tapes, specialty dressings, and skin treatments that will reinforce and broaden the company's leading market positions and accelerate sales growth.

■ In pharmaceuticals, 3M is a global leader in technologies for delivering medications that are inhaled or absorbed through the skin, and the company is expanding its horizons in new molecule discovery.

■ Hostile conditions lie under any vehicle's hood, but 3M's Dyneon Fluoropolymers withstand the heat. Found in seals, gaskets, O-rings, and hoses in automotive and airplane engines, the company's fluoropolymers outperform the competition when high temperatures and chemicals cross paths. And 3M technology isn't merely under the hood. 3M also makes products for the vehicle's body and cabin that identify, insulate, protect, and bond—such as dimensional graphics, Thinsulate Acoustic Insulation, cabin filters, and super-strong adhesives and tapes that replace screws and rivets. The company is also developing window films that help keep the cabin cool by absorbing ultraviolet light and reflecting infrared light.

■ Post-it Notes were named one of the twentieth century's best products by *Fortune* magazine, and Scotch Tape was listed among the century's 100 best innovations by *BusinessWeek* magazine. Also, 3M ranked as the world's most respected consumer-goods company and fifteenth overall in a survey published by the *Financial Times of London.* Finally, 3M received Achieved Vendor of the Year status from four leaders in the office-supply industry.

- In December of 2001, a writer for *The Wall Street Journal* commented on 3M's progress in the health care realm. Erik Ahlberg said, "During the past several decades, the St. Paul, Minnesota, company has been quietly pouring money into a new line of drugs called immune-response modifiers. The compounds help the body fight a range of serious skin conditions, and some very promising early results have dermatologists and analysts alike itching to learn more.

"The first such product approved by the Food & Drug Administration, a cream to treat genital warts called Aldara, hit the market four years ago and now generates $100 million in annual sales. 3M thinks new uses for Aldara together with new drugs in the same family could bring sales of more than $1 billion by 2010.

"'We certainly put the immune-response modifiers in the blockbuster category,' said Tom Harrison, a vice president for the company's pharmaceutical division. 'We're not talking about one or two new products—it's a new class of chemistry.'"

Total assets: $14,404 million
Current ratio: 1.31
Common shares outstanding: 392 million
Return on 2001 shareholder's equity: 27%

	2001	2000	1999	1998	1997	1996	1995	1994
Revenues (millions)	16079	16724	15659	15021	15070	14236	13460	15079
Net income (millions)	1430	1782	1711	1526	1626	1516	1359	1345
Earnings per share	3.58	4.45	4.21	3.74	3.88	3.63	3.23	3.18
Dividends per share	2.40	2.32	2.24	2.20	2.12	1.92	1.88	1.76
Price High	127.0	122.9	103.4	97.9	105.5	85.9	69.9	57.1
Low	85.9	78.2	69.3	65.6	80.0	61.3	50.8	46.4

GROWTH AND INCOME

National City Corporation

P. O. Box 5756, Dept. 2101 ▫ Cleveland, Ohio 44101-0756 ▫ (800) 622-4204 ▫ Dividend reinvestment plan is available: (800) 622-6757 ▫ Web site: www.national-city.com ▫ Listed: NYSE ▫ Ticker symbol: NCC ▫ S&P rating: A ▫ Value Line financial strength rating: A

Unlike the chief executive officers of most corporations, David A. Daberko had good news to report to National City's shareholders in early 2002.

"In last year's letter, we stated, 'Our primary goal for 2001 and the coming years is the resumption of positive revenue and earnings momentum. The people and strategies are in place to do just that.'

"I am pleased to report that, despite a challenging economic environment and other unforeseen difficulties, National City achieved record revenue and earnings per share in 2001. Revenue grew 12 percent, to $6.2 billion, led by a 16 percent increase in net interest income. Net income was $1.4 billion, and earnings were $2.27 per share, the highest in our 156-year history."

Mr. Daberko went on to say, "Our capital position is very strong, even as total assets surpassed the $100 billion level for the first time in our history. Loan loss reserves, essentially a form of capital, were also bolstered during the year, and we remain vigilant in the identification, monitoring, and disposition of problem loan assets. The balance sheet is in excellent shape as we embark on the new year."

Company Profile

National City provides broad-based banking and financial services to about 8.5 million consumers in Ohio, Pennsylvania, Kentucky, Michigan, Illinois, and Indiana. Services are delivered through more than 1,100 branch offices and more than 1,600 ATMs. A growing number of customers choose the convenience of National City's online banking service at *www.national-city.com*. Enhancements completed in 2000 have increased the Web site's versatility, functionality, ease of use, and interconnectivity.

Since David A. Daberko was named chairman and CEO of National City Corporation in mid-1995, the company, once known only to Ohioans, has more than doubled in size through acquisitions.

National City subsidiaries provide financial services that meet a wide range of customer needs, including commercial and retail banking, trust and investment services, item processing, mortgage banking, and credit card processing.

Retail Banking

The retail banking business includes the deposit-gathering branch franchise, along with lending to individuals and small businesses. Lending activities include residential mortgages, indirect and direct consumer installment loans, leasing, credit cards, and student lending.

Fee-Based Businesses

The fee-based businesses include institutional trust, mortgage banking, and item processing.

- Institutional trust includes employee benefit administration, mutual fund management, charitable and endowment services, and custodial services.
- Mortgage banking includes the origination of mortgages through retail offices and broker networks and mortgage servicing.
- Item processing is conducted by National City's majority-owned subsidiary, National Processing, Inc. (NYSE:NAP), and includes merchant credit card processing, airline ticket processing, check guarantee services, and receivables and payables processing services.

Customer Needs and Preferences

To gain insight into customer preferences, National City has been making substantial investments in data warehouse technology to more effectively capture and manage customer information. This capability has already resulted in more effective cross-selling and has given the bank tools to better understand and predict customer needs and preferences.

The bank is well aware that customer demand for financial services transcends traditional time-and-place limitations. To that end, the company initiated a multi-year plan to reconfigure its branch delivery system—reducing traditional, full-service branches while expanding nontraditional alternatives. This includes in-store locations, limited-service facilities, and off-site ATMs—which, along with better call-center capability, make it easier and more convenient for customers to do business with National City.

Shortcomings to Bear in Mind

- In early 2002, Mr. Daberko freely admitted that the recession has left its mark. He said, "The faltering economy created difficulties for many borrowers, both corporate and individual, driving increased loan losses. While our credit performance was better than nearly all of our large bank peers, charge-offs did rise from 46 basis points to 68 basis points. The strong mortgage performance helped to offset the increase in credit costs. We anticipate the cycle will turn for both of these items in 2002." (Note: There are 100 basis points in one percentage point. Thus, twenty-five basis points is the same as one-quarter of one percent.)

- The weakness in the economy that began in late 2000 and has continued into 2002 is hurting corporations of nearly every stripe. Nor are banks immune. A weak economy, for instance, virtually assures an increase in problem assets and loan losses. However, David A. Daberko, the National City CEO, says, "We expect the problems to be manageable and of a lesser scope for National City than for the industry as a whole."

- In recent years, banks have been finding it increasingly difficult to expand revenues. Those with the broadest product mix are more likely to have an easier time registering top-line growth. Savings from cost-cutting efforts, which have propelled earnings for many large banks in recent years, are also becoming more difficult to come by, placing greater emphasis on top-line growth. Loan growth also remains a regional phenomenon, with strength in areas of the Southeast and Midwest, where economies continue to grow at a rate above the national average.

Reasons to Buy

- National City has a solid record of growth. In the 1991–2001 period, earnings per share expanded from $0.91 to $2.27, a compound annual growth rate of 9.6 percent. In the same ten-year span, dividends per share equaled earnings-per-share growth, climbing from $.47 cents to $1.16, a growth rate of 9.5 percent.

- In corporate banking, National City's second-largest business, the bank has worked hard to retain its position as the number-one middle-market lender in its region. The bank's markets have been economically vibrant, as evidenced by low rates of unemployment and significant growth in small and medium-size businesses over the past several years. The bank's decentralized system of credit approval permits quick responsiveness to customer needs. At the same time, the company's product capability is second to none. For example, National City introduced an innovative lending product, Corporate Select, that uses built-in interest-rate protection options inside a conventional loan. This helps companies manage risk in a seamless, straightforward manner. Corporate Select offers a competitive advantage in winning and strengthening customer relationships. There is no comparable product currently available in the market. Through initiatives such as these and with a strong team of relationship managers, National City has been able to maintain or increase market share in virtually all of its markets. What's more, the company has been particularly successful in western Pennsylvania, which it entered through the merger with Integra Financial Corporation.

- National City is one of the five top originators of federally guaranteed student loans in the country. What's more, in dealer finance, the company is ranked as the fifth-largest noncaptive originator of retail loans and leases. National City offers competitive credit card products and indirect consumer installment loans and leases for automotive, marine, recreational vehicle, heavy equipment, and property improvement.

- National City is finding that fee-based businesses are growing at a healthy clip, compared with more conventional banking operations.

National Processing, for example, is enjoying a substantial momentum as a leading processor of merchant card transactions as it continues to expand from its strong base of national accounts into midsized and smaller merchants.

- To enhance the overall efficiency of its branch network, National City equipped each office with Retail OnLine in 2001. This branch-system intranet provides immediate access to current retail banking information in a searchable format. Armed with more timely and accurate data, managers and staff are now better able to assist customers with their needs and concerns.

The capabilities of Retail OnLine have also greatly facilitated problem resolution. In 2002, a broader set of initiatives is already under way to redesign branch and call center processes. The goal is to further improve service quality and work flow while reducing back-office operating costs.

- In yet another sector, the revamped www.NationalCity.com received 7.3 million visits, and the number of customers using Online Banking more than doubled, to about 275,000. What's more, www.NationalCity.com was rated the number one business-to-business Web site operated by a bank. It was rated the second-best business-to-business site in the nation by *Business to Business* magazine.

- For the fourth consecutive year, National City's Stock Transfer Group earned the highest customer satisfaction rating from corporate clients, as measured by the annual Group Five, Inc., Shareowner Services Corporate Satisfaction Study. National City is the only company ever to have won this distinction more than once. Additionally, National City again received the SCS/Rutgers University Agent Comparison Survey's TALON Award for being the best midsized stock transfer agent.

In small business, National City is the leader in Small Business Administration loans in its six-state area. The company is ranked number one in Pennsylvania, Michigan, and Indiana; number two in Ohio; and number eleven in the country.

Total assets: $93,110 million
Return on assets in 2001: 1.49%
Common shares outstanding: 606 million
Return on 2001 shareholders' equity: 19.9%

	2001	2000	1999	1998	1997	1996	1995	1994
Loans (millions)	68041	65604	60204	58011	39573	35830	25732	22566
Net income (millions)	1388	1302	1404	1333	807	733	465	429
Earnings per share	2.27	2.13	2.22	2.00	1.83	1.64	1.48	1.32
Dividends per share	1.16	1.14	1.09	.97	.86	.94	.65	.59
Price High	32.7	29.8	37.8	38.8	33.8	23.6	16.9	14.5
Low	23.7	16.0	22.1	28.5	21.3	15.3	12.6	11.9

CONSERVATIVE GROWTH

Nordson Corporation

28601 Clemens Road □ Westlake, Ohio 44145-4551 □ (440) 414-5344 □ Dividend reinvestment plan is available: (800) 622-6757 □ Web site: www.nordson.com □ Fiscal year ends Sunday closest to October 31 □ Listed: NASDAQ □ Ticker symbol: NDSN □ S&P rating: B+ □ Value Line financial strength rating: B+

Nordson started off fiscal 2002 with the introduction of a new self-cleaning powder-coating system that provides ten-minute color changes and an automatic cleaning system; it is put in action with the push of a button. Quick color changes are achieved through such features as a special canopy design, automatic internal booth cleaning, and automatic external gun cleaning.

Nordson is the world's leading producer of precision dispensing equipment that applies adhesives, sealants, and coatings to a broad range of consumer and industrial products during manufacturing operations, helping customers meet quality, productivity, and environmental targets.

"Finishers have long been challenged to efficiently meet the demand for frequent product color changes in today's dynamic manufacturing environment," said John Binder, Marketing Manager, Powder-Coating Systems.

"While conventional powder-coating systems can take as long as forty minutes for color changes, the automatic cleaning technology of the Speedking self-cleaning system significantly reduces downtime which can add up to substantial savings over the course of a year, as well as a faster return on investment."

Company Profile

Nordson products are used around the world in the appliance, automotive, construction, container, converting, electronics, food and beverage, furniture, graphic arts, metal finishing, nonwovens, packaging, and other diverse industries.

Nordson markets its products through its international sales divisions in North America, Europe, Japan, and Pacific South. These organizations are supported by a network of direct operations in thirty-one countries. Consistent with this strategy, more than 50 percent of the company's revenues are generated outside the United States.

Nordson has manufacturing facilities in Ohio, Georgia, Alabama, California, Germany, the Netherlands, and the United Kingdom.

History

The U.S. Automatic Company, the parent of Nordson, was founded in Amherst, Ohio, in 1909. Initially, the company specialized in high-volume, low-cost screw machine parts for the burgeoning automotive industry.

In the years following World War II, Walter Nord, along with sons Eric and Evan, searched for a proprietary product to serve as a basis for future growth. This resulted in the acquisition of patents covering the "hot airless" method of spraying paint and other coating materials. The company later expanded its product line to include air-spray equipment and incorporated the highly efficient electrostatic process in both airless and air-spray painting systems.

Beginning in the late 1960s, Nordson pioneered the technology and equipment for applying powder coatings with the development of the compact and efficient cartridge-type recovery/recycle systems.

Nordson has steadily refined its cartridge-booth technology and is an innovator in all aspects of the powder coating process for both organic and porcelain enamel applications. Today, Nordson is the acknowledged industry leader in powder-coatings systems.

Each year, the worldwide appliance industry transforms millions of square feet of prefinished sheet steel into consumer durables, including refrigerators, ranges, washers, and dryers. Before appliances are assembled, manufacturers use Nordson flat-line powder coating systems to apply flexible porcelain enamel "powder paint" that quickly turns steel into gleaming panels of white, almond, and black metal that can be bent and wrapped to achieve new model designs. The benefit to manufacturers is increased line speed, higher quality, and lower operating costs. Consumers benefit, too: These uniformly coated appliances are more attractive and less prone to corrosion.

Shortcomings to Bear in Mind

- The company's record of growth leaves something to be desired. In the 1991–2001 period, earnings per share advanced from $0.89 to $1.02, which amounts to a compound annual growth rate of 1.4 percent. To be more realistic, the company was hurt by such negative developments as the recession, the global slowdown in the semiconductor and electronics industries, and the translation of foreign earnings, which were the victim of the strong dollar. In the same ten-year span, dividends performed much better, climbing from $0.20 in 1990 to $0.56 in 2000, a growth rate of 10.8 percent. The company has increased its dividend for thirty-eight consecutive years.

Reasons to Buy

- Nordson began fiscal 2001 with the acquisition of EFD, Inc., "an extraordinary company with a history of strong financial performance and broad exposure to high-technology and industrial markets," said Edward P. Campbell, president and CEO. "EFD is an excellent strategic fit with Nordson, as it is the leading producer of precision, low-pressure dispensing systems. With unrivaled strength in technology, product quality, and customer service, EFD significantly expands Nordson's presence in markets possessing above-average growth rates.

  "In addition, Nordson's strength in international distribution opens the door for EFD to accelerate both performance and growth. With the addition of EFD, Nordson's advanced technology business segment increased to 23 percent of annual sales, from 18 percent in fiscal 2000. Strong internal growth—complemented by strategic acquisitions—has allowed this key segment of Nordson to grow at an average annual compound growth rate of more than 40 percent over the past five years."

- Fiscal 2001 marked the successful conclusion of Action 2000, "our two-year initiative to optimize performance and stimulate financial growth," said Nordson CEO Mr. Campbell. "Fortunately, cost-reduction efforts associated with Action 2000—including the aggregate reduction of worldwide headcount by 15 percent and the closure of nine manufacturing plants—were started well in advance of the economic downturn that we experienced in fiscal 2001.

  "Although we anticipate the total cost of Action 2000 to be approximately $26 million, the program has already returned savings of $36 million, with a continuing $40 million anticipated in fiscal 2002. While some of the savings may be reinvested in product development and other growth opportunities when conditions warrant, the majority represent permanent cost reductions."

- Nordson's finishing businesses have always set a high priority on new product developments that enhance customer productivity. As industry continues to demand increased efficiencies and cost controls, these developments are paying off handsomely for the powder coating, liquid finishing, and container businesses.

While powder coating offers distinct advantages over liquid finishing in terms of applying paint to many types of products, liquid technologies have held the lead in quick color change. Now Nordson's newest powder coating system introduces a technology that makes color changes possible in as little as fifteen minutes. "Fast color changes makes Nordson a market winner in powder coating," says Mark Gacka, vice president. "These new offerings allow manufacturers to change colors faster than ever before. And it makes powder coating economical for a wider range of industrial uses."

- Nordson technology delivers precise applications of both hot- and melt-adhesives and cold glue—simultaneously—to tightly seal cases of agricultural products, beverages, and consumer packaged goods. The hot-melt adhesive delivers an instant bond to seal the cases. At the same time, the slower-setting cold glue permeates the paper fiber to ensure that packages remain intact regardless of the environmental conditions. This dual-gluing process ensures that shipments won't be rejected due to carton failure during transit—a substantial customer benefit.

- Nordson's strategy is to participate in the higher-growth segments of the global economy by expanding its expertise to the realms of electronic assembly and printed circuit board coating. In the future, as electronic parts become smaller and labor rates continue to increase in emerging countries, and as electronics assembly become more complex, we will continue to see more highly automated electronic assembly processes. Management is convinced that Nordson will be a major participant in the market for electronics assembly equipment with internally developed products and acquired businesses.

- In early fiscal 2002, Nordson announced the expansion of its powder-coating customer test laboratory in Amherst, Ohio. With the addition of the new testing capabilities, the 14,300-square-foot facility can run six independent customer tests at the same time and provide a complete range of Nordson systems that can accommodate an unlimited number of part configurations.

"In our expanded state-of-the-art customer test facility, we can duplicate any production coating system, using the customer's parts and coating material, and operating at their line speeds," said Herb Turner, vice president, Powder-Coating Systems. "With it, we can provide proof that any Nordson system will meet or exceed our customers' coating requirements."

Total assets: $862 million
Current ratio: 1.02
Common shares outstanding: 33 million
Return on 2001 shareholders' equity: 13%

	2001	2000	1999	1998	1997	1996	1995	1994
Revenues (millions)	731	741	700	661	637	609	581	507
Net income (millions)	25	55	50	47	50	53	53	47
Earnings per share	1.02	1.85	1.48	1.43	1.43	1.46	1.42	1.23
Dividends per share	.56	.52	.48	.44	.40	.36	.32	.28
Price High	32.2	33.0	33.0	26.2	32.5	32.5	30.5	31.5
Low	20.7	18.1	21.5	21.1	22.2	22.8	26.9	26.0

CONSERVATIVE GROWTH

PepsiCo, Incorporated

700 Anderson Hill Road ▫ Purchase, New York 10577-1444 ▫ (914) 253-2711 ▫ Dividend reinvestment plan is available: (800) 226-0083 ▫ Web site: www.pepsico.com ▫ Listed: NYSE ▫ Ticker symbol: PEP ▫ S&P rating: A ▫ Value Line financial strength rating: A+

With the $13.8-billion acquisition of Quaker Oats, PepsiCo added some major brands to its lineup of products in August of 2001. The big prize was Gatorade, a leading sports drink, growing at 11 percent a year. This made PepsiCo the dominant company in the $2.5-billion-a-year sports drink category. "Gatorade would do even better under PepsiCo than it has under Quaker Oats because of better marketing and distribution," said John Sicher, publisher of *Beverage Digest*.

The deal pushed PepsiCo to the forefront of the noncarbonated business, the most dynamic segment of the soft drink industry, and gave PepsiCo control of such well-known foods as Life Cereal, Rice-A-Roni, and Aunt Jemima pancake syrup.

Mr. Sicher said the deal could help Frito-Lay. "Quaker Oats' grain-based snacks could show real growth within the Frito-Lay marketing and distribution system." Quaker officials said Frito-Lay's marketing muscle could grab more shelf space for Quaker cereals and put its granola bars in more vending machines.

Company Profile

PepsiCo is among the most successful consumer products companies in the world, with 2001 revenues of $26.9 billion. PepsiCo brands are among the best known in the world and are available in about 190 countries and territories. The company consists of the following:

• Frito-Lay Company, the largest manufacturer and distributor of snack chips.

• Pepsi-Cola Company, the second-largest soft drink business.

• Tropicana Products, the largest marketer and producer of branded juice.

Some of PepsiCo's brand names are 100 years old, but the corporation is relatively young. It was founded in 1965 through the merger of Pepsi-Cola and Frito-Lay. Tropicana was acquired in 1998.

Frito-Lay Company

Major Frito-Lay products include Ruffles, Lay's, and Doritos brands snack chips. Other major brands include Cheetos cheese-flavored snacks, Tostitos Tortilla chips, Santitas tortilla chips, Rold Gold pretzels, SunChips multigrain snacks, and Wow! fat-free snacks. Frito-Lay also sells a variety of snack dips and cookies, nuts and crackers. Today, Frito-Lay brands account for 58 percent of the domestic snack chip industry.

Often, Frito-Lay products are known by local names, such as Matutano in Spain, Sabritas and Gamesa in Mexico, Elma Chips in Brazil, and Walkers in the United Kingdom. The company markets Frito-Lay brands on a global level and introduces products for local tastes.

Pepsi-Cola Company

At the turn of the last century, Caleb Bradham, a New Bern, North Carolina, druggist, first formulated Pepsi-Cola and founded PepsiCo's beverage business. Today, consumers spend about $32 billion on Pepsi-Cola beverages. Brand Pepsi and other Pepsi Colas—including Diet Pepsi, Pepsi-One, Mountain Dew, Slice, and Mug brands—account for nearly one-third of total soft drink sales in the United States, a consumer market totaling about $58 billion.

In 1992, Pepsi-Cola formed a partnership with Thomas J. Lipton Company. Today, Lipton is the biggest selling ready-to-drink brand in the United States.

Abroad, Pepsi-Cola Company's soft drink operations include the business of Seven-Up International. Pepsi-Cola beverages are available in about 160 countries.

Tropicana Products, Inc.

Anthony Rossi founded Tropicana in 1947 as a Florida fruit packaging business. The company entered the concentrate orange juice business in 1949. In 1954, Rossi pioneered a pasteurization process for orange juice. For the first time, consumers could enjoy the fresh taste of pure not-from-concentrate 100-percent Florida orange juice in a ready-to-serve package.

Today, Tropicana is the world's largest marketer and producer of branded juices, with products available in fifty countries.

Principal brands in North America are Tropicana Pure Premium, Tropicana Season's Best, Dole juices, and Tropicana Twister. Overseas, principal brands include Tropicana Pure Premium and Dole juices, along with Fruvita, Hitchcock, Looza, and Copella. Today, Tropicana Pure Premium is the fourth-largest brand of all food products sold in grocery stores in the United States.

Shortcomings to Bear in Mind

■ The acquisition of Quaker Oats has its negative aspects. Acquiring Quaker's food business comes at a time when consumers are becoming increasingly impatient with sit-down meals. About 11 percent of PepsiCo's business is now in an ailing food business, ranging from pasta to cereal, that grows at a snail's pace of 2 percent a year. On the other hand, there is some speculation that the company may sell the food business in the next year or two. Under current accounting rules, the company must wait two years following an acquisition. In any event, Steven S. Reinemund, PepsiCo's new CEO, says there are no immediate plans to shed this line. "We haven't bought a collection of cats and dogs here," said Mr. Reinemund. "These are great brands. We intend to grow all of it."

■ Betsy McKay, writing for The Wall Street Journal in May of 2001, pointed out some negative factors in the Gatorade acquisition. "Coke, the underdog this time, has plans of its own. In mid-July (2001), the Atlanta beverage giant will launch a makeover of its sleepy PowerAde brand, which after nine years on the shelves has only a 15 percent share of the sports-drink market, compared with Gatorade's 78 percent share, according to *Beverage Digest*, an industry publication.

"Coke sees Powerade as more than just a thirst quencher for the sweating masses. It wants to establish an alternative identity to Gatorade—which focuses on the serious athlete and mainstream sports—by launching a 'fuel for life' system of beverages. The new line, Coke says, will combine the scientific benefits of the sports drink with the energy boost of drinks like Red Bull, made by a private Austrian firm, that is popular with the Gen-X crowd."

- In February of 2002, Betsy McKay wrote another article dealing with Gatorade. "Investors and analysts are closely watching the performance of Gatorade for evidence that PepsiCo's $13.8-billion acquisition of Quaker is going to pay off. The drink makes up only a small portion of PepsiCo's overall business, but its growth has softened in the face of increased competition from Coca-Cola's Powerade."
- The company's growth record is not impressive. In the 1991–2001 period, earnings per share inched ahead from $0.75 to $1.47, a compound annual growth rate of only 7.0 percent. In the same ten-year span, dividends per share expanded at a better clip, rising from $0.23 to $0.58, for a growth rate far ahead of inflation, at 9.7 percent.

Reasons to Buy

- The sports drink Gatorade was the big prize in the company's recent purchase of Quaker Oats. However, management is salivating over the possibilities that Quaker brings for boosting its sales of snacks and fruit drinks. According to Roger A. Enrico, vice chairman of PepsiCo, Quaker's clout in the noncarbonated beverage aisle could also pay dividends by getting retailers to provide shelf space for Tropicana division's growing line of fruit drinks, such as Tropicana Twisters. The market for noncarbonated drinks is about $16 billion, compared with $58 billion for carbonated drinks, but is growing much faster, according to the industry trade publication Beverage Digest. Enrico also says that Quaker's granola bars, rice cakes, and fruit bars are complementary to the Frito-Lay division's industry-leading lineup of salty snacks such as Tostitos corn chips and Lay's potato chips.

- Carbonated drinks, such as Pepsi and Mountain Dew, are still the mainstay of the company's business. However, sales of noncarbonated beverages, such as Aquafina bottled water and SoBe drinks, are expanding at a rapid pace, as consumer's tastes become more diverse.

- With the acquisition of Quaker Oats, Pepsi now has an immense stable of strong brands, thus boosting its clout among retailers. This provides the company with greater advantage in the tussle among beverage companies for hard-to-get space in convenience-store coolers. "When the PepsiCo guy walks into 7-Eleven, they're going to have to pay a lot more attention to him than they do to Coke," one Pepsi bottler said. "He'll have Pepsi, Gatorade, SoBe, and Tropicana. He owns the refrigerator door."

- The Pepsi-Cola Division introduced Dole single-serve juices into vending machines, coolers, and other retail outlets throughout the United States in early 2001. The new Dole products are being distributed by Pepsi bottlers in sixteen-ounce plastic bottles and eleven-and-a-half-ounce cans. The noncarbonated, caffeine-free, single-serve Dole line includes nine natural fruit flavors: Apple, Orange, Pineapple-Citrus, Ruby Red Grapefruit, Cranberry Juice Cocktail, Paradise Blend, Cranberry-Grape,

Orange-Strawberry-Banana, and Strawberry-Kiwi.

- Stephen Sanborn, an analyst with *Value Line Survey*, said in a recent report, "Prospects are also bright for the years out to 2004–06. The Frito-Lay lines both at home and abroad are very strong, and there is good reason to think they will continue to grow as management adds new products on a regular basis. The beverage business, although second to Coca-Cola, is still strong at home, and there is excellent potential in much of the rest of the world."
- Nor is *Value Line* alone in its optimism for PepsiCo. *Standard & Poor's Stock Reports* in late 2001 said, "We continue our buy recommendation on the shares, reflecting our expectation for enhanced profit growth, earnings consistency, and growing free cash flow, in light of the recent acquisition of Quaker Oats. With this acquisition, we believe PEP is poised to consistently deliver 13 percent to 14 percent annual EPS growth. Together with its purchase of South Beach Beverage Co., these acquisitions provide PepsiCo with leading positions in several fast-growing, noncarbonated beverage categories."

Total assets: $18,339 million
Current ratio: 1.82
Common shares outstanding: 1,779 million
Return on 2001 shareholders' equity: 37%

	2001	2000	1999	1998	1997	1996	1995	1994
Revenues (millions)	26940	25480	20367	22348	20917	31645	30421	28472
Net income (millions)	2660	2540	1845	1760	1730	1865	1990	1784
Earnings per share	1.47	1.42	1.23	1.16	1.10	1.17	1.24	1.11
Dividends per share	.58	.56	.54	.52	.49	.45	.39	.35
Price High	50.5	49.9	42.6	44.8	41.3	35.9	29.4	20.6
Low	40.3	29.7	30.1	27.6	28.3	27.3	16.9	14.6

AGGRESSIVE GROWTH

Pfizer, Inc.

235 East 42nd Street □ New York, New York 10017-5755 □ (212) 573-2323 □ Direct dividend reinvestment plan is available: (800) 733-9393 □ Web site: www.pfizer.com □ Listed: NYSE □ Ticker symbol: PFE □ S&P rating: A+ □ Value Line financial strength rating: A++

In early 2002, Karen Katen, executive vice president of the company and president of Pfizer Pharmaceuticals Group, commented on the company's strong showing in 2001. "Pfizer continues to distinguish itself within the industry by its product breadth and depth across multiple major therapeutic categories. Worldwide in the fourth quarter (of 2001), nine products—representing about 79 percent of the company's human pharmaceutical revenues—grew an aggregate 19 percent.

"Eight products generated at least $1 billion of Pfizer revenues in 2001, including three with more than $2 billion, two with more than $3 billion, and one with more than $6 billion. Ten Pfizer products are leaders in their individual therapeutic areas. Our success is due in large part to our ability to both take share and expand markets through the unsurpassed professionalism and productivity of our global medical, marketing, and sales organizations. And we will strengthen our leadership position even in the face of competition.

"A perfect example of this is Lipitor. The leading cholesterol-lowering therapy in the world and the largest-selling pharmaceutical of any kind, Lipitor sales grew 28 percent, to $6.4 billion, in 2001. Lipitor's clinical profile is unparalleled, with outstanding efficacy and safety across its dose range as demonstrated in more than 20 million patient years of experience and more than 300 clinical trials involving more than 44,000 patients."

Company Profile

Pfizer traces its history back to 1849 when Charles Pfizer and Charles Erhart founded the company. In those early days, Pfizer was a chemical firm. Today, it is a leading global pharmaceutical manufacturer, creating and marketing a wide range of prescription drugs.

Pfizer also has an important stake in hospital products, animal health items, and consumer products.

Pfizer's growth over the past half century has been paced by strategic acquisitions, new drug discoveries, and vigorous foreign expansion. Its most recent move involved the giant acquisition of Warner-Lambert in 2000, making the new firm the largest pharmaceutical company in the world.

Shortcomings to Bear in Mind

- One of Pfizer's major drugs is Viagra, currently the leading drug used to treat erectile dysfunction. Sales in 2001 exceeded $1.5 billion. Viagra is among the world's most widely prescribed medications, with over 45 million prescriptions having been written by 500,000 physicians for over 16 million men.

On the horizon, however, two competitors are gearing up to get a piece of the action. Cialis is made by Eli Lilly, and vardenafil is made by Bayer. Both drugs could reach the market in 2002. Some doctors believe the new drugs have some advantages over Viagra. They act in a similar way, but they appear to act faster and cause fewer side effects such as headaches, nasal congestion, flushed face, and blue vision.

Cialis and vardenafil both block an enzyme called phosphodiesterase-5, or PDE-5. In the process, they relax smooth muscle cells in the penis and elsewhere. In causing these muscles to relax, the drugs effectively increase blood flow to the penis. Though they work in similar ways, Cialis, vardenafil, and Viagra are distinctly different entities.

Assuming both drugs are approved and live up to their advance billing, there could be a heated battle to take market share from Viagra. Being there first, of course, is a big advantage. For one thing, Pfizer has conducted more than eighty studies of Viagra, according to Michael Widlitz, a company vice president. "No competitor can hope to ascend this mountain of efficacy and safety data." Drug industry executives estimate that 30 million American men suffer from some degree of erectile dysfunction. However, only a third have tried Viagra, so the potential for continued growth is still there.

- Like most stocks with bright prospects, Pfizer often sells at an elevated price/earnings ratio.
- Pfizer will have more U.S. competition for two of its biggest drugs in 2002. AstraZeneca Plc intends to introduce a Lipitor rival, Crestor, while Eli Lilly is awaiting the U.S. approval of an

impotence drug (Cialis, discussed earlier) that will challenge Pfizer's Viagra.

- In a report issued by Argus Research Corporation, the analyst said, "One situation we are keeping our eye on, however, is the ongoing litigation between Pfizer and the previous users of Rezulin. Approved by the FDA in 1997 for the treatment of Type II diabetes, Rezulin was supplied by the Warner-Lambert Co. until the drug was withdrawn in March 2000 for causing liver failure and deaths." Pfizer's official position on the situation is that they have enough reserves and insurance coverage to handle the Rezulin liability. According to company officials, Rezulin will not have a material adverse effect on Pfizer's financial position.

Reasons to Buy

- While many companies had terrible results in 2001, Pfizer had a banner year. Commenting on the year, Pfizer chairman and CEO Hank McKinnell said, "Pfizer's strong operational momentum continues, as demonstrated by the strength of the fourth quarter. Earnings were propelled by the quarter's double-digit revenue growth, which was the company's highest of the year. Performance drivers included record research and development investments, a robust development pipeline, outstanding current products, superior sales and marketing capabilities, and continuing productivity initiatives.

  "We market eight of the world's thirty largest-selling medicines, more than any other company. We invested an industry-leading $4.8 billion in research and development in 2001 and fully supported our current products."
- "It's very nice to see that they feel so good about their business in light of the fact that other companies have been having difficulty lately," said Steve

Scala, drug industry analyst with S.G. Cowen. Pfizer, unlike Merck and Bristol-Myers, has few patent expirations to contend with, and it has continuing strong growth of most of its important drugs, such as cholesterol-reducer Lipitor and the antidepressant Zoloft."

- "In all my thirty years on Wall Street, I have never seen such a clear separation from the pack," said David Saks of the Saks MedScience Fund at Ladenburg Thalmann. "Pfizer demonstrated a confidence and crispness that is not had by anybody else in the industry. It is top-notch in terms of management, business model, execution, and results."
- Each day, 20,000 people around the world go to work promoting Pfizer products to the medical profession. They fill their "detail" bags with free samples of popular drugs such as Viagra and Zithromax, and they quote favorable conclusions from scientific studies (often company-sponsored) that show how Lipitor is the most potent way to control cholesterol and should be used instead of Merck's Zocor. By nearly all counts, Pfizer employs the industry's largest, and most effective, sales force.

  According to Henry A. McKinnell, Ph.D., who became the company's CEO at the beginning of 2001, "Pfizer has never been stronger and today possesses strengths and capabilities unequaled in the pharmaceutical industry. Our U.S. sales force, for example, was recently ranked as best in class in a survey of physicians, the sixth year in a row for this honor."
- Pfizer's Animal Health Group (AHG) in not only one of the largest in the world, but the group is also noteworthy for the breadth of its product lines and its geographic coverage. Innovative marketing has become an AHG hallmark in its efforts to succeed in a highly competitive market. An independent survey of

U.S. veterinarians, for example, named the Pfizer sales force the best in the industry.

- The company believes that its research and development operations will continue to set the industry standard. Pfizer expects to invest $5.3 billion in research in 2002, once again leading the industry. Over the next five years, said Karen Katen, "we have fifteen new medicines slated for regulatory filing, each one an impressive entry in an area of high medical need. Our development pipeline contains ninety-four new molecular entities and sixty-eight new product enhancements—for a total of 162 ongoing projects."
- Pfizer's revenue from helping market Pharmacia Corp.'s Celebrex pain killer and Eisai Co.'s Aricept drug for Alzheimer's disease rose 18 percent in 2001, to $411 million. Pfizer has been one of the drug industry's leaders in co-promotion agreements, enabling it to profit from sales of medicines developed outside its own laboratories.

Pfizer will help Pharmacia bring a new painkiller, Bextra, to market. Bextra is part of the Cox-2 class of painkillers, designed to be gentler on the stomach. That's because they more precisely target the cyclooxygenase-2 enzyme. The Cox-2 class includes Pharmacia's Celebrex as well as Vioxx and Arcoxia, a new drug made by Merck.

- In 2002, *Standard & Poor's Stock Reports* said, "Revenues are expected to advance 12 percent in 2002, boosted by growth in key lines such as Lipitor cholesterol-lowering agent, Norvasc cardiovascular, Zoloft antidepressant, Neurontin anticonvulsant, Zithromax antibiotic, and Viagra for erectile dysfunction. Sales of Lipitor should advance 20 percent, helped by the recent withdrawal of Bayer's rival Baycol from the market (due to adverse side effects).

"New products such as Geodon for schizophrenia, Relpax anti-migraine agent, and Vfend antifungal should also contribute to top-line growth."

Total assets: $33,510 million
Current ratio: 1.64
Common shares outstanding: 6,314 million
Return on 2001 shareholders' equity: 44.5%

		2001	2000	1999	1998	1997	1996	1995	1994
Revenues (millions)		32259	29574	16204	13544	12504	11306	10021	8281
Net income (millions)		7788	6495	3360	2627	2213	1929	1554	1298
Earnings per share		1.31	1.02	.87	.67	.57	.50	.41	.35
Dividends per share		.44	.36	.31	.25	.23	.20	.17	.16
Price	High	46.8	49.3	50.0	43.0	26.7	15.2	11.1	6.6
	Low	34.0	30.0	31.5	23.7	13.4	10.0	6.2	4.4

INCOME

Philip Morris Companies, Inc.

see Altria Group

INCOME

Piedmont Natural Gas Company, Inc.

Post Office Box 33068 ◻ Charlotte, North Carolina 28233 ◻ (704) 364-3483 ext. 6438 ◻ Dividend
reinvestment program is available: (800) 937-5449 ◻ Fiscal year ends October 31 ◻ Listed: NYSE ◻ Web site:
www.piedmontng.com ◻ Ticker symbol: PNY ◻ S&P rating: A- ◻ Value Line financial strength rating: B++

Piedmont Natural Gas's customer base has increased at a rate of more than 5 percent per year over the last five years, compared with an industry average of about 2 percent. This exceptional growth has largely been a function of new home construction, enhanced by a regional economy that is among the fastest-growing in the nation.

A key factor in further growth is Piedmont's low saturation of its market—it serves only 45 percent of its potential heating market. According to one analyst, "We believe that future customer growth levels will remain well above the industry average for the foreseeable future."

Company Profile

Incorporated in 1950, Piedmont Natural Gas is an energy services company that is primarily engaged in the transportation, distribution, and sale of natural gas as well as the sale of propane to residential, commercial, and industrial customers in North Carolina, South Carolina, and Tennessee.

The company is the second-largest natural gas utility in the Southeast, serving over 710,000 natural gas customers. Piedmont Natural Gas and its nonutility subsidiaries and divisions are also engaged in acquiring, marketing, transporting, and storing natural gas for large-volume customers, in retailing residential and commercial gas appliances, and in selling propane to over 480,000 customers in twenty-eight states.

An unregulated subsidiary of the company is an equity participant in a venture that markets natural gas to an additional 476,000 customers in Georgia, the first state in the venture's eight-state Southeastern market to open to retail competition for natural gas.

Piedmont is engaged in other business interests that are not subject to state utility regulation. Those include the sale of propane and investments in a natural gas pipeline; an interstate liquefied natural gas (LNG) storage facility; and marketing natural gas and other energy products and services to deregulated markets.

Shortcomings to Bear in Mind

- The company has benefited from extraordinary growth in its service territory. However, customer growth can be a double-edged sword, as it is expensive to continuously expand an underground pipe system to keep up with new construction. On the other hand, Piedmont has effectively lowered its customer connection cost to about $1,800, a significant decline over prior years. Analysts, moreover, expect this cost to continue to decline, which would contribute to future earnings growth.

- Record-high wholesale natural gas prices made 2001 "One of Piedmont's most challenging," said Ware F. Schiefer, president and CEO. These high prices "put tremendous pressure on the ability of many customers to pay their gas bills. Early in the year, the company began an extensive consumer education program in an attempt to forewarn our customers about higher winter gas prices.

"Also during the year, we instituted new payment options to assist customers in dealing with their higher gas bills, and we increased our contributions to nonprofit organizations that help low-income customers with their energy bill payments. Record cold weather in November and December only made matters worse for our customers, many of whom then reacted to the higher gas bills by reducing their gas consumption."

On a more positive note, the winter of 2001–2002 was much warmer, and residential customers received bills that are far lower that those of the prior winter.

Reasons to Buy

- Piedmont Natural gas has increased its dividend for 23 consecutive years. In the 1992–2001 period, dividends expanded from $0.91 per share to $1.52, a compound annual growth rate of 5.9 percent, or well ahead of the pace of inflation.

- The slowing economy has somewhat reduced overall customer growth. In spite of the downturn, however, new home construction remained strong in 2001 in Piedmont's service area. Customer additions grew at a healthy rate of 4.4 percent, or about three times the national average for natural gas utilities.

   In the residential markets, Piedmont gained 27,600 new customers in 2001, of which 21,700 were from new construction activity. Customer additions resulting from existing homeowner conversions amounted to 5,900 for the year. Interestingly, 82 percent of all residential customers added during 2001 were customers who will consume natural gas throughout the year, not merely during the winter heating season.

   According to Mr. Schiefer, "High market shares in this important sector continue to demonstrate the benefits of our marketing efforts and emphasize the importance of the company's trade ally relationships, a key element of our overall sales and marketing strategies."

- The company's nonutility activities continued to expand in 2001, contributing $9.8 million to net income for the year, or 15 percent of total net income. Through a subsidiary, the company's SouthStar joint venture holds a 39 percent market share in Georgia's deregulated retail gas market, and SouthStar was the largest nonutility contributor to earnings in 2001. Doing business as Georgia Natural Gas Services, SouthStar accounted for $5.2 million of Piedmont's net income, more than three times its contribution the prior year.

- Piedmont reached another milestone in its nonutility strategy in 2001, when the company announced its investment in a joint venture with Dominion Resources. The Greenbrier Pipeline will be a $497 million, 263-mile pipeline connecting significant gas production and storage regions to North Carolina to domestic markets in the Southeast. This pipeline is owned 33 percent by Piedmont and 67 percent by Dominion. According to Mr. Schiefer, "The capacity of this line will help serve the growing needs of gas utilities in the Southeast and provide a source of supply of power generation projects that are planned for the region."

- In fiscal 2002, Piedmont Natural Gas announced that it would build, own, and operate a natural gas pipeline that will deliver supplies to a 640-megawatt power plant in Cherokee County, South Carolina. The Mill Creek Plant, owned by Duke Energy Company, is scheduled to go into operation by June 2003. The eight simple-cycle combustion turbines at the Mill Creek plant are designed to operate as a "peaking" facility, providing power primarily during periods when customer use is at it greatest—during the hottest or coldest days of the year.

The agreement marks Piedmont's fifth contract for power generation-related pipeline investments for the Carolinas and its second such project with Duke Power, a subsidiary of Duke Energy. Piedmont already serves Duke Power's Lincoln County plant in North Carolina. Through these five agreements, Piedmont will have invested over $10 million to deliver natural gas to over 4,500 megawatts of generating capacity in the Carolinas by 2003.

■ Piedmont Natural Gas enjoys an economically robust and diverse service area that is among the fastest growing in the nation. The company's three-state service area consists of the Piedmont region of the Carolinas—Charlotte, Salisbury, Greensboro, Winston-Salem, High Point, Burlington, and Hickory in North Carolina and Anderson, Greenville, and Spartanburg in South Carolina—and the metropolitan area of Nashville, Tennessee. Both *Plant Sites and Parks* and *Site Selection* magazines continue to rank the Carolinas and Tennessee among the best in the nation for business relocation and expansion and business climate.

At the center of the Piedmont Carolinas area is the greater Charlotte urban region—sixth largest in the nation—with over six million people within a 100-mile radius. Charlotte is the nation's second-largest financial center. It is headquarters for Bank of America, the nation's largest bank, and for First Union National bank, the sixth largest. Wachovia Corporation, the nation's sixteenth-largest bank, is headquartered in Winston-Salem.

Charlotte/Douglas International Airport, with over 500 flights per day and 23 million passengers annually, is U.S. Airways' largest hub and the twentieth busiest airport in the world.

The Nashville region is a diverse center of a retail trading area of over two million people, where health care is the largest industry. It is also home to major transportation, music, publishing, printing, financial, insurance, and communications companies as well as twenty colleges and universities.

■ An important factor in analyzing any public utility is the region's regulatory environment. In Piedmont's states, regulators have generally been supportive of the company's regulatory needs over the past few years. In the opinion of Daniel M. Fidell and Tracey W. McMillin, analysts with A.G. Edwards, "Our conclusion is based on several factors, such as purchased gas and weather normalization mechanisms in rates that serve to smooth the impact of changes in gas prices and abnormal weather conditions. In addition, PNY has benefited from fair and timely rate relief in the past to recover costs associated with extensive system growth."

Total assets: $1,395 million
Current ratio: 1.17
Common shares outstanding: 32 million
Return on 2001 shareholders' equity: 11.7%

	2001	2000	1999	1998	1997	1996	1995	1994
Revenues (millions)	1108	830	686	765	776	685	505	575
Net income (millions)	65	64	58	60	55	49	40	36
Earnings per share	2.02	2.01	1.86	1.96	1.85	1.67	1.45	1.35
Dividends per share	1.52	1.44	1.36	1.28	1.21	1.15	1.09	1.01
Price High	38.0	39.4	36.6	36.1	36.4	25.8	24.9	23.4
Low	29.2	28.6	27.9	22.0	20.5	18.3	18.0	18.8

Pitney Bowes, Inc.

1 Elmcroft Road □ Stamford, CT 06926-0700 □ (203) 351-6349 □ Dividend reinvestment plan is available: (800) 648-8170 □ Web site: www.pitneybowes.com □ Listed: NYSE □ Ticker symbol: PBI □ S&P rating: A+ □ Value Line financial strength rating: A

In 2001, Pitney Bowes acquired Danka Services International (DSI), a wholly owned subsidiary of Danka Business Systems PLC, for $290 million. It is now part of Pitney Bowes Management Services, a leading provider of facilities management services for the business-support functions of creating, processing, storage, retrieval, distribution, and tracking of information, messages, documents, and packages.

"Acquiring DSI is in accord with our mission to provide leading-edge, global, integrated mail, and document-management solutions," said Michael J. Critelli, CEO of Pitney Bowes. "More than ever, today's corporations see their documents as strategic assets and understand that information sharing, through efficient document imaging, distribution, management can 'unlock' this value and build distinct competitive advantage.

"From outgoing and incoming mail and messaging management, document creation production, to distribution, archiving and retrieval, Pitney Bowes Management Services provides a variety of ways to input, access, and manage documents, giving customers tools to match their tasks, processes, and their individual work habits," said Critelli.

DSI began operations in 1991 as Kodak Imaging Services (a division of Eastman Kodak). The company was acquired by Danka in 1996 and became Danka Services International. Today, DSI has about 330 customer operations and employs about 3,400 people in the United States, Canada, the United Kingdom, Ireland, France, Italy, Denmark, Sweden, Germany, Norway, the Netherlands, and Belgium.

Pitney Bowes Management Services today represents more than 15 percent of Pitney Bowes' consolidated revenue and is among the fastest-growing components of the business. Combined, Pitney Bowes Management Services and DSI will produce nearly $1 billion in annualized revenue, making it one of the largest players in its market.

"DSI has a solid track record of providing customers with leading-edge technology, process management expertise, and turnkey people-friendly solutions," said Randy Miller, who will remain with the combined companies as president.

Company Profile

A pioneer and world leader in mailing systems, Pitney Bowes is a multinational manufacturing and marketing company that provides mailing, shipping, dictating, copying, and facsimile systems; item identification and tracking systems and supplies; mailroom, reprographics, and related management services; and product financing.

The key to Pitney Bowes will probably continue to be consistency rather than spectacular growth, in view of the maturity of its highly profitable postage-meter rental business and the moderate growth of some of its other annuity revenues, such as service.

On the other hand, analysts believe that the stock has limited downside risk; it should appeal largely to long-term investors.

Pitney Bowes is best known as the worldwide leader in mailing systems. It markets a full line of mailing systems, shipping and weighing systems, addressing systems, production mail systems, folding and inserting systems, and mailing software.

Pitney Bowes Software Systems, a division of Mailing Systems located in Illinois, offers a full range of advanced software and services for business communications, and marketing and mailing applications to *Fortune* 1000 companies.

Shipping and Weighing Systems (SWS) provides parcel and freight information and automation systems for the shipping and transportation management functions of the logistics market.

SWS products are marketed through Mailing Systems' worldwide distribution channels, with particular emphasis on North America. Service is provided by specially trained service representatives and a National Remote Diagnostic Center.

Pitney Bowes Transportation Software, a division of Pitney Bowes located in Minnesota, markets and develops logistics management solutions and provides consulting services.

Other Businesses of Pitney Bowes

The company's other businesses are also important. A brief description of each follows.

Pitney Bowes Management Services (PBMS) is a leading provider of facilities management services for the business support functions of creating, processing, storage, retrieval, distribution, and tracking of information, messages, documents, and packages.

Using the latest available technology, PBMS manages mail centers, copy and reprographic centers, facsimile services, electronic printing and imaging services, and records management services for customers across the United States, as well as in Canada and the United Kingdom.

Pitney Bowes Facsimile Systems is a leading supplier of high-quality facsimile equipment to the business market. It is the only facsimile system supplier in the United States that markets solely through its own direct sales force nationwide.

Pitney Bowes' Copier Systems concentrates on serving larger corporations with multiunit installations of its full line of equipment.

Pitney Bowes Financial Services provides lease-financing programs for customers who use products marketed by Pitney Bowes companies.

Shortcomings to Bear in Mind

- Several small newcomers are racing to develop a computer-generated stamp that would replace the old, expensive system of stamping inky, eagle-adorned postmarks onto envelopes. The new "stamps" would include a bold, black bar code below the traditional postmark. Instead of going to the post office to purchase postage in bulk, users would save time by simply ordering and downloading stamps off the Internet and printing them onto envelopes.

  On the other hand, Pitney postage meters still dominate the domestic market, despite aggressive competition from digitally savvy companies like Neopost and Francotyp-Postalia AG of Germany. And analysts expect Pitney Bowes to garner 30 percent of the international postage meter market by 2004, up from about 14 percent at present.

Reasons to Buy

- In early 2002, Pitney Bowes CEO Critelli said, "During the fourth quarter, we successfully completed the spin-off of Imagistics International, Inc., to shareholders and also completed the acquisition of Secap SA, a leading provider of digital mailing and paper-handling systems in France. Both of these transactions enhance our strategy of delivering shareholder value by providing leading-edge global, integrated mail and document-management solutions to organizations of all sizes."

- Some observers are concerned that the volume of mail may be declining, as people rely more on the telephone and their connection with the Internet.

Mr. Critelli, responding to this concern, says, "Outside experts confirm our internal findings that mail volumes worldwide will continue to increase for the next ten years. Lots of paper-based communication is going away, but it is more than being offset by growth engines."

According to Mr. Critelli, there is explosive growth in direct mail marketing. To be sure, individual mailings are falling a couple of percent each year. On the other hand, direct mail is climbing at a far faster pace, between 6 and 8 percent a year. As a result, says the Pitney CEO, the overall volume of mail is going up each year. What's more, the same trend is visible in other developed markets. In the developing world, moreover, the growth of mail is even more explosive. China, for example, is registering increases of 25 percent a year.

- Pitney Bowes has a consistent record of earnings growth. In the 1991–2001 period, earnings per share advanced from $0.90 to $2.26, an annual compound growth rate of 9.6 percent. In the same ten-year stretch, dividends per share climbed from $0.35 to $1.16, a growth rate of 12.7 percent. What's more, the dividend was raised every year.

- As the largest business unit of Pitney Bowes, Mailing Systems is the world leader in helping customers to manage their messages through mailing solutions. These systems are marketed to businesses of all sizes—from the smallest office to *Fortune* 500 companies. With over 2 million customers worldwide, Pitney Bowes Mailing Systems is focused on keeping business messages moving and its customers ahead of the curve.

With products such as the DocuMatch Integrated Mail System, Paragon II Mail Processor, and the AddressRight System, large mailers are provided the tools they need to drive their businesses and enhance competitiveness. The Galaxy Mailing System and Series 3 Folder and Inserter address similar needs in midsize organizations. With DirectNet, a hybrid mailing service, the company is able to assist customers of all sizes with value-added capabilities to improve the efficiency and impact of their messaging applications.

- Pitney Bowes has a number of businesses that lag behind the economic cycle, but they should also resist a downturn. About two-thirds of total revenues come from annuity sources such as postage meter rentals, rentals of other mailing and business equipment, facilities management and rentals, finance, service, and supply revenues.

- Patents and other intellectual property will be more valuable than ever in the Internet era. Pitney Bowes has been ranked in the top 200 of domestic patents issued for more than a decade. The company holds more than 3,000 active patents worldwide—more than 200 on Internet concepts alone.

- In February of 2002, an analyst with *Standard & Poor's Stock Reports* had some favorable comments on Pitney Bowes. "The shares have significantly outperformed the broader market over the past year, rising over 20 percent, compared with declines for the major indexes. These results reflect an investor shift to the relative safety of a company with a large percentage of recurring revenues, a leadership position in its market, and a healthy dividend of close to 3 percent. In addition, competitors from the e-business marketplace have struggled, and thus we do not believe Internet mailing is a major near-term threat to PBI."

Total assets: $7,901 million
Current ratio: 1.02
Common shares outstanding: 244 million
Return on 2001 shareholders' equity: 42.5%

	2001	2000	1999	1998	1997	1996	1995	1994
Revenues (millions)	4122	3881	3812	4221	4100	3859	3555	3271
Net income (millions)	514	563	533	568	526	469	408	348
Earnings per share	2.26	2.19	1.96	2.03	1.80	1.56	1.34	1.11
Dividends per share	1.16	1.14	1.02	.90	.80	.69	.60	.52
Price High	44.7	54.1	73.3	66.4	45.8	30.7	24.1	23.2
Low	32.0	24.0	40.9	42.2	26.8	20.9	15.0	14.6

CONSERVATIVE GROWTH

Praxair, Inc.

39 Old Ridgebury Road □ Danbury, CT 06810-5113 □ (203) 837-2073 □ Dividend reinvestment plan is available: (800) 432-0140 □ Web site: www.praxair.com □ Listed: NYSE □ Ticker symbol: PX □ S&P rating: A □ Value Line financial strength rating: B++

In a 2001 conference call sponsored by J. P. Morgan Securities, Inc., analysts interviewed John Campbell, a well-respected industrial gases consultant and publisher of the insightful monthly, *CryoGas International.*

Mr. Campbell commented on Praxair, saying, "The gases industry has historically performed well relative to the rest of the chemical sector during economic hard landings." To illustrate the point, he went back to 1991, a period of weakness in the economy. He said, "Praxair's U.S. gases operating income actually increased in 1991. We think that the relatively stable nature of pricing in the gases industry is why the industry does well during periods of soft economic growth."

In another part of the interview, Mr. Campbell said, "Praxair had one of the best CEOs in the retired Bill Lichtenberger, but they have a dynamo in the new CEO, Dennis Reilley, who came from DuPont last year (2000). Praxair has a significant focus on shareholder value, growing key end markets with unique offerings, lowering capital intensity with a higher service content, and a focus on generating price improvements. Key market focuses for Praxair include surface technologies, health care, metals technologies, food and beverage, distributor type business."

Company Profile

Praxair serves a diverse group of industries through the production, sale, and distribution of industrial gases and high-performance surface coatings, along with related services, materials, and systems.

Praxair, which was spun off to Union Carbide shareholders in June 1992, is the largest producer of industrial gases in North and South America; it is the third-largest company of its kind in the world.

Praxair's major customers include industries such as aerospace, chemicals, electronics, food processing, health care, glass, metal fabrication, petroleum, primary metals, as well as pulp and paper companies.

As a pioneer in the industrial gases industry, Praxair has been a leader in developing a wide range of proprietary and patented applications and supply-system technology.

The company's primary industrial gases products are atmospheric gases (oxygen, nitrogen, argon, and rare gases) and process gases (helium, hydrogen, electronics gases, and acetylene). Praxair also designs, engineers, and supervises construction of cryogenic and noncryogenic supply systems.

Praxair Surface Technologies provides metallic and ceramic coatings and powders used on metal surfaces to resist wear, high temperatures, and corrosion. Aircraft engine manufacturers are its primary market, but it serves others, including the printing, textile, chemical, and primary metals markets. Praxair also provides aircraft engine and airframe component overhaul services.

The company was founded in the United States in 1907 as Linde Air Products Company.

Shortcomings to Bear in Mind

- *Standard & Poor's Stock Reports* in early 2002 was concerned about two Praxair weaknesses: "Results in Brazil (10 percent of sales) will continue to be hurt by mandated power curtailments, although less than in the second half of 2001, and currency rates may turn favorable in the second quarter.

"The Surface Technologies will be hurt by an anticipated decline in commercial aircraft engine production and servicing, partly offset by greater military orders."

- The recession is curtailing industrial gas consumption by such important customers as the steel industry.

Reasons to Buy

- At the end of 2001, Nestle USA, Inc., selected Praxair to provide engineering services in the design and installation of a carbon dioxide (CO_2) mechanical refrigeration-based food freezing system for Nestle's new state-of-the-art frozen foods plant in Jonesboro, Arkansas. The refrigeration system will employ Praxair's patented CO_2 Mechanical Refrigeration technology, which allows food processors to operate their freezing systems at temperatures below traditional ammonia-based refrigeration systems, at the same time eliminating the presence of ammonia in their processing rooms.

  According to Michael Sinicropi, director of Praxair Food Technologies, "Our patented technology is another new offering in Praxair's portfolio of low-temperature freezing and chilling systems for the food industry. These offerings help to increase productivity while enabling processors to more easily comply with safety and environmental regulations."

- In early 2002, *Standard & Poor's Stock Reports* said, "We also view favorably additional restructuring actions announced by the company. PX will concentrate on several less capital-intensive, faster-growing global markets, in addition to core industrial gases. We believe investors will view these actions positively, despite continuing concerns about the economy."

- Praxair acquired Interwest Home

Medical, Inc., in 2001 for $42 million plus the assumption of debt. The deal enables Praxair to expand its delivery of health care products and services in the Rocky Mountain region. Interwest Home Medical, which rents and sells home oxygen, respiratory equipment, and other home medical equipment, has twenty-five branch locations in Utah, Arizona, Idaho, Nevada, Colorado, Alaska, and California.

- Hydrogen is part of a comprehensive portfolio of bulk and specialty gases, technologies, and services that Praxair provides refining and chemical customers worldwide. For example, Praxair supplies more than fifty refineries and petrochemical plants from its 280 miles of pipeline along the Texas and Louisiana Gulf Coast. Other Praxair pipeline enclaves serving these industries are situated in Ecorse, Michigan; Edmonton, Alberta, Canada; Salvador, Brazil; Antwerp, Belgium; and Beijing, China.

- In addition to helium for fiber optics, Praxair's $400-million electronics portfolio includes semiconductor materials and services, electronic assembly applications, and specialty materials being developed by Praxair Surface Technologies. One of Praxair's fastest-growing businesses, Praxair Semiconductor Materials, builds and manages advanced gas systems in Asia, Europe, and North America, helping chip manufacturers lower the cost of ownership, reduce environmental impact, and improve productivity.

- Beyond its longstanding supply of pure oxygen and bulk storage equipment to hospitals and other medical facilities worldwide, Praxair delivers respiratory therapy gases and equipment as well as a host of on-site gas-management services, including asset, inventory, transaction, and distribution management. Praxair's home oxygen services, moreover, provide respiratory patients with life support, as well as therapies to help with sleep disorders or other illnesses in the home environment.

- Praxair's Surface Technologies develops high-performance coatings and allied technologies that provide resistance to wear, high temperatures, corrosion, and fatigue for metal parts. More recently, it has diversified into materials that answer the needs of the rapidly evolving electronics industry, adding to the already considerable portfolio of products and services offered by Praxair Semiconductor Materials.

- Praxair Metals Technologies was formed in 2000 to develop and commercialize technologies and services to the global metals industry. The organization may be new, but Praxair has been bringing innovations to the metals industry for most of its ninety-year history. The majority of the world's stainless steel producers, for instance, use Praxair's argon-oxygen-decarburization technology. Oxy-fuel combustion, postcombustion, hot-oxygen-injection, slag splashing, and tundish inerting technologies are just a few more examples. Praxair holds more than 275 patents for steel-making technologies.

- The addition of carbon dioxide to Praxair's portfolio opens up new avenues for growth in relatively noncyclical markets, including food preservation, beverage carbonation, and water treatment. Looking ahead, increased demand for beverage carbonation and water treatment, particularly in emerging South American and Asian markets, promises to generate continued growth. Supplying global beverage-carbonation customers also leads to opportunities in new markets for other Praxair products and technology. Use of carbon dioxide in new food-preservation markets, such as bakery goods and dairy products, also is on the verge of rapid growth.

- In recent years, Praxair has developed noncryogenic air-separation technology, allowing lower-cost delivery to customers who have smaller volume needs. By sacrificing a small amount of purity, these customers can purchase a gas that meets customer needs at a discount to the cost of traditional supplies of product in cryogenic liquid form. This product is less expensive for Praxair to produce—and thus higher-margined relative to "cryo" liquid. Not least, demand is growing dramatically.

- Praxair sees opportunities to differentiate its offering in the food and beverage segment, based on the need for higher standards of food safety. Praxair

is bringing the U.S. poultry processing industry the potential to save more than 15 billion gallons of water and $70 million each year through a water recycling system that helps increase production and reduce water consumption without compromising food safety.

- The sparkle in soft drinks, the freshness of pastries, the crunch in an apple—chances are, Praxair carbon dioxide or nitrogen had something to do with all of it. At Praxair's Food Technology Laboratory—the only one of its kind in the industry—technologies and equipment are developed and tested to assist bakers, meat processors, and specialty foods producers deliver products that retain their taste and freshness.

Total assets: $7,715 million
Current ratio: 1.07
Common shares outstanding: 161 million
Return on 2001 shareholders' equity: 17.9%

		2001	2000	1999	1998	1997	1996	1995	1994
Revenues (millions)		5158	5043	4639	4833	4735	4449	3146	2711
Net income (millions)		432	480	441	425	416	335	262	203
Earnings per share		2.64	2.98	2.72	2.60	2.53	2.11	1.82	1.45
Dividends per share		.68	.62	.56	.50	.44	.38	.32	.28
Price	High	55.8	54.9	58.1	53.9	58.0	50.1	34.1	24.5
	Low	36.5	30.3	32.0	30.7	39.3	31.5	19.8	16.3

CONSERVATIVE GROWTH

The Procter & Gamble Company

Post Office Box 599 ◻ Cincinnati, Ohio 45201-0599 ◻ (513) 983-2414 ◻ Direct dividend reinvestment plan is available: (800) 764-7483 ◻ Web site: www.pg.com ◻ Listed: NYSE ◻ Fiscal year ends June 30 ◻ Ticker symbol: PG ◻ S&P rating: A ◻ Value Line financial strength rating: A++

In late 2001, Procter & Gamble received Justice Department approval for its $4.95 billion purchase of the Clairol line of hair-care products, its biggest-ever acquisition. With this move, Procter & Gamble gained such brands as Herbal Essences and

Aussie, in addition to all Clairol hair-care products. Procter & Gamble is a major force in the $4.1 billion U.S. mass-market hair-care segment and boasts such brands as Pantene, Head & Shoulders, Pert, Physique, and Vidal Sassoon.

The company doesn't disclose the extent of its hair-care products. However, its beauty-care division overall has annual sales of more than $7 billion. This includes skin care, cosmetics, deodorants, and other products, in addition to hair care. Its beauty products include Olay, Max Factor, Cover Girl, Giorgio, and Hugo Boss.

Clairol's hair-color brands, which include Nice 'n Easy, Hydrience, Natural Instincts, and Miss Clairol, generate about $1.6 billion in annual revenues. Clairol controls a solid 39 percent of the hair-coloring market, according to A.C. Nielsen, the market research concern. L'Oreal SA is the leader, with a 50 percent share.

The addition of Clairol provides Procter & Gamble with a significant entry into the hair-coloring business, a new sector for the Cincinnati consumer-products company and one that is expanding faster than the shampoo market. Over the past five years, the global hair-color business has grown at a 4-to-6 percent clip, or about double the pace of shampoo, conditioners, and styling aids.

Company Profile

Procter & Gamble dates back to 1837, when William Procter and James Gamble began making soap and candles in Cincinnati. The company's first major product introduction took place in 1879, when it launched Ivory soap. Since then, Procter & Gamble has traditionally created a host of blockbuster products that have made the company a cash-generating machine.

Procter & Gamble is a uniquely diversified consumer-products company with a strong global presence. Procter & Gamble today markets its broad line of products to nearly 5 billion consumers in more than 140 countries.

Procter & Gamble is a recognized leader in the development, manufacturing, and marketing of superior quality laundry, cleaning, paper, personal care, food,

beverage, and health care products, including prescription pharmaceuticals.

Among the company's more than 300 brands are Tide, Always, Whisper, Didronel, Pro-V, Oil of Olay, Pringles, Ariel, Crest, Pampers, Pantene, Vicks, Bold, Dawn, Head & Shoulders, Cascade, Iams, Zest, Bounty, Comet, Scope, Old Spice, Folgers, Charmin, Tampax, Downy, Cheer, and Prell.

Procter & Gamble is a huge company, with 2001 sales of $39 billion. In the same fiscal year (which ended June 30, 2001), earnings per share advanced from $2.95 to $3.12. Dividends also climbed—as they have for many years—from $1.28 to $1.40.

Shortcomings to Bear in Mind

- In comments made by Standard & Poor's in late 2001, the analyst said, "We believe price increases will be difficult for the company to implement, due to severe competition in all of its industry segments. We expect a stabilization of raw material prices and better cost-control to lead to improved margins. Operating margins should widen slightly, benefiting from a restructuring program that will streamline operations and improve new product flow. These gains are expected to be partly offset by higher marketing and advertisement expenses, related to new product launches."

- Emily Nelson, writing for *The Wall Street Journal* in the spring of 2001, was critical of the company's acquisition of Clairol. She said, "Procter & Gamble Co. has a mess at home. So, how can the maker of Tide, Mr. Clean, and Bounty be thinking of adding something else to worry about?

"P&G Chief Executive, A. G. Lafley is in the midst of cutting 17,400 jobs, shedding big food brands, and playing catch-up to rivals in paper goods. Yet the company is bidding about $4 billion to

$4.5 billion to buy Clairol from Bristol-Myers Squibb Co, in what would be P&G's largest-ever acquisition. P&G would get a hefty management challenge: integrating Clairol's five factories and marketing the brands, which have been on the auction block since last fall and face tough hair-color competition from rivals L'Oreal SA and Revlon, Inc."

Reasons to Buy

- In 2001, Procter & Gamble made progress in its domestic market. A year earlier, only three of its top ten U.S. brands were expanding market share. At the end of fiscal 2001, eight of ten were growing share. This progress wasn't limited to the United States.
  - In Latin America, 3-percent volume growth propelled earnings to record levels.
  - Profits rebounded in China during the year, and market shares are now growing broadly.
  - Elsewhere in Asia, according to CEO A. G. Lafley, "We grew volume in virtually every country; in the Philippines, for example, our Fabric and Home Care business turned in an exceptional year with record volume and profits, while regaining volume-share leadership."
  - In Central and Eastern Europe, Russia bounced back from the 1998 economic and currency crises; "volume, sales and market shares are all rebounding with solid profits," said Mr. Lafley.
- In 2000, P&G had five of the top new U.S. consumer products, as reported in the Information Resources, Inc., annual study. Over the past eight years, moreover, the company has averaged three to four in the top ten new items each year. In fact, over the last four years, P&G launched thirteen new products in the United States, each of which has exceeded $100 million in sales. Finally, the company now has eleven brands with more than a billion dollars in annual sales, including Iams pet foods, Tide, Pampers, Ariel, Bounty, Charmin, Pringles, Folgers, and Downy.

- In a recent U.S. survey by Cannondale Associates, retailers were asked to rank manufacturers on a number of competencies. P&G was ranked number one in virtually every category:
  - Clearest company strategy
  - Brands most important to retailers
  - Best brand-marketers overall
  - Most innovative marketing programs
- The company is making a concerted effort to woo Hispanic consumers. In one recent twelve-month period, for instance, Procter & Gamble distributed 4.5 million copies of its promotional magazine *Avanzando con tu Familia*, or *Getting Ahead with Your family*. That amounts to one for every two Latino households. P&G's goal is to build a fire under some brands that are lagging. The company leads in various categories of the Hispanic market, including detergents and shampoos, but some key brands are not up to snuff, including P&G's Cover Girl and Dawn, its dishwashing detergent.

  The company views Hispanics as an underserved market of 32 million people—a market that is growing fast. Over the next fifty years, the Hispanic population will grow by 100 million, according to U.S. census estimates, contributing more than half of the country's population increase. What's more, Hispanics are getting more affluent. Mean household income has expanded by 13.4 percent (adjusted for inflation) in the past decade, to close to $40,500. Finally, Latinos tend to spend big on the type of products that the company sells, such as diapers and shampoo.

- Procter & Gamble is known for product innovation. More than 8,000 scientists and researchers are accelerating the pace of new products. The company has a global network of eighteen technical centers in nine countries on four continents. What's more, P&G holds more than 27,000 patents and applies for 3,000 more each year. Not surprisingly, the company is among the ten patent-producing companies in the world—well ahead of any other consumer-products manufacturer.
- Today, about half of P&G's sales come from North America, yet 95 percent of the world's population lives *outside* that region.

  According to recently retired CEO John Pepper, "If we can achieve these levels of success around the world in just our existing businesses, we'll more than double our current sales and profits."

  "This tremendous potential for growth exists in category after category," states Procter & Gamble's annual report. Capitalizing on this potential will not be easy, but the company will pursue it by staying focused on the company's key value and globalization strategies while placing particular emphasis on three fundamental areas.

- Better products at more competitive prices.
- Deeper, broader cost control.
- Faster, more effective globalization.
- Procter & Gamble believes in product quality. One of the reasons given for the company's problems in 2000 is its refusal to get into the lower-quality, lower-cost private-label business. That just goes against the grain.

  Procter & Gamble believes that the consumer will reward even minor product advantages, and it will not launch a brand if it does not have a competitive advantage. Then, it will continually improve its products and make every effort to maintain that advantage. Tide, for example, has been improved more than seventy times over the years.

- In mid-2001, Procter & Gamble and media group Viacom entered into a broad marketing agreement under which the consumer products giant can now market its brands across the whole spectrum of Viacom television outlets. This unusual one-stop shopping pact enables Procter & Gamble to promote its products on Viacom television and cable outlets such as CBS, MTV, and Comedy Central.

Total assets: $34,387 million
Current ratio: 1.11
Common shares outstanding: 1,296 million
Return on 2001 shareholders' equity: 36.6%

		2001	2000	1999	1998	1997	1996	1995	1994
Revenues (millions)		39244	39951	38125	37154	35764	35284	33434	30296
Net income (millions)		4397	4230	4148	3780	3415	3046	2645	2211
Earnings per share		3.12	2.95	2.85	2.56	2.28	2.15	1.86	1.55
Dividends per share		1.40	1.28	1.14	1.01	.90	.80	.70	.62
Price	High	81.72	118.4	115.6	94.8	83.4	55.5	44.8	32.3
	Low	55.96	52.8	82.0	65.1	51.8	39.7	30.3	25.6

Safeway, Inc.

5918 Stoneridge Mall Road ◻ Pleasanton, California 94566-3229 ◻ (925) 467-3136 ◻ Dividend reinvestment plan is not available ◻ Web site: www.safeway.com ◻ Listed: NYSE ◻ Ticker symbol: SWY ◻ S&P rating: B+ ◻ Value Line financial strength rating: B++

"The top three players—Kroger, Albertson's, and Safeway—have all benefited from industry-wide consolidation and heightened consumer demand for convenience products," said *Money* magazine in its March 2002 issue. "Our pick, Safeway, the third-biggest by revenue, has vastly improved margins to become the most profitable of the big chains.

"As much as a supermarket can be, Safeway has been on fire under the direction of CEO Steve Burd, boosting earnings an average of 20 percent a year for the past five years by increasing same-store sales, promoting aggressively, and making moderate-size acquisitions of regional chains."

Company Profile

Safeway was first incorporated in 1926, upon payment of a $960 tax and a $15 recording fee to the state of Maryland. However, the company traces its roots back to 1915 and the small Idaho town of American Falls, where Marion B. Skaggs bought his father's tiny grocery store for $1,088. At only 576 square feet in overall size, Mr. Skaggs's first store was minuscule compared to the company's 55,000-square-foot prototype superstore today.

Less than eleven years after that first purchase, with the help of his five brothers and other pioneering grocers, Skaggs built his fledgling organization to 428 grocery stores and meat markets spanning ten western states. In 1926, these units merged with the 322 former Sam Seelig stores in southern California (which had adopted the name "Safeway" the previous year).

Safeway, Inc., is one of the largest food and drug retailers in North America. At the end of 2001, the company operated 1,773 stores in the Western, Southwestern, Rocky Mountain, and mid-Atlantic regions of the United States and Canada. The company's retail operations are situated principally in California, Oregon, Washington, Alaska, Colorado, Arizona, Texas, the Chicago metropolitan area, and the mid-Atlantic region.

The company's Canadian retail operations are situated principally in British Columbia, Alberta, Manitoba, and Saskatchewan.

Safeway also holds a 49 percent interest in Casa Ley, S.A., de C.V., which at the end of 2001 operated ninety-nine food and general merchandise stores in western Mexico.

Each of Safeway's twelve retail operating areas is served by a regional distribution center consisting of one or more facilities. The company has sixteen distribution/warehousing centers (thirteen in the United States, and three in Canada), which collectively provide the majority of all products to Safeway stores. The principal function of manufacturing operations is to purchase, manufacture, and process private-label merchandise sold in Safeway stores.

In 2001, Safeway acquired Genuardi's Family Markets, Inc., which at the close of the transaction operated thirty-nine stores in Pennsylvania, Delaware, and New Jersey.

Safeway's average store size is about 44,000 square feet. Safeway's primary new store prototype is 55,000 square feet and is designed both to accommodate changing customer needs and to achieve certain operating efficiencies.

Most stores offer a wide selection of both food and general merchandise and feature a variety of specialty departments, such as bakery, delicatessen, floral, and pharmacy.

At the end of 2001, the company owned about one-third of its stores and leased its remaining outlets. In recent years, Safeway has preferred ownership because it provides control and flexibility with respect to financing terms, remodeling, expansions, and closures.

Shortcomings to Bear in Mind

- Safeway has a rather leveraged balance sheet, with only 52 percent of its capitalization in shareholders' equity. However, coverage of debt interest is adequate at 5.2 times.
- *Value Line Survey* was somewhat critical of Safeway in a report issued in November of 2001. The analyst, Robert M. Greene, CFA, said, "Safeway's same-store sales trends have slowed during 2001. Identical-store sales were up 0.8 percent in the September quarter, a far cry from the consistent 3-percent-plus gains enjoyed during the late Nineties. The sales weakness is confined to three of Safeway's ten operating regions. These areas have experienced a high level of competitive-store openings of late, though these pressures are likely to moderate over the next two years. The company has developed a number of sales-building strategies, but thus far these efforts have been largely thwarted by increased competition."

Reasons to Buy

- Almost 85 percent of the company's sales come from stores situated in areas

growing faster than the national average in the United States and Canada. By concentrating the majority of its capital spending in attractive, high-growth areas where the company commands strong market positions, CEO Steven A. Burd believes, "we enhance our prospects for long-term sales growth and operating margin improvement."

- In 2001, the company acquired Genuardi's Family Markets, Inc., with thirty-nine stores in Pennsylvania, Delaware, and New Jersey. One of the region's leading supermarket chains, Genuardi's is renowned for superior-quality perishables and great customer service. According to Mr. Burd, "Its operating philosophy and corporate culture should mesh well with Safeway's."
- At about the same time, the company purchased eleven ABCO stores in Arizona to complement Safeway's eighty-nine-store Phoenix Division. Mr. Burd says, "Acquisitions continue to be a key element of our long-term growth strategy."
- Safeway believes its greatest opportunity for meaningful long-term growth revolves around the acquisition of other established supermarket companies that are either the leading or second-leading chains in their respective market regions or that offer room for improvement in operating performance. This strategy proved successful with the 1997 acquisition of Vons, Inc., and such acquisitions as Dominick's (acquired in late 1998), Carr-Gottstein Foods (1999), and Randall's in the fall of 1999.
- During the past eight years, Safeway has consistently ranked among the industry's leaders in the following key measures of financial performance: same-store sales growth, cost reduction, working capital management, operating

cash flow margin expansion, and earnings-per-share growth.

- Safeway has developed a line of more
than 1,100 premium corporate brand
products since 1993 under the "Safeway
Select" banner. The award-winning
Safeway Select line is designed to offer
premium quality products that the company believes are equal or superior in
quality to comparable bestselling nationally advertised brands or that are unique
to the category and not available from
national brand manufacturers.

  The Safeway Select line of products
includes carbonated soft drinks; unique
salsas; the Indulgence line of cookies
and other sweets; the Verdi line of fresh
and frozen pastas, pasta sauces, and
olive oils; Artisan fresh-baked breads;
Twice-the-Fruit yogurt; NutraBalance
dog food; Ultra laundry detergents and
dish soaps; and Softly paper products.

  The Safeway Select line also includes
an extensive array of ice creams, frozen
yogurts, and sorbets; Healthy Advantage
items, such as low-fat ice creams and
low-fat cereal bars; and Gourmet Club
frozen entrees and hors d'oeuvres. In
addition, Safeway has repackaged over
2,500 corporate brand products primarily under the Safeway, Lucerne, and
Mrs. Wright's labels.

- Safeway has an exceptional record
of growth. Over the past 10 years
(1991–2001), earnings per share climbed
from $.29 to $2.50, a compound annual
growth rate of 24 percent. What's more,
earnings per share dipped only once in
this span.

- Safeway stores have been able to hold
their own in all of the markets in which
they operate, including those areas
where Wal-Mart and Target have

opened supercenters that sell food and
have hurt other grocers.

- Christopher Helman, writing for *Forbes*
magazine in early 2002, said, "Ross
Margolies, manager of Salomon Smith
Barney Asset Management's Salomon
Capital fund, expects more good news
from Safeway. The chain is adept at
luring customers with dozens of ridicu-
lously cheap weekly specials like a New
York strip steak for $2.99 a pound.

  "As for expansion: With its store
base firmly in the West (under such
names as Vons, Randalls, and
Dominick's), Safeway has only just
begun expanding to the eastern U.S.,
buying Norristown, Pa-based Genuardi's Family Markets."

- Supercenters, such as those opened by
Wal-Mart, are less of a threat to
Safeway. According to CEO Steven
Burd, 70 percent of Safeway's stores are
in urban areas, where megastores are
less likely to set up shop. Mr. Burd says,
"When a supercenter does come in, it
kills off the undercapitalized, small,
independent regional supermarket company." Whatever business Safeway loses
to supercenters, he adds, it regains from
the demise of smaller grocers.

- Mr. Burd has ambitious plans to cut
$1.6 billion from Safeway's costs over
the next five years and to invest those
savings in promotion, new product lines
such as natural foods, and other sales
boosters. What's more, the chain has
been boosting the sale of more profitable
private-label goods. Safeway has also
been lowering costs from theft and food
spoilage. Finally, Mr. Burd is thinking of
diversifying by acquiring companies outside the grocery business.

Total assets: $15,965 million
Current ratio: .83
Common shares outstanding: 505 million
Return on 2001 shareholders' equity: 19.5%

	2001	2000	1999	1998	1997	1996	1995	1994
Revenues (millions)	34301	31977	28860	24484	17269	16398	15627	15215
Net income (millions)	1284	1092	971	807	622	461	326	250
Earnings per share	2.50	2.13	1.88	1.59	1.25	.97	.68	.51
Dividends per share: Safeway does not pay a dividend								
Price High	61.4	62.7	62.4	61.4	31.7	22.7	12.9	8.0
Low	37.4	30.8	29.3	30.5	21.1	11.3	7.7	4.8

GROWTH AND INCOME

SBC Communications Incorporated

175 East Houston, Room 8-A-60 □ San Antonio, Texas 78205 □ (210) 351-2100 □ Direct dividend reinvestment plan is available: (800) 351-7221 □ Web site: www.sbc.com □ Listed: NYSE □ Ticker symbol: SBC □ S&P rating: A- □ Value Line financial strength rating: A+

For many decades, AT&T was the essence of the telephone industry. Although there were many other telephone companies—hundreds, in fact—Ma Bell was what came to mind when you dialed your telephone.

That all ended in 1984 when the federal government decreed that AT&T could keep its Bell Labs and long-distance service but had to divest the Bell companies that provided local telephone service. At the stroke of a pen, this brought forth seven Regional Bell Operating Companies, often known as the Baby Bells. The term hardly fits these huge companies, since none had less than $10 billion in annual revenues.

With the passage of time, there are no longer seven. In 1997, Southwestern Bell (now SBC Communications) acquired Pacific Bell, with local service in California. In 1998, SBC acquired an independent company, Southern New England Telecommunications, for $4.4 billion in stock. In still another Baby Bell elimination, Bell Atlantic acquired NYNEX, with operations in New York and New England. Of the seven Regional Bell operating companies spawned in 1984, only three are left standing: SBC Communications, Bell Atlantic (now Verizon), and BellSouth.

In October of 1999, SBC acquired still another Baby Bell, Ameritech, for $62 billion in stock. Based in Chicago, Ameritech provides local phone service in five Midwestern states: Illinois, Michigan, Ohio, Indiana, and Wisconsin. SBC shareholders now own 56 percent of the combined company, while former Ameritech shareholders hold 44 percent.

Company Profile

SBC Communications now ranks first among U.S. telecommunications providers with 61 million access lines and second with over 20 million domestic wireless subscribers.

As of late 1999, SBC Communications became one of the thirty stocks in the Dow Jones Industrial Average. As you might surmise, SBC is *not* an industrial company—it's clearly a public utility—and might more properly have been included in the Dow Jones Utility Average. Moreover, the same thing could be said of AT&T, which has been a component of the Industrial Average since 1939, when it replaced IBM. To atone for their egregious prewar blunder, some kindly souls let IBM back into the Average in 1979.

As now constituted, SBC Communications serves 61.3 million access lines in high-growth regions. It also reaches more than 113 million potential domestic wireless customers and has equity stakes in international telecommunications businesses reaching more than 375 million potential customers.

International operations include a 10 percent interest in Telefonos de Mexico; cable and telecommunications operations in the United Kingdom and Chile; wireless operations in France, South Korea, and South Africa. SBC also has a long-distance alliance and cable television operations in Israel. Additional ventures were formed in 1997 with Switzerland, South Korea, and Taiwan. What's more, the company has joined with thirteen other international companies to build a trans-Pacific fiber-optic cable for long-distance traffic between the United States and China, which was completed in 2000. Finally, in 1998, SBC and eleven partners agreed to build an undersea communications pipeline between the United States and Japan, for operation in mid-2000.

Shortcomings to Bear in Mind

- Argus Research Corporation pointed out that "The local market has also been suffering from general economic conditions in the access line counts that have been falling recently (late 2001), but the real economic effects for the RBOC's (regional Bell Operating Companies) is felt through the loss of vertical services to these customers. Consumers and businesses alike are eliminating additional access lines and such add-on services as conference calling, call forwarding, and other services deemed non-core to their average usage. Part of this is due to technology shifts as more customers gain high-speed Internet access and shift additional line focus toward cell phone usage."

Reasons to Buy

- On the other hand, the Argus report was not entirely negative. The analyst had this to say. "SBC has a strong balance sheet, very responsive and experienced management, network assets that are valuable and almost impossible to duplicate in most of its service region, a majority share in Cingular wireless (which will likely be spun off around the end of 2002), and strong ties to the Latin American markets. The Latin American markets look to become one of the best growth markets for telecom services in the world over the next decade."
- In late 2001, the company named former U.S. Secretary of Commerce William M. Daley to the newly created post of president, a move that underscores the importance that SBC has placed on promoting its regulatory agenda. Mr. Daley is the brother of Chicago's mayor.

"I thought it was a great opportunity to work with a world-class company," said Mr. Daley, who took over his post on December 1, 2001.

Mr. Daley, age fifty-three, has no telecommunications experience. However, his political background includes serving as chairman of Al Gore's presidential campaign. He also has extensive political connections in the Midwest, where SBC's service problems have irritated politicians and consumers alike.

Commenting on the appointment, Jeffrey Halpern, an analyst with Sanford C. Bernstein & Company, said, "This helps SBC put a powerful figure in the regulatory seat." In the past, SBC has been increasingly vocal in its objection to regulations that it says stifle growth. What's more, the company is promoting legislation that would abolish some of those regulations.
- Ever since the Baby Bells emerged from the old AT&T in 1984, theirs has been a cozy club. With their mutually exclusive territories, they have reaped the

fruits of their dominance as relatively friendly neighbors. Now, however, that truce has come apart at the seams. SBC has invaded the territories of BellSouth, Verizon (which includes what used to be Bell Atlantic and Nynex), and Qwest Communications (which includes what used to be U.S. West). In so doing, SBC hopes to siphon off $1 billion in annual revenue from its Bell brethren.

- Federal regulators gave the stamp of approval to a joint venture between SBC Communications and BellSouth to create the nation's second-largest wireless phone service. The venture, which was sanctioned in the fall of 2000, created a domestic wireless enterprise with more than 19 million customers, second only to Verizon Wireless. The new company Cingular will have combined revenue of at least $10 billion, with operations in forty of the nation's fifty largest markets. To obtain the approval of the FCC, the two Bell companies had to divest wireless operations in Louisiana, Indianapolis, and Los Angeles. SBC owns 60 percent of Cingular.

  BellSouth and SBC say the joint venture enables them to better compete by offering customers everything from wireless Internet access and interactive messaging, to attractive national rate plans and a host of other services. Analysts believe that wireless penetration in the United States, now about 30 percent, will reach 70 percent—perhaps 80 percent—within ten years.

- In the biggest move by a major local phone company into the torrid electronic-commerce business, SBC acquired Sterling Commerce for $3.9 billion in 2000. Based in Dallas, Texas, Sterling provides software that enables businesses to electronically transmit orders, invoices, and payment data to suppliers.

  Sterling, which had revenues of $561 million in fiscal 1999, provides electronic-commerce systems to over 45,000 customers worldwide, including many large corporations such as Wal-Mart, Johnson & Johnson, and Sony. Sterling's revenue growth in 2000 is targeted at 20 percent, with 27 percent forecast for 2001.

  SBC's CEO, Edward E. Whitacre Jr., said that the move into high-margin e-business services helps convince customers and investors that his company is more than a fuddy-duddy Baby Bell stuck in slow-growing traditional telephone markets.

- Cisco Systems, the data networking company, announced in 2000 that it had entered into a multibillion-dollar alliance with SBC Communications. Under the agreement, SBC will be among the biggest buyers of Cisco's routers and switches that are used to build the Internet's infrastructure. It is one of the first times that Cisco has closely aligned itself with a traditional phone company. It will provide equipment to send information over five different networking platforms, including digital subscriber lines, which are faster than dial-up modems, and other services that can transmit data, voice, and video. The two companies hope to develop products to make it easier for Internet users to switch between different Internet service providers as well as to create a local area network.

- SBC Communications won federal approval to offer long-distance phone service to consumers in Kansas and Oklahoma, becoming the first local phone company created with the 1984 breakup of AT&T to offer interstate service in multiple states. On March 7, 2001, the company was able to begin selling service in those states. It had been estimated that consumers in Oklahoma had been spending $220 million a year on long distance, while those in Kansas were spending about $175 million, prior to the invasion on their turf of SBC Communications. In the summer of 2000, moreover, the company got a similar decision in the state of Texas, where it acquired a million new customers after only three months in that state.

- In a report issued in early 2002, Justin Hellman, writing for *Value Line Survey*, said, "DSL (digital subscriber lines) and long distance ought to be the key drivers of top-line growth over the next few years. DSL is the phone company's version of high-speed Internet access.

Although the company plans to slow its deployment of DSL service, due to unexpected regulatory obstacles that have made the rollout costlier, it should still continue to add subscribers at a healthy pace of roughly 150,000 per quarter. (It currently has a subscriber base of 1.2 million.) These additions will likely push annual DSL revenues past the $1 billion by the end of 2002."

- In early 2002, CEO Edward E. Whitacre Jr. pointed out the company's prospects for the future. He said that SBC's financial goals for 2002 include maintaining the company's industry-leading credit rating and generating solid free cash flow. Because of its strong cash flow, SBC has been able to take several steps to enhance shareholder value, including paying shareholders $3.5 billion in dividends during 2001, repurchasing more than 47 million shares of its common stock during that year through a previous repurchase program, and authorizing in November 2001 an additional repurchase program enabling SBC to buy back up to 100 million shares of its common stock. When a company buys back its own stock, it tends to increase per-share earnings, other factors being equal.

Total assets: $97,980 million
Current ratio: 0.55
Common shares outstanding: 3,362 million
Return on 2001 shareholders' equity: 23.5%

	2001	2000	1999	1998	1997	1996	1995	1994
Revenues (millions)	54301	53313	48960	45323	25044	13898	12670	11619
Net income (millions)	7954	7746	7439	7690	3364	2101	1889	1649
Earnings per share	2.35	2.26	2.15	2.08	1.84	1.73	1.55	1.37
Dividends per share	1.02	1.01	.97	.94	.89	.86	.83	.79
Price High	53.1	59.0	59.9	54.9	38.1	30.1	29.3	22.1
Low	36.5	34.8	44.1	35.0	24.6	23.0	19.8	18.4

GROWTH AND INCOME

The Sherwin-Williams Company

101 Prospect Avenue, N.W. ▫ Cleveland, Ohio 44115-1075 ▫ (216) 566-2102 ▫ Dividend reinvestment program available: (866) 537-8703 ▫ Web site: www.sherwin.com ▫ Listed: NYSE ▫ Ticker symbol: SHW ▫ S&P rating: A ▫ Value Line financial strength rating: A

In 2001, Sherwin-Williams generated sales of $5.07 billion, a decline of 2.8 percent. Net income came in at $263.2 million, compared with $309.7 million in 2000.

Earnings per share dipped to $1.68, from $1.90 the prior year.

Obviously, Sherwin-Williams is not bragging about these developments.

However, there were some signs of strength—and that strength is likely to continue as the economy comes back to life in 2002 and 2003.

According to CEO Christopher M. Connor, "This past year, through excellent management of working capital, we increased free cash flow by $145.65 million, to a record $388.09 million. We define free cash flow as net operating cash available after dividend payments and capital expenditures.

"Two factors contributed heavily to this strong performance. We reduced accounts receivable and inventory levels by a combined $133.63 million and decreased days outstanding on both accounts receivable balances and inventory. Our selling, general, and administrative expenses were lower year over year for the first time in twenty years. This was accomplished while still making significant investments in our company. We also were able to reduce headcount through thoughtful and responsible management of our human resource needs.

"Our increased cash flow was used to further strengthen, stabilize, and secure our company in a number of ways. We retired $123.06 million of debt and increased our year-end cash position by $115.92 million. We also used the cash to make an important acquisition in our Paint Stores Segment by purchasing the net assets of the Mautz Paint Company, including their thirty-three paint stores in the Midwest. Additionally, we bought back 6.7 million shares of the company's common stock on the open market."

Company Profile

Sherwin-Williams is a global producer of paints and coatings. Since Henry Sherwin and Edward Williams founded the company in 1886, the company has taken the lead in service and product advances. From developing dry chemical pigments, brushable lacquers, and synthetic enamels to being the first paint company to offer emulsified finish, Sherwin-Williams has continually pushed the envelope of coatings technology.

Today, the pioneering spirit at Sherwin-Williams lives on, with the formulation of new products that are more durable, longer lasting, easier to apply, and friendlier to the environment. As an alternative to traditional solvent-based polymers, the company's technical staff has developed coatings with waterborne and high-solids resins that are Volatile Organic Compound (VOC)-compliant and that exceed application and performance expectations.

Sherwin-Williams has a stake in the manufacture, distribution, and sale of coatings and related products to professional, industrial, commercial, and retail customers, primarily in North and South America.

The company's Paint Store Segment consists of 2,573 company-operated specialty paint stores. They are situated in the forty-eight states, Puerto Rico, the Virgin Islands, Mexico, and Canada. In 2001, the company expanded its Paint Stores Segment by 3.3 percent, adding a net of eighty-five new outlets.

The Paint Stores Segment sells paint, wall coverings, floor coverings, window treatments, industrial maintenance products and finishes, and assorted tools. These products are marketed to the do-it-yourself, professional painting, industrial maintenance, and home building markets as well as to manufacturers of products that require a factory finish.

The Consumer Segment makes architectural paints, stains, varnishes, industrial maintenance products, wood finishing products, paint applicators, corrosion inhibitors, and paint-related products. These products are sold to third-party customers and the Paint Store Segment.

The Automotive Finishes Segment

develops, manufactures, and distributes a variety of motor vehicle finish, refinish, and touch-up products.

The International Coatings Segment develops, licenses, manufactures, and distributes a variety of paint, coatings, and related products worldwide.

Shortcomings to Bear in Mind

- The domestic paint and coatings industry has annual revenues of about $16.6 billion and sells 1.3 billion gallons of paint a year. However, annual unit growth has not been impressive. It has ranged between 1.6 percent and 3.4 percent in recent years. As a result, Sherwin-Williams's strategy is to expand its business through acquisitions—which is a difficult task, since the industry is highly fragmented. There are scores of small companies but precious few large ones.

  The largest acquisitions to date have been Pratt & Lambert United, Inc. (1996), enhancing the company's access to the independent dealer and mass merchandising distribution channels in the United States; and Thompson Minwax Holding Corporation (1997), providing leading brands in the stain and varnish sector.
- International sales have been hurt by a strong dollar and weak economies abroad.
- During the recession of 2001, the do-it-yourself market was sluggish. This may reflect an increased tendency of consumers to switch to having the work done by professional painters.

Reasons to Buy

- In the final weeks of 2001, margins began to improve, partly because of cost cutting. In addition, they are being helped by lower material, administrative overhead, and interest expenses. What's more, margins are expected to improve still further.

- As noted earlier, the company continued its acquisition strategy with the purchase of the Mautz Paint Company in 2001. In March of 2002, Sherwin-Williams acquired the assets of Johnson Paints, Inc., of Ft. Myers, Florida. Johnson Paints manufactures and sells paint and related products under the Flex Bon(r) brand through twenty-four company-owned stores and a dealer network located in south Florida, primarily on the southwest coast and in the Miami area.

  Commenting on the acquisition, Mr. Connor said, "We are pleased that the Flex Bon organization has joined our company and are excited about the opportunities that the Flex Bon business presents us in the growing south Florida market."
- As mentioned earlier, many do-it-yourselfers are shifting the burden to professionals. Part of this is because they are getting older. In addition, many are too busy with their careers to take on additional chores at home. On the other hand, this is not entirely a negative development, since these painting contractors "purchase almost all of the products they need from the paint store channel," said Mr. Connor. "Therefore, our 2,573 company paint stores in North America and the Caribbean give us a significant advantage over all other paint store competitors serving professional customers."
- In 2001, the company continued to strengthen its leadership position in the industrial and marine coatings business. Mr. Connor said, "We gained market share by introducing new product technology aimed at specific focus markets. Our expanded business with the U.S. Navy is one example of our growing customer base for industrial and marine coatings."
- In 2001, the Automotive Finishes Segment completed its first full year in its

350,000-square-foot world headquarters in Warrensville Heights, Ohio. In the words of Mr. Connor, "This investment in technology and facilities is already paying dividends by improving our customer relationships and service. Our customer loyalty program, the A-Plus Club, has an enrollment of more than 750 customers. We are excited about our growing and highly visible participation in NASCAR as the paint supplier to nearly twenty racing teams in 2001. Automotive Finishes Segment customers can also avail themselves of numerous e-business options at our highly interactive Web site.

"The Automotive Finishes Segment has developed a comprehensive distribution platform that includes 174 company-operated branches, thousands of automotive finish distributors, and a presence in nearly thirty countries through subsidiaries and licensing agreements."

■ In recent years, The Paint Stores Segment has sharpened the focus of its product development and store merchandising efforts on the needs of some key customer segments. "This customer-focused approach helps ensure the success of our new products," said Alfred Lewis, City Manager, Paint Stores Group in Chicago.

"Our new Cashmere interior wall paint is a good example. Its ease of application saves residential painting contractors time and effort. Its smooth, stipple-free finish appeals to upscale homeowners. This combination of benefits made Cashmere paint an overnight success and will propel its growth and popularity for years to come.

"Other examples include Harmony, a low-odor, low-VOC wall paint that minimizes disruption in occupied areas; AquaClad Water-Based Alkyd, a one-coat waterborne industrial and marine topcoat; and a Sher-Wood product line extension to help production wood finishers comply with ever-tightening environmental regulations. Each of the twenty-one new products introduced by the Paint Stores Group in 2001 builds on our reputation as an innovator and technology leader."

Total assets: $3,628 million
Current ratio: 1.32
Common shares outstanding: 154 million
Return on 2001 shareholders' equity: 18.9%

		2001	2000	1999	1998	1997	1996	1995	1994
Revenues (millions)		5066	5212	5004	4934	4881	4133	3274	3100
Net income (millions)		263	16	304	273	261	229	201	187
Earnings per share		1.68	.10	1.80	1.57	1.50	1.33	1.17	1.07
Dividends per share		.58	.54	.48	.45	.50	.35	.32	.28
Price	High	28.2	27.6	32.9	37.9	33.4	28.9	20.8	17.9
	Low	19.7	17.1	18.8	19.4	24.1	19.5	16.0	14.8

AGGRESSIVE GROWTH

Stryker Corporation

Post Office Box 4085 □ Kalamazoo, Michigan 49003-4085 □ (616) 385-2600 □ Web site: www.strykercorp.com □ Listed: NYSE □ Dividend reinvestment plan is not available □ Ticker symbol: SYK □ S&P rating: B+ □ Value Line financial strength rating: A

In 2001, Stryker achieved a goal it has been seeking for twenty years. The company received marketing approval for OP-1 (osteogenic protein-1), its proprietary bone-growth factor, in three key regions of the world—the United States, Australia, and the European Union.

These approvals were the first for any bone morphogenic protein in all three jurisdictions, and they led to Stryker's creation of the Biotech, Spine, and Trauma Group. This group has a global focus in product development and manufacturing. More than 60 percent of its products are sold abroad. According to CEO John W. Brown, "We expect that this new structure will further accelerate the fast-growing spine and trauma divisions of the company, and that it will enable us to enhance future opportunities for synergy between spine and trauma products and OP-1."

Each of Stryker's three specific approval indications for OP-1 involves nonunion—or difficult-to-heal—fractures of long bones. The OP-1 is mixed with a collagen carrier and wetted to form a paste that is surgically implanted into the fracture gap.

Australia, where OP-1 has been employed for several years on a compassionate-use basis, issued the broadest approval, covering the treatment of long-bone fractures secondary to trauma. The European authorization covers the treatment of nonunion of the tibia of at least nine months in duration, secondary to trauma, in skeletally mature patients for whom autograft has failed or is not feasible.

In the United States, the FDA approved OP-1 as a humanitarian-use device, one that may be used to treat conditions that are manifested in fewer than 4,000 patients in the United States per year. The approved indications in the United States are as an alternative to autograft in recalcitrant long-bone nonunions where autograft is not feasible

and alternative treatments have failed.

Now that marketing approvals have been granted, physicians must be convinced to use the Stryker product. While the company has developed sales strategies appropriate to each regional market, they all share the primary objective of educating orthopedic surgeons about the efficacy of OP-1. In the United States and Australia, the company has developed specialist sales forces. In Europe, Stryker is selling on a country-by-country basis via a specially trained group of its trauma sales representatives.

Meanwhile, Stryker continues to seek approval for broader indications for OP-1, including posterolateral spine fusion. In the opinion of Mr. Brown, "The market for posterolateral spine treatment is large and growing. The current clinical investigations of OP-1 could lead both to better outcomes for patients and cost savings for the health care system."

Company Profile

Dr. Homer H. Stryker, a leading orthopedic surgeon and the inventor of several orthopedic products, founded Stryker Corporation in 1941. The company now ranks as a dominant player in a $12-billion global orthopedics industry. Stryker has a significant market share in such sectors as artificial hips, prosthetic knees, and trauma products.

Stryker develops, manufactures, and markets specialty surgical and medical products worldwide. These products include orthopedic implants, trauma systems, powered surgical instruments, endoscopic systems, and patient care and handling equipment.

Through a network of 302 centers in twenty-six states, Stryker's Physiotherapy Associates division provides physical, occupational, and speech therapy to orthopedic and neurology patients. The physical therapy business represents a solid complementary business for Stryker, in view of the high number of its surgeon customers who prescribe physical therapy following orthopedic surgery.

A major component of Stryker's success is the optimal use of resources in manufacturing and distribution. Taking advantage of both information technology and leading-edge workflow management practices, the company monitors quality and service levels at its sixteen plants throughout North America and Europe for continuous improvement. This attention to operations has resulted in the inclusion of Stryker facilities in the elite *Industry Week* Best Plants list twice in the last three years. The Stryker Instruments plant in Kalamazoo, Michigan, was named one of the Best Plants in 2000, and the Howmedica Osteonics facility in Allendale, New Jersey, was honored in 1998.

Shortcomings to Bear in Mind

- In the past ten years (1991–2001), Stryker's earnings per share advanced without a dip from $0.18 to $1.34, a compound annual growth rate of 22.2 percent. It's hard to find a company growing at this kind of pace that you can buy for a reasonable PE ratio, and Stryker is no exception. Nor can you invest in Stryker at a bargain-basement share price. It is nearly always selling at a premium to the market. Let's hope it continues to be worth it.

Reasons to Buy

- In a year that frustrated many companies in a variety of industries, Stryker continued its winning ways. According to Mr. Brown, "We have exceeded our goal of at least 20 percent net earnings growth, which we believe is the best test of our ability to execute." In 2001, net sales rose 14 percent, to $2.6 billion. Earnings before an extraordinary item increased 23 percent, to $272 million. Diluted earnings per share (which

assumes the conversion of convertible securities), increased a lusty 22 percent, to $1.34.

- Stryker Spine entered the cervical-fixation market in 2001 with the Reflex system, which generated excellent customer acceptance here at home as well as in Europe. This innovative product addresses the increasing demand for fixation products for the upper part of the spine. The Reflex system features Stryker's proprietary TMZF advanced alloy material, a one-step locking system and simple-to-use instrument technology.

- Stryker Trauma's T2 nailing system, launched in the second half of 2001 in the United States, Europe, and Japan, provides a wide range of fracture repair options for long bones, using a common set of instruments. The expertise of the same engineering team and manufacturing personnel who created the well-established best-in-class Gamma family of nails for hip fractures was leveraged to facilitate rapid development of the T2.

According to a company spokesman, "It earned immediate favorable response from our customers. In addition, Stryker Trauma further specialized its three production plants in Switzerland and Germany, fine-tuned inventory control, and initiated a dedicated sales force in Japan's largest cities."

- In hip and knee implants, Stryker offers comprehensive lines to fill every need, from early intervention to revision. By using the same geometrics and instrumentation throughout the line, "we offer the surgeon both ease of use and greater intraoperative choice. In 2001—its first full year on the market—our Scorpio TS revision knee system achieved stellar sales growth."

The Scorpio TX is designed to work with the Modular Rotating Hinge (MRH)—also introduced in 2001—and the Modular Revision System (MRS).

Using a single set of bone cuts, the surgeon can begin the procedure and then choose the most appropriate of these three implants, depending on the amount of bone remaining.

According to a company spokesman, "We have taken a similar approach to addressing regional needs, particularly in Japan, which has different size, range-of-motion, and flexion requirements than the United States and Europe. In 2000, we adapted our Scorpio knee for Japan, branding it Superflex, and in 2001, we did the same with our Eon and Secur-fit hips, known as Super Eon and Super Secur-fit in their Japanese versions."

■ Analysts believe that industry trends are setting the stage for continued growth for Stryker in the years ahead. Virtually all market dynamics point in that direction. The following sections describe the key factors.

- The population as a whole is aging. In fact, the target population for orthopedic implants for knees and hips is expected to increase 68 percent in the next nine years, according to a report issued by Gerard Klauer Mattison & Company, Inc., a brokerage firm headquartered in New York City.

- Mild inflation in average selling prices for orthopedic implants in the United States compares favorably to the declining price environment of the past decade.

- Consolidation among orthopedic implant and device manufacturers over the past few years has greatly decreased the number of competitors in sectors such as orthopedic implants, spinal devices, arthroscopy products, and other orthopedic products. This serves to consolidate market share and mitigates price competition.

- Advances in orthopedic technology—much of which has taken place in the past decade—have markedly decreased operating and recovery times. These advances have decreased the amount of time a surgeon must spend with each patient, thus giving the surgeon more time to perform more operations in a period. Consequently, according to the Gerard Klauer Mattison report, "we believe that procedural volume will increase."

For its part, Stryker has set itself up to benefit from these microeconomic dynamics, according to the report issued by the same brokerage house. "For example, Stryker has strategically used acquisitions over the past few years to broaden and deepen its product portfolio. Furthermore, innovation in orthopedic implants and instrumentation has provided the company with certain competitive advantages that should be important ingredients for gaining market share in the coming years."

Total assets: $2,424 million
Current ratio: 1.86
Common shares outstanding: 196 million
Return on 2001 shareholders' equity: 28.4%

	2001	2000	1999	1998	1997	1996	1995	1994
Revenues (millions)	2602	2289	2104	1103	980	910	872	682
Net income (millions)	272	221	161	150	125	101	87	72
Earnings per share	1.34	1.10	.81	.77	.64	.52	.45	.38
Dividends per share	.10	.07	.07	.06	.06	.05	.02	.02
Price High	63.20	57.8	36.6	27.9	22.7	16.1	14.6	9.4
Low	43.3	43.3	22.2	15.5	12.1	9.9	9.0	5.9

CONSERVATIVE GROWTH

Sysco Corporation

1390 Enclave Parkway ◻ Houston, Texas 77077-2099 ◻ (281) 584-1458 ◻ Web site: www.sysco.com ◻
Dividend reinvestment plan is available: (800) 730-4001 ◻ Fiscal year ends the Saturday closest to June 30 ◻
Listed: NYSE ◻ Ticker symbol: SYY ◻ Standard & Poor's rating: A+ ◻ Value Line financial strength rating: A+

With the advent of two household incomes, with both husband and wife working outside the home, it is not surprising that no one wants to come home after eight hours at the office and still have to face cooking supper (not to mention cleaning up after the repast).

Today, about half of Americans' food dollars are spent on meals prepared away from home. That figure far surpasses the 37 percent that was spent on away-from-home meals in 1972. It reveals how heavily our society now depends on foodservice operations to satisfy consumers' nutritional needs by providing a variety of quality meals at affordable prices.

The Sygma Network, Inc., Sysco's chain restaurant distribution company, operates thirteen locations across the United States. It generated sales of $2.42 billion in fiscal 2001. Each Sygma center inventories 300 to 400 items per customer and supplies multiple locations for one to five chain restaurant "concepts," or customers, it serves.

During fiscal 2001, Sygma secured a distribution agreement to serve 264 Applebee's, Inc., restaurants in Indiana, Michigan, New England, Ohio, and western Pennsylvania.

Company Profile

As they go about their lives, many people encounter the familiar Sysco trucks, bearing giant blue lettering, delivering products to customers. Few are aware, however, of Sysco's far-reaching influence on meals served daily throughout North America. As the continent's largest marketer and distributor of foodservice products, Sysco operates 124 distribution facilities that serve more than 370,000 restaurants, hotels, schools, hospitals, retirement homes, and other locations where food is prepared to be eaten on the premises or taken away and enjoyed in the comfort of the diner's chosen environment.

Sysco is by far the largest company in the foodservice distribution industry. In sales, Sysco dwarfs its two chief competitors, US Foodservice and Performance Food Group,

The company's operations break down as follows: restaurants (65 percent sales), hospitals and nursing homes (10 percent), schools and colleges (6 percent), hotels and motels (5 percent), and other (14 percent).

With annual sales in 2001 of $21.8 billion, Sysco distributes a wide variety of fresh and frozen meats, seafood, poultry, and fruits and vegetables, plus bakery products, canned and dry foods, paper and disposables, sanitation items, dairy foods, beverages, kitchen and tabletop equipment, and medical and surgical supplies.

Sysco's innovations in food technology, packaging, and transportation provide customers with quality products, delivered on time, in excellent condition and at reasonable prices.

Shortcomings to Bear in Mind

- During a recession, it's possible that more food will be prepared at home, and restaurants will see some empty tables. In response to this idea, Mark Husson, a food retail analyst with Merrill Lynch said, "I don't think the economy will take a shuddering downward turn, but if it does, we can't rely on people's collective memory of how to cook. People think it's their God-given right to eat in restaurants."

- At the end of the second quarter of fiscal 2002, CEO Charles H. Cotros addressed the concern that investors have had concerning the slump in travel-related businesses. "As has widely been reported, many travel and resort destination cities experienced a considerable downturn in demand. Our specialty businesses, which serve the hotels, theme parks and other travel-related industries in certain areas, were also impacted. On the other hand, pockets of the country not dependent on such business reported continued growth, somewhat offsetting the weakness in tourism locations. We are seeing business in the major destination cities slowly increasing, which bodes well for all our companies, as well as our specialty meat, produce, and hotel supply operations."

Reasons to Buy

- Whether they're dining in an upscale restaurant or picking up pasta as the entree for a meal at home, people spend less time on food preparation than ever before. They want variety and flavor in the foods they choose to eat, yet their time to prepare meals is constantly in competition with work and leisure activities. More than ever, people are turning to meals prepared away from home for greater convenience, quality, and, most of all, choice.

  This trend started in World War II, as women began to work outside the home. Business cafeterias, coffee shops, school lunchrooms, and restaurants broadened the range of dining choices for people who were used to much simpler fare. Twenty-five years

ago, not many consumers could identify kiwi fruit. During the past three decades, foodservice offerings have moved from fruit cocktail with a cherry on top to kiwi and other exotic fare; from steak and potatoes to fajitas with all the trimmings.

- As the largest distributor of foodservice products in North America, Sysco assists customers in creating a vast array of dining choices. Menus have greatly improved since the days when a French chef named Boulanger offered a choice of soups, or "restorative," to patrons who paused at his inn to refresh themselves as they traveled during the 1700s. The sign in French read "restaurant," and his establishment may have been the first to offer a menu.

  Today's diverse menu choices could not have been imagined then—raspberries from Australia served fresh in Wisconsin in January; gourmet pesto sauce rich with garlic, fresh basil, and pine nuts delivered to a Vancouver chef's doorstep; or artfully prepared hearts of lettuce served in an Arizona college cafeteria each day. Providing choices from soup to nuts and everything in between, Sysco leads the way in helping chefs in restaurants, schools, business cafeterias, health care locations, lodging, and other facilities increase the variety and quality of food choices in North America.

- Sysco is the largest produce purchaser in the foodservice distribution industry. Produce sales represented 9 percent of total corporate sales in fiscal 2001. According to Tom Lankford, executive vice president, Foodservice Operations, "Our solid supplier relationships, quality assurance strength, and the ability to deliver the products ordered at the specified time have been crucial to the success of Sysco's fresh produce operations, including Sysco Natural and FreshPoint produce."

- In January of 2001, Sysco announced the signing of a multiyear contract with the Ross Products Division of Abbott Laboratories, one of the nation's leading pharmaceutical companies. The agreement provided Sysco an exclusive access to Abbott's Nutra-Balance brand name for use in marketing and sales of nutritional products that Sysco distributes to hospitals, nursing homes, and other medical and extended-care facilities.

  "Sysco's market share in the food-service long-term health care segment is experiencing continued growth," said Richard J. Schnieders, the company's president and chief operating officer. "This joint marketing strategy will further enhance our 'one-stop-shopping' concept and provide additional efficiencies to our valued health care customers."

- Unlike some of its competitors, who order all their products from headquarters, Mr. Cotros encourages his seventy-eight branches to reach their own decisions about which products to carry and how to price them. Sysco's 6,500 sales representatives carry laptop computers that can instantly place orders and confirm inventory. By contract, smaller distributors still take orders with pads and pencils and are often unsure which items are on the warehouse shelf.

- Sysco keeps margins high by selling products under its own label, a strategy it began a year after its founding. It saves on national advertising and passes some of the savings along to its customers. Its private-label business carries an estimated 24 percent gross margin, or 10 percent more than it earns on national brands.

- Sysco has an exceptional record of growth. In the past ten years (1991–2001), earnings per share advanced from $0.21 to $0.88 (with no dips along the way), a compound annual growth rate of 15.4 percent. In the same decade, dividends per share climbed from $0.03 to $0.28, a growth rate of 25.0 percent.

- Many of Sysco's operations have been the result of acquisitions. For instance, Sysco acquired Guest Supply in January of 2001. This move complemented Sysco's existing hospitality market business and increased the product offerings available to Sysco's customers. Guest Supply is the leading national full-service provider of hotel operating supplies to the $7-billion lodging industry. It provides about 19,000 hotel and resort customers with a full range of personal care amenities, room accessories, housekeeping supplies, paper products, furniture, and textiles.

  Acquisitions to enhance geographic coverage or broaden product offerings were components of Sysco's growth strategy during fiscal 2001 "and will continue to be important going forward," according to CEO Charles H. Cotros. Five companies with combined annual sales volume of $706 million were acquired in 2001, including two custom-cutting meat companies, two Canadian broadline operations, and a specialty supplier to the hospitality and lodging industry. In addition, Sysco completed the purchase of another specialty meat company, Fulton Provision Co., at the beginning of fiscal 2002.

- Although acquisitions played a vital role in establishing geographic footholds in Sysco's early years, the company's sustained growth in market share primarily reflects internally generated sales increases within each market served.

- Each day, the drivers of Sysco's nearly 5,800 delivery vehicles crisscross the cities and counties of North America to deliver more than two million cases of product. From the back alley door of a small deli in Los Angeles to the loading dock of a major hospital in St. Louis, Sysco distributes a range of 275,000 products systemwide that have been transported by rail, trucked in, or flown from points near and far around the globe to Sysco warehouses. That foods are shipped daily so reliably and accurately is possible only because of advances in computer technology, transportation, refrigeration, and warehousing.

In the 1970s, the typical fleet unit was a twelve- to sixteen-foot truck with modest refrigeration capabilities. Frozen and dry goods were the primary commodities of the foodservice industry. Today's twenty-eight-to-thirty-six-foot, single-axle trucks typically have three separate food storage compartments with the most reliable mechanical refrigeration systems available.

Total assets: $5,469 million
Current ratio: 1.43
Common shares outstanding: 673 million
Return on 2001 shareholders' equity: 31%

	2001	2000	1999	1998	1997	1996	1995	1994
Revenues (millions)	21784	19303	17423	15328	14455	13395	12118	10942
Net income (millions)	597	454	362	325	302	277	252	217
Earnings per share	.88	.68	.54	.48	.43	.38	.34	.30
Dividends per share	.28	.22	.19	.16	.15	.12	.10	.08
Price High	30.1	30.4	20.6	14.4	11.8	9.0	8.2	7.3
Low	21.8	13.1	12.5	10.0	7.3	6.9	6.2	5.3

AGGRESSIVE GROWTH

Target Corporation

777 Nicollet Mall □ Minneapolis, Minnesota 55402 □ (612) 761-6735 □ Direct dividend reinvestment plan is available: (888) 268-0203 □ Web site: www.target.com □ Fiscal year ends Saturday closest to January 31 of following year □ Listed: NYSE □ Ticker symbol: TGT □ S&P rating: A □ Value Line financial strength rating: A

Among the 1,055 Target units are ninety-two larger stores called SuperTargets, which started appearing on the scene in 2000. These 175,000-square-foot facilities devote 30,000 square feet to high-quality groceries.

According to CEO Robert J. Ulrich, "SuperTarget supplements the tremendous growth opportunities provided by our traditional discount stores and raises the potential to strengthen our brand in key markets. By combining a high-quality, full-line grocery assortment with our general merchandise offering, SuperTarget creates a convenient one-stop shopping

experience for our guests. Like Target, SuperTarget strives to set itself apart from competitors and be preferred by guests. Our merchandising is innovative and differentiated and is focused on delivering fashion and freshness.

"Our assortment includes natural and organic products, choice beef and top-grade produce, as well as premium brands, such as Krispy Kreme doughnuts, Starbucks coffee, Fannie May chocolates, Philippe Starck organic foods, and La Brea breads.

"In addition, our expanding private-label line of Archer Farms items provides a high-quality, low-priced alternative to similar, nationally branded grocery products."

Company Profile

Target is the nation's fourth-largest general merchandise retailer, specializing in large-store formats, including discount stores, moderate-priced promotional stores, and traditional department stores. The company operates Target stores, Marshall Field's, and Mervyn's stores.

At the end of fiscal 2001, the company operated 1,055 Target discount stores (accounting for 83 percent of retail sales). The Target operation is the company's strongest retail franchise and is its growth vehicle for the future. Most of the remaining units operate under Mervyn's banner. These 264 outlets handle soft goods (10 percent of sales). Finally, the department store segment consists mostly of sixty Marshall Field's department stores and four home-furnishing units (7 percent of annual sales).

Target stores are situated largely in such states as California, Texas, Florida, and the upper Middle West. Mervyn's are clustered largely in California and Texas.

In 2000, the company formed target.direct, the direct merchandising and electronic retailing organization. The business combines the e-commerce team of Target with its direct merchandising unit into one integrated organization. The target.direct organization operates seven Web sites, which support the store and catalog brands in an online environment. The organization also produces six retail catalogs.

Shortcomings to Bear in Mind

- *Standard & Poor's Stock Reports* sounded a negative note in its December 2001 report. "New merchandising strategies and a cost-reduction program resulted in improved profitability at Mervyn's in fiscal 2001, but in an overcrowded retail market, there is little opportunity for growth. Weak sales and high markdowns have hurt profitability at the department stores. Cash flow from Mervyn's and the department stores is being used to fund Target's aggressive expansion."
- The company's balance sheet is not impressive. Less than half of its capitalization is in stockholders' equity.
- The retail business is always subject to competitive pressures from such outstanding companies as Bed Bath & Beyond, Wal-Mart, Costco, Lowe's, and Home Depot.

Reasons to Buy

- Unlike many companies, 2001 was a good one for Target. Earnings per share advanced 13 percent to $1.56, and revenues rose to $39.9 billion, for a gain of 8.1 percent over the prior year. More of the same is in store for 2002, said CEO Bob Ulrich. "We are extremely pleased with overall results in fiscal 2001, particularly the strength of our fourth quarter. In 2002, we will continue to manage our business with a disciplined approach and, over the long-term, we remain confident in our ability to achieve average annual earnings per share growth of 15 percent."
- Target has an outstanding record of growth. In the last ten years (1991–2001), earnings per share climbed from $0.31 to $1.56, a compound annual growth rate of 17.5 percent. In the same period, dividends advanced from $0.12 to $0.22, a growth rate of only 6.2 percent. Although not exactly impressive, the small dividend is indicative of a growth stock. In 2001, the company paid out only 14.1 percent of earnings, plowing the rest into new outlets.
- Target intends to accelerate its store-opening program in fiscal 2002. Augmenting this plan is the opening of

thirty-five former Montgomery Ward stores, acquired in 2001. In all, Target's selling space should expand by 12 percent in 2002, a nice jump over the 8.2 percent pace of the prior year. The capital budget of $3.4 billion for both fiscal 2001 and 2002 is 55 percent greater than the average of the preceding two years. That increase reflects the purchase and renovation of the Montgomery Ward units and the rollout of SuperTarget stores.

According to Mr. Ulrich, "This acquisition provides an excellent opportunity for Target to secure prime real estate in a large number of premier markets, including California, where sufficient, desirable property is difficult to find. We intend to extensively renovate these stores to ensure that they fully reflect our Target brand, and expect the majority of these locations to open as Target stores during 2002."

- The company's primary growth comes from new store expansion within the Target Stores division. Through a combination of net new discount stores and new SuperTarget stores, the company plans to continue adding an average of 8 to 10 percent retail square footage annually. In the words of CEO Bob Ulrich, "We continue to build out less penetrated markets, such as Boston, New York, and Philadelphia, that provide substantial growth opportunities because of the dense population and the favorable demographics of potential guests.

"We also continue to introduce Target into entirely new markets, such as our entry into Portland, Maine, in the fall of 2001. But increasingly, Target is expanding its store density in more mature markets, such as Atlanta, Phoenix, and Dallas/Fort Worth, reflecting our growing recognition and strength of the Target brand in major

metropolitan areas across the United States.

"In fact, despite more than doubling our presence in Minnesota in the past ten years, and operating more square footage per capita in Minnesota than in any other state, Target continues to strengthen its Minnesota store base and has added five new stores in 2001. This ability to build additional stores even in well-established markets, and enhance our financial performance, gives us confidence that Target can continue to grow profitably for many years to come."

- Store expansion is only part of the whole story, according to Mr. Ulrich. "In addition to store expansion, the growth of our Target stores division is propelled by our ability to protect and enhance our distinctive brand character. We strive to provide our guests with a stopping experience that is consistently better than, and different from, their experiences at our competitors' stores.

"By offering innovative, well-designed merchandise, compelling prices, and clean, attractive stores, we deliver the excitement and value that our guests expect and demand. In 2000, we introduced Philips Kitchen Appliances, Martex domestics, and Liz Claiborne fashions, among other brands. And in 2001, our assortment of new, exclusive products included Mossimo apparel, Waverly home furnishings, and Eddie Bauer camping gear."

- The company is also benefiting from its credit card business. Mr. Ulrich said, "Our financial services, including our credit card operations, are integral components of our overall strategy and meaningful contributors to our annual revenue and profit growth. Over the past five years, pre-tax contribution from this business has grown at a compound annual rate of 17 percent, and our return on investment has also risen sharply.

"To sustain this growth, we continue to reinforce the use of our own proprietary cards as the preferred method of payment by investing in guest loyalty and rewards programs at all three of our retail segments. In addition, we are expanding our offering of gift cards; pro-

viding access to integrated banking, brokerage, and investment planning services through our alliance with E*Trade; and leveraging guest interactions throughout our organization to create a comprehensive database that will help us strengthen our long-term relationship with our guests."

Total assets: $19,490 million
Current ratio: 1.42
Common shares outstanding: 903 million
Return on 2001 shareholders' equity: 18%

	2001	2000	1999	1998	1997	1996	1995	1994
Revenues (millions)	39888	36903	33702	30662	27487	25371	23516	21311
Net income (millions)	1368	1264	1185	962	775	555	311	434
Earnings per share	1.56	1.38	1.27	1.02	.82	.59	.32	.46
Dividends per share	.22	.21	.20	.18	.17	.16	.15	.14
Price High	41.7	39.2	38.5	27.1	18.5	10.2	6.7	7.2
Low	26.0	21.6	25.0	15.7	9.0	5.8	5.3	5.4

AGGRESSIVE GROWTH

Tenet Healthcare Corporation

3820 State Street ❑ Santa Barbara, CA 93105 ❑ Listed: NYSE ❑ (805) 563-7188 ❑ Dividend reinvestment plan is not available ❑ Fiscal year ends May 31 ❑ Web site: www.tenethealth.com ❑ Ticker symbol: THC ❑ S&P rating: B ❑ Value Line financial strength rating: B

Tenet Healthcare Corporation, a leading operator of hospitals and other related facilities, is showing solid growth in recent years, despite the impact of the recession and the effects of terrorism.

Tenet's strong performance continued into fiscal 2002, with a 43 percent increase in earnings in the second quarter. "We continue to experience the strongest fundamentals and prospects we can remember," said Jeffrey C. Barbakow, Tenet's chairman and CEO. "Our strategies are driving top-line growth. We have achieved across-the-board improvement in all measures of profitability and returns, and expect further improvement. Strong cash flow results in de-leveraging, which in

turn leads to lower interest expense, thus improving earnings growth even more.

"At the same time, we have resumed growth opportunities through strategic acquisitions, which add to our already strong internal growth."

In the same quarter, admissions to Tenet hospitals rose 5.9 percent overall and 2.3 percent on a same-facility basis. However, unit revenues, measured by same-facility net inpatient revenue per admission, climbed 14.9 percent, compared with the same quarter of 2001. This strength is spurred in large part by the success of Tenet's strategy to boost such profitable services such as cardiology, orthopedics, and neurology.

"Emphasizing the growth of these and other specialty services has led us to convert sub-acute beds in many of our hospitals to higher acuity medical/surgical and critical care beds," said Mr. Barbakow. "This has the effect of replacing lower-revenue services with high-revenue services, with a very positive result in unit revenue."

Company Profile

Tenet Healthcare Corporation, a nationwide provider of health care services, owns and operates 116 acute care hospitals and related businesses serving communities in seventeen states. Tenet, which employs 113,500 people, provides central support services to hospitals from a Dallas-based operations center.

Tenet's acute-care hospitals, with 28,786 licensed beds, offer a wide array of medical services and serve as the anchors for its regional health care delivery networks. These regional delivery networks, designed to provide a full spectrum of care throughout a community or region, may include specialty hospitals, outpatient surgery centers, home health agencies, rehabilitation hospitals, psychiatric hospitals, and long-term care.

Highlights of 2001

By nearly any measure, fiscal 2001 (ended May 31, 2001) was the most successful year in Tenet's history. Here are some of the company's accomplishments in that year:

- Earnings per share from operations (excluding special items) were up 27.1 percent over the prior year, to $2.30. Net income from operations (before special items) was up 32.3 percent, to $752.6 million.
- Admissions grew 3.6 percent on a same-facility basis over the prior year, or well above Tenet's historical average of about 2 percent.

- Cash flow from operations was $1.82 billion, up 109 percent over 2000, setting a record for the company.
- For the year, Tenet reduced its debt by a "remarkable" $1.45 billion—another company record. This brought the company's debt-to-equity ratio down to 0.83, from 1.40 just one year earlier.
- Tenet reported significant improvement in virtually all measures of profitability, including operating margins, pretax margins, net income margins, return on assets, and return on equity.

According to Mr. Barbakow, "Among the many factors that contributed to these excellent financial and operating results were continuing strong commercial pricing, a much-improved government reimbursement climate, and our own company-wide initiatives to improve operational performance and grow our acute-care business."

Shortcomings to Bear in Mind

- According to Value Line Survey, "Labor-cost inflation remains a problem, particularly in the area of nursing, where a nationwide shortage persists."
- The company's balance sheet has been leveraged in recent years, and thus its debt has been below average in quality. However, of late, the company has been reducing its debt, and its bond ratings have improved.

Reasons to Buy

- Value Line Survey ranks Tenet above average (2) in the category of Timeliness. The analyst said, "On the operating side, the aging of the baby-boomer generation augurs well for hospital admissions for years to come. The pricing environment is also very encouraging, pursuant to the Balanced Budget Refinement Act, which has enhanced Medicare payments."

- From time to time, Tenet divests hospitals that are not essential to strategic objectives. For the most part, these divested facilities are smaller, less profitable, and not part of an integrated health care delivery system. In 2001, the company sold one general hospital and three long-term care facilities. Tenet closed one long-term care facility and combined the operations of one rehabilitation hospital with the operations of a general hospital. As an offset, Tenet acquired two general hospitals the same year.

- During the second quarter of fiscal 2002, Tenet's bonds were upgraded by Standard & Poor's, Moody's, and Fitch, the three leading rating agencies. According to Mr. Barbakow, "It was an ideal time to move from a high-yield to investment-grade issuer. We were able to refinance a significant portion of our long-term debt in a historically low-rate environment." As a result, the company will benefit from significantly lower interest expense in future years. Tenet estimates fiscal 2002 interest expense will total about $330 million—down by about $125 million from the prior year.

- *Standard & Poor's Stock Reports* had some favorable comments in early 2002, "We are maintaining our buy recommendation on THC and believe the company's operating strategies will allow for three-year average earnings growth of 23 percent. Positive operating trends include surging inpatient revenues per admission, rising occupancy levels, expanding operating margins, and falling bad debt levels."

- "Another success has been our focus on core services at our hospitals—areas like cardiology, neurology, and orthopedics—that are increasing in demand by the aging 83-million-strong baby boomer generation," said Mr. Barbakow. "Our highest rate of admissions growth is now among the baby boomer age groups, and we expect that trend to continue. Admissions for the fifty-one-to-sixty age group were up 10 percent over the prior year, and admissions for the forty-one-to-fifty age group increased 8 percent in 2001.

"We are investing in facilities and equipment and selectively recruiting physicians who specialize in these high-acuity services to help our hospitals meet the health care needs of what will be the largest elderly population in U.S. history.

"For example, at Centinela Hospital Medical Center in Los Angeles, a major new cardiology center, the Tommy Lasorda Heart Institute, and a new arthritis institute that focuses primarily on joint replacement and other orthopedic procedure helped increase overall admissions in fiscal 2001 by 8.1 percent, in a market that is not seeing significant population growth. The number of open-heart surgeries performed at Centinela increased 61 percent since fiscal 1999.

"There are similar examples throughout the company. Overall, admissions in cardiac services were up almost 8 percent in fiscal 2001 over the prior year. Orthopedic and neurology admissions were up almost 7 percent. Additionally, we're expanding capacity where it makes sense. We have a number of expansion projects under way, including a brand-new hospital in Bartlett, near Memphis, a new ten-story USC University Hospital in Los Angeles and a new pavilion at Piedmont Medical Center in Rock Hill, South Carolina."

- As noted above, one problem confronting hospitals is the shortage of nurses. Tenet is having success in dealing with this problem. "Our Employer of Choice initiative is designed to help recruit and retain nurses at our hospitals by offering a wide range of programs and benefits, including online continuing education courses and leadership training," said Mr. Barbakow.

"Several of our hospitals were guiding beacons for this initiative in fiscal 2001. Saint Mary's Regional Medical Center in Russellville, Arkansas, almost halved its nurse vacancy rate in fiscal 2001 after implementing a number of Employer of Choice programs, including a tuition-reimbursement and bonus program that rewards potential employees for the length of time they're willing to commit to a Tenet career."

Total assets: $12,995 million
Current ratio: 1.57
Common shares outstanding: 325 million
Return on 2001 shareholders' equity: 14.8%

	2001	2000	1999	1998	1997	1996	1995	1994
Revenues (millions)	12053	11414	10880	9895	8691	5559	3318	2967
Net income (millions)	752	569	519	537	444	271	200	209
Earnings per share	2.30	1.81	1.65	1.73	1.46	1.27	1.09	1.19
Dividends per share	Nil	—	—	—	—	—	—	—
Price High	62.8	45.8	27.2	40.9	34.9	23.8	20.8	19.5
Low	37.0	16.9	15.4	23.8	21.4	18.1	13.5	12.5

CONSERVATIVE GROWTH

UnitedHealth Group, Inc.

9900 Bren Road East □ Minneapolis, Minnesota 55343 □ Listed: NYSE □ (952) 936-7265 □ Dividend reinvestment plan is not available □ Web site: www.unitedhealthgroup.com □ Ticker symbol: UNH □ S&P rating: A □ Value Line financial strength rating: A

"We believe in choice and direct access to broad, diverse, and fully qualified care providers and health resources," said William W. McGuire, M.D., chairman and CEO of UnitedHealth Group in 2001. "Accordingly, we offer a full range of option-rich benefit designs that enable customers to make choices based on their needs."

Dr. McGuire went on to say, "Today, we serve more than 16 million individuals for general medical care and specialized needs, and an additional 18 million people through Specialized Care Services alone. In addition, by leveraging the buying power of nearly 35 million Americans, UnitedHealth Group can access the best resources at the best prices—making care more affordable for the consumer and fair to the care-giving community.

"We believe in simplifying the health care experience and have made significant and sustained investments to do just that. We have adopted streamlined, more consistent processes and designed simpler, more understandable products and services, and we are using advanced system technologies to automate and speed health care interactions, simplify administrative functions, advance information, and lower costs."

Corporate Profile

UnitedHealth Group is a U.S. leader in health care management, providing a broad range of health care products and services, including health maintenance organizations (HMOs), point of service (POS) plans, preferred provider organizations (PPOs), and managed fee for service programs. It also offers managed behavioral health services, utilization management, workers' compensation, and disability management services, specialized provider networks, and third-party administration services. Here are its four segments.

- UnitedHealth care coordinates network-based health and well-being services on behalf of local employers and consumers in six broad regional markets, including commercial, Medicare, and Medicaid products and services.

- Ovations offers health and well-being services for Americans age fifty and older and their families, including Medicare supplement insurance, hospital indemnity coverage, and pharmacy services for members of the health insurance program of AARP. Ovations also provides health and well-being services for elderly, vulnerable, and chronically ill populations through Evercare.

- Uniprise provides network-based health and well-being services, business-to-business infrastructure services, consumer connectivity and service, and technology support services for large employers and health plans.

- Specialized Care Services offers a comprehensive array of specialized benefits, networks, services, and resources to help consumers improve their health and well-being, including employee assistance/counseling programs, mental health/substance abuse services, solid organ transplant programs and related services, twenty-four-hour health and well-being information services and publications, dental benefits, vision care benefits, life, accident, and critical illness benefits, and chiropractic, physical therapy, and complementary medicine benefits.

Ingenix serves providers, payers, employers, governments, pharmaceutical companies, medical device manufacturers, and academic and other research institutions through two divisions. Ingenix Health Intelligence offers business-to-business publications as well as data and software analytic products. Ingenix Pharmaceutical Services is a global drug development and marketing services organization offering clinical trial management services, consulting services, medical education, and epidemiological and economic research.

Shortcomings to Bear in Mind

- In 2001, a few insiders, such as officers and board members, sold stock in the company. During that same period there were no buyers.

Reasons to Buy

- I'm not the only person who likes UnitedHealth Group. Here are some of the company's recent awards:
  - *Fortune* magazine (April 16, 2001) ranked UnitedHealth Group Number ninety-one in the 2001 rankings of the 500 largest U.S. corporations, based on 2000 revenues. *Fortune* also ranked UnitedHealth Group number two in the health care industry (based on 2000 revenues).
  - UnitedHealth Group Chairman and CEO Bill McGuire was ranked number twenty-six in *Worth* magazine's Top 50 CEO list (May 2001). The magazine selected business leaders based on their foresight, judgment, and competitive edge.
  - The company was ranked number twelve on *Barron's* 500 (April 23, 2001), a report card that grades companies' overall performance for investors.
  - *Fortune* magazine has ranked UnitedHealth Group the first or second

most admired health care company in America every year since 1995.

- For the second consecutive year, CareData, the health care division of J.D. Power and Associates (September 19, 2000), ranked United-Health care the number one managed health care organization in a member satisfaction survey of leading national health plans.
- *Computerworld* magazine (June 4, 2001) listed UnitedHealth Group in its annual list of the 100 Best Places to Work in IT for the eighth consecutive year.

■ *Value Line Survey* ranked United-Health Group above average in the category of Timeliness in December of 2001. The analyst said, "The huge health care concern's extraordinary vitality is broadbased, with contributions coming from many quarters. All four business segments are generating double-digit top-line gains, fueled by a consolidated, same-facility year-to-date increase of 14 percent." The analyst also pointed out, "Concurrently, operating margins continue to expand appreciably, reflecting management actions both to improve productivity through the substitution of technology for labor and to shift product mix towards higher-margin fee business."

■ *Standard & Poor's Stock Reports* was equally impressed with the company. In 2002, its analyst said, "We have upgraded UNH to accumulate from hold, based on its strong, consistent performance. The Health Care Services unit continues to produce solid results. Rapid growth of nonhealth care units (Uniprise, Ingenix, and Specialty Care Services) provides a significant portion of earnings growth, and offers diversification to weather economic weakness. We continue to see UNH as well positioned to benefit in all economic environments. We believe margins widened slightly in 2001, and look for additional expansion in 2002, as UNH raises commercial premiums above medical cost trends and reduces its administrative cost ratio."

■ In the past ten years (1991–2001) earnings per share advanced sharply, from $0.30 to $2.76, a compound annual growth rate of 24.9 percent. The only exception was 1996, when earnings fell from $1.06 to $0.88.

■ Since its inception, UnitedHealth Group and its affiliated companies have led the marketplace by introducing key innovations that make health care services more accessible and affordable for customers, improving the quality and coordination of health care services, and help individuals and their physicians make more informed health care decisions.

Time Line of Selected Highlights and Innovations

■ 1974. Charter Med Incorporated is founded by a group of physicians and other health care professionals.

■ 1977. United Health Care Corporation is created and acquires Charter Med Incorporated.

■ 1979. United Health Care Corporation introduces the first network-based health plan for seniors and participates in the earliest experiments with offering a private-market alternative for Medicare.

■ 1984. United Health Care Corporation becomes a publicly traded company.

■ 1989. William W. McGuire, M.D., assumes leadership of the company. Annual revenues are just over $400 million. (Today, they are over $24 billion.)

■ 1995. The company acquires The Metra-Health Companies, Inc., for $1.65 billion. MetraHealth is a privately held company that was formed by combining the group health care operations of The Travelers Insurance Company and Metropolitan Life Insurance Company.

- 1996. The company's patented artificial intelligence system AdjudiPro, which is entered into the permanent research collection of the Smithsonian Institution, is awarded the CIO Enterprise Value Award.
- 1998. United Health Care Corporation becomes known as UnitedHealth Group and launches a strategic realignment

into independent but strategically linked business segments—UnitedHealth care, Ovations, Uniprise, Specialized Care Services, and Ingenix.

- 1998. The first release of Clinical Profiles takes place. Clinical Profiles, produced by Ingenix, provides network physicians with data comparing their clinical practices to nationally accepted benchmarks for care.
- 2001. UnitedHealth Group is a highly diversified family of companies with revenues exceeding $23 billion.

Total assets: $12,102 million
Current ratio: .63
Common shares outstanding: 312 million
Return on 2001 shareholders' equity: 23.5%

		2001	2000	1999	1998	1997	1996	1995	1994
Revenues (millions)		23454	21122	19562	17355	11794	10074	5671	3651
Net income (millions)		913	705	563	509	460	356	383	310
Earnings per share		2.79	2.10	1.59	1.31	.88	1.06	.89	.62
Dividends per share		.03	.02	.02	.02	.02	.02	.02	.02
Price	High	72.8	63.4	35.0	37.0	30.1	34.5	32.8	27.7
	Low	50.5	23.2	19.7	14.8	21.2	15.0	17.1	18.6

CONSERVATIVE GROWTH

United Technologies Corporation

One Financial Plaza □ Hartford, Connecticut 06101 □ (860) 728-7575 □ Listed: NYSE □ Dividend reinvestment plan is available: (800) 519-3111 □ Web site: www.utc.com □ Ticker symbol: UTX □ S&P rating: B+ □ Value Line Financial Strength A++

Late in 2001, France's Dassault Aviation selected a Pratt & Whitney unit in Canada—a United Technologies business—to power its new Falcon 7X business jet in a deal that could mean more than $3 billion in business for the company. Just days earlier, Pratt & Whitney received some good news from the Pentagon. It was told that it would receive more than $4 billion over the next ten years to develop the first engine for Lockheed Martin, which got the nod to build the Joint Strike Fighter.

Analysts said the added revenue from

the two contracts couldn't come at a more propitious time. "As long as I have known Pratt & Whitney, it has been a tough road" for it in the commercial engine business, said Sam Pearlstein, an analyst with Wachovia Securities. "Their military engine business has been very strong, and the Joint Strike Fighter award only adds to it."

Company Profile

United Technologies provides high-technology products to the aerospace and building systems industries throughout the world. Its companies are industry leaders and include Pratt & Whitney, Carrier, Otis, Sikorsky, International Fuel Cells, and Hamilton Sundstrand. Sikorsky and Hamilton Sundstrand make up the Flight Systems segment.

Pratt & Whitney

Products and Services

Large and small commercial and military jet engines, spare parts and product support, specialized engine maintenance, and overhaul and repair services for airlines, air forces, and corporate fleets; rocket engines and space propulsion systems; and industrial gas turbines.

Primary Customers

Pratt & Whitney's primary customers include commercial airlines and aircraft-leasing companies; commercial and corporate aircraft manufacturers; the U.S. government, including NASA and the military services; and regional and commuter airlines.

Carrier

Products and Services

Carrier's products and services include heating, ventilating, and air conditioning (HVAC) equipment for commercial, industrial, and residential buildings; HVAC replacement parts and services; building controls; and commercial, industrial, and transport refrigeration equipment.

Carrier emphasizes energy-efficient, quiet operation and environmental stewardship in its new residential and commercial products. The new WeatherMaker residential air conditioner using Puron, a nonozone-depleting refrigerant, provides the domestic market with low operating costs and sound levels—about the same as a refrigerator's. The Puron unit gives Carrier a healthy lead over competitors as chlorine-free refrigerants become the standard.

Primary Customers

Carrier's primary customers include mechanical and building contractors; homeowners, building owners, developers and retailers; architects and building consultants; transportation and refrigeration companies; and shipping operations.

Otis

Products and Services

Otis products and services include elevators, escalators, moving walks, and shuttle systems as well as related installation, maintenance, repair services, and modernization products and service for elevators and escalators.

Primary Customers

Otis primary customers include mechanical and building contractors; building owners and developers; homeowners; and architects and building consultants.

Flight Systems

Products and Services

Flight Systems products and services include aircraft electrical and power distribution systems; engine and flight controls; propulsion systems; environmental controls for aircraft, spacecraft, and submarines; auxiliary power units; space life support systems; industrial products, including mechanical power transmissions, compressors, metering devices, and fluid handling equipment; military and commercial helicopters, spare parts, and civil helicopter operations; and maintenance services for helicopters and fixed-wing aircraft.

Primary Customers

Flight Systems primary customers include the U.S. government, including NASA, the FAA, and the military services; non-U.S. governments; aerospace and defense prime contractors; commercial airlines; aircraft and jet engine manufacturers; oil and gas exploration companies; mining and water companies; construction companies; and hospitals and charters.

Highlights of 2001

- Carrier's 2001 revenues grew by 6 percent, almost entirely due to acquisitions. Operating profit, however, was down a modest 4 percent. Operating profit reflected growth in Asia and Europe that was more than offset by poor market conditions in global refrigeration, North American commercial HVAC, and Latin America, along with performance problems in acquired entities, particularly commercial refrigeration.

- Pratt & Whitey's 2001 operating profit increased a healthy 14 percent on a 4 percent expansion in revenue, reflecting the benefit of previous cost-reduction actions.

- The Otis elevator unit, which is highly profitable and expected to be a major factor in enabling United Technologies to withstand what are expected to a be a couple years of tough years in the aviation sphere, turned in superb results in 2001. Operating profits advanced 17 percent on a 3 percent gain in revenues. However, the strong dollar was a negative factor. At constant foreign exchange rates, Otis's operating profit increased 20 percent on a 7 percent increase in sales.

- There was also good news at Flight Systems in 2001. Operating profit climbed 14 percent on a 6 percent increase in sales. These results were enhanced by increases at Hamilton Sundstrand and higher helicopter shipments at Sikorsky. During the year, Hamilton Sundstrand was awarded contracts for air management and actuation systems for the new Airbus A380 aircraft as well as engine controls and electrical systems on the Joint Strike Fighter. Sikorsky delivered 92 aircraft in 2001, significantly more than the seventy deliveries the prior year.

Shortcomings to Bear in Mind

- *Value Line Survey* is lukewarm about United Technologies. In late 2001, its analyst, Daniel L. Marks, said, "United Technologies' shares do not seem particularly attractive at this time. While increased military spending and FASB 142, which eliminates goodwill amortization, will likely give a boost to the company's bottom line in 2002, its near-term earnings prospects still remain unexciting."

- J. Lynn Lunsford, writing for *The Wall Street Journal* in 2001, said, "One of the first stops on every guided tour of Pratt & Whitney's jet-engine factory is a working miniature model of the JT8D, the engine that made Pratt the ruler of the jet age. But that was more than thirty years ago.

  "Today, many of those engines are on airplanes that are headed for the graveyard, and Pratt is struggling to shake off a widely held perception that it has lost its edge. In the last two years, the subsidiary of Hartford-based United Technologies Corp. has been trying to regain its footing against rivals General Electric Co.'s General Electric Aircraft Engines and Rolls-Royce PLC. They have used their newer technology and formidable financial backing during the 1980s and 1990s to become key engine suppliers on most of the new jetliners coming out of Seattle. Pratt, which once owned 90 percent of the world's large-jet-engine market, today clings to about a third."

Reasons to Buy

- Despite the impacts of September 11, earnings per share increased 8 percent in 2001. They have increased at a compound annual rate of 21 percent since 1993. Available cash flow was strong once again. In the words of CEO George David, "We like high cash flow because it funds acquisitions, which add to growth and strengthen our industry-leading companies. It also funds share repurchases, which reduce the common share count and add to earnings per share.

"Available cash flow in 2001 was $1.9 billion and equal to 98 percent of net income. Over the last five years, available cash flow has totaled $8 billion, 105 percent of net income. Over this same period, acquisitions have totaled $10 billion and share repurchases nearly $4 billion."

- Mr. David went on to say, "We had extraordinary contract wins in 2001. Chief among these was the lead engine placement on the Joint Strike Fighter (JSF), called by many the largest military procurement ever. We won the electric generation/distribution system on the same aircraft. Over the JSF jet aircraft program, UTC business may exceed $50 billion. We are also the sole-source engine builder for the twin-engine F-22 Raptor fighter, currently beginning production."

- Through internal growth and acquisition, Carrier's commercial refrigeration business has become a leader in the highly fragmented $17-billion global industry. Carrier's acquisition of Electrolux Commercial Refrigeration will broaden its offerings to supermarkets, convenience stores, and food and beverage markets, particularly in Europe. A new transport refrigeration unit, the Vector, can cool a trailer from 30° C to minus 20° C twice as fast as a conventional unit can.

- In early 2002, Hawaiian Airlines signed a twenty-year agreement with Pratt & Whitney to provide a fleet-management program for the airline's PW4060-powered 767-300ER aircraft. The agreement covers thirty-six engines and has an estimated value of $325 million.

The full-scale overhaul and maintenance work will be performed at Pratt & Whitney's Cheshire Engine Center in Connecticut. The center is currently capable of overhauling JT9D, PW2000, PW4000, F117, and V2500 engine models. Pratt & Whitney Aftermarket Services offers overhaul and repair services at nearly thirty locations around the world.

- Pratt & Whitney scored a major coup in being chosen by the Pentagon as the lead engine supplier on both versions of the Joint Strike Fighter, as well as the F-22 fighter, two of the military's highest-profile new programs. Pratt is also tapping into markets it once chose to leave to others, aggressively seeking commercial-engine overhaul and maintenance business that could be valued at more than $1 billion a year. What's more, the company also has seized on an opportunity provided by the nation's power woes. It expects to sell fifty-four modified JT8D engines for industrial electric generation for major power companies in need of cheap and quickly obtainable electric power.

Total assets: $26.9 billion
Current ratio: 1.25
Return on 2001 equity: 24.2%
Common shares outstanding: 470 million

	2001	2000	1999	1998	1997	1996	1995	1994
Revenues (millions)	27897	26583	24127	25715	24713	23512	22802	21197
Net income (millions)	1938	1808	841	1255	1072	906	750	616
Earnings per share	3.83	3.55	1.65	2.53	2.11	1.73	1.43	1.16
Dividends per share	.90	.83	.76	.70	.62	.55	.52	.48
Price High	87.5	79.8	78.0	56.2	44.5	35.2	24.5	18.0
Low	40.1	46.5	51.6	33.5	32.6	22.7	15.6	13.8

Varian Medical Systems, Inc.

3100 Hansen Way ◻ Palo Alto, California 94304-1038 ◻ (650) 424-5782 ◻ Dividend reinvestment plan is not available ◻ Web site: www.varian.com ◻ Fiscal year ends on Friday nearest September 30 ◻ Ticker symbol: VAR ◻ S&P rating: B+ ◻ Value Line financial strength rating: B++

Fiscal year 2001 was another stellar year for Varian Medical Systems. In the words of CEO Richard M. Levy, "We look forward to having another excellent year in fiscal 2002, with continuing growth opportunities in cancer treatment and X-ray imaging markets as well as emerging opportunities in new markets. Our numbers highlight the fiscal 2001 story:

• "Net earnings were $1.05 per diluted share—37 percent higher than comparative fiscal 2000 earnings—before a one-time charge for the write-off of our dpiX investment and the cumulative net effect of an accounting change (SAB 101).

• "Reported annual sales were $774 million, up 14 percent from comparative fiscal 2000 results.

• "Net orders were $858 million, up 13 percent from the previous year.

• "Reported year-end backlog stood at a record $598 million, up 16 percent.

• "Cash levels were $219 million, up $136 million."

Company Profile

Varian Medical Systems is the world's leading manufacturer of integrated radiotherapy systems for treating cancer and other diseases; it is also a leading supplier of X-ray tubes for imaging in medical, scientific, and industrial applications. Established in 1948, the company has manufacturing sites in North America and Europe and in forty sales and support offices worldwide.

In 1999, the company (formerly Varian Associates, Inc.) reorganized itself into three separate publicly traded companies by spinning off two of its businesses to stockholders via a tax-free distribution.

Since then, the company has significantly broadened its product and business offerings, acquired new businesses, and set records for sales and net orders. More importantly, Varian put itself at the forefront of a radiotherapy revolution that is making a dramatic difference in the struggle against cancer.

About three out of every ten people will be afflicted with some form of cancer. The good news is that their chances of surviving, of beating cancer, have greatly improved, thanks to recent advances in radiation therapy—many of which have been led by Varian Medical Systems.

The company is composed of three segments.

Varian Oncology Systems

Varian Oncology Systems is the world's leading supplier of radiotherapy systems for treating cancer. Its integrated medical systems include linear accelerators and accessories and a broad range of interconnected software tools for planning and delivering the sophisticated radiation treatments available to cancer patients. Thousands of patients all over the world are treated daily on Varian systems. Oncology Systems works closely with health care professionals in community clinics, hospitals, and universities to improve cancer outcomes. The business unit also supplies linear accelerators for industrial inspection applications.

Varian X-Ray Products

Varian X-Ray Products is the world's premier independent supplier of X-ray tubes, serving manufacturers of radiology equipment and industrial inspection equipment, as well as a distributor of replacement tubes. This business provides the industry's broadest selection of X-ray tubes expressly designed for the most advanced diagnostic applications, including CT scanning, radiography, and mammography. These products meet evolving requirements for improved resolution, faster patient throughput, longer tube life, smaller dimensions, and greater cost efficiency. X-Ray Products also supplies a new line of amorphous silicon flat-panel X-ray detectors for medical and industrial applications.

Ginzton Technology Center

The Ginzton Technology Center acts as Varian Medical Systems' research and development facility for breakthrough technologies. The Center also operates a growing brachytherapy business for the delivery of internal radiation to treat cancer and cardiovascular disease. In addition to brachytherapy, current efforts are focused on next-generation imaging systems and advanced targeting technologies for radiotherapy. The Center is also investigating the combination of radiotherapy with other treatment modalities, such as bioengineered gene delivery systems.

Shortcomings to Bear in Mind

- Investors are well aware that Varian Medical has a bright future—they have pushed the company's PE ratio to lofty levels. You might want to wait for a sinking spell before you buy shares in this strong growth company.

Reasons to Buy

- *Value Line Survey* had a few kind words to say about Varian Medical Systems in fiscal 2002. "Oncology systems are Varian's dominant product. The company's cancer care equipment is tops in the field, and its use is growing rapidly. Indeed, the SAB 101 deferral adds $51 million to backlog, which

reached $598 million at the end of fiscal 2001. And, as the installed base of equipment grows, so do Varian's locked-in revenues, for which the service portion is now up to a $150 million annual rate."

- For its part, *Standard & Poor's Stock Reports* also added some favorable comments: "We continue to recommend accumulating the shares. VAR is poised for another year of consistent revenue and earnings growth in FY 02. For more than thirty years, it has been the leading maker of clinical linear accelerators (hardware systems to deliver radiation therapy to the cancer site), dominating both U.S. and worldwide markets. VAR's large and growing order backlog provides excellent visibility for future results."

- In the year 2000, more than 6 million people worldwide succumbed to cancer. Nearly twice as many more were diagnosed with the disease. In some countries, cancer is a leading cause of death among children. Mostly though, it is a disease primarily of aging, with people fifty-five or older—the "baby boomers"—now accounting for nearly 80 percent of diagnosed cases. In the United States, the chances that you'll eventually develop cancer are one in three if you are female, one in two if you are male. In a very real sense, cancer victimizes not only patients but also their families and friends, colleagues and neighbors. Ultimately, the disease affects us all. The social and economic costs are staggering.

The fact is that half of U.S. patients receive radiotherapy as part of their treatment. Now, thanks to the new technology that Varian Medical Systems has helped to develop, radiotherapy is poised to play an even stronger role in cancer treatment, and many more patients could be cured by it. It's technology that is being implemented in all corners of the world.

■ With certain cancers, the odds of surviving are improving markedly, thanks to the growing use of a radiotherapy advance called intensity modulated radiation therapy, or IMRT. IMRT is being used to treat head and neck, breast, prostate, pancreatic, lung, liver, and central nervous system cancers. IMRT makes it possible for a larger and more effective dose of radiation to be delivered directly to the tumor, greatly sparing surrounding, healthy tissues. This is expected to result in a higher likelihood of cure with lower complication rates.

The clinical outcomes using IMRT are extremely promising. A study of early stage prostate cancer has shown that the higher radiation doses possible with IMRT have the potential to double the rate of tumor control to more than 95 percent. Using IMRT, clinicians were able to deliver high doses while reducing the rate of normal tissue complications from 10 percent to 2 percent. Similar results have been reported by doctors using IMRT to treat cancers of the head and neck.

Varian Medical Systems has joined forces with GE Medical Systems to combine the latest in diagnostic imaging results with advanced radiotherapy technologies in what are called See & Treat Cancer Care imaging and treatment tools. This approach enables physicians to see the distribution of malignant cells more clearly and treat them more effectively with precisely targeted radiation doses using IMRT.

■ Varian Medical Systems has long been the world's leading supplier of radiotherapy equipment. Now, the company's SmartBeam IMRT system, the culmination of twelve years and $300 million in development effort, is already making a difference for thousands of patients.

Today, a little more than 500 of the world's 5,700 radiotherapy centers for cancer treatment have acquired a set of integrated tools for SmartBeam IMRT from Varian Medical Systems.

Almost one-fifth of them are now offering it to their patients, and many others are close behind.

In addition to promising outcomes and public demand for better care, new Medicare and Medicaid reimbursement rates are expected to help accelerate the rapid adoption of IMRT by both hospitals and free-standing cancer centers in the United States. In international markets, public health systems are under pressure to reduce patients' waiting periods by updating systems with more effective treatment technology that can treat more patients.

IMRT will probably be available in all major cancer centers within the next five years, according to a prediction made in 2001 by Soren Bentzen, a leading international cancer expert from Gray Laboratory Cancer Research in London.

Total assets: $759 million
Current ratio: 2.27
Common shares outstanding: 67 million
Return on 2001 shareholders' equity: 19.2%

	2001	2000	1999	1998	1997	1996	1995	1994
Revenues (millions)	774	690	590	1422	1426	1599	1576	1552
Net income (millions)	68	53	8	74	82	122	106	79
Earnings per share	1.05	.82	.14	1.22	1.83	1.91	1.51	1.11
Dividends per share	Nil	Nil	.05	.20	.18	.15	.17	.12
Price High	38.6	35.5	21.5	29.2	33.5	31.4	28.7	19.6
Low	27.0	14.2	8.1	15.8	22.9	20.3	17.3	14.1

Vectren Corporation

20 N.W. Fourth Street ◻ Evansville, Indiana 47708 ◻ (812) 491-4205 ◻ Dividend reinvestment plan is available: (800) 622-6757 ◻ Web site: www.vectren.com ◻ Listed: NYSE ◻ Ticker symbol: VVC ◻ S&P rating: B+ ◻ Value Line financial strength rating: A

Unlike many power companies, Vectren's electric utility (Southern Indiana Gas & Electric Company, or SIGECO) strives to provide low-cost and environmentally sound electric generation. Since 1995, the company has had sulfur dioxide (SO_2) scrubbers installed on 85 percent of its coal-fired capacity, far exceeding government standards.

In addition, Vectren is participating in an updated State Implementation Plan (SIP) to reduce nitrogen oxide (NO_X) emissions from power generating plants, as part of an EPA plan to reduce ozone throughout the United States. Vectren will be committing about $160 million in capital expenditures over four years, including about $40 million in 2001, to bring its plants into compliance with standards set for 2004.

What's more, the company's coal-burning plants are already low producers of nitrogen oxide because of steps that the utility took in recent years to retrofit its plants with pollution-control equipment. Previous expenditures of about $20 million already have cut nitrogen oxide emissions by 50 percent. Finally, the new program will install additional nitrogen oxide technology on the company's four largest electric generating units that will reduce these emissions by 85 percent, compared with the levels of 1990.

Company Profile

Vectren Corporation was created in March of 2000 with the merger of two Indiana public utilities: Indiana Energy, Inc. (a natural gas distributor), and SIGCORP, Inc. (primarily an electric utility).

The name "Vectren" was dreamed up as a combination of the words "vector" (forward direction) and "energy." According to the annual report, "It connotes a company moving in new directions, consistent with its core energy industry skills, to create growing value for its shareholders." Frankly, I was happy with its old name of Southern Indiana Gas & Electric. But when it teamed up with Indiana Energy, something had to give. Regardless of the name, both parts of the company are excellent utilities, at least in part because the State of Indiana has a commission that treats utilities fairly—most states don't.

Regulated Operations

Energy Delivery provides gas and/or electricity to about one million customers in adjoining service territories that cover nearly two-thirds of Indiana and west-central Ohio.

In the words of a company spokesman, "We continue to be one of the most stable and lowest-cost providers of electricity in the nation. Our operating expenses are approximately 40 percent below the national average and rank in the lowest 10 percent in the country, according to the latest data available.

"Our cost and pricing advantages make us very competitive in the wholesale power markets and provide an incentive for businesses to locate and expand in our service territories. Toyota, for example, one of our largest electric customers, is expanding its manufacturing plant near Evansville during 2002, adding approximately 1,600 jobs to the southwestern Indiana economy."

Power Supply provides and markets low-cost wholesale power in southwestern Indiana, from 1,448 megawatts of total capacity and a reserve margin target of 15 percent.

In 2001, Vectren's regulated operations produced $65.8 million of income before nonrecurring items, or 74 percent of Vectren's total income.

Nonregulated Businesses

Vectren is involved in nonregulated activities through these primary business groups, as follows:

- Energy Marketing & Services markets natural gas and provides energy management, including performance contracting services.

- Utility Infrastructure Services provides underground construction, facilities locating, and meter reading.

At the end of 2001, the company had a record number of construction crews in place and achieved record construction revenues, with projects concentrated in the Midwest and Southeast. According to a company spokesman, "We believe there is a large backlog of aging infrastructure in these regions that utilities and other companies must replace in the years ahead. With the strong trend among utilities toward outsourcing construction projects, we are optimistic about the prospects for this business group."

- Broadband is invested in broadband communication services, such as analog and digital cable television; high-speed Internet and data services; and advanced local and long-distance telephone services.

- Coal Mining mines and sells coal to Vectren's utility operations and to other parties. This group generates IRS Code Section 29 investment tax credits relating to the production of coal-based synthetic fuels.

This group supplies Vectren utilities with 2.6 million tons of coal at fixed prices, helping the company remain one of the lowest-cost generators of electricity in the nation. In addition, coal reserves are conservatively estimated at 45 million tons, representing a valuable long-term asset for Vectren.

- Other businesses make investments in energy-related opportunities. This general group also includes utility services; municipal broadband consulting, retail, and real estate leveraged lease investments.

In 2001, Vectren's nonregulated business group accounted for income before nonrecurring items of $21.9 million, or 24 percent of the company's total income. Nonregulated businesses and investments represented about 12 percent of Vectren's assets at the end of 2001.

Shortcomings to Bear in Mind

- Electric and natural gas utilities are both subject to a sharp earnings impact from the weather. If the summer is hot, electric utilities benefit, since they sell more power for air conditioning. In the winter, both types of utilities enjoy robust profits when the weather is cold. This is particularly true for natural gas distributors, since the bulk of their sales are for space heating. A mild winter can hurt earnings severely. Unfortunately, the weather is extremely difficult to forecast.

- A number of negative factors hurt Vectren in 2001, including high natural gas prices, unusually warm winter weather, and a contracting economy. Lost margins and increased expenses, including uncollectible accounts expense resulting from the extraordinarily high natural gas costs early in the year, reduced net income before nonrecurring items by nearly $13 million. Additionally, winter weather that was 9 percent warmer than in 2000 reduced demand for energy and reduced net income by about $11 million. However, a portion of these decreases—about $10 million—was offset by savings realized as a result of management's focused cost reduction measures, following the merger and the solid performance of Vectren's nonregulated businesses.

Reasons to Buy

- Vectren's nonregulated business group continued its impressive performance again in 2001, contributing $21.9 million in net income before nonrecurring items, compared to $17.8 million in 2000 and $12.5 million in 1999.

  The company's two principal nonregulated businesses did extremely well in 2001. According to CEO Niel C. Ellerbrook, "Our energy marketing and services businesses contributed earnings before nonrecurring items of $11.9 million in 2001, up 65 percent from the year before as a result primarily of price volatility in the natural gas marketplace and our disciplined trading operations.

  "Our coal mining business, which supplies coal to our electric utility and other utility companies, contributed earnings before nonrecurring items of $13.5 million in 2001, up from $4.6 million the year before. Our second of two mines became fully operational early in the second quarter of the year and contributed to a 173 percent increase in our coal output for the year, which accounted for most of the increased coal earnings."

- Vectren's broadband business offers services such as analog and digital cable television; high-speed Internet and data services; and advanced local and long-distance telephone services to residential and commercial customers in the Evanston, Indiana, area. This business performed well in 2001, generating positive earnings before interest, taxes and depreciation, and amortization in both the third and fourth quarters of 2001.

  According to Mr. Ellerbrook, "We have achieved impressive penetration rates in our service area and are pleased that many customers have subscribed to multiple services. The number of revenue-generating units, or total number of services provided, climbed over 25 percent, to approximately 75,000.

  "We continue to plan for expansion of our broadband communication services into Indianapolis and Dayton, in partnership with Utilicom Networks, LLC, our Evansville partner, but only if suitable debt financing becomes available to fully fund the projects before construction begins."

- In contrast to the well-publicized electric energy experience in California, Vectren continues to provide a reliable flow of low-cost electricity to its customers in southern Indiana. Ownership of its own highly efficient coal mines, which will supply about 75 percent of the fuel for the company's electricity generating units, has helped Vectren maintain this enviable position.

- Vectren has allocated substantial future capital expenditures for building new gas-powered, peak-load generating units and meeting newly promulgated emission-control requirements for its coal-fired generating units. These expenditures will assure the company's continued ability to maintain system reliability, meet its environmental responsibilities, and deliver low prices to consumers. The new gas-powered units will assure an adequate reserve margin to meet the growing needs of customers in its service region for the foreseeable future.

Total assets: $2,857 million
Current ratio: 0.84
Common shares outstanding: 68 million
Return on 2001 shareholders' equity: 10.5%

	2001	2000	1999	1998	1997	1996	1995	1994
Revenues (millions)	2170	1649	1068	998	972	965	404	475
Net income (millions)	64	109	91	87	68	84	33	34
Earnings per share	1.34	1.78	1.48	1.41	1.10	1.36	1.09	1.15
Dividends per share	1.03	.98	.94	.90	.88	.85	.80	.77
Price High	24.4	26.5	24.6	26.4	25.8	22.0	18.1	17.5
Low	19.8	15.0	17.6	19.6	17.1	17.0	13.2	13.1

GROWTH AND INCOME

Verizon Communications

1095 Avenue of the Americas □ New York, New York 10036 □ (212) 395-1842 □ Direct dividend reinvestment plan is available: (800) 631-2355 □ Web site: www.verizon.com □ Ticker symbol: VZ □ S&P rating: B+ □ Value Line financial strength rating: A+

Verizon Wireless and Cingular Wireless, two of the country's biggest cellular companies, captured new shares of airwaves in such cities as Boston and New York in a federal government auction that ended in January of 2001.

The auction, which began in December of 2000, was a key step in the attempts of wireless phone firms to venture into new territories and expand their services in markets that were previously plagued by overcrowded airwaves. Of the eighty-seven companies that participated in the auction, thirty-five won licenses.

For its part, Verizon paid $8.8 billion for about a quarter of the 422 licenses available in 195 markets across the country, from New York, Boston, and Washington, D.C., to Seattle and Los Angeles.

Company Profile

Verizon is well positioned to capitalize on the "new economy" growth trends that are shaping communications around the world. Verizon is all of the following:

• The nation's largest local exchange carrier, covering one-third of the country.

• The nation's largest wireless company, with 29 million customers.

• The world's largest print and Internet directory business.

• A major competitor in high-growth international markets, with a presence extending to forty-five countries in the Americas, Europe, Asia, and the Pacific.

Verizon Communications, formed by the merger of Bell Atlantic and GTE, is one the world's leading providers of high-growth communications services. Verizon companies are the largest providers of wireless communications in the United States, with more than 132 million access line equivalents and more than 29 million wireless customers. Verizon is also the world's largest provider of print and on-line directory information. A *Fortune* 100 company with more than 247,000 employees and about $67 billion in revenues, Verizon's global presence extends to forty-five countries in the Americas, Europe, Asia, and the Pacific.

In April of 2000, the company and Vodafone Group Plc completed its agreement to combine U.S. wireless assets, including cellular, PCS, and paging operations. For its part, Vodafone Group Plc contributed its U.S. wireless operations to an existing Bell Atlantic partnership in exchange for a 65.1 percent interest in the partnership. Bell Atlantic retained a 34.9 percent interest.

On June 30, 2000, Bell Atlantic and GTE completed a merger. With the closing of the merger, the combined company began doing business as Verizon.

Here is a brief description of Verizon's operations.

Domestic Telecom

With nearly 132 million access line equivalents in sixty-seven of the top 100 domestic markets, and nine of the top ten, Verizon reaches one-third of the nation's households, more than one-third of *Fortune* 500 companies, as well as the federal government.

Domestic Wireless

Verizon Wireless is the nation's largest wireless communications provider, with more than 29 million wireless voice and data customers. The company's footprint covers nearly 90 percent of the population, forty-nine of the top fifty and ninety-six of the top 100 U.S. markets.

International

Verizon has wireline and wireless operations in the Americas, Europe, Asia, and the Pacific, and a global presence, which extends into forty-five countries, including FLAG, the world's longest undersea fiber-optic cable.

Information Services

Verizon Information Services is a world-leading print and online directory publisher and content provider. In addition to print directories, Verizon Information Services produces and markets *www.SuperPages.com*, the Internet's preeminent only directory and shopping resource. The Web site *www.SuperPages.com* provides Yellow Pages and directory services to AltaVista, MSN, Lycos, Excite, InfoSpace, Ask Jeeves, BigFoot, HotBot, Tripos, and Angelfire.

Highlights of 2001

- A 59-percent increase in long-distance customers year-over-year, with approximately 40 percent of the customer base coming from New York, Massachusetts, and Pennsylvania.
- A 122-percent increase in digital subscriber line (DSL) customers while improving customer service.
- A 21.2-percent increase in data transport revenues; total data revenues exceed $7 billion.
- Continued industry-leading cost control, with the Domestic Telecom unit showing a year-over-year decline in expenses, including three consecutive quarters of cash expense reductions.
- Technology deployment that enabled the launch of the nation's first major next-generation, 1XRTT wireless network and expanded the company's DSL reach to central offices serving 79 percent of access lines.
- A 22.8-percent year-over-year increase in proportionate international wireless customers, including a 1.8 million increase year-over-year, to 9.6 million total.
- Year-end totals: 29.4 million domestic wireless customers, 7.4 million long-distance customers, 1.2 million DSL customers; $17.4 billion in capital expenditures.

Shortcomings to Bear in Mind

- More than three years after introducing the nation's first all-in-one phone plans, a unit of Verizon Communications pulled the plug on the offering, forcing 370,000 customers nationwide to switch their local and long-distance service to less attractive options.

The plans, which offered local and long-distance phone service for a flat monthly fee, were originally touted as a groundbreaking effort to simplify phone service and spur competition in local markets. But after losing $100 million a year on the effort and making little headway in drawing customers away from local powerhouses such as Pacific Bell and BellSouth, Verizon decided to throw in the towel on the plan, known as Verizon OneSource.

- In the past ten years (1991–2001), the company's growth has been lackluster. In that span, earnings per share advanced from $1.71 to $3.00, an annual compound growth rate of only 5.8 percent. In the same period, dividends expanded at a snail's pace, from $1.26 to $1.54, a growth rate of 2.0 percent. On the other hand, since this Verizon is designated a Growth and Income stock, modest growth should not be considered a serious shortcoming.

Reasons to Buy

- In early 2001, the company announced that it would create a multinational network to serve large businesses, pitting itself more directly against global long-distance companies such as AT&T, British Telecommunications, and France Telecom SA.

  Prior to making this move, Verizon had been hampered in its ability to offer full service to global corporations because it was not able to reach some business hubs directly. As a consequence, rather than handing off phone and data communications bound for Europe, Asia, or Latin America to other carriers as it had been doing, Verizon decided to invest $1 billion over five years, installing its own transmission equipment and buying capacity on undersea and underground cables, enabling the company to keep that business for itself.

The new communications network will use cables owned by flag Telecom Holdings Ltd. and Metromedia Fiber Network, Inc., companies in which Verizon holds an ownership stake. Once the network is up and running, the company expects to save at least $300 million over five years because it won't have to lease lines to carry traffic outside the United States.

- A ruling by the FCC in March of 2001 granted Verizon permission to charge market-driven prices for some special services it offers to customers. This ruling, moreover, gave Verizon the same flexibility that its competitors already had. What's more, the FCC ruling affected dedicated point-to-point services purchased by large business customers and long-distance carriers for telecommunications services between states.

  For example, these services include dedicated high-speed lines that customers were using to connect to multiple locations across the country. Before the action by the FCC, the company's prices for these services were controlled by price regulations. Finally, the ruling affected the company's offerings in such metropolitan areas as New York, Washington, D.C., Philadelphia, Tampa, Dallas–Fort Worth, and Los Angeles.

- Kenneth A. Nugent, an analyst with *Value Line Survey*, had some good things to say about Verizon in early 2002. "The good news continues to roll in from the Federal Communications Commission. During the September (2001) interim, Verizon received the go-ahead from the FCC to offer long-distance service in the approximately $3 billion Pennsylvania market, making it the fourth state in the Northeast where VZ has been given the green light to offer such service. We now look for the company to focus on gaining approval in New Jersey, and Verizon seems on track to offer long-distance throughout its operating region by the end of 2002."

- Argus Research Corporation pointed out at the beginning of 2002 that "Transition costs from the GTE merger should end by the end of this year (2002). The company is running ahead of plan in realizing merger synergies. Verizon realized some $900 million of synergies in 2001 and fully expects to get to its goal of $2 billion in annual savings by 2003. The company has realized total savings of $1.4 billion since the merger closed.

In another section of this report, the analyst said, "Verizon continues to appear to be the premier vehicle of choice for investment in the troubled telecom sector. This is a very large, established company with a myriad of operations across nearly every business line associated with telecommunications. Verizon has substantial financial flexibility and is likely to benefit from regulatory relief for some of its growing business lines shortly following the conclusion of this year's elections."

- Finally, *Forbes Magazine* praised Verizon in its November 26, 2001 issue. "Who's the rightful heir to the premier spot in conservative portfolios that was once held by AT&T? Not AT&T, which has turned into a risky cable stock. In its stead, says Morgan Roberts of Manchester Capital Management, consider Verizon for growth and safety.

"Verizon (NYSE:VZ) blankets the nation with 63 million local lines and 28 million wireless accounts in 97 of the 100 largest U.S. cities.

"The company has done well expanding its turf. In Massachusetts, for example, Verizon snared 475,000 long-distance accounts, almost 20 percent of the market, in just six months of offering the service."

Total assets: 165 billion
Current ratio: 0.60
Common shares outstanding: 2,714 million
Return on 2001 shareholders' equity: 22%

	2001	2000	1999	1998	1997	1996	1995	1994
Revenues (millions)	67190	64707	33174	31566	30457	13081	13430	13791
Net income (millions)	8247	8000	4621	4228	3710	1739	1700	1543
Earnings per share	3.00	2.91	3.01	2.72	2.48	1.98	1.94	1.77
Dividends per share	1.54	1.54	1.54	1.54	1.49	1.43	1.40	1.38
Price High	57.4	66.0	69.5	61.2	45.9	37.4	34.4	29.8
Low	43.8	39.1	50.6	40.4	28.4	27.6	24.2	24.2

GROWTH AND INCOME

Wachovia Corporation

One First Union Center ▫ Charlotte, North Carolina 28288-0206 ▫ (704) 374-2137 ▫ Dividend reinvestment plan is available: (800) 347-1246 ▫ Web site: www.firstunion.com ▫ Listed: NYSE ▫ Ticker symbol: WB ▫ S&P rating: A- ▫ Value Line financial strength rating: B++

Wachovia, a leading banking institution headquartered in Charlotte, North Carolina, has taken aggressive action to strengthen credit reserves and slow the growth of nonperforming assets in an era of economic uncertainty.

According to a company spokesman, "our diversified business model and proactive portfolio management actions place us in a better position today than during previous downturns, with stronger reserves, increased capital, and less reliance on spread income (the difference between the cost of capital and the income received from loans).

"More than 90 percent of our $57 billion consumer loan portfolio is secured by real estate, and loan-to-value ratios, averaging 75 percent. We exited the credit card business and the indirect auto lending and leasing business, and ceased origination of subprime equity loans in 2000. Our $116 billion commercial loan portfolio is broadly diversified by geography, product, and industry concentration, as well as by loan size."

Company Profile

Wachovia Corporation, created through the September 1, 2001, merger of First Union and the former Wachovia, had assets of $330 billion and stockholders' equity of $28 billion at the end of 2001.

Wachovia is a leading provider of financial services to 20 million retail, brokerage, and corporate customers throughout the East Coast and the nation. Wachovia is the nation's fourth-largest banking company, based on assets. It operates 2,800 full-service banking offices and 4,700 automated teller machines under the First Union and Wachovia names in eleven East Coast states and Washington, D.C.

As the nation's fifth-largest full-service retail broker dealer, based on client assets, the company offers full-service brokerage offices in forty-nine states. Wachovia also provides global services through more than thirty international offices. Online banking and brokerage products and services are available through *www.wachovia.com* and *www.firstunion.com*. Direct telephone

banking is available at (800) 413-7898.

Here are some profiles of the bank's principal operations and highlights and accomplishments in 2001:

General Bank
- Leading retail and commercial bank on the East Coast.
- Improved customer satisfaction scores for eleven straight quarters.
- Improved efficiency for five straight quarters.
- Served 9 million households, representing nearly one-quarter of in-footprint market.
- Served 900,000 small business relationships, representing 13 percent of in-footprint market.
- Fifth-largest Small Business Administration lender in the nation.
- Mortgage company generated record volume and superior customer service ratings.

Corporate and Investment Bank
- Emphasis on cost control and focused strategies held the line on expense growth.
- Focused on improving risk-adjusted returns on capital and improved market penetration of noncredit products across a broad corporate relationship spectrum.
- Top Ten provider of lead-arranged leveraged loan syndications, asset-backed finance high-yield debt, convertible bonds, and equity underwriting.
- Second-largest provider of cash and treasury management services in the nation.
- Number one structured products servicer.

Capital Management
- Complete investment product offering resulted in growth in assets under management.
- Balance of transaction-based and recurring fee revenue generated solid

results in a difficult market.

- Record $2.5 billion in Evergreen mutual funds were sold through third-party broker dealers.

- Evergreen Investments awarded the prestigious Dalbar Mutual Fund Service Award for the third year in a row.

- Brokerage Group created efficiencies and better client service by converting to one operating platform.

- The 401(k) business greatly enhanced its operating systems by introducing Nowtrac(k), fully integrated processing that positions Wachovia for dynamic growth.

Wealth Management

- Ended year with $78 billion in assets under management.

- Ranked as one of the largest wealth managers in the United States.

- Ranked sixth-best private bank in *Worth Magazine's* Reader's Choice Award.

- Second-largest personal trust provider.

- Thirteenth-largest insurance broker and third largest among banks.

- Leading charitable service provider.

- Top Five provider of planned-giving services.

Shortcomings to Bear in Mind

■ In early 2002, Wachovia was ordered to pay $276 million in damages to a Maryland man who persuaded a state jury that the institution defrauded his software company and used his ideas to start a $2.4 billion business. In one of the largest verdicts ever by a Maryland jury, jurors awarded $76 million in compensatory damages and $200 million in punitive damages, according to an article in the *Baltimore Sun*. For its part, Wachovia says it will appeal the verdict.

Scott Steele, owner of the Steele Software Systems Corporation, claimed Wachovia stole his idea for a computerized system that helped the bank speed up its loan approval process. He worked under contract for First Union in 1997 and 1998, when the bank created a new company called GreenLink that used many of Steele's methods, the *Baltimore Sun* article said.

Reasons to Buy

■ Wachovia is gathering an increasing share of client assets. In 2001, the bank attracted roughly $20 billion of net new money, including $5 billion in new core deposits, $11 billion in sales of mutual funds, and $3 billion in sales of annuities.

■ The company is winning new business. Today, Wachovia ranks number one or number two in deposit share in all six of its regional marketplaces. Wachovia serves more than a third of commercial and small businesses in that sector. According to CEO G. Kennedy Thompson, "We also moved up in League Table rankings—for example, Wachovia now ranks among the Top Ten in leverage loan syndications, asset-backed finance, convertible bonds, high-yield debt, and equity underwriting."

■ Prior to the merger in the fall of 2001, both companies substantially completed significant restructuring plans—on time, on budget, and as promised. In the words of Mr. Thompson, "To recap briefly, we divested businesses that had minimal connection to our growth strategy, those without scale or competitive strength, and those with limited growth prospects.

"We exited credit card servicing, mortgage servicing, and auto leasing; closed The Money Store and sold eighty-four nonstrategic branch offices. As a result of these decisions, we have little exposure to current areas of concern in consumer lending, such as credit cards and subprime consumer loans."

■ As now constituted, Wachovia has a

number of powerful franchises, including the following:
- 20 million customers.
- 4 million customers enrolled online.
- Nineteenth-largest mutual fund provider.
- Second-largest personal loan provider.
- Third-largest bank insurance annuity provider.
- Second-largest treasury services provider.
- Leading middle-market mergers and acquisition adviser.
- Top Ten debt and equity underwriter.
- Number one retail banking franchise on the East Coast.
- Number three commercial lender in the nation.
- Number five full-service retail brokerage firm in the nation.

■ Wachovia's number one operational goal is to ensure that "we continually improve the service that our customers experience," according to a spokesman.

"Service quality is monitored constantly and measured through 60,000 customer surveys quarterly. Based on these surveys, customer satisfaction has improved for eleven straight quarters."

The spokesman went on to say, "In addition to focusing on fast and friendly service, we also develop new products and services, with customer satisfaction in mind. For example, check imaging capability gives customers the opportunity to instantaneously view online the actual checks that have cleared their account. This reduces the need to retrieve and mail photocopies of checks, providing faster service to customers and reducing expense for the company. The former Wachovia was one of the pioneers in this field, and the service has now been rolled out for all customers of the combined company."

Wachovia led its industry peer group with a score of 72 percent in the University of Michigan Business School's 2001 American Customer Satisfaction Index.

Total assets: $330 billion
Common shares outstanding: 1,361 million
Return on 2001 shareholders' equity: 7.4%

	2001	2000	1999	1998	1997	1996	1995	1994
Net interest inc (millions)	7775	7437	7452	7277	5743	4996	4635	3034
Net income (millions)	1619	138	3223	2891	1896	1499	1013	925
Earnings per share	1.45	.12	3.33	2.95	2.99	2.68	2.93	2.49
Dividends per share	1.20	1.92	1.88	1.58	1.22	1.10	.98	.86
Price High	36.6	38.9	65.8	65.9	53.0	38.9	29.8	24.0
Low	25.2	23.5	32.0	40.9	36.3	25.6	20.7	19.5

AGGRESSIVE GROWTH

Walgreen Company

200 Wilmot Road □ Mail Stop #2261 □ Deerfield, Illinois 60015 □ (847) 914-2922 □ Direct Dividend reinvestment program is available: (888) 290-7264 □ Fiscal year ends August 31 □ Web site: www.walgreens.com □ Ticker symbol: WAG □ S&P rating: A+ □ Value Line financial strength rating: A+

A *Wall Street Journal* reporter recently told Walgreen's management, "We don't write about Walgreens much because you're so boringly consistent." To this statement, an official of the company replied, "Well, if twenty-seven years of consecutive earnings growth—and thirteen straight years of increased store openings—equal 'boring,' we'll take that adjective any day."

Company Profile

Walgreen Co., commonly known as Walgreens, is one of the fastest-growing retailers in the United States, and leads the chain drugstore industry in sales and profits. Sales for 2001 reached $24.6 billion, produced by 3,520 stores in forty-three states and Puerto Rico.

Founded in 1901, Walgreens today has 130,000 employees The company's drugstores serve more than 3 million customers daily and average $6.8 million in annual sales per unit. That's $628 per square foot, among the highest in the industry. Walgreens has paid dividends in every quarter since 1933 and has raised the dividend in each of the past twenty-five years.

Stand-Alone Stores

Competition from the supermarkets has convinced Walgreens that the best strategy is to build stand-alone stores. Since the rise of managed care, many pharmacy customers now make only minimal copayments for prescriptions. That leaves convenience as the major factor in choosing a pharmacy. The free-standing format makes room for drive-thru windows, which provide a speedy way for drugstore customers to pick up or drop off prescriptions.

On the other hand, the company's stand-alone strategy is more expensive. Walgreens insists on building its units on corner lots near an intersection with a traffic light. Such leases normally cost more than a site in a strip mall.

More Than a Pharmacy

Home meal replacement has become a $100-billion business industrywide. In the company's food section, Walgreens carries staples as well as frozen dinners, desserts, and pizzas. In some stores, expanded food sections carry such items as fruit and ready-to-eat salads.

In the photo department, the company builds loyalty through a wide selection of products and the service of trained technicians. Walgreens experimented with one-hour photo service as early as 1982, but it was in the mid-1990s before, according to CEO Dan Jorndt, "We really figured it out." Since 1998, one-hour processing has been available chain-wide, made profitable by "our high volume of business. We've introduced several digital photo products that are selling well and are evaluating the long-term impact of digital on the mass market."

Shortcomings to Bear in Mind

- Often, Walgreens chooses a free-standing location on the site of an existing strip center—for instance, a piece of the mall parking lot. For the property's owners, this usually means an opportunity to charge more for the stand-alone space while renting out the old strip center space. Increasingly, however, supermarkets and other big retailers are starting to put exclusionary provisions in their leases, prohibiting a drugstore from occupying free-standing space on shopping center properties they anchor. Walgreen management says it has encountered such provisions but insists that they aren't yet "a real problem."
- According to one analyst, "gross margins are likely to narrow as Walgreen becomes more aggressive on pricing, in order to continue to gain market share from other drug, supermarket, and mass merchandise retailers. Gross margins could also come under pressure as an increase in third-party prescription sales as a percentage of total pharmacy sales drives pharmacy sales to nearly 58 percent of

total sales." On the other hand, says the analyst, "operating margins should widen, aided by improved expense control and greater sales leverage."

- The stock has performed so well in recent years that its P/E multiple is well above average, sometimes as high as thirty-five times earnings.

Reasons to Buy

- *Value Line Survey* gave a thumbs-up to Walgreens in its January 2002 issue, "Walgreen's long-term profit potential is enhanced by an aggressive expansion strategy. The drug chain opened a record 474 new stores in fiscal 2001, for a net addition of 355 stores, after relocations and closings. At year-end, Walgreen operated 3,520 units, which included 2,535 freestanding locations and 2,424 with drive-through pharmacies. This year (2002), management has its sights set on opening another 475 new drugstores. Walgreen's longer-term expansion plan, which we consider achievable, projects 6,000 outlets by 2010. Too, the company's leading-edge drugstore technologies should provide a competitive edge in the decade ahead."

- In a recent issue put out by the Argus Research Corporation, the analyst said, "We view Walgreens as a good defensive stock in this market, with a relatively high degree of visibility on sales growth, based on solid demand throughout the decade.

    "Favorable demographics include 77 million aging baby boomers (forty-five to sixty-four years old) and their estimated increased usage. For instance, the typical forty-year-old takes six-plus prescriptions annually; at fifty it reaches eight; at sixty the annual rate is eleven; and at seventy the number of prescriptions reaches fifteen."

- Some investors are concerned that the company is diluting sales by putting stores so close together, "just cannibalizing yourself." To that concern, Mr. Bernauer replied, "I haven't gone to a party in two years where that question hasn't come up. The answer is yes—when we open a store very near another one, the old store usually sees a drop in sales. But in virtually every case, it builds back to its original volume and beyond. Here's the scenario: as you add stores, overall sales in the market increase, while expenses are spread over a larger base. Bottom line, *profitability* increases. Our most profitable markets are the ones where we've built the strongest market share."

- Investors are also wondering about e-commerce. They ask, "Is there a long-term future?" To this concern, Mr. Bernauer said, "Though there's a lot of carnage on the early e-commerce road, we definitely see a future for *www.walgreens.com.* That's not, however, in "delivered-to-your-door" merchandise. Frankly, we never thought there would be a big demand for prescriptions by mail, and we were correct—well over 90 percent of prescription orders placed through our Web site are for store pickup. It's not convenient, when you need a prescription or a few drugstore items, to wait three days for it to show up.

    "What *does* excite us is using the Internet to provide better service and information. We're already communicating by e-mail with nearly 20,000 prescription customers per day."

- The company's new pharmacy system, Intercom Plus, is now up and running in all Walgreens stores across the country. This system—costing over $150 million—has raised Walgreens service and productivity to a new level. While providing increased patient access to Walgreens pharmacists, it also substantially raises the number of prescriptions each store can efficiently dispense.

- Walgreens management is heartened by the increase in prescription usage in the United States, due to the dramatic aging of the population. Between 1995 and 2005, the number of people aged fifty-five or older in the United States will grow at a compound rate of 3.8 percent—double the rate of the rest of the population. The good news for Walgreens is that these graying Americans need twice as many prescriptions per year as the rest of the population.

■ Every corner of the Walgreens strategy is focused on convenience: how fast people get into the store—or served in the drive-thru pharmacy; how fast they get out; how easily they find what they came to buy; how well Walgreens clerks remind them of what they are forgetting to buy.

■ Food departments are another example. Recently, a major grocery chain cited drugstores as a reason behind disappointing sales gains: "Fill-in shopping needs," said the grocery CEO, "are increasingly being satisfied in convenience and drugstores." Walgreens, with highly convenient, on-the-way-home locations, is on the receiving end of this trend.

■ According to the company's 2001 annual report, "As baby boomers retire, they'll migrate to states like Arizona, Florida, Georgia, Texas, and the Carolinas. Walgreens will be ready for them. By the end of 2002, we'll have 1,617 stores in the Sunbelt, with plans for continued expansion. And as the number of people sixty-five years and older skyrockets, dollars spent on

prescriptions will also swell—rising almost 40 percent by 2006. Just since 1996, prescriptions have jumped from 45 percent of Walgreens' total sales to nearly 58 percent.

"But the challenge for everyone in the business is the number of pharmacists, which will increase only 5.4 percent in the same time period. That means that by 2006 our pharmacists will be filling 40 percent more prescriptions than they do today.

"To handle this jump, we'll continue to improve our technology, training systems, and physical work environments, already recognized as superior within the industry. By being more efficient, we plan to increase the average number of prescriptions filled per store from 300 to more than 400 per day in the next five years.

"Other boosts to the prescription business are the influx of new drugs and the generic availability of highly prescribed drugs like Prozac. As branded drugs go generic, prices for customers are lowered significantly, and both managed-care companies and retailers benefit as well."

■ With stores in forty-three states and Puerto Rico, Walgreens has a base of customers that covers more of the United States than any other drugstore chain. The company's national coverage is a major advantage in negotiations with managed-care pharmacy companies.

Total assets: $8,834 million
Current ratio: 1.46
Common shares outstanding: 1,021 million
Return on 2001 shareholders' equity: 18.8%

		2001	2000	1999	1998	1997	1996	1995	1994
Revenues (millions)		24623	21207	17839	15307	13363	11778	10395	9235
Net income (millions)		872	756	624	514	436	372	321	282
Earnings per share		.85	.74	.62	.51	.44	.38	.33	.29
Dividends per share		.14	.14	.13	.13	.12	.11	.10	.09
Price	High	45.3	45.8	33.9	30.2	16.8	10.9	7.8	5.7
	Low	28.7	22.1	22.7	14.8	9.6	7.3	5.4	4.2

AGGRESSIVE GROWTH

Wal-Mart Stores, Inc.

702 SW Eighth Street □ Post Office Box 116 □ Bentonville, AR 72716-8611 □ (501) 273-8446 □ Direct Dividend reinvestment plan is available: (800) 438-6278 □ Web site: www.walmart.com □ Listed: NYSE □ Fiscal year ends January 31 □ Ticker symbol: WMT □ S&P rating: A+ □ Value Line financial strength rating: A++

Wal-Mart did not appear to be a corporate colossus in 1962. That was the year that Sam Walton opened his first store in Rogers, Arkansas, with a sign saying "Wal-Mart Discount City. We sell for less." In the decades since, Wal-Mart has evolved into a $200-billion-a-year empire by selling—at a discount, of course—prodigious quantities of all manner of items, from clothing, food, hardware, and eyeglasses to Kleenex, toothbrushes, pots and pans, and pharmaceuticals.

An essential key to Wal-Mart's success, says H. Lee Scott Jr., the company's CEO, is "driving unnecessary costs out of businesses."

To keep prices at rock bottom, the company insists that its 65,000 suppliers become leaner machines that examine every farthing they spend. This ruthless drive to whittle away fat has clearly reshaped the practices of businesses that deal with Wal-Mart, as well as those that compete against them. Wal-Mart's strategies for holding costs in check—the use of cutting-edge technology, innovative logistics, reliance on imported goods, and a nonunion workforce—are becoming industry standards.

Company Profile

Wal-Mart is the world's number one retailer—larger than Sears, Kmart, and J. C. Penney combined. The company operates nearly 3,500 facilities in the United States and more than 1,100 units in the following countries: Mexico (551), Puerto Rico (17), Canada (196), Argentina (11), Brazil (23), China (19), Korea (9),

Germany (95), and the United Kingdom (250). More than 100 million customers per week visit Wal-Mart Stores.

Wal-Mart operates four different retail concepts.

Wal-Mart Discount Stores. Since founder Sam Walton opened his first store in 1962, Wal-Mart has built more than 1,600 discount stores in the United States. The stores range in size from 40,000 to 125,000 square feet and carry 80,000 different items, including family apparel, automotive products, health and beauty aids, home furnishings, electronics, hardware, toys, sporting goods, lawn and garden items, pet supplies, jewelry, and housewares.

Wal-Mart Supercenters. Developed in 1988 to meet the growing demand for one-stop family shopping, Wal-Mart supercenters today number more than 1,050 nationwide and are open twenty-four hours a day. Supercenters save their customers time and money by combining full grocery lines and general merchandise under one roof. These units range in size from 109,000 to 230,000 square feet and carry 100,000 different items, 30,000 of which are grocery products.

Wal-Mart Neighborhood Markets. These stores offer groceries, pharmaceuticals, and general merchandise. Generally, these units are situated in markets with Wal-Mart Supercenters, supplementing a strong food distribution network and providing added convenience while maintaining Wal-Mart's everyday low prices. First opened in 1998, Neighborhood Markets range from 42,000 to 55,000 square feet and feature a wide variety of products, including fresh produce, deli foods, fresh meat and dairy items, health and beauty aids, one-hour photo, and drive-through pharmacies, to name a few.

Sam's Clubs. The nation's leading members-only warehouse club offers a broad selection of general merchandise and large-volume items at value prices. Since 1983, Sam's Club has been the preferred choice for small businesses, families, or anyone looking for great prices on name-brand products. Ranging in size from 110,000 to 130,000 square feet, the 500 Sam's Clubs nationwide offer merchandise for both office and personal use, bulk paper products, furniture, computer hardware and software, groceries, television sets, and clothing. A nominal membership fee ($30 per year for businesses and $35 for individuals) helps defray operating costs and keeps prices exceptionally low.

Shortcomings to Bear in Mind

- At 192,000 square feet, Wal-Mart Supercenters are about the size of four football fields. Wal-Mart quickly found that some customers have trouble navigating them. According to one shopper, "The stores are too big. It takes too long to get around." On the other hand, the store's "really good prices" keep them coming back, but the shopper warns, "We've just about decided we'll go somewhere else and pay more not to have to go through all the hassle."
- Wal-Mart, whose trademark policy is "everyday low prices," has been pricing its merchandise more aggressively in response to heavier discounting from Kmart, Target, and other competitors. As an offset, it's looking to pare expenses, speed up deliveries, and strengthen its clothing lines. "We are paranoid," said CEO Lee Scott, who, along with other executives, shops

competitors once a week. "Everyone is getting better." Mr. Scott, a twenty-two-year Wal-Mart veteran, rose through the ranks to become CEO in January of 2000.

Reasons to Buy

- Wal-Mart's success is no secret. The company was named "Retailer of the Century" by *Discount Store News*; it made *Fortune* magazine's lists of the "Most Admired Companies in America" and the "100 Best Companies to Work For" and was ranked on *Financial Times* "Most Respected in the World" list.
- Not content with its vast empire, Wal-Mart has ambitious plans to add more outlets in the fiscal year that began February 1, 2002. Domestically, the Wal-Mart division plans to open about fifty new discount stores and 180 to 185 new Supercenters. This represents an acceleration of Supercenter unit expansion and reflects the strong consumer acceptance and financial results from this format.

  The company will further expand its Neighborhood Market concept by adding about fifteen to twenty new units. The Sam's Club division will open fifty to fifty-five domestic clubs, about half of which will be relocations or expansions of existing clubs. The division will also continue its aggressive remodeling program with about 100 projects in the fiscal year.

  Outside the United States, Wal-Mart International plans to open 120 to 130 units in existing markets. Projects are scheduled to open in each country in which the company operates and will include new stores and clubs as well as relocations of a few existing units. These announced units will also include several restaurants, department stores, and supermarkets in Mexico.

According to Mr. Scott, "The planned square footage for the coming year represents approximately 46 million square feet of new retail space, which will be the largest square footage increase in the company's history and a 9 percent increase over the fiscal 2002 total."

- In March of 2002, the company made its first foray into the $3.9 trillion Japanese economy by buying a minority interest in a Japanese retailer, Seiyu Ltd. Wal-Mart invested $46.5 million to acquire 6.1 percent of Seiyu, the nation's fifth-largest supermarket chain, with $8.5 billion in annual sales.

  However, this is just the beginning. Wal-Mart could eventually raise its stake to 66.7 percent. "The retail industry has been in a very difficult state for the last few years," said Masao Kiuchi, president of the Japanese company. "We have been restructuring and making dramatic changes, but we thought it was necessary to find a strong business partner like Wal-Mart."

- Wal-Mart makes a concerted effort to find out precisely what its customers want. To do this, the company relies on information technology. It does this by collecting and analyzing internally developed information, which it calls "data-mining." It has been doing this since 1990.

  The result, by now, is an enormous database of purchasing information that enables management to place the right item in the right store at the right time. The company's computer system receives 8.4 million updates every minute on the items that customers take home—and the relationship between the items in each basket.

  Many retailers talk a good game when it comes to mining data at cash registers as a way to build sales. Wal-Mart, since it has been doing this for the past dozen years, is sitting on an information trove so vast and detailed that it far exceeds what many manufacturers know about their own products. What's more, Wal-Mart's database is second in size only to that of the U.S. government's, says one analyst. Wal-Mart also collects "market-basket data" from customer receipts at all of its stores, so it knows what products are likely to be purchased together. The company receives about 100,000 queries a week from suppliers and its own buyers looking for purchase patterns or checking a product.

  Wal-Mart plans to use the data in its new Neighborhood Markets. Equipped with a drive-through pharmacy and selling both dry goods and perishables, the stores are a little smaller than typical suburban supermarkets. They are much smaller than Wal-Mart's Supercenters, the massive grocery-discount store combinations that Wal-Mart began opening in 1987.

  This kind of information has significant value in and of itself. According to management, "Consider Wal-Mart's ability to keep the shelves stocked with exactly what customers want most, but still be able to keep inventories under tight control. Consider the common banana—so common, in fact, that the grocery carts of America contain bananas more often than any other single item. So why not make it easy for a shopper to remember bananas? In Wal-Mart grocery departments, bananas can be found not just in the produce section, but in the cereal and dairy aisles too."

- Wal-Mart has leaned some painful lessons about consumers, regulators, and suppliers around the world. Through trial and error, the company has quietly built a powerful force outside the United States. It's now the biggest retailer in Canada and Mexico.

- The bankruptcy of Kmart creates fresh opportunities for Wal-Mart to lure to its aisles price-conscious shoppers.
- *Value Line Survey* is convinced that Wal-Mart's growth is still vibrant. Analyst David R. Cohen said, "We look for earnings to advance at a 13 percent to 15 percent pace over the three to five years subsequent to fiscal 2001. Sales ought to advance at a 12 percent pace over this period, based on planned selling-space expansion of 8 percent to 9 percent and modest comparable-store sales gains. Key factors that should help boost the operating margins include rapid growth of Wal-Mart's private-label brands, expanded service offerings at International, and a healthier domestic economy."

Total assets: $83,375 million
Current ratio: 1.02
Common shares outstanding: 4,467 million
Return on 2001 shareholders' equity: 18.5%

	2001	2000	1999	1998	1997	1996	1995	1994
Revenues (millions)	217799	191329	165013	137634	117958	104859	93627	82494
Net income (millions)	6671	6295	5377	4430	3526	3056	2740	2681
Earnings per share	1.49	1.40	1.28	0.99	0.78	0.67	0.60	0.59
Dividends per share	.28	.24	.20	0.16	0.14	0.11	0.10	0.09
Price High	58.8	68.9	70.3	41.4	21.0	14.2	13.8	14.6
Low	41.5	41.4	38.7	18.8	11.0	9.6	10.2	10.6

INCOME

Washington Real Estate Investment Trust

6110 Executive Boulevard, Suite 800 ▫ Rockville, Maryland 20852 ▫ (800) 565-9748 ▫ Listed: NYSE ▫ Direct Dividend reinvestment plan is available: (800) 278-4353 ▫ Web site: www.writ.com ▫ Ticker symbol: WRE ▫ S&P rating: Not rated ▫ Value Line Financial Strength B++

Washington Real Estate Investment Trust has had an enviable record. Over the past twenty-eight years, the Trust's shareholders earned a compound annual rate of return of 18.5 percent. This compares favorably to the total returns (stock appreciation plus dividends) of 13.0 percent for the S&P 500 and 12.6 percent for the real estate investment trust industry over the same period.

What's more, the company's record is consistent. Washington Real Estate Investment Trust has produced positive earnings every year since its inception. As of the end of 2001, the Trust had completed a streak of thirty-six consecutive years of increased earnings per share and twenty-nine years of funds from operations (FFO) share growth—all during a span of four recessions. What's more, the company's dividend was increased thirty-six times during this thirty-two-year period, a record unmatched by any other publicly traded real estate investment trust.

Company Profile

Washington Real Estate Investment Trust, founded in 1960, invests in a diversified range of income-producing properties. Management's purpose is to acquire and manage real estate investments in markets it knows well and to protect the company's assets from the risk of owning a single property type, such as apartments, office buildings, industrial parks, or shopping centers.

Washington Real Estate Investment Trust achieves its objectives by owning properties in four different categories. The Trust's properties are primarily situated within a two-hour radius of Washington, D.C., stretching from Philadelphia in the north to Richmond, Virginia, in the south. Its diversified portfolio at the end of 2001 consisted of twenty-three office buildings, ten retail shopping centers, nine apartment complexes, and sixteen industrial distribution centers.

Shortcomings to Bear in Mind

■ Investors may be concerned that the economy's weakness in 2001 would have a negative impact on Washington Real Estate Investment Trust. According to CEO Edmund B. Cronin Jr., "Historically, the greater Washington-Baltimore economy has outperformed the national economy in all economic cycles. I see no reason today why history will not repeat itself. Greater Washington's economic engines in a softening economy as well as during growth periods are the federal government and the technology industry. The latter has a risk profile substantially lower than many of those on the West Coast and in New England.

"One aspect of this lower risk profile is that the greater Washington-Baltimore technology sector achieves 38 percent of its sales to the federal government, as compared to 5 percent in Silicon Valley. That, along with the fact that federal government spending will continue to grow, provides a platform for a soft landing in this region."

Reasons to Buy

■ The greater Washington, D.C., economy is a unique blend of "old economy" service companies and "new economy" high-technology growth companies, anchored by the very significant federal government presence. On the growth side are the following considerations:

● Washington Dulles International Airport and Baltimore-Washington International Airport were ranked number one and two in passenger growth in 1999, the most recent year for which data are available.

● The greater Washington, D.C., region ranks first in the United States in high-tech and bio-tech employment.

● George Mason University Center for Regional Analysis (GMU) projects economic growth in the region of 4.1 percent in 2001, substantially higher than the projection for the nation as a whole.

● Federal spending in this region has increased every year for twenty consecutive years, even in years when federal spending has decreased nationally. GMU projects federal spending in the region will grow by 3 percent per year.

While growth is very important from an investment perspective, economic stability is equally important. In this context, no other region in the country can compete with the greater Washington, D.C., region.

● Federal government spending accounts for 31 percent of the area's gross regional product.

● The greater Washington, D.C., region is not exposed to new or old economy manufacturing fluctuations.

● Greater Washington, D.C., is home to thirty-two colleges and universities, several of which have world-class reputations at both the undergraduate and graduate levels.

■ MAE East, situated in Tysons Corner, Virginia, is one of only two Internet convergence centers in the United States. The presence of MAE East and the thousands of high-tech firms in the area has spawned a concentration of data centers in the region where large Internet and other high-tech firms process tremendous amounts of data. As a result, it is estimated that up to 60 percent of the world's Internet traffic flows through Northern Virginia.

This concentration of high-tech companies has served to attract even more high-tech firms. Companies such as www.Amazon.com, Cisco Systems, and Global Crossing have all set up shop in the Washington-Baltimore market.

The region's real estate markets are the beneficiaries of this growth. Vacancies are extremely low, and rental rate growth is very strong.

- Prior to acquiring a property, Washington Real Estate Investment Trust performs extensive inspections, tests, and financial analyses to gain confidence about the property's future operating performance as well as any required near-term improvements and long-term capital expenditures. Upon completion of this evaluation, the company develops well-informed operating projections for the property. Accordingly, when the company announces an acquisition and its anticipated return on investment, it is confident that the property will meet or exceed its projections.

- Washington Real Estate Investment Trust has always recognized the value of capital improvements to remain competitive, increase revenues, reduce operating costs, and maintain and increase the value of its properties.

- Funds from operations (FFO) per-share growth is the most widely recognized earnings performance measure in the REIT industry. Washington Real Estate Investment Trust has outperformed industry average FFO per-share growth by over 400 basis points over the last three years. (One percentage point equals 100 basis points.) The extent of the Trust's out-performance, moreover, has increased in each of the last three years. The company's average 13.5 per share growth over the past three years is one of the highest in the industry.

- Another common REIT industry performance measure is core portfolio net operating income (or NOI) growth, or same store NOI growth. NOI represents real estate portfolio income before interest expense, depreciation, and corporate general and administrative expenses.

Core portfolio NOI growth excludes income attributable to new acquisitions and developments. It is therefore a good measure of how a company's existing portfolio performed in the most recent period as compared to the prior period. The Trust's core portfolio NOI growth is among the highest in the industry and dramatically higher than the REIT industry overall. Using this NOI measure, Washington Real Estate Investment Trust had average annual growth of 8.5 percent in the past three years, compared with the industry's 5.6 percent.

Total assets: $632 million
Current ratio: not relevant
Return on 2001 equity: 15%
Common shares outstanding: 39 million

	2001	2000	1999	1998	1997	1996	1995	1994
Revenues (millions)	148	135	119	104	79	66	53	46
Net income (millions)	52	45	44	41	30	28	26	23
Funds from operations	1.92	1.79	1.57	1.39	1.23	1.13	1.05	.96
Earnings per share	1.27	1.16	1.02	.96	.90	.88	.88	.82
Dividends per share	1.31	1.23	1.16	1.11	1.07	1.03	.99	.92
Price High	25.5	25.0	18.8	18.8	19.6	17.5	16.6	21.1
Low	20.8	14.3	13.8	15.1	15.5	15.3	13.9	14.9

Weingarten Realty Investors

2600 Citadel Plaza Drive ◻ Post Office Box 924133 ◻ Houston, Texas 77292-4133 ◻ (713) 866-6054 ◻ Direct Dividend reinvestment program available: (888) 887-2966 ◻ Web site: www.weingarten.com ◻ Listed: NYSE ◻ Ticker symbol: WRI ◻ S&P rating: not rated ◻ Value Line financial strength rating: B++

Weingarten Realty Investors announced early in 2002 that it had acquired Outland Business Center, situated in Memphis, Tennessee. The industrial portfolio consists of five buildings totaling 407,200 square feet, situated on about twenty-eight acres. The Tennessee property was developed from 1987 to 1989.

The Outland Business Center is 90-percent leased. The center's major tenants include VSA, Inc. (International Multifoods), ADT Security Services, Inc., LCI/Quest, Krone Farm Equipment, and Porteous Fasteners.

According to CEO Drew Alexander, with the acquisition of Outland Business Center, the company now has four industrial properties in Memphis, which collectively total 1.1 million square feet. Other Weingarten properties in Memphis include Southwide Warehouse, Thomas Street Warehouse, and Crowfarn Drive Warehouse.

Company Profile

Weingarten Realty Investors is an equity-based real estate investment trust (REIT). The company focuses primarily on the development, acquisition, and long-term ownership of anchored neighborhood, community shopping centers and, to a lesser degree, industrial properties.

At the end of 2001, the Weingarten portfolio included 287 income-producing properties in eighteen states spanning the southern half of the United States from coast to coast. Included in the portfolio are 228 neighborhood and community shopping centers, fifty-seven industrial properties, one apartment complex, and one office building, aggregating 35.7 million square feet.

Founded in 1948, Weingarten restructured itself into a real estate investment trust and was first listed on the New York Stock Exchange in 1985. Its performance as a public company has been among the best in the industry. This performance is a product of fifty years of real estate experience (in both growth and recessionary cycles), combined with a seasoned management team focused on specific segments of real estate. In addition to developing and acquiring properties, Weingarten adds value to them through consistent, high-quality operations that incorporate renovation, retailer recycling, and ongoing asset management.

Some History

Weingarten Realty Investors was founded in 1948 with two part-time employees, $60,000 in cash, and a portfolio of supermarket buildings totaling 51,000 square feet. The company was created to develop free-standing stores for J. Weingarten, Inc., a fast-growing grocery chain that was owned by the Weingarten family.

In addition to developing the stores, the company was charged with acquiring raw land for future development and expansion. As a result, management was in an ideal position to take advantage of the trend to develop "clusters of stores" as the evolution of the "shopping center" began to take shape in the early 1950s.

As Weingarten began its new course, it focused on the neighborhood and community shopping center that ranged in size from 100,000 to 400,000 square feet and was "anchored" primarily by supermarkets. This practice continues today, with the company now focusing on certain industrial properties as well.

In 1980, the J. Weingarten supermarket chain was sold, and the realty company began to diversify and expand its relationships with other grocers and general retailers throughout the United States. Today, it boasts a diversified roster of over 2,900 different tenants, many with multiple locations.

During the fifty-three years of Weingarten's existence, the company has emerged as one of the largest REITs listed on the NYSE. Its portfolio has expanded from four properties to 287 at year-end 2001. The company's square footage has increased from 51,000 to nearly 36 million, and the company has expanded its holdings from one city and one state to more than fifty-five cities in eighteen states. Likewise, Weingarten's revenue, funds from operations, and dividends have increased significantly over the fifteen years that it has been a REIT.

Funds from Operations: A Definition

Investors in common stock use "net income" as a key measure of profitability. However, in measuring a REIT, most investors prefer the term "funds from operations," or FFO. This is because earnings and expenses of a real estate investment trust must be looked at differently.

The Securities and Exchange Commission has a blanket requirement that all publicly traded companies file audited financial statements. On a financial statement, the term "net income" has a meaning that is clearly defined under generally accepted accounting principles. Since a REIT falls under the classification of a publicly traded company, net income therefore appears on a REIT's audited financial statement.

For a REIT, however, this figure is less meaningful as a measure of operating success than it is for other types of corporations. The reason is that, in accounting, real estate "depreciation" is always treated as an expense. In the real world, most well-maintained quality properties have *retained* their value over the years. This is because of rising land values. It could also be said to result from steadily rising rental income, property upgrades, and higher costs for new construction for competing properties. Whatever the reason, a REIT's net income, since it suffers from a large depreciation expense, is a less-than-meaningful measure of how a REIT's operations have actually fared. It is because of this reasoning that FFO is often a better way to judge a real estate investment trust than traditional net income. You will note that I have used this alternative term in the table at the end of the article.

Shortcomings to Bear in Mind

- Weingarten Realty Investors is primarily an income stock, which often yields 6 percent or more. In terms of growth, however, it is not exciting. In the 1991–2001 period, funds from operations advanced from $1.48 to $3.04, a compound annual growth rate of only 7.5 percent. Similarly, dividends during this ten-year span advanced from $1.28 to $2.11, a growth rate of 5.1 percent.
- There is no way to avoid risk completely. Real estate ownership and management, like any other business, is subject to all sorts of risks. Mall REITs, for instance, are subject to the changing tastes and lifestyles of consumers.

Reasons to Buy

- Acquisitions and new developments in 2001 added 6.1 million square feet to the portfolio, bringing the total portfolio to 35.7 million square feet. These transactions represent an investment of $518.6 million for the year.

In recapping the year, Drew Alexander, president and CEO of Weingarten, said, "This was an exceptional year for Weingarten Realty in all respects. We now have a coast-to-coast presence in the southern half of the United States."

Mr. Alexander also noted that the company made its entrance into the California market early in 2001 through the acquisition of nineteen properties situated primarily in the Sacramento/Bay area and in southern California. He said, "We have found this clustering of locations allows us to manage our properties more effectively and provide more overall value to our merchants."

During the year, Weingarten also acquired six retail properties in Florida, four in the Memphis market, and one in North Carolina. The total of all shopping center acquisitions for 2001 aggregates 4.6 million square feet. In addition, the acquisition of four industrial properties during 2001 totaled about 1.5 million square feet.

- With respect to new development, Weingarten had twenty retail sites in various stages of development at the end of 2001. These properties will add 1.8 million square feet to the portfolio and will represent a total expected investment of $223 million. Mr. Alexander said that four of these properties have recently come online, comprising 200,000 square feet and a total investment of $26 million. The company anticipates the remaining developments will come online during the rest of 2002 and 2003.

- In early 2002, *Value Line Survey* spoke highly of Weingarten. Its analyst, Milton Schlein, said, "Weingarten Realty has a long and impressive record. It is one of the oldest companies in the REIT group. More significant for the investor is its growth record. Share earnings and dividends have advanced at a good clip over the last fifteen years, with few down years over this period.

  "And the returns on capital and equity have been generally well above the group average. Moreover, the trust has achieved these results while maintaining a good financial position, adding to the safety of the dividend and providing the means for future growth. As a result of these strengths, the dividends have risen every year since 1987, even in periods when reported earnings declined."

- Mr. Alexander noted that the company's core portfolio of neighborhood and community shopping centers is quite stable due to the core tenant base of retailers that provide basic, everyday necessities such as groceries and drugs. Although the occupancy rates were 92.2 percent, down slightly from 93.0 percent at the end of 2000, Weingarten reported the completion of 966 new leases or renewals for the year that totaled 4.9 million square feet. Additionally, rental rates increased an average of 10.5 percent on a same-space basis; net of capital costs, the average increase was 7.8 percent. Net operating income on a same-property basis increased 3.5 percent for 2001, as compared to the prior year.

Total assets: $2,096 million
Current ratio: NM*
Common shares outstanding: 49 million
Return on 2001 shareholders' equity: 12%

	2001	2000	1999	1998	1997	1996	1995	1994
Rental inc. (millions)	309	243	223	195	169	145	125	112
Net income (millions)	108.5	79.0	96.3	61.8	55.0	53.9	44.8	43.8
Funds from operations per share	3.04	2.83	2.62	2.40	2.21	2.06	1.88	1.81
Dividends per share	2.10	2.00	1.89	1.79	1.71	1.65	1.60	1.52
Price High	33.8	30.0	30.4	31.3	30.4	27.2	25.7	27.0
Low	25.9	23.1	24.7	23.9	25.9	22.9	22.3	21.9

* Not meaningful

AGGRESSIVE GROWTH

WellPoint Health Networks, Inc.

1 WellPoint Way ◻ Thousand Oaks, CA 91362 ◻ Listed: NYSE ◻ (805) 557-6789 ◻ Dividend reinvestment plan is not available ◻ Web site: www.wellpoint.com ◻ Ticker symbol: WLP ◻ S&P rating: B+ ◻ Value Line financial strength rating: B+

Early in 2002, WellPoint Health Networks, a managed-care organization that operates health maintenance organizations (HMOs) and preferred provider organizations (PPOs), among other specialized products, made a major acquisition with the purchase of RightCHOICE Managed Care, for which it paid $1.3 billion in cash and stock. At the end of 2001, RightCHOICE plans totaled 3 million members, with annual revenues of $66.4 million.

RightCHOICE, the largest provider of health care benefits in Missouri, is the parent company of Blue Cross and Blue Shield of Missouri and HealthLink, a subsidiary that provides network rental, administrative services, workers' compensation, and other nonunderwritten health benefit programs in Missouri and six neighboring states.

According to *Standard & Poor's Stock Reports*, "We see premium revenues climbing about 34 percent in 2002, on the full-year inclusion of RightCHOICE (RIT), 5 percent to 7 percent organic enrollment growth, and commercial rate hikes averaging 10 percent in California and slightly higher elsewhere."

The same report also said, "We view WLP as one of the best-positioned managed health care companies, in part due to its consistent, high-quality earnings."

Company Profile

WellPoint is one of the nation's largest publicly traded health care companies. The company serves the needs of more than 12 million members and about 45 million specialty members nationwide through Blue Cross of California, Blue Cross and Blue Shield of Georgia, Blue Cross and Blue Shield of Missouri, HealthLink, and UNICRE.

Launched in 1992, the company was founded to operate Blue Cross of California's managed care business. In 1996, WellPoint and Blue Cross of California merged into a single stockholder-owned company, WellPoint Health Networks.

WellPoint's strategy is to offer a diversified mix of products that preserve member choice at competitive prices while focusing on the development of new hybrid plans that take advantage of the best characteristics of traditional managed care and innovative open-access models. The Well-Point family of companies employs about 16,300 full-time associates in more than eighty offices throughout the country.

Consumers want a choice of products and providers, and they want more control over their health care decisions. Employers also want the maximum amount of cost control, but they are more sensitive to employee needs in today's high-employment economy.

WellPoint has created a variety of PPOs, HMOs, and various hybrid and specialty network-based dental and health care services that combine the attributes consumers find attractive with effective cost-control techniques.

By geographic markets, members are located in California (58 percent), Georgia (19 percent), Illinois (5.3 percent), Texas (3.8 percent), and other states (13 percent). Membership includes the acquisition of RightCHOICE, which added 3 million members, primarily in the Midwest.

WLP provides health care services through a network of about 31,000 primary-care and specialized physicians and about 427 hospitals in California. Outside of that state, it provides services through a network of 92,700 primary-care and specialized physicians and 870 hospitals.

Through its specialty-care networks, WellPoint provides pharmacy (32 million members), dental (2.6 million), and utilization management services (1.8 million), as well as life insurance (2.3 million), products to individuals covered through disability insurance (546,000), and behavior health (5.1 million).

WellPoint has been awarded contracts to offer Medi-Cal care programs to various California counties. Under these programs, WellPoint provides health care coverage to Medi-Cal program members and the California Department of Health Services pays

WellPoint a fixed payment per member per month. In 2000, the company formed a newly licensed health maintenance organization, UNICARE, Health Plan of Oklahoma, Inc., to cover SoonerCare Plus Medicaid members in central Oklahoma. Also in 2000, the company entered a joint venture with Medical Card Systems, Inc., to pursue contracts under the Health Reform Program in Puerto Rico.

WellPoint also offers Medicare supplemental plans, which typically pay the difference between health care cost incurred and the amount paid by Medicare when the PPO and HMO provider networks are used.

Shortcomings to Bear in Mind

- During 2001, a few of the insiders, such as officers and board members, sold at least part of their holdings in the company. Even so, the stock continued to advance.

- According to Randy Shrikishun, an analyst with *Value Line Investment Survey*, "uncertainties in health care pricing are a risk factor that some investors should avoid."

Reasons to Buy

- In 2001, revenues grew an impressive 35 percent to $12.4 billion. Net income per share advanced to $3.15, up from $2.65 in 2000, a gain of 18.9 percent. In California, its biggest state, medical membership was driven by strong performance in the company's large group segment, which added over 348,000 new members, or an increase of 9.2 percent for the year.

- "WellPoint's financial strength and the quality of our earnings is reflected in the $1.2 billion increase in cash and investments on our balance sheet during the year (2001)," said David C. Colby, WellPoint's chief financial officer. "Due to this strong cash flow, we reduced the company's debt-to-total-capital ratio from 33.8 percent, immediately after the Cerulean merger in the first quarter, to 28.2 percent by year-end."

- In 2002, WellPoint topped *Fortune* magazine's annual list for an unprecedented four-year running as America's most admired health care company.
- WellPoint was named to *www.Forbes.com* and *Forbes* magazine's Platinum List for the third year in a row in 2002. The company is currently listed as the best-performing corporation in health insurance.
- Leonard D. Schaeffer, WellPoint's chairman and CEO, was named one of America's best CEOs for the third year in a row by *Worth* magazine. Mr. Schaeffer was also named one of the top twenty-five managers of 2000 by *BusinessWeek* magazine.
- In the past eight years (1993–2001), earnings per share climbed from $.94 to $3.15 for a compound annual growth rate of 16.3 percent. There were no dips along the way. Despite the fact that the company has an exceptional growth rate, its P/E ratio is less than the market.
- WellPoint's growth in 2001 was enhanced by the acquisition of Cerulean Companies, Inc.—the parent of Blue Cross and Blue Shield of Georgia, which added 1.9 million members. Membership in the company's medical plans was over 10.1 million at the end of 2001, compared with 7.9 million a year earlier. Deals like this are an indicator of the impact that future takeovers may have on the company's revenue and profit growth.

Over the years, WellPoint has made a number of such moves. In 1996, for instance, the company acquired the group life and health division of Massachusetts Mutual Life Insurance Company, and the group health and related life business of John Hancock Mutual Life Insurance company in 1997.

In 2000, the company acquired Rush Prudential Health Plans of Illinois and PrecisionRx, a mail-service pharmacy fulfillment center in Texas.

- Membership in RightCHOICE's plans totaled 3 million at the end of 2001, compared with 2.7 million at the end of 2000. "Our merger with RightCHOICE allows us to build on the success of Blue Cross and Blue Shield in Missouri, HealthLink, and WellPoint's UNICARE brand," said Mr. Schaeffer. "RightCHOICE's excellent growth in both the nonrisk and underwritten businesses underscores the company's operational excellence and strong competitive positioning."
- Membership growth at Blue Cross and Blue Shield of Missouri, which includes both risk and nonrisk products, was driven by a focus on improving penetration in the larger group market, continued success of the BlueCard program, and strong persistency levels of existing membership due to a continued focus on providing superior customer service.

Total assets: $7,223 million
Current ratio: 1.44
Return on 2001 equity: 19.5%
Common shares outstanding: 128 million

	2001	2000	1999	1998	1997	1996	1995	1994
Revenues (millions)	12429	9229	7485	6478	5796	4170	3107	2792
Net income (millions)	415	342	297	264	223	214	214	213
Earnings per share	3.15	2.65	2.19	1.88	1.61	1.61	1.08	1.07
Dividends per share	Nil	—	—	—	—	—	—	—
Price High	61.4	60.8	48.5	43.9	30.6	19.6	18.5	18.5
Low	40.8	28.5	24.1	21.0	16.3	11.7	13.5	12.1

WGL Holdings, Inc.

1100 H Street, N.W. ◻ Washington, D.C., 20080 ◻ (202) 624-6410 ◻ Dividend reinvestment program is available: (888) 269-8845 ◻ Fiscal year ends September 30 ◻ Listed: NYSE ◻ Web site: www.wglholdings.com ◻ Ticker symbol: WGL ◻ S&P rating: A- ◻ Value Line financial strength rating: A

Washington Gas Light (the principal subsidiary of WGL Holdings, Inc.) provides natural gas to an area that is blessed with a number of advantages over most other geographic regions.

The company's service territory, which includes the Washington, D.C., metropolitan area and surrounding regions in Maryland and Virginia, comprises the fourth-largest economy in the nation. The WGL region leads the nation in many measures of economic activity. The company has the second-highest average household income level of the top ten market areas in the country. The company has more high-technology companies, more computer science and engineering professionals, and the highest percentage of residents with a college degree. Despite a nationwide economic slowdown, regional indicators remain strong, reflecting a solid and stable federal presence, thriving defense and consulting businesses, and a diverse and vibrant commercial sector.

Company Profile

As of November 2000, WGL Holdings, Inc., became the parent company for Washington Gas Light Company and other subsidiaries that operated under Washington Gas prior to this restructuring. The new company holds Washington Gas and a well-balanced group of growing and successful energy-related retail businesses that includes the following: natural gas and power marketing; consumer financing; and commercial and residential heating, ventilating and air conditioning services.

Washington Gas Light Company is the local natural gas distribution company that provides natural gas service to more than 920,000 residential, commercial, and industrial customers throughout metropolitan Washington, D.C., and the surrounding region, including parts of Maryland, Virginia, and West Virginia. The company, which serves an area of 6,648 square miles, has been providing natural gas to the D.C. region for 153 years.

Hampshire Gas Company is the regulated natural gas storage business that serves Washington Gas.

American Combustion Industries, Inc. (ACI), is a full-service mechanical and electrical contractor involved in the installation and service of HVAC systems. ACI specializes in large-scale commercial and federal installations, including power plants and cogeneration systems.

Washington Gas Energy Systems, Inc., is in the business of providing turnkey design/build renovation projects to the commercial and federal markets. Washington Gas Energy Systems specializes in the innovative engineering and design of cost-saving energy systems.

Washington Gas Energy Services, Inc., is a retail energy marketing company that serves the greater Washington, D.C., area and beyond to Baltimore, Maryland, and Richmond, Virginia. The company markets natural gas and electricity to consumers at competitive prices.

Brandywood Estates, Inc., is a partner, along with a major developer, in a venture designed to develop land for sale or lease in Prince George's County, Maryland.

WG Maritime Plaza I, Inc., holds a partnership interest in the first phase of the development of a twelve-acre parcel of land in Washington, D.C.

Washington Gas Consumer Services, Inc., evaluates and performs unregulated functions. None of those actions is being performed at present.

Crab Run Gas Company is an exploration and production subsidiary whose assets are being managed by an Oklahoma-based limited partnership.

Primary Investors, LLC, operating as Primary MultiCraft, currently provides essential residential and light commercial HVAC and plumbing services. The company also engages in the installation, retrofit, and service of equipment related to those services.

Highlights of 2001
- The company achieved record net income of $85.9 million from its core utility business. The improvement resulted largely from colder-than-normal weather, new customer additions, and improved efficiency in operations.
- WGL's solid business strategy and strong operating environment enabled company shareholders to enjoy good stock performance. In the fiscal year ended September 30, 2001, the stock provided shareholders a positive total return of 4.62 percent, or far better than the S&P 500 (which was down 26.64 percent) and the Dow Jones Utility Average (down 21.96 percent in the same period).
- WGL added nearly 28,000 new customer meters to its natural gas distribution system, a growth rate of 3.2 percent, nearly three times the national average for natural gas utilities.
- WGL sold 1.9 billion kilowatt hours of electricity to 44,000 customers.
- The company increased net income for commercial HVAC operations by 56 percent.
- WGL has paid dividends for 150 consecutive years.
- As of 2001, WGL has increased dividends for twenty-five consecutive years.

Shortcomings to Bear in Mind
- Natural gas utilities thrive when the winter weather is severe, but they suffer when the temperature is above normal. In the first quarter of fiscal 2002, for instance, net income dipped to $30.2 million in the three months ended December 31, 2001. By contrast, the company earned $50.4 million in the corresponding quarter of the prior year. What it amounts to is this: the company's utility operations are weather-sensitive, and a significant portion of its revenue comes from deliveries of natural gas to residential heating customers.

Commenting on the poor quarter, CEO James H. DeGraffenreidt Jr., said, "We are pleased that the company's weather insurance policy helped mitigate the effect of the unusually warm winter weather experienced in our utility's service territory. Although our results this quarter were hurt by a 30.9-percent decline in firm gas deliveries to customers, we were able to offset a large part of this impact by recording $6.6 million in weather insurance compensation."

Reasons to Buy
- Natural gas remains the fuel of choice in 92 percent of new homes being constructed, clearly reflecting the region's preference for comfort, reliability, and efficiency. This preference helps drive the robust growth of Washington Gas, the company's core business, which added 28,000 new customers in fiscal 2001, bringing the number of utility customers served to more than 920,000.

Current forecasts predict the company's growth will remain strong for at least another decade.

What's more, utility operations also continue to increase throughput per household. By leveraging customers' preferences for natural gas, management has increased the number of burner tips per household by more than 30 percent to 3.9, up from 2.9 only a few years ago.

- The company's franchise area possesses a significant number of conversion opportunities for Washington Gas Light to pursue. Conversion takes place when owners of older homes that use some other energy source (typically electricity or fuel oil) for their space heating are persuaded to convert to natural gas. The company now has about two-thirds of the business in existing structures in its service territory.

The conversion potential is a legacy of events that took place during the 1970s. This was when natural gas was perceived to be in short supply. To "cure" the problem, WGL's regulators imposed a moratorium on new gas hookups. This ruling prohibited Washington Gas from investing in facilities to serve new customers. With natural gas denied to them, home-owners turned to electricity. Electric heat pumps became a popular alternative for heating new homes built during the mid to late 1970s. As a consequence, a thick ring composed of thousands of electrically heated homes sprung up around the company's service territory. Washington Gas calls this an "electric doughnut."

When the moratorium was lifted in 1980, WGL had to make large capital investments to extend its gas line beyond the doughnut so that it could provide service to new customers in the growing parts of its franchise area.

Meanwhile, the electric heat pumps are now nearing the end of their useful lives. Consequently, with the favorable economics and greater effectiveness of natural gas heating, coupled with the presence of natural gas mains crossing through the area, the aging electric doughnut provides Washington Gas with a significant opportunity to tap into these lines to recapture this business from the electric company.

- In October of 2001, tenants began moving into the first section of Maritime Plaza, a commercial development project built on a twelve-acre site owned by Washington Gas on the Anacostia riverfront in the District of Columbia. Once used by the company for manufacturing gas, the site had a number of environmental issues. Employees found an innovative use for the property, transforming an underutilized asset into a commercial success that benefits many groups.

The company formed a joint venture with a real estate development firm, Lincoln Property Company, to develop the site and manage the buildings. Subject to regulatory review, the company will receive revenue from the ground lease and a portion of any net profits.

Maritime Plaza is part of one of the largest economic development projects in Washington, D.C. Situated across from the Washington Navy Yard, Maritime Plaza's initial phases respond to the need for office space for Navy contractors. Future phases will be constructed as the development of southeast Washington encourages other types of businesses to locate in this convenient sector of the city, just blocks from Capitol Hill. Plans for the entire project include 900,000 square feet of office space, constructed in five phases.

Total assets: $2,081 million
Current ratio: 1.09
Common shares outstanding: 47 million
Return on 2001 shareholders' equity: 11.0%

	2001	2000	1999	1998	1997	1996	1995	1994
Revenues (millions)	1940	1249	972	1040	1056	970	829	915
Net income (millions)	84	83	67	69	82	82	63	60
Earnings per share	1.75	1.79	1.47	1.54	1.85	1.85	1.45	1.42
Dividends per share	1.26	1.24	1.22	1.20	1.17	1.14	1.12	1.11
Price High	30.5	31.5	29.4	30.8	31.4	25.0	22.4	21.3
Low	25.3	21.8	21.0	23.1	20.9	19.1	16.1	16.0

CONSERVATIVE GROWTH

Wyeth
(formerly American Home Products Corp.)

Five Giralda Farms ▫ Madison, NJ 07940 ▫ Listed: NYSE ▫ (973) 660-5340 ▫ Dividend reinvestment plan is available: (800) 565-2067 ▫ Web site: www.wyeth.com ▫ Ticker symbol: WYE ▫ S&P rating: B ▫ Value Line financial strength rating: A+

More than any other pharmaceutical company, American Home Products, which changed its name to Wyeth in March of 2001, is a vastly different enterprise than it was a few years ago. According to Scott Hensley, writing in *The Wall Street Journal*, "If American Home can position itself on the cutting edge of pharmaceutical science, it would mark a big change from its traditional image as a frugal marketer of second-tier medicines. A decade ago, American Home was a mundane conglomerate of consumer-product companies that once hawked Wheatena breakfast cereal alongside over-the-counter remedies and a few prescription drugs. Since then, it has shed a host of businesses to concentrate on drugs and vaccines for humans and animals.

"Now American Home seems to be hitting its stride. In the past two years, American Home has rolled out nine new products. An unexpected highlight was Protonix, a heartburn drug priced at a discount to the crowded field, that has surprised analysts with its strong sales, exceeding $160 million in the first quarter of this year."

The new name, incidentally, is indicative of the transformation that has taken place. "We are changing the name to reflect an important transition in the company's history," said Lowell Weiner, a spokesman for the company. "Over the years, AHP has strategically evolved from a holding company with diversified businesses to a world leader with research-based pharmaceutical products. The Wyeth brand conveys who we are and our position in the global pharmaceutical industry."

The name Wyeth was selected because it was the name of the company's largest subsidiary, a leading manufacturer of ethical drugs, or those sold on prescription. One of the oldest prescription medicine businesses, Wyeth was founded in 1860 and acquired by American Home Products in 1931.

Company Profile

Wyeth is a global leader in pharmaceuticals, consumer health care products, and animal health products. Its products are sold in more than 150 countries. Wyeth's worldwide resources encompass more than 48,000 employees, manufacturing facilities on five continents, and one of the industry's broadest research and development programs, representing all three major discovery and development platforms—small molecules, proteins, and vaccines.

Wyeth's broad, growing lines of prescription drugs, vaccines, nutritionals, over-the-counter medications, and medical devices benefit health care worldwide. Among the company's leading products are such names as Triphasal, Norplant, Premarin, Cordarone, Naprelan, Orudis, Advil, Anacin, Dimetap, Robitussin, Preparation H, Centrum vitamins, Primatene, SMA, Lodine, and Effexor.

Shortcomings to Bear in Mind

- In 2001, worldwide animal health product net revenue decreased 2 percent. The decline, according to the company, "was due primarily to a general weakening in the livestock markets globally, and continuing concern about foot-and-mouth and mad-cow disease, offset by the domestic launch in June 2001, of ProHeart 6, a new single-dose, canine heartworm preventative product that provides six months of continuous heartworm protection."
- Worldwide consumer health care net revenue decreased 1 percent in 2001. A spokesman for the company said, "The decrease was due primarily to lower sales of cough/cold/allergy products, partially offset by higher sales of Caltrate, Advil, and Centrum products. Additionally, the 2001 full-year decrease was impacted by divestitures of two international non-core products that occurred in early 2001, as well as lower sales of Flexagen, offset in part by increased sales of ChapStick."

Reasons to Buy

- Wyeth had a good year in 2001, particularly with its ethical drugs. Worldwide human pharmaceutical net revenue increased 10 percent in the fourth quarter

as well as for the full year. The increase was due primarily to higher sales of Protonix, Effexor XR, and Premarin products, and occurred despite lower sales of Meningitec, Ziac (due to generic competition), and generic products. Also contributing to increased full-year sales were Prevnar and Cordarone I.V.

- In the January 2002 edition of *Value Line Survey*, the analyst said, "The company recently formed another strategic alliance with Elan Corporation, a leading bio-pharmaceutical and drug-delivery firm. Under terms of the agreement, Wyeth will contribute the U.S. marketing rights to the highly successful Sonata, for individuals suffering from sleep disorders. Elan will, in turn, use its propriety drug-delivery technologies to develop new formulations of Sonata, and will be responsible for the sales, marketing, and distribution of that product in the United States. We believe this strategy augurs well for the company, as it appears that the sleep-disorder market will continue to expand at a rapid pace."
- An important clue to how a drug company can perform in the future revolves around the drugs that will ultimately be approved for sale. For its part, Wyeth has a pipeline with 160 experimental compounds encompassing a wide range of therapeutic categories. Key pipeline products include Mylotarg, a treatment for relapsed acute myeloid leukemia; Rapamune, used to prevent kidney transplant rejection; Enbrel for early stage rheumatoid arthritis and congestive heart failure; FluMist intranasal influenza vaccine; low-dose Premarin and Totelle hormone replacement therapies; Retagabline antiepileptic agent; PTP-112 for type 2 diabetes; and rPSGL-lg for acute myocardial infarction (heart attack).
- Robert Essner, president and CEO of Wyeth, in commenting on the outlook for 2002 and beyond, said, "Our

prospects for growth have never been stronger; we are poised to achieve double-digit revenue and earnings growth. The performance of our core products, with their strong patent protection, new product introductions anticipated this year, and expanded manufacturing capability will drive this robust growth. We remain confident that we will deliver strong results in 2002 and beyond."

- Wyeth specializes in therapy sectors of critical need, including women's health, cardiovascular diseases, gastrointestinal diseases, infectious diseases, transplantation and immunology, hemophilia, oncology, vaccines, and neuroscience. The company focuses research and development on three key technologies: small molecules, conjugate vaccines, and recombinant proteins.

- Wyeth seems to be turning the corner on litigation related to the diet drug known as "fen-phen," which has been a source of investor concern since 1997. During 2001, the company said it paid $4.1 billion to settle diet-drug cases, bringing the total to $8.2 billion. Finally, Wyeth reiterated that it is confident that its reserves of $12.25 billion are adequate to deal with future losses from litigation. In mid-2001, a federal appeals court in Philadelphia dismissed the last appeal by a patient challenging the national settlement.

- Pharmaceutical companies have one major worry: drugs that go off patent. When that happens, firms that make generic copies jump in and slash prices, which normally reduces revenues drastically in short order. According to Barbara Ryan, an analyst with Deutsche Banc Alex. Brown, "It's a pretty strong portfolio of existing drugs, and there's minimal exposure to generics." Mr. Essner concurred. He said the company's patents look unbreachable for the next seven or eight years, making Wyeth one of the best-protected drug makers.

- Premarin and its family of products are the most prescribed medications in the United States. Considering that Premarin has been on the market for nearly sixty years, this leadership position is particularly noteworthy. And now there are new opportunities to use Premarin as a springboard to expand the company's women's health care franchise.

Research provides increasing evidence of the potential consequences of estrogen deficiency on bone mineral density, cardiovascular health, and cognitive functioning. Wyeth-Ayerst, through its Women's Health Research Institute, is at the forefront of research in hormone replacement and estrogens. Currently, the company is pursuing Phase III studies of lower doses of Prempro to determine its benefits on bone and on menopausal symptoms.

Trimegestone, a new progestin for hormone replacement and contraception, is undergoing evaluations in combination with Premarin, as well as with 17 B-estradiol for hormone replacement and with ethinyl estradiol for contraception.

Total assets: $21,092 million
Current ratio: 1.42
Common shares outstanding: 1,319 million
Return on 2001 shareholders equity: Not Meaningful

	2001	2000	1999	1998	1997	1996	1995	1994
Revenues (millions)	14129	13263	11881	13463	14196	14088	13376	8966
Net income (millions)	2285	loss	2133	2474	2160	1883	1338	1528
Earnings per share	1.72	loss	1.61	1.85	1.67	1.48	1.10	1.24
Dividends per share	.92	.92	.91	.87	.86	.79	.76	.74
Price High	63.8	65.3	70.3	58.8	42.4	33.3	25.0	16.8
Low	52.0	39.4	36.5	37.8	28.5	23.5	15.4	13.8

Index of Stocks by Category

Income

About the Author

John Slatter has a varied investment background and has served as a stock broker, securities analyst, and portfolio strategist. He is now a consultant with Prim Asset Management, a firm in Cleveland, Ohio, that manages investment portfolios on a fee basis.

Mr. Slatter has written hundreds of articles for such publications as *Barron's*, *Physician's Management*, *Ophthalmology Times*, and *Better Investing*, as well as for brokerage firms he has worked for, including Hugh Johnson & Company and First Union Securities. His books include: *Safe Investing*, *Straight Talk About Stock Investing*, and six prior editions of *The 100 Best Stocks You Can Buy*.

Mr. Slatter has also been quoted in such periodicals as the *Cleveland Plain Dealer*, the *New York Times*, the *Gannett News Service*, the *Burlington Free Press*, the *Wall Street Journal*, the *Cincinnati Enquirer*, the *Toledo Blade*, the *Christian Science Monitor*, *Money Magazine*, the *Dayton Daily News*, and the *Buffalo News*. He has been quoted in a number of books, including *The Dividend Investor* and *Stocks for the Long Run*, and he has also been interviewed by a number of radio stations, as well as by the daily television program, CNBC (Today's Business).

In August of 1988, John Slatter was featured in *The Wall Street Journal* concerning his innovative investment strategy that calls for investing in the ten highest-yielding stocks in the Dow Jones Industrial Average. This approach to stock selection is sometimes referred as *The Dogs of the Dow*, a pejorative reference that Mr. Slatter does *not* believe is justified, since the stocks with high yields have, in the past, included such blue chips as Merck, IBM, 3M, General Electric, AT&T, Caterpillar, DuPont, Exxon, J. P. Morgan Chase, and Altria Group.

John Slatter may be reached by calling (802) 879-4154 (during business hours only) or by writing him at 70 Beech Street, Essex Junction, Vermont 05452. His e-mail address is *john.slatter@verizon.net* and his fax number is (802) 878-1171.

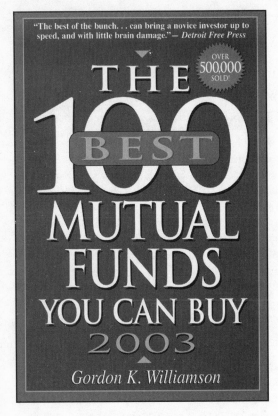

"The best of the bunch. . . can bring a novice investor up to speed, and with little brain damage." — *Detroit Free Press*

OVER 500,000 SOLD!

THE 100 BEST MUTUAL FUNDS YOU CAN BUY 2003

Gordon K. Williamson

Mutual funds are the best investment vehicle developed in the last century. They are easy to purchase and redeem, require simple recordkeeping, are less risky than stocks, and can perform superbly. It's all a matter of finding the right fund.

For the 2003 edition of this bestselling guide, noted financial planner Gordon Williamson has thoroughly reanalyzed every one of the more than 15,000 mutual funds available to consumers to determine an authoritative ranking of the best 100. The result is a brand-new list of offerings for the savvy investor, with easy-to-follow star ratings and performance rankings.

The 100 Best Mutual Funds You Can Buy, 2003 brings you the best choices for:

✦ Growth funds
✦ Global funds
✦ Technology stock funds
✦ Tax-free funds

You'll find everything you need here, in one handy volume. This is the only resource to rate each fund annually for long-term performance, management stability, risk sensitivity, up-market and down-market performance, tax minimization, and predictability of returns. Completely revised and updated, The *100 Best Mutual Funds You Can Buy, 2003* is the guide you'll rely on-year after year.

Trade Paperback, $14.95
6" x 9 ¼", 320 pages
ISBN: 1-58062-754-4

To order, call 1-800-872-5627, or visit us at *www.adamsmedia.com*!